S0-EDK-754

Essays on the Korean Economy Vol. I

PLANNING MODEL AND MACROECONOMIC POLICY ISSUES

Edited by
Chuk Kyo Kim

1977

KOREA DEVELOPMENT INSTITUTE

Seoul, Korea

The Korea Development Institute was established on March 11, 1971 by President Park Chung Hee. KDI systematically conducts research on policy matters concerning the overall national economy, helps develop the nation's five-year plans, and assists in policy making.

KDI is a non-profit corporate organization operated on an endowment fund. For this reason, its autonomy and independence are guaranteed to the maximum possible extent in the performance of its policy-oriented research activities.

The results of research conducted by KDI will be published and distributed. The contents of report, however, will represent the opinion of the person in charge of the respective research, and shall not be construed as an official opinion of the Institute.

Distributed Outside Korea by
The University Press of Hawaii

ISBN 0–8248–0546–1

FOREWORD

The Korea Development Institute has produced a large number of policy-oriented research papers since its inception in 1971. These papers cover a wide range of issues, but many are out of print, while demand for them is increasing as more interest is being shown in the Korean economy both at home and abroad. We therefore feel that it is appropriate to select some of these papers and publish them together.

The twenty-three papers brought together in these two volumes were the result of long-term studies undertaken by economists affiliated with the Korea Development Institute, either as full-time fellows of the Institute or as visiting fellows. These papers have been written at different times, so that some of them may be less relevant to today's Korea. However, since all of them analyze various aspects of the Korean economy at one time or another in its process of growth, they will help readers to understand the nature of the Korean development process and issues facing the Korean economy. We hope that the studies contained in these two volumes will also be useful in assessing prospects for other developing countries.

The interpretations and conclusions in each of the papers are those of the author or authors and do not necessarily represent the official views of the Korea Development Institute.

Mahn Je Kim
President,
Korea Development Institute

INTRODUCTION

In spite of its lack of natural resources and heavy defense burden, Korea has achieved phenomenal growth since it launched the First Five-Year Economic Development Plan in 1962. We feel that Korea's entire development experience is therefore of great value and interest, firstly, because understanding the past will enable us to design a better future, and secondly, because the lessons emerging from Korea's past experience may be helpful to other developing countries.

As a policy-oriented research organization, the Korea Development Institute has played an instrumental role in helping the government to formulate and evaluate various development strategies and other key economic policies. In this process our Institute has been engaged in a number of research works related to economic policy issues. The twenty-three papers collected in these two volumes represent the results of some of these studies which have not yet been published in monograph form.

Before introducing the main content of each paper, a few editorial words may be in order. Although some of the papers had to be revised and updated, they have all been published in their original form except for minor editorial changes. We deleted "Korea" from the original titles of some papers to avoid unnecessary repetition, since it is evident that all the papers deal with one aspect or another of the Korean economy. Furthermore, although all authors had included acknowledgements thanking many people for their helpful comments, criticisms and assistance, the editor, with the permission of the authors, chose to omit them in these volumes. However, this does not mean that these unacknowledged contributions are forgotten.

The first volume, "Planning Model and Macroeconomic Policy Issues," contains thirteen papers that are divided into four major parts. The three papers in Part I present planning models which were used for short-term as well as long-term planning purposes. The paper by Hee-yhon Song attempts to build a quarterly econometric forecasting model, the first attempt of this kind in Korea. Although the model is still in an experimental stage, it was quite helpful in formulating the annual plan. Yoon Hyung Kim constructs a 53-sector interindustry model and produces sectoral projections for the Fourth Plan period (1977–81). Four alternative projections are made under different assumptions concerning export expansion and the extent of import substitution. Yung Bong Kim presents an aggregate GNP account model for the overall resources budget in which a financial variable is used as a determinant of levels of aggregate demand and supply.

Part II, "Inflation and Savings Behavior," includes four papers. Mahn Je Kim and Yung Chul Park analyze savings behavior in Korea based on the data for the 1953–72 period in an attempt to formulate a framework for projecting the domestic saving propensity for the 1973–81 period. In doing so, they utilize both McKinnon's and the neo-Keynesian models, and their projections indicate that a saving propensity target of 27 percent for 1981 should be relatively easy to attain. Kwang Suk Kim's study uses family budget data in testing various hypotheses regarding household savings behavior. He finds, among other things, that the marginal saving rate of average farm households is higher than the rate for various occupational groups in urban areas, although the average saving rate is generally lower than that of urban households. Il SaKong's paper provides an overview of the current state of corporate finance and the recent development of the capital market which has been playing an increasingly important role in Korea.

Part III contains three papers related to the "Fiscal Structure" of Korea. Chuk Kyo Kim finds that there were displacement effects in the time pattern of government expenditure influenced by two major disruptions, the Korean war and a sharp decline in foreign aid after 1962. Since the former tended to shift the level of government expenditure upward whereas the latter had a downward effect, evidence cannot be found of a increasing expenditure share in GNP as income increases over time. The next paper by Chong Kee Park undertakes a quantitative assessment of the short-run direct tax revenue outlook for 1972 and 1973 through an income elasticity approach. Wan Soon Kim investigates the intergovernmental fiscal relations and shows that subventions to the provincial governments have not been adequate to alleviate the divergency between their needs and capacities. He then suggests an alternative revenue sharing method by which financial requirements for acceptable minimum levels of service are met.

Part IV, "Foreign Exchange and Trade Policies," deals with the vital issue of external policies for economic development. Wontack Hong's paper investigates the growth and associated shifts in the trade pattern of the Korean economy. It also attempts to project a possibly efficient export pattern which might serve as a guideline for Korea's path of export expansion in the future. The paper by Suk Tai Suh probes the nature of the Korean incentive system and concludes that it is a combination of an export-oriented system and an import substitution system although the former overshadows the latter. He also argues that the protective tariff structure may have caused some distortions in the efficient growth path of the economy and therefore that trade liberalization should be further enhanced. Bon Ho Koo studies the adverse effects resulting from a multiple exchange rate system and then attempts to show, contrary to the gap theory and other pessimistic views, that maintenance of a proper unified exchange rate can serve as a powerful policy measure in restoring both internal and external balance in Korea.

Volume II contains the remaining ten papers which are concerned with "Industrial and Social Development Issues." The four papers in Part I, "Pricing Policy and Demand Analysis," are the results of studies of several individual industries. Along with a brief historical review of rice policy, Pal Yong Moon evaluates the various issues in the formulation of foodgrain policy, with particular emphasis on the interrelation of the objectives and constraints within which the government support programs are operated. He points out that the effort to save rice through price policy and other administrative measures is self-limiting and that the only long-range solution is to increase domestic production by attaining higher yields per unit area. Pal Yong Moon's second paper attempts to develop a set of foodgrain pricing models that permit simultaneous consideration of the various goals of economic development in Korea. He applies this model to find the self-sufficiency level of rice prices and shows the trade-offs among different objectives due to alternative pricing for rice. Heeyhon Song attempts to develop forecasting models for demand and prices of steel products. The last paper by Kyu Sik Lee measures the elasticity of capital-labor substitution for the Korean electricity and transportation sector, and finds that the elasticity of substitution obtained from the Bruno model is substantially lower than that obtained by the ACMS method. This low elasticity of substitution is, according to Lee, greatly affected by the policy- induced factor market distortion.

Part II presents three papers dealing with "Regional and Urban Problems." Byung Nak Song and Raymond Struyk analyze the status of Korean housing and argue for certain government policies which would achieve the objectives of reducing the acute housing shortage, including provision of quality housing above the minimum standard, and the promotion of an increased rate of homeownership. Byung Nak Song's next paper attempts to study the growth process of the Seoul metropolitan region by analyzing the distribution and movement of jobs and industry in the region in comparison to the growth pattern of major metropolitan areas in the United States. He finds that the spatial growth pattern of the Seoul metropolitan area is similar to that of major urban areas in the United States. Sung Hwan Ban undertakes a review of the New Community Movement (Saemaul Undong) which was launched in 1971 as a comprehensive rural development program aimed at increasing the income of farm and fishery households and improving their living conditions. He describes the evolution of the movement, the main contents of its programs, and analyzes the performance of the movement during the period from its initiation to 1974.

Part III, "Education, Health and Income Distribution," contains three papers on social development, which has been rather neglected but is now considered to be extremely important in the context of recent Korean development. The paper on health by Chong Kee Park examines the organization of health care, the magnitude of national health expenditures, the advantages and disadvantages of the conventional fee-for-service system and the role of the social security system in financing health care in Korea. Chang Young Jeong's article attempts to estimate social marginal rates of return on investment in different levels of education and in physical capital within the framework of cost-benefit analysis. He finds that the social marginal rates of return on investment in education are relatively lower than the rates of return on physical capital, implying that there has been over-investment in human capital relative to physical capital. His second finding is that the additional social rate of return sharply decreases for high school graduates who finished college. This leads him to conclude that the heavy subsidization for national and public colleges should be reexamined. Hakchung Choo documents historical reasons for relatively equitable income distribution in Korea since 1945, which is, according to him, attributable to the prevention of income-generating wealth concentration.

It is hoped that by reading these papers the reader can obtain a better understanding of both the issues that Korea has faced during its development process and the main characteristics of its economic structure and policies. While these papers are the result of individual research, it is our hope that they fit together and, as a whole, furnish a significant addition to the reader's knowledge of the Korean economy.

Chuk Kyo Kim
Director,
Second Research Department

March 1977

TABLE OF CONTENTS

PART III. FISCAL STRUCTURE

PART IV. FOREIGN EXCHANGE AND TRADE POLICIES

PART I

PLANNING MODELS

AN ECONOMETRIC FORECASTING MODEL OF THE KOREAN ECONOMY

*Heeyhon Song**

I. Introduction

Since the major revision of the Korean national income accounts in 1967, a number of annual macro-econometric models have been developed, some of which have already been published.[1] However, no applicable quarterly macro-model could have been constructed until very recently, for the quarterly national income statistics have only been available since July 1971. In July 1972, a quarterly macro-model was presented at the KDI symposium[2] and another quarterly model was constructed by the Bank of Korea.[3]

The primary objective of this research is to estimate the structural equations of the Korean economy in rather aggregate forms, so that they could eventually be used as a short-term forecasting tool. The simulation of some of the economic processes through the model makes it possible to experiment with the ultimate consequences of alternative sets of policy adjustments. An accurate projection with a given set of policy decisions will be a great help in formulating the Korean annual plan (*i.e.*, the Overall Resources Budget).

---

* Senior Fellow at the Korea Development Institute. This paper was presented at the Korea Development Institute—Development Advisory Service (Harvard University) Conference, Seoul, Oct. 10–12, 1973.

[1] M. J. Kim and D. W. Nam (1968); I. Adelman and M. J. Kim (1969); D. R. Norton (1969); and M. J. Kim (1969).

[2] Heeyhon Song (1972).

[3] the Bank of Korea (1972).

The model consists essentially of two parts: (1) the description of an aggregate demand structure by linear equations, and (2) the specifications of an aggregate production function by non-linear forms. Since only real data are available for the quarterly national income statistics (1965 constant won), the model is specified in real terms. To handle the combined model of linear and non-linear relationships, a flexible procedure, *i.e.*, a recursive and iterative solution, has been adopted. The solution proceeds period by period with iteration adjustment. Although the model is relatively small, 15 stochastic equations and 10 identities, its forecasting ability seems powerful.

This paper is divided into four major sections. The estimated equations which are believed to be the most reliable descriptions of the structure of the Korean economy are presented first. Next, the nature of the equations is discussed in terms of economic experience and statistical validity. The third section tests the performance of the model with the dynamic simulation experiments, along with the forcasts for 1972, 1973 and 1974. Finally, the paper closes with some concluding remarks.

II. The Model

The observed sample data include the quarters from I-1963 to IV-1972. The included sample data are specified for each equation. For lagged values some earlier quarters were used. The model is in essence a recursive system, except for the simultaneous relation among demand for money, value added in the non-primary sector, and the level of the wholesale price index. From a statistical point of view, the recursive system makes it acceptable to use ordinary least squares to estimate the structural parameters if there is no correlation between error terms of each equation in the system. Because of the autocorrelation problem, the Cochrane-Orcutt iterative technique was used to eliminate first-degree autocorrelations of the residuals.

1. The Basic Model

In matrix form, the basic model can be expressed as follows:

$$A\ Y_t + \Delta Y_{t-T} + B_1 X_{1t} + B_2 X_{2t} + e_t = 0$$

where A is a square matrix, Y_t is a vector of endogenous variables,

Table 1. *Matrices of Coefficients*

A-Matrix

Endogenous Variables

	1 C^p	2 C	3 I^h	4 I^{meq}	5 I^{nho}	6 I^f	7 I^{na}	8 K^{na}	9 ST^h	10 L^{na}	11 P	12 V^{na}	13 V	14 TD	15 I^i	16 I	17 M^i	18 M^{meq}	19 M^c	20 M	21 E^c	22 E	23 T^{dr}	24 T^{idr}	25 V^d	26 SD
C^p	−1																									
C	1	−1																								
I^h			−1																							
I^{meq}				−1																						
I^{nho}					−1																					
I^f			1	1	1	−1																				
I^{na}						a	−1																			
K^{na}							1	−1																		
ST^h			1						−1																	
L^{na}										−1																
P											−1	a														
V^{na}											a	−1														
V												1	−1													
TD													1	−1												
I^i												a			−1											
I						1									1	−1										
M^i											a	a					−1									
M^{meq}											a							−1								
M^c																	1	1	−1							
M																			1	−1						
E^c											a										−1					
E																					1	−1				
T^{dr}												a											−1			
T^{idr}												a												−1		
V^d													1										−1		−1	
SD	−1												1			−1				1		−1				−1

Table 1. (Continued)
Δ-Matrix
Lagged Endogenous Variables

	V^{na}_{-1}	V^{na}_{-2}	V^{na}_{-3}	V^{na}_{-4}	V^{na}_{-5}	V^{na}_{-6}	V^{na}_{-7} V^{na}_{-9}	K^{na}_{-1}	ST^{h}_{-1}	ST^{h}_{-2}	P_{-3} P_{-6}	MSN_{-1} MSN_{-3}
C^p		δ	δ	δ	δ							
C												
I^h		δ	δ	δ	δ					δ		
I^{meq}	δ	δ	δ	δ								
I^{nho}		δ	δ	δ	δ	δ	δ					
I^f												
I^{na}												
K^{na}								1				
ST^h									1			
L^{na}												
P	δ	δ										δ
V^{na}												
V								δ				
TD	δ	δ	δ								δ	
I^i												
I												
M^i												
M^{meq}		δ	δ	δ	δ							
M^c												
M												
E^c												
E												
T^{dr}												
T^{idr}												
V^d												
SD												

Table 1. (Continued)

	B_1-Matrix Policy Variables										B_2-Matrix Other Exogenous Variables								Error terms
	C^g	I^g	R	MSN	ER^s	ER^b	S^b	TR	P^r	P^u	V^a	M^g	M^s	E^s	V^{ujr}	P^{fw}	P^{fx}	FL	
C^p																			e_1
C	1																		
I^h																			e_2
I^{meq}																		β_2	e_3
I^{nho}																		β_2	e_4
I^f		1																	
I^{na}																			
K^{na}																			
ST^h																			
L^{na}																			e_5
P				β_1	β_1				β_1	β_1									e_6
V^{na}				β_1															e_7
V											1								
TD				β_1							β_2								e_8
I^i																			e_9
I																			
M^i					β_1			β_1									β_2		e_{10}
M^{meq}					β_1			β_1									β_2		e_{11}
M^c												1							
M													1						
E^c						β_1	β_1								β_2	β_2			e_{12}
E														1					
T^{dr}																			e_{13}
T^{idr}																			e_{14}
V^d																			
SD																			

Y_{t-T} is a vector of lagged endogenous variables, X_{1t} and X_{2t} are vectors of exogenous variables, e_t is a vector of error terms, and Δ, B_1 and B_2 are matrices (See Table 1). The exogenous variables X_{1t} are called policy variables and X_{2t} are other exogenous variables. The list of all variables is presented in the next section.

2. *List of Variables*

A. Endogenous Variables

V = Total value added, billions of 1965 won
NV = Total value added, billions of current won
V^{na} = Total value added in the non-primary sector (industries other than agriculture, forestry and fishery), billions of 1965 won
sV^{na} = Seasonally adjusted value added in the non-primary sector, billions of 1965 won
$V^{na\prime}$ = Percent change in V^{na} from the past to the current quarter
$sV^{na\prime}$ = Percent change in sV^{na} from the past to the current quarter
V^m = Total value added in manufacturing, billions of 1965 won
sV^m = Seasonally adjusted value added in manufacturing, billions of 1965 won
V^d = Total disposable income, billions of 1965 won
C = Total consumption expenditures, billions of 1965 won
C^p = Private consumption expenditures, billions of 1965 won
MSN = Currency in circulation and total demand deposits, billions of current won
MSN' = Percent changes in MSN from the past to the current quarter
MS = Currency in circulation and total demand deposits, billions of constant won, deflated by wholesale price index (1965 = 100)
TD = Demand for time and savings deposits
I = Gross domestic investment, billions of 1965 won
I^f = Total fixed capital formation, billions of 1965 won
I^{na} = Fixed capital formation in the non-primary sector, billions of 1965 won
I^h = Fixed capital formation in residential buildings, billions of 1965 won
I^{nho} = Fixed capital formation in non-residential buildings and others, billions of 1965 won

I^{meq} = Fixed capital formation in machinery and equipment, billions of 1965 won
I^{i} = Increase in stocks, billions of 1965 won
M = Total imports, billions of 1965 won
M^{c} = Total commodity imports, billions of 1965 won
M^{meq} = Imports of machinery and equipment, billions of 1965 won
M^{i} = Imports of intermediate goods, billions of 1965 won
E = Total exports, billions of 1965 won
E^{c} = Total commodity exports, billions of 1965 won
X^{cr} = Total commodity exports, millions of 1970 constant U.S. dollars (in real terms)
$EMER$ = Real effective import exchange rate, $(ER^{s} + TR) \times P^{fx}/P^{w}$
$EXER$ = Real effective export exchange rate, $(ER^{b} + S^{b}) \times P^{fw}/P^{w}$
L^{na} = Employment in the non-primary sector, million persons
P^{w} = Wholesale price index for all commodities (1970 = 100)
P' = Percent change in P_{w} from the past to the current quarter
P^{c} = Seoul consumer price index (1965=100)
T^{dr} = Direct tax revenue, billions of 1965 won
T^{idr} = Indirect tax revenue, billions of 1965 won
K^{na} = Capital stock in the non-primary sector at end-of-quarter, billions of 1965 won
ST^{h} = Residential building stock at end-of-quarter, billions of 1965 won

B. Exogenous Variables

i) Policy Variables

C^{g} = Government consumption expenditures, billions of 1965 won
I^{g} = Government investment, billions of 1965 won
R = Interest rate on one-year time deposits
ER^{s} = Exchange rates of won to U.S. dollar, selling rate
ER^{b} = Exchange rates of won to U.S. dollar, buying rate
TR = Tariff rate $\left(= \dfrac{\text{Total customs duty}}{\text{Total commodity imports}}\right)$
S^{b} = Subsidies per dollar export
MSN = Currency and demand deposits, billions of current won (could be treated as exogenous)

P^r = Price of rice index (1970 = 100)
$P^{r'}$ = Percent change in P^r from the past to the current quarter
P^u = Public utility price index (1970 = 100)
$P^{u'}$ = Percent change in P^u from the past to the current quarter

ii) Other Exogenous Variables

V^a = Total value added in agriculture, fishery, and forestry, billions of 1975 won
M^g = Grain imports, billions of 1965 won
M^s = Service imports, including factor payments, billions of 1965 won
E^s = Service exports, including factor receipts, billions of 1965 won
V^{ujr} = Real GNP index of the U.S. and Japan weighted by Korea's commodity exports (1970 = 100)
$ER^{s'}$ = Percent change in ER^s from the past to the current quarter
P^{fw} = Wholesale price index of U.S. and Japan weighted by Korea's commodity exports (1970 = 100)
P^{fx} = Export price index of U.S. and Japan weighted by Korea's commodity exports (1970 = 100)
P^{fm} = Wholesale price index of U.S. and Japan weighted by Korea's commodity imports (1972 = 100)
FL = Inflow of long-term foreign loans, billions of 1965 won
t = Time in units of quarters
D_1 = 1 in the first quarter, 0 otherwise
D_2 = 1 in the second quarter, 0 otherwise
D_3 = 1 in the third quarter, 0 otherwise
D_4 = 1 in the fourth quarter, 0 otherwise

3. *Estimated Structural Equations and Identities*

In the equations written below the figures in the parentheses under coefficients are t-statistics. R^2 is the coefficient of multiple correlation and DW is the Durbin-Watson statistic measuring serial correlation of residuals. In the process of choosing structural equations, in addition to statistical validity and size of estimated parameters, forecasting ability tested by dynamic simulation also has been taken into account.

A. Estimated Structural Equations

$$(1\text{–}1)\ \ln\left(\frac{V^{na}}{L^{na}}\right) = \underset{(-1.77)}{-1.6675} + \underset{(4.71)}{0.5625} \ln\left(\frac{K^{na}_{-1}}{L^{na}}\right) + \underset{(4.70)}{0.2939} \ln wMS$$

$$+ \underset{(1.63)}{0.0056}\, t + \underset{(12.45)}{0.1948}\, D2 + \underset{(11.71)}{0.1367}\, D3 + \underset{(11.21)}{0.1559}\, D4$$

$R^2 = 0.9911$ $DW = 2.0351$
Sample period = 1966 1/4 — 1972 4/4

where $wMS = 0.58\ MS + 0.33\ MS_{-1} + 0.09\ MS_{-2}$

$$(2\text{–}1)\ L^{na} = \underset{(15.29)}{3.1091} + \underset{(9.0)}{0.0072}\, sV^{na}_{-1} - \underset{(-5.54)}{0.2675}\, D1 - \underset{(-11.32)}{0.6031}\, D2$$

$$- \underset{(-4.95)}{0.2284}\, D3$$

$R^2 = 0.9632$ $DW = 1.8407$
Sample period = 1965 1/4 — 1972 4/4

$$(3\text{–}1)\ C^p = \underset{(0.65)}{4.2363} + \underset{(13.09)}{0.1763}\, V^d_{-2} + \underset{(13.91)}{0.1843}\, V^d_{-3} + \underset{(24.37)}{0.3151}\, V^d_{-4}$$

$$+ \underset{(14.46)}{0.2002}\, V^d_{-5}$$

$R^2 = 0.9824$ $DW = 1.8655$
Sample period = 1965 1/4 — 1972 4/4

$$(4\text{–}1)\ I^h = \underset{(5.12)}{175.140} - \underset{(-5.12)}{0.1542}\, ST^h_{-2} + \underset{(6.44)}{0.1757}\, wVNAX_{-2} - \underset{(-7.70)}{4.3626}\, D1$$

$R^2 = 0.8651$ $DW = 1.9407$
Sample period = 1964 1/4 — 1972 4/4

where $wVNAX = 0.3967\ V^{na} + 0.2999\ V^{na}_{-1} + 0.2013\ V^{na}_{-2} + 0.1030\ V^{na}_{-3}$

$$(4\text{–}2)\ I^{meq} = \underset{(3.10)}{6.0375} + \underset{(7.34)}{0.5006}\, FL + \underset{(4.61)}{0.5816}\, wVNACF_{-1} - \underset{(-2.11)}{2.9792}\, D1$$

$R^2 = 0.9429$ $DW = 1.9296$
Sample period = 1963 1/4 — 1972 4/4

where $wVNACF = 0.2912\ VNAC + 0.2637\ VNAC_{-1} + 0.2363\ VNAC_{-2} + 0.2088\ VNAC_{-3}$

$VNAC = V^{na} - V^{na}_{-4}$

$$\text{(4–3)}\ I^{nho} = \underset{(4.84)}{6.9218} + \underset{(2.13)}{0.1551}\ FL + \underset{(3.66)}{0.4925}\ wVNACA_{-2} - \underset{(-5.14)}{6.2566}\ D1$$

$R^2 = 0.8816 \qquad DW = 2.0218$
Sample period = 1963 1/4 — 1972 4/4

where $wVNACA = 0.1543\ VNAC + 0.1459\ VNAC_{-1} + 0.1376\ VNAC_{-2} + 0.1292\ VNAC_{-3} + 0.1208\ VNAC_{-4} + 01124\ VNAC_{-5} + 0.1041\ VNAC_{-6} + 0.0957\ VNAC_{-7}$

$$\text{(4–4)}\ I^{i} = \underset{(-8.30)}{-45.2704} + \underset{(1.13)}{0.2195}\ VNAC + \underset{(2.34)}{0.6257}\ VAC + \underset{(22.16)}{165.042}\ D4$$

$R^2 = 0.9583 \qquad DW = 1.8681$
Sample period = 1964 1/4 — 1972 4/4

where $VAC = V^{a} - V^{a}_{-4}$

$$\text{(5–1)}\ M^{meq} = \underset{(3.11)}{53.5847} + \underset{(13.53)}{0.2274}\ wVNAY_{-2} - \underset{(-4.16)}{0.1921}\ (ER^{s} + TR) \times \frac{Pfx}{Pw}$$

$R^2 = 0.9347 \qquad DW = 1.9653$
Sample period = 1964 1/4 — 1972 4/4

where $wVNAY = 0.355\ V^{na} + 0.2852\ V^{na}_{-1} + 0.215\ V^{na}_{-1} + 0.1448\ V^{na}_{-3}$

$$\text{(5–2)}\ M^{i} = \underset{(-1.35)}{-11.0433} + \underset{(29.79)}{0.3751}\ V^{na} - \underset{(-1.27)}{0.0314}\ (ER^{s} + TR) \times \frac{Pfx}{Pw}$$

$R^2 = 0.9709 \qquad DW = 1.8654$
Sample period = 1963 1/4 — 1972 4/4

$$\text{(6–1)}\ \ln\left(\frac{X^c}{Pfw}\right) = \underset{(-16.65)}{-25.426} + \underset{(34.27)}{4.479}\ \ln V^{ujr} + \underset{(5.56)}{1.692}\ \ln\left[(ER^{b} + S^{b}) \times \frac{Pfw}{Pw}\right] - \underset{(-7.79)}{0.230}\ D1 - \underset{(-3.19)}{0.090}\ D3$$

$R^2 = 0.9910 \qquad DW = 1.9343$
Sample period = 1965 1/4 — 1972 4/4

$$(7\text{–}1)\ \ln MSN = \underset{(-3.40)}{-0.7068} + \underset{(17.54)}{0.3340} \ln NV + \underset{(14.47)}{0.2750} \ln NV_{-1}$$
$$+ \underset{(13.29)}{0.2474} \ln NV_{-2} + \underset{(17.29)}{0.3147} \ln NV_{-3} - \underset{(3.52)}{0.1831} \ln R$$
$$- \underset{(-6.49)}{0.2254} \ln MWP_{-2}$$

$R^2 = 0.9967 \qquad DW = 2.0375$
Sample period = 1962 3/4 — 1972 4/4

where $MWP = 0.197\ P + 0.289\ P_{-1} + 0.296\ P_{-2} + 0.218\ P_{-3}$

$$P = \frac{Pc - Pc_{-4}}{Pc_{-4}} \times 100$$

$$(7\text{–}2)\ \ln TD = \underset{(-11.53)}{-8.2418} + \underset{(20.01)}{0.5804} \ln NV + \underset{(18.08)}{0.5243} \ln NV_{-1}$$
$$+ \underset{(18.99)}{0.5316} \ln NV_{-2} + \underset{(20.14)}{0.5840} \ln NV_{-3} + \underset{(4.79)}{0.4785} \ln R$$
$$\underset{(-6.90)}{-0.4626} \ln TWP_{-3}$$

$R^2 = 0.9990 \qquad DW = 1.52$
Sample period = 1963 1/4 — 1972 4/4

where $TWP_{-3} = 0.207\ P_{-3} + 0.229\ P_{-4} + 0.360\ P_{-5} + 0.204\ P_{-6}$

$$(8\text{–}1)\ P' = \underset{(-1.24)}{-0.4570} - \underset{(-2.34)}{0.1611}\ wsV^{na'} + \underset{(4.44)}{0.1857}\ wMSN' + \underset{(7.95)}{0.3699}\ wER^{s'}$$
$$+ \underset{(9.49)}{0.1133}\ P^{r'} + \underset{(7.50)}{0.2376}\ P^{u'}$$

$R^2 = 0.9300 \qquad DW = 1.8790$
Sample period = 1966 1/4 — 1972 4/4

where $wsV^{na'} = 0.25\ sV^{na'} + 0.44\ sV^{na'}_{-1} + 0.31\ sV^{na'}_{-2}$

$wMSN' = 0.35\ MSN'_{-1} + 0.37\ MSN'_{-2} + 0.28\ MSN'_{-3}$

$wER^{s} = 0.2727\ ER^{s'} + 0.7273\ ER^{s'}_{-1}$

$$P' = \frac{Pw - Pw_{-1}}{Pw_{-1}} \times 100$$

$$(9\text{–}1)\ \ln T^{dr} = \underset{(-0.47)}{-0.5173} + \underset{(9.70)}{1.7802} \ln V^{na} - \underset{(-1.38)}{0.0966}\, D1 - \underset{(-2.57)}{0.1610}\, D3$$

$R^2 = 0.9178$ $DW = 2.3932$

Sample period = 1965 1/4 — 1972 4/4

$$(9\text{–}2)\ \ln T^{idr} = \underset{(-11.25)}{-6.0535} + \underset{(16.47)}{1.6397} \ln V^{na} - \underset{(-0.86)}{0.0508}\, D1$$

$R^2 = 0.9404$ $DW = 2.1301$
Sample period = 1965 1/4 — 1972 4/4

B. Identities

(6–1) $C = C^p + C^g$

(7–1) $I^f = I^{meq} + I^h + I^{nho} + I^g$

(8–1) $I = I^f + I^i$

(9–1) $M^c = M^{meq} + M^i + M^g$

(10–1) $M = M^c + M^s$

(11–1) $E = E^c + E^s$

(12–1) $V = V^{na} + V^a$

(13–1) $V = C + I + E - M + SD$ (statistical discrepancy)

(14–1) $V^d = V - T^{dr}$

(15–1) $I^{na} = 0.925\, I^f$

(16–1) $K^{na} = 0.9935\, K^{na}_{-1} + I^{na}$

(17–1) $ST^h = ST^h_{-1} + I^h$

III. Discussion of the Equations

1. Aggregate Production Functions

Only one aggregate production function was estimated for the non-primary sector. Because of the lack of quarterly data, no attempt has been made to estimate disaggregated production functions.

The type of production function estimated here represents a relationship between real output and input of utilized capital stock, man-hours worked, and a technological time trend. Since the data for man-hours worked were not available, employment was taken as labor input. The estimation of capital utilization is particularly difficult in Korea due partly to the shortage of information. It was not possible, for the present, to adopt the Wharton School index of capacity utilization.[4]

It could be quite controversial to introduce real money balances into a neo-classical production function as a factor input. Several writers have argued that real money balances are a factor of production because they affect productivity by facilitating transactions, exchange, and specialization.[5]

Sinai and Stokes' article[6] tested the hypothesis that real money balances have been mistakenly omitted from the production function. They found that real money balances, regardless of definition, entered significantly into a Cobb-Douglas production function as a separate factor input like capital and labor inputs. The main rationale for including real money balances in the production function in their article is the increment of "economic efficiency" of a monetary economy compared with a barter economy. Thus, the marginal product of money balances is the increased output obtained as a consequence of an increase in real money balances which releases additional labor and capital services for utilization of production instead of exchange. Finally their results support the view that real money balances are a producer's good.[7]

It is very true that real cash balances make it possible to combine factor inputs more efficiently so that they relate to total factor productivity. With additional real cash balances, output can be increased with the same amount of capital and labor inputs. This increased output is caused by additional "effective" amounts of both capital and labor inputs. By improving production conditions in general, additional real money balances make it possible to enhance effective production capacity with the same amount of capital and labor inputs. Thus, the role of real cash balances in production should be distinguished from the role of capital and labor

[4] L. R. Klein (1964), pp. 23–24.

[5] M. J. Bailey (1962), pp. 54–56; M. I. Nadiri (1970), p. 1153; M. I. Nadiri (1969), p. 175; D. Levhari and D. Patinkin (1968), pp. 737–740; and J. Tobin (1965), pp. 671–684.

[6] A. Sinai and H. H. Stokes (1972).

[7] D. Levhari and D. Patinkin (1968).

inputs. Real cash balances in the process of aggregate production are like lubricating oil. Lubricating oil is essential for the smooth operation of a machine. Thus, it enhances a machine's effective production capacity. No doubt, lubricating oil is a prominent factor in the efficient operation of the machine, but lubricating oil itself is not a part of the machine.

In this paper, a linear and homogeneous Cobb-Douglas production function was assumed. A multi-collinearity problem between employment and stock variables made it difficult to estimate the production function of non-constant returns to scale. Hicks-neutral technical progress can be written as follows:

$$O = e^{mt} K^{\alpha} L^{1-\alpha} \ldots\ldots\ldots\ldots\ldots\ldots\ldots\ldots\ldots\ldots (1)$$

where O = output
L = labor
K = capital
t = time
m = rate of disembodied or neutral technical change
α = elasticity of output with respect to capital ($O < \alpha < 1$).

By introducing λ into (1):

$$V = e^{mt} (\lambda K)^{\alpha} (\lambda L)^{1-\alpha} \ldots\ldots\ldots\ldots\ldots\ldots\ldots\ldots (2)$$

where λ = multiplier of both capital and labor due to availability of real money balances
λK and λL = "effective" capital stock and labor force respectively
V = *ex post* output under the assumption of existence of λ.

Let us assume that:

$$\lambda = MS^{\gamma} \ldots\ldots\ldots\ldots\ldots\ldots\ldots\ldots\ldots\ldots\ldots (3)$$

where MS = real money balances and $0 < \gamma < 1$.
This implies that the increment of mulitplier, λ, decreases as an equal amount of real money balances increases, i. e.,

$$\frac{d\lambda}{dMS} = \gamma\, MS^{\gamma-1} = \frac{\gamma}{MS^{1-\gamma}}$$

where $-1 < \gamma - 1 < 0$.

The above assumption is reasonable because the marginal contribution of additional real cash balances in regard to K and L would decrease as an equal amount of real money balances increases.

Hence the hypothesized Cobb-Douglas production function with constant returns to scale has taken the following form from equations (2) and (3), *i.e.*,

$$V = e^{mt}(MS^{\gamma}K)^{\alpha}(MS^{\gamma}L)^{1-\alpha}u$$

where u = disturbance term

So $V = e^{mt}\, K^{\alpha}L^{1-\alpha}\, MS^{\gamma}\, u$ ....(4)

where γ = elasticity of output with respect to real money balances.

By dividing equation (4), both sides, by L:

$$\frac{V}{L} = e^{mt}\left(\frac{K}{L}\right)^{\alpha} MS^{\gamma}\, u \quad \ldots\ldots\ldots\ldots\ldots\ldots(5)$$

Equation (5) was estimated in log linear form as

$$\ln\left(\frac{V}{L}\right) = mt + \alpha \ln\left(\frac{K}{L}\right) + \gamma \ln MS + \ln u$$

With real money balances (currency in circulation and demand deposits) weighted by a polynomial distributed lag technique,[8] Cobb-Douglas type non-primary sector production functions were estimated in log linear form. Equation (1–1) shows that the coefficient of real money balances is highly significant along with the coefficient of per capita capital stock. The shares of capital and labor inputs were 56.2 percent and 43.7 percent, respectively. These figures are very close to actuality. The average actual share of compensation of employees out of the total value added in the non-primary sector was 42.8 percent, according to input-output tables for 1966, 1968 and 1970.

The annual average of the marginal real productivity of capital implied by the coefficient of K, 0.562, was approximately 14 percent. By adding 11 percent of average annual inflation over the sample period,[9] the

[8] See footnote 17.

[9] Over the last seven years, 1966–1972, the average annual rate of increase in the wholesale and consumer price indexes were about 9 and 12 percent, respectively.

annual marginal productivity of capital in current money value was approximately 24 percent. This magnitude seems reasonable, considering general market rates of interest on a long-term loan. Similarly, the annual average of the marginal real productivity of labor implied by the coefficient of L, 0.438 was 84,500 won (in 1965 constant prices). This magnitude is quite reasonable, because the average annual wage earnings in the non-primary sector was approximately 79,500 won (in 1965 constant prices), according to input-output tables for 1966, 1968 and 1970.

The marginal product of real money balances implied by the coefficient of MS, 0.29, was 1.69. This means that a one won increase in purchasing power over capital and labor is associated with about a 1.7 unit increase in real output of the non-primary sector. This magnitude is about four times larger than that for the private sector of the U.S. economy estimated by Sinai and Stokes.[10]

The larger magnitude in Korea than in the U.S., of the marginal product of real cash balances can perhaps be justified as follows: (i) The market rate of interest on short-term loans in Korea over the sample period was about 4 times higher than that in the U.S.[11] (ii) In the U.S. the average ratio of output of the private sector to real money balances was about 2.5, while that of the non-primary sector in Korea was about 6.1. (iii) While the input data for capital and labor used in this study were not corrected for quality change and rate of utilization as mentioned earlier, Sinai and Stokes used the corrected data taken from a recent study by Christensen and Jorgenson.[12] (iv) Moreover, in a fast growing economy where abundant labor is available, such as in the Korean economy, marginal real money balances can contribute to increasing "economic efficiency" much more effectively than in advanced nations, *i.e.*, the adoption of existing modern production techniques, business organization and a commercial system makes it possible to increase total productivity much faster than in advanced nations. Thus, a relatively large number of factor inputs can be released from the traditional methods of production and distribution.[13] At present, however, the author is not sure whether this magnitude of marginal product of real balances is consistent with the behavior

---

[10] A Sinai and H. H. Stokes (1972), p. 294.

[11] The annual average bank rate of interest on major short-term loans over the sample period was higher than 20 percent before some additional costs, and the average interest rate in the unorganized money market was not lower than 35 percent.

[12] L. R. Christenson and D. W. Jorgenson (1970).

[13] Over the sample period, the average annual real growth of the non-primary sector was 14.8 percent.

of firms in Korea.

The following equation is the result of estimating a Cobb-Douglas production function without real money balances.

$$\ln\left(\frac{V^{na}}{L^{na}}\right) = \underset{(0.99)}{1.007} + \underset{(1.97)}{0.293} \ln\left(\frac{K^{na}_{-1}}{L^{na}}\right) + \underset{(18.73)}{0.021}\, t + \underset{(11.40)}{0.209}\, D2 + \underset{(8.62)}{0.124}\, D3 + \underset{(8.83)}{0.138}\, D4$$

$R^2 = 0.984$ $\quad DW = 2.078$

Sample period = 1966 1/4 — 1972 4/4

The above equation without real money balances is inferior to the equation with real balances with respect to the goodness of fit and the size of the estimated coefficients. The capital share was too small and the share of labor was too large. While 58.8 percent of the average annual growth of the non-primary sector was explained by trend variables in the equation without real money balances, 15.6 percent was explained by trend variables and about 42 percent by real money balances in the equation with real money balances (1–1). In other words, the trend variable is much more significant in an equation without money balances but loses its significance when real balances are included. This result implies that real money balances have a significant independent effect on productivity.[14]

Factor contributions to growth in the non-primary sector imputed by the coefficients of the two production functions, with and without real money balances, are compared in Table 2.

2. *Employment Equation*

Because the amount of labor demanded was assumed to be mainly determined by output produced, employment was made a function of lagged output. Equation (2–1) implied that the marginal employment output ratio was 1800 (= 7200/4) workers per one billion 1965 constant won, and the marginal output-employment ratio was about 550,000 won (in 1965 constant price) per worker. Real wage was not significant enough to explain the level of employment.

3. *Consumption Equation*

Only one aggregate private consumption function was considered in

[14] A. Sinai and H. H. Stokes (1972), p. 294.

Table 2. Factor Contribution to Growth in the Non-Primary Sector, 1966–1972

	Equation with real money balances			Equation without real money balances		
	Elasticity	Average annual increasing rate (%)	Contribution rate (%)	Elasticity	Average annual increasing rate (%)	Contribution rate(%)
Average annual growth rate of the non-primary sector	—	—	14.8 (100.0)	—	—	14.8 (100.0)
Capital stock	0.56	5.9	3.30 (22.3)	0.29	5.9	1.71 (11.6)
Labor	0.44	6.0	2.64 (17.8)	0.71	6.0	4.26 (28.8)
Real money balances	0.29	21.6	6.26 (42.3)	—	—	—
Time trend	0.0226*	—	2.26 (15.3)	0.0866*	—	8.66 (58.5)
Disturbance term	—	—	0.34 (2.3)	—	—	0.17 (1.1)

Notes: ( ) composition ratio
* Converted from quarterly growth rate to annual growth rate

this model due to the lack of appropriate quarterly information for disaggregated consumption expenditures. While assuming consumption was dependent on lagged incomes, some qualifications were introduced, that is, income was adjusted for taxes.

The coefficients on lagged disposable income were highly significant ranging back five quarters. There was no significant relation between current consumption and current income according to the estimated equations. It seems that a short-run lag effect exists as a result of psychological and institutional reasons.[15] The magnitude of the fourth quarter lagged income coefficient was the largest among the four lags. The reason may be that the fourth quarter lag coefficient explains the spending habits in the same quarter of the previous year. According to equation (3–1), the *MPC* with respect to disposable income was approximately 0.876, which

[15] G. Ackley (1961), pp. 255–257.

was very reasonable.

4. Investment Equations

A version of the flexible accelerator originated by Chenery and Koyck[16] was adopted. The determinants of investment included changes in output and the availability of foreign capital. Since a large amount of investment goods had to be financed either by grants or by loans from abroad, the availability of foreign financing has been a critical determinant of desired capital formation, especially in machinery and equipment. The time structure of the investment process was taken into account by use of the Almon polynomial distributed lag structure.[17]

Four investment equations were considered as behavioral equations: (1) residential construction (I^h), (2) investment in machinery and equipment (I^{meq}), (3) non-residential and other construction (I^{nho}), and (4) inventory investment (I^i). Government construction (I^g) was exogenously estimated through the magnitudes of government direct investment and development loans.

Residential building construction was assumed to depend positively on income and negatively on the housing stock—that is, at higher incomes more is spent for housing, and the larger the housing stocks at any given level of income, the less is allocated to shelter. The seasonal dummy variable for the first quarter was significantly included in the equation, because of undesirable weather conditions for construction.

Investment in machinery and equipment was dependent upon changes in both non-primary output and the inflow of long-term foreign loans. The foreign capital inflow was such a dominant determinant in this category of investment that the relative role of an accelerator version was markedly diminished as compared with other categories of the investment. An accelerator version of investment function was also assumed for expenditures in non-residential buildings and other construction. It was assumed that the larger the outputs, the more additional inventory was accumulated.

5. Imports Equations

Total imports are disaggregated into (1) machinery and equipment,

[16] D. W. Jorgenson (1971).

[17] S. Almon (1968) and S. Robinson (1970).

(2) intermediate commodities (total commodity imports minus imports of machinery and equipment and grain), (3) grain, and (4) services including factor income. Imports of grain and services are treated as exogenous variables.

Imports of machinery and equipment were strongly related to expectation of the future output and real effective import prices. The weighted average of the lagged non-primary sector outputs was used as the proxy variable of the expectation. Imports of intermediate materials were directly related to current output.

The import elasticity of machinery and equipment with respect to the real effective exchange rate implied by equation (5–1) was 2.4 and that of intermediate commodities implied by equation (5–2) was 0.21. Since about 50 percent of total imported raw materials are used for exports, and a minimum level of raw material imports is associated with a certain level of production, the import of intermediate commodities is less sensitive to price compared with the import of machinery and equipment. The level of import price is sensitively related to capital costs because it affects the flow of expected rate of net returns.

The import elasticities of both machinery and equipment and intermediate commodities with respect to the output of the non–primary sector range from 1.4 to 1.5. These magnitudes agreed well with the actual observations. The imports of the above two groups increased at an annual rate of about 20 percent, about 1.4 times higher than the growth of the non-primary sector.

6. Export Equation

Export was explained in terms of export demand by the major importing countries and relative price. The weighted index of real GNP of the U.S. and Japan was taken as a proxy variable of the demand for export. The real effective export exchange rate was used as a relative price variable. Seasonal dummy variables for both the first and second quarter were also included to explain seasonal variations of exports. Commodity exports were treated as an endogenous variable, and other services and factor incomes were treated as exogenous variables, as is done in the import equation.

As expected, commodity exports were highly sensitive to the rate of change in real GNP of the U.S. and Japan. The major reason might be, (i) in 1972, for example, about 75 percent of the total commodity exports were shipped to the U.S. and Japan, and (ii) most of the export commodities are not only still unfamiliar products to import customers but occupy a marginal share of the major importers, commodity markets. The elasticity of commodity exports with respect to the relative price implied by the coefficient of the real effective exchange rate should be given special attention, because this magnitude indicates the degree of the international competitive position of the Korean export.[18]

7. *Demand for Money Equations*[19]

The demand for money, and time and savings deposits was explained in terms of the total wealth to be held, the return to holding liquid financial assets, and alternative forms of financial and non-financial wealth.

Particular emphasis was placed upon the analysis of the effects of both changes in the interest rate and the rate of inflation on the variation of demand for money and other liquid assets.[20] We have therefore selected the following forms of functional relationships for narrowly defined money and time and savings deposits:

$$MSN = f(NV, R, P)$$
$$TD = f(NV, R, P)$$

where:

MSN = money (currency + demand deposits) in current billion won

NV = Gross National Product in current billion won

R = interest rate on one-year time deposits

P = percentage change in Consumer Price

TD = time and savings deposits in current billion won.

GNP represents wealth and income variables. The interest rate on one-year time deposits is used as a return to holding money substitute, *i.e.*, highly liquid financial assets. The percentage change in the Consumer Price Index in a lagged form is considered as a proxy variable for the expected rate of inflation which can explain the cost of holding money against the return on other forms of wealth, particularly real assets. Since narrowly defined money and time and savings deposits have quite different be-

[18] M. Tatemoto, *et. al.* (1967), p. 24.

[19] M. J. Kim, Heeyhon Song, and K. S. Kim (1973).

[20] G. C. Chow(1966); F. Liu(1970); H. D. Dickson, *et. al.*(1972); J. A. Lybeck(1972); and A. A. Shapiro (1973).

havioral relationships in regard to changes in the interest rate, the demand for money equations were separately estimated.

After experimenting with various lagged forms for GNP, interest rate and the rate of inflation, we have selected equation (7–1) on the basis of statistical fitness and size of estimated parameters. Quarterly GNP in current prices was constructed by multiplying real GNP by the Consumer Price Index for the corresponding quarter, and the expected rate of inflation was represented by a four-quarter weighted moving average of percent changes in the Consumer Price Index lagged two quarters. The weights for the specified lags of the price expectation variable are the normalized values of the regression coefficients for the appropriate lags of P.

As expected, the elasticity of income came out slightly higher than unity, approximately 1.2. Interest rate elasticity for money turned out to be nearly -0.2 and the elasticity of the rate of price expectation was -0.23. Thus the short-run variation of the demand for money was explained by other than income variables.

The same functional form as the demand for money equation was used for time and savings deposits. The income elasticity implied by equation (7–2) was approximately 2.2 which is much higher than that of narrowly defined money. The elasticity for the interest rate on one-year time deposits is 0.50, indicating a strong effect of the interest rate on this asset. In addition, the elasticity for the expected rate of inflation is -0.46 which is also very large.[21]

8. Price Equation

In order to explain short-term variations of the wholesale price or rate of inflation in Korea, an attempt was made to develop a Harberger–type dynamic model of inflation.[22]

The rate of quarterly changes in the wholesale price index was taken as a dependent variable to be explained. It would be advisable not to take the level of the price index as a dependent variable because of the strong upward trends in the variables under consideration.

The short-term variations of the wholesale price were explained in terms of changes in money supply and income, and three more explanatory determinants, namely, changes in the foreign exchange rate, public utility prices and the price of rice. These three variables are treated as explanatory

[21] M. J. Kim, H. Song and K. S. Kim (1973), p. 5

[22] A. C. Harberger (1963).

variables, because the changes in them are very strongly dependent upon policy decisions, at least over a short-term period of less than a couple of years. In fact, these three variables are components of the wholesale price, *i.e.*, lagged prices by policy decisions. Therefore, in the analysis of a long-term trend of price changes or inflation, these three variables should not be treated as explanatory variables. Perhaps, as the quantity theory of money tells us, a long-term trend of price movement can be explained by changes in both the nominal money supply and the availability of goods and services, along with the velocity of money.

A detailed examination was made in order to inquire into the dynamic paths of increases in the nominal money supply, real output, and foreign exchange rate in order to take into account their full effect upon the short-term changes in wholesale prices. The output of the non-primary sector was used instead of a GNP measure because of undesirable fluctuations of agricultural outputs.

The result for the wholesale price index using quarterly data is summarized in equation (8–1). The explanatory power of this equation is excellent and the resulting sizes of the coefficients appear reasonable. Equation (8–1) suggests that it takes about a full year for an increase in the nominal money supply to have its full influence on the wholesale price index,[23] and something like two and three quarters for the exchange rate and income, respectively.

The coefficient of change in real output in terms of the GNP base was about a quarter (= 0.161 × 1.54),[24] indicating that a 10 percent rise in real GNP, other things being equal, causes a short-term fall of about 2.5 percent in the price level. The coefficient of the lagged changes in the money supply is nearly one-fifth, indicating that a 10 percent increase in the quantity of money causes a short-term rise of 2.0 percent in the price level, other things being equal.

The size of the coefficient of foreign exchange, 0.37, is acceptable because nearly 40 percent of the total weight of the wholesale price index is accounted for by internationally traded goods. A 10 percent devaluation, for example, would virtually automatically raise the price index by about 4.0 percent. The magnitude of the coefficient of public utility prices, 0.24, did not seem unreasonable. About 13 percent of the total weight of the wholesale price index is accounted for by public utility items,

[23] Harberger suggested about two years in his study of "Dynamics of Inflation in Chile."

[24] During the sample period, the real growth rate of the nonprimary sector was about 1.54 times as high as that of real GNP.

the indirect cost-push effects attributable to utility prices are estimated to be about 5 percent, and about 6 percent would be the psychological effect of the changes in utility prices as a signal of a general price rise. The weight of the price of rice in the wholesale price index is about 10 percent, indicating that a 10 percent increase in the price of rice would automatically raise the price index by about one percent. Thus, the size of coefficients of the price of rice variable, 0.11, was very reasonable.

The roles of wage rate and price expectation were assumed to be somewhat significant in determining changes in price, but we failed to include them in the final equation. It seems that the wage rate in Korea is led by the general price rise, instead of the other way around, due to the existence of a large labor force. It seemed that the role of expectation in the price rise in Korea was prominent, but it was difficult to prove it empirically.

In a long-term analysis of inflation, the expected elasticities of both aggregate outputs and nominal money balances would be about one. However, in the short-term analysis of price change in this paper, the elasticities of both output and money stock implied by equation (8–1) ranged from approximately 0.20 to 0.25. These magnitudes appear reasonable. Since approximately 75 percent of short-term variations in the general price level are explained by the commodities related to the three policy variables (exchange rate, utility prices and price of rice), about a quarter of the changes in the general price are left to be explained by the changes in aggregate output and nominal money stock.

9. Tax Equations

There are two types of taxes in this model: direct tax and indirect tax. Tax revenues were explained in terms of the value added in the non-primary sector. In order to eliminate the effect of price increases from the estimation of the tax equations, all variables used were expressed in real terms. Tax revenues series were uniformly deflated by the wholesale price index.

The elasticities of direct and indirect tax revenues with respect to the output of the non-primary sector were about 1.80 and 1.64, according to equations (9–1) and (9–2), respectively. Over the sample period, direct and indirect tax revenues actually increased 1.84 and 1.66 times as fast as the average growth of the non-primary sector, respectively.

[25] See C. K. Park (1972) and W. S. Kim (1972) for the disaggregated direct and indirect tax equations along with elaborate discussions.

IV. Some Applications

In the trial calculations using the present model, two types of *ex post* tests were tried along with *ex ante* forecasts for the years 1972, 1973, and 1974.

1. Ex Post Test of the Model

Ex post simulation has the advantage of testing the forecasting ability of the model. Since good estimates of the predetermined exogenous variables are available, one can avoid errors in the assumptions for the exogenous variables.

The first type of test provides interpolation from 1971 to 1972. By inserting predetermined variables into the first quarter of 1971, the system was recursively solved with iterations through the fourth quarter of 1972. Exogenous variables were assigned their actual values for the corresponding quarter's solution, but lagged endogeous variables were generated within the model after starting from given initial conditions. GNP imputed from the demand side was equated with total outputs generated from production functions by treating the differences as a category of inventory plus statistical discrepancy. The equation for inventory investment was not used for the simulation because its forecasting power was very poor. The supply of money was treated as an exogenous policy variable. The results of this simulation experiment are given in Table 3.

The second type of test provides extrapolation beyond the terminal sample data, IV–1970, for the years 1971 and 1972. A new set of equations based on sample data, I-1963—IV-1970, was estimated (See Table 7). *Ex post* extrapolations of a model outside the sample data provide better tests than do *ex post* calculations using internal sample data.[26]

The system again recursively solved in the same way as for the first test. Again the exogenous variables were assigned their actual values for each quarter's solution, and the lagged endogenous variables were estimated within the system. The *ex post* extrapolations were in most cases almost as good as the *ex post* interpolations in terms of forecasting ability. The results are shown in Table 4. It should be mentioned that the testing period of years, 1971 and 1972, were a recession period, recording very low real GNP growth rates of 10.5 and 7.8 percent in 1965 constant

[26] L. R. Klein (1964), p. 32.

Table 3. *Actual and Simulated Values of Selected Variables, 1971–1972 (ex post interpolation of internal sample data)*

(billion won at 1965 prices)

		V^{na}			sV^{na}		
		Actual	Computed	Error term (%)	Actual	Computed	Error term (%)
		(A)	(B)	$\frac{(B)-(A)}{(A)}$	(A)	(B)	$\frac{(B)-(A)}{(A)}$
1971	I	257.81	257.69	−1.21	1158.68	1144.67	−1.21
	II	307.70	304.82	−0.94	1205.60	1190.70	−1.24
	III	305.02	304.43	−0.19	1198.76	1196.19	−0.21
	IV	311.74	319.15	+2.38	1167.80	1195.32	+2.36
	Total	1182.27 (12.1)	1183.09 (12.2)	+0.07	1182.71 (12.5)	1181.72 (12.4)	−0.08
1972	I	242.67	274.97	+0.84	1225.80	1235.82	+0.82
	II	325.00	328.51	+1.08	1268.36	1281.99	+1.07
	III	334.39	334.74	+0.11	1314.36	1315.40	+0.08
	IV	363.62	367.93	+0.19	1362.64	1379.31	+1.22
	Total	1295.68 (9.6)	1306.18 (10.5)	+0.81	1292.79 (9.3)	1303.13 (10.2)	+0.80

		E^c			M^c		
		Actual	Computed	Error term(%)	Actual	Computed	Error term (%)
		(A)	(B)	$\frac{(B)-(A)}{(A)}$	(A)	(B)	$\frac{(B)-(A)}{(A)}$
1971	I	56.53	54.42	−3.73	135.21	134.72	−0.36
	II	76.36	74.22	−2.80	175.06	171.62	−1.97
	III	76.54	78.42	+2.45	169.60	165.35	−2.51
	IV	91.06	87.71	−3.68	155.58	158.37	+1.79
	Total	300.49	294.77	−1.90	635.45	630.06	−0.85
1972	I	77.39	78.05	+0.85	135.24	139.56	+3.19
	II	105.05	108.94	+3.70	174.94	175.33	+0.22
	III	122.93	120.80	−1.73	171.71	177.12	+3.15
	IV	139.41	144.46	+3.62	187.45	185.02	−1.30
	Total	444.78	452.25	+1.68	669.34	677.03	+1.15

Table 3. (Continued)

		I^h			I^{meq}		
		Actual (A)	Computed (B)	Error term (%) $\frac{(B)-(A)}{(A)}$	Actual (A)	Computed (B)	Error term (%) $\frac{(B)-(A)}{(A)}$
1971	I	5.58	5.95	+6.63	47.78	44.67	−6.51
	II	12.72	11.90	−6.45	54.40	51.76	−4.85
	III	12.10	11.54	−4.63	57.42	55.74	−2.93
	IV	7.36	7.86	+6.79	44.76	47.55	+6.23
	Total	37.76	37.25	−1.36	204.36	199.72	−2.27
1972	I	4.14	4.49	+8.45	40.36	41.28	+2.28
	II	10.34	10.94	+5.80	48.95	48.76	−0.39
	III	9.87	9.41	−4.66	45.78	48.55	+6.05
	IV	8.00	8.42	+6.89	46.00	49.08	+6.70
	Total	32.35	33.26	+2.81	181.09	187.67	+3.63

		P^w		
		Actual (A)	Computed (B)	Error term (%) $\frac{(B)-(A)}{(A)}$
1971	I	154.40	152.30	−1.36
	II	158.00	155.95	−1.30
	III	162.50	159.47	−1.86
	IV	171.50	169.07	−1.42
1972	I	178.10	175.65	−1.38
	II	184.25	182.03	−1.20
	III	186.56	184.88	−0.90
	IV	186.41	187.34	+0.50

Note: ( ) Annual growth rate of V^{na}, percent.

Table 4. *Actual and Simulated Values of Selected Variables, 1971–1972 (ex post extrapolation outside the sample data)*

(billion won at 1965 prices)

		V^{na}			sV^{na}		
		Actual	Computed	Error term (%)	Actual	Computed	Error term (%)
		(A)	*(B)*	$\frac{(B)-(A)}{(A)}$	*(A)*	*(B)*	$\frac{(B)-(A)}{(A)}$
1971	I	257.81	258.00	+0.07	1158.68	1159.55	+0.08
	II	307.70	308.10	+0.13	1205.60	1203.52	−0.17
	III	305.02	306.41	+0.46	1198.76	1203.97	+0.43
	IV	311.74	315.37	+1.16	1167.80	1200.27	+2.78
	Total	1182.27 (12·1)	1187.88 (12.7)	+0.47	1182.71 (12.5)	1191.83 (13.3)	+0.77
1972	I	272.67	276.06	+1.24	1225.80	1240.72	+1.22
	II	325.00	329.35	+1.34	1268.36	1285.27	+1.33
	III	334.39	338.05	+1.09	1314.36	1328.29	+1.06
	IV	363.39	367.67	+1.18	1362.64	1378.33	+1.15
	Total	1295.68 (9.6)	1311.13 (10.9)	+1.19	1292.79 (9.3)	1308.15 (10.6)	+1.19

		E^c			M^c		
		Actual	Computed	Error term (%)	Actual	Computed	Error term (%)
		(A)	*(B)*	$\frac{(B)-(A)}{(A)}$	*(A)*	*(B)*	$\frac{(B)-(A)}{(A)}$
1971	I	56.53	57.95	+2.51	135.21	131.35	−2.85
	II	76.36	78.46	+2.75	175.06	169.67	−3.08
	III	76.54	79.80	+4.26	169.60	157.30	−7.25
	IV	91.06	91.90	+0.92	155.58	157.29	+1.10
	Total	300.49	308.11	+2.54	635.45	615.61	−3.12
1972	I	77.39	79.20	+2.34	135.24	139.43	+3.10
	II	105.05	108.24	+3.04	174.94	173.11	−1.05
	III	122.93	128.48	+4.51	171.71	174.38	+1.55
	IV	139.41	143.85	+3.18	187.45	181.11	−3.38
	Total	444.78	459.77	+3.37	669.34	668.03	−0.20

Table 4. (Continued)

		I^h			I^{meq}		
		Actual	Computed	Error term (%)	Actual	Computed	Error term (%)
		(A)	*(B)*	$\frac{(B)-(A)}{(A)}$	*(A)*	*(B)*	$\frac{(B)-(A)}{(A)}$
1971	I	5.58	5.92	+6.09	47.78	44.68	−6.49
	II	12.72	12.15	−4.48	54.40	53.76	−1.18
	III	12.10	11.81	−2.40	57.42	59.86	+4.25
	IV	7.36	8.13	+10.46	44.76	50.07	+11.86
	Total	37.76	38.01	+0.66	204.36	208.37	+1.96
1972	I	4.14	4.39	+6.04	40.36	41.63	+3.15
	II	10.34	10.83	+4.74	48.95	48.03	−1.88
	III	9.87	9.69	−1.82	45.78	48.87	+6.75
	IV	8.00	8.83	+10.38	46.00	47.31	+2.85
	Total	32.35	33.74	+4.30	181.09	185.84	+2.62

		P^w		
		Actual	Computed	Error term (%)
		(A)	*(B)*	$\frac{(B)-(A)}{(A)}$
1971	I	154.40	153.10	−0.84
	I	158.00	156.34	−1.05
	III	162.50	160.59	−1.18
	IV	171.50	169.26	−1.31
1972	I	178.10	176.30	−1.01
	II	184.25	182.42	−0.99
	III	186.56	185.19	−0.73
	IV	186.41	187.82	+0.76

Note: ( ) Annual growth rate of V^{na}, percent.

Figure 1. Actual and Simulated Annual Growth Rates of GNP, 1971–1972 (ex post interpolation of internal sample data)

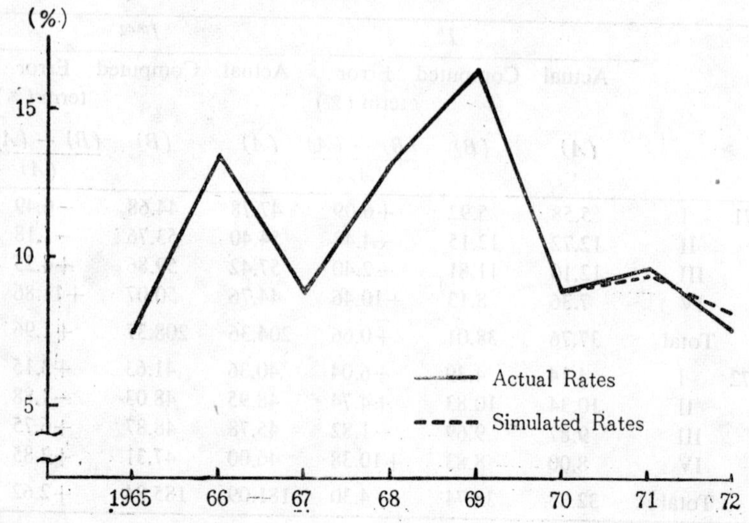

Figure 2. Actual and Simulated Annual Growth Rates of GNP, 1971–1972 (ex post extrapolation of outside sample data)

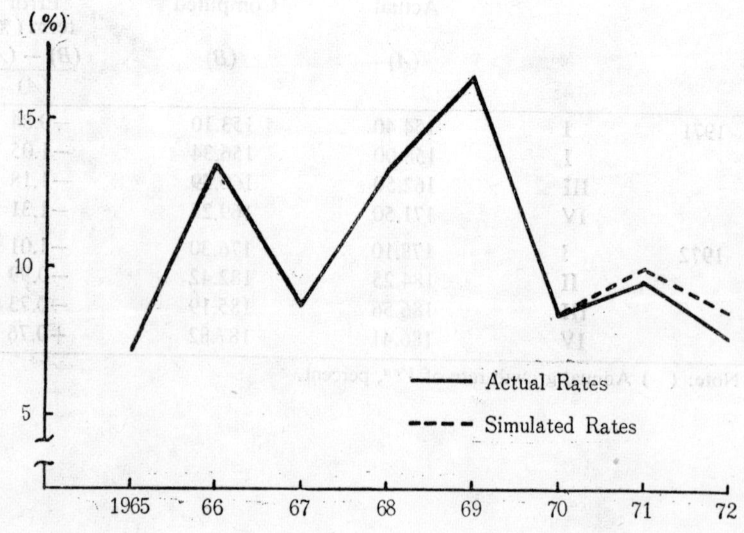

price.[27]

The estimates of V^{na} were very close to, although slightly larger than, the actuals. The annual increasing rates of GNP were also calculated and compared with actuals in Figures 1 and 2. The forecasts hit the turning point (trough) quite well. Although the quarterly estimates of trade volumes were not as close to the actuals as the estimates of the V^{na} were, the annual sum of the quarterly forecasts of trade volumes was fairly close to the actuals. The wholesale price indexes were slightly underestimated throughout the testing period. The main reason would be overestimations of V^{na} in the solution of the model.

As expected, investments were most poorly estimated. Except for the equation for machinery and equipment, the other investment equations were rather poor in terms of specification and statistical validity.

2. Ex Ante Forecasts

For the predictions of the years 1972 and 1973, the model was extrapolated beyond the terminal sample data, IV-1971. These predictions were completed in March 1972 and presented to the Economic Planning Board as a guide in revising and formulating the Overall Resources Budget (Korean annual plan) of 1972 and 1973.[28] According to the model forecasts, the annual rate of GNP growth in 1972 was expected to be down to about eight percent,[29] the lowest growth rate since 1966. In 1973, however, the economy was predicted to recover from the expected trough of 1972, achieving an annual growth rate of about nine percent.[30]

The latest forecasts for 1973 and 1974 were 15.6 and 12.7 percent, respectively. The primary reasons for a high rate of economic growth in 1973 are a rapid increase in export demand, a high rate of increase in industrial investment, and active housing construction. Assuming a lower increasing rate of exports in 1974 than in 1973, the GNP growth rate of 1974 was forecasted to be about three percent lower than that of 1973. Table 5 shows the results of forecasts for 1973 and 1974 in terms of a semi-annual base. The predetermined exogenous variables used in the forecasts for 1973 and 1974 are shown in Table 6.

---

[27] The average real GNP growth rate during the last seven years was 11.1 percent according to real GNP measures in 1965 constant price.

[28] Korea Development Institute, *Growth Strategy for Overall Resources Budget Plan,* Seoul, March 1972.

[29] The actual growth rate of GNP for 1972 is 7.8 percent according to real GNP measures in 1965 constant won (= 7.0 percent in 1970 constant won).

[30] H. Song (1972), pp. 38–39.

Table 5. *Macro-Variables, Actuals and Forecasts(in billion won, at 1970 constant prices)*

	1972		1973						1974					
	Annual		First-half year		Second-half year		Annual		First-half year		Second-half year		Annual	
	Amount	Increase rate(%)	Amount	Increase rate(%)	Amount	Increase rate(%)	Amount	Increase rate(%)	Amount	Increase rate(%)	Amount	Increase rate(%)	Amount	Increase rate(%)
I. Gross National Product	3023.6	7.0	1444.7	19.3	2050.6	13.2	3495.3	15.6	1674.0	15.9	2268.7	10.6	3942.7	12.8
1. Agriculture	760.9	1.7	179.2	5.5	632.5	7.0	811.7	6.7	190.5	6.3	657.7	4.0	848.2	4.5
2. Non-Primary	2262.7	8.9	1265.5	21.5	1418.1	16.1	2683.6	18.6	1483.5	17.2	1611.0	13.6	3094.5	15.3
II. Expenditure on GNP														
1. Consumption Expenditure	2551.6	6.7	1351.0	11.2	1478.4	10.6	2829.4	10.9	1501.0	11.1	1648.1	11.5	3149.1	11.3
2. Gross Domestic Fixed Capital Formation	659.1	−3.2	399.7	33.5	476.2	32.4	875.9	32.9	498.8	24.8	589.7	23.8	1088.5	24.3
3. Imports	859.7	5.1	560.8	41.0	694.9	50.4	1255.7	46.1	739.8	31.9	894.7	28.8	1634.5	30.2
Commodities (millions of U.S. dollars)*	2429.0	3.6	1614.1	44.4	2015.9	53.9	3630.0	49.4	2145.2	32.9	2617.4	29.8	4762.6	31.2
4. Exports	691.6	37.8	496.3	70.3	585.2	46.2	1081.5	56.4	645.7	30.1	783.7	33.9	1429.4	32.2
Commodities (millions of U.S. dollars)*	1729.2	46.9	1253.5	76.7	1534.0	50.4	2787.5	61.2	1667.4	33.0	2098.5	36.8	3765.9	35.1
5. Increase in Stocks, and Statistical Discrepancy	−19.0		−241.5		205.7		−35.8		−231.7		141.9		−89.8	
III. Balance of Payments Deficit (millions of U.S. dollars)*	541.0	−46.9	207.6	−39.3	353.1	77.5	560.7	3.6	302.8	45.9	357.4	1.2	660.2	17.7
IV. Per Capita GNP	303	10.2					345	13.9					384	11.3
(U.S. dollars)*	(303)	10.2					(363)	19.8					(432)	19.0

Notes: * In 1972 constant U.S. dollars
( ) In current U.S. dollars

Table 6. *Predetermined Exogenous Variables Used in the Forecasts, 1973–1974*

Units		V^a	FL	C^g	I^g
		billions of 1965 won	billions of 1965 won	billions of 1965 won	billions of 1965 won
1973	I	30.07	71.97	31.03	8.41
	II	60.68	78.67	37.55	18.89
	III	46.89	81.25	41.73	20.45
	IV	277.27	75.47	48.74	22.84
1974	I	32.95	67.54	34.93	9.68
	II	65.44	73.18	40.51	21.81
	III	51.00	81.16	44.40	22.02
	IV	284.20	76.52	51.86	26.29

Units		E^s	M^s	M^g	V^{ujr}
		billions of 1965 won	billions of 1965 won	billions of 1965 won	1970 = 100
1973	I	47.40	41.50	22.06	117.40
	II	69.80	47.65	29.49	119.16
	III	69.30	53.89	29.47	120.33
	IV	66.93	57.96	35.22	121.90
1074	I	57.15	50.79	27.00	122.55
	II	93.26	77.53	36.10	125.67
	III	98.70	77.45	36.07	128.52
	IV	93.11	80.64	43.11	132.06

Units		P^{fm}	P^{fm}	P^{fx}	ER^b
		1970 = 100	1972 = 100	1970 = 100	won/dollar
1973	I	112.91	111.80	124.79	436.45
	II	117.91	118.30	132.05	436.45
	III	119.59	125.20	139.75	436.45
	IV	121.16	127.40	142.20	436.45
1974	I	123.58	131.20	145.04	436.45
	II	126.00	135.20	147.89	436.45
	III	128.43	139.20	150.73	436.45
	IV	130.86	140.10	153.58	436.45

Table 6. (Continued)

Units		ER^s	P^r	P^u	t
		won/dollar	1970 = 100	1970 = 100	
1973	I	419.50	167.01	129.35	53
	II	427.81	168.05	129.35	54
	III	427.81	168.55	129.35	55
	IV	427.81	176.45	129.35	56
1974	I	427.81	176.45	129.35	57
	II	427.81	177.45	129.35	58
	III	427.81	178.45	129.35	59
	IV	427.81	185.50	129.35	60

V. Concluding Remarks

The present paper is a progress report and will be only one contribution to a series of Korean macro-models. The ancestors of this model have been used to make a number of annual forecasts, providing helpful tools in formulating the national economic plans. Since it was our first experience in building a quarterly model of the Korean economy, it will set the stage for more work and further improvements in the future.

The limitation of our quarterly data is one of the most serious problems in developing short-term forecasting models. Disaggregated production functions for manufacturing, social overhead and service industries, can be estimated when quarterly data on capital stock are available. Inventory might have to be subdivided into agricultural and non-agricultural groups, and imported raw materials and other imports. Consumption expenditures might also be needed to disaggregate into durable, non-durable, and service consumption expenditures.

Investment equations are especially unsatisfactory and we need to develop better ways to estimate those equations. Prediction of the inflow of long-term foreign loans is also very difficult, yet it is a very significant determinant of fixed capital formation over the sample period. The inflow of long-term foreign loans was dependent largely upon government policy decisions and international economic and political conditions. However, it should eventually be treated as an endogenous variable because inflow of foreign loans is determined by investment demand and availability of domestic resources.

It would be desirable to introduce the supply of money function, since

Table 7. Estimated Structural Equations (Based on Sample Data up to 1970 4/4)

(1–1) $\ln\left(\frac{V^{na}}{L^{na}}\right) = -0.8165 + 0.5204 \ln\left(\frac{K^{na}_{-1}}{L^{na}}\right) + 0.1596 \ln wMS$
$\qquad (-0.92) \quad (3.94) \quad (2.52)$

$+ 0.0211\, t + 0.1903\, D2 + 0.1284\, D3 + 0.1529\, D4$
$\qquad (3.10) \quad (10.51) \quad (9.44) \quad (10.50)$

$R_2 = 0.9877 \qquad DW = 2.1793$
Sample period = 1964 1/4 — 1970 4/4

(2–1) $L^{na} = 2.7587 + 0.00945\, sVNA_{-2} - 0.2360\, D1 - 0.6106\, D2 - 0.2452\, D3$
$\qquad (13.43) \quad (8.57) \quad (-3.56) \quad (-8.48) \quad (-3.88)$

$R^2 = 0.9496 \qquad DW = 1.8863$
Sample period = 1964 1/4 — 1970 4/4

(3–1) $C^p = 9.0129 + 0.1546\, V^d_{-2} + 0.1586\, V^d_{-3} + 0.3221\, V^d_{-4} + 0.2257\, V^d_{-5}$
$\qquad (1.22) \quad (9.97) \quad (10.48) \quad (21.79) \quad (13.35)$

$R^2 = 0.9713 \qquad DW = 1.8567$
Sample period = 1964 1/4 — 1970 4/4

(4–1) $I^h = 145.548 - 0.1291\, ST^h_{-2} + 0.1581\, wVNAX_{-2} - 3.5944\, D1$
$\qquad (1.81) \quad (-1.85) \quad (2.83) \quad (-6.34)$

$R^2 = 0.8716 \qquad DW = 1.9111$
Sample period = 1964 1/4 — 1970 4/4

(4–2) $I^{meq} = 6.3038 + 0.4754\, FL + 0.5713\, wVNCF_{-1} - 3.3894\, D1$
$\qquad (4.25) \quad (5.16) \quad (4.00) \quad (-2.58)$

$R^2 = 0.9545 \qquad DW = 2.0476$
Sample period = 1962 1/4 — 1970 4/4

(4–3) $I^{nho} = 6.7421 + 0.4461\, wVNACA_{-2} + 0.2202\, FL - 5.7685\, D1$
$\qquad (4.40) \quad (2.71) \quad (2.36) \quad (-4.43)$

$R^2 = 0.8928 \qquad DW = 1.9234$
Sample period = 1963 1/4 — 1970 4/4

(5–1) $M^{meq} = 72.4433 + 0.2018\, wVNAY_{-2} - 0.2337\, (ER^s + TR) \times \frac{P^{fx}}{P^w}$
$\qquad (2.96) \quad (6.11) \quad (-4.02)$

$R^2 = 0.9459 \qquad DW = 1.8620$
Sample period = 1964 1/4 — 1970 4/4

(5–2) $M^i = -9.5840 + 0.3636\, VNA - 0.0309\, (ER^s + TR) \times \frac{P^{fx}}{P^w}$
$\qquad (-1.09) \quad (20.41) \quad (-1.25)$

$R^2 = 0.9454 \qquad DW = 1.8928$
Sample period = 1963 1/4 — 1970 4/4

Table 7. (Continued)

$$(6\text{–}1)\ \ln\left(\frac{X^c}{Pfw}\right) = \underset{(-13.66)}{36.3683} + \underset{(57.64)}{4.5734} \ln V^{ujr}$$

$$+ \underset{(7.88)}{3.4462} \ln (ER^b + S^b) \times \frac{Pfw}{P^w} - \underset{(-6.99)}{0.2444}\, D1 - \underset{(-2.69)}{0.0895}\, D3$$

$R^2 = 0.9914$ $DW = 2.0140$
Sample period = 1965 1/4 — 1970 4/4

$$(7\text{–}1)\ \ln MSN = \underset{(-1.82)}{-0.5567} + \underset{(16.29)}{0.3358} \ln NV + \underset{(14.02)}{0.2820} \ln NV_{-1}$$

$$+ \underset{(12.14)}{0.2440} \ln NV_{-2} + \underset{(14.44)}{0.2964} \ln NV_{-3} - \underset{(-3.41)}{0.1821} \ln R$$

$$- \underset{(-5.13)}{0.2541} \ln MWP_{-2}$$

$R^2 = 0.9963$ $DW = 2.001$
Sample period = 1963 1/4 — 1970 4/4

$$(8\text{–}1)\ P' = \underset{(-1.89)}{-0.704} - \underset{(-2.14)}{0.165}\, wsV^{na} + \underset{(5.80)}{0.232}\, wMSN' + \underset{(8.25)}{0.363}\, wER^{s'}$$

$$+ \underset{(12.10)}{0.121}\, P^{r'} + \underset{(8.70)}{0.200}\, P^{u'}.$$

$R^2 = 0.935$ $DW = 1.69$
Sample period = 1965 1/4 — 1970 4/4

the role of monetary policy is very important in economic fluctuations, growth, and stabilization. Exogenous treatment of the government sector (government consumption, investments and loans, and tax revenues), is not desirable. It will be sensible to distinguish between induced government expenditures and autonomous categories. Then some equations can also be developed for the induced part of the expenditures.

All these improvements require substantial research work, but they are all feasible and can be added to the basic system presented here.

REFERENCES

1. Ackley, Gardner, *Macroeconomic Theory*, New York: Macmillan Company, 1961.
2. Adelman, Irma and Mahn Je, Kim, "Econometric Model of the Korean Economy," in Irma Adelman (ed.), *A Practical Approach to Development Planning*, Baltimore: Johns Hopkins

University Press, 1969.
3. Almon, Shirley, "The Distributed Lag Between Capital Appropriations and Expenditures," in Arnold Zellner (ed.), *Reading in Economic Statistics and Econometrics*, Boston: Little, Brown and Company, 1968, pp. 559–570.
4. Bailey, Martin J., *National Income and the Price Level*, New York: McGraw-Hill Book Company, Inc., 1962.
5. The Bank of Korea, "Quarterly Econometric Model of the Korean Economy," *Monthly Report of Economic Research*, August 1972, pp. 37–68.
6. Brown, T.M., "A Forecast Determination of National Product, Employment, and Price Level in Canada, from an Econometric Model," in *Models of Income and Wealth*, Vol. 28, National Bureau of Economic Research, Princeton: Princeton University Press, 1964, pp. 23–24.
7. Chow, Gregory C., "On the Long-Run and Short-Run Demand for Money," *Journal of Political Economy*, April 1966, pp. 111–131.
8. Christenson, L.R. and D.W. Jorgenson, "U.S. Real Product and Real Factor Input, 1929–1967," *Review of Income and Wealth*, March 1970, pp. 19–50.
9. Dickson, Harold D. and Dennis R. Starleaf, "Polynomial Distributed Lag Structures in the Demand Function for Money," *Journal of Finance*, December 1972, pp. 1035–1043.
10. Eisner, Robert, "Investment Plans and Realizations," *American Economic Review*, May 1962, pp. 190–203.
11. Evans, Michael K. and Lawrence R. Klein, *The Wharton Econometric Forecasting Model*, Philadelphia: University of Pennsylvania, 1968.
12. Harberger, Arnold C., "The Dynamics of Inflation in Chile," in Carl Christ, *et al., Measurement in Economics: Studies in Mathematical Economics and Econometrics*, in Memory of Yehuda Grunfeld, Stanford: Stanford University Press, 1963, pp. 219–250.
13. Ichimura, S., L.R. Klein, S. Koizumi, K. Sato, and Y. Shinkai, *An Econometric Analysis of Postwar Japanese Economy: Chapter II. Outline of the Osaka Model*, Discussion Paper No. 6, The Center for Southeast Asia Studies, Kyoto, Japan: Kyoto University, 1967.
14. Jorgenson, Dale W., "Econometric Studies of Investment Behavior: A Survey," *Journal of Economic Literature*, Vol. IX, No.3 (De-

cember 1971), pp. 1111–1147.

15. Jorgenson, Dale W. Jerald, Hunter, and M. Ishang Nadiri, "A Comparison of Alternative Economic Models of Quarterly Investment Behavior," *Econometrica*, Vol. 38, March 1970.
16. Kim, Mahn Je and Duck Woo Nam, *A Statistical Model for Monetary Management: The Case of Korea, 1956–67,* A Paper Presented to the Third Far Eastern Meeting of the Econometric Society, June 27–29, 1968.
17. _______, and S.Y. Lee, *A Macro-Econometric Model of the Korean Economy*, Economic Research Series No. 8, Seoul: Sogang College, 1969.
18. Kim, Mahn Je, Heeyhon Song, and Kwang Suk Kim, *Revised Note on Monetary Forecasts for 1973*, Working Paper 7301, Seoul: Korea Development Institute, January 1973.
19. Kim, Wan Soon, *A Simple Projection Model of Indirect Tax Revenue*, Working Paper 7205, Seoul: Korea Development Institute, June 1972.
20. Klein, Lawrence R., "Postwar Quarterly Model: Description and Applications," *in Models of Income Determination*, Studies in Income and Wealth, Vol. 28, National Bureau of Economic Research, Princeton: Princeton University Press, 1964, pp. 23–24.
21. _______, "What Kind of Macroeconometric Model for Developing Economies?," in Arnold Zellner (ed.), *Reading in Economic Statistics and Econometrics*, Boston: Little, Brown and Company, 1968, pp. 559–570.
22. Korea Development Institute, Growth Strategy for *Overall Resources Budget Plan*, Seoul, March 1972.
23. _______, *1973 and 1974 Projection for the Korean Economy*, Seoul, September 1973.
24. Levhari, D. and D. Patinkin, "The Role of Money in a Simple Growth Model," *American Economic Review*, Sept. 1968, pp. 713–754.
25. Liu, Fu-Chi, *The Demand for Money*, Economic Paper, Series No. 7, Taipei: The Institute of Economics, Academia Sinica, June 1970.
26. Lybeck, Johan A., "A Note on the Short-Run Demand for Money in Sweden," *Swedish Journal of Economics*, December 1972, pp. 459–467.
27. Nadiri, M. I., "Some Approaches to the Theory and Measurement of Total Factor Productivity: A Survey," *Journal of Economic Literature*, 8 (December 1970), pp. 1137–1178.

28. Nadiri, M. I., "The Determinants of Real Cash Balances in the U.S. Total Manufacturing Sector," *Quarterly Journal of Economics*, 83 (May 1969), pp. 173–196.
29. Nerlove, Marc, "A Quarterly Econometric Model for the United Kingdom: A Review Article," *American Economic Review*, March 1962, pp. 54–174.
30. Norton, D. Roger, *An Econometric Model of Korea 1956–67*, (Mimeographed), 1969.
31. Park, Chong Kee, *A Forecasting Model for Revenue Estimations of Direct Taxes*, Working Paper 7210, Seoul: Korea Development Institute, June 1972.
32. Robinson, Sherman, *Polynomial Approximation of Distributed Lag Structures*, Discussion Paper No. 1, Department of Economics, London School of Economics, June 1970.
33. Shapiro, A. A., "Inflation, Lags, and the Demand for Money," *International Economic Review*, February 1973, pp. 81–96.
34. Simon, Julian L. and Dennis J. Aigner, "Cross-Section and Time-Series Tests of the Permanent-Income Hypothesis," *American Economic Review*, Vol. IX, No. 3 (June 1970), pp. 341–351.
35. Sinai, Allen and Houston H. Stokes, "Real Money Balances: An Omitted Variable from the Production Function?" *Review of Economics and Statistics*, August 1972 pp. 290–296.
36. Song, Heeyhon, *An Econometric Forecasting Model of the Korean Economy*," Working Paper 7212, Seoul: Korea Development Institute, June 1972.
37. Suits, Daniel B., "Forecasting and Analysis with an Econometric Model," *American Economic Review*, March 1962, pp. 104–132.
38. Tatemoto, Masahiro, Tadao Uchida, and Tsunehike Watanabe, "A Stabilization Model for the Postwar-Japanese Economy: 1954–62," *International Economic Review*, February 1967, pp. 13–44.
39. Tobin, James, "Money and Economic Growth," *Econometrica*, Vol. 33, No. 4 (October 1965), pp. 671–684.
40. Wallis, Kenneth F., "Some Recent Developments in Applied Econometrics," *Journal of Economic Literature*, Vol. VII, No. 4 (September 1969), pp. 771–796.
41. Zellner, Arnold, "The Short-Run Consumption Function," *Econometrica*, Vol. 25, 1965, pp. 552–67.
42. ________, D. A. Huang, and L. C. Chau, "Further Analysis of the Short-Run Consumption Function with Emphasis on the Role of Liquid Assets," *Econometrica*, Vol. 33, 1965, pp. 571–581.

A 53-SECTOR INTERINDUSTRY PROJECTION MODEL, 1974 — 1981

*Yoon Hyung Kim**

I. Introduction

In the preparation of Korea's Fourth Five-Year Plan a 53-sector interindustry model has been constructed to analyze long-run structural changes in the Korean economy. In particular, the model examines the effects on sectoral output, employment, investment and import requirements resulting from assumed structural changes in consumption and export patterns as well as in import substitution.

The model may be regarded as a "requirements analysis". Given targets on consumption and exports derived from the macro-model, the following questions are to be studied in this paper within the consistent accounting framework of the 1970 input-output table compiled by the Bank of Korea in 1973:

1) how much should be produced in each sector in each year of the plan (1977–1981), with the emphasis on heavy and chemical industries?
2) how much should be invested to increase the capital stock in each sector in each year, with the emphasis on heavy and chemical industries?

The simulation will be run with a variety of exogenous projections of consumption, import substitution and exports with close attention being paid to the sectoral investment levels over time implied by different plans.

---

* Senior Fellow at the Korea Development Institute. This paper was originally published in July 1975 as KDI Working Paper No. 7505.

These sectoral investment levels are then compared to planned investment and efforts are made to shift the sectoral composition of investment.

The next section is devoted to the mathematical formulation of a 53-sector interindustry model. In the third section, we give a detailed discussion of the solution technique we use. The fourth section explains the development of the data. In the final section of the paper, the numerical results are presented.

II. The Model

The purpose of constructing an intersectoral consistency model is to project sectoral output and hence, investment and import requirements consistent with the macroeconomic variables.

The main idea underlying the model is the one that is often used in the open, dynamic Leontief approach namely the linking of gross outputs to final demands via the input-output table. Consumption and export demands are projected outside the model and introduced exogenously. Import substitution becomes a policy variable to relax the balance-of-payments constraint when the latter becomes binding. This determines the import substitution targets. The rest of the final demands are related in some simple ways to gross outputs. Thus, sectoral output requirements consistent with export and import substitution targets can be found by solving the difference equation for outputs.

Briefly, the model is triggered by the exogenous estimates of final demand for consumption (private and government) and exports. In this model, gross output and investment are simultaneously determined. Import and employment requirements have been endogenously estimated through import coefficient matrices and labor coefficients, respectively.

The 1973 interindustry flow table has not yet been prepared. Therefore, a 53-sector interindustry model has been built around the Bank of Korea's 1970 input-output table, which splits imports into the two categories, "competitive" and "noncompetitive", by a detailed I-O breakdown. Accordingly, final demand projections have been made at 1970 prices. The resulting sectoral output, investment and import requirements are then converted to 1974 prices by using the proper sectoral price deflators. We have also reduced energy input coefficients for all sectors by a uniform rate of 10 percent, on the basis of the nation-wide 10 percent energy saving campaign.

The fundamental balance equations in the I-O accounting framework are as follows (for each sector i in each time period t):

$$(1)\ X_i(t) = \Sigma_j X_{ij}^d(t) + C_i^d(t) + G_i^d(t) + V_i^d(t) + H_i^d(t) + E_i(t) + S_i(t),$$

$$(2)\ M_i^c(t) = \Sigma_j X_{ij}^c(t) + C_i^c(t) + G_i^c(t) + V_i^c(t) + H_i^c(t) - S_i(t),$$

$$(3)\ M_i^n(t) = \Sigma_j X_{ij}^n(t) + C_i^n(t) + G_i^n(t) + V_i^n(t) + H_i^n(t),$$

where X_i is the gross output level from sector i,
M_i is imports into sector i,
X_{ij} is intermediate sales from sector i to sector j,
C_i is the private consumption demand for products of sector i,
G_i is government expenditures for products of sector i,
V_i is investment demand for sector i products induced by output increases,
H_i is inventory accumulation demand for sector i,
E_i is exports from sector i,
S_i is import substitution of commodity i.

Here the superscripts d, c and n on M_i, X_{ij}, C_i, V_i and H_i denote domestic deliveries, "competitive" and "noncompetitive" imports, respectively. Note that the volume indices of quantities and sales are in 1970 base year prices. The underlying assumptions of our demand-supply equality (1) are that there are no joint products and that output is not thrown away.

The essential part of our consistency planning model is first to project intermediate and final demands in the balance equations (1)–(3) over the planning period 1971–1981; given 1970 base year output levels, next, sectoral outputs for the planning years are computed from the demand-supply equality (1); finally, import requirements are calculated from the balance equations (2) and (3). For each component of demands, we must either specify its relationships to outputs or project it exogenously.

1. Intermediate Demand

Total intermediate inputs in each sector are the sum of domestic goods, competitive imports, and noncompetitive imports:

$$(4)\ X_{ij}(t) = X_{ij}^d(t) + X_{ij}^c(t) + X_{ij}^n(t).$$

We shall adopt the usual hypothesis of fixed production coefficients for intermediate deliveries. Thus,

(5) $X_{ij}(t) = a_{ij}(t)\, X_j(t)$,

(6) $X^c_{ij}(t) = a^c_{ij}(t)\, X_j(t)$,

(7) $X^n_{ij}(t) = a^n_{ij}(t)\, X_j(t)$,

where the input-output coefficients, a_{ij}, represent current account interindustry demands on item i per unit output of process j.

The a_{ij}'s, a^c_{ij}'s, and a^n_{ij}'s are derived from a 1970 base year input-output table but take into account predictable technical changes in the input of heavy and chemical industries and import substitution targets over the planning period 1971–1981.

Domestic coefficients for intermediate inputs are obtained as a residual after subtracting import coefficients from the total:

$$\begin{aligned}(8)\ X^d_{ij}(t) &= X_{ij}(t) - X^c_{ij}(t) - X^n_{ij}(t) && \text{(from (4))}\\ &= [a_{ij}(t) - a^c_{ij}(t) - a^n_{ij}(t)]\, X_j(t) && \text{(from (5)–(6))}\\ &= a^d_{ij}(t)\, X_j(t).\end{aligned}$$

2. Private Consumption Demand

Aggregate private consumption growth targets are set up as goals of the Fourth Five-Year Plan by the Economic Planning Board (EPB). Sectoral consumption levels are obtained by assuming a constant expenditure elasticity for each good during the planning period:

$$(9)\ C_i(t) = \eta_i\, \bar{c}(t)^{\varepsilon i},$$

Where C_i is household consumption expenditures of the ith commodity,
η_i is a constant,
ε_i is Engel elasticity,
$\bar{c}$ is aggregate consumption expenditures.

Engel elasticities ε_i's are estimated from log-linear regressions. Since the $C_i(t)$ resulting from (9) usually will not add up to $\bar{c}(t)$, the consumption function is linearized around the base year (1970) consumption pattern:

$$(10)\ C_i(t) = (1 - \varepsilon_i^*)\, \bar{c}_i(1970) + \varepsilon_i^* \left[\frac{\bar{C}_i(1970)}{\bar{c}(1970)}\right] c(t),$$

where $\varepsilon_i^* = \rho\varepsilon_i$ is such that $\sum_i \varepsilon_i^*\, \bar{C}_i\,(1970) = \bar{c}(1970)$.

Private consumption expenditures in each sector consist of the three components, domestic goods, competitive imports and noncompetitive imports:

$$(11)\ C_i(t) = C_i^d(t) + C_i^c(t) + C_i^n(t).$$

Given exogenous projections of sectoral consumption levels and import coefficients, imported consumption expenditures by commodity are computed as follows:

$$(12)\ C_i^c(t) = \alpha_i^c\, C_i(t),$$

$$(13)\ C_i^n(t) = \alpha_i^n\, C_i(t),$$

where α_i's are taken from a 1970 base year I-O table.

Finally, $C_i^d(t)$ is obtained as a residual after subtracting imported consumption demand from the total:

$$\begin{aligned}(14)\ C_i^d(t) &= [1 - \alpha_i^c - \alpha_i^n]\, C_i(t) \\ &= \alpha_i^d\, C_i(t).\end{aligned}$$

3. *Government Consumption Demand*

Projections of government consumption demands are based on a target level of aggregate government consumption set by the EPB. Sectoral consumption levels are obtained by assuming fixed proportions of aggregate consumption:

$$(15)\ G_i(t) = \omega_i \bar{g}(t),$$

where ω_i's are derived from a 1970 base year table,
$\bar{g}$ is aggregate government consumption expenditure.

Sectoral consumption expenditures are composed of domestic goods, competitive imports, and noncompetitive imports:

$$(16)\ G_i(t) = G_i^d(t) + G_i^c(t) + G_i^n(t),$$

whence, using estimated import coefficients, we derive

$$(17)\ G_i^c(t) = \beta_i^c\, G_i(t),$$

$$(18)\ G_i^n(t) = \beta_i^n\, G_i(t),$$

$$\begin{aligned}(19)\ G_i^d(t) &= [1 - \beta_i^c - \beta_i^n]\, G_i(t) \\ &= \beta_i^d\, G_i(t),\end{aligned}$$

where β_i's are derived from a 1970 base year table.

4. Induced Fixed Investment Demand

Total fixed investment goods in each sector are the sum of domestic goods, competitive imports, and noncompetitive imports:

$$(20)\ V_i(t) = V_i^d(t) + V_i^c(t) + V_i^n(t),$$

whence, using estimated import coefficients for fixed investment demand, we obtain

$$(21)\ V_i^c(t) = \gamma_i^c V_i(t),$$

$$(22)\ V_i^n(t) = \gamma_i^n V_i(t),$$

$$(23)\ V_i^d(t) = [1 - \gamma_i^c - \gamma_i^n]\, V_i(t) = \gamma_i^d V_i(t).$$

The γ_i's are taken from a 1970 base year input-output table.

Finally, to forecast sectoral fixed investment demand, $V_i(t)$, over the planning period, we shall adopt the commonly used assumption that in each year, the induced fixed investment demand is generated through an accelerator relationship, *i.e.*, through multiplying capital coefficients by future output increases:

$$(24)\ V_i(t) = \Sigma_j b_{ij} [X_j(t + q_j) - X_j(t + q_j - 1)],$$

where b_{ij} is fixed capital account demands on item i per unit increase in output of process j,
q_j is a gestation lag in investment demand of sector j.

This relationship is designed to explore some specific effects of time lags between investment and output. In a growing economy, a shortened lag has an equivalent effect to a reduction in the capital-output ratio.

For each of the 53 sectors, a gestation lag of 1–3 years has been assumed over the planning period.

Finally, substituting $V_i(t)$ from (24) into (23), we derive the structural relationship between V_i^d and X_i's as follows:

$$(25)\ V_i^d(t) = \Sigma_j b_{ij} [1 - \gamma_i^c - \gamma_i^n][X_j(t + q_j) - X_j(t + q_j - 1)] = \Sigma_j b_{ij}\, \gamma_i^d [X_j(t + q_j) - X_j(t + q_j - 1)].$$

5. *Induced Inventory Investment Demand*

Just as in fixed investment demand, induced inventory investment demand is generated through multiplying inventory coefficients by output increases. Thus,

$$(26)\ H_i(t) = H_i^d(t) + H_i^c(t) + H_i^n(t) = \sum_j s_{ij}[X_j(t+1) - X_j(t)],$$

where s_{ij} is the amount of item i required as inventory in period t-1 to produce one unit of item j in period t.

Using estimated import coefficients for inventory accumulation demand, we derive H_i^d as a function of X_j's:

$$(27)\ H_i^d(t) = \sum_j s_{ij}[1 - \delta_i^c - \delta_i^n][X_j(t+1) - X_j(t)],$$
$$= \sum_j s_{ij}\, \delta_i^d[X_j(t+1) - X_j(t)],$$

where δ_i's are obtained from a 1970 base year table.

6. *Export Demand*

Export demand is given exogenously and we will use two sets of demand figures—high and low export totals—made up on the basis of the plan guideline and KDI's export demand studies. The composition of export demand is obtained partly by KDI's export demand studies and partly by studying the trend during the years 1970–1974.

Thus, estimates of different commodities and services are determined outside the model structure, and

$$(28)\ E_i(t) = \bar{E}_i(t).$$

Exports are an important part of the model and it is important to experiment with high and low export demands assuming an unchanged composition. By comparing the two solutions, the choice between export promotion and import substitution can be made within the model solution.

7. *Import Substitution*

Import substitution is treated like final demand and is reflected in changes to the various import coefficients in the model. The import coefficients are reduced suitably in cases of import substitution, the extent of reduction being judged by the feasibility of increased domestic production in the individual sector, including the investment goods sector, on the basis of information provided in the long-term sectoral investment plan (1973–81) developed by the EPB. Reductions in import coefficients have been matched by appropriate increases in the demand for domestic inputs.

It would be very difficult to specify changes in individual import coefficients. At this stage, we confine import substitution only to competitive imports and define the target rate of import substitution in sector i to be f_i such that

$$(29)\ S_i(t) = f_i[\Sigma_j X_{ij}^c(t) + C_i^c(t) + G_i^c(t) + V_i^c(t) + H_i^c(t)],$$
$$= \Sigma_j f_i \cdot a_{ij}^c(t) \cdot X_j(t) + f_i \cdot \alpha_i^c \cdot C_i(t)$$
$$+ f_i \cdot \beta_i^c \cdot G_i(t) + f_i \cdot \gamma_i^c \cdot V_i(t) + f_i \cdot \delta_i^c \cdot H_i(t).$$

8. The Model in the Difference Equation Form

It remains now only to put together the complete model in a form which can be solved by a high speed computer.

Substituting $X_{ij}^d(t)$ from (8), $C_i^d(t)$ from (14), $G_i^d(t)$ from (19), $V_i^d(t)$ from (25), $H_i^d(t)$ from (27), $E_i(t)$ from (28) and $S_i(t)$ from (29) into the basic demand-supply equality (1), we obtain the following difference equation for sectoral output $X_i(t)$:

$$(30)\ X_i(t) = \Sigma_j[a_{ij}^d(t) + f_i \cdot a_{ij}^c(t)]\, X_j(t)$$
$$+ \Sigma_j b_{ij} \cdot [\gamma_i^d + f_i \cdot \gamma_i^c][X_j(t + q_j) - X_j(t + q_j - 1)]$$
$$+ \Sigma_j s_{ij}[\delta_i^d + f_i \cdot \delta_i^c][X_j(t + 1) - X_j - (t)]$$
$$+ [(\alpha_i^d + f_i \cdot \alpha_i^c)\, \bar{C}_i(t) + (\beta_i^d + f_i \cdot \beta_i^c)\, \bar{G}_i(t) + \bar{E}_i(t)].$$

9. Summary Statement of the Model

The various predictive equations in the model are collected here.
Output Requirements:

$$(31)\ X_i(t) = \Sigma_j\, \tilde{a}_{ij}(t)\, X_j(t)$$
$$+ \Sigma_j\, \tilde{b}_{ij}[X_j(t + q_j) - X_j(t + q_j - 1)]$$
$$+ \Sigma_j\, \tilde{s}_{ij}[X_j(t + 1) - X_j(t)] + \bar{D}_i(t),$$

where $\tilde{a}_{ij}(t) = a^d_{ij}(t) + f_i \cdot a^c_{ij}(t)$,

$$\tilde{b}_{ij} = b_{ij}[\gamma^d_i + f_i \cdot \gamma^c_i],$$

$$\tilde{s}_{ij} = s_{ij}[\delta^d_i + f_i \cdot \delta^c_i],$$

$$\bar{D}_i(t) = (\alpha^d_i + f_i \cdot \alpha^c_i)\bar{C}_i(t) + (\beta^d_i + f_i \cdot \beta^c_i)\bar{G}_i(t) + \bar{E}_i(t).$$

Fixed Investment Requirements:

(32) $V_i(t) = \sum_j b_{ij}[X_j(t + q_j) - X_j(t + q_j - 1)]$.

Inventory Investment Requirements:

(33) $H_i(t) = \sum_j s_{ij}[X_j(t + 1) - X_j(t)]$.

Competitive Import Requirements:

(34) $M^c_i(t) = \sum_j (1 - f_i)\, a^c_{ij}(t)\, X_j(t) + (1 - f_i)\, \alpha^c_i \cdot \bar{C}_i(t) + (1 - f_i)\, \beta^c_i \cdot G_i(t) + (1 - f_i)\, \gamma^c_i \cdot V_i(t) + (1 - f_i)\, \delta^c_i \cdot H_i(t)$.

Noncompetitive Import Requirements:

(35) $M^n_i(t) = \sum_j a^n_{ij}(t) + \alpha^n_i \cdot C_i(t) + \beta^n_i \cdot G_i(t) + \gamma^n_i \cdot V_i(t) + \delta^n_i \cdot H_i(t)$.

Employment Requirements:

(36) $L_i(t) = l_i(1 + \gamma_i)^t X_i(t)$,

where $L_i(t)$ is amount of labor required for the year t,
l_i is labor coefficient of sector i in the base-year,
γ_i is annual compound growth rate of labor coefficient in sector i between 1963 and 1970.

III. Solution Process

For simplicity, the length of the investment gestation period is assumed to be uniform for all sectors and equal to one year. Then, the dynamic input-output model specified by equation (31) turns out to be a linear first order matrix differential equation:

(37) $X(t) = A(t)\, X(t) + B(t)\, \dot{X}(t) + \bar{D}(t),$

where $A = (\tilde{a}_{ij}),$

$B = (\tilde{b}_{ij} + \tilde{s}_{ij}).$

The matrix differential equation (37) would define a forward recursive relationship for $X(t)$, if the B-matrix could be inverted. In general, the investment coefficient matrix B is singular. This singularity problem can be circumvented through the use of a matrix-partitioning procedure.

This approach of integrating forward in time from the initial conditions may generate reasonable outputs at time one and two but soon thereafter inordinately large or negative output levels due to the inherent, intrinsic instability property of the Leontief dynamic model.[1]

In contrast to the forward integrating approach, the dynamic inverse approach developed by Leontief is a recursive procedure for solving (37) backward from given terminal conditions. Leontief's method avoids the instability problem but ignores problems of consistency with initial conditions. While consistency can be obtained through iterative selection of terminal conditions, the dynamic inverse approach is not very useful as a forecasting tool, because iterative selection of terminal conditions would be computationally difficult for a model with many sectors.[2]

A successive approximation procedure for solving the model (37) was employed to avoid instability and inconsistency problems. For backward recursion, we have

(38) $X(t) = Q(t)\, \bar{D}(t) + Q(t)\, B\, \dot{X}(t),$

where $Q(t) = [I - A(t)]^{-1}.$

To start the iteration, the first approximation for outputs is given by

(39) $X^{(0)}(t) = Q(t)\bar{D}(t),\ t = 1, \ldots, T,$

where the superscript on $X(t)$ denotes the step in the iteration process and T is the terminal year. Then, by least squares, we fit a polynomial to the investment term, $B\dot{X}^{(0)}(t)$. With this term fixed, we solve equation (38) for $X^{(1)}(t)$, approximate $B\dot{X}^{(1)}(t)$ by a polynomial, put it back into equation (38) and repeat the process.[3]

[1] Many formal discussions of the instability of the Leontief Dynamic Model are available in the literature. An excellent analysis is given by Jorgenson [1961].

[2] See Leontief [1970] and Kendrick [1972].

[3] For a more complete discussion, see Almon [1966].

When fifth-degree polynomials were applied to the time series of computed increments in the capital and inventory stocks, $B\dot{X}(t)$, the above iterative process converged to the unique solution. Apparently, this has proved far more successful than the rigid accelerator investment models that have been attempted previously at KDI.

IV. Development of the Data

In this section, we will discuss the derivations of the numerical data used in the sectoral model. Two types of data are required to define the technology of production and also to estimate the demands for output.

1. Production Data

The production data are a set of ratios for each sector that indicate input requirements per unit of output.

A. Current Account Input-Output Coeffcients

The 1973 interindustry flow table has not yet been prepared. Therefore, the input-output coefficients used in the FFYP model are those from the 1970 153-order input-output matrix compiled by the Bank of Korea.

We have, however, found it desirable to perform some aggregation of sectors in order to reduce the computational work and to estimate demand coefficients. The resulting sector classification is presented in Annex Table 1. Central to the classification of production activity in the model is its fine classifications for heavy and chemical industries. In addition, social development sectors are classified into water and sanitary services, housing, education and health for the purpose of facilitating social development planning.

Our 53-order transactions table is adjusted for scraps. The treatment of scrap in the tables for 1960, 1963, 1966 and 1968 is identical. A new method of handling scrap was, however, introduced in the 1970 table. Consequently, we converted the Bank of Korea's original 1970 table to conform to the previous years' convention, since the information required to convert the earlier tables to the 1970 convention does not exist.

Since the input-output coefficient does change over time, it would be desirable to update the input-output coefficient for the long-term projections. The use of past years' input-output coefficients in a projection model will lead to sizable errors if major changes in the economy's structure are anticipated. Due to time limits and resource constraints, we have adjusted only energy input coefficients by reducing a uniform rate of 10 percent for all sectors, on the basis of the nation-wide 10percent energy saving campaign. The rest of the input-output coefficients of the 1970 transaction matrix have been directly used for the years 1974–1981.

B. Capital Coefficients

The endogenous treatment of capital formation in an interindustry model raises a number of practical problems, because of the non-availability of reliable information on an incremental capital coefficients matrix for a model involving 53 sectors. Considerable efforts in this direction have already been made in Korea.

Dr. Byung-Nak Song of KDI has constructed a Korean capital coefficients matrix for a 52-sector interindustry model based on:

(1) the Bank of Korea's estimates on annual ICOR's for 11 sectors,
(2) the 1968 National Wealth Survey conducted by Professor Kee Chun Han of Yonsei University,
(3) the EPB's 1963, 1966, 1968 and 1970 Mining and Manufacturing Censuses.

In addition, the 1973 National Wealth Survey Data are currently being compiled by Dr. Hak Chung Choo of KDI. In the future, we can expect more reliable information on a capital coefficients matrix.

In the present exercise, most of the capital coefficients of Dr. Song's capital matrix have been directly used for the FFYP model. Capital coefficients of heavy and chemical industries and the electricity sector have been appropriately increased in order to reflect longer investment gestation lags in the future. The resulting capital coefficients matrix is presented in Annex Table 2.

C. Inventory-Output Coefficient Matrix

Until recently, official data on the capital and inventory coefficients in Korea have not been available. In 1969, however, for the first time in its history, the Korean government attempted to fill this gap by means of the 1968 National Wealth Survey. Using this survey data, Professor Kee Chun Han has recently estimated Korea's aggregate inventory-output coefficients by sector for 1968, as listed in Table 1.

Before using Professor Han's inventory coefficients to construct an inventory coefficient matrix, it is better to check on the reliability of Professor Han's figures.

Table 1. Aggregate Inventory-Output Coefficients

Sector	Coefficients
1. Agriculture & Forestry	.06336
2. Fishery	.01794
3. Coal	.08811
4. Metallic Ores	.26609
5. Non-Metallic Minerals	.04872
6. Processed Foods	.08459
7. Beverage & Tobacco	.20006
8. Fiber Spinning	.29111
9. Fabrics	.23795
10. Finished Textiles	.10318
11. Leather & Leather Products	.18686
12. Lumber & Plywood	.16122
13. Wood Products & Furniture	.19596
14. Pulp, Paper & Paper Products	.10940
15. Printing & Publishing	.09563
16. Inorganic Chemicals	.05353
17. Organic Chemicals	.13945
18. Chemical Fertilizers	.25334
19. Synthetic Resin & Chemical Fibers	.01006
20. Other Chemicals	.29814
21. Petroleum Products	.20767
22. Coal Products	.08376
23. Rubber Products	.29525
24. Cement	.29087
25. Glass, Clay & Stone Products	.14177
26. Iron & Steel	.15928
27. Rolled Steel	.28183
28. Steel Pipes & Plated Steel	.03251
29. Cast & Forged Steel	.09644
30. Non-Ferrous Metals	.05360
31. Metallic Products	.20519
32. Non-Electrical Machinery	.12553
33. Industrial Electrical Machinery	.18573
34. Electronics	.09046
35. Household Electrical Machinery	.15886
36. Shipbuilding & Repairing	.39001
37. Railroad Transport	.15888

Table 1. *(Continued)*

Sector	Coefficients
38. Motor Vehicles	.08514
39. Precision & Optical Products	.33582
40. Other Manufacturing	.20992
41. Residence & Building	.01070
42. Public & Other Construction	.03871
43. Electricity	.01246
44. Water & Sanitary Service	.01675
45. Banking & Insurance	.00106
46. Housing	.00044
47. Communication	.01029
48. Transport & Storage	.01161
49. Commerce	.34723
50. Education	.00900
51. Health	.00517
52. Other Services	.02610
53. Scrap & Unclassifiable	.25427
Total	.120486

For the 1970 base year, the growth rate of output $\Delta x/x$ is about 12 percent and the value added ratio is approximately .5427. Hence, using Professor Han's aggregate inventory coefficient $s/x = .12$, the inventory change-output ratio is

$$\frac{\Delta s}{x} = \frac{\Delta s}{\Delta x} \times \frac{\Delta x}{x}$$

$$= .12 \times .12$$

$$= .0144$$

This figure may be compared with .0147, which is computed from a 1970 I-O table.

Next, since for the year 1970 the value added ratio v/x is about 5427, the inventory change-value added ratio is computed as follows:

Table 2. *Labor Input Coefficients*

(persons per million won of output)

Sector	(1) Labor Coefficients	(2) Annual Growth Rate(%) 1963–1970	(3) Annual Growth Rate (%)
1. Agriculture & Forestry	5.338	−8.73	−2.00
2. Fishery	2.707	−14.29	−2.00
3. Coal	1.538	−6.37	−3.59
4. Metallic Ores	1.027	−14.55	−3.59
5. Non-Metallic Minerals	2.442	2.66	−3.59
6. Processed Foods	0.646	−6.44	−5.85
7. Beverage & Tobacco	0.293	2.77	−5.85
8. Fiber Spinning	0.604	−4.36	−5.85
9. Fabrics	1.017	−6.40	−5.85
10. Finished Textiles	1.131	−5.57	−5.85
11. Leather & Leather Products	1.095	−3.13	−5.85
12. Lumber & Plywood	0.523	−2.66	−5.85
13. Wood Products & Furniture	1.753	−3.10	−5.85
14. Pulp, Paper & Paper Products	0.563	0.05	−5.85
15. Printing & Publishing	1.038	−3.47	−5.85
16. Inorganic Chemicals	0.680	−0.71	−5.85
17. Organic Chemicals	0.351	−1.79	−5.85
18. Chemical Fertilizers	0.179	−16.58	−5.85
19. Synthetic Resin & Chemical Fibers	0.529	−23.07	−5.85
20. Other Chemicals	0.485	−5.88	−5.85
21. Petroleum Products	0.043	−28.00	−5.85
22. Coal Products	0.390	−12.86	−5.85
23. Rubber Products	0.913	−4.58	−5.85
24. Cement	0.136	−6.11	−5.85
25. Glass, Clay & Stone Products	1.748	−6.14	−5.85
26. Iron & Steel	0.255	−16.17	−5.85
27. Rolled Steel	0.298	1.70	−5.85
28. Steel Pipes & Plated Steel	0.293	−8.29	−5.85
29. Cast Forged Steel	0.606	−5.13	−5.85
30. Non-Ferrous Metals	0.394	−5.33	−5.85
31. Metallic Products	1.057	−5.88	−5.85
32. Non-Electrical Machinery	1.074	−5.12	−5.85

Table 2. *(Continued)*

Sector	(1) Labor Coefficients	(2) Annual Growth Rate(%) 1963–1970	(3) Annual Growth Rate (%)
33. Industrial Electrical Machinery	0.595	−1.26	−5.85
34. Electronics	0.586	−10.88	−5.85
35. Household Electrical Machinery	0.918	−10.03	−5.85
36. Shipbuilding & Repairing	0.862	−2.93	−5.85
37. Railroad Transport	0.502	−2.02	−5.85
38. Motor Vehicles	0.460	−17.59	−5.84
39. Precision & Optical Products	0.885	−10.95	−5.85
40. Other Manufacturing	1.349	−2.82	−5.85
41. Residence & Building	0.654	−10.34	−5.85
42. Public & Other Construction	0.868	−10.68	−5.85
43. Electricity	0.229	−14.44	−5.85
44. Water & Sanitary Service	1.577	−7.47	−5.85
45. Banking & Insurance	0.987	0.34	−3.69
46. Housing	0.088	5.62	−3.69
47. Communication	1.192	−5.24	−5.85
48. Transport & Storage	1.136	−10.05	−5.85
49. Commerce	2.337	−6.01	−5.85
50. Education	1.991	5.35	−5.35
51. Health	0.952	5.24	−5.24
52. Other Services	1.743	−8.45	−5.80
53. Scrap & Unclassifiable	—	—	0.00

$$\frac{\Delta s}{v} = \frac{\Delta s}{.5427x}$$
$$= \frac{1}{.5427} \times \frac{\Delta s}{x}$$
$$= \frac{1}{.5427} \times .0144$$
$$= .0265$$

On the other hand, the inventory change-value added ratio $\Delta s/v$ from the national income account is approximately .0315 for 1969, .0211 for 1970, and .0241 for 1971.

Thus, we can safely conclude that at least the aggregate inventory coefficient figure of professor Han is compatible with both the 1970 I-O table and the national income account. As to professor Han's sectoral inventory coefficient figures, it is hard to check whether or not these coefficients are reasonable numbers due to the lack of data.

In view of the compatibility of professor Han's aggregate coefficient with the 1970 I-O table and the national income account, we decided to use professor Han's inventory coefficients to construct an inventory-output coefficient matrix. That is, the aggregate inventory-output ratio in each sector is distributed along a column in the proportions of the non-service elements of the corresponding column in the input-output matrix.

The inventory-output coefficients matrix is presented in Annex Table 3.

D. Labor Coefficients

The weakest data in the FFYP model are those concerned with labor inputs. This reflects the fact that data on labor inputs in Korea are available only for very broad aggregates or in the form of point estimates. There are no detailed time series estimates for labor inputs.

Labor input coefficients of 53 sectors, as shown in Column 1 of Table 2, come from the Bank of Korea's 1970 input-output table. The situation regarding sectoral labor productivity is even worse as there are presently no reliable data for Korea. The absence of readily available data of reasonable quality on labor productivity was largely responsible for omitting labor from the development planning model for Korea.

For the first time in Korea, Dr. Sookon Kim of KDI attempted to fill this gap by computing the annual compound growth rate of the labor input coefficient between 1963 and 1970, which is shown in Column 2 of Table 2. However, labor productivity in some sectors turned out to be greater than the output growth rate. In particular, labor requirements for the petroleum industry turned out to be near to zero in 1981.

For experimental purposes, Dr. Kim's revised estimates are adopted in the model. The figures are presented in Column 3 of Table 2.

2. *Demand Data*

To specify the demands for output, the following have to be estimated for each period.

A. Private Consumption

In order to forecast sectoral household consumption expenditures for each year of the planning period, the Engel elasticities were estimated partly from time series data[4], and partly from 1973 cross-section household-budget survey data compiled by the Bureau of Statistics of the EPB. The Engel elasticities are presented in Table 3. Where time series and cross section data are lacking on Sectors 16, 17, and 53, we use the elasticity of Sector 20 (other chemical products) for Sectors 16 and 17 (inorganic and organic chemicals). For Sector 53 (scrap and unclassifiable), we assume that the 1970 year's share of scrap and unclassifiable items in total expenditures will prevail for the entire planning period.

The aggregate private consumption for each year of the plan period (1977–1981), as shown in Table 4, is derived from the aggregate plan.

With the Engel elasticities and aggregate consumption data in hand, we have projected sectoral private consumption for the next ten years from the 1970 base year figures. The results, which are shown in Annex Table 4, provide an indication of the important changes which are likely to take place in the seventies. As evidenced by the index number on the last two columns, the demand for food (Sectors 1, 2 and 6) record rather limited increases, whereas expenditures on household durables (Sectors 13, 31–35), fuel and electric power (Sectors 21, 22, 43) and transport and communications (Sectors 38, 47, 48) expand at a rate considerably higher than the average.

---

[4] The 1960–1970 time series data on sectoral household consumption expenditures are constructed by Mr. Wee Suk Kang, Research Department, Bank of Korea. The Sources of sectoral consumption figures for the years 1960, '63, '66 and '68 are the private consumption columns of the corresponding year's input-output table. For the rest of the years, sectoral consumption expenditure figures are derived from cross-section household-budget survey data. The deflator used is the disaggregated commodity price index.

Table 3. Engel Elasticities

Sector	Elasticities
1. Agriculture & Forestry	.2
2. Fishery	.5217
3. Coal	.3042
4. Metallic Ores	0.0
5. Non-Metallic Minerals	.3495
6. Processed Foods	1.016
7. Beverage & Tobacco	.9486
8. Fiber Spinning	3.0-7
9. Fabrics	1.5267
10. Finished Textiles	1.233
11. Leather & Leather Products	1.539
12. Lumber & Plywood	1.6644
13. Wood Products & Furniture	1.6644
14. Pulp, Paper & Paper Products	2.242
15. Printing & Publishing	2.313
16. Inorganic Chemicals	3.3832
17. Organic Chemicals	3.3832
18. Chemical Fertilizers	0.0
19. Synthetic Resin & Chemical Fibers	3.3832
20. Other Chemicals	3.3832
21. Petroleum Products	3.3832
22. Coal Products	1.3715
23. Rubber Products	.6871
24. Cement	0.0
25. Glass, Clay & Stone Products	.897
26. Iron & Steel	0.0
27. Rolled Steel	0.0
28. Steel Pipes & Plated Steel	0.0
29. Cast & Forged Steel	0.0
30. Non-Ferrous Metals	0.0
31. Metallic Products	3.4339
32. Non-Electrical Machinery	3.4339
33. Industrial Electrical Machinery	3.4339
34. Electronics	3.8098
35. Household Electrical Machinery	3.4339
36. Shipbuilding & Repairing	0.0
37. Railroad Transport	0.0

Table 3. *(Continued)*

Sector	Elasticities
38. Motor Vehicles	3.8098
39. Precision & Optical Products	3.4339
40. Other Manufacturing	1.559
41. Residence & Building	0.0
42. Public & Other Construction	0.0
43. Electricity	1.452
44. Water & Sanitary Service	1.052
45. Banking & Insurance	.6682
46. Housing	.6682
47. Communication	1.9392
48. Transport & Storage	1.035
49. Commerce	0.0
50. Education	1.035
51. Health	1.035
52. Other Services	1.035
53. Scrap & Unclassifiable	0.0

Table 4. *Projections of Aggregate Consumption for 1974–1981*

(million won at 1970 prices)

Year	Aggregate Private Consumption (1)	Aggregate Government Spending (2)	Aggregate Government Consumption (3)	Government Value Added (4)
1970	1,884.3	281.8	144.6	137.2
1971	2,080.1	331.9	160.1	151.8
1972	2,226.0	325.6	167.1	158.5
1973	2,415.8	336.6	172.7	163.9
1974	2,557.6	381.4	195.7	185.7
1975	2,661.8	427.2	219.2	208.0
1976	2,770.4	510.5	262.0	248.5
1977	2,914.7	577.9	296.6	281.3
1978	3,123.3	636.8	326.8	310.0
1979	3,342.1	704.3	361.4	342.9
1980	3,569.6	779.0	399.8	379.2
1981	3,815.2	860.0	441.3	418.7

Note: Column (2) is the sum of columns (3) and (4).

Table 5. Structures and Elasticities of Private Consumption Expenditure from 1970 to 1981

Sector	Share (%)		
	1970	1976	1981
1. Agriculture & Forestry	31.05	23.52	19.14
2. Fishery	2.04	1.79	1.65
3. Coal	0.00	0.00	0.00
4. Metallic Ores	0.00	0.00	0.00
5. Non-Metallic Minerals	0.13	0.11	0.09
6. Processed Foods	10.23	10.83	11.17
7. Beverage & Tobacco	5.98	6.18	6.30
8. Fiber Spinning	0.21	0.36	0.45
9. Fabrics	1.09	1.35	1.50
10. Finished Textiles	5.89	6.68	7.17
11. Leather & Leather Products	0.46	0.57	0.63
12. Lumber & Plywood	0.00	0.00	0.00
13. Wood Products & Furniture	0.11	0.13	0.15
14. Pulp, Paper & Paper Products	0.06	0.09	0.11
15. Printing & Publishing	0.62	0.92	1.10
16. Inorganic Chemicals	0.00	0.00	0.00
17. Organic Chemicals	0.00	0.00	0.00
18. Chemical Fertilizers	0.00	0.00	0.00
19. Synthetic Resin & Chemical Fibers	0.59	1.07	1.35
20. Other Chemicals	1.95	3.53	4.46
21. Petroleum Products	0.16	0.30	0.38
22. Coal Products	1.41	1.67	1.82
23. Rubber Products	0.35	0.33	0.32
24. Cement	0.00	0.00	0.00
25. Glass, Clay & Stone Products	0.06	0.06	0.06
26. Iron & Steel	0.00	0.00	0.00
27. Rolled Steel	0.00	0.00	0.00
28. Steel Pipes & Plated Steel	0.00	0.00	0.00
29. Cast & Forged Steel	0.00	0.00	0.00
30. Non-Ferrous Metals	0.00	0.00	0.00
31. Metallic Products	0.32	0.59	0.74
32. Non-Electrical Machinery	0.04	0.08	0.10
33. Industrial Electrical Machinery	0.02	0.04	0.05
34. Electronics	0.43	0.83	1.06
35. Household Electrical Machinery	0.20	0.37	0.47

Table 5. *(Continued)*

Sector	Share (%)		
	1970	1976	1981
36. Shipbuilding & Repairing	0.00	0.00	0.00
37. Railroad Transport	0.00	0.00	0.00
38. Motor Vehicles	0.25	0.50	0.64
39. Precision & Optical Products	0.37	0.68	0.86
40. Other Manufacturing	1.04	1.30	1.45
41. Residence & Building	0.00	0.00	0.00
42. Public & Other Construction	0.00	0.00	0.00
43. Electricity	0.66	0.80	0.88
44. Water & Sanitary Service	0.16	0.17	0.18
45. Banking & Insurance	0.63	0.58	0.56
46. Housing	5.40	5.04	4.83
47. Communication	0.49	0.68	0.78
48. Transport & Storage	6.69	7.12	7.38
49. Commerce	8.00	8.00	8.00
50. Education	1.81	1.93	1.99
51. Health	2.33	2.48	2.57
52. Other Services	8.67	9.23	9.56
53. Scrap & Unclassifiable	0.07	0.08	0.07
Total	100.00	100.00	100.00

These structural changes can be seen even more clearly in Table 5, which indicates the sectoral composition of total expenditure and the elasticity values during the projection periods. According to the table, the share of agriculture and mining (Sectors 1, 2, 3, 5) gradually declines from 33.22 percent in 1970 to 20.88 percent in 1981. This reduction will lead to an increase in the shares of other sectors, especially marked in heavy and chemical industry (Sectors 16–39). The share of light industry, as is shown in Table 5, gradually rises from 25.69 percent in 1970 to 30.03 percent in 1981; for heavy and chemical industry, from 6.15 percent to 12.31 percent; for social overhead capital, from 14.03 percent to 14.61 percent; for services and others, from 20.88 percent to 22.19 percent.

B. Government Consumption

Predictions of sectoral government consumption expenditures require total government consumption figures and consumption proportions. Total government consumption expenditures, as shown in Table 4, are

Table 6. Government Consumption Proportions

Sector	Proportions (%)
1. Agriculture & Forestry	.969
2. Fishery	.013
3. Coal	.139
4. Metallic Ores	.0
5. Non-Metallic Minerals	.018
6. Processed Foods	1.521
7. Beverage & Tobacco	.064
8. Fiber Spinning	.003
9. Fabrics	.049
10. Finished Textiles	.176
11. Leather & Leather Products	.010
12. Lumber & Plywood	.041
13. Wood Products & Furniture	.064
14. Pulp, Paper & Paper Products	.518
15. Printing & Publishing	2.773
16. Inorganic Chemicals	.056
17. Organic Chemicals	.027
18. Chemical Fertilizers	.066
19. Synthetic Resin & Chemical Fibers	.054
20. Other Chemicals	1.286
21. Petroleum Products	2.638
22. Coal Products	.388
23. Rubber Products	.386
24. Cement	.077
25. Glass, Clay & Stone Products	.054
26. Iron & Steel	.0
27. Rolled Steel	.0
28. Steel Pipes & Plated Steel	.0
29. Cast & Forged Steel	.001
30. Non-Ferrous Metals	.009
31. Metallic Products	.305
32. Non-Electrical Machinery	.351
33. Industrial Electrical Machinery	.201
34. Electronics	.236
35. Household Electrical Machinery	.121
36. Shipbuilding & Repairing	.099

Table 6. (*Continued*)

Sector	Proportions (%)
37. Railroad Transport	.0
38. Motor Vehicles	.333
39. Precision & Optical Products	.553
40. Other Manufacturing	.130
41. Residence & Building	1.168
42. Public & Other Construction	4.767
43. Electricity	1.032
44. Water & Sanitary Service	.674
45. Banking & Insurance	2.149
46. Real Estate	.0
47. Communication	1.682
48. Transport & Storage	4.220
49. Commerce	1.924
50. Education	50.969
51. Health	3.688
52. Other Services	13.052
53. Scrap & Unclassifiable	.955
Total	100.00

estimated by utilizing total government spending projections derived from the EPB's aggregate plan and the share of government value added from the 1970 I-O table. Finally, consumption proportions are taken from a 1970 base year input-output table. The proportions are presented in Table 6.

C. Import Coefficients for Final Demands and Target Rates of Import Substitution

The sources of import coefficients are the final demand columns of the 1970 input-output table. These import coefficients are presented in Table 7. Columns 1 and 5 of Table 7 are competitive and noncompetitive import coefficients for private consumption, respectively; columns 2 and 6, for government consumption; column 3 and 7, for fixed investment demand; columns 4 and 8, for inventory accumulation demand.

The target rates of import substitution, as shown in Table 8, are judged by the feasibility of increased domestic production in the individual sector, including the investment goods sector, on the basis of information provided in the long-term sectoral investment plan (1973–1981) developed by the Economic Planning Board.

Table 7. Import Coefficients for Final Demands

Sector	Competitive (%)				Noncompetitive (%)			
	α^c (1)	β^c (2)	γ^c (3)	δ^c (4)	α^n (5)	β^n (6)	γ^n (7)	δ^n (8)
1. Agriculture & Forestry	7.8048	6.0880	2.3296	6.1503	.0498	0.	0.	10.0781
2. Fishery	0.2484	0.	0.	0.	0.	0.	0.	0.
3. Coal	15.7895	0.1950	0.	0.	0.	0.	0.	3.4615
4. Metallic Ores	0.	0.	0.	1.0181	0.	0.	0.	0.
5. Non-Metallic Minerals	17.1670	0.	0.	1.5200	0.	0.	0.	84.9700
6. Processed Foods	2.8126	3.7745	0.	1.5546	0.	0.	0.	34.6989
7. Beverage & Tobacco	0.3188	0.	0.	0.2750	0.	0.	0.	.7300
8. Fiber Spinning	0.3526	0.	0.	10.2250	0.	0.	0.	.4031
9. Fabrics	5.3182	0.	0.	16.9546	0.	0.	0.	0.
10. Finished Textiles	0.2477	0.	3.1286	0.	0.	.2316	3.3314	0.
11. Leather & Leather Products	0.0902	0.	0.	0.	0.	0.	0.	0.
12. Lumber & Plywood	0.	0.	0.	0.	0.	0.	0.	0.
13. Wood Products & Furniture	1.5591	13.3404	12.5049	0.5080	0.	0.	0.	0.
14. Pulp, Paper & Paper Products	8.4247	1.3255	0.	1.8212	0.	.3805	0.	5.0994
15. Printing & Publishing	2.8725	2.5970	0.	3.5983	0.	0.	0.	0.
16. Inorganic Chemicals	0.	27.2838	0.	18.9500	0.	6.6991	0.	11.9600
17. Organic Chemicals	0.	27.9898	0.	2.1304	0.	21.1196	0.	88.9135
18. Chemical Fertilizers	0.	0.	0.	0.4957	0.	0.	0.	11.2590
19. Synthetic Resin & Chemical Fibers	0.6285	0.	0.	4.7171	.1620	7.4813	0.	34.6524
20. Other Chemicals	1.8188	3.0745	0.	6.9810	.9558	6.1384	0.	4.7637
21. Petroleum products	14.2480	3.9325	0.	7.4501	0.	0.	0.	0.
22. Coal Products	0.	0.0350	0.	0.	0.	0.	0.	0.
23. Rubber Products	0.1491	4.0281	0.	11.3090	0.	0.	100.0000	0.
24. Cement	0.	0.	0.	0.	0.	0.	0.	0.
25. Glass, Clay & Stone Products	11.5307	12.6566	0.	40.7716	0.	0.	0.	0.

26. Iron & Steel	0.	0.	0.	4.7600	0.	0.	0.	0.
27. Rolled Steel	0.	0.	0.	0.0078	0.	0.	0.	8.5038
28. Steel Pipes & Plated Steel	0.	0.	0.	10.9148	0.	0.	0.	0.
29. Cast & Forged Steel	0.	0.	0.	0.	0.	0.	0.	0.
30. Non-Ferrous Metals	0.	0.	0.	0.	0.	0.	0.	0.
31. Metallic Products	11.5735	8.5390	2.9183	17.0813	0.	1.1786	.0391	0.
32. Non-Electrical Machinery	48.9669	34.9206	78.2865	48.7271	0.	22.9385	9.2998	3.0063
33. Industrial Electrical Machinery	3.9687	3.6737	54.7919	17.7560	0.	0.	26.9962	0.
34. Electronics	16.5869	32.6990	19.3479	72.5085	.2848	1.4994	21.4530	3.8893
35. Household Electrical Machinery	12.9047	3.0337	15.2675	7.8512	0.	.0562	3.7103	0.
36. Shipbuilding & Repairing	0.	96.3574	86.1487	21.0697	0.	0.	2.5308	0.
37. Railroad Transport	0.	0.	41.2309	0.	0.	0.	5.8808	0.
38. Motor Vehicles	6.4366	7.3529	7.5476	6.1556	0.	0.	11.8536	23.0513
39. Precision & Optical Products	24.9479	88.8520	59.6172	65.8853	0.	2.1509	30.4938	0.
40. Other Manufacturing	12.8650	0.	7.8277	0.	0.	0.	0.	0.
41. Residence & Building	0.	0.	0.	0.	0.	0.	0.	0.
42. Public & Other Construction	0.	0.	0.	0.	0.	0.	0.	0.
43. Electricity	0.	4.1793	0.	0.	0.	0.	0.	0.
44. Water & Sanitary Service	0.	3.8489	0.	0.	0.	0.	0.	0.
45. Banking & Insurance	0.	1.1696	0.	0.	0.	0.	0.	0.
46. Housing	0.	0.	0.	0.	0.	0.	0.	0.
47. Communication	2.5172	8.6693	0.	0.	0.	0.	0.	0.
48. Transport & Storage	0.2438	13.3143	0.	0.	0.	0.	0.	0.
49. Commerce	0.	0.	0.	0.	0.	0.	0.	0.
50. Education	0.	0.	0.	0.	0.	0.	0.	0.
51. Health	0.	0.	0.	0.	0.	0.	0.	0.
52. Other Services	0.6129	3.1779	0.	0.	0.	0.	0.	0.
53. Scrap & Unclassifiable	80.0067	81.4230	0.	0.	0.	0.	0.	0.

Table 8. Target Rates of Import Substitution

Sector	Rate of Import Substitution (%)
1. Agriculture & Forestry	5
2. Fishery	0
3. Coal	0
4. Metallic Ores	0
5. Non-Metallic Minerals	0
6. Processed Foods	0
7. Beverage & Tobacco	0
8. Fiber Spinning	50
9. Fabrics	50
10. Finished Textiles	0
11. Leather & Leather Products	0
12. Lumber & Plywood	0
13. Wood Products & Furniture	0
14. Pulp, Paper & Paper Products	0
15. Printing & Publishing	0
16. Inorganic Chemicals	0
17. Organic Chemicals	0
18. Chemical Fertilizers	0
19. Synthetic Resin & Chemical Fibers	50
20. Other Chemicals	0
21. Petroleum Products	0
22. Coal Products	0
23. Rubber Products	0
24. Cement	0
25. Glass, Clay & Stone Products	0
26. Iron & Steel	30
27. Rolled Steel	30
28. Steel Pipes & Plated Steel	30
29. Cast & Forged Steel	30
30. Non-Ferrous Metals	10
31. Metallic Products	30
32. Non-Electrical Machinery	30
33. Industrial Electrical Machinery	30
34. Electronics	20
35. Household Electrical Machinery	0
36. Shipbuilding & Repairing	30
37. Railroad Transport	0

Table 8. *(Continued)*

Sector	Rate of Import Substitution (%)
38. Motor Vehicles	0
39. Precision & Optical Products	0
40. Other Manufacturing	0
41. Residence & Building	0
42. Public & Other Construction	0
43. Electricity	0
44. Water & Sanitary Service	0
45. Banking & Insurance	0
46. Housing	0
47. Communication	0
48. Transport & Storage	0
49. Commerce	0
50. Education	0
51. Health	0
52. Other Services	0
53. Scrap & Unclassifiable	0

D. Export Projections (1974–1981)

Export commodities are first grouped into eight commodity groups: primary products, processed food, textiles and clothing, miscellaneous manufactures, chemicals, steel and metal products, machinery and electronics. Subsequently, group projections were made on the basis of Dr. Wontack Hong's econometric model. A detailed breakdown within each commodity group has been made on the basis of composition trend as revealed by longitudinal analysis of past data (1970–1974). The structure of export commodities thus estimated is presented in Table 9.

On the other hand, export projections for different services have been obtained partly by using the EPB's projections and partly by studying trends during the years 1970–1974. The resulting composition of services is also shown in Table 9.

Exports are an important part of the model and it is important to experiment with high and low export demands assuming an unchanged composition. Export projections are based on two overall target figures for 1981 commodity exports: the EPB's 12.7 billion dollars and Dr. Hong's 13.5 billion dollars.

We projected the export patterns of 1974 and 1981 only. The export patterns of the in-between years are obtained by computing annual com-

Table 9. Export Structures

Sector	Share (%)	
	1974	1981
1. Agriculture & Forestry	2.13	1.11
2. Fishery	1.69	1.00
3. Coal	0.10	0.05
4. Metallic Ores	0.66	0.32
5. Non-Metallic Minerals	0.55	0.32
6. Processed Foods	4.45	2.97
7. Beverage & Tobacco	0.02	0.02
8. Fiber Spinning	4.20	3.14
9. Fabrics	6.66	8.12
10. Finished Textiles	23.72	18.45
11. Leather & Leather Products	1.82	1.60
12. Lumber & Plywood	7.46	4.57
13. Wood Products & Furniture	1.29	1.03
14. Pulp, Paper & Paper Products	1.00	0.68
15. Printing & Publishing	0.50	0.63
16. Inorganic Chemicals	0.16	0.10
17. Organic Chemicals	0.79	0.41
18. Chemical Fertilizers	0.01	0.58
19. Synthetic Resin & Chemical Fibers	0.81	1.84
20. Other Chemicals	0.95	0.51
21. Petroleum Products	0.87	0.37
22. Coal Products	0.00	0.00
23. Rubber Products	3.17	1.95
24. Cement	0.66	1.95
25. Glass, Clay & Stone Products	0.60	0.55
26. Iron & Steel	0.91	0.67
27. Rolled Steel	5.38	4.16
28. Steel Pipes & Plated Steel	1.81	3.33
29. Cast & Forged Steel	0.37	1.29
30. Non-Ferrous Metals	0.26	0.19
31. Metallic Products	3.00	2.25
32. Non-Electrical Machinery	1.75	2.28
33. Industrial Electrical Machinery	1.21	1.87
34. Electronics	9.15	12.29
35. Household Electrical Machinery	0.94	1.43
36. Shipbuilding & Repairing	1.63	8.66

Table 9. *(Continued)*

Sector	Share (%) 1974	Share (%) 1981
37. Railroad Transport	0.23	0.39
38. Motor Vehicles	0.81	1.77
39. Precision & Optical Products	1.38	2.92
40. Other Manufacturing	6.87	4.18
Total	100.00	100.00
41. Residence & Building	0.00	0.00
42. Public & Other Construction	6.54	7.45
43. Electricity	2.66	3.00
44. Water & Sanitary Service	0.17	0.20
45. Banking & Insurance	0.66	0.75
46. Housing	0.00	0.00
47. Communication	0.61	0.69
48. Transport & Storage	34.79	39.67
49. Commerce	26.81	16.58
50. Education	0.00	0.00
51. Health	0.00	0.00
52. Other Services	8.25	9.43
53. Scrap & Unclassifiable	19.50	22.23
Total	100.00	100.00

pound growth rates between 1974 and 1981. The export vectors thus estimated are presented in Annex Table 5 in the case of 12.7 billion dollars and in Annex Table 6 in the case of 13.5 billion dollars.

V. Discussion On Results

The 1973 input-output table has not yet been prepared. Therefore, a 53-sector interindustry model has been built using the Bank of Korea's 1970 input-output table. Accordingly, final demand projections have been made at 1970 prices. The resulting sectoral output, investment and import requirements are then converted to 1974 prices by using the proper sectoral price deflators.

Four alternative projections were made under different assumptions concerning export expansion and the extent of import substitution in the textile, chemical, metal and machinery sectors. The results under the various alternative assumptions are shown in Table 10. GNP projections under the alternative assumptions are presented in Table 11, while other macroeconomic results are given in Table 12.

Table 10. Description of Alternative Variants of the Model

Group No.	Case No.	1981 Export Target (million dollars in 1974 prices)	Import Substitution
I	IA	12,667	without import subst.
	IB	12,667	with import subst.
II	IIA	13,500	without import subst.
	IIB	13,500	with import subst.

Case IB assumes 1981 commodity exports of 12.7 billion dollars, a 7.3 percent per annum increase in consumption expenditures, and the effect of import substitution. Case IB, as is shown in Table 11, yields a projected compound GNP growth rate of 8.6 percent per annum for the period 1974–81. This is consistent with the results for the macroeconomic model.

Case IIB differs from Case IB only in assuming a higher export level of 13.5 billion dollars. Under these conditions, gross output increases at 9.5 percent per annum during the period 1975–1981, which, as expected, is a slightly higher rate than case IB. Compared with Case IB, as is shown in Table 12, Case IIB generates more employment but also requires more investment. In addition, the balance of payments problem is slightly improved. In order to compare Case IB and Case IIB, two other projections were made.

Case IA assumes that commodity exports increase to 12.7 billion dollars and consumption expenditures grow at 7.3 percent per annum, but, unlike Cases IB and IIB, the effects of further import substitution were not considered. Case IA indicates that Korea can achieve a 9.2percent growth rate per annum, but will face a serious balance of payments deficit, as shown in row (8) of Table 12.

Finally, Case IIA assumes commodity exports of 13.5 billion dollars with all other assumptions the same as in Case IA. Note that Cases IA and

Table 11. Gross National Product Accounts of Alternative Cases

(billion won at 1974 prices)

	1974	1981				
		EPB	IA	IB	IIA	IIB
Private Consumption	4,905.5	7,317.6	7,317.6	7,317.6	7,317.6	7,317.6
Gov't Consumption	729.3	1,644.4	1,644.4	1,644.4	1,644.4	1,644.4
Inventories Change	418.9	177.9	321.2	346.3	337.1	363.0
Fixed Investment	1,727.3	3,261.8	3,030.0	3,217.5	3,119.0	3,312.2
Exports	2,086.0	5,994.8	5,994.8	5,994.8	6,331.3	6,331.3
Imports	2,857.2	5,747.2	6,538.1	5,886.6	6,772.1	6,095.2
Gross Domestic Product	7,009.8	12,649.3	11,769.9	12,634.0	11,977.3	12,873.3
Net Factor Income	-67.0	-304.6	-304.6	-304.6	-304.6	-304.6
Gross National Product	6,942.8	12,344.7	11,455.3	12,329.4	11.672.7	12,568.7
GNP Growth Rate in 1974–81 (%)		8.6	7.4	8.6	7.7	8.9

Table 12. Macroeconomic Results of Alternative Cases

(period: 1975–1981)

Macro Indicators	Alternatives			
	IA	IB	IIA	IIB
Gross Output Increments (billion won in 1974 prices)	10,900.4	11,748.4	11,422.0	12,317.7
Output Growth Rate (%)	9.2	9.4	9.3	9.5
Employment Increments (thousand persons)	2,996	3,235	3,162	4,073
Cumulated Investment Requirements (billion won in 1974 prices)	16,886.0	17,524.0	17,191.4	17,846.7
Cumulated Import Requirements (billion dollars in 1974 prices)	84.6	76.6	86.9	78.8
ICOR[1]				
—Total	2.74	2.79	2.76	2.81
—Manufacturing	2.89	2.95	2.91	2.97
Import Share of Capital Equipment (%)	67.3	52.1	66.2	52.1
Cumulated Balance of Payment Deficit (billion dollars in 1974 prices)	16.4	8.5	16.2	8.1

Note: [1] $I_t/[GDP_{t+1} - GDP_t]$.

Table 13. Sectoral Gross Output Levels (Case IB)

(billion won at 1974 prices)

Sector	1970	1974	1981	Annual Growth Rate (%) 1970–74	1974–81
1. Agriculture & Forestry	1,803.1	2,169.6	2,885.2	4.73	4.16
2. Fishery	77.1	107.7	154.0	8.72	5.24
3. Coal	55.9	83.0	150.9	10.39	8.91
4. Metallic Ores	32.7	35.6	72.4	2.15	10.67
5. Non-Metallic Minerals	54.0	70.4	140.2	6.85	10.34
6. Processed Foods	538.5	803.5	1,255.3	10.52	6.58
7. Beverage & Tobacco	245.3	350.7	557.5	9.35	6.85
8. Fiber Spinning	169.0	337.4	701.6	18.87	11.02
9 Fabrics	138.4	298.5	681.2	21.19	12.51
10 Finished Textiles	273.7	550.1	1,046.4	19.07	9.62
11. Leather & Leather Products	26.7	79.5	163.8	31.36	10.88
12. Lumber & Plywood	120.1	191.9	371.0	12.43	9.88
13. Wood Products & Furniture	27.5	54.0	109.0	18.38	10.68
14. Pulp, Paper & Paper Products	104.4	176.5	347.0	14.93	10.14
15. Printing & Publishing	68.1	120.4	24.71	15.31	10.82
16. Inorganic Chemicals	29.5	49.3	104.2	13.70	11.28
17. Organic Chemicals	21.2	56.2	104.6	17.60	9.28
18. Chemical Fertilizers	46.2	52.4	92.3	3.20	8.42
19. Synthetic Resin & Chemical Fibers	172.5	336.7	770.2	18.20	12.55
20. Other Chemicals	129.5	240.9	459.1	16.79	9.65
21. Petroleum Products	427.7	657.1	1,288.6	11.33	10.10
22. Coal Products	68.8	102.3	173.1	10.43	7.80
23. Rubber Products	50.6	111.6	200.4	21.86	8.72
24. Cement	80.7	93.5	238.4	3.75	14.31
25. Glass, Clay & Stone Products	61.5	84.1	170.2	8.14	10.60
26. Iron & Steel	48.9	112.2	262.1	23.08	12.89
27. Rolled Steel	148.0	317.3	765.1	21.00	13.40
28. Steel Pipes & Plated Steel	28.2	67.3	233.5	24.29	19.45

Table 13. *(Continued)*

Sector	1970	1974	1981	Annual Crowth Rate (%) 1970–74	1974–81
29. Cast & Forged Steel	29.1	49.5	170.5	14.20	19.32
30. Non-Ferrous Metals	48.3	80.7	188.3	13.69	12.87
31. Metallic Products	73.6	142.1	293.4	17.88	10.91
32. Non-Electrical Machinery	116.4	162.8	369.9	8.75	12.44
33. Industrial Electrical Machinery	69.9	105.9	265.3	10.94	14.02
34. Electronics	65.3	191.6	595.9	30.88	17.60
35. Household Electrical Machinery	18.4	38.1	113.0	19.96	16.80
36. Shipbuilding & Repairing	53.5	84.1	500.3	11.97	29.01
37. Railroad Transport	12.2	25.3	59.5	20.00	13.00
38. Motor Vehicles	115.2	175.6	376.9	10.80	11.71
39. Precision & Optical Products	15.9	46.7	167.0	30.91	19.97
40. Other Manufacturing	118.5	193.9	329.8	13.10	7.88
41. Residence & Building	463.8	536.3	992.5	3.70	9.19
42. Public & Other Construction	211.6	243.8	481.5	3.60	10.21
43. Electricity	90.0	145.5	303.4	12.76	11.07
44. Water & Sanitary Service	25.8	39.7	75.3	11.38	9.58
45. Banking & Insurance	145.5	223.1	434.4	11.28	9.99
46. Housing	173.9	277.5	315.0	6.95	4.76
47. Communication	43.2	70.2	136.7	12.91	9.99
48. Transport & Storage	464.4	672.9	1,353.3	9.71	10.50
49. Commerce	820.5	1,239.1	2,257.7	10.86	8.95
50. Education	213.2	299.6	595.5	8.88	10.31
51. Health	97.9	142.0	228.4	9.74	7.03
52. Other Services	694.5	1,021,9	1,846.7	10.14	8.82
53. Scrap & Unclassifiable	147.9	232.7	598.8	12.00	13.65
Total	9,474.4	14,098.4	26,764.9	10.45	9.59

Table 14. Sectoral Value Added (Case IB)

(billion won at 1974 prices)

Sector	1974	1981	Annual Growth Rate (%) 1974–81
1. Agriculture & Forestry	1,594.6	2,120.6	4.2
2. Fishery	65.3	93.3	5.2
3. Coal	60.2	109.2	8.0
4. Metallic Ores	25.3	51.5	10.7
5. Non-Metallic Minerals	56.1	111.8	10.4
6. Processed Foods	213.5	333.5	6.6
7. Beverage & Tobacco	197.7	314.3	6.8
8. Fiber Spinning	85.8	178.4	11.0
9. Fabrics	77.4	176.7	12.5
10. Finished Textiles	150.7	286.6	9.6
11. Leather & Leather Products	26.1	53.9	10.9
12. Lumber & Plywood	41.4	80.1	9.9
13. Wood Products & Furniture	20.1	40.9	10.7
14. Pulp, Paper & Paper Products	47.8	94.0	10.1
15. Printing & Publishing	46.1	94.7	10.8
16. Inorganic Chemicals	17.5	37.1	11.3
17. Organic Chemicals	16.2	30.0	9.2
18. Chemical Fertilizers	20.8	36.6	8.4
19. Synthetic Resin & Chemical Fibers	120.9	276.6	12.6
20. Other Chemicals	79.3	151.1	9.6
21. Petroleum Products	257.6	505.1	10.1
22. Coal Products	17.1	29.0	7.8
23. Rubber Products	27.2	49.9	8.8
24. Cement	36.9	94.3	14.3
25. Glass, Clay & Stone Products	35.3	71.5	10.6
26. Iron & Steel	15.6	36.5	12.9
27. Rolled Steel	54.0	130.3	13.4
28. Steel Pipes & Plated Steel	11.6	40.3	19.5
29. Cast & Forged Steel	14.9	51.2	19.3
30. Non-Ferrous Metals	17.8	41.5	12.9
31. Metallic Products	34.8	71.9	10.9
32. Non-Electrical Machinery	55.0	124.9	12.4
33. Industrial Electrical Machinery	29.3	73.4	14.0
34. Electronics	66.6	207.2	17.6

Table 14. (Continued)

Sector	1974	Annual Growth Rate (%) 1981	1974–81
35. Household Electrical Machinery	14.6	43.5	16.9
36. Shipbuilding & Repairing	30.0	178.5	29.0
37. Railroad Transport	5.7	13.4	13.0
38. Motor Vehicles	56.4	121.8	11.6
39. Precision & Optical Products	14.2	50.6	19.9
40. Other Manufacturing	81.3	138.3	7.9
41. Residence & Building	193.4	358.0	9.2
42. Public & Other Construction	99.4	195.7	10.2
43. Electricity	98.2	204.9	11.1
44. Water & Sanitary Service	22.0	41.8	9.6
45. Banking & Insurance	176.3	343.3	10.0
46. Housing	195.9	217.2	4.8
47. Communication	58.3	113.4	10.0
48. Transport & Storage	414.8	834.2	10.5
49. Commerce	1,030.8	1,878.1	8.9
50. Education	234.3	465.8	10.3
51. Health	85.5	137.4	7.0
52. Other Services	659.6	1,191.9	8.8
53. Scrap & Unclassifiable	74.5	182.3	13.6
Total	7,181.7	12,960.8	8.8

IIA are basically a continuation of the past Korean development strategy. Case IIA produces more employment and a more rapid GNP growth rate with smaller investment resources as compared with the other projections, but it also encounters a larger deficit in the balance of payments due to greater import dependency. This is more or less the story of the development path of the Korean economy over the last ten years.

As already mentioned, Case IB has been chosen as the variant most consistent with the Fourth Five-Year Plan. The projections of sectoral gross output and investment and import requirements are presented in Tables 13–16 for Case IB which is consistent with the macroeconomic model. Finally, export projections for different commodities are shown in Table 17 under the assumption that 1981 commodity exports total 12.7 billion dollars.

Table 15. Sectoral Gross Fixed Investment Requirements (Case IB)

(billion won at 1974 prices)

Sector	1970–1974		1975–1976		1977–1981	
	Amounts	Share (%)	Amounts	Share (%)	Amounts	Share (%)
1. Agriculture & Forestry	555.7	7.8	253.5	6.4	868.1	6.4
2. Fishery	127.7	1.8	42.0	1.1	137.4	1.0
3. Coal	60.4	.9	32.2	.8	112.7	.8
4. Metallic Ores	11.8	.2	13.6	.3	42.9	.3
5. Non-Metallic Minerals	30.1	.4	28.7	.7	79.9	.6
6. Processed Foods	106.7	1.5	37.3	.9	135.1	1.0
7. Beverage & Tobacco	30.7	.4	12.7	.3	46.5	.3
8. Fiber Spinning	251.1	3.5	105.3	2.7	362.7	2.7
9. Fabrics	137.0	1.9	60.3	1.5	217.6	1.6
10. Finished Textiles	109.6	1.6	42.0	1.1	138.4	1.0
11. Leather & Leather Products	20.1	.3	9.2	.2	27.2	.2
12. Lumber & Plywood	32.2	.5	10.5	.3	39.5	.3
13. Wood Products & Furniture	11.2	.2	6.0	.2	16.4	.1
14. Pulp, Paper & Paper Products	93.7	1.3	49.0	1.2	157.8	1.2
15. Printing & Publishing	37.1	.5	15.8	.4	60.9	.5
16. Inorganic Chemicals	42.2	.6	26.2	.7	84.5	.6
17. Organic Chemicals	43.2	.6	13.5	.3	45.7	.3
18. Chemical Fertilizers	18.4	.3	8.6	.2	62.6	.5
19. Synthetic Resin & Chemical Fibers	254.7	3.6	114.7	2.9	447.6	3.3
20. Other Chemicals	42.2	.6	16.8	.4	61.4	.5
21. Petroleum Products	318.6	4.5	186.6	4.7	617.1	4.5
22. Coal Products	19.5	.3	8.6	2.	31.0	.2
23. Rubber Products	63.6	.9	20.2	.5	63.1	.5
24. Cement	59.0	.8	90.1	2.3	298.4	2.2
25. Glass, Clay & Stone Products	15.8	.2	13.2	.3	40.0	.3
26. Iron & Steel	78.3	1.1	49.9	1.3	145.9	1.1
27. Rolled Steel	250.4	3.5	156.1	4.0	479.5	3.5
28. Steel Pipes & Plated Steel	8.7	.1	7.8	.2	30.3	.2

Table 15. (*Continued*)

Sector	1970–1974		1965–1976		1977–1981	
	Amount	Share (%)	Amount	Share (%)	Amount	Share (%)
29. Cast & Forged Steel	20.1	.3	20.5	.5	88.7	.7
30. Non-Ferrous Metals	46.9	.7	35.9	.9	108.9	.8
31. Metallic Products	53.0	.8	32.6	.8	88.0	.6
32. Non-Electrical Machinery	43.9	.6	42.9	1.1	119.7	.9
33. Industrial Electrical Machinery	19.6	.3	19.6	.5	58.8	.4
34. Electronics	38.2	.5	20.6	.5	78.9	.6
35. Household Electrical Machinery	8.0	.1	7.0	.2	22.1	.2
36. Shipbuilding & Repairing	57.6	.8	100.3	2.5	491.0	3.6
37. Railroad Transport	11.5	.2	7.7	.2	21.3	.2
38. Motor Vehicles	26.2	.4	22.6	.6	62.5	.5
39. Precision & Optical Productions	14.9	.2	10.8	.3	43.0	.3
40. Other Manufacturing	26.5	.4	12.3	.3	34.6	.3
41. Residence & Building	8.2	.1	11.0	.3	25.8	.2
42. Public & Other Construction	39.1	.6	41.2	1.0	81.6	.6
43. Electricity	497.8	7.0	288.3	7.3	1,002.6	7.3
44. Water & Sanitary Service	107.1	1.5	56.9	1.4	198.9	1.5
45. Banking & Insurance	36.8	.5	21.2	.5	70.6	.5
46. Housing	759.1	10.7	265.4	6.7	1,014.9	7.4
47. Communication	82.4	1.2	41.9	1.1	147.0	1.1
48. Transport & Storage	1,294.7	19.7	906.4	22.9	3,192.4	23.4
49. Commerce	258.6	3.7	140.7	3.6	443.8	3.3
50. Education	196.8	2.8	150.1	3.8	501.4	3.7
51. Health	63.1	.9	25.9	.7	95.9	.7
52. Other Services	451.1	6.4	238.8	6.0	830.4	6.1
53. Scrap & Unclassifiable	0.	0.	0.	0.	0.	0.
Total	7,090.9	100.0	3,950.9	100.0	13,673.0	100.0

Table 16. Commodity Import Requirements (Case IB)

(million dollars at 1974 prices)

Sector	1974	1981
1. Agriculture & Forestry	1,506.5	2,666.0
2. Fishery	1.4	2.7
3. Coal	1.0	2.5
4. Metallic Ores	13.7	34.2
5. Non-Metallic Minerals	730.9	1,445.4
6. Processed Foods	176.6	292.5
7. Beverage & Tobacco	3.6	5.4
8. Fiber Spinning	58.5	123.1
9. Fabrics	132.1	255.3
10. Finished Textiles	6.3	12.7
11. Leather & Leather Products	7.2	15.0
12. Lumber & Plywood	4.9	18.9
13. Wood Products & Furniture	4.3	9.2
14. Pulp, Paper & Paper Products	120.3	248.0
15. Printing & Publishing	10.8	21.1
16. Inorganic Chemicals	85.7	184.6
17. Organic Chemicals	401.1	845.8
18. Chemical Fertilizers	6.4	9.1
19. Synthetic Resin & Chemical Fibers	350.7	758.7
20. Other Chemicals	202.0	393.1
21. Petroleum Products	40.0	79.9
22. Coal Products	11.6	29.8
23. Rubber Products	47.5	76.3
24. Cement	.3	.3
25. Glass, Clay & Stone Products	20.2	48.3
26. Iron & Steel	21.0	50.5
27. Rolled Steel	258.7	727.8
28. Steel Pipes & Plated Steel	20.0	42.1
29. Cast & Forged Steel	9.5	20.5
30. Non-Ferrous Metals	96.9	245.8
31. Metallic Products	119.0	245.7
32. Non-Electrical Machinery	719.8	1,412.9
33. Industrial Electrical Machinery	217.4	421.5
34. Electronics	299.5	808.2
35. Household Electrical Machinery	14.5	35.4
36. Shipbuilding & Repairing	283.7	584.5
37. Railroad Transport	34.1	64.5
38. Motor Vehicles	299.5	618.0
39. Precision & Optical Products	151.9	337.4
40. Other Manufacturing	18.8	32.7
Total	6,507.9	13,225.4

Table 17. Commodity Export Projections: Case of 12.7 billion dollars

(million dollars at 1974 prices)

Sector	1970	1974	1981
1. Agriculture & Forestry	37.5	76.3	107.8
2. Fishery	34.5	70.0	117.7
3. Coal	5.1	3.8	4.7
4. Metallic Ores	71.9	41.4	54.5
5. Non-Metallic Minerals	14.4	25.4	40.5
6. Processed Foods	68.1	184.9	332.3
7. Beverage & Tobacco	1.3	0.9	1.6
8. Fiber Spinning	82.0	183.5	370.5
9. Fabrics	75.2	291.2	956.9
10. Finished Textiles	374.7	1,037.0	2,173.5
11. Leather & Leather Products	3.0	57.9	137.1
12. Lumber & Plywood	103.6	227.0	374.9
13. Wood Products & Furniture	4.6	38.7	83.7
14. Pulp, Paper & Paper Products	5.6	43.2	79.0
15. Printing & Publishing	1.0	21.5	73.7
16. Inorganic Chemicals	2.8	12.5	20.4
17. Organic Chemicals	1.9	61.1	86.1
18. Chemical Fertilizers	18.3	0.9	121.9
19. Synthetic Resin & Chemical Fibers	9.2	63.0	383.4
20. Other Chemicals	22.0	72.7	106.5
21. Petroleum Products	40.8	115.1	132.4
22. Coal Products	8.5	0	0
23. Rubber Products	30.9	147.6	245.0
24. Cement	13.6	54.0	428.3
25. Glass, Clay & Stone Products	5.3	38.9	95.8
26. Iron & Steel	6.7	51.8	103.9
27. Rolled Steel	19.7	307.5	641.0
28. Steel Pipes & Plated Steel	0.7	103.6	513.2
29. Cast & Forged Steel	0.7	21.2	198.4
30. Non-Ferrous Metals	9.5	12.1	24.5
31. Metallic Products	22.2	140.5	283.5
32. Non-Electrical Machinery	12.9	82.9	289.9
33. Industrial Electrical Machinery	12.4	57.1	237.9
34. Electronics	62.2	432.1	1,564.0
35. Household Electrical Machinery	4.0	44.5	182.2
36. Shipbuilding & Repairing	5.2	79.3	1,137.7
37. Railroad Transport	0	11.4	51.6
38. Motor Vehicles	12.2	39.7	233.1
39. Precision & Optical Products	3.8	53.9	306.6
40. Other Manufacturing	140.2	229.9	377.3
Total	1,348.2	4,537.0	12,667.0

REFERENCES

1. Adelman, Irma, and Erick Thorbecke, eds., *The Theory and Design of Economic Development,* Baltimore: Johns Hopkins University Press, 1966.
2. Almon, Clopper, *The American Economy to 1975,* New York: Harper & Row Publishers, 1966.
3. Bank of Korea, *National Income Statistics,* Seoul, 1960 through 1974.
4. _______ , Input-Output Table and Supporting Materials for 1960, 1963, 1966, 1968 and 1970, Seoul: Research Department, various years.
5. Choo, Hakchung, "Recommendations for the 1973 Capital Stock Estimation," Seoul: Korea Development Institute, 1973. (mineographed)
6. Eckaus, Richard S. and Kirit S. Parikh, *Planning for Growth: Multisectoral, Intertemporal Models Applied to India,* Cambridge: MIT Press, 1968.
7. Ecomomic Planning Board and the Korea Development Bank, *Report on Mining and Manufacturing Census,* 1963 through 1970.
8. _______ , *Annual Report on the Family Income and Expenditure Survey,* 1968 through 1974.
9. Goreux, Louis M. and Alan S. Manne, eds., *Multi-Level Planning: Case Studies in Mexico,* Amsterdam: North-Holland, 1973.
10. Han, Kee Chun, *Estimates of Korean Capital and Inventory Coefficients in 1968,* Seoul: Yonsei University Press, 1970.
11. Hong, Wontack, "A Projection of Korea's Trade Pattern: 1977–86," Seoul: Korea Development Institute, 1975. (mimeographed)
12. Jorgenson, Dale W., "A Dual Stability Theorem," *Econometrica* 28: 982–99, 1960.
13. Kendrick, David, "On the Leontief Dynamic Inverse," *Quarterly Journal of Economics* 86: 693–96, 1972.
14. Leontief, Wassily, "The Dynamic Inverse," in A. Carter and A. Brody, ed., *Contributions to Input-Output Analysis,* Amsterdam: North-Holland, 1970.
15. Song, Byung Nak, "Observation on Korean Capital Coefficients with International Comparisons," Seoul: Korea Development Institute, 1974. (mimeographed)

Annex Table 1. Sectoral Classification in the Model

KDI Classification		BOK 1970 Classification	
Sector No.	Sector	Sector No.	Sector
1.	Agriculture & Forestry	1.	Rice
		2.	Barley & wheat
		3.	Other grains
		4.	Potatoes
		5.	Vegetables
		6.	Fruits
		7.	Flax, hemp & oil-bearing crops
		8.	Leaf tobacco & beverage crops
		9.	Miscellaneous industrial crops
		10.	Livestock & livestock products
		11.	Sericulture
		12.	Forest planting & conservation
		13.	Forest products
2.	Fishery	14.	Marine fishing
		15.	Coastal & inland aquaculture
3.	Coal	16.	Coal
4.	Metallic Ores	17.	Iron ores
		18.	Tungsten ores
		19.	Lead & zinc ores
		20.	Other nonferrous metal ores
5.	Non-Metallic Minerals	21.	Stone, clay & sand
		22.	Crude salt
		23.	Ceramic raw materials
		24.	Graphite
		25.	Other nonmetallic minerals
6.	Processed Foods	26.	Slaughtering, meat & dairy products
		27.	Vegetable & fruit processing
		28.	Canning & processing of sea foods
		29.	Grain polishing
		30.	Flour milling
		31.	Confectionery & bakery products
		32.	Sugar
		33.	Seasonings
		34.	Animal, vegetable oils & fats & processed products

Annex Table 1. (Continued)

KDI Classification		BOK 1970 Classification	
Sector No.	Sector	Sector No.	Sector
		35.	Prepared feeds for livestock
		36.	Other food preparations
7.	Beverage & Tobacco	37.	Alcoholic beverages
		38.	Beverages
		39.	Tobacco
8.	Fiber Spinning	40.	Cotton yarn
		41.	Silk yarn
		42.	Wool yarn
		43.	Ramie & flax yarn
		44.	Chemical fibre yarn
		45.	Other fibre yarn
9.	Fabrics	46.	Cotton fabrics
		47.	Silk fabrics
		48.	Wool fabrics
		49.	Hemp fabrics
		50.	Chemical fabrics
		51.	Dyeing & finishing
10.	Finished Textiles	52.	Knit goods
		53.	Rope & fishing nets
		54.	Apparel & accessories
		55.	Miscellaneous fabricated textile products
11.	Leather & Leather Products	56.	Leather & fur
		57.	Leather products
12.	Lumber & Plywood	58.	Lumber
		59.	Plywood
13.	Wood Products & Furniture	60.	Wood products
		61.	Wooden furniture
14.	Pulp, Paper & Paper Products	62.	Pulp
		63.	Paper
		64.	Paper products
15.	Printing & Publishing	65.	Printing & Publishing

Annex Table 1. (Continued)

KDI Classification		BOK 1970 Classification	
Sector No.	Sector	Sector No.	Sector
16.	Inorganic Chemicals	66.	Sulfuric & hydrochloric acids
		67.	Calcium carbide
		68.	Sodium products
		69.	Industrial compressed gas
		70.	Other inorganic chemicals
17.	Organic Chemicals	71.	Basic petrochemical products
		72.	Acyclic intermediates
		73.	Cyclic intermediates
		74.	Other organic chemicals
18.	Chemical Fertilizers	75.	Chemical fertilizers
19.	Synthetic Resin & Chemical Fibers	79.	Synthetic resins
		80.	Plastic products
		81.	Chemical fibres
20.	Other Chemicals	76.	Drugs & medicines
		77.	Cosmetics & tooth paste & powder
		78.	Agricultural chemicals
		82.	Explosives & pyrotechnic products
		83.	Paints & allied products
		84.	Soap & surface active agents
		85.	Other chemical products
21.	Petroleum Products	86.	Petroleum refining & related products
22.	Coal Products	87.	Coal products
23.	Rubber Products	88.	Rubber products
24.	Cement	92.	Cement
25.	Glass, Clay & Stone Products	89.	Pottery products
		90.	Glass & glass products
		91.	Structural clay products
		93.	Concrete products
		94.	Other nonmetallic mineral products
26.	Iron & Steel	95.	Pig iron
		96.	Raw steel
		97.	Ferroalloys

Annex Table 1. (Continued)

KDI Classification		BOK 1970 Classification	
Sector No.	Sector	Sector No.	Sector
27.	Rolled Steel	98.	Steel rolling & drawing
28.	Steel Pipes & Plated Steel	99.	Steel pipes & galvanized steel products
29.	Cast & Forged Steel	100.	Steel castings & forgings
30.	Non-Ferrous Metals	101.	Nonferrous metal ingots
		102.	Primary nonferrous metal products
31.	Metallic Products	103.	Metal furniture
		104.	Structural metal products
		105.	Other metal products
32.	Non-Electrical Machinery	106.	Prime movers & boilers
		107.	Metalworking machinery
		108.	Special industry machinery
		109.	Office & service industry machines
		110.	General industrial machinery & equipment
		111.	Household appliances
		112.	General machinery parts
33.	Industrial Electrical Machinery	113.	Electric transmission & distribution equipment & electrical industrial apparatus
34.	Electronics	114.	Radio, television & communication equipment & electronic components
35.	Household Electrical Machinery	115.	Household electric appliances
		116.	Miscellaneous electrical equipment & supplies
36.	Shipbuilding & Repairing	117.	Shipbuilding & repairing
37.	Railroad Transport	118.	Railroad transportation equipment
38.	Motor Vehicles	119.	Motor vehicles & parts
		120.	Automobile repair
		121.	Other transportation equipment
39.	Precision & Optical Products	122.	Measuring, medical & optical instruments

Annex Table 1. (Continued)

KDI Classification		BOK 1970 Classification	
Sector No.	Sector	Sector No.	Sector
40.	Other Manufacturing	123.	Miscellaneous manufacturing
41.	Residence & Building	124.	Residential buildings
		125.	Nonresidential buildings
		126.	Buildings maintenance
42.	Public & Other Construction	127.	Public utilities construction
		128.	Other construction
43.	Electricity	129.	Electric utilities
44.	Water & Sanitary Service	130.	Water services
		147.	Sanitary services
45.	Banking & Insurance	131.	Financing
		132.	Insurance
46.	Housing	133.	Real estate
47.	Communication	134.	Communications
48.	Transport & Storage	135.	Railroad transportation
		136.	Highway transportation
		137.	Water transportation
		138.	Air transportation
		139.	Loading & unloading
		140.	Warehousing
49.	Commerce	141.	Wholesale & retail trade
50.	Education	143.	Educational services
51.	Health	144.	Medical and health services
52.	Other Services	142.	Government services
		145.	Other social services
		146.	Business services
		148.	Amusement & cultural services
		149.	Restaurants & Hotels
		150.	Personal Services
		151.	Office supplies
		152.	Business consumption
53.	Scrap & Unclassifiable	153.	Unclassifiable

Annex Table 2. Capital-Output Coefficient Matrix

(to *j* sector)	1	2	3	4	5	6	7	8	9
(from *i* sector)	*A. & F.*	*Fi.*	*Coal*	*M.O.*	*N.M.*	*P.F.*	*B. & T.*	*F.S.*	*Fab.*
1. Agriculture & Forestry	.181	0.	0.	0.	0.	0.	0.	0.	0.
2. Fishery	0.	0.	0.	0.	0.	0.	0.	0.	0.
3. Coal	0.	0.	0.	0.	0.	0.	0.	0.	0.
4. Metallic Ores	0.	0.	0.	0.	0.	0.	0.	0.	0.
5. Non-Metallic Minerals	0.	0.	0.	0.	0.	0.	0.	0.	0.
6. Processed Foods	0.	0.	0.	0.	0.	0.	0.	0.	0.
7. Beverage & Tobacco	0.	0.	0.	0.	0.	0.	0.	0.	0.
8. Fiber Spinning	0.	0.	0.	0.	0.	0.	0.	0.	0.
9. Fabrics	0.	0.	0.	0.	0.	0.	0.	0.	0.
10. Finished Textiles	0.	.098	0.	0.	0.	0.	0.	0.	0.
11. Leather & Leather Products	0.	0.	0.	0.	0.	0.	0.	0.	0.
12. Lumber & Plywood	0.	0.	0.	0.	0.	0.	0.	0.	0.
13. Wood Products & Furniture	0.	.003	.008	.008	.021	.004	.004	.008	.002
14. Pulp, Paper & Paper Products	0.	0.	0.	0.	0.	0.	0.	0.	0.
15. Printing & Publishing	0.	0.	0.	0.	0.	0.	0.	0.	0.
16. Inorganic Chemicals	0.	0.	0.	0.	0.	0.	0.	0.	0.
17. Organic Chemicals	0.	0.	0.	0.	0.	0.	0.	0.	0.
18. Chemical Fertilizers	0.	0.	0.	0.	0.	0.	0.	0.	0.
19. Synthetic Resin & Chemical Fibers	0.	0.	0.	0.	0.	0.	0.	0.	0.
20. Other Chemicals	0.	0.	0.	0.	0.	0.	0.	0.	0.
21. Petroleum Products	0.	0.	0.	0.	0.	0.	0.	0.	0.
22. Coal Products	0.	0.	0.	0.	0.	0.	0.	0.	0.
23. Rubber Products	0.	0.	0.	0.	0.	0.	0.	0.	0.
24. Cement	0.	0.	0.	0.	0.	0.	0.	0.	0.
25. Glass, Clay & Stone Products	0.	0.	0.	0.	0.	0.	0.	0.	0.

26. Iron & Steel	0.	0.	0.	0.	0.	0.	0.	0.	0.
27. Rolled Steel	0.	0.	0.	0.	0.	0.	0.	0.	0.
28. Steel Pipes & Plated Steel	0.	0.	0.	0.	0.	0.	0.	0.	0.
29. Cast & Forged Steel	0.	0.	0.	0.	0.	0.	0.	0.	0.
30. Non-Ferrous Metals	0.	0.	0.	0.	0.	0.	0.	0.	0.
31. Metallic Products	0.	.003	.025	.013	.019	.005	.003	.006	.002
32. Non-Electrical Machinery	.104	.133	.413	.440	.422	.126	.064	.500	.282
33. Industrial Electrical Machinery	.104	.133	.004	.020	.007	.001	.001	.001	.004
34. Electronics	0.	0.	.001	.002	0.	.017	0.	.002	0.
35. Household Electrical Machinery	0.	0.	.001	0.	.001	.001	0.	0.	.001
36. Shipbuilding & Repairing	0.	2.131	0.	0.	.441	.002	0.	0.	0.
37. Railroad Transport	0.	0.	.071	.070	.028	0.	0.	0.	0.
38. Motor Vehicles	.080	0.	.224	.329	.152	.042	.044	.058	.062
39. Precision & Optical Products	0.	0.	0.	0.	.003	.001	0.	.003	0.
40. Other Manufacturing	0.	0.	0.	0.	.001	0.	0.	0.	0.
41. Residence & Building	.643	0.	1.247	.613	.416	.151	.143	.656	.345
42. Public & Other Construction	.299	1.077	0.	0.	0.	0.	0.	0.	0.
43. Electricity	0.	0.	0.	0.	0.	0.	0.	0.	0.
44. Water & Sanitary Service	0.	0.	0.	0.	0.	0.	0.	0.	0.
45. Banking & Insurance	0.	0.	0.	0.	0.	0.	0.	0.	0.
46. Housing	0.	0.	0.	0.	0.	0.	0.	0.	0.
47. Communication	0.	0.	0.	0.	0.	0.	0.	0.	0.
48. Transport & Storage	0.	0.	0.	0.	0.	0.	0.	0.	0.
49. Commerce	.054	.138	.075	.055	.057	.013	.010	.048	.027
50. Education	0.	0.	0.	0.	0.	0.	0.	0.	0.
51. Health	0.	0.	0.	0.	0.	0.	0.	0.	0.
52. Other Services	0.	0.	0.	0.	0.	0.	0.	0.	0.
53. Scrap & Unclassifiable	0.	0.	0.	0.	0.	0.	0.	0.	0.
Total	1.465	3.717	2.069	1.551	1.568	.362	.270	1.282	.726

Annex Table 2. (Continued)

(to *j* sector) (from *i* sector)	10 *F.T.*	11 *L.&L.P.*	12 *L.&P.*	13 *W.P.&F.*	14 *P.P&P.F.*	15 *P.&P.*	16 *I.C.*	17 *O.C.*	18 *C.F.*
1. Agriculture & Forestry	0.	0.	0.	0.	0.	0.	0.	0.	0.
2. Fishery	0.	0.	0.	0.	0.	0.	0.	0.	0.
3. Coal	0.	0.	0.	0.	0.	0.	0.	0.	0.
4. Metallic Ores	0.	0.	0.	0.	0.	0.	0.	0.	0.
5. Non-Metallic Minerals	0.	0.	0.	0.	0.	0.	0.	0.	0.
6. Processed Foods	0.	0.	0.	0.	0.	0.	0.	0.	0.
7. Beverage & Tobacco	0.	0.	0.	0.	0.	0.	0.	0.	0.
8. Fiber Spinning	0.	0.	0.	0.	0.	0.	0.	0.	0.
9. Fabrics	0.	0.	0.	0.	0.	0.	0.	0.	0.
10. Finished Textiles	0.	0.	0.	0.	0.	0.	0.	0.	0.
11. Leather & Leather Products	0.	0.	0.	0.	0.	0.	0.	0.	0.
12. Lumber & Plywood	0.	0.	0.	0.	0.	0.	0.	0.	0.
13. Wood Products & Furniture	.003	.007	.007	.005	.027	.053	.032	.012	.004
14. Pulp, Paper & Paper Products	0.	0.	0.	0.	0.	0.	0.	0.	0.
15. Printing & Publishing	0.	0.	0.	0.	0.	0.	0.	0.	0.
16. Inorganic Chemicals	0.	0.	0.	0.	0.	0.	0.	0.	0.
17. Organic Chemicals	0.	0.	0.	0.	0.	0.	0.	0.	0.
18. Chemical Fertilizers	0.	0.	0.	0.	0.	0.	0.	0.	0.
19. Synthetic Resin & Chemical Fibers	0.	0.	0.	0.	0.	0.	0.	0.	0.
20. Other Chemicals	0.	0.	0.	0.	0.	0.	0.	0.	0.
21. Petroleum Products	0.	0.	0.	0.	0.	0.	0.	0.	0.
22. Coal Products	0.	0.	0.	0.	0.	0.	0.	0.	0.
23. Rubber Products	0.	0.	0.	0.	0.	0.	0.	0.	0.
24. Cement	0.	0.	0.	0.	0.	0.	0.	0.	0.
25. Glass, Clay & Stone Products	0.	0.	0.	0.	0.	0.	0.	0.	0.

26. Iron & Steel	0.	0.	0.	0.	0.	0.	0.	0.	0.
27. Rolled Steel	0.	0.	0.	0.	0.	0.	0.	0.	0.
28. Steel Pipes & Plated Steel	0.	0.	0.	0.	0.	0.	0.	0.	0.
29. Cast & Forged Steel	0.	0.	0.	0.	0.	0.	0.	0.	0.
30. Non-Ferrous Metals	0.	0.	0.	0.	0.	0.	0.	0.	0.
31. Metallic Products	.005	.007	.008	.010	.005	.016	.016	.012	.027
32. Non-Electrical Machinery	.165	.100	.141	.100	.631	.221	.436	.583	.733
33. Industrial Electrical Machinery	.002	.014	.015	.001	.007	.028	.009	.012	0.
34. Electronics	0.	.001	.001	.001	0.	.001	.002	.033	.001
35. Household Electrical Machinery	.007	.010	.001	0.	0.	0.	0.	0.	0.
36. Shipbuilding & Repairing	0.	0.	0.	0.	0.	0.	0.	0.	0.
37. Railroad Transport	0.	0.	0.	0.	0.	0.	0.	0.	0.
38. Motor Vehicles	.022	.065	.020	.063	.073	.069	.112	.066	.090
39. Precision & Optical Products	.001	0.	0.	0.	.001	.002	.001	.020	.001
40. Other Manufacturing	0.	0.	0.	0.	0.	0.	0.	0.	0.
41. Residence & Building	.138	.184	.092	.206	.404	.180	1.313	.352	.891
42. Public & Other Construction	0.	0.	0.	0.	0.	0.	0.	0.	0.
43. Electricity	0.	0.	0.	0.	0.	0.	0.	0.	0.
44. Water & Sanitary Service	0.	0.	0.	0.	0.	0.	0.	0.	0.
45. Banking & Insurance	0.	0.	0.	0.	0.	0.	0.	0.	0.
46. Housing	0.	0.	0.	0.	0.	0.	0.	0.	0.
47. Communication	0.	0.	0.	0.	0.	0.	0.	0.	0.
48. Transport & Storage	0.	0.	0.	0.	0.	0.	0.	0.	0.
49. Commerce	.013	.015	.011	.015	.044	.022	.074	.042	.070
50. Education	0.	0.	0.	0.	0.	0.	0.	0.	0.
51. Health	0.	0.	0.	0.	0.	0.	0.	0.	0.
52. Other Services	0.	0.	0.	0.	0.	0.	0.	0.	0.
53. Scrap & Unclassifiable	0.	0.	0.	0.	0.	0.	0.	0.	0.
Total	.357	.403	.295	.397	1.192	.593	1.995	1.133	1.816

Annex Table 2. *(Continued)*

(to *j* sector)	19	20	21	22	23	24	25	26	27
(from *i* sector)	*S.R.&C.F.*	*O.C.*	*P.P.*	*C.P.*	*R.P.*	*Cement*	*G.C.&S.P.*	*I.&S.*	*R.S.*
1. Agriculture & Forestry	0.	0.	0.	0.	0.	0.	0.	0.	0.
2. Fishery	0.	0.	0.	0.	0.	0.	0.	0.	0.
3. Coal	0.	0.	0.	0.	0.	0.	0.	0.	0.
4. Metallic Ores	0.	0.	0.	0.	0.	0.	0.	0.	0.
5. Non-Metallic Minerals	0.	0.	0.	0.	0.	0.	0.	0.	0.
6. Processed Foods	0.	0.	0.	0.	0.	0.	0.	0.	0.
7. Beverage & Tobacco	0.	0.	0.	0.	0.	0.	0.	0.	0.
8. Fiber Spinning	0.	0.	0.	0.	0.	0.	0.	0.	0.
9. Fabrics	0.	0.	0.	0.	0.	0.	0.	0.	0.
10. Finished Textiles	0.	0.	0.	0.	0.	0.	0.	0.	0.
11. Leather & Leather Products	0.	0.	0.	0.	0.	0.	0.	0.	0.
12. Lumber & Plywood	0.	0.	0.	0.	0.	0.	0.	0.	0.
13. Wood Products & Furniture	.016	.007	.011	.004	.018	.003	.006	.007	.004
14. Pulp, Paper & Paper Products	0.	0.	0.	0.	0.	0.	0.	0.	0.
15. Printing & Publishing	0.	0.	0.	0.	0.	0.	0.	0.	0.
16. Inorganic Chemicals	0.	0.	0.	0.	0.	0.	0.	0.	0.
17. Organic Chemicals	0.	0.	0.	0.	0.	0.	0.	0.	0.
18. Chemical Fertilizers	0.	0.	0.	0.	0.	0.	0.	01	0.
19. Synthetic Resin & Chemical Fibers	0.	0.	0.	0.	0.	0.	0.	0.	0.
20. Other Chemicals	0.	0.	0.	0.	0.	0.	0.	0.	0.
21. Petroleum Products	0.	0.	0.	0.	0.	0.	0.	0.	0.
22. Coal Products	0.	0.	0.	0.	0.	0.	0.	0.	0.
23. Rubber Products	0.	0.	0.	0.	0.	0.	0.	0.	0.
24. Cement	0.	0.	0.	0.	0.	0.	0.	0.	0.
25. Glass, Clay & Stone Products	0.	0.	0.	0.	0.	0.	0.	0.	0.

26. Iron & Steel	0.	0.	0.	0.	0.	0.	0.	0.	0.
27. Rolled Steel	0.	0.	0.	0.	0.	0.	0.	0.	0.
28. Steel Pipes & Plated Steel	0.	0.	0.	0.	0.	0.	0.	0.	0.
29. Cast & Forged Steel	0.	0.	0.	0.	0.	0.	0.	0.	0.
30. Non-Ferrous Metals	0.	0.	0.	0.	0.	0.	0.	0.	0.
31. Metallic Products	.027	.015	.004	.007	.022	.006	.021	.030	.006
32. Non-Electrical Machinery	.708	.091	.315	.162	.491	.771	.228	.817	.354
33. Industrial Electrical Machinery	.002	.003	0.	.013	.004	0.	.004	.020	0.
34. Electronics	0.	.001	0.	0.	0.	.002	.001	.003	0.
35. Household Electrical Machinery	.120	0.	0.	0.	0.	0.	0.	0.	0.
36. Shipbuilding & Repairing	0.	0.	.187	0.	0.	0.	0.	0.	.014
37. Railroad Transport	0.	0.	0.	.026	0.	.131	0.	.002	.069
38. Motor Vehicles	.048	.045	.244	.138	.053	.532	.080	.009	.269
39. Precision & Optical Products	.005	.012	0.	0.	0.	0.	.013	.005	.002
40. Other Manufacturing	0.	0.	0.	0.	0.	0.	0.	0.	0.
41. Residence & Building	.312	.156	.450	.163	.300	1.189	.245	.338	.641
42. Public & Other Construction	0.	0.	0.	0.	0.	0.	0.	0.	0.
43. Electricity	0.	0.	0.	0.	0.	0.	0.	0.	0.
44. Water & Sanitary Service	0.	0.	0.	0.	0.	0.	0.	0.	0.
45. Banking & Insurance	0.	0.	0.	0.	0.	0.	0.	0.	0.
46. Housing	0.	0.	0.	0.	0.	0.	0.	0.	0.
47. Communication	0.	0.	0.	0.	0.	0.	0.	0.	0.
48. Transport & Storage	0.	0.	0.	0.	0.	0.	0.	0.	0.
49. Commerce	.048	.013	.047	.019	.034	.097	.023	.047	.050
50. Education	0.	0.	0.	0.	0.	0.	0.	0.	0.
51. Health	0.	0.	0.	0.	0.	0.	0.	0.	0.
52. Other Services	0.	0.	0.	0.	0.	0.	0.	0.	0.
53. Scrap & Unclassifiable	0.	0.	0.	0.	0.	0.	0.	0.	0.
Total	1.286	.343	1.257	.534	.921	2.733	.620	1.278	1.410

Annex Table 2. (Continued)

(to *j* sector) / (from *i* sector)	28 *S.P.&P.S.*	29 *C.&F.S.*	30 *Non-F.M.*	31 *M.P.*	32 *Non-E.M.*	33 *I.E.M.*	34 *Elec.*	35 *H.E.M.*	36 *S.&R.*
1. Agriculture & Forestry	0.	0.	0.	0.	0.	0.	0.	0.	0.
2. Fishery	0.	0.	0.	0.	0.	0.	0.	0.	0.
3. Coal	0.	0.	0.	0.	0.	0.	0.	0.	0.
4. Metallic Ores	0.	0.	0.	0.	0.	0.	0.	0.	0.
5. Non-Metallic Minerals	0.	0.	0.	0.	0.	0.	0.	0.	0.
6. Processed Foods	0.	0.	0.	0.	0.	0.	0.	0.	0.
7. Beverage & Tobacco	0.	0.	0.	0.	0.	0.	0.	0.	0.
8. Fiber Spinning	0.	0.	0.	0.	0.	0.	0.	0.	0.
9. Fabrics	0.	0.	0.	0.	0.	0.	0.	0.	0.
10. Finished Textiles	0.	0.	0.	0.	0.	0.	0.	0.	0.
11. Leather & Leather Products	0.	0.	0.	0.	0.	0.	0.	0.	0.
12. Lumber & Plywood	0.	0.	0.	0.	0.	0.	0.	0.	0.
13. Wood Products & Furniture	0.	.004	.016	.010	.010	.007	.005	.005	.062
14. Pulp, Paper & Paper Products	0.	0.	0.	0.	0.	0.	0.	0.	0.
15. Printing & Publishing	0.	0.	0.	0.	0.	0.	0.	0.	0.
16. Inorganic Chemicals	0.	0.	0.	0.	0.	0.	0.	0.	0.
17. Organic Chemicals	0.	0.	0.	0.	0.	0.	0.	0.	0.
18. Chemical Fertilizers	0.	0.	0.	0.	0.	0.	0.	0.	0.
19. Synthetic Resin & Chemical Fibers	0.	0.	0.	0.	0.	0.	0.	0.	0.
20. Other Chemicals	0.	0.	0.	0.	0.	0.	0.	0.	0.
21. Petroleum Products	0.	0.	0.	0.	0.	0.	0.	0.	0.
22. Coal Products	0.	0.	0.	0.	0.	0.	0.	0.	0.
23. Rubber Products	0.	0.	0.	0.	0.	0.	0.	0.	0.
24. Cement	0.	0.	0.	0.	0.	0.	0.	0.	0.
25. Glass, Clay & Stone Products	0.	0.	0.	0.	0.	0.	0.	0.	0.

26. Iron & Steel	0.	0.	0.	0.	0.	0.	0.	0.	0.
27. Rolled Steel	0.	0.	0.	0.	0.	0.	0.	0.	0.
28. Steel Pipes & Plated Steel	0.	0.	0.	0.	0.	0.	0.	0.	0.
29. Cast & Forged Steel	0.	0.	0.	0.	0.	0.	0.	0.	0.
30. Non-Ferrous Metals	0.	0.	0.	0.	0.	0.	0.	0.	0.
31. Metallic Products	.001	.034	.024	.021	.035	.005	.005	.007	.079
32. Non-Electrical Machinery	.105	.519	.732	.401	.381	.179	.032	.136	.505
33. Industrial Electrical Machinery	.003	.003	.058	.010	.004	.001	.005	.004	.002
34. Electronics	0.	.001	.004	.001	.001	0.	.074	.001	.003
35. Household Electrical Machinery	0.	0.	.003	.001	.001	.001	0.	0.	.012
36. Shipbuilding & Repairing	0.	0.	0.	0.	0.	0.	.011	0.	.048
37. Railroad Transport	.003	.007	.028	0.	0.	0.	0.	0.	0.
38. Motor Vehicles	.016	.038	.168	.040	.109	.047	.012	.029	.057
39. Precision & Optical Products	.001	0.	.006	.001	.002	.002	.003	.002	.001
40. Other Manufacturing	0.	0.	0.	0.	0.	0.	0.	0.	0.
41. Residence & Building	.083	.249	.267	.269	.230	.238	.093	.193	.548
42. Public & Other Construction	0.	0.	0.	0.	0.	0.	0.	0.	0.
43. Electricity	0.	0.	0.	0.	0.	0.	0.	0.	0.
44. Water & Sanitary Service	0.	0.	0.	0.	0.	0.	0.	0.	0.
45. Banking & Insurance	0.	0.	0.	0.	0.	0.	0.	0.	0.
46. Housing	0.	0.	0.	0.	0.	0.	0.	0.	0.
47. Communication	0.	0.	0.	0.	0.	0.	0.	0.	0.
48. Transport & Storage	0.	0.	0.	0.	0.	0.	0.	0.	0.
49. Commerce	.008	.033	.049	.029	.030	.019	.009	.015	.054
50. Education	0.	0.	0.	0.	0.	0.	0.	0.	0.
51. Health	0.	0.	0.	0.	0.	0.	0.	0.	0.
52. Other Services	0.	0.	0.	0.	0.	0.	0.	0.	0.
53. Scrap & Unclassifiable	0.	0.	0.	0.	0.	0.	0.	0.	0.
Total	.222	.889	1.354	.782	.804	.499	.248	.392	1.461

Annex Table 2. *(Continued)*

(to *j* sector) / (from *i* sector)	37 *R.T.*	38 *M.V.*	39 *P.&O.P.*	40 *O.M.*	41 *R.&B.*	42 *P.&O.C.*	43 *Elect.*	44 *W.&S.S.*	45 *B.&I.*
1. Agriculture & Forestry	0.	0.	0.	0.	0.	0.	0.	0.	0.
2. Fishery	0.	0.	0.	0.	0.	0.	0.	0.	0.
3. Coal	0.	0.	0.	0.	0.	0.	0.	0.	0.
4. Metallic Ores	0.	0.	0.	0.	0.	0.	0.	0.	0.
5. Non-Metallic Minerals	0.	0.	0.	0.	0.	0.	0.	0.	0.
6. Processed Foods	0.	0.	0.	0.	0.	0.	0.	0.	0.
7. Beverage & Tobacco	0.	0.	0.	0.	0.	0.	0.	0.	0.
8. Fiber Spinning	0.	0.	0.	0.	0.	0.	0.	0.	0.
9. Fabrics	0.	0.	0.	0.	0.	0.	0.	0.	0.
10. Finished Textiles	0.	0.	0.	0.	0.	0.	0.	0.	0.
11. Leather & Leather Products	0.	0.	0.	0.	0.	0.	0.	0.	0.
12. Lumber & Plywood	0.	0.	0.	0.	0.	0.	0.	0.	0.
13. Wood Products & Furniture	.005	.015	.014	.007	0.	.003	.001	.003	.001
14. Pulp, Paper & Paper Products	0.	0.	0.	0.	0.	0.	0.	0.	0.
15. Printing & Publishing	0.	0.	0.	0.	0.	0.	0.	0.	0.
16. Inorganic Chemicals	0.	0.	0.	0.	0.	0.	0.	0.	0.
17. Organic Chemicals	0.	0.	0.	0.	0.	0.	0.	0.	0.
18. Chemical Fertilizers	0.	0.	0.	0.	0.	0.	0.	0.	0.
19. Synthetic Resin & Chemical Fibers	0.	0.	0.	0.	0.	0.	0.	0.	0.
20. Other Chemicals	0.	0.	0.	0.	0.	0.	0.	0.	0.
21. Petroleum Products	0.	0.	0.	0.	0.	0.	0.	0.	0.
22. Coal Products	0.	0.	0.	0.	0.	0.	0.	0.	0.
23. Rubber Products	0.	0.	0.	0.	0.	0.	0.	0.	0.
24. Cement	0.	0.	0.	0.	0.	0.	0.	0.	0.
25. Glass, Clay & Stone Products	0.	0.	0.	0.	0.	0.	0.	0.	0.

26. Iron & Steel	0.	0.	0.	0.	0.	0.	0.	0.	0.
27. Rolled Steel	0.	0.	0.	0.	0.	0.	0.	0.	0.
28. Steel Pipes & Plated Steel	0.	0.	0.	0.	0.	0.	0.	0.	0.
29. Cast & Forged Steel	0.	0.	0.	0.	0.	0.	0.	0.	0.
30. Non-Ferrous Metals	0.	0.	0.	0.	0.	0.	0.	0.	0.
31. Metallic Products	.036	.014	.014	.015	0.	.004	.002	.005	.003
32. Non-Electrical Machinery	.083	.157	.137	.078	.002	.072	1.027	.268	.019
33. Industrial Electrical Machinery	.120	.002	.004	.001	.002	.072	1.027	.268	.019
34. Electronics	0.	.001	.001	0.	.002	.072	1.027	.268	.019
35. Household Electrical Machinery	.004	0.	.002	.002	0.	0.	0.	0.	0.
36. Shipbuilding & Repairing	0.	0.	0.	0.	0.	0.	0.	0.	0.
37. Railroad Transport	.042	0.	0.	0.	0.	.020	0.	0.	0.
38. Motor Vehicles	0.	.074	.030	.042	.004	.086	.164	.312	.022
39. Precision & Optical Products	.001	.005	.005	.005	.001	.071	.982	.185	.015
40. Other Manufacturing	0.	0.	0.	0.	0.	0.	0.	0.	0.
41. Residence & Building	.536	.141	.223	.174	0.	.116	0.	0.	.315
42. Public & Other Construction	0.	0.	0.	0.	.069	0.	3.544	5.439	0.
43. Electricity	0.	0.	0.	0.	0.	0.	0.	0.	0.
44. Water & Sanitary Service	0.	0.	0.	0.	0.	0.	0.	0.	0.
45. Banking & Insurance	0.	0.	0.	0.	0.	0.	0.	0.	0.
46. Housing	0.	0.	0.	0.	0.	0.	0.	0.	0.
47. Communication	0.	0.	0.	0.	0.	0.	0.	0.	0.
48. Transport & Storage	0.	0.	0.	0.	0.	0.	0.	0.	0.
49. Commerce	.031	.016	.017	.013	.003	.019	.300	.260	.016
50. Education	0.	0.	0.	0.	0.	0.	0.	0.	0.
51. Health	0.	0.	0.	0.	0.	0.	0.	0.	0.
52. Other Services	0.	0.	0.	0.	0.	0.	0.	0.	0.
53. Scrap & Unclassifiable	0.	0.	0.	0.	0.	0.	0.	0.	0.
Total	.858	.425	.447	.337	.082	.537	8.074	7.008	.430

Annex Table 2. (Continued)

(to *j* sector) / (from *i* sector)	46 *Housing*	47 *Commun.*	48 *T. &S.*	49 *Commerce*	50 *Education*	51 *Health*	52 *O. S.*	53 *S. & Uncla.*
1. Agriculture & Forestry	0.	0.	0.	0.	0.	0.	0.	0.
2. Fishery	0.	0.	0.	0.	0.	0.	0.	0.
3. Coal	0.	0.	0.	0.	0.	0.	0.	0.
4. Metallic Ores	0.	0.	0.	0.	0.	0.	0.	0.
5. Non-Metallic Minerals	0.	0.	0.	0.	0.	0.	0.	0.
6. Processed Foods	0.	0.	0.	0.	0.	0.	0.	0.
7. Beverage & Tobacco	0.	0.	0.	0.	0.	p.	0.	0.
8. Fiber Spinning	0.	0.	0.	0.	0.	0.	0.	0.
9. Fabrics	0.	0.	0.	0.	0.	0.	0.	0.
10. Finished Textiles	.003	.001	0.	0.	0.	0.	0.	0.
11. Leather & Leather Products	0.	0.	0.	0.	0.	0.	0.	0.
12. Lumber & Plywood	0.	0.	0.	0.	0.	0.	0.	0.
13. Wood Products & Furniture	0.37	0.09	.003	.001	.002	0.01	.001	0.
14. Pulp, Paper & Paper Products	0.	0.	0.	0.	0.	0.	0.	0.
15. Printing & Publishing	0.	0.	0.	0.	0.	0.	0.	0.
16. Inorganic Chemicals	0.	0.	0.	0.	0.	0.	0.	0.
17, Organic Chemicals	0.	0.	0.	0.	0.	0.	0.	0.
18. Chemical Fertilizers	0.	0.	0.	0.	0.	0.	0.	0.
19. Synthetic Resin & Chemical Fibers	0.	0.	0.	0.	0.	0.	0.	0.
20. Other Chemicals	0.	0.	0.	0.	0.	0.	0.	0.
21. Petroleum Products	0.	0.	0.	0.	0.	0.	0.	0.
22. Coal Products	0.	0.	0.	0.	0.	0.	0.	0.
23. Rubber Products	0.	0.	0.	0.	0.	0.	0.	0.
24. Cement	0.	0.	0.	0.	0.	0.	0.	0.
25. Glass, Clay & Stone Products	0.	0.	0.	0.	0.	0.	0.	0.

26. Iron & Steel	0.	0.	0.	0.	0.	0.	0.	0.
27. Rolled Steel	0.	0.	0.	0.	0.	0.	0.	0.
28. Steel Pipes & Plated Steel	0.	0.	0.	0.	0.	0.	0.	0.
29. Cast & Forged Steel	0.	0.	0.	0.	0.	0.	0.	0.
30. Non-Ferrous Metals	0.	0.	0.	0.	0.	0.	0.	0.
31. Metallic Products	.079	.016	.006	.001	.004	.002	.002	0.
32. Non-Electrical Machinery	.603	.188	.170	.031	.117	.072	.069	0.
33. Industrial Electrical Machinery	.603	.188	.170	.031	.117	.072	.069	0.
34. Electronics	.603	.188	.170	.031	.117	.072	.069	0.
35. Household Electrical Machinery	0.	0.	0.	0.	0.	0.	0.	0.
36. Shipbuilding & Repairing	0.	0.	1.420	0.	0.	0.	0.	0.
37. Railroad Transport	0.	0.	.167	0.	0.	0.	0.	0.
38. Motor Vehicles	.697	.102	.651	.038	.144	.089	.084	0.
39. Precision & Optical Products	.462	.162	.127	.025	.096	.059	.056	0.
40. Other Manufacturing	.020	0.	0.	0.	0.	0.	0.	0.
41. Residence & Building	9.809	0.	.311	.194	.737	.455	.431	0.
42. Public & Other Construction	0.	1.814	2.529	.194	.737	.455	.431	0.
43. Electricity	0.	0.	0.	0.	0.	0.	0.	0.
44. Water & Sanitary Service	0.	0.	0.	0.	0.	0.	0.	0.
45. Banking & Insurance	0.	0.	0.	0.	0.	0.	0.	0.
46. Housing	0.	0.	0.	0.	0.	0.	0.	0.
47. Communication	0.	0.	0.	0.	0.	0.	0.	0.
48. Transport & Storage	0.	0.	0.	0.	0.	0.	0.	0.
49. Commerce	.498	.103	.215	0.21	.080			
50. Education	0.	0.	0.	0.	0.	0.	0.	0.
51. Health	0.	0.	0.	0.	0.	0.	0.	0.
52. Other Services	0.	0.	0.	0.	0.	0.	0.	0.
53. Scrap & Unclassifiable	0.	0.	0.	0.	0.	0.	0.	0.
Total	13.414	2.771	.938	.567	2.153	1.329	1.259	0.

Annex Table 3. *Inventory–Output Coefficient Matrix*

(to *j* sector) (from *i* sector)	1 *A. & F.*	2 *Fi.*	3 *Coal*	4 *M. O.*	5 *N. M.*	6 *P. F.*	7 *B. & T.*	8 *F. S.*	9 *Fab.*
1. Agriculture & Forestry	.032	0.	.026	.011	.003	.051	.061	.166	0.
2. Fishery	0.	.001	0.	0.	0.	.004	0.	0.	0.
3. Coal	0.	0.	.001	.004	0.	0.	0.	0.	0.
4. Metallic Ores	0.	0.	0.	0.	0.	0.	0.	0.	0.
5. Non-Metallic Minerals	0.	0.	0.	0.	.001	0.	0.	0.	0.
6. Processed Foods	.013	.001	0.	0.	0.	.016	.032	0.	.001
7. Beverage & Tobacco	0.	0.	0.	0.	0.	0.	.041	0.	0.
8. Fiber Spinning	0.	0.	0.	0.	0.	0.	0.	.008	.121
9. Fabrics	0.	0.	0.	.001	0.	0.	0.	.007	.011
10. Finished Textiles	0.	.005	0.	.005	.001	.001	0.	0.	0.
11. Leather & Leather Products	0.	0.	0.	0.	0.	0.	0.	0.	0.
12. Lumber & Plywood	0.	0.	0.	.002	0.	0.	0.	0.	0.
13. Wood Products & Furniture	0.	.001	0.	0.	0.	0.	.005	.002	0.
14. Pulp, Paper & Paper Products	0.	0.	0.	.002	0.	.001	.008	0.	.001
15. Printing & Publishing	0.	0.	.001	.003	0.	0.	.001	0.	0.
16. Inorganic Chemicals	0.	0.	.001	.031	.001	.001	0.	.008	.002
17. Organic Chemicals	0.	0.	.002	.008	0.	.001	.003	0.	.010
18. Chemical Fertilizers	.009	0.	0.	0.	0.	0.	0.	.071	0.
19. Synthetic Resin & Chemical Fibers	0.	0.	0.	0.	0.	.001	.001	0.	.062
20. Other Chemicals	.002	.004	.017	.061	.009	.001	.004	.003	.002
21. Petroleum Products	0.	0.	.004	.019	.010	.001	.003	0.	.004
22. Coal Products	0.	0.	0.	.001	0.	0.	0.	0.	0.
23. Rubber Products	0.	0.	.002	.010	.010	0.	0.	0.	0.
24. Cement	0.	0.	0.	.001	0.	0.	0.	0.	0.
25. Glass, Clay & Stone Products	0.	0.	0.	.002	0.	0.	.012	0.	0.

26. Iron & Steel	0.	0.	0.	0.	0.	0.	0.	0.	0.
27. Rolled Steel	0.	0.	.008	.011	.001	0.	0.	0.	0.
28. Steel Pipes & Plated Steel	0.	0.	.001	.002	0.	0.	0.	0.	0.
29. Cast & Forged Steel	0.	0.	0.	.013	0.	0.	0.	0.	0.
30. Non-Ferrous Metals	0.	0.	0.	0.	0.	0.	0.	.001	0.
31. Metallic Products	.001	0.	.004	.017	.006	.001	.003	.001	.001
32. Non-Electrical Machinery	0.	.001	.006	.023	.003	0.	.001	0.	.003
33. Industrial Electrical Machinery	0.	0.	.003	.007	.001	0.	0.	0.	0.
34. Electronics	0.	0.	0.	0.	0.	0.	0.	0.	0.
35. Household Electrical Machinery	0.	0.	.001	.001	0.	0.	0.	0.	0.
36. Shipbuilding & Repairing	0.	.001	0.	0.	0.	0.	0.	0.	0.
37. Railroad Transport	0.	0.	.001	.001	0.	0.	0.	0.	0.
38. Motor Vehicles	0.	0.	.002	.009	.003	0.	.001	0.	0.
39. Precision & Optical Products	0.	0.	0.	0.	0.	0.	0.	0.	0.
40. Other Manufacturing	.001	0.	0.	.003	.004	.001	.008	.001	0.
41. Residence & Building	0.	0.	0.	0.	0.	0.	0.	0.	0.
42. Public & Other Construction	0.	0.	0.	0.	0.	0.	0.	0.	0.
43. Electricity	0.	0.	0.	0.	0.	0.	0.	0.	0.
44. Water & Sanitary Service	0.	0.	0.	0.	0.	0.	0.	0.	0.
45. Banking & Insurance	0.	0.	0.	0.	0.	0.	0.	0.	0.
46. Housing	0.	0.	0.	0.	0.	0.	0.	0.	0.
47. Communication	0.	0.	0.	0.	0.	0.	0.	0.	0.
48. Transport & Storage	0.	0.	0.	0.	0.	0.	0.	0.	0.
49. Commerce	.004	.001	.006	.018	.003	.006	.013	.020	.016
50. Education	0.	0.	0.	0.	0.	0.	0.	0.	0.
51. Health	0.	0.	0.	0.	0.	0.	0.	0.	0.
52. Other Services	0.	0.	0.	0.	0.	0.	0.	0.	0.
53. Scrap & Unclassifiable	0.	0.	0.	0.	0.	0.	0.	0.	0.
Total	.063	.018	.088	.266	.049	.085	.200	.291	.238

Annex Table 3. *(Continued)*

(to *j* sector)	10	11	12	13	14	15	16	17	18
(from *i* sector)	*F.T.*	*L.&L.P.*	*L.&.P.*	*W.P.&F.*	*P.P.&P.F.*	*P. & P.*	*I.C.*	*O.C.*	*C.F.*
1. Agriculture & Forestry	.001	.003	.131	.023	.009	0.	0.	0.	0.
2. Fishery	0.	0.	0.	.006	0.	0.	0.	0.	0.
3. Coal	0.	0.	0.	0.	0.	0.	.003	0.	.001
4. Metallic Ores	0.	0.	0.	0.	0.	0.	0.	0.	0.
5. Non-Metallic Minerals	0.	0.	0.	0.	0.	0.	.015	.008	.040
6. Processed Foods	0.	.046	.001	0.	.001	0.	0.	.009	.006
7. Beverage & Tobacco	0.	0.	0.	0.	0.	0.	0.	0.	0.
8. Fiber Spinning	.030	.001	0.	0.	.002	0.	0.	0.	0.
9. Fabrics	.051	.002	0.	.002	0.	0.	0.	.001	0.
10. Finished Textiles	.002	.003	0.	.001	.001	0.	0.	.001	.004
11. Leather & Leather Products	.001	.073	0.	0.	0.	0.	0.	0.	0.
12. Lumber & Plywood	0.	0.	.004	.015	0.	0.	0.	0.	0.
13. Wood Products & Furniture	0.	0.	0.	.002	0.	0.	0.	0.	0.
14. Pulp, Paper & Paper Products	.001	0.	0.	.001	.073	.069	.001	.002	.003
15. Printing & Publishing	0.	0.	0.	.002	0.	.006	0.	0.	.001
16. Inorganic Chemicals	0.	.002	0.	0.	.002	0.	.012	.012	.021
17. Organic Chemicals	0.	0.	.005	0.	.002	0.	.004	.082	.002
18. Chemical Fertilizers	0.	0.	.002	0.	0.	0.	0.	0.	.003
19. Synthetic Resin & Chemical Fibers	.008	.016	0.	.002	.001	0.	0.	0.	0.
20. Other Chemicals	0.	.006	.001	.013	.003	.006	.004	.003	.015
21. Petroleum Products	0.	.002	.002	.004	.002	.002	.003	.006	.101
22. Coal Products	0.	0.	0.	0.	0.	0.	.001	0.	.001
23. Rubber Products	0.	.013	0.	0.	0.	0.	0.	0.	.001
24. Cement	0.	0.	0.	0.	0.	0.	0.	0.	0.
25. Glass, Clay & Stone Products	0.	0.	0.	.007	.001	0.	.001	0.	.001

26. Iron & Steel	0.	0.	0.	0.	0.	0.	0.	0.	0.
27. Rolled Steel	0.	.001	0.	0.	0.	0.	0.	0.	0.
28. Steel Pipes & Plated Steel	0.	0.	0.	0.	0.	0.	0.	0.	0.
29. Cast & Forged Steel	0.	0.	0.	0.	0.	0.	0.	0.	0.
30. Non-Ferrous Metals	0.	0.	0.	0.	0.	.001	0.	0.	0.
31. Metallic Products	0.	.004	.001	.013	.002	.001	.003	.002	.002
32. Non-Electrical Machinery	.001	.001	.001	.001	.001	.001	.0	.001	.001
33. Industrial Electrical Machinery	0.	0.	0.	0.	0.	0.	0.	0.	0.
34. Electronics	0.	0.	0.	0.	0.	0.	0.	0.	0.
35. Household Electrical Machinery..	0.	0.	0.	0.	0.	0.	0.	0.	0.
36. Shipbuilding & Repairing	0.	0.	0.	0.	0.	0.	0.	0.	0.
37. Railroad Transport	0.	0.	0.	0.	0.	0.	0.	0.	0.
38. Motor Vehicles	0.	0.	0.	0.	0.	0.	.001	.001	.001
39. Precision & Optical Products	0.	0.	0.	0.	0.	0.	0.	0.	0.
40. Other Manufacturing	0.	.001	0.	0.	0.	0.	0.	0.	0.
41. Residence & Building	0.	0.	0.	0.	0.	0.	0.	0.	0.
42. Public & Other Construction	0.	0.	0.	0.	0.	0.	0.	0.	0.
43. Electricity	0.	0.	0.	0.	0.	0.	0.	0.	0.
44. Water & Sanitary Service	0.	0.	0.	0.	0.	0.	0(	0.	0.
45. Banking & Insurance	0.	0.	0.	0.	0.	0.	0.	0.	0.
46. Housing	0.	0.	0.	0.	0.	0.	0.	0.	0.
47. Communication	0.	0.	0.	0.	0.	0.	0.	0.	0.
48. Transport & Storage	0.	0.	0.	0.	0.	0.	0.	0.	0.
49. Commerce	.007	.013	.011	.013	.007	.006	.004	.009	.017
50. Education	0.	0.	0.	0.	0.	0.	0.	0.	0.
51. Health	0.	0.	0.	0.	0'	0.	0.	0.	0.
52. Other Services	0.	0.	0.	0.	0.	0.	0.	0.	0.
53. Scrap & Unclassifiable	0.	0.	0.	0.	0.	0.	0.	0.	0.
Total	.103	.187	.161	.196	.109	.096	.054	.139	.253

Annex Table 3. (Continued)

(to *j* sector) / (from *i* sector)	19 *S.R.&C.F.*	20 *O.C.*	21 *P.P.*	22 *C.P.*	23 *R.P.*	24 *Cement*	25 *G.C.&S.P.*	26 *I.&S.*	27 *R.S.*
1. Agriculture & Forestry	0.	.004	0.	0.	.077	0.	.001	0.	0.
2. Fishery	0.	0.	0.	0.	0.	0.	0.	0.	0.
3. Coal	O.	0.	0.	.075	0.	.003	.010	.010	.001
4. Metallic Ores	0.	0.	0.	0.	0.	.011	0.	.011	0.
5. Non-Metallic Minerals	0.	.001	.175	0.	0.	.073	.053	.005	.001
6. Processed Foods	0.	.035	0.	0.	0.	0.	0.	0.	0.
7. Beverage & Tobacco	0.	0.	0.	0.	0.	0.	0.	0.	0.
8. Fiber Spinning	0.	.001	0.	0.	.005	0.	0.	0.	0.
9. Fabrics	0.	0.	0.	0.	.038	0.	0.	0.	0.
10. Finished Textiles	0.	.001	.001	0.	.002	.001	0.	0.	0.
11. Leather & Leather Products	0.	.001	0.	0.	.002	0.	0.	0.	0.
12. Lumber & Plywood	0.	0.	0.	0.	0.	.003	0.	0.	0.
13. Wood Products & Furniture	0.	.003	0.	0.	0.	0.	.001	0.	0.
14. Pulp, Paper & Paper Products	0.	.018	0.	0.	.003	.038	.004	0.	.001
15. Printing & Publishing	0.	.002	0.	0.	0.	.001	0.	0.	0.
16. Inorangic Chemicals	0.	.013	0.	0.	.012	.012	.018	.004	.002
17. Organic Chemicals	.003	.064	.002	0.	.104	0.	.002	0.	0.
18. Chemical Fertilizers	0.	0.	0.	0.	0.	0.	0.	0.	0.
19. Synthetic Resin & Chemical Fibers	.005	.007	0.	0.	.005	0.	0.	0.	0.
20. Other Chemicals	0.	.097	.004	0.	.086	.001	.004	0.	0.
21. Petroleum Products	0.	.005	.006	.001	.010	.042	.013	.004	.005
22. Coal Products	0.	0.	0.	0.	0.	0.	0.	.011	.001
23. Rubber Products	0.	.001	0.	0.	.012	.001	.001	0.	0.
24. Cement	0.	0.	0.	0.	0.	.046	.011	0.	0.
25. Glass, Clay & Stone Products	0.	.010	0.	0.	0.	.004	.003	.019	.004

26. Iron & Steel	0.	0.	0.	0.	0.	0.	0.	.071	.177
27. Rolled Steel	0.	0.	0.	0.	0.	.014	.001	.002	.066
28. Steel Pipes & Plated Steel	0.	0.	0.	0.	0.	0.	0.	.001	.001
29. Cast & Forged Steel	0.	0.	0.	0.	0.	.006	.001	.001	.001
30. Non-Ferrous Metals	0.	.005	0.	0.	0.	0.	0.	0.	0.
31. Metallic Products	0.	.006	.002	0.	.002	.010	.002	.002	.001
32. Non-Electrical Machinery	0.	0.	.001	.001	.003	.003	.002	.001	.001
33. Industrial Electrical Machinery	0.	0.	.001	0.	0.	0.	0.	.003	0.
34. Electronics	0.	0.	0.	0.	0.	0.	0.	0.	0.
35. Household Electrical Machinery	0.	0.	0.	0.	0.	0.	0.	0.	0.
36. Shipbuilding & Repairing	0.	0.	0.	0.	0.	0.	0.	0.	0.
37. Railroad Transport	0.	0.	0.	0.	0.	0.	0.	0.	0.
38. Motor Vehicles	0.	.001	.001	.001	.001	.002	.001	.001	.001
39. Precision & Optical Products	0.	0.	0.	0.	0.	0.	0.	0.	0.
40. Other Manufacturing	0.	0.	0.	0.	0.	0.	.002	0.	0.
41. Residence & Building	0.	0.	0.	0.	0.	0.	0.	0.	0.
42. Public & Other Construction	0.	0.	0.	0.	0.	0.	0.	0.	0.
43. Electricity	0.	0.	0.	0.	0.	0.	0.	0.	0.
44. Water & Sanitary Service	0.	0.	0.	0.	0.	0.	0.	0.	0.
45. Banking & Insurance	0.	0.	0.	0.	0.	0.	0.	0.	0.
46. Housing	0.	0.	0.	0.	0.	0.	0.	0.	0.
47. Communication	0.	0.	0.	0.	0.	0.	0.	0.	0.
48. Transport & Storage	0.	0.	0.	0.	0.	0.	0.	0.	0.
49. Commerce	.001	.020	.014	.006	.020	.020	.010	.011	.019
50. Education	0.	0.	0.	0.	0.	0.	0.	0.	0.
51. Health	0.	0.	0.	0.	0.	0.	0.	0.	0.
52. Other Services	0.	0.	0.	0.	0.	0.	0.	0.	0.
53. Scrap & Unclassifiable	0.	0.	0.	0.	0.	0.	0.	0.	0.
Total	.010	.298	.208	.084	.295	.291	.142	.159	.282

Annex Table 3. (Continued)

(to *j* sector)	28	29	30	31	32	33	34	35	36
(from *i* sector)	*S.P.&P.S.*	*C.&F.S.*	*Non-F.M.*	*M.P.*	*Non-E.M.*	*I.E.M.*	*Elec.*	*H.E.M.*	*S.&R.*
1. Agriculture & Forestry	0.	0.	0.	0.	0.	0.	0.	0.	0.
2. Fishery	0.	0.	0.	0.	0.	0.	0.	0.	0.
3. Coal	0.	.011	.001	0.	.001	0.	0.	0.	0.
4. Metallic Ores	0.	.002	.027	.001	0.	0.	0.	0.	0.
5. Non-Metallic Minerals	0.	.003	0.	0.	.002	0.	.001	0.	0.
6. Processed Foods	0.	0.	0.	0.	0.	0.	0.	0.	0.
7. Beverage & Tobacco	0.	0.	0.	0.	0.	0.	0.	0.	0.
8. Fiber Spinning	0.	0.	0.	0.	0.	.002	0.	0.	0.
9. Fabrics	0.	0.	0.	0.	0.	0.	0.	0.	0.
10. Finished Textiles	0.	0.	0.	.001	.001	0.	0.	0.	.001
11. Leather & Leather Products	0.	0.	0.	0.	0.	0.	0.	0.	0.
12. Lumber & Plywood	0.	0.	0.	.002	.001	.002	0.	0.	.056
13. Wood Products & Furniture	0.	0.	0.	0.	.001	0.	.002	.002	.001
14. Pulp, Paper & Paper Products	0.	0.	0.	.001	. 001	.007	.002	.006	.0
15. Printing & Publishing	0.	0.	0.	.001	0.	0.	0.	.001	.001
16. Inorganic Chemicals	0.	.002	.004	.002	.001	.002	.001	.003	.C06
17. Organic Chemicals	0.	0.	0.	.003	0.	.002	.001	.004	0.
18. Chemical Fertilizers	0.	0.	0.	0.	0.	0.	0.	0.	0.
19. Synthetic Resin & Chemical Fibers	0.	0.	0.	.003	.002	.008	.003	.009	0.
20. Other Chemicals	0.	.001	0.	.003	.001	.002	.001	.002	.003
21. Petroleum Products	0.	.003	.001	.004	.002	.004	.001	.004	.002
22. Coal Products	0.	.005	.001	0.	0.	.001	0.	0.	0.
23. Rubber Products	0.	0.	0.	0.	.001	.001	.001	.001	.001
24. Cement	0.	0.	0.	0.	0.	.003	0.	0.	.001
25. Glass, Clay & Stone Products	0.	.006	.001	.001	.002	.002	.001	.015	.003

26. Iron & Steel	0.	.040	0.	.003	.011	.018	0.	0.	0.
27. Rolled Steel	.026	.004	0.	.094	.024	.001	.002	.009	.142
28. Steel Pipes & Plated Steel	0.	.001	0.	.020	.003	.002	0.	.001	.007
29. Cast & Forged Steel	0.	.005	0.	.007	.020	.089	0.	.011	.001
30. Non-Ferrous Metals	.002	.001	.012	.026	.010	.004	.003	.024	.002
31. Metallic Products	0.	.002	0.	.015	.008	.003	.002	.013	.009
32. Non-Electrical Machinery	0.	.001	0.	.002	.003	.017	0.	.005	.052
33. Industrial Electrical Machinery	0.	0.	0.	0.	0.	.003	.004	.018	.012
34. Electronics	0.	0.	0.	0.	0.	0.	.057	.010	.012
35. Household Electrical Machinery	0.	0.	0.	0.	0.	0.	0.	0.81	0.02
36. Shipbuilding & Repairing	0.	0.	0.	0.	0.	0.	0.	0.	0.47
37. Railroad Transport	0.	0.	0.	0.	0.	0.	0.	0.	0.
38. Motor Vehicles	0.	.001	0.	.001	.001	0.	0.	.001	.001
39. Precision & Optical Products	0.	0.	0.	.001	0.	0.	0.	.001	0.
40. Other Manufacturing	0.	0.	0.	0.	0.	0.	0.	0.	.001
41. Residence & Building	0.	0.	0.	0.	0.	0.	0.	0.	0.
42. Public & Other Construction	0.	0.	0.	0.	0.	0.	0.	0.	0.
43. Electricity	0.	0.	0.	0.	0.	0.	0.	0.	0.
44. Water & Sanitary Service	0.	0.	0.	0.	0.	0.	0.	0.	0.
45. Banking & Insurance	0.	0.	0.	0.	0.	0.	0.	0.	0.
46. Housing	0.	0.	0.	0.	0.	0.	0.	0.	0.
47. Communication	0.	0.	0.	0.	0.	0.	0.	0.	0.
48. Transport & Storage	0.	0.	0.	0.	0.	0.	0.	0.	0.
49. Commerce	.002	.007	.004	.014	.008	.013	.006	.011	.026
50. Education	0.	0.	0.	0.	0.	0.	0.	0.	0.
51. Health	0.	0.	0.	0.	0.	0.	0.	0.	0.
52. Other Services	0.	0.	0.	0.	0.	0.	0.	0.	0.
53. Scrap & Unclassifiable	0.	0.	0.	0.	0.	0.	0.	0.	0.
Total	.033	.096	.054	.205	.126	.186	.090	.159	.390

Annex Table 3. (Continued)

(to *j* sector) (from *i* sector)	37 *R.T.*	38 *M.V.*	39 *P.&O.P.*	40 *O.M.*	41 *R.&.B.*	42 *P.&O.C.*	43 *Elect.*	44 *W.&S.S.*	45 *B.&T.*
1. Agriculture & Forestry	0.	0.	0.	.032	0.	.001	0.	0.	0.
2. Fishery	0.	0.	0.	.001	0.	0.	0.	0.	0.
3. Coal	.001	0.	0.	0.	0.	0.	.002	0.	0.
4. Metallic Ores	0.	0.	0.	0.	0.	0.	0.	0.	0.
5. Non-Metallic Minerals	0.	0.	0.	.001	0.	.002	0.	0.	0.
6. Processed Foods	0.	0.	0.	0.004	0.	0.	0.	0.	0.
7. Beverage & Tobacco	0.	0.	0.	0.	0.	0.	0.	0.	0.
8. Fiber Spinning	0.	0.	0.	.003	0.	0.	0.	0.	0.
9. Fabrics	.003	0.	0.	.004	0.	0.	0.	0.	0.
10. Finished Textiles	.001	0.	0.	.011	0.	0.	0.	.001	0.
11. Leather & Leather Products	.001	0.	0.	.003	0.	0.	0.	0.	0.
12. Lumber & Plywood	.002	.001	.005	.003	.002	.002	0.	0.	0.
13. Wood Products & Furniture	0.	0.	.001	.001	0.	0.	0.	0.	0.
14. Pulp, Paper & Paper Products	0.	0.	.005	.004	0.	0.	0.	0.	0.
15. Printing & Publishing	.001	0.	.001	.001	0.	0.	0.	.001	.001
16. Inorganic Chemicals	.001	.001	.004	.002	0.	0.	0.	.002	0.
17. Organic Chemicals	0.	0.	0.	.003	0.	0.	0.	0.	0.
18. Chemical Fertilizers	0.	0.	0.	0.	0.	0.	0.	0.	0.
19. Synthetic Resin & Chemical Fibers	.003	.001	.010	.085	0.	0.	0.	0.	0.
20. Other Chemicals	.004	.001	.008	.003	0.	0.	0.	0.	0.
21. Petroleum Products	.002	.002	.003	.001	0.	.003	.008	.004	0.
22. Coal Products	.001	0.	.001	.001	0.	0.	0.	0.	0.
23. Rubber Products	.003	.005	0.	.002	0.	0.	0.	.001	0.
24. Cement	0.	0.	0.	0.	.002	.006	0.	0.	0.
25. Glass, Clay & Stone Products	.003	.001	.013	.001	.001	.011	0.	0.	0.

26. Iron & Steel	.006	.001	.001	0.	0.	0.	0.	0.	0.
27. Rolled Steel	.020	.010	.018	.004	.001	.005	0.	0.	0.
28. Steel Pipes & Plated Steel	.004	.002	.001	0.	0.	.002	0.	0.	0.
29. Cast & Forged Steel	.001	.001	.008	.001	0.	0.	0.	0.	0.
30. Non-Ferrous Metals	.009	.001	.026	.016	0.	0.	0.	0.	0.
31. Metallic Products	.012	.002	.006	.003	.001	.003	0.	0.	0.
32. Non-Electrical Machinery	.011	0.	.001	.003	0.	.002	0.	.001	0.
33. Industrial Electrical Machinery	.007	.002	.002	0.	0.	.007	0.	.001	0.
34. Electronics	.001	0.	.001	0.	0.	.001	0.	0.	0.
35. Household Electrical Machinery	0.	0.	0.	0.	0.	0.	0.	0.	0.
36. Shipbuilding & Repairing	0.	0.	0.	0.	0.	0.	0.	0.	0.
37. Railroad Transport	.049	0.	0.	0.	0.	0.	0.	0.	0.
38. Motor Vehicles	.002	.047	.001	0.	0.	0.	0.	.002	0.
39. Precision & Optical Products	0.	0.	.196	0.	0.	0.	0.	.002	0.
40. Other Manufacturing	0.	0.	0.	.001	0.	0.	0.	0.	0.
41. Residence & Building	0.	0.	0.	0.	0.	0.	0.	0.	0.
42. Public & Other Construction	0.	0.	0.	0.	0.	0.	0.	0.	0.
43. Electricity	0.	0.	0.	0.	0.	0.	0.	0.	0.
44. Water & Sanitary Service	0.	0.	0.	0.	0.	0.	0.	0.	0.
45. Banking & Insurance	0.	0.	0.	0.	0.	0.	0.	0.	0.
46. Housing	0.	0.	0.	0.	0.	0.	0.	0.	0.
47. Communication	0.	0.	0.	0.	0.	0.	0.	0.	0.
48. Transport & Storage	0.	0.	0.	0.	0.	0.	0.	0.	0.
49. Commerce	.011	.006	.023	.014	.001	.003	.001	.001	0.
50. Education	0.	0.	0.	0.	0.	0.	0.	0.	0.
51. Health	0.	0.	0.	0.	0.	0.	0.	0.	0.
52. Other Services	0.	0.	0.	0.	0.	0.	0.	0.	0.
53. Scrap & Unclassifiable	0.	0.	0.	0.	0.	0.	0.	0.	0.
Total	.390	.085	.336	.210	.011	.039	.012	.017	.001

Annex Table 3. (Continued)

(from *i* sector) (to *j* sector)	46 *Housing*	47 *Commun.*	48 *T.&S.*	49 *Commerce*	50 *Education*	51 *Health*	52 *O.S.*	53 *S.&Uncla.*
1. Agriculture & Forestry	0.	0.	0.	.002	0.	.001	.002	.099
2. Fishery	0.	0.	0.	0.	0.	0.	0.	0.
3. Coal	0.	0.	0.	0.	0.	0.	0.	0.
4. Metallic Ores	0.	0.	0.	0.	0.	0.	0.	.003
5. Non-Metallic Minerals	0.	0.	0.	.003	0.	0.	0.	.002
6. Processed Foods	0.	0.	0.	.003	0.	0.	.002	.006
7. Beverage & Tobacco	0.	0.	0.	0.	0.	0.	.009	.027
8. Fiber Spinning	0.	0.	0.	0.	0.	0.	0.	.011
9. Fabrics	0.	0.	0.	.002	0.	0.	0.	.010
10. Finished Textiles	0.	.001	0.	.041	0.	0.	.001	.007
11. Leather & Leather Products	0.	0.	0.	0.	0.	0.	0.	0.
12. Lumber & Plywood	0.	0.	0.	.008	0.	0.	0.	.003
13. Wood Products & Furniture	0.	0.	0.	.006	0.	0.	0.	.001
14. Pulp, Paper & Paper Products	0.	0.	0.	.066	.001	0.	.001	.003
15. Printing & Publishing	0.	.002	0.	.017	.003	0.	.002	.005
16. Inorganic Chemicals	0.	0.	0.	.001	0.	0.	0.	.002
17. Organic Chemicals	0.	0.	0.	0.	0.	0.	0.	0.
18. Chemical Fertilizers	0.	0.	0.	0.	0.	0.	0.	.001
19. Synthetic Resin & Chemical Fibers	0.	0.	0.	.009	0.	0.	0.	.012
20. Other Chemicals	0.	0.	0.	.010	0.	.003	.002	.006
21. Petroleum Products	0.	.001	.005	.030	.001	0.	.001	.006
22. Coal Products	0.	0.	0.	.034	0.	0.	.001	0.
23. Rubber Products	0.	0.	.001	.017	0.	0.	0.	.001
24. Cement	0.	0.	0.	.007	0.	0.	0.	.001
25. Glass, Clay & Stone Products	0.	0.	0.	.008	0.	0.	0.	.004

26. Iron & Steel	0.	0.	0.	0.	0.	0.	0.	0.
27. Rolled Steel	0.	0.	0.	0.	0.	0.	0.	.004
28. Steel Pipes & Plated Steel	0.	0.	0.	0.	0.	0.	0.	.002
29. Cast & Forged Steel	0.	0.	.001	0.	0.	0.	0.	0.
30. Non-Ferrous Metals	0.	0.	0.	.001	0.	0.	0.	.001
31. Metallic Products	0.	0.	0.	.003	0.	0.	0.	.005
32. Non-Electrical Machinery	0.	0.	0.	.004	0.	0.	0.	.005
33. Industrial Electrical Machinery	0.	.002	0.	.003	0.	0.	0.	.002
34. Electronics	0.	.001	0.	.003	0.	0.	0.	.003
35. Household Electrical Machinery	0.	0.	0.	.005	0.	0.	0.	.001
36. Shipbuilding & Repairing	0.	0.	.001	0.	0.	0.	0.	.001
37. Railroad Transport	0.	0.	.001	0.	0.	0.	0.	.001
38. Motor Vehicles	0.	0.	.002	.014	0.	0.	0.	.002
39. Precision & Optical Products	0.	0.	0.	.003	0.	0.	0.	0.
40. Other Manufacturing	0.	0.	0.	.024	0.	0.	.001	0.
41. Residence & Building	0.	0.	0.	0.	0.	0.	0.	0.
42. Public & Other Construction	0.	0.	0.	0.	0.	0.	0.	0.
43. Electricity	0.	0.	0.	0.	0.	0.	0.	0.
44. Water & Sanitary Service	0.	0.	0.	0.	0.	0.	0.	0.
45. Banking & Insurance	0.	0.	0.	0.	0.	0.	0.	0.
46. Housing	0.	0.	0.	0.	0.	0.	0.	0.
47. Communication	0.	0.	0.	0.	0.	0.	0.	0.
48. Transport & Storage	0.	.001	.001	.023	.001	0.	.002	.017
49. Commerce	0.	0.	0.	0.	0.	0.	0.	0.
50. Education	0.	0.	0.	0.	0.	0.	0.	0.
51. Health	0.	0.	0.	0.	0.	0.	0.	0.
52. Other Services	0.	0.	0.	0.	0.	0.	0.	0.
53. Scrap & Unclassifiable	0.	0.	0.	0.	0.	0.	0.	0.
Total	0.	.010	.011	.347	.009	.004	.026	.0254

Annex Table 4. Projections of Private Consumption Expenditures in 1976 and 1981, at 1970 prices

Sector	Expenditure				
	Absolute Value (in billion won)			Index (1970 = 100)	
	1970	1976	1981	1976	1981
1. Agriculture & Forestry	585.1	651.6	730.1	111.4	124.8
2. Fishery	38.5	49.7	62.9	129.1	163.4
3. Coal	0.0	0.0	0.0	0.0	0.0
4. Metallic Ores	0.0	0.0	0.0	0.0	0.0
5. Non-Metallic Minerals	2.5	3.0	3.6	120.0	144.0
6. Processed Foods	192.8	299.9	426.2	155.6	221.1
7. Beverage & Tobacco	112.7	171.3	240.5	152.0	213.4
8. Fiber Spinning	4.0	10.1	17.2	252.5	430.0
9. Fabrics	20.6	37.4	57.1	181.6	278.2
10. Finished Textiles	111.0	185.1	272.4	166.8	245.4
11. Leather & Leather Products	8.7	15.8	24.2	181.6	278.2
12. Lumber & Plywood	0.0	0.1	0.1	0.0	0.0
13. Wood Products & Furniture	2.0	3.7	5.8	185.0	290.0
14. Pulp, Paper & Paper Products	1.2	2.6	4.3	123.8	204.8
15. Printing & Publishing	11.6	25.5	41.9	219.8	361.2
16. Inorganic Chemicals	0.0	0.0	0.0	0.0	0.0
17. Organic Chemicals	0.0	0.0	0.0	0.0	0.0
18. Chemical Fertilizers	0.0	0.0	0.0	0.0	0.0
19. Synthetic Resin & Chemical Fibers	11.1	29.7	51.5	267.6	464.0
20. Other Chemicals	36.7	97.9	170.0	266.8	463.2
21. Petroleum Products	3.1	8.3	14.5	267.7	467.7
22. Coal Products	26.6	46.3	69.4	174.1	260.9
23. Rubber Products	6.6	9.1	12.1	137.9	183.3
24. Cement	0.0	0.0	0.0	0.0	0.0
25. Glass, Clay & Stone Products	1.1	1.6	2.2	145.5	200.0

26. Iron & Steel	0.0	0.0	0.0	0.0	0.0
27. Rolled Steel	0.0	0.0	0.0	0.0	0.0
28. Steel Pipes & Plated Steel	0.0	0.0	0.0	0.0	0.0
29. Cast & Forged Steel	0.0	0.0	0.0	0.0	0.0
30. Non-Ferrous Metals	0.0	0.0	0.0	0.0	0.0
31. Metallic Products	6.1	16.3	28.4	267.2	465.6
32. Non-Electrical Machinery	0.8	2.2	3.9	275.0	487.5
33. Industrial Electrical Machinery	0.4	1.1	2.0	275.0	500.0
34. Electronics	8.1	23.0	40.6	284.0	501.2
35. Household Electrical Machinery	3.8	10.3	17.9	271.1	471.1
36. Shipbuilding & Repairing	0.0	0.0	0.0	0.0	0.0
37. Railroad Transport	0.0	0.0	0.0	0.0	0.0
38. Motor Vehicles	4.8	13.8	24.3	287.5	506.3
39. Precision & Optical Products	7.0	18.9	32.9	270.0	470.0
40. Other Manufacturing	19.6	36.0	55.2	183.7	281.6
41. Residence & Building	0.0	0.0	0.0	0.0	0.0
42 Public & Other Construction	0.0	0.0	0.0	0.0	0.0
43. Electricity	12.4	22.1	33.5	178.2	270.2
44. Water & Sanitary Service	3.1	4.8	6.9	154.8	222.6
45. Banking & Insurance	11.8	16.2	21.4	137.3	181.4
46. Housing	101.7	139.5	184.1	137.2	181.0
47. Communication	9.3	18.8	29.9	202.2	321.5
48. Transport & Storage	126.0	197.3	281.4	156.6	223.3
49. Commerce	150.7	221.6	305.2	147.1	202.5
50. Education	34.1	53.4	76.1	156.6	223.2
51. Health	43.9	68.8	98.1	156.7	223.5
52. Other Services	163.3	255.7	364.6	156.6	223.3
53. Scrap & Unclassifiable	1.4	2.1	2.8	150.0	200.0
Total	1,884.3	2,770.4	3,815.2		

Annex Table 5. 1981 Export Projection: Case of 12.7 billion dollars

(billion dollars at 1970 prices)

Sector	1974	1976	1981
1. Agriculture & Forestry	18.3	20.5	27.2
2. Fishery	14.5	16.8	24.4
3. Coal	0.9	1.0	1.2
4. Metallic Ores	5.7	6.2	7.9
5. Non-Metallic Minerals	4.7	5.4	7.9
6. Processed Foods	38.3	46.0	72.6
7. Beverage & Tobacco	0.2	0.2	0.4
8. Fiber Spinning	36.1	44.8	76.9
9. Fabrics	57.3	81.7	198.6
10. Finished Textiles	204.1	256.0	451.1
11. Leather & Leather Products	15.7	20.4	39.2
12. Lumber & Plywood	64.2	75.2	111.8
13. Wood Products & Furniture	11.1	14.1	25.3
14. Pulp, Paper & Paper Products	8.6	10.3	16.6
15. Printing & Publishing	4.3	6.2	15.5
16. Inorganic Chemicals	1.4	1.6	2.4
17. Organic Chemicals	6.8	7.6	10.1
18. Chemical Fertilizers	0.1	0.4	14.3
19. Synthetic Resin & Chemical Fibers	7.0	11.9	45.0
20. Other Chemicals	8.2	9.2	12.5
21. Petroleum Products	7.5	7.9	9.1
22. Coal Products	0.0	0.0	0.0
23. Rubber Products	27.3	32.1	47.8
24. Cement	5.7	10.4	47.7
25. Glass, Clay & Stone Products	5.2	6.8	13.5
26. Iron & Steel	7.8	9.6	16.5
27. Rolled Steel	46.3	58.0	101.8
28. Steel Pipes & Plated Steel	15.6	25.0	81.5
29. Cast & Forged Steel	3.2	6.1	31.5
30. Non-Ferrous Metals	2.2	2.7	4.7
31. Industrial Electrical Machinery	25.8	32.0	54.9
32. Non-Electrical Machinery	15.1	21.9	55.7
33. Industrial Electrical Machinery	10.4	15.9	45.7
34. Electronics	78.7	115.4	300.5
35. Household Electrical Machinery	8.1	12.3	35.0
36. Shipbuilding & Repairing	14.0	30.5	211.8
37. Railroad Transport	2.0	2.1	9.6

Annex Table 5. (Continued)

Sector	1974	1976	1981
38. Motor Vehicles	7.0	11.7	43.4
39. Precision & Optical Products	11.9	19.9	71.4
40. Other Manufacturing	59.1	69.1	102.3
41. Residence & Building	0.0	0.0	0.0
42. Public & Other Construction	11.8	18.2	40.9
43. Electricity	4.8	7.3	16.5
44. Water & Sanitary Service	0.3	0.5	1.1
45. Banking Insurance	1.2	1.8	4.1
46. Housing	0.0	0.0	0.0
47. Communication	1.1	1.7	3.8
48. Transport & Storage	62.8	96.9	217.9
49. Commerce	48.4	65.4	91.1
50. Education	0.0	0.0	0.0
51. Health	0.0	0.0	0.0
52. Other Services	14.9	23.0	51.8
53. Scrap & Unclassifiable	35.2	54.3	122.1
Total	1040.5	1395.3	2994.7

Annex Table 6. 1981 Export Projection: Case of 13.5 billion dollars
(billion dollars at 1970 Prices)

Sector	1974	1976	1981
1. Agriculture & Forestry	18.3	20.9	29.1
2. Fishery	14.5	17.2	26.1
3. Coal	0.9	1.0	1.3
4. Metallic Ores	5.7	6.4	8.5
5. Non-Metallic Minerals	4.7	5.5	8.5
6. Processed Foods	38.3	46.8	77.5
7. Beverage & Tobacco	0.2	0.2	0.4
8. Fiber Spinning	36.1	45.7	82.1
9. Fabrics	57.3	83.3	212.1
10. Finished Textiles	204.1	260.9	481.8
11. Leather & Leather Products	15.7	20.8	41.9
12. Lumber & Plywood	64.2	76.7	119.4
13. Wood Products & Furniture	11.1	14.3	27.0
14. Pulp, Paper & Paper Products	8.6	10.5	17.7
15. Printing & Publishing	4.3	6.3	16.6
16. Inorganic Chemicals	1.4	1.7	2.6

Annex Table 6. *(Continued)*

Sector	1974	1976	1981
17. Organic Chemicals	6.8	7.7	10.8
18. Chemical Fertilizers	0.1	0.4	15.3
19. Synthetic Resin & Chemical Fibers	7.0	12.1	48.1
20. Other Chemicals	8.2	9.4	13.4
21. Petroleum Products	7.5	8.1	9.8
22. Coal Products	0.0	0.0	0.0
23. Rubber Products	27.3	32.7	51.0
24. Cement	5.7	10.6	50.9
25. Glass, Clay & Stone Products	5.2	6.9	14.4
26. Iron & Steel	7.8	9.8	17.6
27. Rolled Steel	46.3	59.1	108.8
28. Steel Pipes & Plated Steel	15.6	25.5	87.0
29. Cast & Forged Steel	3.2	6.2	33.7
30. Non-Ferrous Metals	2.2	2.8	5.0
31. Metallic Products	25.8	32.6	58.6
32. Non-Electrical Machinery	15.1	22.4	59.5
33. Industrial Electrical Machinery	10.4	16.2	48.9
34. Electronics	78.7	117.6	321.0
35. Household Electrical Machinery	8.1	12.5	37.4
36. Shipbuilding & Repairing	14.0	31.0	226.3
37. Railroad Transport	2.0	3.2	10.3
38. Motor Vehicles	7.0	12.0	46.4
39. Precision & Optical Products	11.9	20.3	76.2
40. Other Manufacturing	59.1	70.4	109.3
41. Residence & Building	0.0	0.0	0.9
42. Public & Other Construction	11.8	18.2	40.9
43. Electricity	4.8	7.3	16.5
44. Water & Sanitary Service	0.3	0.5	1.1
45. Banking & Insurance	1.2	1.8	4.1
46. Housing	0.0	0.0	0.0
47. Communication	1.1	1.7	3.8
48. Transport & Storage	62.8	96.9	217.9
49. Commerce	48.4	65.4	91.1
50. Education	0.0	0.0	0.0
51. Health	0.0	0.0	0.0
52. Other Services	14.9	23.0	51.8
53. Scrap & Unclassifiable	35.2	54.3	122.1
Total	1040.5	1416.8	3161.5

A MACRO-ECONOMIC MODEL FOR THE OVERALL RESOURCES BUDGET

*Yung Bong Kim**

I. Introduction

Since 1967, when the revised set of national income data were released by the Bank of Korea, a number of domestic and foreign economists have involved themselves in building macro-economic models for Korea.[1] They were largely financed and developed for the purpose of finding inter-relations among economic variables which could be used for the formulation of economic development plans.

It is generally agreed, however, that the major contribution of earlier works can be found in the advancement of economic science in Korea rather than in policy implementation. Efforts devoted to the development of scientific economic models have not fully paid off in practical planning due to data insufficiency and frequent structural change of the economy. Although estimates on macro-economic variables such as overall rates of growth of output, investment, savings, exports and imports were critical in designing and executing development programs, lack of confidence in the statistical base and in their performance has limited application of aggregate models to economic planning. Except for some overall resource budgeting, guesswork and estimates obtained by sectoral models were more

* Senior Fellow at the Korea Development Institute (KDI). This paper was presented at the First International Symposium sponsored by KDI, Seoul, July 5–11, 1972.

[1] I. Adelman and M. J. Kim (1969); M. J. Kim and D. W. Nam (1968); R. D. Norton (1969); and Research Institute for Economics and Business, *An Econometric Model for the Korean Economy* (Seoul: Sogang College, Feb. 1968).

frequently used to derive macro-estimates.

As we expect that a greater reliance would be placed upon the estimates of an aggregate model in future planning work, it becomes increasingly necessary to develop a macro-economic model which would reveal the long-term structural trend of the economy. It is still early to develop such a model because of incomplete data and a short sample period. This paper, therefore, intends to be another model building exercise, hoping that some of its findings may be of use for the construction of improved macro-economic models.

This paper attempts to put together more available information, data and techniques, and to apply some macro-economic theories to practical model building in Korea. It is a main objective of this paper to do annual projections, which, if possible, reflect the apparent recent down-turning trend of the economy.

The model assumes two separate systems in the determination of income; it forecasts an output level solely determined by production processes, and GNP on the demand side is determined by estimating the level of investment, consumption and imports, respectively. The *ex ante* gap between them should be interpreted as an inflationary or deflationary gap, indicating that precautionary financial and fiscal measures should be taken. For this, powerful financial intermediation is allowed to influence the level of GNP both on demand and production sides. Financial variables function as an input in production, and, with taxes, determine the level of investment and, in turn, imports.

The inclusion of such powerful financial intermediation, in which the Government is a main agent, increases the practical value of the model for planning purposes, unless we are bothered by possible arguments against its use from a theoretical point of view. A financial variable necessarily enters the system as a policy variable for attaining overall equilibrium of the economy, unless we propose a closed system, in which there is little interdependence between monetary and real sectors except that monetary policy could affect the attainment of short-run equilibrium of the price level. The intervention of a financial variable in the production function, meanwhile, erases a dichotomy between the supply and demand sides of the system, since monetary policy affects the level of investment and import.

A fuller description of the structural equations, and their data, estimation and theoretical background are presented in Section II of this paper. Economic projections for 1972 and 1973 are done in Section III of this paper. Section IV presents a conclusion with suggestions and discussions for the Third Five-Year Plan and its execution.

II. The Model

Selection of the sample size is considered to be very important in the model specification as it greatly affects the value of coefficients of the structural equations. Those which were derived from the larger sample size have rich statistical properties but do not seem to reflect the real economic structure of Korea; the converse case is true for those from the smaller sample size. In this section, therefore, we present two sets of structural equations for comparison, estimations of which were obtained by applying least square methods, based upon the data of 1957–1971 and those of 1960–1971. An even shorter sample period 1965–1971, was required for the estimation of some import and investment equations because of the importance of those variables in the most recent years.

Each set of structural equations is designed to have two income determination systems expressing GNP on the expenditure or demand side and on the industrial origin or production side. The two systems approach GNP from different angles, and are mutually independent since a variable which is a dependent variable in one system is treated as exogenous if it enters in the other system as an independent variable. The gap thus obtained reflects *ex ante* disequilibrium between the aggregate demand and supply, which should disappear *ex post* through adequate adjustments.

The model contains 19 statistical equations, 14 identities, 33 endogenous variables, 7 exogenous policy variables, and 31 exogenous and lagged endogenous variables.

1. The Data

Basic data were mainly obtained from the publications of the Bank of Korea except for the data on employment and capital stock.

Because of discontinuity and incomparability in the series of employment data, it was necessary to construct a new series which covers the period 1957–1971. The work was done by KDI research staff. The 1963–1970 series published by the Bureau of Statistics, Economic Planning Board, was appropriately extended based upon the information obtained from the *1960 Population and Housing Census of Korea* and the earlier series on employment published by the Bureau of Statistics, Ministry of Internal Affairs.

The capital stock series was constructed by K. S. Lee (1971), Senior Fellow, KDI, using the stock figures obtained from *Estimates of Korean Capital and Inventory Coefficients in 1968* by K. C. Han as a base.

All values, unless otherwise specified, were expressed in terms of billions of won at 1965 prices. For those values which were only available in terms of current prices or dollars, appropriate deflators were used for the conversion. For instance, money supply was deflated by the wholesale price index, government revenue was deflated by the weighted index of the government consumption deflator and the government fixed capital formation deflator, and dollar values were converted by multiplying 265.4, the 1965 par value of the dollar in terms of won.

2. *List of Variables*

A. Endogenous Variables

V^a : Value added in agriculture, forestry, and fishing
V^m : Value added in mining and manufacturing
V^o : Value added in electricity, construction, water, sanitary service, transportation, storage and communications
V^s : Value added in wholesale and retail trades, banking and insurance, ownership of dwellings, public administration, defence, education and other services
V : GNP
C : Total consumption
C^p : Private consumption
C^g : Government consumption
I : Gross domestic capital formation
I^f : Gross domestic fixed capital formation
I^a : Gross fixed investment in the primary sector
I^m : Gross fixed investment in the mining and manufacturing sector
I^o : Gross fixed investment in the social overhead sector
I^s : Gross fixed investment in the service sector
I^i : Increase in stocks
M^k : Imports of machinery and equipment
M^d : Imports of intermediate goods for domestic use
M^x : Imports of intermediate goods for export
M^f : Imports of fuel
$M^g_{c.i.f.}$: Total imports of goods at CIF

$M^g_{f.o.b.}$: Total imports of goods at FOB
M : Total imports
V^{na} : Value added in the non-agricultural sector
S^g : Government saving, deflated by gross domestic capital formation deflator
K^a : Beginning-of-year capital stock in the primary sector
K^m : Beginning-of-year capital stock in the mining and manufacturing sector
K^o : Beginning-of-year capital stock in the social overhead sector
K^s : Beginning-of-year capital stock in the service sector
D^a : Depreciation allowance for fixed capital in the primary sector
D^m : Depreciation allowance for fixed capital in the mining and manufacturing sector
D^o : Depreciation allowance for fixed capital in the social overhead sector
D^s : Depreciation allowance for fixed capital in the service sector

B. Exogenous Policy Variables

MS : Money supply outstanding
GR : Government revenue
DT : Direct tax, deflated by the GNP deflator
P^m : Exchange rate on imports
$PiFPiw$: Domestic fuel price index, deflated by the wholesale price index
Mgr : Imports of grains
X^g : Total exports of goods

C. Exogenous Variables

L^a : Employment in the primary sector, thousands of persons
L^m : Employment in the mining and manufacturing sector
L^o : Employment in the social overhead sector
L^s : Employment in the service sector
V^f : Net factor income from the rest of the world
Fe : Fertilizer consumed, ten thousands of metric tons
M^s : Imports of service
X^s : Exports of service
t : Time trend (the first year of the sample period-1)
D^w : Weather dummy variable

3. Production Functions

Four sectoral production functions, for the primary, mining and manufacturing, social overhead, and service sectors were estimated in order to obtain the industrial origin of GNP or aggregate supply. Each sectoral function is of the Cobb-Douglas type, implying unitary factor substitution and homogeneity.

The estimation of these production functions represented an attempt to refine and develop existing production theories in the field of macroeconomic research on Korea. Each of them assumes three inputs for production: fixed capital, labor and liquid assets, except for the primary sector where fertilizer application is included instead of money. Lack of data and inconsistency had delayed estimation of a Cobb-Douglas type production function, with all these variables, for Korea.

The most distinctive feature of these production functions is the inclusion of a financial variable as an explanatory variable. To my knowledge attempts to estimate such production functions have yet to appear in the economic literature, on the subject. Therefore, some justification and elaboration is required.

Generally, monetary phenomena have been studied for short-run equilibrium analysis in empirical research work. Recently, a group of monetary economists led by the University of Chicago Professors have endeavored to integrate the monetary sector with the real sector in a model of economic growth.[2]

Those theories, however, largely start from the proposition that cash balances influence consumption, saving, and investment behavior by affecting utility functions and portfolio choices. Although a difference in assumptions is apparent between these theories and our production function, it suggests to us a possibility of utilizing the money factor for the explanation of output growth.

Three basic assumptions underlie this incorporation of a financial variable, *MS*, into the neo-classical production function. They are:

1) A production unit is equipped with fixed capital goods and working capital. They are mutually substitutable within the finite planning horizon, and the ratio between them is planned according to the profit maximization principle of an individual firm.

---

[2] M. Sidrauski (1966, 1969); J. G. Johnson (1966), pp. 265–287; M. Friedman (1953); J. G. Gurley and E. S. Shaw (1960); J. Tobin (1965), pp. 676–684; and D. Patinkin (1965).

2) Production activity of an individual firm is greatly affected by the availability of liquid assets. Disregarding the constraints of demand for output, a firm would expand or contract its production according to its credit availability. *MS* is considered as the proxy variable of the aggregate liquid assets of the production units, private or public.

3) *MS* yields its own marginal products. Returns to the services rendered by *MS* are paid as interest and dividend payments, which are, in turn, based upon the social opportunity cost of money.

Thus the general form of our new production function is:

$$\text{(i)}\quad V = AL^{\alpha}K^{\beta}MS^{\gamma}$$

$$\text{where } 1 > \alpha > 0,\ 1 > \beta > 0,\ 1 > \gamma > 0$$

$$\text{and } \alpha + \beta + \gamma = 1$$

giving:

$$\text{(ii)}\quad V = AL^{\alpha}(K^{\beta/(1-\alpha)}MS^{1-\beta/(1-\alpha)})^{1-\alpha}$$

$$\text{(iii)}\quad = AL^{\alpha}[K(MS/K)^{1-\beta/(1-\alpha)}]^{1-\alpha}$$

In equation (i), *MS* is defined as an independent factor of production, to be substituted freely for *L* and *K*, with its marginal products expressed as:

$$\frac{\partial V}{\partial MS} = \gamma\frac{V}{MS} = (1 - \alpha - \beta)\frac{V}{MS}$$

where the value of γ is determined independently from *L* and *K*.

Equation (ii) defines *MS* as working capital which is substitutable only for *K*, the fixed capital goods. This only decomposes a firm's assets into two different types of capital for the comparison of their different productivities. Thus the marginal product of *MS* is:

$$\frac{\partial V}{\partial MS} = \frac{\partial V}{\partial K}\cdot\frac{\partial K}{\partial MS} = (1 - \alpha)\frac{V}{K}\left(1 - \frac{b}{1-\alpha}\right)\frac{K}{MS}$$

$$= (1 - \alpha - \beta)\frac{V}{MS}$$

where *K* is defined as total capital or $MS + K$. Although the outcome is the same as that of equation (i), its implications are different in that it assumes two broadly defined factors of production, but not the homogeneity of one of those factors whereas equation (i) assumes three factors of production.[3]

Equation (i) assumes two factors of production, where K is defined as real fixed capital, and MS as the capacity utilization variable of capital goods. MS contributes to production only to the extent that it increases the rate of utilization of capital goods, and its services are paid from the share of capital. Therefore, unless MS/K is not assumed to affect utilization, that is $\gamma = 0$, the rate of utilization reaches the maximum when $MS/K = 1$.

Whether to treat this financial variable as a factor of production, distinguished as an alternative asset to real capital, as in equation (ii), or as an independent factor from capital or labor, as in equation (i), is a hypothesis to be further developed theoretically. M. J. Bailey shares this position, and states:

> Whether or not cash balances are a variable independently influencing the relation between consumption and income, there is no question that they are a factor of production. . . . To some extent it is clearly true that real cash balances are a factor of production; they reduce the other resources required for a given level of production, by facilitating payments. . . . Cash balances held by business firms are obviously a productive service similar to any other. . . . It should be noted that the proposition that real cash balances are a factor of production, which is necessarily true, is distinct from the proposition that they are a function in the consumption function, which need not be true.[4]

It is quite reasonable to assume that the financial variable is a factor of production. From a micro-economic standpoint, it is the working capital that constrains the level of production. Government fiscal and monetary policies are largely aimed at stimulating production and stabilizing the economy. Such is especially true in the Korean economy, where the government development plans lead the growth path of the private sector, and import, fiscal and financial policies are considered as a choice between

---

[3] The same can also be done for the labor factor by disaggregating it according to skill classification, or for capital goods, by decomposing machinery according to its efficiency, such as domestic-made or imported in the dual economy. Therefore, if the homogeneity of capital factors is assumed, that is, $\beta = \gamma$, then it becomes the usual neoclassical two-factor production function, and only the definition of capital differs from that of equation (ii).

[4] M. J. Bailey (1962), pp. 59–61.

growth and stabilization.[5]

For those who take a less positive position on the role of the financial variable in the production function, it may be interpreted as a mere capacity utilization variable as in equation (iii).[6] Techniques that utilize capacity adjustment variables describing the rate of utilization have occasionally been used for the estimation of production functions.[7] This increases efficiency in estimating structural equations and projections. Introduction of the weather variable and fertilizer application falls in this group.

A. Production Function of the Primary Sector

Primary sector value added was assumed to be a function of beginning-of-year capital stock, labor, fertilizer application and weather conditions. In addition to the two basic factors of production, an intermediate input, chemical fertilizer application, entered in the production function as an explanatory variable which influences factor productivity change.

The land variable was not used in the equation due to its characteristic of fixed supply, but its productivity change was explained by fertilizer input and weather conditions. The weather dummy is chosen by extrapolating time series data of agricultural output such that it takes values of -1, 0, and $+1$ for unfavorable, neutral, and favorable weather conditions.

$$\text{(1A)}\ \log \frac{V^a}{L^a} = \underset{(0.146)^*}{-0.455} + \underset{(0.013)}{0.030}\, D^w + \underset{(0.062)}{0.621} \log \frac{K^a}{L^a} + \underset{(0.027)}{0.067} \log \frac{Fe}{L^a}$$

$$R^2 = 0.969\ (1957\text{–}1971)^{**}$$

$$\text{(1B)}\ \log \frac{V^a}{L^a} = \underset{(0.121)}{-0.666} + \underset{(0.011)}{0.052}\, D^w + \underset{(0.046)}{0.566} \log \frac{K^a}{L^a} + \underset{(0.019)}{0.056} \log \frac{Fe}{L^a}$$

$$R^2 = 0.982\ (1060\text{–}1971)$$

[5] In addition, it was impossible to estimate the Cobb-Douglas type production functions without introducing this variable. Data inconsistency was often blamed for its failure. But the new production functions fit very well, which may both demonstrate the relevance of introducing the financial variable and improve our confidence in our statistical data.

[6] This is only a conceptual difference; the extent that *MS* affects the production function (the deduced coefficient of *MS*) is the same for each equation: This, however, reduces the chance of being involved in criticism concerning the definitions and assumptions of the production function.

[7] L. R. Klein, *et. al.* (1961), pp. 51–52; and I. Adelman and M. J. Kim in I. Adelman ed. (1969), pp. 80–81.

* The number in parentheses denotes standard error of each coefficient.

** This denotes the sample observation period.

The obtained function indicates relatively low marginal productivity of labor (MPL), which explains the labor intensive nature of Korean agriculture. Outward migration of labor and capital formation in the agricultural sector, however, has raised MPL by 67 percent, from 14,960 won to 24,950 won, over the sample period 1957–1971. Meanwhile, output has grown by 63 percent, and marginal productivity of capital (MPK) decreased by 20 percent. Whereas growth of capital stock was the largest factor in output growth, accounting for 94 percent of the annual output growth rate of 3.6 percent, the contribution on the part of labor has been negative.[8]

Fertilizer input was also an important determinant of agricultural production which accounted for the rest of output growth. During the late 1950's and early 1960's fertilizer input was especially significant in inducing output growth of this sector.[9]

The estimated function also determined the dependency of agricultural production upon weather conditions, indicating a 6 percent range of output fluctuation between good-crop and bad-crop years.

Comparing two estimates of the production function based on samples of different sizes, we find that the coefficients for capital and fertilizer are decreasing, and those for labor and the dummy variable increasing. This accords with our general observation that the efficiency of capital and fertilizer is decreasing due to continuing capital formation and chemical fertilizer application, and that labor productivity is increasing due to the slower rate of growth of the labor force than that of capital stock and fertilizer use. The higher coefficient for the weather dummy seems to reflect the more abrupt change in weather conditions in the 1960's.

B. Production function of the mining and manufacturing sector

This sector production function incorporates money supply and technical change into the general Cobb-Douglas type production function. The function assumes a constant ratio of money supply to the holding of liquid assets of each sector over the sample period.

$$\text{(2A)}\ \log \frac{V^m}{L^m} = \underset{(0.28)}{-1.562} + \underset{(0.29)}{0.641} \log \frac{K^m}{L^m} + \underset{(0.12)}{0.133} \log \frac{MS}{L^m} + \underset{(0.017)}{0.0743}\, t$$

$$R^2 = 0.945\ (1957\text{–}1971)$$

[8] See Appendix I for the detail.
[9] See Appendix I.

$$\text{(2B)}\ \log \frac{V^m}{L^m} = \underset{(0.13)}{-1.334} + \underset{(0.15)}{0.657} \log \frac{K^m}{L^m} + \underset{(0.064)}{0.164} \log \frac{MS}{L^m} + \underset{(0.0092)}{0.0842\, t}$$

$$R^2 = 0.988\ (1960\text{–}1971)$$

It was found that the growth elasticity of output was 0.641, 0.226, and 0.133 with respect to fixed capital, labor, and money supply, respectively.

As discussed in the previous pages, the coefficient for money supply has different implications depending upon the definition of this variable. Treating this variable as working capital, the coefficient for capital in the broad sense was 0.774, where it was 0.641 for fixed capital and 0.133 for working capital. If we regard MS/K as a capacity utilization variable for fixed capital, the coefficient for fixed capital was 0.774, where the coefficient for MS/K was 0.465. For each case, the production function was reduced to the following forms:

$$\text{(2Aa)}\ V^m = 0.210e^{.074t}\, L^{m.226}\, (K^{m.828} MS^{.172})^{.774}$$

and

$$\text{(2Ab)}\ V^m = 0.210e^{.074t}\, L^{m.226} \left(K^m \left(\frac{MS}{K^m} \right)^{.465} \right)^{.774}$$

A relatively low coefficient for labor as compared with that of capital as a whole reflects the production structure of developing countries. The capital-output ratio has been steadily decreasing, from 5 in 1957 to 1.5 in 1971, implying utilization of existing capital stock during the sample period with the aid of an expansionary monetary policy. Marginal productivity of working capital (MPMS), accordingly decreased by 2 percent, while MPL has increased by 127 percent, from 34,000 won to 77,400 won, and MPK by 259 percent.

The average annual growth rate of 14.7 percent during the sample period may be divided into a contribution of 12.8 percent for labor, 21.8 percent through fixed capital formation, 13.7 percent through growth of money supply, and 50.6 percent from the total productivity factor.[10] Assuming this total productivity increase is equally distributed, the contribution ratio becomes 45 percent for capital, 27 percent for labor, and 28 percent for money supply. The contribution of capital was especially high since the mid-1960's; it accounted for 29.7 percent of the annual output growth during 1965–1971 against only 13.5 percent during 1957–1965.

[10] See Appendix I.

Elasticity of output growth with respect to labor is lower in equation (2B) than that in equation (2A). This reflects faster growth of MPK than that of MPL due to labor absorption.

C. Production Function for the Social Overhead Sector

Output of this sector was also assumed to be a function of labor, fixed capital, money supply and technical progress.

$$\text{(3A)} \log\frac{V^o}{L^o} = \underset{(0.413)}{-2.548} + \underset{(0.244)}{0.848} \log\frac{K^o}{L^o} + \underset{(0.158)}{0.053} \log\frac{MS}{L^o} + \underset{(0.011)}{0.077}\, t$$

$$R^2 = 0.924 \text{ (1957–1971)}$$

$$\text{(3B)} \log\frac{V^o}{L^o} = \underset{(0.45)}{-2.184} + \underset{(0.31)}{0.629} \log\frac{K^o}{L^o} + \underset{(0.19)}{0.110} \log\frac{MS}{L^o} + \underset{(0.012)}{0.079}\, t$$

$$R^2 = 0.928 \text{ (1960–1971)}$$

As in the case of the production function for mining and manufacturing, equation (3A) was reduced to:

$$\text{(3Aa)} \quad V^o = 0.0782\, e^{.077t} L^{o\,.099} (K^{o.941}\, MS^{.059})^{.901}$$

$$\text{and (3Ab)} \quad V^o = 0.0782\ e^{.077t} L^{o\,.099}\left(K^o\left(\frac{MS}{K^o}\right)^{.059}\right)^{.901}$$

The growth elasticities of output were found to be 0.848, 0.099, and 0.053 with respect to fixed capital, labor, and money supply. The effect of capital formation in inducing production was dominant while that of labor and of money supply was negligible, which should have been largely due to the shortage of production capacity and full capacity operation in this sector.

Equation (3A), however, does not seem to reflect the real production structure of this sector at present, since this shortage has disappeared as a result of the sizeable capital formation in this sector during the second half of the 1960's. This can be seen more clearly by a comparison of the two production functions; equation (3B), the estimation of which relied more upon the recent behavior of variables, shows much higher coefficients for labor and money supply, and a lower one for net capital stock.

During the period 1957–1971, the capital-output ratio decreased from 13.7 to 5.4. MPL went up by 128 percent, MPK by 154 percent and MPMS by 1 percent. The average growth rate of output in this sector of 14.9

percent was mostly attributable to the growth of capital-stock, explaining 40.8 percent of output growth against 5.3 percent for employment increase, 5.0 percent for money supply and the rest for total factor productivity[11]

D. Production Function for the Service Sector

Production in this sector was related to capital stock, labor and the money supply.[12]

$$\text{(4A)}\quad \log\frac{V^s}{L^s} = \underset{(0.18)}{-0.736} + \underset{(0.094)}{0.213}\log\frac{K^s}{L^s} + \underset{(0.054)}{0.376}\log\frac{MS}{L^s}{}^{13}$$

$$R^2 = 0.809\ (1957\text{—}1971)$$

giving:

$$\text{(4Aa)}\quad V^s = 0.497\, L^{s.411}\,(K^{s.362}\, MS^{.638})^{.589}$$

and

$$\text{(4Ab)}\quad V^s = 0.479\, L^{s.411}\left(K^s\left(\frac{MS}{K^s}\right)^{1.506}\right)^{.589}$$

The growth elasticity of output was found to be 0.213 for fixed capital, 0.411 for labor and 0.376 for money supply. This indicates that increases in liquid assets and employment largely expanded output in this sector during the sample period.

The effect of *MS* in inducing output is so strong in this sector that it cannot be safely regarded as a mere capacity utilization variable. In fact, the even higher coefficient for money supply than that of fixed capital indicates that liquid assets are an even more important factor of production than fixed capital. Credit availability was an especially constraining factor

---

11 See Appendix I.

12 In view of the fact that this sector is generally regarded as a sponge sector for other sectors, the trend variable was deliberately not used in the estimation.

13 The alternative function gives:

$$\text{(4B)}\quad \log\frac{V^s}{L^s} = \underset{(0.15)}{-0.794} - \underset{(0.10)}{0.051}\log\frac{K^s}{L^s} + \underset{(0.044)}{0.369}\log\frac{MS}{L^s}\qquad \underset{(1960\text{–}1971)}{R^2 = 0.924}$$

which indicates negative MPK. Although a low correlation between capital and value added in this sector was expected, this extraordinarily low coefficient for capital has limited practical usefulness in this function.

during the earlier phase of Korean economic development. As the tight credit condition has been eased, MPMS in 1971 has decreased to two-fifths of the 1957 level. This expansion of credit supply accounted for 70.3 percent of the growth of value-added in the sector against 25.8 percent from the employment increase and 3.9 percent from the growth of capital stock.

The low coefficient for the capital stock indicates a relative abundance of capital stock in the earlier stage of the sample period. Despite the fact that further fixed capital formation was continued sufficiently to reduce the capital-output ratio to 4.4 in 1971 from 10 in 1961, MPK still went up by 126 percent, because the money supply was growing faster than capital. MPL, however, did not rise so fast, probably because of the relatively high MPL during the initial period and the high growth of employment in this sector.

4. Depreciation Equations

A fixed marginal rate of depreciation to the beginning-of-year capital stock was applied in the estimation of the depreciation equations. Data for the depreciation allowance for fixed capital were taken as a proxy variable for depreciation and obsolescence, as no other information was available.

(5A) $D^a = -7.632 + 0.069\,K^a \qquad R^2 = 0.981$
$\qquad (0.485) \quad (0.0028) \qquad (1957\text{–}1970)$

(5B) $D^a = -8.141 + 0.072\,K^a \qquad R^2 = 0.980$
$\qquad (0.64) \quad (0.0035) \qquad (1960\text{–}1970)$

(6A) $D^m = -49.031 + 0.147\,K^m \qquad R^2 = 0.984$
$\qquad (2.49) \quad (0.0054) \qquad (1957\text{–}1970)$

(6B) $D^m = -52.057 + 0.152\,K^m \qquad R^2 = 0.990$
$\qquad (2.49) \quad (0.0052) \qquad (1960\text{–}1970)$

(7A) $D^o = -10.219 + 0042\,K^o \qquad R^2 = 0.915$
$\qquad (2.04) \quad (0.0037) \qquad (1957\text{–}1970)$

(7B) $D^o = -9.576 + 0.041\,K^o \qquad R^2 = 0.893$
$\qquad (2.79) \quad (0.0048) \qquad (1960\text{–}1970)$

(8A) $D^s = -72.419 + 0.045\,K^s \qquad R^2 = 0.926$
$\qquad (7.28) \quad (0.0037) \qquad (1957\text{–}1970)$

(8B) $D^s = -81.158 + 0.050\,K^s \qquad R^2 = 0.943$
$\qquad (8.09) \qquad (0.0041) \qquad (1960\text{–}1970)$

Any of these equations shows a high marginal rate of depreciation which may imply a relatively high rate of obsolescence and substitution of machinery in the economy.

5. *Consumption Functions*

Consumption expenditures were disaggregated into private consumption and public consumption. Such disaggregation was necessary in view of differences in consumption behavior between the two sectors.

A. Private Consumption Expenditure

In an attempt to determine the different consumption patterns of the rural and non-rural sectors, income was disaggregated into agricultural income and non-agricultural income. The hypothesis of different marginal propensities to consume is worth a test in view of the dualistic nature of living standards between urban and rural dwellers.

Further, the Duesenberry-Modigliani type ratchet effect was tested so as to measure consumption response to current income and previous consumption. Hence the function takes the form:

$$C_t^p = c_1 Y_t^a + c_2 Y_t^{na} + c_3 C_{t-1}^p + a$$

where Y^a and Y^{na} represent rural income and urban income. MPC is approximately $c_1 / 1 - c_3$ for the rural sector and $c_2 / 1 - c_3$ for the non-rural sector, if it is assumed that relative income levels are constant over time.[14]

---

[14] MPC for the rural sector is: $\frac{\partial C_t^p}{\partial Y} = c_1 + c_3 \frac{\partial C_{t-1}}{\partial Y_t^a}$

where $C_{t-1}^p = C_1 Y_{t-1}^a + C_2 Y_{t-1}^{na} + c_3 C_{t-2}^p + a$
If all past incomes are assumed to be equal, then it properly reduces to:

$$\frac{\partial C_t^p}{\partial Y_t^a} = c_1(c + c_3 + c_3^2 \ldots) = c\left(\frac{1}{1 - c_3}\right) \text{ since } \frac{\partial C_{t-1}^p}{\partial Y_{t-1}^a} = c_1 + c_3 \frac{\partial C_{t-2}^p}{\partial Y_{t-1}}$$

And the same applies to MPC for the non-rural sector. As this assumtion is not relevant in the Korean context where past incomes were on the rising trend, MPC for sector *i* should be less than $c_i\left(\frac{1}{1 - c_3}\right)$. It can only be used as an approximate to MPC.

In both cases agricultural output and non-agricultural output were used as proxy variables to rural and non-rural income. A further adjustment was made by deducting direct taxes from non-agricultural output on the assumption that direct taxes do not affect the disposable income level of the rural sector but do affect that of the urban sector and that indirect taxes and transfers affect income levels of the two sectors proportionally. Two stage least squares were also applied in the estimation only for the purpose of reference.[15]

$$\text{(9Aa)}\quad C^p = \underset{(37.64)}{90.143} + \underset{(0.11)}{0.496}\,(V^{na}\text{-}DT) + \underset{(0.10)}{0.160}\,V^a + \underset{(0.16)}{0.459}\,C^p_{-1}$$
$$R^2 = 0.999\ (1957\text{–}1971)$$

$$\text{(9Ab)}\quad C^p = \underset{(23.31)}{182.643} + \underset{(0.021)}{0.800}\,(V^{na}\text{-}DT) + \underset{(0.11)}{0.311}\,V^a \quad \underset{(1957\text{–}1971)}{R^2 = 0.9987}$$

$$\text{(TSLX)}\quad C^p = \underset{(40.01)}{181.556} + \underset{(0.037)}{0.800}\,(V^{na}\text{-}DT) + \underset{(0.19)}{0.316}\,V^a \quad \underset{(1957\text{–}1971)}{R^2 = 0.9996}$$

$$\text{(9Ba)}\quad C^p = \underset{(62.07)}{107.993} + \underset{(0.16)}{0.529}\,(V^{na}\text{-}DT) + \underset{(0.12)}{0.14}\,V^a + \underset{(0.23)}{0.412}\,C^p_{-1}$$
$$R^2 = 0.999\ (1960\text{–}1971)$$

$$\text{(9Bb)}\quad C^p = \underset{(29.04)}{210.162} + \underset{(0.022)}{0.809}\,(V^{na}\text{-}DT) + \underset{(0.13)}{0.213}\,V^a \quad \underset{(1960\text{–}1971)}{R^2 = 0.9987}$$

$$\text{(TSLS)}\quad C^p = \underset{(41.87)}{210.223} + \underset{(0.032)}{0.809}\,(V^{na}\text{-}DT) + \underset{(0.18)}{0.211}\,V^a \quad \underset{(1960\text{–}1971)}{R^2 = 0.997}$$

It was observed that the MPC of the non-rural sector is between 0.8–0.9, whereas that of the rural sector is around 0.3, indicating a highly dualistic consumption structure.[16] It was further found that such unbalanced consumption patterns are a continuing characteristic in Korea, as we com-

[15] TSLS estimators are inefficient in a case where the predetermined variables are lagged endogeneous variables, since the residuals of the regression equations were highly correlated. Moreover, it was hard to expect the efficiency of TSLS in obtaining consistent estimators because of a relatively short sample observation period. Considering their mutual interdependence, significance and multicollinearities, the following variables were selected for the TSLS estimation: C^g, I, $M^x + M^{sv}$, X^g, $M^{gr} + M^f\ PiFPiw$, V^a.

[16] The marginal propensities to consume are derived as 0.92 for the non-rural sector and 0.30 for the rural sector from equation (9Aa).

pare two groups of estimated consumption functions based upon different sample observations.

B. Government Consumption Expenditure

Government expenditure was related to government revenue.[17]

$$\text{(10A)}\quad C^g = \underset{(1.98)}{49.505} + \underset{(0.015)}{0.331}\, GR \qquad R^2 = 0.975\ (1957\text{–}1971)$$

$$\text{(10B)}\quad C^g = \underset{(2.59)}{47.835} + \underset{(0.018)}{0.339}\, GR \qquad R^2 = 0.974\ (1960\text{–}1971)$$

6. Investment Functions

In accordance with the policy orientation of this model, the fixed capital formation function was designed to focus on the effects of shocks from outside and to have maximum forecasting capacity. Therefore, emphasis was given to estimating significant coefficients for financial variables such as government non-consumption expenditure and money supply.

Sectoral disaggregation of fixed capital formation was in line with that of production. Except for the mining and manufacturing sector, each sectoral function was of the accelerator type, including past change of output and the lagged endogenous variable. A lagged endogenous variable was introduced in the equation in order to supplement the limitation of this

---

[17] Attempts were made to estimate other equations with additional variables such as a lagged endogenous variable and number of government employees (N^g). They are:

$$C^g = \underset{(8.35)}{13.923} + \underset{(0.043)}{0.150}\, GR + \underset{(0.16)}{0.683}\, C^g_{-1} \qquad R^2 = 0.974\ (1957\text{–}1971)$$

$$C^g = \underset{(12.65)}{67.232} + \underset{(0.055)}{0.406}\, GR + \underset{(0.060)}{0.085}\, N^g \qquad R^2 = 0.978\ (1957\text{–}1971)$$

$$C^g = \underset{(18.83)}{6.192} + \underset{(0.088)}{0.115}\, GR + \underset{(0.051)}{0.024}\, N^g + \underset{(0.20)}{0.736}\, C^g_{-1} \qquad R^2 = 0.990\ (1957\text{–}1971)$$

$$C^g = \underset{(8.93)}{13.713} + \underset{(0.048)}{0.158}\, GR + \underset{(0.17)}{0.672}\, C^g_{-1} \qquad R^2 = 0.990\ (1960\text{–}1971)$$

$$C^g = \underset{(16.65)}{63.232} + \underset{(0.065)}{0.397}\, GR - \underset{(0.075)}{0.070}\, N^g \qquad R^2 = 0.976\ (1960\text{–}1971)$$

$$C^g = \underset{(21.03)}{-2.699} + \underset{(0.095)}{0.087}\, GR + \underset{(0.059)}{0.051}\, N^g + \underset{(0.21)}{0.075}\, C^g_{-1} \qquad R^2 = 0.991\ (1960\text{–}1971)$$

Although the fitting of each equation was good, they did not give stable estimators as the sample sizes differ.

equation in explaining variations of investment demand caused by under- or over-utilization of capacity. Thus the general form of the equation is:

$$I_t = v_1 \Delta V_{t-1} + v_2 I_{t-1} + a$$

If it is assumed that past income changes are constant over time, the investment accelerator becomes $v_1 / 1 - v_2$.[18]

A. Gross Fixed Investment in the Primary Sector

Investment demand in this sector was assumed to be determined by the investment level of the previous year, past changes of value added in this sector and government non-consumption expenditures. Because of a wide range of fluctuations of agricultural output in the past, averages of the change in agricultural production in the last two years were used to determine the accelerator coefficient. The financial condition of this sector was assumed to be affected by the non-consumption expenditures, but only slightly by the money supply.

$$\text{(11A)} \quad \underset{(3.07)}{I^a = 6.411} + \underset{(0.06)}{0.120\, S^g} + \underset{(0.33)}{0.334\, I^a} + \underset{(0.07)}{0.093} \frac{(\Delta V^a_{t-1} + \Delta V^a_{t-2})}{2}$$

$$R^2 = 0.922 \text{ (1957–1971)}$$

$$\text{(11B)} \quad \underset{(3.69)}{I^a = 6.981} + \underset{(0.06)}{0.121\, S^g} + \underset{(0.38)}{0.300\, I^a_{-1}} + \underset{(0.09)}{0.108} \frac{(\Delta V^a_{t-1} + \Delta V^a_{t-2})}{2}$$

$$R^2 = 0.904 \text{ (1960–1971)}$$

Investment levels in this sector appear to be greatly dependent upon the direction of government fiscal policies, especially government investment. The investment accelerator is between 0.09–0.15, indicating a lack of self-financing ability for capital formation in this sector. The high coefficient for its own lagged value represents a positive dynamic adjustment in the investment demand for agricultural output. The equation as a whole re-

---

[18] $I_t = v_1 \Delta V_{t-1} + V_2 I_{t-1} + a$

which expands to:

$$I_t = \sum_{1=0}^{\infty} (v_1 v_2^t \Delta V_{t-t-1} + v^t a)$$

If $\Delta V_{t-1} = \Delta V_{t-2} = \ldots = \Delta V_{t-t-1}$, then:

$$I_t = \sum_{1=0}^{\infty} (v_1 v_2^t \Delta V_{t-1} + V^t a) = \frac{v_1}{1 - v_2} (\Delta V_{t-1} + a)$$

flects, rather, the autonomous nature of this investment.

B. Gross Fixed Investment in the Mining and Manufacturing Sector

The investment demand equation of this sector was assumed to be a function of the lagged value of imports of capital goods and the money supply. As priority was given to obtaining a significant coefficient for the financial variable in the equation, it was necessary to omit some variables with theoretical justification on account of the strong multicollinearity with the money supply[19]. Besides, the past investment behavior appeared to have a strong tendency to catch up with the trend, which had limited the use of lagged values of investment and past changes of production.

In this equation, past levels of imports of capital goods were substituted for past changes in value added for the evaluation of the accelerator coefficient in this sector. As will be seen in the import equations, imports of capital goods are, in turn, determined by the level of fixed investment. Therefore, it may be said that this model assumes a multiplier-accelerator relationship between imports of capital goods and investment in the mining and manufacturing sector.

$$\text{(12A)}\; I^m = \underset{(13.32)}{2.920} + \underset{(0.29)}{0.206}\, M^k_{-1} + \underset{(0.31)}{0.389}\, MS \qquad \underset{(1957\text{–}1971)}{R^2 = 0.858}$$

$$\text{(12B)}\; I^m = \underset{(19.77)}{3.296} + \underset{(0.38)}{0.169}\, M^k_{-1} + \underset{(0.42)}{0.416}\, MS \qquad \underset{(1960\text{–}1971)}{R^2 = 0.838}$$

The estimated equation indicates that investment demand in this sector is largely determined by the availability of domestic financing. The equation also shows that the accelerator coefficient of imports of capital goods in inducing capital formation in this sector is 0.2, which reflects a rather low dependency of investment demand upon the availability of imported

---

19 Alternative equations which were estimated but dropped in the model specification because of these reasons are:

$$I^m = 6.746 + \underset{(0.533)}{1.156}\, \Delta V^m_{-1} + \underset{(0.113)}{0.082}\, (MS + S^g) \qquad \underset{(1960\text{–}1970)}{R^2 = 0.9005}$$

$$I^m = 6.021 + \underset{(0.343)}{1.401}\, \Delta V^m_{-1} + \underset{(0.129)}{0.077}\, MS \qquad \underset{(1955\text{–}1970)}{R^2 = 0.914}$$

$$I^m = -0.539 + \underset{(0.185)}{0.388} M^k_{-1} + \underset{(0.435)}{2.070}\, MS - \underset{(8.286)}{8.173}\, \Delta V^m_{-1} \qquad \underset{(1957\text{–}1971)}{R^2 = 0.954}$$

$$I^m = -0.615 + \underset{(0.255)}{0.480}\, M^k_{-1} + \underset{(0.508)}{2.060}\, MS - \underset{(12.609)}{12.541}\, \Delta V^m_{-1} \qquad \underset{(1960\text{–}1971)}{R^2 = 0.947}$$

machineries. Comparison of the two equations based upon different sample observations further indicates that the dependency of the investment demand upon financial availability is higher and that upon imports availability is lower in the recent period.

C. Gross Fixed Investment in the Social Overhead Sector

Fixed investment in social overhead was related to the change in non-agricultural production in the previous year, the lagged value of investment of the sector, and government non-consumption expenditures. In consideration of the public nature of this investment and the externalities it involves, the availability of government finance and the change in non-agricultural production were assumed to affect investment demand in this sector.

$$\text{(13A)} \quad I^o = \underset{(8.81)}{22.016} + \underset{(0.30)}{0.877}\, S^g + \underset{(0.19)}{0.034}\, I^o_{-1} + \underset{(0.26)}{0.368}\, V^{na}_{-1}$$

$$R^2 = 0.974 \ (1957\text{–}1971)$$

$$\text{(13B)} \quad I^o = \underset{(10.45)}{22.055} + \underset{(0.40)}{0.941}\, S^g + \underset{(0.23)}{0.014}\, I^o_{-1} + \underset{(0.33)}{0.341}\, V^{na}_{-1}$$

$$R^2 = 0.969 \ (1960\text{–}1971)$$

$$\text{(13C)} \quad I^o = \underset{(14.13)}{6.245} + \underset{(0.35)}{0.074}\, I^o_{-1} + \underset{(0.62)}{0.634}\, \Delta V^{na}_{-1} + \underset{(1.20)}{1.025}\, S^g$$

$$R^2 = 0.968 \ (1965\text{–}1971)$$

The estimated coefficients differ a great deal in these three equations indicating that the function relationship has been changing in the last 15 years. This sector was initially endowed with little capital stock, and sizeable investment has followed subsequently, especially during the second half of the 1960's, which has resulted in sufficient and probably excess capacity in this sector.

The investment accelerator coefficient lay between 0.34–0.63 with respect to the change in non-agricultural value added, and the multiplier between 0.88–1.03 with respect to government financing during the sample periods. It may be said that there was little dynamic adjustment in the behavior of investment demand in this sector.

D. Gross Fixed Investment in the Service Sector

Investment demand was assumed to be derived from this sector's production change in the previous year and availability of financing.

$$\text{(14A)} \quad I^s = -5.880 + 0.322\,\Delta V^s_{-1} + 0.359\,MS + 0.438\,I^s_{-1}$$

$$R^2 = 0.986 \text{ (1957–1971)}$$

$$\text{(14B)} \quad I^s = \underset{(5.36)}{-5.901} + \underset{(0.25)}{0.347}\,\Delta V^s_{-1} + \underset{(0.22)}{0.381}\,MS + \underset{(0.36)}{0.434}\,I^s_{-1}$$

$$R^2 = 0.983 \text{ (1960–1971)}$$

The functional relationship was quite consistent in the two sample periods. The accelerator coefficient with respect to the past change of its own production is 0.32. The high coefficient for money supply, 0.36, indicates heavy dependency of its investment demand upon financial availability. The coefficient for the lagged term represents a dynamic response of investment in this year conpared to that in the previous year: an initial rise calls for a subsequent secondary rise.

E. Changes in Inventory

Accumulation of inventory was related to the change in agricultural production and in non-agricultural production. In general, the statistical fits were poor, probably because of inaccuracies in data.

$$\text{(15A)} \quad I^i = \underset{(4.28)}{-0.142} + \underset{(0.14)}{0.483}\Delta V^a + \underset{(0.11)}{0.478}\Delta V^m$$

$$R^2 = 0.704 \text{ (1957–1971)}$$

$$\text{(15B)} \quad I^i = -4.122 + 0.457\,\Delta V^a + 0.556\,\Delta V^m$$

$$R^2 = 0.781 \text{ (1960–1971)}$$

The dependency of inventory accumulation upon the production changes in the agricultural sector and in the mining and manufacturing sector are both 0.48. But the dependency upon changes in mining and manufacturing production becomes higher according to equation (15B), which probably reflects the more round-about production and sales structure of the sector in the recent period.

7. *Import Functions*

Total imports are disaggregated into 6 categories: (1) imports of machinery and equipment, (2) intermediate goods for domestic demand, (3) intermediate goods for exports, (4) fuels, (5) grains and (6) services, of which the last two categories were treated as exogenous. Import functions in general are designed to evaluate the elasticity of price variables and the marginal propensity to import with respect to production, export, or fixed investment, and the dynamic response of this year's imports to the previous level of imports. The price variable was computed in the following way:

$$P^m = (OER + TMR) \cdot \frac{PI^x_{us\ jap}}{PI^w}$$

p^m: Real exchange rate on imports

OER: Official exchange rate

TMR: Amount of effective tariffs per dollar-import, which takes account of (1) actual tariff collection, (2) foreign exchange tax, (3) tariff exemption and (4) premiums for exports.[20]

$PI^x_{us\ jap}$: Export price index of the U.S. and Japan, weighted by the amount of imports from each country, 1965–100

PI^w: Domestic wholesale price index, 1965=100, which should reflect the real and relative exchange rate on imports.

A. Imports of Machinery and Equipment

In this category imports were related to the level of fixed investment and the exchange rate on imports, and account was taken of dynamic response. Imports of capital goods were greatly increased in recent years, which might have entailed changes in the structural relationship. Therefore, a long-term observation of samples did not appear, so as to increase the reliability of the estimated equations. Rather, an estimation based upon a short sample period would give a better analysis for imports of capital goods.

(16A) $M^k = 1.656 + 0.443\ I^f - 0.095\ P^m + 0.028\ M^k_{-1}$
$\qquad\qquad(13.30)\quad(0.066)\qquad(0.060)\qquad(0.16)$

$R^2 = 0.986\ (1957–1971)$

(16B) $M^k = 30.009 + 0.441\ I^f - 0.200\ P^m + 0.026\ M^k_{-1}$
$\qquad\qquad(33.89)\quad(0.073)\qquad(0.13)\qquad(0.18)$

$R^2 = 0.985\ (1960–1971)$

[20] The figures were obtained from K. S. Kim (1971).

$$\text{(16C)}\quad M^k = \underset{(259.15)}{37.845} + \underset{(0.33)}{0.553}\, I^f - \underset{(0.79)}{0.291}\, P^m - \underset{(0.56)}{0.183}\, M^k_{-1}$$

$$R^2 = 0.978 \; (1965\text{–}1971)$$

Equation (16C) indicates that the marginal propensity to import with respect to fixed investment lies between 0.47–0.55, taking account of the coefficient for lagged terms.[21]

Dependency of domestic fixed investment upon foreign capital goods was greater in the recent period, as the third equation indicates. The exchange rate elasticity for this category of imports is −0.69. The negative sign of the coefficient for the lagged term in equation (16C) reflects the effect of accumulation in both investment and imports of machinery and equipment.

B. Imports of Intermediate Goods for Domestic Demand

Imports of this category were assumed to be a function of value added in mining and manufacturing and the exchange rate, and dynamic adjustments were also taken into account.

$$\text{(17A)}\quad M^d = \underset{(22.81)}{98.883} + \underset{(0.067)}{0.417}\, V^m - \underset{(0.068)}{0.254}\, P^m - \underset{(0.22)}{0.197}\, M^d_{-1}$$

$$R^2 = 0.981 \; (1957\text{–}1971)$$

$$\text{(17B)}\quad M^d = \underset{(26.36)}{120.606} + \underset{(0.063)}{0.385}\, V^m - \underset{(0.070)}{0.340}\, P^m - \underset{(0.21)}{0.106}\, M^d_{-1}$$

$$R^2 = 0.987 \; (1957\text{–}1971)$$

Equation (17A) indicates that the marginal propensity to import, with respect to value added in mining and manufacturing lies between 0.35–0.42, and that the average elasticity with respect to the exchange rate is −0.63, which is lower than expected. However, equation (17B), based upon a shorter sample period, gives a lower marginal propensity to import and a higher exchange rate elasticity, indicating the effect of import substitution in the recent period. The coefficient for lagged terms represents the effect of accumulation in imports of intermediate goods for domestic uses.

---

[21] The same operation as in footnote 18 applies to the computation of the marginal propensity to import here. That is, if the level of imports of capital goods is assumed to be the same for every period, MPM with respect to fixed investment is 0.47 for equation (16C), 0.46 for equation (16A), and 0.45 for equation (16B).

C. Imports of Intermediate Goods for Exports

In this category, the import function took account of the import dependency of export goods and the exchange rate. Only a very short sample observation was done in the estimation of the structural equation in view of the significance of this variable in the recent period.

$$(18)\quad M^x = \underset{(15.68)}{15.518} + \underset{(0.0095)}{0.448}\, X^g - \underset{(0.056)}{0.068}\, P^m$$

$$R^2 = 0.999\ (1965\text{–}1971)$$

The coefficient for export goods indicates the marginal dependency of exports upon imports of raw materials and intermediate goods. The marginal earning ratio for the export industry is 0.45 and the exchange rate elasticity for imports of these goods is −0.06. The elasticity is low because the exchange rate affects trade in both directions: a high exchange rate stimulates exports, which results in greater demand for intermediate goods, but restrains imports of these goods. The estimated equation indicates that the import substitution effects more than offset the export effects, so that a higher exchange rate would result in an absolute decrease in imports of intermediate goods for export demand.

D. Imports of Fuels

Imports of fuels were related to value-added in non-agriculture and relative price of fuels. Because petroleum accounts for almost all imports in this category, the domestic wholesale price index was deflated by the overall wholesale price index in order to represent the price variable in this equation.

$$(19A)\quad M^f = \underset{(5.43)}{-10.566} + \underset{(0.0038)}{0.044}\, V^{na} + \underset{(4.26)}{0.218}\, PiFPiw$$

$$R^2 = 0.928\ (1957\text{–}1971)$$

$$(TSLS)\quad M^f = \underset{(5.29)}{-10.649} + \underset{(0.0037)}{0.044}\, V^{na} + \underset{(4.13)}{0.228}\, PiFPiw$$

$$R^2 = 0.932\ (1957\text{–}1971)$$

$$(19B)\quad M^f = \underset{(6.53)}{-24.880} + \underset{(0.0041)}{0.052}\, V^{na} + \underset{(4.40)}{8.274}\, PiFPiw$$

$$R^2 = 0.960\ (1960\text{–}1971)$$

$$(TSLS)\quad M^f = \underset{(6.29)}{-25.056} + \underset{(0.0040)}{0.052}\, V^{na} + \underset{(4.23)}{8.334}\, PiFPiw$$

$$R^2 = 0.963 \ (1960\text{–}1971)$$

$$\text{(19C)} \quad M^f = \underset{(11.73)}{-45.615} + \underset{(0.0039)}{0.059} V^{na} + \underset{(12.46)}{24.461} \ PiFPiw$$

$$R^2 = 0.983 \ (1965\text{–}1971)$$

As the demand for energy expanded in recent years, imports of fuels rose sharply, which resulted in a major burden in the balance of payments. The negative constant terms further indicate that this demand is exploding. According to equation (19C), which appears to reflect the present trend most relevantly, the price elasticity is 0.9, indicating that, regardless of fuel prices, import demand for fuels is increasing, but high fuel prices induce domestic suppliers to import more.

8. Identities

$$\text{(20)} \quad V = V^a + V^m + V^o + V^s + V^f$$

$$\text{(21)} \quad V = C + I + X - M$$

$$\text{(22)} \quad C = C^g + C^p$$

$$\text{(23)} \quad I^f = I^a + I^m + I^o + I^s$$

$$\text{(24)} \quad I = I^f + I^i$$

$$\text{(25)} \quad M^g_{c.i.f.} = M^k + M^d + M^x + M^f + M^{gr}$$

$$\text{(26)} \quad M^g_{f.o.b.} = M^g_{c.i.f.} - (m^g_{c.i.f.} - M^g_{f.o.b.})$$

$$\text{(27)} \quad M = M^g_{f.o.b.} + M^s$$

$$\text{(28)} \quad V^{na} = V - V^a$$

$$\text{(29)} \quad S^g = GR - C^g$$

$$\text{(30)} \quad K^a = K^a_{t-1} - D^a_{t-1} + I^a_{t-1}$$

$$\text{(31)} \quad K^m = K^m_{t-1} - D^m_{t-1} + I^a_{t-1}$$

$$\text{(32)} \quad K^o = K^o_{t-1} - D^o_{t-1} + I^o_{t-1}$$

$$\text{(33)} \quad K^s = K^s_{t-1} - D^s_{t-1} + I^s_{t-1}$$

III. The Model as a Forecasting Instrument

The model itself presents an over-indentified system in the determination of GNP, as it estimates aggregate demand and production from two alternative approaches. The *ex ante* gap which thereby resulted from two levels of GNP can be minimized by simulation of policy variables, but it cannot possibly disappear *ex post* because of the stochastic estimation of the equations.

Since the major purpose of the model is to forecast future values of the unknowns with precision, a single set of policy variables is given such that it represents the most probable policy implementation in the short-term planning period. The model, then, forecasts two values of GNP, the lesser of which may be regarded as a constraint on the other. Those figures, however, should not differ greatly, since the major policy variable, *MS*, affects the levels of the two estimates of GNP in the same direction. Values of the exogenous variables for the forecasts of 1972 and 1973 are presented in Table 1.

Value-added in non-agriculture, which is an explanatory variable in the formulation of the consumption and imports-of-fuels functions, has to be generated from the demand side such that:

$$\hat{V}^{na} = \hat{C} + \hat{I} + X - \hat{M} - \hat{V}^{a}$$

where $\hat{V}^{na}$, $\hat{C}$, $\hat{I}$, $\hat{M}$ and $\hat{V}^{a}$ represent the estimated values of those variables.

In practice, however, V^{na} was obtained from estimates of GNP from the production side, because V^{na} obtained by simultaneous estimation of consumption and imports appeared greatly deviant from V^{na} obtained from production functions. These values are supposed to be identical *ex post*, but different *ex ante* because of differences in the structural relations and the accumulation of errors in the stochastic equations. As it was reasoned that it was predominantly the latter terms, especially those which resulted from the estimation of GNP on the demand side, which caused this deviation, the value of V^{na} was obtained from the income determination system of the production side in order to increase the efficiency in forecasting.

Each function was presented with a few alternative equations in the model description section. Each equation has different properties and implications in representing a structural relation, and a certain subjective judgment inevitably entered into the selection of equations for the forecast.

In the case of the production functions, it was considered that an estimation based upon the larger sample observation, as noted "A" after the equation number, better reflected the production structure in Korea. As consistency of forecasting was desired, projections of most of the other

Table 1. Values of the Exogenous Variables

(billion won at 1965 prices)

	1971	1972	1973	Sources
MS	203.59	217.84	246.16	a
GR	246.96	262.84	283.16	b
DI	83.34	84.75	91.30	c
P^m	265.74	265.74	265.74	
$PiFPiw$	0.91	0.91	0.91	
Mgr	80.68	71.51	53.08	ORB figures
X^g	299.90	380.85	482.23	ORB figures
V^f	2.26	−22.26	−31.82	d
Fe	125.24	127.80	130.41	2.043%
M^s	114.92	147.03	163.49	ORB figures
X^s	130.58	116.78	119.96	ORB figures
D^w	0	0	0	
$M^g{}_{c.i.f.} - M^g{}_{f.o.b.}$	55.55	69.21	74.77	105 of $M^g{}_{c.i.f.}$
L^a	4,708.50	4,586.55	4,467.76	−2.5%
L^m	1,375.25	1,395.88	1,416.82	1.50%
L^o	713.25	758.11	805.80	6.29%
L^s	2,910.75	3,110.14	3,323.18	6.85%

Notes:

a. 20% nominal growth rate for 1972 and 1973.

b. 20% nominal growth rate for 1972 and 15% for 1973.

c. FY 1972 Budget figure, and 15% nominal growth rate for 1973.
(a, b, c, all assume 13% price increase rate for 1972 and 7% for 1973).

d. Projected figures from:

$V = V^{fr} - V^{fp}$

$V^{fr} = IY^r - 0.842 + 0.322\ GOSVC^r$

$V^{fp} = IY^p - 1.731 + 0.317\ GOSVC^p$

V^{fr} : Factor income from the rest of the world
V^{fp} : Factor income paid to the rest of the world
IY^r : Interest receipt from the rest of the world
IY^p : Interest payment to the rest of the world
$GOSVC^r$: Government and other service receipt
$GOSVC^p$: Government and other service payment

values were also made on the basis of equations based upon a larger sample period, 1957–1971. In the forecasts of imports of intermediate goods for exports and fuels, however, equations estimated for the period 1965–1971 were used, taking account of the rapid structural changes in these demands. Consumption expenditures were forecasted on the basis of equation (9Aa).

Estimated values from these equations are further adjusted in consideration of the over-estimating tendency of these equations in very recent years. The statistical equations reflect very strongly the rising trends of the Korean economy in the 1960's, but the economy has apparently been settling back since 1971. There is no way to know whether this recess will continue or be only a temporary phenomenon. For a short-term forecasting model like this one, however, this tendency has to be corrected in one way or another.

Except for the projections of value added in the primary and manufacturing sectors, which took account of the first difference of fitted values, the projections were carried out by taking account of recent trends. Tables 2 and 3 present the projections of macro-variables: the GNP growth rate was expected to be 7.4 percent in 1972 and 9.5 percent in 1973. The projection, as a whole, appears quite reasonable, as it indicates a retardation of the growth rate of GNP for 1972 due to lack of investment demand and slower growth of production in the social overhead and service sectors. It further shows recovery of the economy in 1973 due to a general improvement in economic activity.

IV. Conclusion

This study has presented a macro-model for the analysis of the Korean economy. Based upon the model and with some forecasting techniques employed, projections were made in order to view future levels of economic activities in Korea. At this stage in the development of the model, however, they do not provide a comfortable base for normative inferences on policy issues. For the practical values of this model to be realized for planning purposes, the model has to be further developed along the lines of the suggestions made below.

First, a weakness of this model is that it hypothesizes a positive influence of financial variables without taking account of effects of financial intermediation on the behavior of prices and various deflators. In order to

Table 2. Projection of Gross National Product

(billion 1965 won and million current dollars)

	1971			1972			1973		
	Preliminary Value	Composition (%)	Growth Rate (%)	Projected Value	Composition (%)	Growth Rate (%)	Projected Value	Composition (%)	Growth Rate (%)
Expenditure on GNP	1566.91	100.0	10.2	1682.32	100.0	7.4	1858.44	100.0	10.5
Consumption	1338.31	85.4	11.2	1456.96	86.6	8.9	1590.52	85.6	9.2
Investment	483.46	30.9	6.1	497.65	29.6	2.9	502.11	27.0	0.9
Fixed Investment	438.54	28.0	5.2	461.62	27.4	5.3	469.00	25.2	1.6
Exports	430.48	27.5	17.6	497.63	29.6	15.6	602.19	32.4	21.0
($)	(1622.00)			(1875.00)			(2269.00)		
Goods	299.90	19.1	28.1	380.85	22.6	27.0	482.25	25.9	26.6
($)	(1130.00)			(1435.00)			(1817.00)		
Imports	694.82	44.3	20.0	769.92	45.8	10.8	836.38	45.0	8.6
($)	(2618.00)			(2900.98)			(3151.39)		
Goods	579.00	37.0	21.1	622.89	37.0	7.4	672.89	36.2	8.0
($)	(2185.00)			(2346.99)			(2535.38)		
Net Imports	264.34	16.9	24.1	272.29	16.2	3.0	234.19	12.6	−14.0
($)	(996.00)			(1025.96)			(882.40)		
Statistical Discrepancy	9.48	0.6							
Industrial origin of GNP	1566.91	100.0	10.2	1684.57	100.0	7.5	1845.70	100.0	9.6
Agriculture, Fishery and Forestry	376.45	24.0	2.5	393.72	23.4	4.6	411.75	22.3	4.6
Mining and Manufacturing	471.17	30.1	18.3	535.52	31.8	13.7	610.85	33.1	14.1
Social Overhead	198.78	12.7	6.7	206.73	12.3	4.0	212.70	11.5	2.9
Service	518.26	33.1	12.6	570.86	33.9	10.1	642.22	34.8	12.5
Net factor income from R.O.W	2.25	0.1		−22.26	−1.3		−31.82	−1.7	

Table 3. Comparison of Preliminary Values and Projected Values

(billion won at 1965 prices)

	1971		1972	1973
	Preliminary Value	Projected Value	Projected Value	Projected Value
C	1338.31	1319.45	1456.96	1590.52
C^p	1196.62	1184.88	1302.52	1420.79
C^g	141.69	134.57	154.44	169.73
I	483.46	463.56	497.65	502.11
I^f	438.54	424.55	461.62	649.00
I^a	32.51	29.24	35.89	41.97
I^m	109.55	99.16	116.56	124.60
I^o	158.39	160.94	165.83	157.21
I^s	138.09	135.21	143.34	145.20
I^i	44.92	39.01	36.03	33.11
M^{cif}	635.45	594.36	692.10	747.66
M^k	181.91	155.35	188.64	187.70
M^d	191.83	181.98	208.90	230.63
M^x	131.37	129.48	165.00	206.42
M^f	49.66	46.87	58.05	69.83
V	1566.91	1557.59	1684.57	1845.70
V^a	376.45	382.02	393.72	411.75
V^m	471.17	454.78	535.52	610.85
V^o	198.78	201.18	206.73	212.70
V^s	518.26	517.36	570.86	642.22

improve the efficiency of the model, it would be worthwhile to attempt to adjust the model so that it contains a set of deflators and price equations which are interrelated with other structural equations. In this case, statistical equations which explain the behavior of national account variables are to be estimated on the basis of values specified at current prices.

Second, it has to avoid the use of the money supply as a proxy variable for the liquid assets and the availability of financing for production and investment. It is desirable to disaggregate the money supply by sectors or to obtain relevant data to represent such sectoral allocation, since government financial policies are actually formulated to direct optimum resource allocation.

Third, the model has a limitation in the analysis and projection of the economy because of the exogenous treatment of many variables. Although it is not necessarily desirable to have a sophisticated system, some variables such as some important categories of exports of goods and services, imports of grains and services, and tax revenues should preferably be expressed as functions of more basic economic variables.

Finally, it is also desirable to disaggregate private consumption expenditure by type of expenditures or even by sectors in view of long-term shifts in preferences and different consumption patterns among regions.

Appendix. Growth of Capital Stock, Employment, and the Money Supply, and Their Contribution to the Growth of the Economy.

The hypothesis of a Cobb-Douglas type production function for the Korean economy enables us to analyze factor contributions to growth in the past. This analysis is worthwhile as we can observe the productivity change which resulted from a variation of factor proportion. The general growth equation is derived from a production function in which:

$$\frac{\Delta V}{V} = \lambda + \alpha_k \frac{\Delta K}{K} + \alpha_L \frac{\Delta L}{L} + \alpha_{MS} \frac{\Delta MS}{MS}$$

where λ is the coefficient for t; α_K, α_L and α_{MS} are output growth elasticities with respect to K, L and MS.

The average annual growth rates of factors and their contributions to growth are presented in Tables 4 to 8.

In the primary sector, growth of the capital stock was the most important contributing factor, explaining 94 percent of the growth of production. Comparison of factor contributions during sub-periods indicates that the contribution of the capital stock is increasing while that of employment is decreasing. The level of growth of fertilizer input was found to be an important factor during the period 1957–1961.

Fifty-two per cent growth in mining and manufacturing production is explained by the total productivity or residual factor. But this percentage is decreasing while those of other factors are increasing.

As expected, growth of social overhead production is mainly explained by the growth of the capital stock, especially during the latter half of the 1960. Here again, much of the growth is not explained by either capital stock, employment or financial availability.

Increases in capital stock were not found to be a significant factor in the

Table 4. Average Annual Growth Rates (%) of V, K, L and Fe and Contributions of K, L Fe and D^w to Growth (%); the Primary Sector.

	1957–1961	1961–1965	1965–1968	1968–1971	1957–1965	1965–1971	1957–1965
$\Delta V^a/V^a$	3.883	3.791	2.013	4.400	3.838	3.200	3.564
$\Delta K^a/K^a$	3.164	4.258	7.413	7.370	3.573	7.392	5.193
$\Delta L^a/L^a$	0.744	0.232	−0.915	−1.075	0.487	−0.994	−0.151
$\Delta Fe/Fe$	14.550	1.900	4.495	2.038	8.040	3.261	5.965
ΔD^w	−18.90	0	25.99	25.99	−9.05	0	−5.08
a. $\Delta \hat{V}^a/\hat{V}^a$	2.605	2.843	3.840	5.157	2.638	4.498	3.426
b. $\alpha_k \Delta K^a/K^a$	1.965	2.644	4.603	4.577	2.219	4.590	3.225
c. $\alpha_L \Delta L^a/L^a$	0.232	0.072	−0.285	−0.335	0.152	−0.310	−0.047
d. $\alpha_{Fe} \Delta Fe/Fe$	0.975	0.127	0.301	0.136	0.539	0.218	0.400
e. $\lambda \Delta D^w$	−0.567	0	−0.779	0.779	−0.272	0	−0.152
b/a	75.43	93.00	119.87	88.75	84.12	102.05	94.13
c/a	8.91	2.53	−7.42	−6.50	5.76	−6.89	−1.37
d/a	37.43	4.47	7.84	2.64	20.43	4.85	11.68
e/a	−21.77	0	−20.29	15.11	−10.31	0	−4.44

Note: $\alpha_k = 0.621$ $\alpha_L = 0.312$ $\alpha_{Fe} = 0.067$ $\lambda = 0.03$

growth of value added in the service sector. Rather, availability of financing is the most important factor, which is quite conceivable in view of the importance of working capital in trade. Employment growth also contributed to the growth of this sector significantly.

For the economy as a whole, it was found that the contribution of capital stock has been increasing which may reflect an increasing rate of utilization of capacity with the additional supply of other inputs. Assuming that the total factor productivity is explained proportionally to the relative importance of other factors, growth of the capital stock has contributed 41 percent of the 8.3 percent average annual growth of the economy during the sample period. Employment growth and an increase in the availability of financing, meanwhile, explained 18 percent and 39 percent of this economic growth.

Table 5. Average Annual Growth Rates (%) of V, K, L and MS and Contributions of K, L, MS and t to Growth (%); The Mining and Manufacturing Sector.

	1957–1961	1961–1965	1965–1968	1968–1971	1957–1965	1965–1971	1957–1971
$\Delta V^m/V^m$	7.301	14.505	21.073	16.544	10.845	20.032	14.693
$\Delta K^m/K^m$	2.678	2.430	7.578	8.636	2.555	8.106	4.898
$\Delta L^m/L^m$	3.269	14.011	13.755	2.025	8.506	7.730	8.173
$\Delta MS/MS$	17.362	0.658	26.290	21.003	8.691	23.618	14.854
a. $\Delta \hat{V}^m/\hat{V}^m$	12.195	12.242	18.893	16.217	12.146	17.514	14.393
b. $\alpha_k \Delta K^m/K^m$	1.717	1.558	4.857	5.536	1.638	5.196	3.140
c. $\alpha_L \Delta L^m/L^m$	0.739	3.166	3.109	0.458	1.922	1.747	1.847
d. $\alpha_{MS} \Delta MS/MS$	2.309	0.088	3.497	2.793	1.156	3.141	1.976
e. t	7.43	7.43	7.43	7.43	7.43	7.43	7.43
b/a	14.08	12.73	25.71	34.14	13.49	29.67	21.82
c/a	6.06	25.86	16.46	2.82	15.82	9.92	12.83
d/a	18.93	0.72	18.51	17.22	9.52	17.93	13.73
e/a	60.93	60.69	39.33	45.82	61.17	42.42	51.62
b/(b+c+d)	36.03	32.38	42.37	63.00	34.73	51.53	45.10
c/(b+c+d)	15.51	65.79	27.12	5.21	40.75	17.32	26.53
d/(b+c+d)	48.46	1.83	30.51	31.79	24.51	31.15	28.38

Note: $\alpha_k = 0.641$ $\alpha_L = 0.226$ $\alpha_{MS} = 0.133$

Table 6. Average Annual Growth Rates (%) of V, K, L and MS and Contributions of K, L, MS and t to Growth (%); The Social Overhead Sector.

	1957–1961	1961–1965	1965–1968	1968–1971	1957–1965	1965–1971	1957–1971
$\Delta V^o/V^o$	8.444	15.660	22.890	15.209	11.994	18.981	14.940
$\Delta K^o/K^o$	2.525	4.674	8.424	17.867	3.595	13.047	7.545
$\Delta L^o/L^o$	11.088	7.432	6.984	7.509	9.245	7.247	8.348
$\Delta MS/MS$	17.362	0.658	26.290	21.003	8.691	23.618	14.854
a. $\Delta \hat{V}^o/\hat{V}^o$	11.839	12.415	16.908	24.687	12.713	20.713	15.695
b. $\alpha_K \Delta K^o/K^o$	2.141	3.964	7.144	15.151	3.049	11.064	6.398
c. $\alpha_L \Delta L^o/L^o$	1.098	0.736	0.691	0.743	0.915	0.717	0.830
d. $\alpha_{MS} \Delta MS/MS$	0.920	0.035	1.393	1.113	0.461	1.252	0.787
e. t	7.68	7.68	7.68	7.68	7.68	7.68	7.68
b/a	18.18	31.93	42.25	61.37	25.19	53.42	40.76
c/a	9.27	5.93	4.09	3.01	7.56	3.46	5.29
d/a	7.77	0.28	8.24	4.51	3.81	6.01	5.01
e/a	64.87	61.86	45.42	31.11	63.44	37.08	48.93
b/(b + c + d)	51.48	83.72	77.42	89.09	68.90	84.89	79.83
c/(b + c + d)	26.40	15.54	7.49	4.37	20.68	5.50	10.36
d/(b + c + d)	22.12	0.74	15.10	6.54	10.42	9.61	9.82

Note: $\alpha_k = 0.848$ $\alpha_L = 0.099$ $\alpha_{MS} = 0.053$

Table 7. Average Annual Growth Rates (%) of V, K, L and MS and Contributions of K, L, MS to Growth (%); The Service Sector

	1957–1961	1961–1965	1965–1968	1968–1971	1957–1965	1965–1971	1957–1971
$\Delta V^s/V^s$	2.740	5.570	12.076	12.436	4.145	12.256	7.547
$\Delta K^s/K^s$	0.388	0.700	1.472	3.890	0.543	2.673	1.451
$\Delta L^s/L^s$	4.616	5.335	5.159	4.805	4.975	4.982	4.978
$\Delta MS/MS$	17.362	0.658	26.290	21.003	8.691	23.618	14.854
a. $\Delta \hat{V}^s/\hat{V}^s$	8.508	2.589	12.319	10.701	5.429	11.497	7.940
b. $\alpha_K \Delta K^s/K^s$	0.038	0.149	0.314	0.829	0.116	0.569	0.309
c. $\alpha_L \Delta L^s/L^s$	1.897	2.193	2.120	1.975	2.045	2.048	2.046
d. $\alpha_{MS} \Delta MS/MS$	6.528	0.247	9.885	7.897	3.268	8.880	5.585
b/a	0.98	5.76	2.55	7.75	2.14	4.95	3.89
c/a	22.30	84.70	17.21	18.46	37.67	17.81	25.77
d/a	76.73	9.54	80.24	73.80	60.20	77.24	70.34

Note: $\alpha_K = 0.213$ $\alpha_L = 0.411$ $\alpha_{MS} = 0.376$

Table 8. *Average Annual Growth Rates (%) of V and Contribution of K, L, MS, Fe, D^w and to Growth (%); The Korean Economy.*

	1957–1961	1961–1965	1965–1968	1968–1971	1957–1965	1965–1971	1957–1971
$\Delta V/V$	4.222	7.049	11.455	12.291	5.627	11.871	8.259
V^a/V	43.56	40.22	33.97	26.31	41.89	30.14	36.86
V^m/V	14.59	18.03	22.76	28.23	16.31	25.50	20.24
V^o/V	6.18	7.76	10.47	12.97	6.97	11.72	9.01
V^s/V	35.67	33.99	32.80	32.49	34.83	32.64	33.89
a. $\Delta\hat{V}/\hat{V}$	6.680	5.263	11.415	12.614	5.821	12.003	8.281
b. K	1.268	1.703	3.520	5.001	1.450	4.191	2.505
c. L	0.953	1.402	1.379	0.779	1.153	1.105	1.125
d. MS	2.722	0.171	4.184	3.499	1.359	3.846	2.364
e. Fe	0.425	0.051	0.102	0.036	0.226	0.066	0.147
f. D^w	−0.247	0	−0.265	0.205	−0.114	0	−0.056
g. t	1.559	1.936	2.495	3.094	1.747	2.795	2.196
b/a	19.98	32.36	30.84	39.65	24.91	34.92	30.25
c/a	14.27	26.64	12.08	6.18	19.81	9.21	13.59
d/a	40.75	3.25	36.65	27.74	23.35	32.04	28.55
e/a	6.36	0.97	0.89	0.29	3.88	0.55	1.78
f/a	−3.70	0	−2.32	1.63	−1.96	0	−0.68
b/(b+c+d+e+f)	24.76	51.19	39.46	52.53	35.59	45.51	41.17
c/(b+c+d+e+f)	18.61	42.14	15.46	8.18	28.30	12.00	18.49
d/(b+c+d+e+f)	53.15	5.14	46.91	36.75	33.36	41.77	38.85
e/(b+c+d+e+f)	8.30	1.53	1.14	0.38	5.55	0.72	2.42
f/(b+c+d+e+f)	−4.82	0	−2.97	2.15	−2.80	0	−0.92

REFERENCES

1. Adelman, I. and M. J. Kim, "An Econometric Model of the Korean Economy," in Irma Adelman, ed., *A Practical Approach to Development Planning*, Baltimore: Johns Hopkins University Press, 1969.
2. M. J. Bailey, *National Income and the Price Level*, New York: Mc Graw-Hill, 1962.
3. Friedman, M., *Essays in Positive Economics*, Chicago: University of Chicago Press, 1953.
4. Gurley, J. G. and E. S. Shaw, *Money in a Theory of Finance*, New York: The Brookings Institution, 1960.
5. Han, K. C., *Estimates of Korean Capital and Inventory Coefficients in 1968*, Seoul: Yonsei University, 1970.
6. Johnson, J. C., "The Neo-Classical One Sector Growth Model; A Geometrical Exposition and Extension to a Monetary Economy, *Econometrica*, Vol. 33, No. 131, 1966.
7. Kim, K. S., *Trade & Industrial Policy in Korea, 1945–1970*, 1971, (mimeographed).
8. Kim, M.J. and D.W.Nam, *A Statistical Model for Monetary Management; The Case of Korea, 1956–67*, 1968.
9. Klein, L. R., R. J. Ball, A. Hazlewood, and P. Vandome, *An Econometric Model of the United Kingdom*, Oxford: Basil Blackwell Mott, Ltd., 1961.
10. Lee, K. S., *The Bruno Production Function, Factor Market Disequilibrium, and Factor Contributions to Growth in the Korean Industrial Sectors*, Seoul: Korea Development Institute, 1971.
11. Norton, R. D., *An Econometric Model of Korea, 1956–67*, 1969, (mimeographed).
12. Patinkin, D., *Money, Interest and Prices*, 2nd ed., New York: Harper and Row, 1965.
13. Research Institute for Economics and Business, *An Econometric Model for the Korean Economy*, Seoul: Sogang College, February 1968.
14. Sidrauski, M., "Rational Choice and Patterns of Growth," *Journal of Political Economics*, Vol. 77, No. 4 (July/August 1969).
15. Sidrauski, M., *Growth in a Monetary Economy*, 1966, (mimeographed).
16. Tobin, J., "Money and Economic Growth," *Econometrica*, October 1965.

PART II

INFLATION AND SAVINGS BEHAVIOR

A STUDY ON THE SAVINGS BEHAVIOR, 1953—1972

Mahn Je Kim &
*Yung Chul Park**

I. Introduction

Economics literature abounds with hypotheses on the nature of savings behavior and empirical studies that examine the validity of these hypotheses both in less developed countries (LDCs) and advanced countries. However, most of these hypotheses have been developed for advanced countries and may not necessarily be relevant to LDCs whose institutional and structural characteristics are vastly different from those of advanced countries. Aside from this theoretical issue, there is the practical problem of the paucity of reliable and consistent data in LDCs that makes it difficult to test these hypotheses and obtain reasonable results.

The empirical literature on savings behavior in LDCs may be divided into two categories. In the first category are the studies that empirically examine various hypotheses developed for advanced countries. Belonging to the second category are the reduced form equations studies and ad-hoc equations studies that regress domestic savings against a set of explanatory variables without specifying the causal relationships between the independent and dependent variables.

The explanatory variables used in these studies also vary a great deal,

* The authors are respectively President of the Korea Development Institute, and Visiting Fellow at KDI and Professor of Economics at Korea University. This is a revised version of a paper presented at the KDI–DAS (Harvard University) Conference, Seoul, October 10–12, 1973.

but most researchers seem to emphasize real variables such as GNP, per capita income, the growth rate, and permanent income as the major determinants of real savings and tend to ignore financial variables such as the stock of money, financial assets, the rates of interest and domestic credit.[1] There are a few studies that examine the effects of these financial variables but they often fail to specify how these variables influence savings behavior.

Fiscal policy, in particular, change in the level and structure of taxes, has been regarded as the most reliable means of mobilizing domestic real savings and promoting growth. Monetary and financial policies, on the other hand, have been relegated to a minor role in the saving-investment process. However, fiscal policy as a means of mobilizing domestic savings is subject to many limitations. The administrative difficulties and waste involved in tax policy would be enormous; also distortions in resource allocation associated with taxes cannot be ignored. Moreover, a heavy reliance on fiscal policy, if it is carried to the extreme, has the tendency of ignoring policy measures that would induce people to save more voluntarily and placing too much emphasis on various coercive measures, which are hardly effective.

In recent years, there has been a growing number of theoretical studies which analyze the role of money and financial institutions in the saving and investment process and in economic development.

The writings of Gurley, Shaw, Cameron, Goldsmith, Patrick, and McKinnon[2] suggest that financial development (i) encourages savers to

[1] For a comprehensive survey of the literature, see R.F. Mikesell and J.E. Zinser, "The Nature of the Savings Function in Developing Countries: A Survey of the Theoretical and Empirical Literature," *Journal of Economic Literature*, Mar. 1973, pp. 1–26.

[2] J. G. Gurley and E. S. Shaw, "Financial Aspects of Economic Development," *American Economic Review*, Sept. 1955. See also his "Financial Intermediaries and the Saving-Investment Process," *Journal of Finance*, May 1965, *Money in a Theory of Finance* (Washington, D.C.: The Brookings Institution, 1960), and "Financial Structure and Economic Development," *Economic Development and Cultural Change*, April 1967; Rondo Cameron, "Theoretical Bases of a Comparative Study of the Role of Financial Institutions," in the *Conference of Economic History*, Aix-en Province, France, 1962; Robert L. Bennet, "Financial Innovation and Structural Change in the Early Stage of Industrialization: Mexico, 1945–59," *Journal of Finance*, Dec. 1963; H. Patrick, "Financial Development and Economic Growth in Underdeveloped Countries," *Economic Development and Cultural Change*, Jan. 1966; Raymond W. Goldsmith, *Financial Structure and Development* (New Haven: Yale University Press, 1969); R.I. McKinnon, *Money and Capital in Economic Development* (Washington, D.C: The Brookings Institution, 1973). See also his "Money, Growth, and the Pro-

hold their savings in the form of financial, rather than unproductive tangible, assets; (ii) ensures efficient allocation of savings to most productive investments and (iii) provides incentives for increased savings. This view suggests a much broader role of, and scope for, money and financial policies in the context of economic development and implies that policy makers should encourage proper formation and expansion of the financial sector.

The Korean government recently announced a set of rather ambitious economic targets: by the early 1980's, the government hopes to reach the level of $1,000 per capita income and $10 billion in exports. The attainment of these targets requires a new development strategy involving, among other things, changes in industrial structures and mobilization and efficient allocation of domestic resources. The government also made public its detailed economic planning for the 1970's consistent with these targets. According to this planning, the domestic saving ratio must be raised from the present level of 14.5 percent to 27.1 percent in 1981, that is, the ratio must be doubled over a ten-year period.

The major objective of this study is to examine whether such an increase in the saving ratio can be expected in the course of economic development in the 1970's.

Section II and III develop a framework of analysis which focus on the role of money and financial institutions as an intermediary between savers and investors in the saving-investment process. In Section IV, we analyze the past savings behavior in Korea in comparison to Taiwan and Japan—two countries with an exceptionally high saving ratio—together with an empirical analysis of the savings functions derived from our theoretical analysis and projections of the saving ratios for the period 1973–81 using some of the regression equations. Concluding remarks will be found in Section V.

II. The Role of Financial Variables in the Saving-Investment Process

1. Debt-Intermediation View of Money

Broadly speaking, there are two different views on money, finance, and

pensity to Save: An Iconoclastic View," April 1973, unpublished manuscript; and Edward S. Shaw, *Financial Deepening in Economic Development* (New York: Oxford University Press, 1973).

economic growth. The first view may be represented by a large and ever growing volume of literature on the neoclassical and Keynesian theories of money and growth. The advocates of these theories—Friedman, H. Johnson, Tobin, J. Stein, and Mundell[3] view money as a substitute for completely malleable capital goods in the asset portfolios and assume that the markets for primary securities and capital goods are perfectly competitive. In such a framework, the role of money is limited to essentially a medium of exchange and the role of financial institutions as an intermediary between savers and investors is completely redundant.

Neoclassical and Keynesian growth models are largely inapplicable to the problems of developing economies (LDCs) because the assumptions of these models are irrelevant to these economies. For instance, these models imply that an increase in the real return to holding money could reduce the rate of capital formation as it induces people to substitute capital for money in their portfolios—a proposition based on the assumptions that capital markets operate perfectly and costlessly and that inputs including capital goods are perfectly divisible with constant returns to scale. However, in most LDCs, a more realistic view would be that capital and primary securities markets do not exist; even if these markets are present, they are so fragmented and rudimentary that they hardly perform the role of mobilizing savings and allocating them to investment. The predominance of firm-households and the agricultural sector in LDCs also suggest that indivisibilities in investment are of considerable importance. When these characteristic features of LDCs are properly taken into consideration, the role of money as a financial asset is broadened and becomes significant in the saving-investment process. In fact, contrary to the neoclassical argument, it can be shown that an increase in the real rate of return on money could raise the rate of capital accumulation. The experience of some LDCs which have pursued high deposit rate

[3] For the literature on the neo-classical and Keynesian theories of monetary growth, see J.L. Stein, *Money and Capacity Growth* (New York and London: Columbia University Press, 1971), pp. 265–67; Allan H. Meltzer, "Money, Intermediation and Growth," *Journal of Economic Literature*, March 1969, pp. 40–56; D. Levhari and D. Patinkin, "The Role of Money in a Simple Growth Model," *American Economic Review*, Sept. 1968, pp. 713–53; "The Role of Money in a Simple Growth Model: Reply," *American Economic Review*, March 1972, p. 185; J. Harkness, "The Role of Money in a Simple Growth Model: Comment," *American Economic Review*, March 1972, pp. 177–79; also the comment on the same paper by R. Ramanathan, *American Economic Review*, March 1972, pp.180–184; D.K. Foley and M. Sidrauski, *Monetary and Fiscal Policy in a Growing Economy* (London: The MacMillan Company, Collier MacMillan Limited).

policies in recent years seems to bear out this argument.

The second view, which may be called the Debt-Intermediation view of monetary theory, stresses the role of money as a store of value and as a vehicle of capital accumulation and of financial institutions as an intermediary between savers and investors in an environment where the crucial neoclassical assumptions do not hold. In this sense, the Debt-Intermediation view appears to be more applicable to the analysis of monetary problems of fragmented economies with poorly developed capital markets.

Although the causal nexus between money and financial institutions on the one hand, and economic development on the other, still remains an unsettled issue in this view, the writings of Gurley, Shaw, Cameron, Patrick, and McKinnon[4] suggest the following relationships between financial development and economic growth:

(1) Financial institutions can encourage a more efficient allocation of a given amount of total assets by bringing about changes in its ownership and in its composition through intermediation among various types of asset holders. The result of such a transformation in the composition of the asset portfolios is not a continued higher rate of growth, but a permanent increase in the level of output, though the full impact of the change may be spread over a period of several years.

(2) Financial institutions can encourage more efficient allocation of a given amount of savings from less to more productive investment. An increase in the allocative efficiency of the economy could raise the rate of economic growth as the increase usually improves the average productivity of capital. A higher growth rate could in turn raise the saving propensity for two reasons. First, the increase in $\Delta Y/Y$ is associated with a relative increase in the transitory component of measured income. Secondly, the increase will induce people to accumulate real cash balances to satisfy their increased needs, or transactions demand, for money. In a financially unsophisticated economy, people may have to save more to maintain a desired money/income ratio.

(3) Financial institutions can induce people to save more by offering a wide variety of financial assets with a higher yield and lower risk. With the terms of the trade-off between saving and consumption more favorable to the former, individuals substitute increased savings for consumption out of

[4] See footnote 2 on page 156

current income.

While the causal nature of the relation between financial institutions and economic development has been analyzed in some detail, mostly in the context of LDCs, the proponents of the DI view have not succeeded in formalizing their theory in a general equilibrium framework. One reason for this is the sheer difficulty of building a mathematical model reflecting the institutional characteristics of fragmented economies. The other reason may be that there still exists a considerable amount of confusion on the precise nature of the interaction between the real and monetary sectors of the economy. In a recent book and a paper, McKinnon attempts to clarify the nature of the relationships between financial and real variables in the saving and investment process.[5] Since we are basically interested in the effects of financial variables on the savings propensity, we will briefly examine his argument.

McKinnon considers a financially underdeveloped economy where broad money is the only financial asset whose demand function is specified as follows:

$$\frac{M}{P} = L\,(y, r - p^*) \quad \text{.......(1)}$$

where M/P = the real stock of broad money, defined as the sum of currency in circulation, demand deposits and savings and time deposits.
y = real income
r = deposit rate of interest
p^* = expected rate of inflation

The partial derivatives of equation (1) are all positive. Corresponding to this simple financial structure, there is a social savings function which can be partitioned as follows:

$$S = \Delta\left(\frac{M}{P}\right) - G + S_p, \quad \text{.......(2)}$$

where S = real private savings
G = the real flow of government seigniorage
S_p = self-financed investment

[5] McKinnon, "Money, Growth, and the Propensity to Save: An Iconoclastic View", *op. cit.*

The first term in equation (2) is that portion of real private savings that goes to acquire real cash balances. McKinnon assumes that G is negatively related to r-p^*, because G rises as r-p^* declines in the adjustment process. S_p is also inversely related to r-p^*, because money and capital are likely to be complements over a certain range of investment opportunities in LDCs.

Differentiating equation (1) with respect to time, we obtain,

$$\Delta\left(\frac{M}{P}\right) = L_1\Delta y + L_2\Delta(r - p^*).$$

On a balanced growth path, $\Delta(r - p^*) = 0$,
so that

$$\Delta\frac{M}{P} = L_1\Delta y \quad \text{.......(3)}$$

Substituting equation (3) into (2) and dividing through both sides of the equation by y, we have

$$\frac{S}{y} = L_1\frac{\Delta y}{y} - \frac{G}{y} + \frac{S_p}{y} \quad \text{.......(4)}$$

If the income elasticity of the demand for money is unity, equation (4) can in general be written as

$$\frac{S}{y} = F\left(\frac{\Delta y}{y}, r - p^*\right) \quad \text{.......(5)}$$

Otherwise, $\frac{S}{y}$ will also depend upon the level of real income, That is,

$$\frac{S}{y} = F\left(\frac{\Delta y}{y}, r - p^*, y\right) \quad \text{.......(5)'}$$

Suppose also that equation (1) can be written as

$$r - p^* = L^*\left(\frac{M}{P}, y\right) \quad \text{.......(6)}$$

Substituting equation (6) into (5), we have

$$\frac{S}{y} = F^*\left(\frac{\Delta y}{y}, \frac{M}{Y}\right) \quad \text{.......(7)[6]}$$

[6] If consumption is a function of permanent income or subject to a distributed lag, then the saving ratio will also depend upon the rate of growth of income. See, S,K. Singh, *Development Economics: Theory and Findings* (Lexington, Mass: D.D. Heath, 1972); K. Yoshihara, "The Growth Rate as a Determinant of the Saving Ratio," *Hitosubashi Journal of Economics*, Feb. 1972, pp. 60–72.

where $\frac{M}{Y}$ is the money-nominal income (Y) ratio.

What we have presented above is essentially the formal structure of McKinnon's view on the role of money and financial intermediation in the context of economic development. The model is by far the most elegant exposition of the *DI* view and certainly has many important implications for appropriate financial policies in LDCs. But the elegance is somewhat marred by the internal inconsistency and conceptual difficulties of its logical structure. First, it is not altogether clear whether it is legitimate to transform the identity (equation 2) into a behaviorial relationship (equation 5). If such a transformation is feasible, then one should be able to show that the resulting function is consistent with the intertemporal utility maximization of consumption expenditure. McKinnon has little to say on this. Nor does he specify how the demand for money function (equation 1) is derived. Therefore, there is no way of knowing whether the saving ratio function corresponds to an economic units' choice between current and future consumption. Secondly, the inverse relationship between G and $r\text{-}p^*$ is not based upon any assumptions concerning government behavior, but the result of an adjustment process of the economy. This aspect of the model suggests that the saving ratio function is partly a reduced-form type equation. Thirdly, McKinnon fails to consider the relationship between domestic savings and the supply of unorganized credit. Correctly specified, the saving identity equation (2) should include a change in the supply of credit to the unorganized money market by the private sector. This is because unorganized credit is an important asset in the portfolios of wealth owners in LDCs. In most of the LDCs, the unorganized money market absorbs a substantial portion of domestic savings and caters to the credit needs of small scale industries and the agricultural sector. It is true that much of unorganized credit would be diverted to the financing of consumption expenditure, but still it performs the role of mobilizing savings and channelling them to investment. An increase in the real deposit rate then may increase the demand for money, but the increase in the demand for money may be realized entirely by an equal reduction in the supply of unorganized credit in so far as the supply depends upon the real deposit rate. In that event, that is, when money and unorganized credit are good substitutes in the asset portfolios, the increase in the real deposit rate cannot increase domestic savings. This is another reason why equation 5 may not be a behavioral relationship.

However, the validity of McKinnon's thesis is based, not so much on the internal logical structure, as on his intuitive view on the role of money in a poor fragmented economy. He believes that money and real capital goods are the only vehicles of savings and that these two assets are complementary to each other. Hence any changes in the demand for money will directly influence the saving ratio. The conceptual problems we have pointed out are serious, but to the extent that McKinnon's central thesis is intuitively appealing, perhaps it is justifiable to verify its validity by looking at the historical experience of some LDCs.

In our empirical analysis, we will estimate equations (5) and (7). However, it must be pointed out that the estimated equations are meaningful only under a set of very restrictive assumptions and thus must be interpreted with caution. First, as we have noted, the saving propensity equations are neither behavioral functions nor reduced form equations: they are a hybrid of the two. Secondly, the saving functions are subject to a simultaneous equation bias: $\Delta y/y$ and M/y are endogenous variables jointly determined with S/y in a general equilibrium framework. One way of avoiding this bias could be to assume that foreign savings, which account for a substantial portion of total savings in most of the LDCs, are an exogenous variable and that a given change in M at time t affects the price level with a lag. Thirdly, we have the problem of identification: we do not know whether we are estimating a savings function or an investment function.

2. *Intermediation Efficiency of the Banking Industry and Domestic Savings*

The DI view places its major emphasis on financial development but little on economic efficiency of financial institutions in mobilizing domestic savings. The implicit assumption here is that the efficiency of these institutions improves as the financial sector of the economy expands. This may not be true, however. In the early stages of economic development, the financial sector is rather small and financial institutions that make up the sector are likely to be inefficient. As financial development takes place, the actual size of this sector may increase, but the intermediation efficiency of financial institutions may not improve.

For a given degree of financial sophistication, an increase in the real deposit rate on money could be regarded as an increase in the real return to saving so long as money is a store of value. As the exchange ratio between future consumption and present consumption becomes favorable to the former, individuals could save more out of current income. This interest rate effect on savings would be stronger if the asset choice of individual savers is restricted to either holding money or capital goods as is likely the case in LDCs. Increased savings resulting from the increase in the real deposit rate will then be transformed into an equivalent amount of investment through bank intermediation, if one assumes that banks are efficient in their role of intermediation. However, just like any other economic units, banks may not allocate the mobilized savings to the most productive investments, thereby generating a positive discrepancy between potential and realized savings. The wastage involved in the intermediation process could be greater, the more imperfect the banking industry is.

To clarify this point, let us assume that the government raises r. Other things being equal, the increase in r will induce people to save more in the form of money. The resulting increase in the demand for bank deposits expands the intermediation capacity of banks. As an intermediary, however, banks could divert some of the mobilized savings to the financing of consumption expenditure, and working capital requirements. In the long-run, such a composition of the bank loan portfolios would tend to put the economy on a lower growth path than when bank resources were largely channelled to the financing of fixed investments of business firms. The effects of alternative compositions of the bank portfolios on the saving propensity would be explained by the growth rate in McKinnon's model, but in other frameworks one has to consider another variable reflecting efficiency of the banking industry. In order to account for the impact of changes in the intermediation efficiency of the banking sector on the saving ratio, we will assume that domestic savings (S_d) can be decomposed into two parts. Type one savings (S_1), which are referred to as self-financed investment, depend on income alone and require no financial intermediation. Type two savings (S_2) are held in financial assets and depend upon income and the interest rates on these assets. Unlike S_1, however, the extent of realization of S_2 depends upon the efficiency of the existing financial institution. Suppose S_1 and S_2 can be specified as follows:

$$S_1 = sY \quad \text{(8)}$$

$$S_2 = S(Y, r\text{-}p^*, X) \quad \text{(9)}$$

where X is a variable reflecting the degree of economic efficiency of the financial sector. Then,

$$S_d = sY + S^*(r - p^*, X)Y$$

$$= [s + S^*(r - p^*, X)]Y \quad \text{(10)}$$

In general,

$$\frac{S_d}{Y} = S_d(r - p^*, X) \quad \text{.................................(11)}$$

As before, we may substitute M/Y for $r-p^*$ in the above equation. In reality, X can not be observed directly, so that one must use a proxy for X. We examined L_M/L, L_M/M, L_I/M, L_I/L. (L_M is the amount of total bank loan L that is channelled to the manufacturing industry and L_I is fixed investment loans.) Among these, L_M/M appears to be most significant, but hardly a satisfactory one.

III. Alternative Views on the Factors Determining the Saving Ratio

As we have already noted in Section I, a number of factors other than various income variables have been suggested as the likely determinants of the saving ratio. Among these, we have examined three variables that we consider relevant to our purpose of projection. They are exports, foreign savings, and a variable representing the development of the manufacturing industry.

1. Exports and Savings

Several studies have examined the significance of exports as an argument for a savings function and found a positive relationship between the two, each study utilizing a different specification of the domestic savings function. We have tested all of the specifications suggested by these studies but the results are highly unsatisfactory. The basic problem was collinearity between the independent variables of the savings function which makes it difficult to determine the significance of exports as an independent variable.

2. Development of the Manufacturing Industry and Domestic Savings

In a recent study on the Korean economy, Shimomura[7] argues that the

[7] Osamu Shimomura, *Some Suggestions for Stabilization of the Korean Economy*, Research Report No. 8, KDI, Aug. 1972.

key to a high rate of growth in a stable environment lies in a conscientious government policy that encourages investment in the manufacturing sector. In the course of the argument, he also suggests that such a policy will also raise the saving ratio over time for the following reasons. First, the capital output ratio of the manufacturing industries is relatively lower than that of other industries in the economy. One would then expect that a given increase in investment in the manufacturing sector would result in a larger increase in output than in other industrial sectors. Such an increase in output would have the effect of slowing down the rate of inflation which would in turn increase the real return on holding money.

Second, concentrated investment in the M sector would lead to an expansion of the export and import-substitution industry. This expansion would in turn reduce the chronic BOP deficits experienced by most of the LDCs and subsequently relax the BOP constraint on economic growth. Improvement in the BOP position would allow the authorities to maintain their exchange rates at equilibrium values and thus avoid the overvaluation of currencies that inhibits the flow of savings to investment through financial channels.

Thirdly, manufacturing industries are relatively more labor intensive than others so that they have a larger capacity for absorbing surplus labor in LDCs. Since they are also high technology industries, development of this sector could provide a strong impetus for a rapid industrialization of the economy. According to Lewis[8], the relative expansion of the capitalist (or modern) sector raises the profits-GNP ratio, which in turn increases the rate of saving and investment.

The preceding discussion suggests that there is likely to be a positive relationship between the saving ratio and the relative development of the manufacturing sector. In order to verify this relationship, we will assume the following saving ratio function.

$$\frac{S_d}{Y} = S_d\left(\frac{M}{Y}, Z\right) \quad \text{.................................} (12)$$

where M/Y explains the significance of financial variables in domestic savings and Z is a variable reflecting the relative importance of the manufacturing sector in the economy. For Z, we have used the ratio of manufac-

[8] A. N. Agarwala and S. P. Singh (editors), W. A. Lewis, "Economic Development with Unlimited Supplies of Labor," in *The Economics of Underdevelopment*, (New York: Oxford University Press, 1958), pp. 400–447.

turing output to GNP, (Y_M/Y), the ratio of fixed investment in the manufacturing sector to total investment, (I_M/I), and I_M/Y. I_M/I was not significant in any of the three countries and we were unable to determine the significance of Y_M/Y because of a high degree of multicollinearity between M/Y and Y_M/Y both in Korea and Taiwan. Only in the case of Japan, the saving function fits the data quite well. However, when we used I_M/Y as a proxy for Z, the linear version of the saving function explained most of the fluctuations in S_d/Y in all three countries. However, it may not be legitimate to treat I_M/Y as an independent variable of S_d/Y, given the definitional relationship between the two. Thus, it is possible that our estimation result reflects correlation rather than causality.

3. *Financial Aspects of Capital Inflows and Domestic Savings*

In capital-scarce LDCs, inflows of foreign savings are expected to supplement and even induce domestic savings and investment. However, in recent years a number of economists have not only questioned the effects foreign savings have on both the saving propensity and the level of savings but also suggested that inflows of savings cause a reduction in domestic savings and the magnitude of this reduction is measurable.[9] As for the possible causes of the negative relationship between S_d and S_F, these economists have presented various arguments, but none of them seems to succeed in specifying a precise mechanism through which foreign savings affect domestic savings. The negative relationship, as Papanek shows, may be in part the result of the accounting convention in which domestic savings are measured by substracting foreign savings from total investment.[10] One could also point to a number of specific circumstances where a low saving rate and a high inflow of foreign savings are likely to have been caused by a poor or deteriorating economic and political situation rather than the former being caused by the latter. Furthermore, most of these empirical studies inevitably suffer from a variety of statistical problems. The state of knowledge on the causality between S_d and S_F seems to be as unclear as it has ever been.

Analyses based on two-gap models by Chenery-Strout and Chenery-

[9] For a survey of the literature on the relationship between foreign capital and domestic savings, see Mikesell and Zinser, *op, cit.*, pp. 12–15; G. F. Papanek, "The Effect of Aid and Other Resource Transfers on Savings and Growth in LDCs," *Economic Journal*, Sept. 1972, pp. 734–950.

[10] Papanek, *op, cit.*, p. 938.

Eckstein[11] suggest that an inflow of foreign capital could indeed reduce domestic savings when the trade-gap is binding. An inflow of foreign savings provides the foreign exchange for additional investment but also serves as a perfect substitute for domestic savings in "financing" investment. In other words, the inflow provides the foreign exchange needed to support a higher level of investment, but at the same time the increase in capital imports increases the deficit on the trade account. Hence, gross domestic savings, *ex post*, do not necessarily rise even though total investment may have increased by the amount of the capital inflow. This must always be true in the accounting sense. What one must know is rather how such an *ex post* result is brought about. Chenery-Eckstein do not provide a satisfactory answer; they simply state that if the prospective trade gap is the larger of the two, actual saving is "assumed" to fall short of potential saving-for example, through lower taxes or more liberal consumer credit.[12]

In what follows, we will show that there exists a definite mechanism through which an inflow of S_F can reduce domestic saving when the *ex ante* trade gap is dominant. For this purpose, we will assume that the rate of investment is exogenously determined to achieve a target rate of growth. In this way we can immediately dispose of the supply side of the model. We also assume that the government authorities can control the growth of M, that the required investment is maintained in part by the supply of bank credit, and that prices are rather flexible. Under these assumptions, suppose the economy in question is in a disequilibrium state characterized by the dominance of the trade gap. This situation corresponds to the Keynesian case of insufficient aggregate demand, which will exert downward pressures on prices. If the gap is filled up by an inflow of foreign savings, then the inflow is most likely to cause an accumulation of foreign reserve assets of the central bank in the short run (If the inflow takes entirely the form of commodity aid and suppliers' credit, there will be no change in the level of foreign reserves). The accumulation would then lead to an expansion of the supply of broad money. If the authorities wish to maintain a constant rate of monetary growth, they have no alternative but to reduce the supply of domestic credit to the government and private sector enough to neutralize the expansion of M resulting from the inflow. In other words, the authorities will have to pursue tight monetary and credit policies to reduce

[11] See, H. B. Chenery and P. Eckstein, "Development Alternatives for Latin America," *Journal of Political Economics*, July/August, 1970, pp. 966–1006. H. B. Chenery and A. Strout, "Foreign Assistance and Economic Development," *Amercian Economic Review*, Sept. 1966, pp. 679–733.

[12] Chenery-Eckstein, *op. cit.*, p. 968.

the rate of increase in the demand for currency, demand and savings deposits. Since the increase in the demand for broad money is equivalent to an equal increase in S_d—though under limited circumstances of LDCs—the government authorities are in fact absorbing domestic savings and keeping them in the form of foreign exchange assets. The level of domestic saving will therefore fall. In this way the inflow of foreign savings restores balance in the output market and eliminates the initial downward pressure on the price level. On the other hand, if the authorities let M expand, the immediate consequence will be to expand the credit-creating capacity of the banking sector. Business firms already receive an adequate supply of bank credit, so that banks will be able to increase their consumption loans and offer favorable terms of credit. The increase in the supply of bank credit will stimulate aggregate demand for goods and services, which will in turn push up the price level. A higher price level will reduce the real supply of M and the real return on money. The adjustment process will continue until the increase in the price level reduces domestic savings enough to restore equilibrium in the output market.

A prerequisite for the verification of the above argument would be to determine whether the economy was subject to a trade gap during the period under consideration. This is not an easy task and no one has produced a satisfactory method. Chenery-Eckstein's method is to regress domestic savings against GNP, S_F, and the share of exports in GNP and then to examine the sign of the coefficient of S_F.[13] If the sign is negative, then the trade gap has been the larger of the two. We have estimated the same equation using data from Korea, Japan, and Taiwan. In the case of Korea, we found that the sign was negative but S_F was insignificant statistically. Both in Japan and Taiwan, the sign was positive, but again S_F was not significant for the period.

Though unsatisfactory, we will use this as evidence that the trade gap was in general greater than the saving gap in Korea during most of the past twenty years[14]. We will then test the negative relationship between

[13] *Ibid.*, p. 97.

[14] A. M. Strout argues that until 1967 the savings gap had been dominant in Korea. His analysis is based upon the following regression equation: $\frac{\Delta I}{\Delta Y} = 0.29 + 1.0 \left(\frac{\Delta S_F}{\Delta y}\right)$ The coefficient of $\frac{\Delta S_F}{\Delta Y}$ takes values of 0 and 1 in theory. When the coefficient is 1, this means that a country's growth is constrained by available foreign resources. Somehow we were not able to reproduce his result. See, A.M. Strout, "Korea's Use of Foreign and Domestic Resources: A Cross-Country Comparison," in I. Adelman (editor), *Practical Approaches to Development Planning: Korea's Second Five-Year Plan* (Baltimore: The Johns Hopkins University Press, 1969), Chapter 11.

S_d/Y and S_F/Y by assuming the following saving functions and fitting the linear versions of these equations:

$$\frac{S_d}{Y}=f\left(\frac{M}{Y},\frac{S_F}{Y}\right) \quad \cdots\cdots(13)$$

$$\frac{S_d}{Y}=h\left(\frac{\Delta y}{y},\frac{M}{S},\frac{S_F}{Y}\right) \quad \cdots\cdots(14)$$

IV. Estimation of the Models

1. *The Savings Behavior in Korea, 1953–72*

Over the period 1953–65, the figures on the saving propensity for Korea record one of the poorest performances among the LDCs in a comparable stage of economic development. The domestic saving ratio actually fell from 9.4 percent in 1953 to 7.5 percent in 1965, although per capita income rose by more than 40 percent during the same period. The saving ratio also fluctuated over a wide margin(See Tables 1 and 3 and Figure 1). The relatively poor performance of the propensity to save in Korea during the period could be attributed to a number of factors. One factor appears to be the government's inability to control inflation and low interest rate policy that kept real return to holding money negative. Another explanation could be the over-valued exchange rates that inhibited the flow of domestic savings to investment through financial channels thereby misallocating savings. A third factor might have been the relatively low manufacturing share in total investment that slowed down the development of export and import-substitution industries(See Tables 3 and 4). A fourth reason may be found in the general political and social instability that plagued the country after the Korean War.

The fluctuation in the saving propensity may be partially accounted for by the general instability of the economy but largely by the fluctuations in the level of agricultural output which depends on the weather. The proportion of agricultural inventories in total output would be greater if the agricultural sector were larger. In an inflationary environment farmers tend to save by accumulating their own inventories as a hedge against the loss of nominal value which they must incur when they hold money or other financial assets. This means that the domestic saving ratio would be sensitive to changes in the level of agricultural output.

A simple observation of the raw data suggests a sharp rise in the savings ratio in 1965 (See Figure 1) the year when the government introduced various monetary reforms. The reform raised the official ceiling rates on bank time deposits from 15 percent to 30 percent thereby raising the real return on money to a positive level for the first time in the post Korean War period. Undoubtedly, the increase attracted a substantial amount of bank saving deposits and diverted the loanable funds that would otherwise have flown into the curb market to the organized credit sector. As a result, there was a significant expansion in the size of the organized financial sector as measured by M/Y ratio which rose from 9 percent in 1964 to 15 percent in 1966. Since the reform in 1965, the M/Y ratio more than doubled over an eight-year period reaching 38.4 percent in 1972 suggesting a continued expansion in the banking sector. At the same time, the growth performance of the economy has been impressive; the economy has been growing approximately 10 percent per annum on the average. Yet, the saving performance has been rather disappointing. Since the monetary reform, the saving ratio rose steadily to 1969 when it was 17.5 percent and thereafter it began to fall reaching 14.6 percent in 1972. One could perhaps entertain a number of explanations for the poor performance in the savings behavior during this period, but the most important ones are likely to be the substantial increase in the inflow of foreign capital that has led to misallocation of domestic savings, the government investment policy that emphasized the social overhead capital goods industries at the expense of other industries, and intermediation inefficiency of the banking industry. In particular, it appears that inflows of foreign savings have had a significant adverse effect on the propensity to save since the 1965 monetary reform in Korea. The reform which raised the deposit rates to a level comparable to the prevailing curb market rates was highly successful in increasing private demand for savings and time deposits. The increase in the deposit rate also attracted a larger inflow of foreign capital in the form of trade credit, cash loans, and direct investment, most of which was used for the financing of long-term business investment. As a result, commercial banks were increasingly diverting most of the mobilized savings to the financing of working capital requirements of business corporations and partly to consumer credit. At the same time, the inflow of foreign capital together with the increase in the demand for bank deposits contributed to a marked increase in the supply of money. The supply of broad money (M) rose by 64 percent, 80 percent, and 62 percent in three successive years after the 1965 monetary reform as compared with a 30 percent annual average rate of increase during the five-year period before the reform. The increase was no doubt excessive and threatened open inflation. To avoid this explosive situation, authorities adopted a restrictive stance on monetary and credit policy. The required reserve ratio on time and savings deposits was raised successively from 10 percent in 1965 to 20 percent in Feb. 1966 and to 25 percent in Nov. 1967; it was not until Nov. 1971 that the ratio was reduced to the 1965 level. At the same time, the required ratio on demand deposits was also raised from 16 percent in 1965 to 20 percent in Feb. 1966. A little more than a year later, the ratio was again raised to an all time high figure of 35 percent (Nov. 1967). Thus, the monetary authorities found themselves pursuing contradictory policies. On the one hand, they raised the nominal deposit rates to a market level to attract more time and savings deposits. On the other hand, they were tightening up the credit conditions so as to restrain the excessive rate of increase in M which resulted from the high deposit rates policy. In other words, the monetary authorities were absorbing much of the mobilized savings and keeping them in the form of foreign exchange reserve rather than allocating them to investment.

In our empirical analysis, we will examine whether the data bear out these interpretations. Over a similar period, we also observe a steady rise in the saving ratio with minor fluctuations around its trend in Taiwan. The savings ratio remained around the 10 percent level until 1960 and began to rise sharply in 1963. The sharp rising trend continued, passing the 30 percent level in 1972. During the 20-year period, the M/Y ratio rose by more than five times—an indication of a fast development in the banking sector. Thus, unlike Korea, we do not observe a divergency between S_d/Y and M/Y ratio in Taiwan.

Another interesting observation in the Taiwanese savings behavior is that, despite the fact that the economy has been growing at a faster pace than in other LDCs, particularly since 1963, the rate of growth does not appear to have had any appreciable impact on the savings behavior. Nor did the inflows of foreign savings have much effect on the savings behavior in Taiwan, suggesting that Taiwan had already reached a self-sufficient stage and confronted no prolonged serious BOP problems in the 1960s. Rather, the gradual increase in I_M/Y appears to have been a more important variable in explaining the Taiwanese savings behavior.

Japan provides another interesting case study of savings behavior. By the early 1950's, Japan had already reached the 20 percent level of the domestic propensity to save which was extremely high compared with other developing countries at that time. The miraculous growth of the Japanese economy since World War II is well known; the increase in the S_d/Y ratio which almost doubled during the 20-year period, seems to confirm this experience. Economists have suggested a number of different explanations for the remarkable increase in the saving ratio in Japan. But in our view, the most important factors responsible for the Japanese saving performance would be found in an equally impressive growth in the organized financial sector and a very high rate of economic growth. The saving ratio doubled while the M/Y ratio also more than doubled over the period 1952–72 which can hardly be a pure coincidence.

As the preceding discussion indicates, the models we have developed in this paper seem to apply well to all three countries. In the following section, we will attempt to estimate some of the savings equations we have derived in section II.

2. *Bases for the Projections of the Savings Behavior for the Period 1973–81*

We have estimated the following savings equations based on our theoretical analyses in Section II using the time-series data for Korea, Japan and Taiwan for the period of 1953–72 and also the pooled time-series and cross-section data of all three countries.

$$\frac{S_d}{Y} = a_0 + a_1\frac{\Delta y}{y} + a_2(r - p^*) \quad \dots\dots(1)$$

$$\frac{S_d}{Y} = b_0 + b_1\frac{\Delta y}{y} + b_2\frac{M}{Y} \quad \dots\dots(2)$$

$$\frac{S_d}{Y} = c_0 + c_1\frac{\Delta y}{y} + c_2\frac{M}{Y} + c_3\frac{S_F}{Y} \quad \dots\dots(3)$$

$$\frac{S_d}{Y} = d_0 + d_1\frac{M}{Y} + d_2\frac{I_M}{Y} \quad \dots\dots(4)$$

$$\frac{S_d}{Y} = e_0 + e_1\frac{M}{Y} + e_2\frac{I_M}{Y} + e_3\frac{S_F}{Y} \quad \dots\dots(5)$$

where S_d/Y is the domestic propensity to save.

We have also estimated the private propensity to save (S_p/Y) using the same independent variables as in the above equations. The regression results of the savings functions for Korea, Taiwan, and Japan are reported in Table 5 and 6.

In all of the equations we have tested, equation (4) explains the savings behavior quite well in all three countries. With the exception of Taiwan, both the growth rate and M/Y in equation (2) appear to be statistically significant. In an effort to avoid some of the statistical problems associated with the use of time-series data, we have also tested equation (2) utilizing the cross-section data of 24 LDCs:

$$\frac{S_d}{Y} = 8.7 + 0.04\frac{\Delta y}{y} + 0.24\frac{M}{Y} \qquad R^2 = 0.43$$
$$\qquad\qquad (0.14) \qquad (1.89) \qquad\qquad DW = 2.27$$

$$\frac{S_d}{Y} = 4.50 + 0.42\frac{M}{Y} \qquad R^2 = .62$$
$$\qquad\qquad (4.9) \qquad\qquad DW = 2.25$$

Data: 1966–1968 average
Source: Various issues of IMF, *International Financial Statistics* and U.N., *National Income Statistics.*

The result indicates that though the growth rate is insignificant, the ratio of broad money to GNP is, beyond any reasonable doubt, an important factor in the savings function in LDCs. On the other hand, the real deposit rate has either a wrong sign or negligible influence on the saving ratios in all three countries. However, the latter result should not be taken literally; it may simply mean that we do not have accurate information on the expectation formation process of the holders of wealth or that r-p^* is not a proper measure of the actual real return on money. Our results on the effects of interest rates on the saving ratio also contradict the findings of at least three recent studies on the savings behavior in Korea. Gilbert Brown[15] finds that various measures of savings and saving ratios are positively related to the rates of interest. His results were statistically significant and R^2's were generally above 0.6. A study by Frank, Kim, and Westphal[16] also shows that the nominal deposit rates and expected rate of inflation are important determinants of savings. Kim's study on inflation in Korea[17] suggests a similar result.

[15] G. Brown, "The Impact of Korea's 1965 Interest Rate Reform on Savings, Investment, and the Balance of Payments," (A paper presented to CENTC Symposium on Central Banking, Monetary Policy and Economic Development, Izmir, Turkey, April 1971).

[16] C. R. Frank, K. S. Kim, and L. E. Westphal, *Foreign Exchange, Trade Policy, and Economic Growth in Korea*, Chapter 8, 1972 (Unpublished manuscript).

[17] K. S. Kim, *The Causes and Effects of Inflation in Korea,* KDI Working Paper 7302, Jan. 1973.

Our results also indicate that the rate of growth is an important determinant of real savings in Korea and Japan but not in Taiwan. Thus, McKinnon's models explain the savings behavior for Korea and Japan quite well but rather poorly for Taiwan where either the growth rate or the real deposit rate has no significant effect on the saving propensity. The Taiwan experience shows that the rate of economic growth, which was relatively high compared with other LDCs over the period (approximately 10 percent per annum on the average), has exerted no measurable impact on savings. Much of the fluctuation in the saving ratio for Taiwan is explained by M/Y and I_M/Y.

As we expected, the ratio of foreign savings to GNP, (S_F/Y), has had a significant adverse effect on the savings behavior in Korea. The phenomenon appears to have been more pronounced since the Monetary Reform in 1965. However, this variable is not an important explanatory variable either in Taiwan or Japan confirming the fact that both countries already reached a self-sufficient stage and confronted no serious prolonged BOP problems in the 1960's.

In our projection of S_d/Y and S_p/Y for the years 1973–81, we have used the regression results of equations (1), (3), (5), (10), (14), (15), and (38). For the values of the independent variables, we relied on the estimates made by the Economic Planning Board (EPB) (for $\Delta y/y$, I_M/Y) and K.S. Kim (for M/Y)[18]

Before going into the discussion of the projected values of S_d/Y and S_p/Y, however, it is necessary to clarify our projection process and its implications for government planning for the 1970's.

The EPB has projected all the key real variables including the saving propensity for the years 1973–81. They are consistent with the government target values of $1,000 per capita income and $10 billion exports in 1980. Whether the government could achieve these target values will depend on the possibility of raising the domestic saving ratio from the present level of approximately 15 percent to 27 percent in 1981. Our

[18] In his projections of M/Y, Kim uses the following regression equation of the demand for money:

$$M = -70.101 + 0.146Y \qquad R^2 = 0.98$$
$$(-3.65) \quad (17.98) \qquad DW = 2.39$$
$$\text{Period} = 1963\text{–}72$$

where M is the stock of broad money and Y is nominal GNP. This equation shows that the income elasticity of the demand for money is approximately 1.35.We have also estimated a variety of demand for money functions for the 1953–72 period. In all of our regression equations, it appears that the elasticity is greater than 2.

projection of S_d/Y is then to examine whether the required saving ratio in the EPB's planning framework can be expected under the assumption that there would be no significant structural changes in the economy.

The EPB planning model which is a version of the Harrod-Domar growth model, begins with a required growth rate of real income for the government target values of per capita income and level of exports in 1980. Given the required growth rate and capital-output ratio of the economy, one could determine a required investment-output ratio. The levels of exports and imports are projected separately for the period. Then the required domestic saving ratio is determined as a residual of the difference between $I/Y - S_F/Y$.

Suppose that the government somehow could maintain the required ratio of investment to income and hence $\Delta y/y$ either by borrowing from foreign sources or relying on domestic savings. Our projection will then show how much domestic savings are expected to be realized when the economy is on that particular growth path. The potential saving ratio may or may not be equal to the required ratio. If the potential ratio is lower than the required ratio, then one could examine alternative policy measures that could be taken to bridge the gap between the two ratios. In the following diagram, suppose the *OE* line depicts a growth path of the economy which corresponds to the government targets in 1980 (*OE* is drawn for a given capital-output ratio). *SS* is the savings function which is positively related to the rate of growth.

Suppose *OB* is the target rate of economic growth. At that rate there exists a positive gap between the required and actual savings propensity by *CD*. Once we know the difference (*CD*) from our projection, then we could go on to examine possible policy measures that could shift the *SS* schedule upwards to *S'S'*.

Our projections of S_d/Y and S_p/Y for the 1972–81 period are based on the coefficients of regression equations (1), (3), (5), (10), (14), (15), and (38) in Tables 5 and 6 and these results are given in Table 7.

For the period 1972–76, the projected annual average values of S_d/Y range from 17.3 percent when we use regression equation (15) to 20.9 percent with the coefficients of regression equation (38), whereas S_p/Y varies from 10.2 percent (KDI projection *C*) to 15.1 percent (KDI projection *G*). For the years 1976–81, our projections show that the possible range of S_d/Y will be from 22 percent (KDI projection *F*) to 29 percent (KDI projection *G*) and S_p/Y from 15 percent (KDI projection *F*) to 20.4 percent (KDI projection *A*).

Thus, the results suggest that EPB's required saving ratio for the years

1972–81 are not unreasonable figures to reach. However, it must be pointed out that our projection process is rather crude and the regression equations are subject to many limitations so that one must interpret these results with caution. The reported results are meant to be suggestive not conclusive.

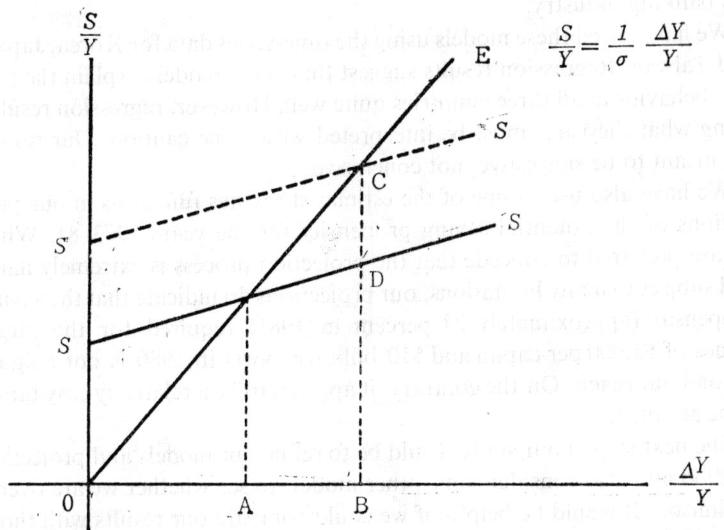

$$\frac{S}{Y}=\frac{S_d}{Y}+\frac{S_F}{Y}=S\left(\frac{\Delta y}{y},\frac{M}{Y}\right)+\frac{S_F}{Y}$$

V. Concluding Remarks

The major objective of this study has been to analyze savings behavior in Korea during the 1953–72 period in comparison to Taiwan and Japan with a view to formulating a framework for our projections of the domestic saving propensity for the years 1973–81.

For a framework of analysis we have developed two models. The first is McKinnon's model which stresses the role of money as a conduit through which capital accumulation takes place in LDCs and the role of financial institutions as an intermediary between savers and investors. The major variables that enter the savings function in McKinnon's model are the rate of growth and the real deposit rate. The latter variable may be substituted for by the money-income ratio (M/Y) under certain assumptions. The second model is based on the Neo-Keynesian view of saving and investment. In this model, real domestic savings depend upon the real return on money and a variable reflecting the intermediation efficiency of the banking industry.

We have tested these models using the time-series data for Korea, Japan and Taiwan. Regression results suggest that these models explain the savings behavior in all three countries quite well. However, regression results, being what they are, must be interpreted with some caution. Our results are meant to be suggestive, not conclusive.

We have also used some of the estimated savings functions in our projections of the potential saving propensity for the years 1973–81. While we are prepared to concede that the projection process is extremely naive and subject to many limitations, our projections do indicate that the saving propensity (approximately 27 percent in 1981) required for the target values of $1,000 per capita and $10 billion exports in 1980 is not a figure beyond our reach. On the contrary, it appears to be a relatively easy target to be attained.

The next step in our study would be to refine our models and projection method and also consider some other models to see whether we are overly optimistic. It would be helpful if we could compare our results with those of other general equilibrium forecasting models, provided, of course, one's preference is such that he still has faith in these econometric models even at this stage of the econometric game.

REFERENCES

1. Bank of Korea, *Economic Statistics Yearbook*, 1972.
2. Bank of Korea, *National Income Statistics Yearbook*, 1972.
3. Bank of Japan, *Economic Statistics Annual*, 1968.
4. Bank of Japan, *Economic Statistics Monthly*, Jan. 1969–Apr. 1973.
5. Bennet, Robert L., "Financial Innovation and Structural Change in the Early Stage of Industrialization: Mexico, 1945–59," *Journal of Finance*, Dec. 1963.

6. Brown, G., "The Impact of Korea's 1965 Interest Rate Reform on Savings, Investment, and the Balance of Payments," (A paper presented to CENTC Symposium on Central Banking Monetary Policy and Economic Development, Izmir, Turkey, April 1971.)
7. Cameron Rondo, "Theoretical Bases of a Comparative Study of the Role of Financial Institutions," in the *Conference of Economic History*, Aix-en Province, France, 1962.
8. Chenery, H. B. and P. Eckstein, "Development Alternatives for Latin America," *Journal of Political Economics*, July/Aug. 1970.
9. Chenery, H. B. and A. Strout, "Foreign Assistance and Economic Development," *American Economic Review*, Sept. 1966.
10. Council for International Economic Cooperation and Development *Taiwan Statistical Yearbook*, 1969 & 1971, Republic of China.
11. Council for International Economic Cooperation and Development *Industry of Free China*, Republic of China, May 1973.
12. Foley, D. K. and M. Sidrauski, *Monetary and Fiscal Policy in a Growing Economy*, London: The MacMillan Company, Collier MacMillan Limited.
13. Frank, C. Jr., K. S. Kim, and L. Westphal, *Foreign Trade Regimes and Economic Development: South Korea*, N. Y.: NBER, 1975.
14. Goldsmith, Raymond W., *Financial Structure and Development*, New Haven: Yale University Press, 1969.
15. Gurley, J. G. and E. S. Shaw, "Financial Aspects of Economic Development," *American Economic Review*, Sept. 1955.
16. Gurley, J. G. and E. S. Shaw, "Financial Intermediaries and the Saving-Investment Process," *Journal of Finance*, May 1956.
17. Gurley, J. G. and E. S. Shaw, *Money in a Theory of Finance*, Washington, D. C.: the Brookings Institution, 1960.
18. Gurley, J. G. and E. S. Shaw, "Financial Structure and Economic Development," *Economic Development and Cultural Change*, April 1967.
19. Harkness, J., "The Role of Money in a Simple Growth Model: Comment," *American Economic Review*, March 1972.
20. IMF, *International Financial Statistics*, various issues.
21. Kim, K. S., *The Causes and Effects of Inflation in Korea*, KDI Working Paper 7302, Jan. 1973.
22. Levhari, D. and D. Patinkin, "The Role of Money in a Simple Growth Model," *American Economic Review*, Sept. 1968.
23. Levhari, D. and D. Patinkin, "The Role of Money in a Simple Growth Model: Reply," *American Economic Review*, March 1972.

24. Lewis, W. A., "Economic Development with Unlimited Supplies of Labor," in *The Economics of Underdevelopment*, A. N. Agarwala and S. P. Singh (editors), New York: Oxford University Press, 1958.
25. McKinnon, R. I., *Money and Capital in Economic Development*, Washington, D. C.: The Brookings Institution, 1973.
26. McKinnon, R. I., "Money, Growth, and the Propensity to Save: An Iconoclastic View," April 1973, unpublished manuscript.
27. Meltzer, Allan H., "Money, Intermediation and Growth," *Journal of Economic Literature*, March 1969.
28. Mikesell, R. F. and J. E. Zinser, "The Nature of the Savings Function in Developing Countries: A Survey of the Theoretical and Empirical Literature," *Journal of Economic Literature*, March 1973, pp. 1–26.
29. Papanek, G. F., "The Effect of Aid and Other Resource Transfers on Savings and Growth in LDCs," Economic Journal Sept. 1972.
30. Patrick, H., "Financial Development and Economic Growth in Underdeveloped Countries," *Economic Development and Cultural Change*, Jan. 1966.
31. Ramanathan, R., "The Role of Money in a Simple Growth Model: Comment," *American Economic Review*, March 1972.
32. Shaw, Edward S., *Financial Deepening in Economic Development*, New York: Oxford University Press, 1973.
33. Shimomura, Osamu, *Some Suggestions for Stabilization of the Korean Economy*, Research Report No. 8, KDI, Aug. 1972.
34. Singh, S. K., *Development Economics: Theory and Findings*, Lexington, Mass: D. D. Heath, 1972.
35. Stein, J. L., *Money and Capital Growth*, New York and London: Columbia University Press, 1971.
36. Strout, A. M., "Korea's Use of Foreign and Domestic Resources: A Cross-Country Comparison," in *Practical Approaches to Development Planning: Korea's Second Five-Year Plan*, I. Adelman, Baltimore: The Johns Hopkins University Press, 1969.
37. U. N. *Yearbook of National Accounts Statistics*, Various issues.
38. Yoshihara, K., "The Growth Rate as a Determinant of the Saving Ratio," *Hitotsubashi Journal of Economics*, Feb. 1972.

APPENDIX

Table 1. Components of Savings, 1965–1971

Year	Domestic Savings Ratio	(General Gov't)	(Corp.)	(Households)	Foreign Savings Ratio
1965	9.6	(1.7)	(4.0)	(1.8)	4.0
1966	13.7	(2.8)	(4.0)	(5.1)	5.8
1967	12.7	(4.1)	(4.1)	(3.8)	7.1
1968	14.5	(6.3)	(4.6)	(2.7)	9.9
1969	17.9	(6.2)	(4.6)	(6.7)	10.3
1970	16.3	(7.0)	(3.9)	(5.5)	9.7
1971	14.6	(6.0)	(3.7)	(4.8)	11.2
Annual Average					
1967–71	15.2	(5.9)	(4.2)	(4.7)	9.6

Source: Bank of Korea, *National Income Statistics Yearbook*, 1972.

Table 2. Savings and Manufacturing Investment Ratios

Year	GNP Growth Rate $\left(\frac{\Delta y}{y}\right)$	Inv't Ratio $\left(\frac{I}{Y}\right)$	Domestic Savings Ratio $\left(\frac{S_d}{Y}\right)$	Broad Money Ratio $\left(\frac{M}{Y}\right)$	Inv't Ratio in Mfg. $\left(\frac{I_M}{Y}\right)$	Domestic Savings to Broad Money Ratio $\left(\frac{S_d}{M}\right)$
1967	7.8	19.8	12.7	20.0	4.5	64.8
1968	12.6	24.4	14.5	25.8	5.3	56.4
1969	15.0	29.7	17.9	32.2	5.2	61.9
1970	7.9	27.2	16.3	34.4	5.0	47.8
1971	9.2	26.5	14.6	34.0	4.6	42.9
Annual Average						
1967–71	10.5	25.5	15.2	29.3	4.9	51.9

Sources: [1] Korea; Bank of Korea, *National Income Statistics Yearbook*, 1972, and *Economic Statistics Yearbook*, 1972;

[2] Japan; Bank of Japan, *Economic Statistics Annual*, 1968, and *Economic Statistics Monthly*, Jan. 1969–April 1973;

[3] Taiwan; Council for International Economic Cooperation & Development, *Taiwan Statistical Yearbook*, Republic of China, and *Industry of Free China*, May 1973.

Table 3. Mobilization of Savings and Prospects

Classification	1957–61	1962–66	1967–71	1972–76[1]	1977–81[1]
GNP Growth Rate	4.7	7.8	10.5	9.5	11.0
Investment Ratio	10.2	14.5	25.5	23.5	26.4
Domestic Savings Ratio	2.7	9.2	15.2	18.1	24.8
(General Gov't)	(−)	(0.7)	(5.9)	5.8	6.8
Foreign Savings Ratio	7.8	6.2	9.6	5.4	1.6

Note: [1] EPB Projections

Source: Bank of Korea, *National Incomes Statistics Yearbook*, 1972.

Table 4. International Comparison of Savings and Manufacturing Investment Ratios

Country	During	GNP Growth Rate (%) $\left(\frac{\Delta y}{y}\right)$	Inv't Ratio (%) $\left(\frac{I}{Y}\right)$	Domestic Savings Ratio (%) $\left(\frac{S_d}{Y}\right)$	Money & Time Deposit Ratio (%) $\left(\frac{M}{Y}\right)$	Mfg. Inv't Ratio (%) $\left(\frac{I_M}{Y}\right)$	Domestic Savings to Broad Money Ratio (%) $\left(\frac{S_d}{M}\right)$	Per Capita GNP ($) $\left(\frac{Y}{N}\right)$	Rate of Change in WPI[1] (%)
Korea	1962–66	7.8	14.5	9.2	12.6	3.2	73.0	131	16.7
	1967–71	10.5	25.5	15.2	29.3	4.9	51.9	257	7.8
Taiwan	1955–59	6.8	17.1	9.5	15.8	2.2	60.1	127	9.1
	1960–64	8.5	19.2	16.2	29.2	3.9	55.5	211	5.9
	1965–69	9.7	24.5	22.1	38.1	6.5	58.0	345	0.2
Japan	1953–57	7.2	27.0	26.2	47.1	5.0	55.6	339	1.1
	1958–63	10.6	34.9	34.3	66.8	8.6	51.5	709	2.2
	1964–70	11.0	42.0	42.6	78.2	7.8	54.5	1,905	1.7
Korea[2]	1972–76	9.5	25.7	19.8	44.3	8.0	42.4	482	3.0
	1977–81	11.0	30.0	27.5	67.3	9.6	40.9	970	3.0

Notes: [1] WPI = Wholesale Price Index

[2] Estimates based on Economic Planning Board Projections. The estimates of M/Y have been made by K.S. Kim at the KDI.

Sources: [1] Korea; BOK, *National Income Statistics Yearbook*, 1972, and *Economic Statistics Yearbook*, 1972;

[2] Japan; Bank of Japan, *Economic Statistics Annual*, 1968, and *Economic Statistics Monthly*, Jan. 1969–April 1973; and

[3] Taiwan; Council for International Economic Cooperation & Development, *Taiwan Statistical Yearbook*, 1969, 1971. Republic of China, and *Industry of Free China*, May 1973.

Table 5. Regressions for the Savings Propensities

Country	Equation Number	Propensities to Save	Intercept	$\frac{\Delta y}{y}$	$\frac{M}{Y}$	$\frac{I_M}{Y}$	$\frac{S_F}{Y}$	r[1]	p^*[2]	$r-p^*$	$\frac{L_M}{M}$	Q[3]	$\bar{R}^2$	DW	Period
Korea	1	$\frac{S_d}{Y}$	−3.33 (−3.95)	0.88 (8.16)	0.31 (7.64)								0.93	1.89	1954–72
	2	″	−4.77 (−2.46)		0.29 (4.17)	2.06 (4.17)							0.87	1.88	1953–72
	3	″	−2.85 (−1.51)	0.76 (4.34)	0.32 (5.80)								0.89	1.66	1961–72
	4	″	0.85 (0.33)	0.86 (5.35)	0.34 (6.89)		−0.52 (−1.91)						0.92	1.95	1961–72
	5	″	3.57 (0.68)		0.37 (3.66)		−0.07 (−0.13)						0.63	0.90	1961–72
	6	″	−2.30 (−0.83)	0.77 (2.54)				0.35 (1.80)	−0.06 (−1.10)				0.76	0.79	1955–72
	7	″	−0.70 (−0.39)	1.07 (4.69)						0.09 (1.62)			0.73	0.94	1955–72
	8	″	−15.30 (−4.69)	0.48 (2.35)				0.40 (3.39)	0.04 (0.62)		0.54 (4.02)		0.93	2.61	1957–71
	9	″	−11.19 (−2.88)	0.94 (5.52)						0.08 (1.21)	0.53 (3.02)		0.87	2.31	1957–71
	10	$\frac{S_p}{Y}$	−5.03 (−3.61)	0.70 (3.86)	0.21 (3.12)								0.73	1.28	1954–72
	11	″	−3.27 (−1.96)	0.95 (4.51)						−0.00 (−0.07)			0.57	0.87	1954–72

12	〃	1.63	0.42	0.10							0.77	2.18	1961–72
		(1.33)	(3.69)	(2.88)									
13	〃		0.53	0.13							0.72	2.05	1961–72
			(6.28)	(3.90)									
14	〃	4.45	0.49	0.11	−0.40						0.87	2.65	1961–72
		(3.01)	(5.27)	(4.02)	(−2.49)								
15	〃	6.01		0.14	−0.14						0.39	1.86	1961–72
		(1.99)		(2.31)	(−0.44)								
16	〃	−7.50	0.99	0.53	−1.14						0.81	1.28	1954–71
		(−4.68)	(4.76)	(3.69)	(−2.42)								
17	〃	−6.41	0.96	0.52	−1.16					−0.73	1.30	1.30	1954–71
		(−1.47)	(3.95)	(3.12)	(−2.35)					(−0.27)			
18	〃	−3.24	0.87			7.06	−0.04				0.63	0.96	1955–71
		(−1.10)	(2.71)			(0.31)	(−0.66)						
19	〃	11.40	0.80			−0.51	0.07			−8.61	0.83	2.25	1955–71
		(2.76)	(3.58)			(−2.51)	(0.15)			(−4.00)			
20	〃	−7.15	0.44					−0.10			0.87	1.74	1957–71
		(−0.86)	(2.12)					(−1.21)					
21	〃	−14.08	0.53			0.17	0.01		0.44		0.88	2.35	1957–71
		(−3.42)	(2.63)			(1.42)	(0.15)		(3.36)				
22	〃	−12.42	0.72					0.04	0.44		0.84	2.32	1957–71
		(−4.12)	(5.43)					(0.75)	(3.22)				

Notes: Figures in parentheses are t ratios.
[1] Nominal interest rate on one-year time deposits
[2] Two year moving average of percentage changes in GNP deflator
[3] A dummy variable ($Q = 1$ for 1953–65, otherwise, $Q = 0$)

Table 6. Regressions for the Savings Propensities

Country	Equation Number	Propensities to Save	Intercept	$\frac{\Delta y}{y}$	$\frac{M}{Y}$	$\frac{I_M}{Y}$	$\frac{S_F}{Y}$	r	p^*	$r - p^*$	Q_1[5]	Q_2[6]	$\bar{R}^2$	DW	Period
Taiwan	23	$\frac{S_d}{Y}$	2.20		0.42	0.57							0.96	1.06	1952–71
			(2.85)		(6.82)	(1.89)									
	24	〃	0.17	0.19	0.51								0.96	1.32	1954–70
			(0.13)	(1.04)	(14.56)										
	25	〃	−0.67	1.86						−0.03			0.49	0.73	1955–70
			(−0.13)	(3.44)						(−0.25)					
	26	〃	47.46	0.04			−9.67	−1.77	0.08				0.96	0.90	1957–72
			(13.00)	(0.17)			(−0.46)	(−10.01)	(0.69)						
	27	〃	17.73	1.28			−1.15			−0.34			0.63	1.56	1957–72
			(2.51)	(2.18)			(−2.04)			(−0.98)					
	28	$\frac{S_p}{Y}$	3.47	0.13	0.39								0.97	2.10	1954–70
			(4.09)	(1.03)	(16.01)										
	29	〃	2.86	1.37									0.51	0.85	1955–70
			(0.75)	(3.54)											
	30	〃	3.19	0.07	0.45		−9.69						0.94	1.19	1957–72
			(2.00)	(0.32)	(9.39)		(−0.50)								
	31	〃	39.04	0.28			7.71	−1.42	0.09				0.91	0.86	1957–72
			(8.54)	(1.00)			(0.29)	(−6.44)	(0.60)						
Japan	32	$\frac{S_d}{Y}$	8.67		0.26	1.02							0.92	1.28	1953–70
			(4.59)		(7.90)	(4.57)									
	33	〃	7.85	0.40	0.32								0.89	1.12	1953–71
			(3.49)	(3.24)	(10.59)										
	34	〃	31.02	0.50						−1.01			0.41	0.84	1954–72
			(9.66)	(1.90)						(−2.17)					

	35	$\frac{S_p}{Y}$	4.51	0.32	0.29					0.88	1.08	1953–71
			(2.12)	(2.78)	(9.86)							
	36	″	24.62	0.42			−0.71			0.32	0.80	1954–72
			(8.33)	(1.66)			(−1.65)					
Cross-Section[4]	37	$\frac{S_a}{Y}$	0.28		0.40	0.79				0.95	0.85	1955–70
			(0.38)		(15.69)	(3.16)						
	38	″	−0.51		0.28	1.13		3.80	6.83	0.97	1.31	1955–70
			(−0.73)		(8.22)	(5.42)		(5.22)	(4.61)			
	39	″	−2.30	0.60	0.44					0.97	1.08	1955–70
			(−2.77)	(6.03)	(30.68)							
	40	″	−2.37	0.35	0.63			2.30	5.77	0.97	1.39	1955–70
			(−3.13)	(12.67)	(7.18)			(3.92)	(3.76)			
	41	″	4.15	1.93			0.08			0.39	0.51	1955–70
			(1.37)	(5.35)			(0.91)					
	42	″	−0.92	1.00			−0.00	10.27	23.72	0.90	0.81	1955–70
			(−0.06)	(5.76)			(−0.07)	(6.35)	(15.61)			
	43	$\frac{S_p}{Y}$	3.79	1.44			0.11			0.29	0.34	1955–70
			(1.33)	(4.22)			(1.25)					
	44	″	−3.22	0.80			−0.03	14.27	22.32	0.92	0.94	1955–70
			(−2.51)	(5.61)			(−0.88)	(10.78)	(17.46)			
	45	″	−3.37	0.56	0.36					0.89	0.47	1955–70
			(−2.41)	(3.30)	(15.38)							
	46	″	−2.37	0.63	0.35			2.80	5.77	0.97	1.39	1955–70
			(−3.13)	(7.18)	(12.67)			(3.92)	(3.76)			

[4] Cross-section and time Series data for Korea, Japan and Taiwan

[5] $Q_1 = 1$ for Taiwan
$= 0$, otherwise

[6] $Q_2 = 1$ for Japan
$= 0$, otherwise

Table 7. *Projections and Asset Profiles of the Saving Propensities for the Years 1972–81*

	Period	$\frac{S}{Y}$	$\frac{S_d}{Y}$	$\frac{S_g}{Y}$	$\frac{S_p}{Y}$	$\frac{S_h^s}{Y}$	$\frac{S_p^*}{Y}$	$\frac{S_F}{Y}$	$\frac{\Delta M}{Y}$	$\frac{M}{Y}$	$\frac{\Delta y}{y}$	$\frac{\Delta M}{M}$	$\frac{I_m}{Y}$
	1962–66	17.3	8.0	1.2	6.8	1.8	5.0	8.3	2.9	13.1	7.8	22.1	3.8
	1967–71	26.6	15.1	6.1	9.0	2.4	6.6	10.6	9.0	30.1	10.5	30.0	4.9
EPB PROJECTION	1972–76	23.5	18.1	5.8	12.3			5.4			9.5		8.0
	1977–81	26.4	24.8	6.8	18.0			1.6			11.0		9.6
KDI PROJECTION A	1972–76	24.2	18.8	5.8	13.0			5.4	9.7	44.3	9.5	21.8	8.0
(Regression Equation No. (1))	1977–81	28.8	27.2	6.8	20.4			1.6	16.2	67.3	11.0	24.0	9.6
KDI PROJECTION B	1972–76	23.7	18.6	5.8	12.8			5.4		44.3	9.5		8.0
(Regression Equation No. (3))	1977–81	28.7	27.1	6.8	20.3			1.6		67.3	11.0		9.6
KDI PROJECTION C	1972–76	23.4	18.0	5.8	12.2			5.4		44.3	9.5		8.0
(Regression Equation No. (5))	1977–81	29.5	27.9	6.8	21.1			1.6		67.3	11.0		9.6
KDI PROJECTION D	1972–76	23.4	18.0	5.8	10.2			5.4		44.3	9.5		8.0
(Regression Equation No. (10))	1977–81	25.2	23.6	6.8	16.8			1.6		67.3	11.0		9.6
KDI PROJECTION E	1972–76	23.0	17.6	5.8	11.8			5.4		44.3	9.5		8.0
(Regression Equation No. (14))	1977–81	25.0	23.4	6.8	16.6			1.6		67.3	11.0		9.6
KDI PROJECTION F	1972–76	22.7	17.3	5.8	11.5			5.4		44.3	9.5		8.0
(Regression Equation No. (15))	1977–81	23.6	22.0	6.8	15.2			1.6		67.3	11.0		9.6
KDI PROJECTION G	1972–76	26.3	20.9	5.8	15.1			5.4		44.3	9.5		8.0
(Regression Equation No. (38))	1977–81	30.8	29.2	6.8	22.4			1.6		67.3	11.0		9.6
Asset Profile of KDI	1972–76	23.0	17.6	5.8	11.8	5.0	6.8	5.4	9.7	44.3	9.5	21.8	8.0
Projection E	1977–81	25.0	25.0	6.8	16.6	11.5	5.1	1.6	16.7	67.3	11.0	24.0	9.6

Figure 1. Korea

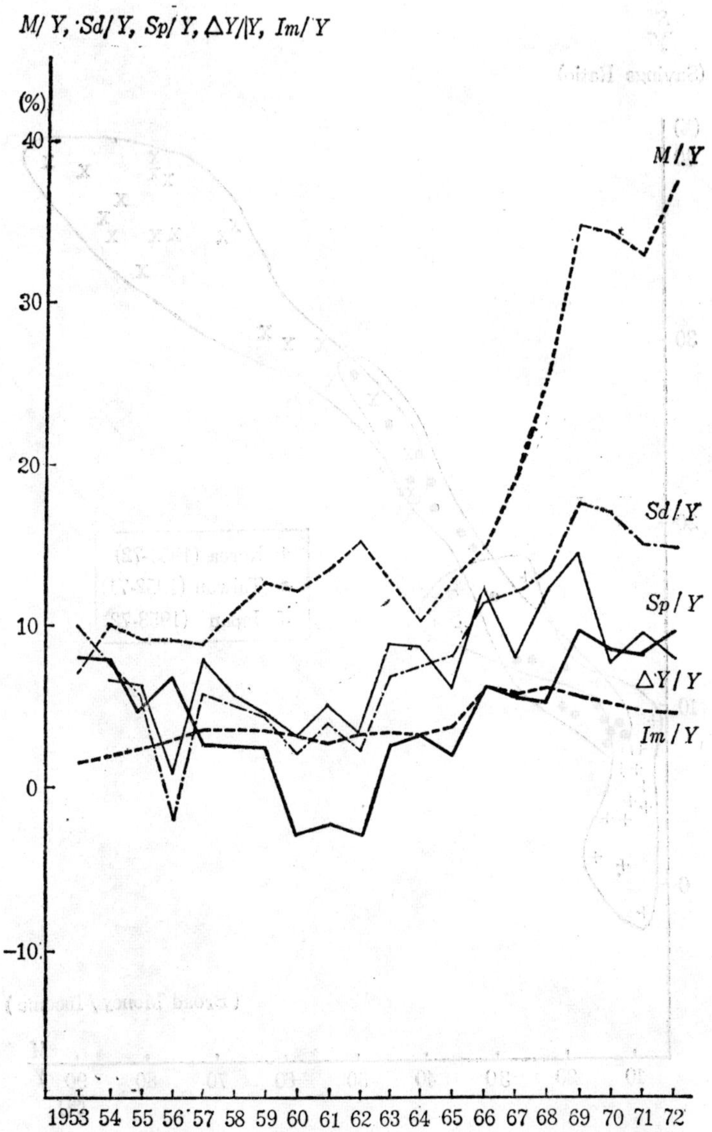

Figure 2. Cross Section-Time Series

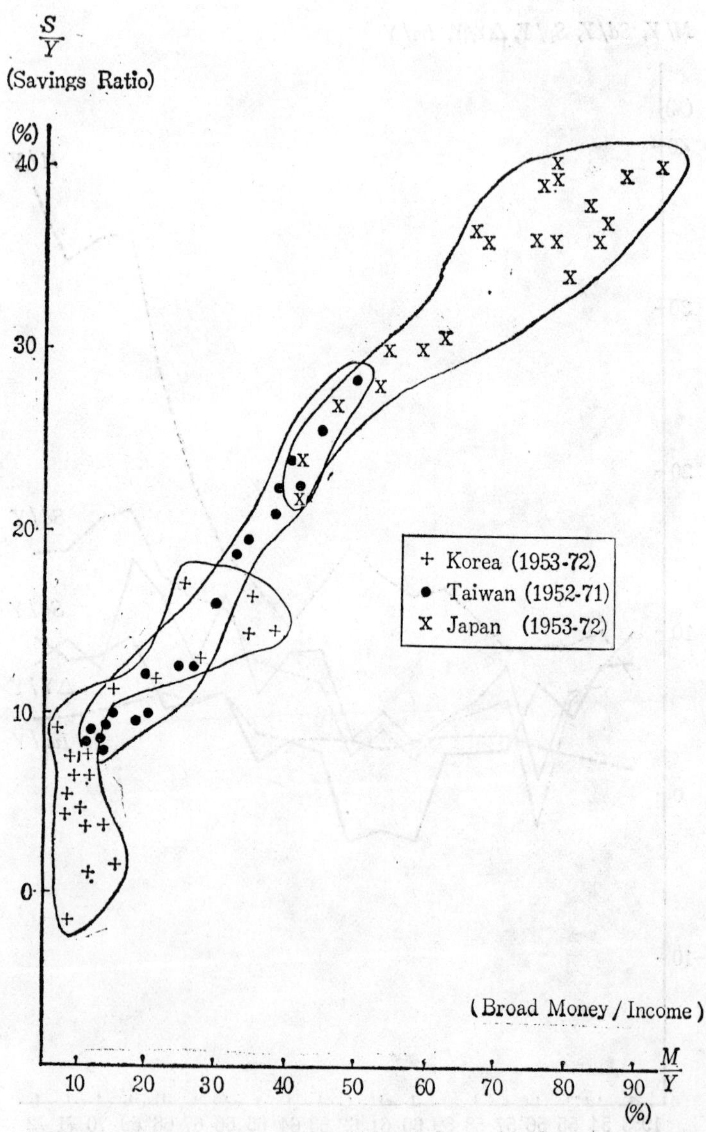

Figure 3. Cross Section-Time Series

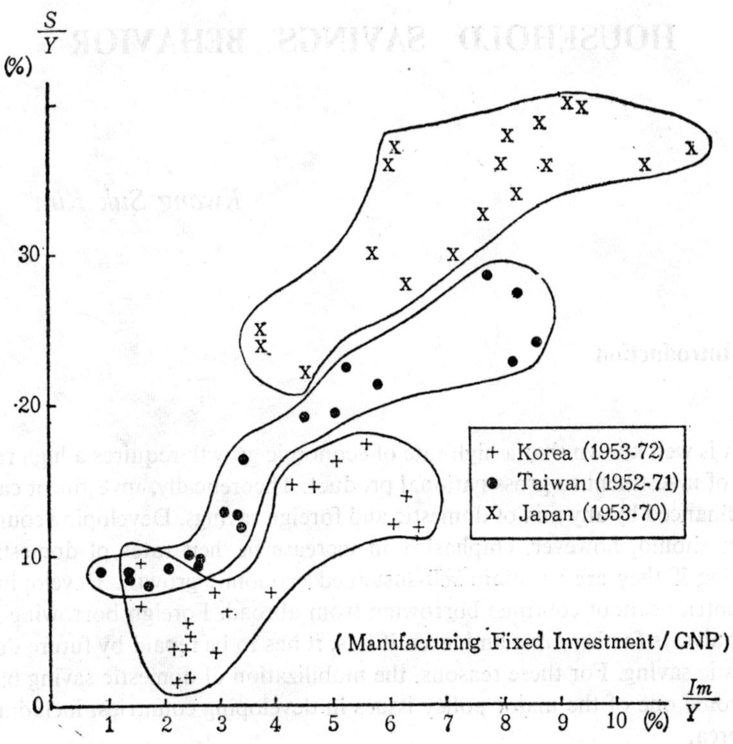

HOUSEHOLD SAVINGS BEHAVIOR

*Kwang Suk Kim**

I. Introduction

It is well known that a high rate of economic growth requires a high ratio of investment to gross national product. Theoretically, investment can be financed by any mix of domestic and foreign savings. Developing countries should, however, emphasize an increase in their rates of domestic saving if they are to attain self-sustained economic growth. Developing countries cannot continue borrowing from abroad. Foreign borrowing is not always forthcoming and, even if it is, it has to be repaid by future domestic saving. For these reasons, the mobilization of domestic saving has become one of the major policy issues in developing countries, including Korea.

Despite the emphasis on increasing domestic saving, it seems that the formulation of policies designed to increase the saving propensity has suffered from a dearth of knowledge regarding the determinants of saving in developing countries. Economic research on the determinants of savings in less developed countries has lagged far behind the pace set in advanced countries. In addition, most of the empirical studies concerning savings behavior in developing countries are based on a macro–formulation of the savings function. Very few studies attempt to deal with the disaggregated

---

* Senior Fellow at the Korea Development Institute. This paper reflects part of the KDI research monograph, *Household Savings Behavior in Korea*, published in Korean in 1975.

sectoral components of saving or to analyze the impact of structural change on aggregate saving. This may be partly due to poor data conditions in most developing countries.

This paper attempts to present an exploratory analysis of household savings behavior in Korea. This analysis is based on grouped time series of both urban and farm family budget survey data. Although there are many problems with the family budget survey, these data provide a superior base for testing hypotheses regarding the household savings function. As pointed out elsewhere[1], the sectoral components of saving (particularly household saving) given in the Bank of Korea's national income accounts do not seem consistent with other comparable economic statistics. In addition, the use of aggregate national accounts data does not allow us to extend our analysis to the impact of structural change on saving within the household sector.

This paper attempts to examine (1) the impact on saving of the source of income and occupation, (2) the impact of the size of family and family dependency rate (ratio of unemployed to total family members), and (3) the life-cycle theory of savings behavior. Our analysis utilizes time series of both urban and farm family budget survey data for a recent decade.[2]

Since the available consistent time series seems too short to experiment with any complicated theoretical formulations, we did not attempt an extensive investigation of the functional form of the household savings function, but used the simple linear form, relating per capita saving to per capita disposable income. In addition, all work was based on the classification of the original family budget survey data as published in the Economic Planning Board's, *Annual Report on the Family Income and Expenditure Survey* (various issues) and the Ministry of Agriculture and Fishery's, *Report on the Results of Farm Economy Survey and Production Cost Survey of Agricultural Products* (various issues). This paper has to be limited, therefore to the testing of hypotheses which are feasible under the given grouping of the data. In this sense, this report should be taken only as a preliminary exploration aimed at providing a useful guide for further study based on better data.

---

[1] See my Interim Report 7306 (KDI).

[2] See Appendix Tables 1–3 for average disposable income per household and saving rates of both urban and farm households during 1965–1973 (or 1964–73 in the case of farm households).

II. Source of Income and Occupation as Determinants of Saving

W. A. Lewis's writing speculates that peasants and entrepreneurs are more thrifty and save more than any other classes of the community. He argues that the salary and wage earning classes save very little "because their mentality is directed towards spending rather than toward saving."[3] Friend and Kravis tried to demonstrate that non-farm entrepreneurs save more than other income groups in the United States. They found that in the U.S., the average saving-income ratio for entrepreneurial groups (except artisans), was well above the national average. In fact, the ratio for owners of unincorporated businesses is in the range of 3 to 4 times the national average. They concluded that entrepreneurs have high saving propensities and account for a high proportion of total saving, at least in prosperous years. Entrepreneurs' saving fluctuates more because their income varies widely depending upon the business cycle.[4]

Kelley and Williamson hypothesized that the source of income and occupation are important determinants of saving and attempted to test this on the basis of a cross-section data for Indonesia. They found that the marginal saving coefficients for non-farm entrepreneurs (traders and owners of businesses) are much higher than the same coefficients for farmers and salary and wage earners.[5]

This hypothesis concerning the different saving propensities of various income and occupation groups may be justified on the following grounds. First, the savings propensities of entrepreneurs may be higher than those of other occupational groups because of capital market imperfections. The entrepreneurs may invest their savings in their own businesses for a higher rate of return than the average rate of return on other group's saving, while the salary and wage earners may in general face a limited outlet for

---

[3] W. A. Lewis speculates further that "the rate of saving is determined not by whether countries are rich or poor, but by the ratio of profits to national income, and both these ratios cease to increase once a certain stage of development has been reached." W. Arthur Lewis, *Theory of Economic Growth* (Pennsylvania: Urwin Univ. Books, 1965), pp. 225–244.

[4] Irwin Friend and Irving B. Kravis, "Enterpreneurial Income, Saving and Investment," *American Economic Review*, June 1957, pp. 270–301.

[5] Allen C. Kelley and Jeffrey G. Williamson, "Household Saving Behavior in the Developing Economies: The Indonesian Case", *Economic Development and Cultural Change*, April 1968, pp. 385–403.

their savings in the form of earning assets. Secondly, the entrepreneurial group has to save more of their current income because this group manages depreciating assets which are their primary source of income. Thirdly, the entrepreneurs may save more because they prefer internal investment in order to maintain control of their assets. Lastly, the marginal savings propensities of the entrepreneurial group may be higher than those of other occupational groups because of greater short-run instability of current income.

This hypothesis attempts to explain the higher saving propensity of the entrepreneurial group compared with all other functional income groups. It may, however, be important to examine the difference in savings propensities among the non-entrepreneurial groups. In order to see whether this hypothesis can be applicable to Korea and to examine the savings propensities of different occupational groups in Korea, we have attempted a regression analysis using time series data for a recent 9 to 10 year period (converted into 1970 constant prices). Since our time series of family budget data for each occupational group is too short to experiment with a complicated savings function, we have formulated a simple linear "per capita" function as shown below.

$$(S/N)_{tj} = \alpha_j + \beta_j(Y/N)_{tj}$$

where S = household saving (disposable income less total consumption expenditures)
N = family size
Y = disposable income

In this saving function, 't' represents time (year) while 'j' is the occupational classification of the household based on the occupation of the family head. One can conceive a more general form of the household saving function by explicitly introducing the family size (N). But since the number of observations was relatively small and the correlation between Y and N clouded the results, we have taken the per capita form. The results of regressions for different occupational groups are shown in Table 1.

Before going into the results of the regressions, it may be important to explain the use of a dummy variable in the savings equations for salary and wage earner's households. The dummy variable (which is 1 for both 1968 and 1969 and zero for all other years) was used to correct the data bias and to eliminate significant first-order serial auto-correlation of the residuals. The regression results indicated a particularly bad fit for 1968 and 1969. We therefore examined the original data and found that average savings of salary and wage earner's households for both 1968 and 1969 could be severely under-estimated compared to the other years due mainly to a change in sampling design.[6]

According to Table 1, the marginal saving propensity (β coefficient) of average urban households was about 16.3 percent during 1965–73, which is much higher than the average saving propensity of the same households at the mean values of both disposable income and savings during the same period. Contrary to our expectation, the marginal saving rate for households other than salary and wage earners, which stands at about 15 percent, is lower than the rate for average salary and wage earner's households. At the same time, the marginal saving rate of sales workers is about 16 percent, while the rate of "other workers", including managers of companies as well as the owners of small shops, is only about 6 percent. This indicates that the marginal saving rate of the entrepreneurial group (other than sales workers) is the lowest among all occupational groups shown, although the regression coefficient for this group is not statistically significant. Although the marginal saving rate of this occupational group is low as compared with other groups, the mean per capita disposable income in 1970 constant prices for this group was the highest.

The lower marginal saving rates for the entrepreneurial group seems to result from the fact that the income data for this group are based on withdrawals from business accounts. Friedman has pointed out the same possibility for some U.S. data.[7] Since there is no clear distinction between a household and a business in the case of unincorporated enterprises, the measured household income for the entrepreneurial group may simply reflect withdrawals from the business accounts. This group tends to withdraw required amounts for current household expenditures while keeping any excess (or earnings over current household expenditures) in the business accounts.

The marginal saving rate of farm households is, however, higher than the rates for various occupational groups in urban areas. The marginal saving rate of farm households (computed from the disposable income and

[6] Not only the total sample size for the urban family budget survey but also the share of the samples selected from Seoul City were unusually larger in both 1968 and 1969 than in the other years. The high share of Seoul is considered to give a downward bias to the savings propensities of the average salary and wage earner's households since the marginal saving propensities of the salary and wage earners in Seoul are lower than those of other urban areas (see Table 2).

[7] Milton Friedman, *A Theory of Consumption Function* (Princeton: Princeton University Press, 1957), pp. 74–75.

Table 1. Estimated Parameters of the Saving Function $S/N = \alpha + \beta Y/N$ by Occupational Group

(sample period: 1965–73 for urban households and 1964–73 for farm households)

Households by Occupational Class	α	β	Dummy	R^2	d	Y/N at mean (won)	APS at mean
A. Urban Households							
1. Salary and wage earners	−634.1 (−3.6)	0.192 (5.6)	−236.3 (−2.6)	.86	1.5	5,099	.057
a. Salary earners	−845.3 (−5.0)	0.213 (7.9)	−339.5 (−4.1)	.93	1.9	6,205	.065
1) Gov't employees	−664.0 (−4.3)	0.187 (6.8)	−220.9 (−2.8)	.90	2.0	5,350	.054
2) Clerical workers	−739.9 (−4.8)	0.207 (8.6)	−376.3 (−4.2)	.94	2.1	6,604	.074
b. Wage earners	−552.3 (−2.5)	0.188 (3.4)	−118.1 (−1.1)	.66	1.5	3,940	.041
1) Regular workers	−544.4 (−2.9)	0.187 (4.4)	−141.7 (−1.4)	.78	1.6	4,317	.054
2) Daily workers	−382.6 (−1.6)	0.154 (2.0)	—	.37	2.4	3,053	.028
2. Other households	−486.2 (−1.6)	0.153 (2.9)	—	.54	1.8	5,730	.069
a. Sales workers	−442.9 (−1.3)	0.161 (2.5)	—	.64	2.6	5,011	.073
b. Other workers	−126.1 (−0.3)	0.062 (1.1)	—	.14	1.3	6,468	.043
3. Average for all households	−545.4 (−4.2)	0.163 (6.9)	—	.87	2.0	5,371	.062
B. Farm Households							
1. Excluding agri. inventories	−7,911.8 (−4.6)	0.258 (5.6)	—	.80	2.4	36,873	.043

Notes: R^2 = Coefficient of determination.
d = Durbin-Watson d statistic.
APS = Average propensity to save.
Y/N = Per capita disposable income in 1970 constant prices. It is in terms of monthly income for urban households, while it is in terms of annual income for farm households.

Figures in parantheses indicate t-ratio. A t-ratio exceeding 2.4 indicates that the regression coefficients are statistically significant at the 5 percent level.

savings data excluding the increase in agricultural inventories) was about 24 percent during the same period.[8] The marginal saving rate of farm households thus calculated is comparable with that of urban households but significantly higher. The real per capita annual disposable income of farm households was significantly lower than the equivalent figure for average urban households.[9]

In the urban salary and wage earner's households, salary earners save more out of their current disposable income than wage earners. Within the salary earner group, clerical workers in non-government organizations seem to save slightly more than government employees. Within the wage earner group, the marginal saving rate of regular workers is a little higher than that of daily workers. It should, however, be noted that the marginal saving rates for the various occupational groups in urban areas generally vary with the level of mean per capita disposable income (See Table 1). In other words, the marginal saving rate is generally higher for the occupational groups with higher per capita disposable income. This implies that in urban salary and wage earners households, the level of per capita disposable income is a more important determinant of household saving than is occupation.

Table 2 compares the estimated parameters of the saving function for Seoul households with those for households in other cities by occupational group. As shown, the marginal saving rate in Seoul is about 3 percentage points lower than that of households in other cities, although the mean value of real per capita disposable income for Seoul households is much higher than that in other urban areas. The marginal saving rate of wage earners in Seoul is significantly lower than that of wage earners in other cities. The marginal saving rate of the entrepreneurial group (other households) in Seoul is also significantly lower than that of the entrepreneurial group in other cities. The lower marginal saving rate in Seoul can be explained either by the permanent income hypothesis or the relative income hypothesis.[10] In any case, it suggests that the rapid immigration of population into Seoul will adversely affect the government policy to increase

---

[8] The increase in agricultural inventories is excluded from farm household saving, since it is considered to be a function of agricultural output and unaffected by the voluntary savings decisions of individual households.

[9] The annual equivalent of real per capita disposable income for average urban households was 64,452 won in 1970 prices (i.e., 5,371 won × 12 months).

[10] Friedman, *op. cit.* (1957). See also Dorothy S. Brady, "Family Savings in Relation to Changes in the Level and Distribution of Income", *Studies in Income and Wealth*, vol. 15 (1952), pp. 103–130.

Table 2. Estimated Parameters of the Saving Function $S/N = \alpha + \beta Y/N$ for Seoul and Other City Households by Occupational Groups, 1965–73

	α	β	Dummy	R^2	d	Y/N at mean (won)	APS at mean
SEOUL							
Average	−533.9	.147	—	.82	2.01	6,294	.062
	(−3.2)	(5.7)					
Salary & wage earners	−665.2	.181	−266.4	.86	1.48	6,157	.063
	(−3.3)	(5.6)	(−2.4)				
Salary earners	−963.6	.216	−470.9	.87	1.61	7,296	.069
	(−3.3)	(5.6)	(−3.4)				
Wage earners	−408.6	.133	−9.154	.76	1.41	4,649	.045
	(−2.8)	(4.3)	(−0.1)				
Other households	−591.3	.156	—	.45	1.65	6,486	.065
	(−1.4)	(2.4)					
OTHER CITIES							
Average	−562.1	.185	—	.86	2.50	4,817	.069
	(−4.0)	(6.5)					
Salary & wage earners	−625.2	.201	−178.5	.84	1.59	4,498	.053
	(−3.6)	(5.4)	(−2.1)				
Salary earners	−800.8	.218	−174.6	.89	2.77	5,411	.063
	(−4.4)	(6.8)	(−2.0)				
Wage earners	−616.0	.217	−157.4	.65	1.60	3,621	.038
	(−2.5)	(3.2)	(−1.3)				
Other households	−620.4	.202	—	.55	1.96	5,237	.084
	(−1.7)	(2.9)					

Note: See notes on Table 1.

domestic saving.

Now it might be interesting to give some observations on the estimated intercepts (α value) of the savings functions for various occupational groups. These intercepts, if statistically significant, should roughly indicate the level of real per capita disposable income at which households stop saving. It should be noted that the zero saving point is given in terms of monthly per capita income for urban households while it is in terms of annual income for farm households. According to Tables 1 and 2, the zero saving points vary by occupational group and between Seoul and other urban households. This variation seems to have some relation to the variations in both the per capita disposable income and the marginal savings rates. In the case of urban households, the average zero saving point of monthly disposable income was 545 won per household member, or about 2,998 won per family (in 1970 prices, taking the average urban family size of 5.5 persons during 1965–73). This zero saving point of about 6,540 won per year for each member of urban households was somewhat lower than the 7,911 won for each member of farm households (See line B1 in Table 1).

III. Analysis of Farm Household Saving

In the previous section we showed that the marginal saving rate of average farm households is greater than that of average urban households in Korea, although the average per capita disposable income for farm households is lower than that for urban households. This result seems to support Tsutomu Noda's findings based on Japanese family budget data for 1952–64. Noda found that the farmer's marginal propensity to save was greater than that of salary and wage earners in Japan. Further, among farmers the marginal saving rate of full-time farmers was higher than that of part-time farmers. He mentioned that these relative marginal saving propensities were "also found in pre-war Japan and (are) due to the entrepreneurial character of farming and the instability of agricultural output."[11]

We now examine farm household savings behavior in some detail. Table 3 presents the estimated parameters of the saving function for farm households by size of cultivated land holdings. We used a simple linear form of the saving function,

$$(S/N)_{tj} = \alpha_j + \beta_j(Y/N)_{tj}$$

where S, Y and N are the same as defined in the previous section and t represents year and j the farm household group classified by size of cultivated land holdings. We have shown the saving function estimated for each class of farm household, excluding agricultural inventories. In other words, the changes in agricultural inventories held by farm households are excluded from both S and Y in estimating the saving function.

As shown in the table, the marginal saving rates of farm households generally become greater as the cultivated land area increases. Except for

---

[11] Tsutomu Noda, "Saving of Farm Households," in Ohkawa, Johnston and Kaneda (ed.), *Agriculture and Economic Growth: Japan's Experience* (Princeton, N.J.: Princeton Univ. Press, 1969), pp. 352–373.

Table 3. Estimated Parameters of the Saving Function $S/N = \alpha + \beta Y/N$ for Farm Households

(sample period: 1964–73)

Farm households by size of cultivated land	α	β	R^2	d	Y/N at mean (won)	APS at mean
a. All farm households	−7,911.8 (−4.61)	.258 (5.61)	.80	2.4	36,873	.043
b. Less than 0.5 chongbo	−3,700.9 (−1.23)	.109 (1.08)	.13	3.0	29,444	.017
c. 0.5 – 1.0	−6,244.0 (−5.25)	.203 (5.64)	.80	0.9	32,653	.012
d. 1.0 – 1.5	−10,068.0 (−2.95)	.321 (3.65)	.62	1.4	38,436	.590
e. 1.5 – 2.0	−10,369.8 (−3.74)	.317 (5.19)	.77	2.5	44,882	.086
f. Over 2.0 chongbo	−15,821.2 (−3.69)	.409 (5.17)	.77	2.9	53,673	.114

Note: See notes on Table 1.

the marginal saving rate of farmers with less than 0.5 chongbo of land, all the marginal saving rates turned out to be statistically significant. This seems to indicate that for farmers with less than 0.5 chongbo of land, saving cannot be explained by the level of per capita disposable income since this group's income is too low for any saving. The coefficient of determination for the regression equation of this particular group was only 13 percent. The average saving propensity of this group at the mean values of disposable income and saving was about zero during 1964–73.

The average saving propensities of farmers also become greater as the cultivated land area increases. This is as expected. Since the cultivated land area largely determines the level of disposable income for each farm household in Korea, those with more land have a higher level of disposable income and, other things being equal, may be able to save a higher proportion of their current income. But can we expect the marginal saving propensities of farmers to increase as the cultivated land area increases? If agricultural inventory investment is included, we can definitely expect the marginal propensities to increase. Farmers with more land will obtain a higher level of agricultural output and will have larger inventories to carry over from one year to the next.

As we have excluded inventory changes, the higher marginal saving propensities of the farmers with more land can be justified in the following manner. Farm households with more land obtain a higher share of their income from cultivated agriculture than do other households, and the saving propensity out of purely agricultural income is higher than the saving propensity out of side-business income. The farm economy survey data for 1964–73 actually indicate that the share of income from agricultural production is generally greater in farm households with more land, while the share of income from side-business and other sources is greater in the households with less land.

In order to see whether or not the farmer's saving propensity out of agricultural income is higher than that out of other income and to test other hypotheses relating to farm household savings behavior, we have specified the following three savings functions:

(1) $S/Y = \alpha + \beta\, Y/N + \gamma\, RDPF$

(2) $S/Y = \alpha + \beta\, Y/N + \gamma\, RDPF + \delta\, EDL$

(3) $S/Y = \alpha + \beta_1\, YA/N + \beta_2\, YO/N + \gamma\, RDPF + \delta\, EDL$

where S = farm household saving (excluding agricultural inventories),

Y = farm household disposable income (excluding the increases in agricultural inventories),

N = family size,

$RDPF$ = dependency rate, i.e., the ratio of unemployed members to total family size,[12]

EDL = educational attainment level of family head (number of years in school),

YA = agricultural income (excluding inventory change),

YO = farmer's income from side-business and other sources less non-consumption expenditure.

In these savings functions we tried to explain the saving ratio instead of the level of per capita saving. Parameters for the savings equations are estimated by the ordinary least-squares method. For this estimate we pooled cross-section and time series data for 1964–73, since the consistent time series is limited to only 10 years. In the case of pooled data we had 50 observations. The results of the regressions are shown below.[13]

[12] See the discussions in Section IV for the hypothesis relating to this dependency rate variable.

[13] Figures in parentheses indicate t-ratio for the regression coefficients.

$$(1)\ S/Y = -7.53 + 0.241\ Y/N + 0.143\ RDPF$$
$$\quad (-6.7) \quad (15.0) \qquad (0.1)$$
$$R^2 = 0.83 \qquad d = 1.8$$

$$(2)\ S/Y = -7.8 + 0.239\ Y/N + 0.157\ RDPF + 0.079\ EDL$$
$$\quad (-1.8) \quad (7.9) \qquad (0.1) \qquad (0.1)$$
$$R^2 = 0.83 \qquad d = 1.9$$

$$(3)\ S/Y = -5.2 + 0.245\ YA/N + 0.110\ YO/N + 0.421\ RDPF - 0.312\ EDL$$
$$\quad (-1.2) \quad (8.5) \qquad (1.9) \qquad (0.3) \qquad (-0.3)$$
$$R^2 = 0.85 \qquad d = 2.0$$

Equations (1) and (2) indicate that per capita disposable income is statistically significant in explaining the farm household saving rate, as expected. When we divided the per capita disposable income of farm households into the income originating from agricultural production and the income from other sources as in equation (3), the regression coefficient for agricultural income turned out to be higher and statistically more significant than the coefficient for other income. Although the coefficient for other income shows a positive sign, it is only marginally significant in explaining the saving rate. This result seems to explain the higher marginal saving propensities of farmers with more cultivated land.

Now we might give an explanation of the regression coefficients for the dependency rate (*RDPF*) and the educational attainment level of the family head (*EDL*). The coefficient for RDPF is not statistically significant in any equation. Contrary to our expectation, the coefficient for RDPF showed a positive sign in all three equations. This may be because the variable combines two conflicting effects on household saving: on the one hand, the burden for consumption expenditures, and on the other, economies of scale in family consumption. The regression coefficient for the educational attainment level of the family head also turned out to be statistically insignificant. This implies that the educational level of the family head does not have any significant effect on farm household saving.

IV. Family Size as a Determinant of Saving

With a given level of household disposable income, we may expect that family size will have a significant effect on household consumption expenditures and savings. Since a given disposable income has to be shared by all members of a family for necessary consumption expenditures, it may be expected that, other things being equal, larger households save a smaller proportion of their disposable income than smaller households. On the other hand, we may expect some economies of scale in consumption of larger households. Thus, family size may be expected to have two conflicting effects on household savings.

Thus far, we have assumed that all members of a family will have the same consumption requirements. However, it is normally expected that the consumption expenditures of a household will vary with its age and sex composition. In order to study accurately the effect of family size on household consumption and savings, it is important to convert all family members into "a unit consumer scale" or "adult equivalence scale." The family size effect, including economies of scale, should be measured in terms of the unit consumer scale. This is, however, not attempted here.[14]

Although it is expected that family size will have a strong influence on household saving behavior, the empirical literature dealing explicitly with the family size effect on saving seems rather scant. Noda formulated the saving function for Japanese farm households, explicitly including family size as shown below.[15]

$$S = a - bN + cY$$

where N represents the family size, and S and Y are average farm household saving and disposable income, respectively. Although he didn't specify his hypothesis on the family size variable, his estimation of parameters for the saving function indicated that the b coefficient was negative and statistically significant. Nevertheless, the regression coefficient for the family size variable didn't seem to be stable. The coefficient showed wide variation depending upon the data base and the specifications of both S and Y. This might have been due to some intercorrelation between Y

[14] The estimation of "adult equivalence scale" is attempted in a separate study undertaken jointly by Kim, Dai Young and myself [see "The Effects of Household Size and Structure and Household Income on Expenditure Patterns," Interim Report 7408 (July 1974), KDI]. When this study completes the estimation of an "adult equivalence scale," we may attempt to reformulate the family size effect on saving. For general understanding of the family size effect on consumption patterns, see Prais and Houthakker, *The Analysis of Family Budgets* (Cambridge : Cambridge University Press, 1971).

[15] Tsutomu Noda, *op. cit.*

and N and the two conflicting effects of family size on saving.

There are some empirical studies dealing with the dependency rate, rather than the family size effect, on savings. Leff formulated the hypothesis that there will be an inverse relation between dependency rates and saving rates. He defined two dependency ratios: one is the percentage of the population aged 14 or less, and the other is the percentage of the population aged 65 or older. His test of the hypothesis on the basis of international cross-section data indicates that the two dependency ratios are statistically significant in explaining the disparity in aggregate saving rates between developed and under-developed countries.[16] In Leff's paper, the dependency rates are defined in terms of total population for his analysis of international cross-section data.

This hypothesis concerning the inverse relationship between the dependency rate and the saving rate can also be applied to analyzing household savings behavior if the dependency rate variables are properly redefined. For the analysis of household savings behavior using family budget data, the dependency rate may be defined as the percentage of family members aged 14 or less and over 65 to total family size. Or, more directly, the variable may be defined as the ratio of unemployed members to total family size as in the case of RDPF variable in the previous section. The first method of defining the dependency rate was impractical since the detailed age composition of family members is not shown in the grouped data published by the responsible government offices. Accordingly, we only utilized the second method on the basis of the grouped family budget data, as shown in Table 4. The Table shows the estimated dependency rates for urban salary and wage earner's households by size of family in 1965 and 1973. We can see that the dependency rates vary closely with family size in Korea.

Since the dependency rates of urban households are closely related to family size in Korea, we might formulate the hypothesis that the family size itself is inversely related to household saving. In order to test this hypothesis, we have used a simple linear per capita form of the saving function for family groups by size of family. The results of regressions using the time series data for 1965–73 are shown in Table 5.

The Table shows that the marginal saving rates of urban salary and wage

[16] Nathaniel H. Leff, "Dependency Rates and Savings Rates," *American Economic Review*, Dec. 1969, pp. 886–896. For criticism of his paper, see Kanhayo L. Gupta, "Dependency Rates and Savings Rates: Comment," *American Economic Review*, June 1971, pp. 469–471, and Nassan A. Adams, "Dependency Rates and Savings Rates: Comment," *American Economic Review*, June 1971, pp. 472–473.

earner's households generally decline as the size of family increases. The marginal saving rate of households with 2 members is about 27 percent, while that of households with more than 9 members is as low as 12 percent. This indicates that with a given level of disposable income, there is an inverse relation between family size and saving. This inverse relation suggests that the size effect of increasing family consumption requirements is overwhelmingly greater than economies of scale in family consumption.

As the family size increases from 2 to 9 persons, the average saving rate at the mean values of per capita disposable income and saving for 1965–73 declined from 10.8 percent to 2.8 percent. The average per capita disposable income also declined in inverse relation to family size. All these results seem to support our observation that an increase in family size mainly increases the family consumption burden, and thus reduces the room for household saving. This implies that family planning efforts will have an important bearing on the household saving drive in Korea.

The intercepts of the regression equations (α coefficient) also gradually decline in inverse relation to family size, although some of the coefficients are statistically not very significant. The α coefficients, if they are significant, should reflect the zero saving point of real per capita disposable income (in 1970 prices). The inverse relation between family size and the α coefficient may imply that there are some economies of scale in consumption due to the increase in family size. We should mention that the α coefficients for households with 2 and 3 members are notably larger than the same coefficients for other households.

V. Life-Cycle Hypothesis and Saving

Modigliani, Brumberg and Ando developed a theory of consumer expenditure based on considerations relating to the life-cycle of income and the consumption needs of households. This theory assumes that an individual consumer's utility is a function of his own consumption in current and future periods. The individual consumer is then assumed to maximize his utility subject to the resources available to him, his resources being the sum of current and discounted future earnings over his life-time and his current net worth. Accordingly, the consumption function of an individual is formulated as,[17]

[17] Albert Ando and Franco Modigliani, "The Life-Cycle Hypothesis of Saving: Aggregate Implications and Test", *American Economic Review*, March 1963, pp. 55–84.

earner's households generally decline as the size of family increases. The marginal saving rate of households with 2 members is about 27 percent, while that of households with more than 9 members is as low as 12 percent. This indicates that with a given level of disposable income, there is an inverse relation between family size and saving. This inverse relation suggests that the size effect of increasing family consumption requirements is overwhelmingly greater than economies of scale in family consumption.

As the family size increases from 2 to 9 persons, the average saving rate at the mean values of per capita disposable income and saving for 1965–72 declined from 10.8 percent to 2.8 percent. The average per capita disposable income also declined in inverse relation to family size. All these results seem to support our observation that an increase in family size mainly increases the family consumption burden, and thus reduces the room for household saving. This implies that family planning efforts will have an important bearing on the household saving drive in Korea.

The intercepts of the regression equations (a coefficient) also gradually decline in inverse relation to family size, although some of the coefficients are statistically not very significant. The a coefficients, if they are significant, should reflect the zero saving point of real per capita disposable income (in 1970 prices). The inverse relation between family size and the a coefficient may imply that there are some economies of scale in consumption due to the increase in family size. We should mention that the a coefficients for households with 2 and 3 members are notably larger than the same coefficients for other households.

V. Life-Cycle Hypothesis and Saving

Modigliani, Brumberg and Ando developed a theory of consumer expenditure based on considerations relating to the life-cycle of income and the consumption needs of households. This theory assumes that an individual consumer's utility is a function of his own consumption in current and future periods. The individual consumer is then assumed to maximize his utility subject to the resources available to him, his resources being the sum of current and discounted future earnings over his lifetime and his current net worth. Accordingly, the consumption function of an individual is formulated as,[7]

[7] Albert Ando and Franco Modigliani, "The Life-Cycle Hypothesis of Saving: Aggregate Implications and Test", *American Economic Review*, March 1963, pp. ...

Table 7. Estimated Parameters of the Saving Function $S/N = \alpha + \beta Y/N$ for Urban Salary and Wage Earner's Households by Age Class of Family Head

(sample period: 1963–73)

Age class	α	β	R^2	d	Y/N at mean	APS at mean
Under 24	−591.2	0.174	0.78	2.39	3,950	0.025
	(−4.6)	(5.7)				
25 — 29	−634.4	0.186	0.76	1.41	5,384	0.069
	(−3.2)	(5.3)				
30 — 34	−686.4	0.196	0.81	1.31	5,289	0.066
	(−4.0)	(6.3)				
35 — 39	−764.8	0.210	0.91	1.05	4,808	0.051
	(−7.1)	(9.8)				
40 — 49	−481.3	0.132	0.72	1.14	4,656	0.029
	(−3.6)	(4.8)				
50 and over	−537.1	0.136	0.38	1.52	4,527	0.018
	(−1.9)	(2.3)				

Note: See notes on Table 1.

thesis.[22] Kelley and Williamson observed that the life-cycle model predicts a rise in marginal propensity to save as the household grows older and that their empirical study for Indonesia supports such a prediction. The reason is that the share of current and expected income from property in total resources increases with the age of family head[23] and the saving propensity out of property income is assumed to be higher than that out of salary and wage income.

As shown in Table 7, the estimated parameters of the saving function for all age groups turned out to be statistically significant except for the age group of "50 and over." The regression coefficient for the "50 and over" group is only marginally significant. The lower significance of the regression coefficient seems to result from the wide dispersions of per capita income and per capita saving by household in this age group.[24] In any case, the regression results show that the marginal saving rates (β coefficients) increase gradually from the youngest age group (under 24) to the 35–39 group and then decline sharply beginning with the 40–49 group. This does not seem fully consistent with the life-cycle hypothesis of saving.

[22] Modigliani and Ando, *op. cit.*

[23] Kelley and Williamson, *op. cit.*

[24] The lower R^2 for the saving equation of this group may support this point (See Table 7).

There may be two interrelated reasons for the low marginal saving rates for the older age groups. One may be that households in the age groups of 40–49 and over 50 have to use a higher proportion of their current income for education of their children, compared with the younger age groups.[25] The other reason, which is related to the one just explained, may have something to do with the traditional family system in Korea. Although the extended family system is no longer prevalent, particularly in urban areas, it seems that some members of the older generations still expect their children to satisfy their income requirements at retirement. In this situation, the life-cycle hypothesis of saving which emphasizes the retirement motive for saving, is inadequate for explaining household savings behavior.

VI. Summary and Implications

We have concentrated our efforts on testing hypotheses relating to household savings behavior. Due to limitations in available family budget data, we used time series data for a recent 9–10 year period. We did not, therefore, attempt to experiment with any complicated form of the saving function but used a simple linear "per capita" form for testing various hypotheses. Accordingly, the results given in this paper should be taken as a preliminary exploration, which should be reexamined on the basis of better data. Our findings and their implications are, however, summarized below:

1. The economic literature dealing with hypotheses on the effect of source of income and occupation on saving propensities generally emphasizes the higher saving propensity of the entrepreneurial group relative to other functional income groups. It was, however, not possible to confirm that the marginal saving rate of the non-farm entrepreneurial group was any higher than that of other functional income groups. The lower saving rate of this group compared to average salary and wage earners in urban areas

[25] For instance, the ratios of family educational expenditure to disposable income for various age groups in 1972 were as follows: 3.1 percent for the "under 24" group, 3.3 percent for the 25–29 group, 3.9 percent for the 30–34 group, 5.4 percent for the 35–39 group, 8.3 percent for the 40–49 group and 8.2 percent for both the 50–59 and the "over 60" groups. The average ratio for all urban salary and wage earner's households was 6.4 percent in 1972. See EPB, *op. cit.*

REFERENCES

1. Adams, N. A., "Dependency Rates and Savings Rates; Comment," *American Economic Review*, June 1971, pp. 472–473.
2. Ando, A. and F. Modigliani, "The 'Life-Cycle' Hypothesis of Saving: Aggregate Implications and Tests," *American Economic Review*, March 1963, pp. 55–84.
3. Brady, D. S., "Family Savings in Relation to Changes in the Level and Distribution of Income," *Studies in Income and Wealth*, Vol. XV, 1952, pp. 103–130.
4. Bruton, H. J., "Contemporary Theorizing on Economic Growth," in Hoselitz, B. F. (ed.), *Theory of Economic Growth*, N. Y.: Free Press, 1960, pp. 239–298.
5. Economic Planning Board, *Annual Report on the Family Income and Expenditures Survey*, various issues.
6. Fisher, J. A., "Family Life-Cycle Analysis in Research on Consumer Behavior," in Clark, L. H. (ed.), *Consumer Behavior*, Vol. II, New York: N. Y. Univ. Press, 1955.
7. Friedman, M., *A Theory of the Consumption Function*, Princeton: Princeton University Press, 1957.
8. Friend, I. and I. B. Kravis, "Entrepreneurial Income, Saving and Investment," *American Economic Review*, June 1957, pp. 270–301.
9. Goldsmith, R. W., *A Study of Saving in the United States*, Vol. I-III, Princeton: Princeton University Press, 1956.
10. Gupta, K. L., "Dependency Rates and Savings Rate; Comment," *American Economic Review*, June 1971, pp. 469–471.
11. Houthakker, H. S., "On Some Determinants of Saving in Developed and Underdeveloped Countries," in Robinson, E. A. G. (ed.), *Problems in Economic Development*, N. Y.: St. Martin Press, 1966.
12. Houthakker, H. S. and L. D. Taylor, *Consumer Demand in the United States*, (2nd ed.), Cambridge, Mass.: Harvard University Press, 1970.
13. Kelley, Allen C. and J. G. Williamson, "Household Saving Behavior in the Developing Economies: The Indonesian Case, *Economic Development and Cultural Change*, Vol. XVI. No. 3, April 1968, pp. 385–403.

APPENDIX

Appendix 1. Average Annual Disposable Income per Household and Saving Rate–Urban and Farm Households

(thousand won)

Year	Average disposable income per household in 1970 prices[1]			Household saving rate (%)		
	Urban	Farm	Average	Urban	Farm	Average
1965	197.6	207.5	202.7	−1.7	1.3(4.4)[2]	−0.2 (1.3)[2]
1966	257.8	214.6	236.1	3.6	1.1(10.5)	2.6 (6.5)
1967	355.2	219.9	286.6	3.9	1.1 (9.8)	2.9 (6.1)
1968	377.9	220.3	300.2	8.6	−0.4(16.1)	5.4(11.3)
1969	377.8	242.5	314.2	6.7	4.3(17.8)	5.8(10.6)
1970	379.0	249.1	323.9	5.2	4.1(15.2)	4.8 (8.4)
1971	405.1	305.4	363.5	7.7	7.9(29.0)	7.8(15.3)
1972	406.5	323.1	372.9	9.4	4.9(24.5)	7.8(14.8)
1973	422.9	328.6	385.0	9.1	7.9(26.2)	8.6(16.0)
% change (1973/1965)	114.0	58.4	89.9			

Sources: EPB, *Annual Report on the Family Income and Expenditure Survey,* various issues, and MAF, *Report on the Results of Farm Household Economy Survey and Production Cost Survey of Agricultural Products,* various issues.

Notes: [1] The disposable income per urban household in current prices was deflated by the national consumer price index, while the disposable income per farm household was deflated by the "Index of Prices, Wages and Charges in Rural Areas" published by National Agricultural Cooperatives Federation(NACF).

[2] Figures in parentheses indicate the ratio of savings to disposable income including farm household saving in the form of agricultural products inventories

Appendix 2. Average Monthly Disposable Income per Household and Saving Rate–Urban Households

(thousand won)

Year	Average disposable income per household in 1970 prices[1]					Household saving rate (%)				
	Salary earner	Wage earner	Average salary & wage earners	Other households	Average for all households	Salary earner	Wage earner	Average salary & wage earners	Other households	Average for all households
1965	21.4	11.6	15.5	17.7	16.4	−0.9	−3.8	−2.0	−1.3	−1.7
1966	26.5	15.2	19.9	23.7	21.5	3.6	1.0	2.8	4.6	3.6
1967	34.2	21.5	27.4	32.3	29.6	5.0	1.9	3.7	4.1	3.9
1968	34.5	21.7	27.7	36.6	31.5	2.5	2.4	2.3	15.0	8.6
1969	36.0	22.6	29.4	34.6	31.5	3.0	2.8	3.0	11.3	6.7
1970	36.0	22.5	29.8	34.0	31.6	6.7	1.4	4.9	5.4	5.2
1971	38.1	23.8	31.5	36.6	33.8	10.3	3.9	8.1	7.4	7.7
1972	38.9	24.8	32.4	35.7	33.9	10.5	10.9	10.7	7.9	9.4
1973	40.5	25.0	33.3	37.7	35.2	11.6	9.8	11.0	7.0	9.1
% change (1973/65)	89.3	115.5	114.8	113.0	114.6	—	—	—	—	—

Sources: EPB, *Annual Report on the Family Income and Expenditure Survey*, various issues.
Note: [1] Deflated by CPI.

Appendix 3. Average Annual Disposable Income per Household and Saving Rate–Farm Households

(thousand won)

Year	Average disposable income per household in 1970 prices[1]						Household saving rate (%)[2]					
	Less than 0.5 Chongbo	0.5–1.0	1.0–1.5	1.5–2.0	Over 2 Chongbo	Average	Less than 0.5 Chongbo	0.5–1.0	1.0–1.5	1.5–2.0	Over 2 Chongbo	Average
1964	167.0	233.9	318.0	439.7	569.1	270.8	−4.2	−2.3	−3.2	6.8	10.2	0.1
1965	134.3	174.9	240.5	316.8	400.6	207.5	−6.0	−2.6	3.2	8.1	9.3	1.4
1966	138.3	178.7	245.5	313.5	440.3	214.6	−4.1	−3.2	1.7	5.2	10.7	1.1
1967	143.1	186.7	244.3	319.7	410.2	219.9	−1.1	−0.9	1.7	2.7	5.3	1.1
1968	146.8	178.7	248.1	316.0	420.4	220.3	−3.3	−2.3	3.1	−0.9	1.6	−0.4
1969	156.8	204.6	270.4	336.5	473.7	242.5	−0.8	2.0	6.7	5.5	9.2	4.3
1970	159.7	207.2	280.4	373.1	457.7	249.1	−1.3	3.3	3.3	11.3	5.3	4.1
1971	181.9	253.6	357.9	444.0	576.8	305.4	−5.0	2.6	9.7	8.8	17.0	7.8
1972	181.6	273.3	393.7	498.1	547.4	323.1	−5.9	3.4	8.8	6.7	9.0	4.9
1973	195.7	274.5	371.1	467.5	657.0	328.6	3.0	5.5	8.9	12.3	11.6	7.8
% change (1973/64)	17.2	17.4	16.7	6.3	15.4	21.3	—	—	—	—	—	—

Sources: MAF, *Report on the Results of Farm Household Economy Survey and Production Cost Survey of Agricultural Products*, various issues.

Notes: [1] Deflated by the Index of Prices, Wages and Charges in Rural Areas published by NACF.

[2] Saving rates excluding saving in the form of agricultural product inventories, which is not considered to be affected by the voluntary saving decisions of farm households.

THE CAUSES AND EFFECTS OF INFLATION

*Kwang Suk Kim**

This paper summarizes my research monograph, *The Causes and Effects of Inflation in Korea* which was published in Korean.[1] Since the monograph was actually completed in 1973, it analyzed the causes and effects of inflation in Korea and examined the stabilization policies of the government during the period 1945–1972, placing particular emphasis on the problems during the post-Korean War period (1955–1972). An epilogue is therefore provided here to follow up major events in 1973–1974.

I. Causes of Inflation

Price increases in Korea have been persistent since 1945, except for a short period of price stability during 1958–1959. During the period of economic disorganization immediately following Korea's liberation from Japan (1945–1949) and during the Korean War (1950–1953), the annual rate of inflation (measured by the Seoul wholesale price index) ranged from 25 to 531 percent. Although the rate of inflation gradually declined in the post-Korean War period, the average annual rate of inflation (measured in terms of the GNP deflator) was about 20 percent from 1954 to 1960. In the early sixties the annual rate of inflation gradually rose to a peak of 32 percent in 1964. Since the annual rate of inflation was stabilized at the 8–14 percent level during the later period, however,

* Senior Fellow at the Korea Development Institute.

[1] Kwang Suk Kim (1973).

the average annual rate for the entire period 1961–1972 was about 15 percent.

It was not possible to conduct an econometric analysis on the causes of inflation from 1945 to 1953 due to lack of available data. On the basis of limited statistics, however, we observed that inflation during 1945–1953 resulted mainly from supply shortages and excessive monetary expansion, owing to the economic disorganization during the immediate post-World War II period and the Korean War.

For the period from 1955 to 1972, we hypothesized that Korean inflation was a "mixed" inflation generated not only by excess demand but also by cost-push and structural factors. The hypothesis was tested by regression analysis using time series data for the period 1955 to 1972. The best results obtained are summarized below.[2]

$$(1)\quad P' = \underset{(1.3)}{5.122} + \underset{(5.0)}{0.651}\,\bar{M}' - \underset{(-2.8)}{1.127}\,TAR' + \underset{(5.5)}{0.681}\,T'$$

$$R^2 = 0.81 \qquad DW = 1.5$$

$$(2)\quad P' = \underset{(0.9)}{3.311} + \underset{(3.8)}{0.500}\,\bar{M}' - \underset{(-2.0)}{0.765}\,TAR' + \underset{(4.8)}{0.566}\,T' + \underset{(2.3)}{0.167}\,\overline{PG'}$$

$$R^2 = 0.87 \qquad DW = 2.1$$

$$(3)\quad T = \underset{(1.6)}{2.316} + \underset{(3.5)}{0.221}\,RL + \underset{(3.2)}{0.076}\,\bar{P}' \qquad R^2 = 0.78 \qquad DW = 1.8$$

where

P' = annual percentage change in GNP deflator;

M'_t = percentage change in year-end nominal money supply[3] between the years t–1 and t;

$\bar{M}'$ = $0.6\,M'_t + 0.4\,M'_{t-1}$;

TAR' = annual percentage change in total available resources (nonagricultural GNP plus net foreign capital inflow for the current year, plus value added in agriculture, forestry and fishery sectors for the previous year) in constant 1965 prices;

$\overline{PG'}$ = two-year moving average of percentage change in wholesale price index for grains;

---

[2] Figures in parentheses indicate the t-ratios and *DW* stands for Durbin-Watson *d* statistic.

[3] The term "money supply" used in this paper indicates narrow money, i.e., demand deposits plus currency in circulation.

T = average monthly turnover rate of demand deposits in commercial banks;
T' = annual percentage change in T;
$\bar{P}'$ = price expectation variable measured in terms of two-year moving average of P' [*i.e.*, $\bar{P}'_t = (P'_{t-1} + P'_t)/2$];
RL = nominal interest rate on ordinary commercial bank loans (%).

To summarize the above results we may say that the consistent, major sources of inflation during the period 1955 to 1972 were: (1) money supply expansion exceeding the demand for real money (which was determined mainly by the real growth rate of total available resources); (2) the percentage change in the turnover rate of demand deposits (which was used as a proxy for price acceleration); and (3) the increase in grain prices. As expected, the turnover rate of demand deposits increases as the domestic interest rate and the expected rate of inflation rise. It was found that changes in both the official foreign exchange rate and real wages are statistically insignificant in explaining inflation during the period 1955 to 1972. Even though rapid increases in the exchange rate and wage rates in certain years should have created some upward pressures on the general price level, our analysis indicates that they were not consistent sources of inflation during the long period from 1955 to 1972.

Recently, there have been some arguments that Korean inflation was caused mainly by cost-push factors. In order to examine the basis for such arguments, an analysis was made from the industrial cost side, using data for 1966–1971. This indicated that the increases in mining and manufacturing producer's prices and overall domestic market prices accompanied a rapid increase in the nominal wage rate exceeding the rise in labor productivity. We could not, however, find any evidence that the rapid increase in the wage rate led the rise in the general price level. Our statistical analysis indicates that the wage increase exceeded the rise in labor productivity primarily because of the rapid growth rate of non-agricultural GNP and the consequent reduction in unemployment. In addition, it was found that there exists a negative correlation between the increase in the wage rate (whether current or lagged one year) and the rate of inflation for the current year. All this suggests that although the increase in wage rates was conspicuously high in recent years, it was caused by the rapid increase in demand for labor which resulted from the high growth rate of the economy, and was not a consistent source of inflation in Korea. This result is also consistent with our finding based on the econometric analysis of inflation for the period 1955–1972.

II. Effects of Inflation [4]

Inflation not only reduced the demand for money but also had an adverse effect on financial savings, while creating a chronic excess demand for bank loans. It was found that inflation also had a significant adverse effect on real domestic savings, particularly on household savings. Although the high interest policy beginning in 1965 mitigated the adverse effects of inflation on both financial and real savings, the high interest rate policy raised the interest costs of domestic loans and increased incentives to borrow from abroad.

It was not possible to test statistically the effect of inflation on private investment, due mainly to incomplete data. However, it is felt that inflation created a bias toward short-lived projects, luxurious houses and land speculation. This bias has been mitigated in recent years by positive government policies for promoting productive long-term investment and preventing real estate speculation.

Inflation had an adverse effect on exports and a positive effect on imports, thereby contributing to increasing trade deficits in Korea. On the other hand, it increased demand for foreign loans by reducing the real interest cost of foreign loans to domestic borrowers. Thus, the effect of inflation on the overall balance of payments was generally negative.

We could not find any significant relationship between the growth rate of GNP (or non-agricultural GNP) and the rate of inflation. It is, however, noted that chronic inflation had a significant impact on the growth path of the economy. Since inflation had an adverse impact on domestic savings, Korean economic growth had to depend largely upon inflows of foreign capital.

As for the effect of inflation on income distribution, it was found that the share of wage income in total national income was generally lower in the period of strong inflation, while the share of non-agricultural business income showed quite the opposite movement. This suggests that some redistribution of income from wage earners to capitalists occurred in Korea when inflation suddenly soared to an extremely high rate. However, such redistribution was gradually corrected when the rate of inflation declined or generally stabilized. It was not possible to test statistically the effects of inflation on property owners or on income distribution by income brac-

[4] See the Appendix for some of the empirical results supporting this summary.

ket. This was due to incomplete data in the former case and the unavailability of data in the latter case.

III. Stabilization Policy

In order to check inflation, the Korean government has been implementing financial stabilization programs ever since 1957, although there was an interruption during 1961–62. However, the inability of monetary authorities to effectively control the money supply and domestic credit, combined with a rule of thumb approach to setting the annual target for monetary expansion, resulted in a large fluctuation in the annual rate of increase of the money supply from 1957 to 72. It was found that this rate had a significant, though lagged, impact on the growth of non-agricultural GNP. This seems to imply that monetary mismanagement was responsible not only for the continuous inflation of the last decade but also at least partly for the economic recessions in 1958, 1961, 1964 and 1971–72.

It is therefore suggested that the government maintain stability in the annual growth rate of the money supply, in order to achieve both price stabilization and stable economic growth. For this purpose, the government should establish annual and quarterly programs for monetary expansion on the basis of short-term forecasts of demand for money, and effectively implement the programs. Short-term monetary forecasts can be made as illustrated in KDI Working Papers 7218 and 7301.[5] Monetary control techniques should also be improved so that any program once established may actually be implemented.

IV. Epilogue

The book dealt with the various aspects of Korean inflation during the period 1945–72. Beginning in 1973, however, Korea was faced with a new type of inflation, which can be described as "imported inflation."

A Presidential Emergency Decree was promulgated on August 3, 1972 and introduced some drastic measures for both activation of the sluggish domestic economy and domestic price stabilization. Following these mea-

[5] M. J. Kim *et. al.* (1972 and 1973).

sures, the economy revived significantly and the domestic price level also seemed relatively stable for a while. A new type of inflationary pressure began to be felt in about the second quarter of 1973 and increased thereafter due mainly to rapid increases in the prices of imported raw materials.

The Reuter's international commodity price index, which had been relatively stable in the past several years, showed an increase of 128.5 percent between the 1972 average and December 1973. The international commodity price index compiled by *the Economist* also indicated a similar trend. Korea's imported raw material price index, which was computed by KDI using the value of Korean imports for 1972 as weights, increased about 118 percent from the average for January-September 1972 to December 1973. In addition, the import price of crude oil has risen almost continuously since 1972, thus making the oil price in 1974 about 378 percent higher than the 1972 level.

Despite the strong cost-push pressures arising from sharp increases in the prices of imported raw materials, Korea was able to restrict the rise in the wholesale price index to about 15 percent from December 1972 to December 1973 (See Table 1). This rate of increase in wholesale prices was relatively low compared with the rates in major industrialized countries during the same period. The 15 percent level of price inflation in 1973 was achieved as a result of strong government measures for price stabilization. Tariff rates on major raw materials and commodity tax rates on some domestic products were reduced in the first half of 1973. The government intensified direct controls on prices. This implied, however, that most of the inflationary pressures created in 1973 were carried over to 1974. The wholesale price index rose about 45 percent between December 1973 and December 1974.

It seems that the future prospect of price stabilization in Korea will largely depend upon what happens to the international prices of raw materials and the inflationary trends in industrialized countries. Since Korea's exports and imports of goods and services already accounted for approximately 32 percent and 36 percent, respectively, of GNP in 1973, it seems that independent domestic policy measures for price stabilization will have only a limited effect. Similarly, Korea's growth prospects will also depend upon the trade and growth policies of major industrialized countries.

Table 1. Prices, Money Supply and GNP, 1972–74

	December 1972 (A)	December 1973 (B)	December 1974 (C)	Percent Increase (B/A)	(C/B)
1. Wholesale Price Index (1970 = 100)	126.2	145.2	210.0	15.1	44.6
Food	138.0	150.0	222.0	8.7	48.0
Non-food	120.8	143.1	204.5	18.5	42.9
2. Seoul Consumer Price Index (1970 = 100)	127.0	136.3	171.8	7.3	26.0
3. WPI for imported goods (1970=100)	125.9	171.0	224.4	35.8	31.2
4. Money Supply (bil. won)	519.4	730.3	945.7	40.6	29.5
5. GNP (1970 bil. won)[1]	3,023.6	3,522.7	3,825.5	16.5	8.6
Agr., forestry & fishery	760.9	803.0	847.6	5.5	5.6
Non-Agr. Sectors	2,262.7	2,719.8	2,977.9	20.2	9.5

Sources: Bank of Korea, *Economic Statistics Yearbook*, 1973–75.
Note: [1] Indicates GNP for respective years.

APPENDIX

Results of Regressions to Test the Effects of Inflation on Specific Aspects

1. Definitions of variables:

1) M = nominal average money supply (demand deposits plus currency in circulation) in year t.

2) $\bar{P}$ = implicit GNP deflator (1965 = 100).

3) $\bar{P}'$ = annual percentage change in P.

4) $\bar{P}'$ = price expectation variable approximated by two-year moving average of P', *i.e.*, $\bar{P}' = (P'_{t-1} + P'_t)/2$.

5) TAR = total available resources measured in terms of 1965 constant prices.

6) RD = nominal interest rate on one-year time deposits.

7) ΔTSD = annual increase in total time and savings deposits plus money in trust, in 1965 constant won.

8) Y = gross national product in 1965 constant won.

9) ΔY = annual increment in Y.
10) SH = real household savings, excluding saving in the form of grain inventories, in constant 1965 won.
11) YH = gross income of household and private non-profit institutions in constant 1965 won.
12) SP = gross private savings in constant 1965 won.
13) MNG = non-grain commodity imports (c.i.f.) in constant 1965 won.
14) YNA = non-agricultural GNP in constant 1965 won.
15) RM = nominal effective exchange rate on imports, in won per dollar.
16) PP = purchasing power parity index; *i.e.*, domestic WPI deflated by the weighted average WPI of Korea's major trade partners (Japan and U.S.).
17) MG = grain imports in constant 1965 won.
18) X = commodity exports (f.o.b.) in constant 1965 won.
19) RX = nominal effective exchange rate on exports, in won per dollar.
20) CK = net imports of foreign commercial loans in 1965 constant won.
21) I = gross domestic fixed investment in 1965 constant won.
22) RLR = real rate of interest on domestic commercial bank loans (nominal loan rate less the rate of inflation lagged one year).
23) RRF = real rate of interest on foreign commercial loans (nominal loan rate less the rate of inflation lagged one year plus a 3 year moving average of annual percentage rates of devaluation).
24) $CKDM$ = dummy variable (1 for 1970 and zero for all other years).

2. Regression equations:

1) $$\log M/P = -4.542 + 1.372 \log TAR - 0.172 \log \bar{P}' - 0.088\,(RD - \bar{P}')$$
$$(-11.01)\quad (21.44)\qquad\qquad (-6.14)\qquad\quad (-4.19)$$
$$R^2 = 0.978 \qquad DW = 1.98 \text{ (Sample period: 1953–72)}$$

2) $$\Delta TSD = -11.835 + 0.526\,\Delta Y + 1.010\,RD - 1.181\,\bar{P}'$$
$$(-0.65)\quad (3.41)\qquad (0.77)\qquad (-2.02)$$
$$R^2 = 0.850 \qquad DW = 1.75 \text{ (Sample period: 1957–71)}$$

3) $SH = -32.709 + 0.037\ YH + 1.726\ RD - 1.075\ \bar{P}'$
$\quad (-4.68) \quad (4.03) \quad (4.21) \quad (-4.17)$

$R^2 = 0.918 \quad DW = 2.25$ (Sample period: 1960–71)

4) $SP = -46.770 + 0.100\ Y + 3.023\ RD - 1.341\ \bar{P}'$
$\quad (-3.98) \quad (6.38) \quad (3.54) \quad (-2.74)$

$R^2 = 0.939 \quad DW = 1.83$ (Sample period: 1957–71)

5) $MNG = -117.278 + 0.630\ YNA - 0.876\ RM + 1.771\ PP$
$\quad (-7.31) \quad (15.23) \quad (-3.36) \quad (1.78)$

$R^2 = 0.992 \quad DW = 1.43$ (Sample period: 1956–71)

6) $MG = -36.491 - 0.409\ RM + 1.810\ PP$
$\quad (-1.80) \quad (-2.51) \quad (3.43)$

$R^2 = 0.846 \quad DW = 1.75$ (Sample period: 1956–71)

7) $X = -170.638 + 0.353\ Y + 0.478\ RX - 2.188\ PP$
$\quad (-9.76) \quad (10.76) \quad (1.98) \quad (2.66)$

$R^2 = 0.992 \quad DW = 1.51$ (Sample period: 1956–71)

8) $CK = -23.764 + 0.263\ I + 148.535\ RLR - 77.732\ RRF$
$\quad (-7.06) \quad (7.86) \quad (2.87) \quad (-2.02)$

$- 27.844\ CKDM$
(-3.06)

$R^2 = 0.985 \quad DW = 2.57$ (Sample period: 1959–70)

REFERENCES

1. Kim, Kwang Suk, *Hankuk Inflation Ui Wonin Gua Gu Yonghyang* (The Causes and Effects of Inflation in Korea), KDI Research Series I, Changmoongak, Seoul, 1973.
2. Kim, M.J., H.Y. Song and K.S. Kim, "A Note on Monetary Forecasts, 1972–73," KDI Working Paper 7218 (1972).
3. ———, "Revised Note on Monetary Forecasts for 1973," KDI Working Paper 7301 (1973).

AN OVERVIEW OF CORPORATE FINANCE AND THE LONG-TERM SECURITIES MARKET

*Il SaKong**

I. Introduction

A necessary, if not sufficient, condition for rapid economic development of a less developed country (LDC) is a sustained high rate of investment. Investment may be financed by domestically mobilized savings and/or transferred foreign savings. The volume of domestic savings available in most LDCs, however, may be insufficient to finance the investment required for rapid economic development. Consequently, it may be unavoidable for LDCs, especially in their earlier stages of development, to rely rather heavily on foreign savings. As development proceeds, however, these LDCs will have to rely more on domestically mobilized savings. Korea seems to fit this pattern well.

During the last decade, Korea achieved a remarkably rapid economic growth. The average real GNP growth rate was 9.2 percent during the 1960s and 11.7 percent during the 1965–1969 period. During these periods, Korea relied heavily on foreign sources of investment. As seen from Table 1, foreign savings financed 78.3 percent of total investment in 1960 and 54.2 percent during the First Five-Year Economic Development Plan period (1962–1966). Its share was reduced to 39.9 percent during the 1967–1971 period (the Second Five-Year Economic Development Plan period). A further reduction to 21 percent is envisaged during the Third Plan

* Senior Fellow at the Korea Development Institute. This paper was Originally published in January 1975 as KDI Working Paper No. 7505

Table 1. *Total Investment and Its Financing Sources*

(billion current won)

Year	Total Investment	National Saving			Foreign Saving[3]	Statistical Discrepancy
		Total	Private[1]	Government[2]		
1960	26.80 (100)	3.54 (13.2)	8.55 (31.9)	−5.01(−18.7)	20.99 (78.3)	2.27 (8.5)
1961	38.79 (100)	11.58 (29.9)	16.88 (43.6)	−5,30(−13.7)	25.29 (65.2)	1.92 (4.9)
1962	45.47 (100)	5.48 (12.0)	10.34 (22.7)	−4.86(−10.7)	37.95 (83.5)	2.04 (4.5)
1963	90.26 (100)	30.49 (33.8)	31.81 (35.3)	−1.32 (−1.5)	52.36 (58.0)	7.41 (8.2)
1964	102.24 (100)	51.94 (50.8)	48.39 (47.3)	3.55 (3.5)	49.13 (48.1)	1.17 (1.1)
1965	121.98 (100)	60.50 (49.6)	46.48 (38.1)	14.02 (11.5)	51.53 (42.2)	9.95 (8.2)
1966	224.48 (100)	122.45 (54.6)	93.37 (41.6)	29.08 (13.0)	87.63 (39.0)	14.40 (6.4)
1967	280.97 (100)	151.81 (54.0)	99.96 (35.6)	51.85 (18.4)	112.86 (40.2)	16.30 (5.8)
1968	427.87 (100)	218.32 (51.0)	117.71 (27.5)	100.61 (23.5)	184.33 (43.1)	25.22 (5.9)
1969	620.70 (100)	365.18 (58.8)	235.63 (37.9)	129.55 (20.9)	229.02 (36.9)	26.50 (4.3)
1970	704.66 (100)	423.20 (60.1)	243.20 (34.6)	180.00 (25.6)	249.31 (35.3)	32.15 (4.6)
1971	805.35 (100)	458.27 (56.9)	268.17 (33.3)	190.10 (23.6)	354.00 (44.0)	−6.92(−0.9)
1972	805.48 (100)	577.31 (71.7)	427.74 (53.1)	149.57 (18.6)	215.03 (26.7)	13.14 (1.6)
1973	1,292.29 (100)	1,087.97 (84.2)	864.68 (66.9)	225.09 (17.4)	198.92 (15.4)	3.60 (0.3)
1974	1,193 (100)	915 (76.7)	624 (52.3)	291 (24.4)	278 (23.3)	
1975	1,426 (100)	1,142 (80.1)	776 (54.4)	366 (25.7)	284 (19.9)	
1976	1,647 (100)	1,383 (84.0)	924 (56.1)	459 (27.9)	264. (16.0)	
1977	2,019 (100)	1,705 (84.4)	1,145 (56.7)	560 (27.7)	314 (15.6)	
1978	2,379 (100)	2,108 (88.6)	1,465 (61.6)	643 (27.0)	271 (11.4)	
1979	2,791 (100)	2,585 (92.6)	1,848 (66.2)	737 (26.4)	206 (7.4)	
1980	3,277 (100)	3,173 (96.8)	2,355 (71.9)	818 (25.0)	104 (3.2)	
1981	3,873 (100)	3,909 (100.9)	2,983 (77.0)	926 (23.9)	−36 (−0.9)	

Source: Bank of Korea, *Monthly Economic Statistics*, September 1974, for the 1960–1973 period, and Economic Planning Board, *Long-Term Perspective of Our Economy*, December 1973, for the 1973–1981 period.

Notes: Figures in parentheses are in percent.

[1] includes unincorporated enterprises, private corporations and government-controlled corporations.

[2] includes both general government and government enterprises.

[3] includes both net borrowings and net transfers from the rest of the world.

period (1972–1976).[1] It will eventually reach minus 0.3 percent in 1981.[1] At the same time, the composition of domestic savings is also expected to change with the share of private savings in total investment reaching 76 percent in 1981. Therefore, the future development of Korea will depend largely on private domestic capital to be mobilized through the domestic financial system. This in turn requires an efficient financial system for the Korean economy.

An efficient financial system may evolve in response to the demand for services of the system generated from the real economy.[2] This "demand-following" phenomenon, in which "finance is essentially passive and permissive in the growth process,"[3] was observed in England during the late eighteenth and early nineteenth century. Today in most developing countries, however, one can easily imagine various obstacles which may inhibit an adequate demand-following response by the financial system. Hence, the "supply-leading" approach of developing a financial system has been followed by some developing countries. Brazilians adopted the strategy of economic development by consciously taking the supply-leading approach since 1964.[4]

Since the interest-rate reform of October, 1965 the Korean government has also been making a strenuous effort to develop the nation's financial markets, institutions and instruments. In particular, various important measures have been taken with regard to the long-term securities market, one important ingredient of the nation's financial system. The primary purpose of this paper is rather modest in that an overview of corporate finance is presented and various aspects of the long-term securities market are described. This study, as such, is not meant to be rigorously analytical but to provide a background for systematic analyses of the overall financial system of the nation in the near future.

---

[1] These figures are from Economic Planning Board, *Long-Term Perspective of Our Economy*, 1973, which was prepared before the recent world oil crisis. Consequently, they will have to be appropriately adjusted upward in the light of the new situation. This adjustment, however, will not change the general picture to a great extent. It is also worthwhile to remind readers of the fact that minus 0.3 percent is on a net basis.

[2] See Hugh T. Patrick, "Financial Development and Economic Growth in Underdeveloped Countries," *Economic Development and Cultural Change*, January 1966.

[3] Patrick, *Ibid.*, p. 175.

[4] For discussions on the financial innovations introduced and their effectiveness, see Walter L. Ness, Jr., "Financial Markets Innovation as a Development Strategy: Initial Results from the Brazilian Experience," *Economic Development and Cultural Change*, April 1975, and David M. Trubek, *Law, Planning and the Development of the Brazilian Capital Market* (Institute of Finance Bulletin No. 72–73, New York University, April 1971).

II. An Overview of Corporate Finance in Korea

During the period 1963–1973, the corporate sector[5] relied primarily on external sources of finance as seen from Table 2. Over 80 percent of total funds were raised externally during the period. Funds from internal sources could have financed only 37 percent of the sector's fixed capital formation, even with the extreme assumption that all retained earnings and depreciation allowances were used for financing fixed capital formation.

Patrick[6] reports that the Japanese corporate sector also relied heavily on external sources of finance during the period when the economy grew so rapidly. Between 1952 and 1967, for example, Japanese real GNP grew at an average annual rate of 9.6 percent. During this period (1954–1967), 68 percent of total funds were provided externally. As shown in the following table, the pattern of the Korean corporate financial structure is similar to that of Japan. Other developed countries, including the U.S., have quite different corporate financial structures. External sources of corporate finance in these countries are far less important.

Even for Japan, corporate gross saving could have financed about 80 percent of the sector's fixed capital formation during the same period. This Japanese experience under a similar growth situation puts the corporate financial structure of Korea into perspective.

Table 4 presents the composition of external sources of finance for the period. As expected, the most important source of finance was banking institutions. Foreign loans were also as important as expected during the period. If we assume that funds from all internal sources, security issues,[7] and foreign sources were used solely for the fixed capital formation, they

---

[5] This includes both private and government-controlled corporations while excluding financial institutions as in the flow-of-funds accounts. This corporate sector was responsible for more than half of total capital formation for the nation during the 1963–1973 period. The government, unincorporated enterprises and financial institutions together make up the rest.

[6] Hugh T. Patrick. "Finance, Capital Markets and Economic Growth in Japan," in Arnold W. Sametz (ed.), *Financial Development and Economic Growth* (New York: New York University Press, 1972).

[7] As discussed in Section IV, security issues here include not only publicly-issued securities but those distributed directly to other spending units. Included here, for example, are stocks distributed to capital contributors at the time of incorporation, and government equity shares in government-controlled corporations.

Table 2. Corporate Sector Sources and Uses of Funds, 1963—1973

(thousand current won)

Sources	1963		1964		1965	
Internal-Total	16,388	(30.5)	20,575	(32.1)	25,066	(26.5)
Net Saving	9,072	(16.9)	10,863	(17.0)	13,486	(14.3)
Capital Consumption Allowance	7,316	(13.6)	9,712	(15.2)	11,580	(12.3)
External-Total	32,840	(61.1)	36,041	(56.3)	62,979	(66.6)
Stocks & Debentures[1]	11,142	(20.7)	8,343	(13.0)	9,621	(10.2)
Domestic Loans[2]	11,059	(20.6)	7,602	(11.9)	29,820	(31.5)
Foreign Loans	8,106	(15.1)	1,813	(2.8)	7,804	(8.3)
Trade Credit	1,025	(1.9)	4,277	(6.7)	4,822	(5.1)
Miscellaneous	1,508	(2.8)	14,006	(21.9)	10,912	(11.5)
Adjustment	4,522	(8.4)	7,391	(11.6)	6,496	(6.9)
Total	53,750	(100.0)	64,007	(100.0)	94,541	(100.0)
Uses	**1963**		**1964**		**1965**	
Real Investment	48,252	(89.8)	48,181	(75.3)	67,541	(71.4)
Fixed Capital Formation	38,214	(71.1)	41,248	(64.4)	47,331	(50.1)
Inventories	10,038	(18.7)	6,933	(10.8)	20,210	(21.4)
Financial Investment	5,498	(10.2)	15,826	(24.7)	27,000	(28.6)
Primary Securities	1,168	(2.2)	11,738	(18.3)	13,624	(14.4)
Stocks & Debentures[1]	300	(0.6)	3,451	(5.4)	4,722	(5.0)
Bonds[3]	98	(0.2)	−278	(−0.4)	−248	(−0.3)
Domestic Loans	—		—		—	
Trade Credit	770	(1.4)	8,565	(13.4)	9,150	(9.7)
Indirect Securities	113	(0.2)	−6	(−0.0)	4,736	(5.0)
Money	−593	(−1.1)	−339	(−0.5)	1,775	(1.9)
Time & Savings Deposits	−4	(−0.0)	132	(0.2)	3,063	(3.2)
Insurance & Trust	710	(1.3)	201	(0.3)	−102	(−0.1)
Miscellaneous	4,217	(7.9)	4,094	(6.4)	8,640	(9.1)
Total	53,750	(100.0)	64,007	(100.0)	94,541	(100.0)
Sources	**1966**		**1967**		**1968**	
Internal-Total	33,059	(21.4)	47,666	(15.8)	67,719	(16.3)
Net Saving	15,581	(10.1)	26,499	(8.8)	25,435	(6.1)
Capital Consumption Allowance	17,478	(11.3)	21,167	(7.0)	42,284	(10.2)
External-Total	119,689	(77.6)	245,384	(81.2)	365,291	(87.9)
Stocks & Debentures[1]	13,293	(8.6)	16,567	(5.5)	32,345	(7.8)
Domestic Loans[2]	35,076	(22.7)	92,995	(30.8)	137,030	(33.0)
Foreign Loans	49,878	(32.3)	66,865	(22.1)	112,182	(27.0)
Trade Credit	8,564	(5.6)	21,487	(7.1)	41,704	(10.0)
Miscellaneous	12,878	(8.4)	47,470	(15.7)	42,030	(10.1)
Adjustment	1,492	(1.0)	9,010	(3.0)	−17,330	(−4.2)
Total	154,240	(100.0)	302,060	(100.0)	415,680	(100.0)

Table 2. (*Continued*)

Uses	1966		1967		1968	
Real Investment	121,598	(78.8)	184,388	(61.0)	256,066	(61.6)
Fixed Capital Formation	109,306	(70.9)	164,413	(54.4)	219,975	(52.9)
Inventories	12,292	(8.0)	19,975	(6.6)	36,091	(8.7)
Financial Investment	32,642	(21.2)	117,672	(39.0)	159,614	(38.4)
Primary Securities	8,823	(5.7)	33,288	(11.0)	69,889	(16.8)
Stocks & Debentures[1]	1,288	(0.8)	7,687	(2.5)	8,045	(1.9)
Bonds[3]	−176	(−0.1)	−150	(−0.1)	1,202	(0.3)
Domestic Loans	—		—		—	
Trade Credit	7,711	(5.0)	25,751	(8.5)	60,642	(14.6)
Indirect Securities	7,840	(5.1)	20,163	(6.7)	44,747	(10.8)
Money	1,752	(1.1)	5,622	(1.9)	3,234	(0.8)
Time & Savings Deposits	4,826	(3.1)	13,897	(4.6)	35,673	(8.6)
Insurance & Trust	1,262	(0.8)	644	(0.2)	5,840	(1.4)
Miscellaneous	15,979	(10.4)	64,221	(21.3)	44,978	(10.8)
Total	154,240	(100.0)	302,060	(100.0)	415,681	(100.0)
Sources	**1969**		**1970**		**1971**	
Internal-Total	89,084	(14.7)	85,023	(13.4)	114,922	(16.7)
Net Saving	27,715	(4.6)	21,622	(3.4)	36,871	(5.4)
Capital-Consump. Allowance	61,369	(10.1)	63,401	(10.0)	78,051	(11.4)
External-Total	556,902	(91.8)	531,453	(83.7)	610,228	(88.9)
Stocks & Debentures[1]	79,504	(13.1)	82,674	(13.0)	110,191	(16.1)
Domestic Loans[2]	187,501	(30.9)	164,352	(25.9)	194’412	(28.3)
Foreign Loans	124,292	(20.5)	131,810	(20.8)	127,815	(18.6)
Trade Credit	61,417	(10.1)	62,641	(9.9)	71,433	(10.4)
Miscellaneous	104,188	(17.2)	89,976	(14.2)	106,377	(15.5)
Adjustment	−39,284	(−6.5)	18,869	(3.0)	−38,491	(−5.6)
Total	606,702	(100.0)	635,345	(100.0)	686,659	(100.0)
Uses	**1969**		**1970**		**1971**	
Real Investment	347,349	(57.3)	379,467	(59.7)	419,904	(61.2)
Fixed Capital Formation	308,071	(50.8)	350,127	(55.1)	393,877	(57.4)
Inventories	39,278	(6.5)	29,340	(4.6)	26,027	(3.8)
Financial Investment[1]	259,353	(42.8)	255,878	(40.3)	266,395	(38.8)
Primary Securities[3]	96,231	(15.9)	94,756	(14.9)	115,147	(16.8)
Stocks & Debentures	18,260	(3.0)	15,838	(2.5)	23,408	(3.4)
Bonds	1,323	(0.2)	3,422	(0.5)	2,165	(0.3)
Domestic Loans	—		—		—	
Trade Credit	76,648	(12.6)	75,496	(11.9)	89,574	(13.0)
Indirect Securities	74,317	(12.3)	80,921	(12.7)	44,512	(6.5)
Money	17,172	(2.8)	28,862	(4.5)	12,124	(1.8)
Time & Savings Deposits	51,935	(8.6)	47,662	(7.5)	28,505	(4.2)
Insurance & Trust	5,210	(0.9)	4,397	(0.7)	3,883	(0.6)
Miscellaneous	88,805	(14.6)	80,201	(12.6)	107,096	(15.6)
Total	606,702	(100.0)	635,345	(100.0)	686,659	(100.0)

Table 2. (*Continued*)

Sources	1972	1973	1963–1973
Internal-Total	173,141 (24.5)	335,500 (27.2)	1,008,143 (20.3) (19.8)
Net Saving	46,215 (6.5)	163,300 (13.2)	396,659 (8.0) (7.8)
Capital-Consumption Allowance	126,926 (18.0)	172,200 (14.0)	611,484 (12.3) (12.0)
External-Total	595,256 (84.3)	930,160 (75.5)	4,086,223 (82.5) (80.2)
Stocks & Debentures[1]	222,488 (31.5)	254,518 (20.7)	840,686 (17.0) (16.5)
Domestic Loans	233,534 (33.1)	448,676 (36.4)	1,542,057 (31.1) (30.3)
Foreign Loans	86,752 (12.3)	178,279 (14.5)	895,596 (18.1) (17.6)
Trade Credit	15,906 (2.3)	15,384 (1.3)	308,660 (6.2) (6.1)
Miscellaneous	36,576 (5.2)	33,303 (2.7)	499,224 (10.1) (9.8)
Adjustment	−62,164(−8.8)	−33,506(−2.7)	−142,995
Total	706,233(100.0)	1,232,154(100.0)	4,951,372(100.0)(100.0)[4]

Uses	1972	1973	1963–1973
Real Investment	429,007 (60.8)	690,800 (56.1)	2,992,553 (60.4)
Fixed Capital Formation	419,716 (59.4)	677,100 (55.0)	2,769,378 (55.9)
Inventories	9,291 (1.3)	13,700 (1.1)	223,175 (4.5)
Financial Investment	277,226 (39.3)	541,354 (43.9)	1,958,458 (39.6)
Primary Securities	114,261 (16.2)	228,720 (18.6)	787,645 (15.9)
Stocks & Debentures	54,181 (7.7)	92,141 (7.5)	229,321 (4.6)
Bonds	3,977 (0.6)	21,629 (1.8)	32,964 (0.7)
Domestic Loans	—	17,975 (1.5)	17,975 (0.4)
Trade Credit	56,103(7.9)	96,975 (7.9)	507,385 (10.3)
Indirect Securities	133,142 (18.9)	241,610 (19.6)	652,095 (13.2)
Money	51,547 (7.3)	109,408 (8.9)	230,564 (4.7)
Time & Savings Deposits	75,279 (10.7)	134,401 (10.9)	395,369 (8.0)
Insurance & Trust	6,316 (0.9)	−2,199(−0.2)	26,162 (0.5)
Miscellaneous	29,823 (4.2)	71,024 (5.8)	519,078 (10.5)
Total	706,233(100.0)	1,232,154(100.0)	4,951,372(100.0)

Sources: Bank of Korea, *Flow of Funds Accounts in Korea, 1963—1970*, 1971, for 1963–1969; Bank of Korea, *Economic Statistics Yearbook, 1973*, for 1970; and Bank of Korea, *Economic Statistics Yearbook, 1974*, and Bank of Korea, *Monthly Economic Statistics*, November 1974, for 1971–1973.

Notes: Figures in parentheses are in percent.

[1] includes equities other than stocks.

[2] includes BOK loans, commercial bank loans, specialized bank loans, insurance and trust loans, government loans, and other loans.

[3] includes all national bonds, educational bonds, telephone bonds, local government bonds, and other government-guaranteed bonds.

[4] percentage distributions excluding adjustments.

Table 3. Percentage Distribution of Sources of Funds for All Corporations

	Korea 1963 — 1973	Japan 1954 — 1967	U.S.A. 1947—1963
Internal-Total	19.8	32.6	65
Net Saving	7.8	12.1	23
Depreciation Allowances	12.0	20.4	42
External-Total	80.2	67.5	35
Security Issues	16.5	8.8	
Domestic Loans	30.3	33.6	
Foreign Loans	17.6	2.0	
Trade Credit	6.1	22.6	
Miscellaneous	9.7	0.5	
Total Sources	100	100	100

Sources: [1] Same as Table 2 for Korea;

[2] Patrick, *op. cit.*, pp. 110–111, for Japan; and

[3] Arnold W. Sametz, "Business Investment Demand," in Murray E. Polakoff (ed.), *Financial Institutions and Markets* (Boston: Houghton Mifflin Co., 1970), p. 271, for the U.S.A.

together, could have financed on the average over 90 percent of the sectoral fixed investment for the period[8] as shown in Table 2. This implies that funds from the remaining sources could have been used primarily for liquidity purposes, inventory investments, and financial portfolio investments. As seen from the uses side of Table 2, 45 percent of total funds could have been used for these purposes.[9]

In relation to this phenomenon, one might argue that the corporate sector not only produced goods and services but performed "financial intermediation" to the extent that it borrowed more than its liquidity and deficit financing needs.[10] It is beyond the scope of the present study

[8] Funds from these sources were more than enough to finance the sectoral fixed investment for 1972 and 1973.

[9] In the case of Japan, this proportion was even higher for the period 1954–1969. Almost 60 percent of total funds were used for other than financing fixed capital formation. Half of these funds were, however, used for financing trade credit. Trade credit financing is not a major element in the Korean case. The difference might have originated from various sources, e.g., different payment customs, and different degrees of information available on credit worthiness.

[10] Gurley and Shaw's discussion on financial growth and mixed asset-debt positions seems to be relevant for this issue. See Gurley, John G., and Edward S. Shaw, *Money in a Theory of Finance* (Washington, D.C.: The Brookings Institutions, 1960), pp. 112–113.

Table 4. Composition of External Sources of Corporate Finance, 1963–1973

(million current won)

	1963	1964	1965	1966	1967	1968
External-Total	32,840(100.0)	36,041(100.0)	62,979(100.0)	119,689(100.0)	245,384(100.0)	365,291(100.0)
Indirect Finance	8,930 (27.2)	4,413 (12.2)	27,586 (43.8)	25,495 (21.3)	69,871 (28.5)	123,732(33.9)
Bank Loans	6,915 (21.1)	4,305 (11.9)	26,318 (41.8)	23,951 (20.0)	68,510 (27.9)	119,345(32.7)
Non-Bank Loans	2,015 (6.1)	108 (0.3)	1,268 (2.0)	1,544 (1.3)	1,361 (0.6)	4,387 (1.2)
Direct Finance	14,296 (43.5)	15,809 (43.9)	16,677 (26.5)	31,438 (26.3)	61,178 (24.9)	87,347 (23.9)
Security Issues	11,142 (33.9)	8,343 (23.2)	9,621 (15.3)	13,293 (11.1)	16,567 (6.8)	32,345 (8.9)
Private Loans	2,129 (6.5)	3,189 (8.9)	2,234 (3.6)	9,581 (8.0)	23,124 (9.4)	13,298 (3.6)
Trade Credit	1,025 (3.1)	4,277 (11.9)	4,822 (7.7)	8,564 (7.2)	21,487 (8.8)	41,704 (11.4)
Miscel-laneous	1,508 (4.6)	14,006 (38.9)	10,912 (17.3)	12,878 (10.8)	47,470 (19.4)	42,030 (11.5)
Foreign Loans	8,106 (24.7)	1,813 (5.0)	7,804 (12.4)	49,878 (41.7)	66,865 (27.3)	112,182 (30.7)

Table 4. (*Continued*)

	1969	1970	1971	1972	1973	1963–1973 Total
External-Total	556,902(100.0)	531,453(100.0)	610,228(100.0)	595,256(100.0)	930,160(100.0)	4,086,223(100.0)
Indirect Finance	165,701 (29.8)	139,052 (26.2)	169,512 (27.8)	258,234 (43.4)	448,276 (48.2)	1,440,802 (35.3)
Bank Loans	141,883 (25.5)	113,081 (21.3)	120,164 (19.7)	167,443 (28.1)	301,627 (32.4)	1,093,542 (26.8)
Non-Bank Loans	23,818 (4.3)	25,971 (4.9)	49,348 (8.1)	90,791 (15.3)	146,649 (15.8)	347,260 (8.5)
Direct Finance	162,721 (29.2)	170,615 (32.1)	206,524 (33.8)	213,694 (35.9)	270,302 (29.1)	1,250,601 (30.6)
Security Issues	79,504 (14.3)	82,674 (15.6)	110,191 (18.1)	222,488 (37.4)	254,518 (27.4)	840,686 (20.6)
Private Loans	21,800 (3.9)	25,300 (4.8)	24,900 (4.1)	−24,700(−4.2)	400 (0.0)	101,255 (2.5)
Trade Credit	61,417 (11.0)	62,641 (11.8)	71,433 (11.7)	15,906 (2.7)	15,384 (1.7)	308,660 (7.6)
Miscel-laneous	104,188 (18.7)	89,976 (16.9)	106,377 (17.4)	36,576 (6.1)	33,303 (3.6)	499,224 (12.2)
Foreign Loans	124,292 (22.3)	131,810 (24.8)	127,815 (21.0)	86,752 (14.6)	178,279 (19.2)	895,596 (21.9)

Source: Same as Table 2.

to examine the extent to which financial intermediation is performed by the sector. It is, however, an important issue to be analyzed in the future, since it has important implications for government policy toward corporate finance, especially privileged bank loans and government-guaranteed foreign loans.

Let us now consider some of the factors which might explain the most salient feature of the corporate financial structure of Korea, the extremely heavy reliance on external sources of finance, especially on borrowing.

Theoretically speaking, availability and/or the relative cost of financing alternatives would be the most important factors in determining the particular corporate financial structure.[11] As already indicated, business corporations make investments financed by internally generated and/or externally acquired funds. The cost of internal funds is the opportunity cost to the stockholders who forego cash dividends. With regard to external funds, the costs of borrowed funds and external equity capital should be separately considered.

The cost of borrowed funds involves out-of-pocket as well as imputed costs: *i.e.*, interest payments and the imputed cost of financial risks borne by stockholders who have claims only on the residual earnings. The cost imputed for financial risks increases with the volume of borrowing. Of course, the increased "leverage" as a result of more borrowing simultaneously raises the expected earnings for stockholders. As compared to the cost (supply price) of equity capital, the cost (supply price) of debt must be lower because of the extra burden of risk carried by stockholders. With an increasing volume of borrowing, however, the gap between equity and debt capital narrows. This is so because both the imputed cost and the direct interest costs for debt increase simultaneously as borrowing proceeds.

The cost of external equity capital is necessarily greater than the cost for internal equity capital. Of course, both external and internal equity have the same opportunity cost. External equity has, however, additional costs such as flotation costs and the imputed costs of disclosure of internal information and management dilution.

As can be seen from Table 2, the volume of internal funds grew quite rapidly during the 1963–1973 period. Since the corporate sector started with such a meager internal fund base, however, it had to rely heavily on external sources under such a rapid growth situation. It is also true that,

---

[11] A good discussion on comparative costs of finance is found in Sametz, *op. cit.*, pp. 260–265.

under these conditions, internal funds could have grown faster and thus increased the proportion of internal equity financing. There were (and still are) some structural or institutional factors which could have contributed to the slower growth of corporate internal funds.

First, for "privately-held corporations,"[12] there is a built-in legal disincentive for retaining earnings. Currently, there is a personal income tax provision by which retained earnings for these corporations are taxed as if they were paid to stockholders as dividends.[13] Since this provision is not applied to "publicly-held corporations," it might be considered as a factor to encourage corporations to go public. It seems to be necessary, however, to find ways by which corporate profit retention for all corporations is encouraged while simultaneously preventing various malpractices. Brazil, for example, encouraged profit retention by allowing corporations to deduct from profits an amount equivalent to that needed for financing working capital increases due to inflation.[14]

Second, we can also find some possible explanations for rather small corporate depreciation allowances. In an inflationary situation, depreciation charges based on book-values would tend to be small and therefore, corporate tax liabilities will be increased accordingly. To help improve this situation, the Asset Revaluation Law was enacted in March 1965. According to the Law, corporations are allowed to revalue their operational fixed assets once every two years at most. The capitalization of the increased asset value is subject to a rather low tax rate.[15] Stock dividends are paid as a result of the asset revaluation and these stock dividends are very popular among shareholders, most of whom seem to consider them as important as cash dividends.

There are, however, alleged reasons for corporations to hesitate to revalue their assets. Publicly-held corporations[16] are not anxious to revalue their assets since the government, as well as the public, would put

[12] Privately-held corporations are those which are not considered to be "publicly-held corporations" defined by the Corporate Income Tax provisions. The definition is provided in the following section. It may be worthwhile to point out at this point, however, that "publicly-held corporations" are not the same as public corporations (or government-controlled corporations).

[13] See Article 2, The Personal Income Tax Law. This tax is not applicable to reserves for investments.

[14] See Ness, Jr., *op. cit.*

[15] Currently, it is three percent.

[16] We will discuss matters related to stock dividends in a following section and indicate why this seemingly fallacious phenomenon occurs. The same phenomenon occurred in Brazil according to Ness. (Ness, Jr., *Ibid.*)

pressure on these corporations to pay out a certain rate of per-share dividends on total shares outstanding. The revaluation tax may also be a factor as the Korean Chamber of Commerce recently recommended reducing the tax rate as a measure for improving the over-leveraged corporate financial structure. On the other hand, it is claimed that non-publicly-held corporations are reluctant to revalue their assets since they are afraid that their increased assets might be used as an arbitrary tax assessment criterion.[17] A comprehensive study on this matter would be worthwhile in order to determine why corporations do not want to revalue as often as they can so that they can increase their depreciation allowance and thus their cash flow.

There are some other factors related directly to relative costs which might discourage internal vis-a-vis external financing. For example, there is a reason (common to most other countries) for corporations to prefer debt to equity financing in general, and that is, that interest payments are considered to be costs for tax purposes while dividends are not. It is also possible that during a period of rapid corporate growth such as the one under consideration, leverage considerations might have encouraged corporations to use debt capital even more liberally. Of course, increased financial risks would have raised the cost of borrowing to a prohibitive level if loan markets were operated competitively. In fact, however, the loan markets, especially bank loans, have been operated under a disequilibrium system.[19]

We will discuss external equity financing in a following section. At this point, however, we can state that a necessary step to help remedy the over-leveraged financial status of Korean corporations is not only to increase external equity financing but also to encourage internal financing.

---

[17] For the definition of the publicly-held corporations, see Section III.

[18] Currently, an "arbitrary tax assessment" is made for non-publicly-held corporations.

[19] Under this situation, of course, the real cost of a loan would include not only interest payments but additional costs of loan acquisition; e.g., under-the-table payments. It is a well-known fact, however, that there have always been long queues for bank loans.

III. Important Policy Measures Taken Recently to Affect The Long-Term Corporate Securities Market

As was indicated earlier, our primary interest in the present study lies in the nation's long-term securities market. The long-term securities market is often described as the "capital market". The latter term, however, is used by different authors to mean different things. Some authors use the term to include all financial markets, both short-term and long-term, while others use the term to indicate the market for long-term funds, including long-term loans as well as long-term securities. The term is used in the present study to indicate only the long-term securities market.[20]

The securities market consists of two sub-markets . . the "new-issue market" and the "trading market". New security issues are made in the new-issue market while seasoned securities are traded in the trading market. The new-issue market performs the economically significant role of mobilizing savings and distributing them to investment alternatives. The trading market, a by-product of the new-issue market, does not involve net new savings and investments, but only reshuffles claims on existing assets. In other words, activities in this market are derived from asset-holders' constant efforts to readjust their portfolios. This trading market is no less important than the new-issue market simply because it is essential to have a well-functioning secondary market for an effective new-issue market. This is so because purchasers of new-issues are guaranteed to have liquidity on their loans in the presence of a well-functioning trading market.

As will be seen from Table 6 in Section IV, the new-issue market for corporate equities was virtually negligible before 1968. There were a few cases of new-issues offered to existing shareholders through their subscription rights. There were no debentures issues at all before 1972. Due primarily to various policy measures to be discussed shortly, the new-issue market has been relatively active only since 1968 for equities, and since 1972 for corporate debentures. The Korea Stock Exchange (KSE)[21]

[20] For a discussion of this term, see U Tun Wai and Hugh T. Patrick, "Stock and Bond Issues and Capital Markets in Less Developed Countries," *IMF Staff Papers,* July 1973, pp. 254–255.

[21] A well-documented history of the Korean securities market is found in the Korea Stock Exchange, *Ten-Year History of Korea Stock Exchange,* 1968. It is also found in the Korea Security Dealers Association, *Twenty-Year History of Korea Security Dealers Association,* 1973.

was established as the nation's securities trading market in March 1956. The principal trading item on the KSE until late 1961 had been government bonds issued during the Korean War. Since late 1961, however, trading of stocks became the primary activity in the market, and at the same time, the KSE became the center of frantic speculation. The speculation was mainly on so-called "security group shares" which consisted of shares of the Korea Stock Exchange itself, and those of the Korea Securities Finance Corporation. The episode of speculations on these shares ended with a stock market crash resulting in a three month closing of the KSE in February 1963.

During this process, many "innocent" participants in the securities market got hurt and the public in general became suspicious about participating in the market. This general public attitude toward the securities market obviously contributed to the depressed market activities in the following period. This low level of activity in the market continued into 1967.

As pointed out earlier, since 1968 the government has taken various measures to promote both new-issue and trading markets. With these governmental efforts, both markets showed some improvements in their performances. Before examining the long-term corporate securities market, it seems worthwhile to review some of the important governmental measures taken to promote the market in the present section.

These measures can be classified into three broad categories: namely, those to stimulate/force business corporations to go public (to increase the supply of corporate securities), those to create demands for corporate securities, and those to make the market more efficient and stable.

The first important measure to be considered here is the introduction in November 1967 of a new concept for corporate income tax purposes. This is the concept of a "publicly-held corporation"[22] which enjoys various privileges over other corporations. For example, publicly-held corporations are treated favorably under the Corporate Income Tax Law. The maximum tax differential vis-a-vis non-publicly-held corporations can be as great as 13 percent.[23]

[22] See Appendix.

[23] Corporate Income Tax Schedule*

Taxable Income (TY)	Other Corporations	Publicly-held Corporations	Difference
$TY < 1$ million won	20	16	4
$1 \leq TY < 5$ million won	30	20	10
$TY \geq 5$ million won	40	27	13

*The amount of tax is calculated incrementally according to the following schedule.

Publicly-held corporations are supposed to calculate their ordinary depreciation allowances according to the depreciation provisions of the Corporate Income Tax Law. In addition, for tax purposes, they are allowed to add 20 percent of their ordinary depreciation allowances so calculated. As pointed out earlier, personal income tax is currently paid on retained earnings of non-publicly-held corporations at the rate of 5 percent just as if they were paid out as dividends. This tax is also exempted for the publicly-held corporations. There are other special privileges for these publicly-held corporations: e.g., instalment payments for corporate income tax are allowed, contributions to various reserves may be treated as costs, and favorable treatment is given when obtaining loans from financial institutions.

In essence, the introduction of this new concept is to induce corporations to go public and therefore to increase the supply of corporate equities to the public.

The November 1968 enactment of "the Law for Promotion of the Capital Market" is another major event in the development of the capital market. This law includes each of the three aspects of demand creation, supply stimulation, and market development. Major factors for an increased demand by the public, for example, are a non-government shareholders dividends guarantee,[24] permission for use of stocks of publicly-held corporations as deposits to the central and local governments and to government-controlled corporations, and personal income tax exemptions of dividend income from publicly-held corporations.[25] In accordance with the Law for Promotion of the Capital Market, the Korea Investment Corporation (KIC) was established to facilitate issuing, distributing and underwriting securities, and to stabilize security prices. The purpose of the establishment of KIC was to stimulate the supply of, and demand for, securities and to help build an efficient capital market.[26]

"The Law for Inducing Business Corporations to go Public" was enacted

---

[24] According to the original Implementation Decree of the Law, non-government shareholders are guaranteed to receive dividend payments at a rate of 10 percent per annum. This was recently revised so that the rate would be the same as the interest rate on a one-year time deposit.

[25] Minority shareholders' (defined as those shareholders who own less than 3/100 of total shares outstanding) dividend income is considered to be non-taxable for income tax purposes (See the Income Tax Law, Article 7). Large shareholders are treated favorably in their integrated income tax calculations (the Income Tax Law, Article 27).

[26] The KIC is permitted to engage in activities of financing (with securities as collateral), investment trust, corporate debenture guarantee, security saving, security loans, and security issues.

in December 1972. This new law has the stated purposes of "encouraging privately-held corporations to go public, facilitating domestic resource mobilization, helping improve the corporate financial structure, and encouraging the public's participation in business enterprises for the national goal of economic development."[27] In fact, the aim is not only to encourage, but to force "appropriate"[28] corporations to go public by punitive measures to be taken against those appropriate corporations not going public. Punitive measures include unfavorable treatment in calculating corporate and personal income tax, and possible limitations set for those corporations in getting loans from financial institutions.

As the title implies this Law is mostly concerned with creating a sufficient supply of good corporate equity shares to the public. As such, the Law includes, in addition to various punitive provisions, the following important privileges given to publicly-held corporations so as to stimulate the supply of corporate equity shares to the public.

Firstly, a special privilege is given to them with regard to their asset revaluation. According to the Law on Asset Revaluation, all corporations are allowed to revalue their operating (but not non-operating) assets once every two years at most. Publicly-held corporations, however, are allowed to revalue their non-operating land just once, and the tax rate on the asset revaluation gain is 27 percent even though according to the provisions of Article 13 of the Asset Revaluation Law it is 40 percent for other corporations.

Secondly, another special provision gives incentives for large shareholders of privately-held corporations to open their corporations to the

---

[27] See Article 1 of the Law.

[28] According to Article 4 of the Law, the Minister of Finance shall select "appropriate corporations" based on the total capital, financial situation, ability to pay dividends, stock trading prospects, the security market trend, etc., from among "eligible corporations" and order these corporations to go public. The Implementation Decree of the Law specifies the conditions required for appropriate corporations. They are if, 1) total equity including reserves is over 50 million won, 2) at least two years have passed since establishment, 3) at least 10 percent dividend payment is expected, and 4) the price of the stock is expected to be above par-value of the stock in view of the stock market situation. An "eligible corporation", in turn, is defined as follows: 1) a corporation which, under the provisions of the Foreign Capital Inducement Law, obtained an authorization for a cash loan contract or a capital equipment procurement contract in excess of its own equity, 2) a corporation with a private loan (including an adjusted private loan according to the August 3rd Presidential Emergency Decree) over 100 million won, 3) a corporation whose loans from financial institutions total 1 billion won or more, and 4) a corporation which is, by its nature, deemed desirable to go public for the economic development of the nation.

public. A tax deduction equivalent to 50 percent of the tax on dividend income included in the integrated personal income tax is allowed for those large shareholders who own less than 30/100 of total shares outstanding.

Another major governmental measure was recently taken. This is the May 29 announcement of "Presidential Special Instruction" of 1975 which prompted the Ministry of Finance to take various measures which are to affect both ends of the capital market and especially the new-issue market. These measures were taken to pressure big businesses into going public and to keep publicly-held shares over 20–30 percent of total shares outstanding. Encouragement is given to allow a majority shareholder only up to 30 percent of the shares as opposed to the present limit of 51 percent. These measures will obviously affect the supply side of the market.

In attempts to stimulate demand for securities due to the announcement of the Instructions, various securities saving schemes were created, securities investment trusts were expanded, securities investment financing was increased, institutional investors' purchase of securities was encouraged, and information regarding securities investments was made more readily available to the public.

To make the new-issue market more efficient, a new underwriting system was introduced with an underwriting fund of 10 billion won (6 billion won for stocks and 4 billion won for corporate debentures). Until recently, there were rare cases of strict underwriting in Korea. Most new issues have been marketed on a stand-by or a best-effort basis. Underwriters designated by the new system consist of the KIG, security firms with equity of over 300 million won, commercial paper dealers, institutions including commercial, trust, and development banks, and insurance companies.

In addition to these measures, various institutional and regulatory reforms have been introduced with regard to the trading market. Most importantly, in February 1969, the futures transaction method of trading was eliminated as it had been primarily responsible for the stock market speculation experienced in the early 1960's. A major trading method reform[29] and new listing system[30] were also introduced in June 1971. These

[29] Currently, most stock transactions are made by the "regular way" method. The regular way transaction is settled through the clearing section of the KSE on the third business day following the day of contract. A few transactions are on a "cash" basis by which the settlement of a contract is made with the delivery of cash and shares through the clearing department of the KSE on the day of contract.

[30] Listing of securities means to designate securities as objects of trading on the KSE. In June 1971, two separate sections of trading in which listed securities are traded were

measures are, in essence, to make the trading market more stable and efficient.

Besides these measures which directly affect the capital market, there have been other governmental actions which affected the market indirectly, e.g., repeated downward adjustments of interest rates started since June 1969.

So far, we have been mostly concerned with measures regarding the corporate equity shares market. What about the market for corporate debentures? Since 1971, the government has attempted to help transfer funds from the private loan market (or curb market) to the organized financial market. For example, an income tax exemption was introduced in December 1971 under the Personal Income Tax Law for the interest income from those corporate debentures sold, or arranged to be sold, by the KIC, trust companies, insurance companies, security firms, and financial institutions such as the Korea Development Bank or Korea Development Financing Corporation, provided their maturities are over one year and the debenture holders have less than 10 percent of total debentures issued. In addition, another measure which directly contributed to the development of the corporate debentures market was the introduction of "the Law for Registering Public and Private Bonds" in January 1970. This Law is to protect bondholders' rights and to facilitate bond issues.

In this section we have considered some of the important policy measures taken to affect favorably the nation's corporate securities market. In sum, these measures were designed to stimulate demand for, and/or supply of, long-term corporate securities. For adopting effective future policy measures, the most important thing is to determine which constraint—demand or supply—is primarily responsible for the currently underdeveloped Korean capital market.[31]

Of course, these policy measures should be adopted after carefully exa-

established. Listing of securities on these sections is based on screening standards such as the years since the establishment of the corporation, the amount of paid-in equity capital, total number of shareholders, dividend payment ability, share distribution status, and the volume of monthly trading. All newly-listed stocks are automatically in Section 2 of the KSE. They are moved to Section 1 as they meet various requirements.

[31]This issue has been well discussed with regard to the Greek capital market. See, for example, George Maniatis, "Reliability of the Equities Market to Finance Industrial Development in Greece," *Economic Development and Cultural Change,* July 1971, and Diomedes D. Psilos, *Capital Market in Greece* (Athens: Center of Economic Research, 1964). Related discussions are also found in U Tun Wai and Hugh Patrick, *op. cit.*

mining their possible impact on the rest of the nation's financial system, since the ultimate goal for these actions is to make the financial system most efficient in mobilizing and allocating resources.

With this background, let us now turn to the following section in which the development of the market during the 1963–1974 period is examined.

IV. Current Development of the Long-Term Corporate Securities Market of Korea

Before describing the current status of the long-term corporate securities market, let us first examine the following table. As indicated earlier, total new-issues from flow-of-funds accounts include both publicly-issued and privately-distributed corporate securities. The following table presents proportions of publicly-issued[32] corporate securities in total new issues. The proportion of securities offered to the public through the capital market has become substantial only since 1972 when major policy measures were taken to encourage/force corporations to go public as discussed in the previous section. This phenomenon can be seen in greater detail in Table 6 which summarizes new-issue market activities during the 1963-the 1st half of 1973 period.

The new-issue market for corporate equities was not active before 1968, being confined to a few cases of new-issues offered to existing shareholders through subscription rights. Substantial portions of these issues were in turn made by the Korea Electric Company (KECO) and commercial banks. Fluctuations in capital-increases by the KECO and commercial banks were primarily responsible for overall fluctuations in total new-issues until very recently, as seen in Table 7.

Let us carefully examine the new-issue market for corporate equities in reference to Table 6. There are, broadly speaking, three ways of issuing new shares for increasing corporate capital: offering shares to 1) existing shareholders by granting subscription rights, 2) selected groups or persons by giving subscription priorities, and 3) the general public. As seen from Table 6, most issues were offered to existing shareholders by granting subscription rights. Issues to employees or other such selected groups are still minimal. New-issues to the general public increased drastically in 1973,

[32]Strictly speaking, public-issues should include only those new-issues offered to the public. Shares distributed to existing shareholders through subscription rights are also considered to be publicly-issued for our discussion purpose here, however.

Table 5. *Public-Issues as Compared to Total New-Issues*

(billion current won)

		Total New-Issues (A)	Public-Issues[1] (B)	B/A × 100
1969	1st qr.	23.63	1.10	4.66
	2nd qr.	19.72	3.85	19.52
	3rd qr.	15.03	1.93	12.84
	4th qr.	21.13	1.32	6.25
	Total	79.51	8.20	10.31
1970	1st qr.	23.15	1.32	5.70
	2nd qr.	28.42	4.21	14.81
	3rd qr.	20.96	0.16	0.76
	4th qr.	10.14	2.60	25.64
	Total	82.67	8.29	10.03
1971	1st qr.	20.84	1.03	4.94
	2nd qr.	23.42	0.47	2.01
	3rd qr.	27.76	0.90	3.24
	4th qr.	38.17	1.32	3.46
	Total	110.19	3.72	3.38
1972	1st qr.	44.40	3.47	7.82
	2nd qr.	35.69	8.52	23.87
	3rd qr.	33.96	7.14	21.02
	4th qr.	117.85	0.93	0.79
	Total	231.90	26.06	11.24
1973	1st qr.	70.78	5.63	7.95
	2nd qr.	59.17	12.58	21.26
	3rd qr.	43.18	19.88	46.04
	4th qr.	81.40	16.20	19.90
	Total	254.53	54.29	21.33
1974	1st qr.	58.01	14.27	24.60
	2nd qr.	62.25	22.10	35.50

Sources: Same as Table 2, for (A), and Korea Stock Exchange, *Stock*, various issues, for (B).

Note: [1] includes stocks distributed through subscription rights.

Table 6. *New-Issue Market Activities, 1963–1974 (1st half)*

(thousand current won)

	STOCKS						Debentures	Total	
	New-Issues			Existing Shares[1]					
Year	Total (A)=(B)+(C)	Offered to the Public (B)	Offered to Existing Shareholders[2] (C)	Total (D)=(E)+(F)	Offered to the Public (E)	Offered to the Public via Auction[3] (F)	(G)	(H)=(A)+(G)	(I)=(A)+(D)+(G)
1963	607,634 (4)	—	607,634 (4)		—	—	—	607,634 (4)	607,634 (4)
1964	368,625 (2)	—	368,625 (2)	27,909	—	27,909	—	368,625 (2)	396,534 (2)
1965	100,038 (1)	—	100,038 (1)	17,236	—	17,236	—	100,038 (1)	117,274 (1)
1966	368,986 (3)	—	368,986 (3)	1,103,654	—	1,103,654	—	368,986 (3)	1,472,640 (3)
1967	1,300,555 (3)	—	1,300,555 (3)	49,598	—	49,598	—	1,300,555 (3)	1,350,153 (3)
1968	20,477,339 (12)	160,000 (2)	20,317,339 (10)	726,641	—	726,641	—	20,477,339 (12)	21,203,980 (12)
1969	8,193,625 (18)	2,210,550 (12)	5,983,075 (6)	15,747	—	15,747	—	8,193,625 (18)	8,209,372 (18)
1970	8,293,323 (22)	2,068,369 (9)	6,224,954 (13)	—	—	—	—	8,293,323 (22)	8,293,323 (22)
1971	2,940,000 (11)	850,000 (4)	2,090,000 (7)	—	—	—	—	2,940,000 (11)	2,940,000 (11)
1972	16,129,715 (37)	3,249,996 (7)	12,879,719 (30)	125,000 (1)	125,000 (1)	—	9,928,000 (35)	26,057,715 (72)	26,182,715 (73)
1973	50,843,697 (88)	17,426,815 (35)	33,416,882 (53)	4,014,500 (10)	3,336,500 (10)	678,000	3,450,000 (12)	54,293,697(100)	58,308,197(110)
1974 I	23,147,392 (36)	8,526,992 (11)	14,620,400 (25)	4,461,116 (6)	4,461,116 (6)	—	13,220,000 (32)	36,367,392 (68)	40,828,508 (74)

Sources: Korea Stock Exchange, *Stock*, various issues and "Stock Market" (daily bulletin), various issues.

Notes: Figures in parentheses are the numbers of issues.

[1] existing shares of privately-held corporations offered to the public.

[2] includes shares of public corporations taken by the government.

[3] auction held in the case of block trading.

Table 7. New-Issues of Corporate Stocks, 1963–1974 (1st half)

(thousand current won)

Year	KECO & Commercial Banks (A)	Total New-Issues (B)	New-Issues Excluding (A)
1963	—	607,634	607,634
1964	—	368,625	368,625
1965	—	100.038	100,038
1966	—	368,986	368,986
1967	516,698	1,300,555	783,857
1968	18,588,153	20,477,339	1,889,186
1969	4,098,739	8,193,625	4,094,886
1970	1,813,365	8,293,323	6,479,958
1971	—	2,940,000	2,940,000
1972	5,448,309	16,129,715	10,681,406
1973	19,081,663	50,843,697	31,762,034
1974	4,995,400	23,147,392	18,151,992

Source: Korea Stock Exchange, *Stock,* September 1974.

especially in the first quarter of the year. This phenomenon was due primarily to the introduction in late 1972 of the Law for Inducing Business Corporations to Go Public and the historical record of the economic expansion of Korea experienced in 1973.[33]

The pricing of new-issues[34] is traditionally on a par-value basis even for those new-issues offered to the general public. Since 1972, however, new-issues with premiums started to appear in Korea.[35]

This pricing of a new-issue with a premium is closer to market-value pricing. In a strict sense, the par-value of a stock is not necessarily related to the "intrinsic value" of the stock involved but is merely a stated figure in the corporate charter. Consequently, it has little economic significance. Despite this fact, however, current pricing is mostly on a par-value basis and dividends are paid according to the par-value of a stock.

In the case of Japan,[36] corporations have traditionally adopted the

[33] The GNP growth rate in real terms was 16.9 percent in 1973.

[34] For discussions on the new-issue pricing and the behavior of newly-issued stocks during 1973, see Il SaKong, "Some Observations on the Securities Market of Korea", KDI Working Paper 7410, 1974.

[35] The average premium for all 33 cases since 1972 was 116 percent.

[36] See Japan Securities Research Institute, *Securities Market in Japan,* Tokyo, Japan, 1973, pp. 21–22.

"partial public offering" method whereby some of the new issues are offered to the general public according to the market price of the stock at the time of their issue and the remainder is allotted to shareholders or other specific persons based on a fixed price. Since the market-value pricing method for an entire block of issue was introduced in January 1969, this pricing method has become increasingly popular and accounted for 69 percent of total paid-in capital increases in 1972.

Of course, there would be various merits of the market-value pricing vis-a-vis par-value pricing method. Among them are: 1) that the issuing company will be able to finance investment at a lower cost, 2) that resources will be allocated more efficiently as financing is to be market-tested, and 3) that purchases of new-issues only for the purpose of short-term capital gain will be eliminated.[37] As an outright underwriting system is widely adopted and the capital market is broadened to leave no room for manipulations, the market-value pricing method should eventually be adopted.

As seen from Table 6, the corporate debentures market did not exist in Korea before 1972. Thanks primarily to various previously discussed government measures favorable to the development of the market, it began operations in 1972. Information on the corporate debentures market since 1972 is summarized in Table 8.

One thing that is very clear at this point is that total domestic savings mobilized through new-issue markets for stocks and debentures are still rather small when compared to total resources mobilized for investment. This can be seen easily from Table 9 in which total stocks and debentures issued are compared to total fixed investment.[38]

Before turning to trading market activities, let us consider stock-dividends originating from the transfer of asset revaluation gains, and/or profit surplus, to capital. As was indicated earlier, according to the Law on Asset Revaluation, corporations are allowed to revalue their operating fixed assets once every two years at most. The following table presents the amounts and cases involved with stock-dividends since 1963.

It was pointed out earlier that for various reasons the majority of listed

[37] As new-issues in general were undervalued in the past, there was an over-subscription phenomenon in the new-issue market of Korea. This over-subscription phenomenon was fanned by a short-term speculative motive among participants in the market. A discussion on this matter is included in SaKong, *op. cit.*

[38] Total fixed investment figures are for both financial and corporate sectors from the flow-of-funds accounts. The reason for including the financial sector was simply that new-issues to be compared with fixed capital formation include those issues made by the financial sector.

Table 8. Corporate Debentures Issues

Year	Classification	Number of Issues	Average Interest Rate[1]	Average Maturity[2]	Total Amount of Issues Involved	Average Amount of Issues Involved[3]
1972	Ordinary Bonds	23	23.8	2	6,278,000	268,608
	Guaranteed Bonds	11	21.6	2	3,350,000	304,545
	Convertible Bonds	1	21.0	2	300,000	300,000
1973	Ordinary Bonds	6	18.0	2	1,750,000	291,667
	Guaranteed Bonds	6	16.2	2	1,700,000	283,333
1974.5.	Ordinary Bonds	17	19.5	2	8,350,000	491,176
	Guaranteed Bonds	19	18.3	2	6,670,000	351,053

Source: Korea Stock Exchange, *Stock,* July 1974.

Notes: Guaranteed debentures are those guaranteed by the KIC and banks.

[1] in percent per annum.

[2] in years.

[3] in thousand current won.

Table 9. Total Stocks and Debentures Issues and Fixed Capital Formation

(billion current won)

Year	Domestic Fixed Investment (A)	Fixed Investment by Corporate and Financial Sectors (B)	Total Stocks & Debentures Issued[1] (C)	(B)/(A) ×100 (D)	(C)/(B) ×100 (E)
1963	68.04	40.76	0.61	59.9	1.5
1964	81.44	42.19	0.37	51.8	0.9
1965	119.17	48.38	0.10	40.6	0.2
1966	208.69	111.71	0.37	53.5	0.3
1967	272.96	168.94	1.30	61.9	0.8
1968	411.66	229.04	20.48	55.6	8.9
1969	552.94	321.25	8.19	58.1	2.6
1970	650.20	370.11	8.29	56.9	2.2
1971	729.72	408.30	2.94	56.0	0.7
1972	780.23	428.72	26.06	55.0	6.1
1973	1,169.43	691.32	54.29	59.1	7.9

Sources: Bank of Korea, *Monthly Economic Statistics,* September 1974, for (A); Same sources for Table 2, for (B); and Korea Stock Exchange, *Stock,* Various issues, for (C).

Note: [1] public-issues as defined earlier.

Table 10. Stock Dividends, 1963–1974 (1st Half)

(thousand current won)

Year	Amount
1963	6,707,742 (8)
1964	4,762,213 (5)
1965	21,200 (1)
1966	8,000 (1)
1967	16,276,441 (11)
1968	22,665,777 (5)
1969	12,012,091 (13)
1970	3,863,326 (11)
1971	3,171,555 (12)
1972	6,340,118 (7)
1973	13,392,366 (16)
1974.I.	40,846,824 (21)

Source: Korea Stock Exchange, *Stock,* Various issues.
Note: Figures in parentheses are the number of cases involved.

corporations did not revalue their assets even once during the 1963–1974 period. It was also indicated that shareholders in Brazil seem to value stock dividends as much as cash dividends. It is the same in Korea. Let us examine the cause of this phenomenon.

A stock dividend, theoretically speaking, does not directly increase stockholders' total wealth nor the net worth of the company.[39] A stock dividend is made to existing stockholders in the same proportion, and consequently, a stockholder's proportional ownership remains unaltered. Since the number of shares of stock outstanding, however, is increased due to a stock dividend, earnings per share would be lowered proportionally even though total earnings available to shareholders would remain the same. Presumably, the market price of the stock will decline if everything else is constant, so that the total market value of each shareholder stays the same. If this is the case, the stock dividend with no cash dividend means nothing but additional stock certificates. Why then, do investors in Korea consider stock dividends worthwhile?

The stock dividend can be valuable to investors if the company promises to maintain the same cash dividend per share even after the stock dividend. This is more or less the case in Korea where dividends are paid as a certain percent of the par-value of a stock. At the same time, pressures are

[39] For a good discussion on the subject, see James C. Van Horne, *Financial Management and Policy* (New Jersey; Prentice-Hall, Inc., 1968), pp. 274–277.

put on corporations by concerned authorities to maintain a certain percentage of dividends. Consequently, investors consider stock dividends valuable. Whether or not the increase in cash dividend per shareholder in fact has a positive effect on shareholder wealth, however, will depend on the trade-off between current dividends and future dividends via growth.

Another possible positive aspect of the stock dividend to existing shareholders might be psychological in the sense that they can sell the entire shares which were originally purchased and still keep some.

Now, let us turn to the trading market for long-term corporate securities in Korea.

Table 11 shows the marked spurt in KSE activity in 1972, and even more dramatically, during 1973.[40] Unusually high average share turnover ratios for earlier years are due primarily to a particular trading method (i.e., the futures transaction method), utilized until recently. This ratio has been recently stabilized at a rather lower level.[41]

The following table presents the distribution over time of listed stock ownership by various groups in Korea. As of July 1974, there were only 204,550 shareholders in Korea according to shareholder lists of companies listed on the Stock Exchange. A large number of these shareholders, however, are counted more than once simply because they own shares in more than one company. According to a survey conducted by the Korea Security Dealers Association in January of last year,[42] 35 percent out of those who held securities at the time of the survey held one security, 33 percent of them held two securities, 27 percent of them held 3 to 10 securities, and 5 percent held more than 10 securities.[43] If we consider this as a reasonable reflection of the shareholder population in Korea, the actual number of shareholders would be much smaller.[44] It might not be too unreasonable

[40] As indicated earlier, various government measures taken and the period's rapid economic expansion were primarily responsible for this phenomenon.

[41] In November 1972, this ratio reached a record high of 120.6 percent on the Tokyo Stock Exchange on an annual basis. Usually, however, it stayed between 30 and 50 percent during the 1960's (See Japan Securities Research Institute, *op. cit.*, p. 43).

[42] Korea Security Dealers Association, *The First Survey Report on the Trend of Security Investment,* January 1974.

[43] The Survey covered not only stocks but bonds.

[44] It is believed that there are some who purchase shares of a company stock under different names to conceal the concentration of ownership of the company stock. Some securities companies also carry their customers' stocks under their names on shareholder lists. Both of these practices put a downward bias into the reported figure, but we consider the bias not to be as substantial as the ownership of multiple stocks by shareholders.

to assume the figure to be around 50,000. What this suggests is that the "penetration ratio" measured by the proportion of the total population[45] is in the neighborhood of 0.1 percent. Even if we take the reported shareholder figure liberally, the penetration ratio is still only 0.6 percent. These ratios indicate the shallowness of stock ownership penetration in Korea.[46] The table also shows that as of July 1974, individuals as a group account for almost 98 percent of total shareholders and the group owned 56 percent of total shares listed.[47] The average number of shares per individual shareholder is calculated to be 1,282 shares, which is rather substantial.

Table 11. Current Status of Listed Stocks on the KSE

As of the end of	Number of Companies Listed (A)	Number of Shareholders (B)	Number of Shares Listed (C)	Paid-in Capital (D)	Total Market Value (E)	Sales Volume (F)
1963	15	14,823	31,973,133	16,971,133	10,024,719	57,653,173
1964	17	13,878	27,021,126	22,228,116	17,084,500	316,617
1965	17	14,820	28,933,103	23,162,409	15,566,077	43,047
1966	24	31,767	42,936,070	32,450,943	19,507,981	48,684
1967	24	33,064	59,446,277	46,083,353	38,475,664	72,029
1968	34	39,986	114,861,833	96,585,361	64,323,410	76,342
1969	42	54,318	141,041,810	119,902,298	86,569,423	98,325
1970	48	76,276	158,965,146	134,292,367	97,922,555	78,384
1971	50	81,923	170,211,718	141,356,684	108,706,133	49,852
1972	66	103,266	209,755,045	174,338,694	245,980,705	83,963
1973	104	199,999	305,053,433	251,620,053	426,246,648	129,800
1974. 7.	122	204,550	439,648,653	344,039,163	489,848,002	11,703
1974. 9.	127	206,187	466,079,752	363,768,407	492,832,989	9,367

[45] Raymond W. Goldsmith, *Financial Structure and Development* (New Haven and London: Yale University Press, 1969), p. 357.

[46] In comparison, as of December 1973, there were 17,580,000 shareholders in Japan according to the National Stock Exchange's, *A Survey of Japanese Stock Distribution,* August 1974. A penetration ratio based on this figure is about 16 percent. The actual penetration for Japan might be estimated to be around 5 to 6 percent. As a matter of fact, Goldsmith's calculation of penetration ratios for Japan included in his book (p. 358) do not consider multiple stock ownership, and that is why the ratio was 6 percent in 1963. According to the New York Stock Exchange, the actual penetration ratio for the U.S. in 1972 was around 16 percent. Since the New York Stock Exchange figure is based on a stock population survey, the calculated ratio reflects actual penetration.

[47] The individual share ownership is on an upward trend.

Table 11. *(Continued)*

As of the end of	Sales Value[1] (G)	Average Number of Shares per Shareholder (H) = (C)/(B)	Average Market Value per Share[2] (I) = (E)/(C)	Average Investment per Shareholder[3] (J) = (H)×(I)	Average Share Turn-Over (K) = (F)/(C) × 100	Average Value Turn-Over (L) = (G)/(E) × 100
1963	25,999,879	2,157	314	677,296	180,317.6	259.4
1964	27,038,985	1,947	632	1,230,504	1,171.7	158.3
1965	9,271,092	1,952	538	1,050,338	148.8	59.6
1966	11,160,405	1,352	454	613,808	113.3	57.2
1967	24,916,661	1,798	647	1,163,251	121.2	64.8
1968	19,984,212	2,873	560	1,608,629	66.5	31.1
1969	41,942,109	2,597	614	1,594,309	69.7	48.5
1970	42,142,031	2,084	616	1,283,792	49.3	43.0
1971	33,775,150	2,078	639	1,327.653	29.3	31.1
1972	70,268,753	2,031	1,173	2,382,611	40.0	28.6
1973	160,129,277	1,525	1,397	2,130,809	42.6	37.6
1974. 7.	12,322,983	2,149	1,114	2,394,371	2.7	2.5
1974. 9.	10,259,266	2,260	1,057	2,389,318	2.0	2.1

Source: Korea Stock Exchange, *Stock*, October 1974.
Notes: [1] in thousand current won
[2] in thousand shares
[3] in current won

Table 12. Distribution of Listed Stock Ownership

Year	Number of	Total	By Group Classification					
			Government & Public Entities	Banking Institutions	Securities Companies	Insurance Cos & Other Legal Persons	Individuals	Foreigners
1963	Shareholders	14,823(100)	12 (0.08)	—	381 (2.57)	464 (3.13)	13,966 (44.22)	—
	Shares held	32,167,088(100)	9,510,219(29.57)	—	4,627,179.4(14.38)	7,215,505.9(22.43)	10,814,183.7(33.62)	—
1964	Shareholders	13,878(100)	12 (0.09)	76 (0.54)	341 (2.40)	433 (3.12)	13,016 (93.79)	—
	Shares held	28,670,658(100)	14,599,278(50.92)	4,609,435.3(16.08)	1,899,640.4 (6.63)	1,923,408.4 (6.71)	5,638,895.9(19.67)	—
1965	Shareholders	14,820(100)	20 (0.13)	63 (0.43)	335 (2.26)	446 (3.01)	13,898 (93.78)	58 (0.39)
	Shares held	28,387,103(100)	16,011,637(55.34)	2,452,663 (8.48)	1,901,120 (6.57)	2,060,472.4 (9.01)	5,903,693.6(20.40)	57,517 (0.20)
1966	Shareholders	31,767(100)	71 (0.22)	68 (0.21)	340 (1.07)	493 (1.55)	30,742 (96.78)	53 (0.17)
	Shares held	42,963,070(100)	27,209,843(63.33)	2,823,048 (6.57)	1,801,035 (4.19)	4,563,647.4(10.62)	6,502,979.6(15.14)	62,517 (0.15)
1967	Shareholders	33,064(100)	75(0.23)	81 (0.24)	324 (0.98)	490 (1.48)	32,038 (96.90)	56 (0.17)
	Shares held	63,710,307(100)	39,641,157(62.22)	4,405,232 (6.91)	1,819,066.8 (2.85)	6,465,444.4(10.15)	11,312,218.8(17.78)	67,188 (0.11)
1968	Shareholders	39,986(100)	71 (0.18)	90 (0.22)	347 (0.87)	1,172 (2.93)	38,239 (95.63)	67 (0.17)
	Shares held	115,481,833(100)	50,568,278(43.79)	23,712,446(20.53)	2,097,729.8 (1.82)	12,816,025.4(11.10)	26,125,969.8(22.62)	161.392 (0.14)
1969	Shareholders	54,318(100)	50 (0.09)	125 (0.23)	517 (0.95)	1 433 (2.64)	52,122 (95.94)	81 (0.15)
	Shares held	143,234,139(100)	59,409,901.4(41.47)	26,754,021(18.68)	2,661,618 (1.86)	14,020,305 (9.79)	40,130,547.6(28.02)	257,746 (0.18)
1970	Shareholders	76,276(100)	59 (0.08)	142 (0.19)	619 (0.81)	1,584 (2.07)	73,774 (96.72)	98 (0.13)
	Shares held	164,654,908(100)	63,930,926.4(38.83)	24,430,794(14.83)	2,641,570.6 (1.61)	16,128,866 (9.79)	57,204,326 (34.74)	318,425 (0.20)
1971	Shareholders	81,923(100)	63 (0.08)	130 (0.16)	649 (0.79)	1,847 (2.25)	79,130 (96.57)	104 (0.13)
	Shares held	175,023,718(100)	62,670,238.4(35.80)	24,420,742(13.95)	2,456,654 (1.41)	18,760,649.6(10.72)	65,604,660.5(37.48)	1,110,773.5(0.64)
1972	Shareholders	103,266(100)	70 (0.46)	147 (0.14)	845 (0.82)	1,962 (1.90)	100,128 (97.00)	114 (0.11)
	Shares held	213,791,456(100)	69,562,068(32.54)	20,212,343 (9.45)	5,608,501 (2.62)	25,909,141 (12.11)	91,131,885 (42.63)	1,367,518 (0.64)
1973	Shareholders	199,999(100)	94 (0.05)	281 (0.14)	1,955 (0.98)	2,430 (1.21)	195,134 (97.57)	105 (0.05)
	Shares held	320,890,733(100)	63,486,100(19.78)	25,250,612 (7.87)	11,483,766 (3.58)	41,826,581 (13.04)	176,995,272 (55.16)	1,848,402 (0.57)
July	Shareholders	204,550(100)	96 (0.05)	357 (0.18)	2,210 (1.08)	2,757 (1.34)	199,016 (97.29)	114 (0.06)
1974	Shares held	452,063,337(100)	76,084,079(16.83)	30,612,901 (6.77)	13,284,064 (2.94)	73,951,095 (16.36)	255,127,756 (56.44)	3,003,442 (0.66)

Source: Korea Stock Exchange, *Stock,* September 1974.

Notes: Figures in parentheses are in percent.

Figures here include those stocks not yet listed but in the process of being listed.

This is due primarily to a few large shareholders in the group as can be seen from the following table 13.

According to this table, 56 percent of the total shareholders, mostly individuals, own only 0.8 percent of shares outstanding, with each individual owning only one to ninety-nine shares. The remaining 33 percent of total shareholders own 100 to 999 shares and as a group they hold only about 4.6 percent of total shares outstanding. These two groups of shareholders, who are mostly individuals, account for 89 percent of the total.

Table 13. Stock Ownership Concentration (as of July 1974)

(unit: percent)

	1–99 Shares	100–1,000 Shares	1,000–10,000 Shares	10,000–100,000 Shares	Over 100,000 Shares
Number of Shareholders	56.08	32.59	9.20	1.89	0.24
Number of Shares	0.76	4.55	12.52	22.77	59.40

Source: Korea Stock Exchange, *Stock*, September 1974.

Table 14. Stocks and Bonds Listed on the KSE (as of December 28, 1974)

	Stocks			Bonds and Debentures		
	1st Section	2nd Section	Total	Public Bonds	Corporate Debentures	Total
Number of Companies	87	41	128	8	42	50
Number of Items[1]	135	86	221	197	54	251
Paid-in Capital[2]	321,162	60,182	381,344			
Balance Outstanding[2]				177,839	22,400	200,239
Sales Value[2,3]	158,986	19,952	178,938			3,175

Source: Korea Stock Exchange, "Stock Market" (daily bulletin), December 28, 1974.

Notes: [1] some companies list several stock or bond issues.
[2] in million current won.
[3] during 1973.

Considering the average market value per share of 1,114 won as of July 1974, their maximum investment is 1,114,000 won. The Korea Security Dealers Association survey previously mentioned also reports that only about 23 percent of investors hold more than one million won worth of shares and about 50 percent of them hold 100,000 won to 500,000 won worth.[48] Institutional investors hold the remaining shares outstanding. This includes the central government and government-controlled corporations which together account for less than three percent of the total shareholders.

Corporate debenture trading on the KSE is rather minimal when compared to total sales value of stocks. As can be seen from Table 14, total public bond and corporate debenture trading together accounted for only about 1.8 percent of total stock trading during 1974.

V. A Concluding Remark

In the capital market savings are transferred from income surplus units to deficit units as capital market instruments (e.g., stocks and bonds) are traded. The supply of such instruments by deficit units (e.g., the business sector), is determined by the relative cost and availability of financing alternatives. On the other hand, the demand for such capital market instruments is based on portfolio considerations on the part of surplus units. As indicated, this study was not intended to do rigorous analyses of financing alternatives available to corporations nor to analyze the portfolio behavior of various economic units. Instead, the primary objective was to describe the actual state of corporate finance and the current development of the capital market of Korea as an important part of the nation's overall financial system. Despite the government's continued effort to develop the capital market by introducing rather innovative measures, the market is still in its infant stage. It is, however, important at this stage for the government to have a balanced look at the overall financial system in adopting an appropriate strategy of financial development for the future. This necessitates more systematic analyses of the nation's financial system as a whole.

[48] This estimation is based on par values or issue prices of stock. Consequently, the market value of their holding might be a bit larger as of July 1974.

REFERENCES

1. Bank of Korea, *Economic Statistics Yearbook*, various issues, Seoul.
2. ________, *Flow of Funds Accounts in Korea, 1963–1970*, Seoul, 1971.
3. ________, *Monthly Economic Statistics*, various issues, Seoul.
4. Economic Planning Board, *Long-Term Perspective of Our Economy*, Seoul, 1973.
5. Goldsmith, Raymond W., *Financial Structure and Development* (New Haven and London: Yale University Press, 1969).
6. Gurley, John G. and Edward S. Shaw, *Money in a Theory of Finance* (Washington, D. C.: The Brookings Institutions, 1960).
7. Japan Securities Research Institute, *Securities Market in Japan*, Tokyo, 1973.
8. Korea Security Dealers Association, *The First Survey Report on the Trend of Security Investment*, Seoul, January 1974.
9. ________, *Twenty-Year History of Korea Security Dealers Association*, Seoul, 1973.
10. Korea Stock Exchange, *Stock*, various issues, Seoul.
11. ________, "Stock Market" (daily bulletin), various issues, Seoul.
12. ________, *Ten-Year History of Korea Stock Exchange*, Seoul, 1968.
13. Maniatis, George, "Reliability of the Equities Market to Finance Industrial Development in Greece," *Economic Development and Cultural Change*, July 1971.
14. National Stock Exchange, *A Survey of Japanese Stock Distribution*, August 1974.
15. Ness, Jr., Walter L., "Financial Markets Innovation as a Development Strategy: Initial Results from the Brazilian Experience," *Economic Development and Cultural Change*, April 1975.
16. Patrick, Hugh T., "Finance, Capital Markets and Economic Growth in Japan," in Sametz, Arnold W. (ed.), *Financial Development and Economic Growth* (New York: New York University Press, 1972).
17. ________, "Financial Development and Economic Growth in Underdeveloped Countries," *Economic Development and Cultural Change*, January 1966.
18. Psilos, Diomedes D., *Capital Market in Greece* (Athens: Center of Economic Research, 1964).
19. SaKong, Il, "Some Observations on the Securities Market of Korea",

KDI Working Paper #7410, 1974.
20. Sametz, Arnold W., "Business Investment Demand," in Polakoff, Murray E. (ed.), *Financial Institutions and Markets* (Boston: Houghton Mifflin Co.), 1970.
21. Trubek, David M., *Law, Planning and the Development of the Brazilian Capital Market*, New York University Institute of Finance Bulletin No. 72–73, April 1971.
22. U Tun Wai and Hugh T. Patrick, "Stock and Bond Issues and Capital Markets in Less Developed Countries," *IMF Staff Papers*, July 1973.
23. Van Horne, James C., *Financial Management and Policy* (New Jersey: Prentice-Hall, Inc., 1968).

APPENDIX

"Publicly-held corporations" are defined as those domestic legal entities whose stock is listed on the KSE or whose capital was raised "publicly" either for the establishment of the corporation or for capital-increase (Article 22 of the Corporate Income Tax Law). At the same time, they must meet the following requirements:

1) The total number of shares held by one shareholder and his "immediate relatives" (defined in the Civil Law) is not to exceed 51/100 of total outstanding shares.

2) Total shares held by minority shareholders (defined as those who own shares less than 3/100 of total shares outstanding) must exceed 30/100 of total shares outstanding less shares held by the Government.

3) The number of minority shareholders is to exceed 200.

In addition, further conditions must be satisfied according to the provision of Article 67 of the Corporate Income Tax Law Implementation Decree, and they are:

1) In case of public offering either for capital-increase or corporate establishment, the total number of shares involved is to exceed 20 percent of the total shares to be issued or outstanding.

2) The stock is to be listed on the KSE within 6 months of the date when the listing requirements are met.

3) The total number of shares traded per month is to be on the average above 2/1000 of the shares outstanding.

These requirements are to be revised according to the tax revision which will become effective in 1975. The revised requirements are as follows:

1) Minority shareholders are defined as those who own less than the value of shares equivalent to the lesser of one percent of total equity (on a par-value basis) or ten million won.

2) The total shares held by minority shareholders shall exceed 40/100 of total shares outstanding. They include shares held by underwriters and employees.

3) The number of minority shareholders shall exceed 300.

4) Monthly average trading shall exceed 0.3 percent of total shares outstanding. In addition, "immediate relatives" are newly defined.

These new requirements are not applicable to currently existing publicly-held corporations until 1977.

PART III

FISCAL STRUCTURE

THE GROWTH PATTERN OF CENTRAL GOVERNMENT EXPENDITURE

*Chuk Kyo Kim**

I. Introduction

The Korean economy has achieved remarkable growth since the early 1960s. The gross national product in real terms rose at an average annual rate of 9.8 percent during the period 1962–1975, and even if we include the post war period 1953–1961, the growth rate of GNP averaged 7.5 percent, which is still very impressive by international comparison.

There is no doubt that this remarkable achievement of the Korean economy over the last two decades is, to a considerable extent, attributable to the aggressive fiscal policy followed by the government. Despite the important role the government played in the development process of the Korean economy, little attempt has been made to analyze the government sector of the economy in a long-term historical context, particularly in the field of government expenditures, where the existing data pose a number of difficulties due to definitional problems and the lack of consistency.

In view of the problems involved in the existing statistical data, the primary purpose of this paper is to present a consistent time series of government expenditures since 1949, which is essential for any kind of govern-

* Senior Fellow at the Korea Development Institute. This is part of the on-going long-term research on the growth and structural changes in government expenditure in Korea, and was originally published in March 1977 as KDI Working Paper No. 7702.

ment sector analysis, and then, on the basis of this time series data, to explain the growth pattern of government expenditure over the past quarter of a century.

II. Statistical and Conceptual Problems

Before we proceed to analyze the long-term growth of government expenditures, it seems necessary to discuss some of the conceptual and statistical problems which are crucial for this kind of study.

To measure correctly the size of the government sector requires first of all a consistent series of government expenditures based on consolidated government accounts. The official budget statistics are not classified in this way at all. In addition, the scope of the government sector, as defined by official budget statistics, (called "general government sector") covers only a part of the budgetary transactions of the government, and its concept has been changed often. For these reasons the time series data on the general government sector are not appropriate for our purposes.

The Bank of Korea (BOK) has been compiling separate statistics on central government expenditures since 1949. They are classified in economic and functional categories and include the detailed data on expenditures of the individual budgetary accounts. We have relied heavily on these Bank of Korea statistics. However, consolidated expenditure figures have only been published by the Bank of Korea since 1967. Therefore, we attempted to calculate the consolidated revenues and expenditures of the central government for the entire period. We did not use the expenditure figures shown in the economic and functional classification of the Bank of Korea because firstly, the BOK classification is based on the national income accounting concept, which is not suitable for government finance statistics, and secondly, double counting, for example, in social security contributions, is not fully eliminated while some types of expenditures, such as contingency expenditures and reserves, are left out.

Since no reliable time series data are available for local government and extra-budgetary transactions before 1967, our attempt was limited to the budgetary account of the central government. Accordingly, the government sector is here defined to cover only the budgetary transactions of central government accounts. In order to obtain net consolidated expenditure figures, inter-departmental and inter-accounts as well as intra-account transactions are all eliminated, and lending activities are shown on a net basis. For those departmental enterprises such as government enterprise special accounts, capital expenditures only are included in our estimates. The distinction between trading and non-trading services of government is a fairly arbitrary one and we simply followed the classification made by the government.[1]

The classification of government expenditures into economic and functional categories has, as indicated already, been available since 1949. There are, however, some definitional and statistical problems in the BOK classification. Therefore, a number of adjustments were made in the BOK figures, particularly for the period from 1949 to 1956.[2] Since we do not follow the SNA concept, for example, no subtraction was made of the sales of goods and services of business-type special accounts other than government enterprise special accounts. Increase in inventories is also excluded and government lending is shown on a net basis in order to make the BOK figures as consistent as possible with our expenditure figures based on the consolidated account. There are, nevertheless, some differences between the two time series, partly due, as already mentioned, to the omission of some types of expenditures and partly due to some double counting which we could not identify. However, the differences are so small that both series can be used interchangeably, as far as the aggregate level of government expenditure in current prices is concerned.

A final important task was to change the money expenditures into real terms, since inflation has been playing such an important role in the Korean economy. In order to minimize the possible distortions arising from the use of an aggregate price index, such as the wholesale price index, or an aggregate GNP deflator, we used separate price indices for different components of government expenditure. The total expenditures are divided into current expenditures, capital expenditures, and transfers

---

[1] Besides six departmental enterprises which are officially classified as government enterprise special accounts, there are certainly some government trading services, such as a national hospital special account, which are not classified as government enterprises. Therefore, the official classification of government enterprise is problematical. This type of governmental trading service is, however, not treated as a departmental enterprise because it has only a negligible impact on the aggregate expenditure level.

[2] The functional and economic classification made by the Bank of Korea between 1949 and 1956 did not take into account the capital expenditures of government enterprise special accounts. In addition, the calculation of wages and salaries and other current expenditures was not consistent with the criteria used in the later period. Therefore, a substantial adjustment was made to the current as well as capital expenditures from 1949 up to 1956.

and subsidies. The current expenditures are further broken down into wages and salaries, and other current expenditures. Furthermore, a separate price index was used for defense expenditures.

The deflators for the current and capital expenditures are taken from the national income statistics, where fairly detailed deflators for each component of government expenditure are available since 1953. However, some adjustment was made in the BOK deflator for wages and salaries, which we find increased too fast between 1953 and 1959. Therefore, the deflator for wages and salaries was revised based on the wage index of civil servants, and a separate deflator was used for the military. The current transfers and subsidies were deflated by the wholesale price index, while capital transfers to the private sector were deflated by the GNP deflator for private capital formation.

III. The Long-Term Growth of Government Expenditure

As Figure 1 indicates, the expenditure of the central government in money terms shows phenomenal growth over the past quarter of a century, i.e., from 88 million won in 1949 to 1,696 billion won in 1975.

There is no doubt that this extremely rapid growth of government expenditure is, to a considerable extent, attributable to the outbreak of war in 1950 and the continuing inflationary trend of the Korean economy throughout the entire period. Particularly notable is the fact that the expenditures of the central government continued to grow except for small interruptions in 1963 and 1973, showing a more or less linear upward movement. In other words, we cannot clearly see the time pattern of expenditure growth by simply looking at the movement of the aggregate spending level. In order to identify the time pattern, therefore, it seems more appropriate to look at the movement of the share of government expenditure in GNP.

As shown in Figure 2, the share of government expenditure rose considerably over the period under study, but it does not follow any linear upward movement over the entire period. Instead, it shows a characteristic time pattern which is different in different stages of social and economic development. Broadly speaking, we can see three distinct stages of expenditure growth, namely, a rapidly rising trend from 1949 up to 1962, a drastic decline in 1963 and 1964, and, finally, a rising trend again up to 1972.

Figure 1. *GNP and Central Government Expenditure (at Current Prices)*

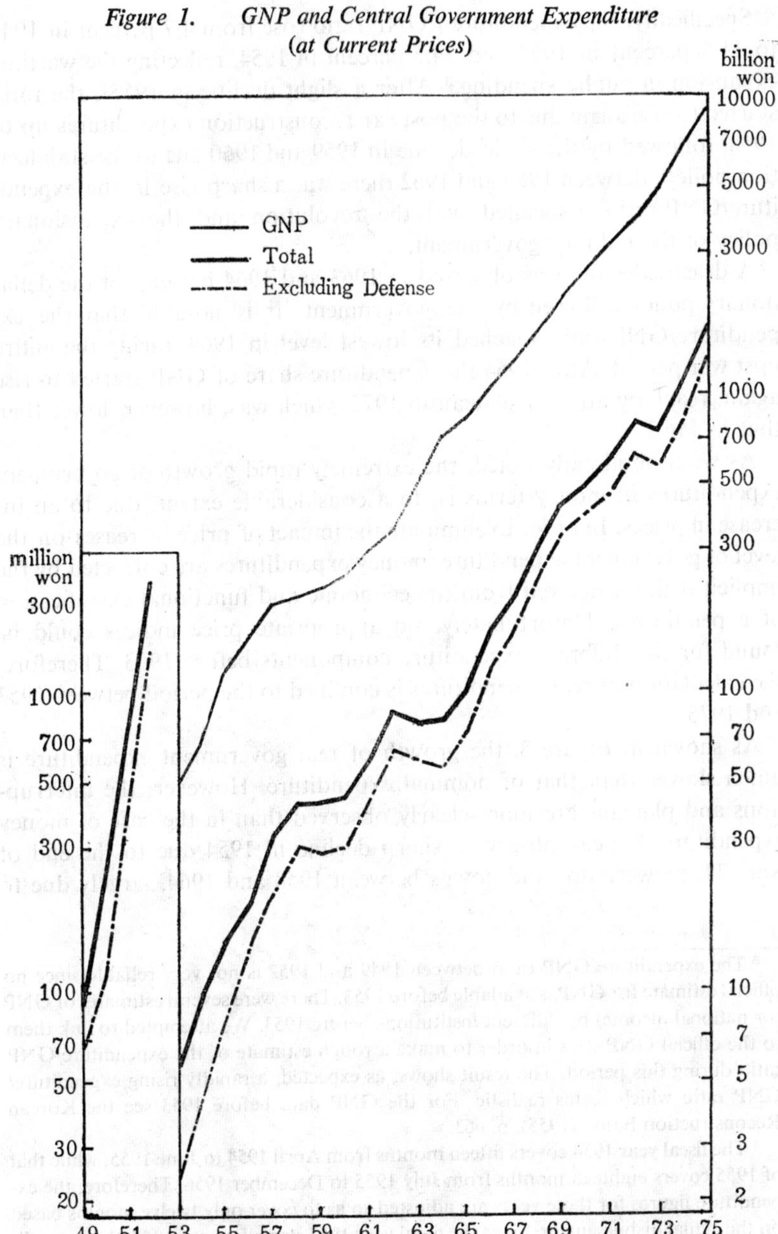

Specifically, the expenditure / GNP ratio rose from 4.7 percent in 1949 to 11.8 percent in 1953 and 14.5 percent in 1954, reflecting the wartime expansion in public spending.[3] After a slight decline in 1955[4], the ratio started to rise again due to the postwar reconstruction expenditures up to 1958, followed by the slight decline in 1959 and 1960 due to the stabilization policy. Between 1960 and 1962 there was a sharp rise in the expenditure/GNP ratio associated with the revolution and the expansionary policy of the military government.

A drastic decline was observed in 1963 and 1964 because of the deflationary policy followed by the government. It is notable that the expenditure/GNP ratio reached its lowest level in 1964 during the entire post war period. After 1964 the expenditure share of GNP started to rise again, reaching another plateau in 1972 which was, however, lower than that in 1962.

As we have already noted, the extremely rapid growth of government expenditures in money terms is, to a considerable extent, due to an increase in prices. In order to eliminate the impact of price increases on the level of government expenditure, money expenditures are corrected by the implicit deflator derived from the economic and functional classification of expenditures. Unfortunately, no appropriate price indices could be found for the different expenditure components before 1953. Therefore, the calculation of real expenditures is confined to the period between 1953 and 1975.

As shown in Figure 3, the growth of real government expenditure is much slower than that of nominal expenditure. However, the interruptions and plateaus are more clearly observed than in the case of money expenditure. We can observe a sharp decline in 1954 due to the end of war. There were ups and downs between 1958 and 1964, largely due to

---

[3] The expenditure/GNP ratio between 1949 and 1952 is not very reliable since no official estimate for GNP is available before 1953. There were several estimates of GNP (or national income) by different institutions before 1953. We attempted to link them to the official GNP data in order to make a rough estimate of the expenditure/GNP ratio during this period. The result shows, as expected, a rapidly rising expenditure/GNP ratio which seems realistic. For the GNP data before 1953 see the Korean Reconstruction Bank, (1955), p. 663.

[4] The fiscal year 1954 covers fifteen months from April 1954 to June 1955, while that of 1955 covers eighteen months from July 1955 to December 1956. Therefore, the expenditure figures for these years are adjusted so as to cover only twelve months based on the actual disbursement. Since the fiscal year 1957 starts January 1957, the expenditure figures for 1956 covers only nine months.

Figure 2. *Central Government Expenditure as Percent of GNP (at Current Prices)*

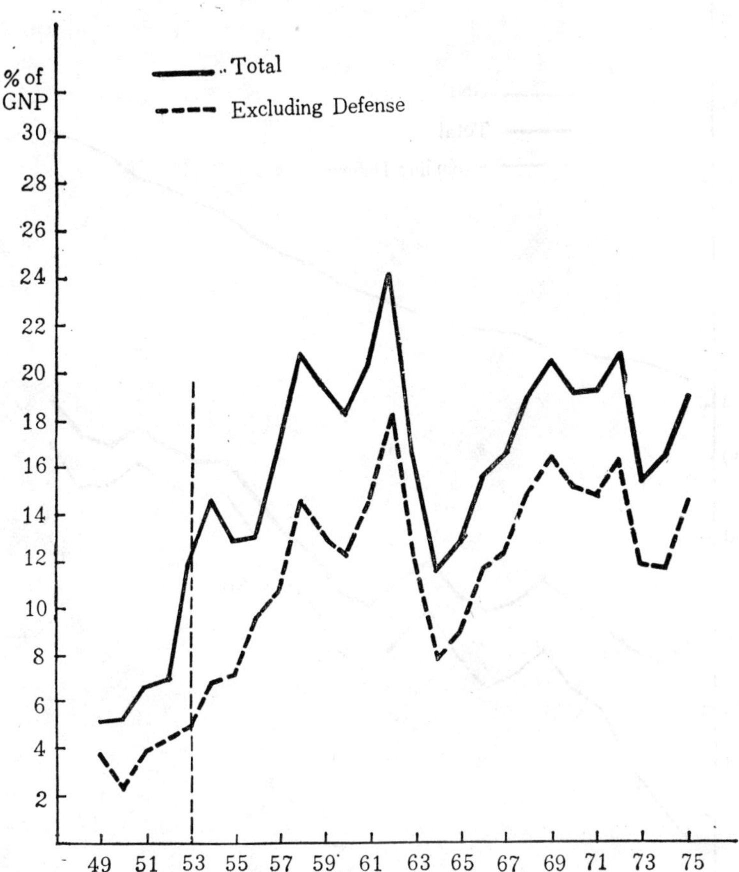

the disruptions resulting from internal revolution and deflationary fiscal policies.

It is also remarkable that non-defense expenditure grew much faster than did total government expenditure over the entire period. This was particularly so between 1953 and 1964 when there was a rapid increase in reconstruction and development expenditure while defense expenditure decreased. The slower growth of total expenditure during this period is

Figure 3. GNP and Central Government Expenditure (at 1970 Constant Prices)

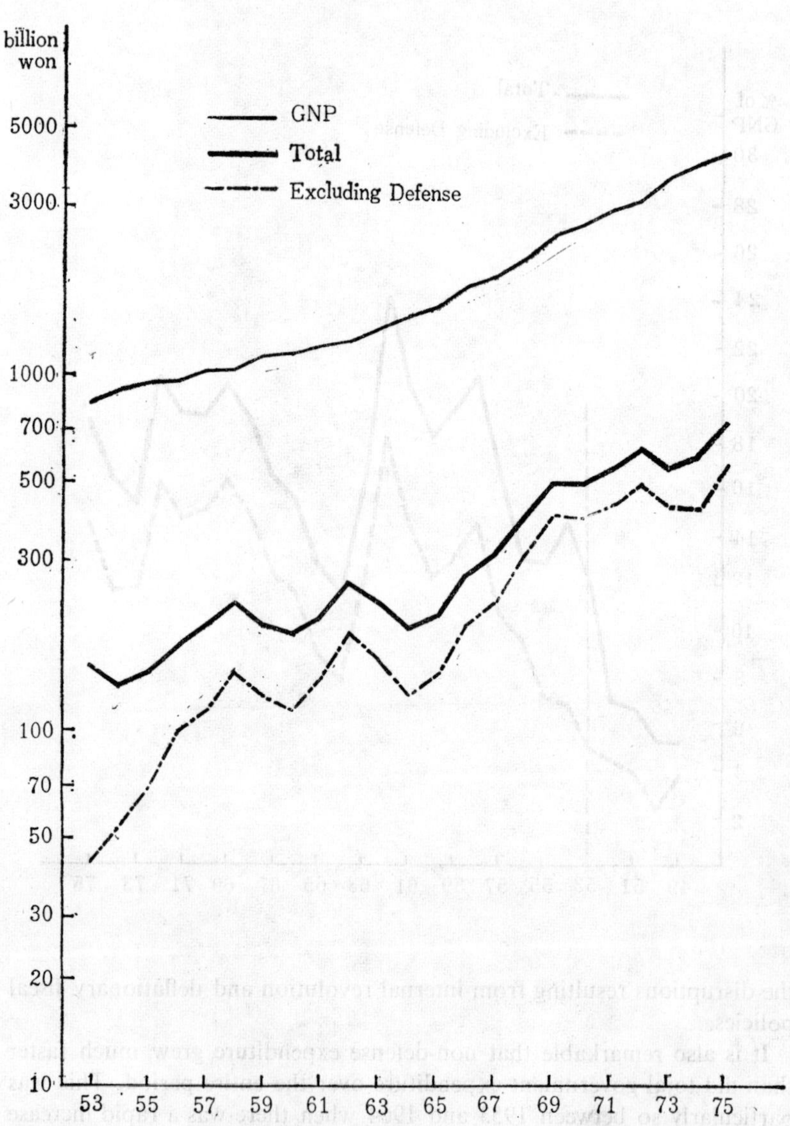

therefore largely due to a decrease in defense expenditure, which on the average accounted for more than 40 percent of total expenditure in real terms between 1953 and 1958.

The expenditure/GNP ratio in real terms has been erratic compared to the money expenditure/GNP ratio between 1953 and 1962 (See Figure 4). Nevertheless, the characteristic time pattern remains basically unchanged, namely; there was a rapid increase in the ratio from 1954 up to 1958 with ups and downs in the subsequent years from 1959 to 1962, and there was a sharp decline in 1963 and 1964 followed by a rising trend up to 1972. There was also a decline in 1973 resulting from the exceptionally high growth of GNP combined with a tight fiscal policy. In other words, there is no clear tendency of an increasing expenditure/GNP ratio over time as far as the aggregate spending level between 1953 and 1975 is concerned. Therefore, we might say that there is no clear evidence of the operation of Wagner's Law over the period under review, though the time period covered may be too short to say anything about the Law.[5]

IV. Time Pattern of Expenditure Growth

The growth pattern observed in the previous section suggests that the temporal behavior of government expenditure can be discussed in terms of disruptions and intervals of rapid growth which seem to be closely related to the growth pattern of the Korean economy. On the basis of this observed pattern, we might divide the whole period into four sub-periods, namely (1) 1950–1953; (2) 1954–1960; (3) 1961–1964; (4) 1965–1972.[6]

The first period 1950 to 1953 are the years of the Korean war during which the government expenditure share of GNP more than doubled, with defense expenditure constituting more than fifty percent of total expenditure. This war time period is followed by the period of expenditure expansion from 1954 to 1960. This is also the period of post war reconstruction during which both GNP and government expenditure underwent a rapid expansion, particularly from 1954 up to 1958. The aggregate government expenditure in real terms rose at 6.1 percent per annum while GNP grew at an annual rate of 4.1 percent between 1954 and 1960. If

[5] For the limitation of Wagner's Law in today's developing countries, see R. A. Musgrave (1969), p. 72.

[6] The years from 1973 to 1975 are omitted for the convenience of discussion.

Figure 4. Central Government Expenditure as Percent of GNP (at 1970 Constant Prices)

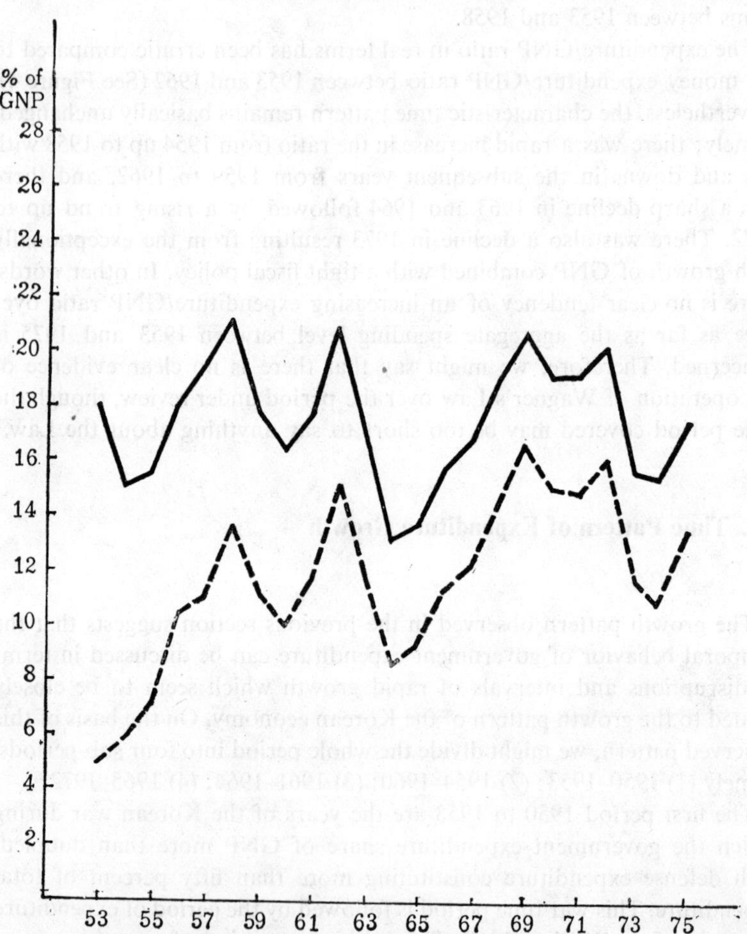

defense expenditures are excluded, the growth of government expenditure is much higher, averaging 15.5 percent per annum(See Table 1).

As a result, the aggregate expenditure/GNP ratio in real terms shows an increasing trend up to 1960, and a sharp increase was observed in the non-defense expenditure share of GNP, which increased from 5.9 percent to 10 percent between 1954 and 1960. Even in per capita terms, the growth rate is striking, 4 percent, compared to 1.8 percent for GNP in the case

Table 1. Growth Rates of GNP, Total Expenditure and Non-Defense Expenditure

Period	GNP	Total Expenditure	Non-Defense Expenditure	Per Capita GNP	Per Capita Total Expenditure	Per Capita Non-Defense Expenditure
1954–60	4.1	6.1	15.5	1.8	4.0	13.3
1961–64	6.8	–1.6	–0.5	3.9	–4.2	–3.2
1965–72	10.3	16.9	19.9	8.2	14.6	17.5
1965–75	10.5	13.7	15.7	8.3	11.4	13.3

Source: See Appendix 2 and 3.

of aggregate expenditure, implying that the income elasticity of expenditure must have been very high during this period.

The third period 1961–1964 is the period of social upheaval and drastic change in economic policy. The military government which came to power in 1961 adopted an expansionary policy and launched the ambitious first five-year development plan in 1962 which resulted in a rapid expansion of government expenditure. The expansionary policy of the military government, however, brought back inflation, which accelerated in the subsequent years.

To cope with the galloping inflation and the increasing revenue constraint due to diminishing foreign aid as a major source of financing, the government followed a deflationary policy in 1963 and 1964, with emphasis given to the elimination of the fiscal deficit, which had been a major source of inflation. The annual financial stabilization program was renewed and the first five-year development plan was scaled down. For the first time since 1949, there was an absolute decline in money government expenditure in 1963 and virtually no increase was made in 1964. In real terms, the government expenditure decreased by 11.6 percent in 1963 and a further decrease of 15.4 percent occurred in 1964. Although the GNP continued to grow at an annual rate of 6.8 percent and despite the substantial increase in 1962, government expenditure decreased at the rate of 1.6 percent per annum between 1961 and 1964, leading to a drastic decline in the expenditure/GNP ratio from 20.7 percent in 1962 to 13.2 percent in 1964. If we look at per capita expenditure, the decline in expenditure is even more striking, averaging 4.2 percent per annum, whereas the per capita GNP maintained a positive growth of 3.9 percent between 1961 and 1964.

After two years of fiscal retrenchment in 1963 and 1964, government expenditure entered the second expansion stage from 1965 to 1972, as the economy regained its growth momentum with relative price stability. Beginning in 1965 the government made serious efforts to increase government revenues, since the tax/GNP ratio continued to decline from 1962 through 1964, while the demand for financing development outlays, which was suppressed during the deflationary years, had been steadily increasing, particularly due to the initiation of the second five-year development plan in 1967.

Thus, a major effort was made to increase tax receipts through an improved tax administration. A new office of national tax administration was established in 1966 and the government undertook a large-scale reform of the internal tax and tariff structure, which was put into effect in 1967. As a result, there was a sharp increase in tax revenues between 1965 and 1972, during which the growth in national tax receipts increased by 36.2 percent annually. The government also adopted a realistic pricing policy for government enterprises, which, together with the improvement of their operational efficiency, made an important contribution to financing development outlays.[7]

Thanks to rapidly increasing tax revenues, coupled with a realistic pricing policy for government enterprises, government expenditure increased very rapidly between 1965 and 1972, showing a 16.8 percent growth rate in real terms, which outstripped the 10.3 percent growth of GNP during the period. Thus, the expenditure/GNP ratio rose from 13.7 percent in 1965 to 20.1 percent in 1972. In per capita terms, the growth rate of government expenditure averaged 14.6 percent compared to 8.2 percent for GNP.

It is notable that both per capita expenditure and per capita income between 1965 and 1975 rose very rapidly, suggesting that government expenditure was increasingly financed by domestic resources. This is in great contrast to the post war period 1954–1960 during which the rapid growth of government expenditure was accompanied by no substantial growth of per capita income, and was financed largely by foreign aid.

V. Determinants of Expenditure Pattern

As we have already noted, Korea has experienced two major disruptions over the past quarter of a century. One was the Korean war from 1950

[7] See S. Kanesa—Thassan (1969). p. 5.

to 1953, which had a far-reaching impact on the growth pattern of government expenditure during the fifties. The other one can be found between 1961 and 1964 when the military revolution, which followed a period of rapid inflation, brought a drastic change in monetary and fiscal policy largely because of a sharp decline in foreign aid during this period. We have also found that the growth pattern of government expenditure has not significantly changed between 1954 and 1975, even if the permanent influences such as increase in income, prices and population are taken into account, suggesting that the specific time pattern of government expenditure during this period might be explained by factors other than these.

In view of the important role these two disruptions have played in shaping the time pattern of expenditure growth, an attempt will be made to measure the effects of these disruptions on the pattern of government expenditure between 1954 and 1975. Although we could observe clear evidence of the displacement effect of war during the immediate post war years, it has not been possible to make any statistical test, since no reliable GNP and deflator data are available for the years before 1953, and also because the pre-war period is too short to test. We are particularly interested in why there was a sharp reduction in the level of government expenditure and its share in GNP in 1963 and 1964, and how this affected the pattern of government expenditure after 1965. For this purpose, the following regression equations[8] are used:

$$E_p = a + bY_p + cD + dDY_p$$

and

$$NE_p = a + bY_p + cD + dDY_p$$

where

E_p = per capita total real expenditure
NE_p = per capita non-defense real expenditure
Y_p = per capita real GNP
D_p = dummy intercept shift variable with a value of 1 for the period 1965–1975 and 0 for the period 1954–1960
DY_p = slope shift between pre-disruption and post-disruption period

The years of the disruption period from 1961 to 1964 are omitted, and

[8] See S. P. Gupta (1967), p. 430; J. M. Bonin, B. W. Finch and J. B. Waters (1968), p. 443.

it is hypothesized that there was a shift in the expenditure pattern after 1965. All the continuous variables are specified in logarithmic form and the equation is estimated for per capita total and per capita non-defense expenditure. The shift is tested against the null hypothesis that it is not associated with the disruption between 1961 and 1964. For the period 1954–1975[9] the following regression equations[10] are obtained:

$$\log E_p = -\underset{(1.79)}{16.2982} + \underset{(2.77)}{2.3590} \log Y_p + \underset{(1.44)}{13.2796}\, D - \underset{(1.45)}{1.2473}\, D \log Y_p \qquad (1)$$

$$R^2 = 0.92$$
$$DW = 1.18$$

and

$$\log NE_p = -\underset{(3.34)}{44.8765} + \underset{(3.96)}{4.9717} \log Y_p + \underset{(2.98)}{40.6991}\, D - \underset{(2.97)}{3.7824}\, D \log Y_p \qquad (2)$$

$$R^2 = 0.92$$
$$DW = 1.42$$

In order to measure the shift effect, the level of government expenditure in the year immediately after the shift, i.e., the year 1965, is calculated with reference to the period 1954–1960. This is subtracted from the level of expenditure in the same year calculated with reference to the period 1965–1975. The antilog of the difference provides a measurement of the change in government expenditure after the shift took place.

The estimated values of per capita total and per capita non-defense expenditures in 1965 with reference to the period 1954–1960 amounted to 12,179 won and 10,926 won, respectively, while those values for the period 1965–1975 amounted to 8,920 won and 6,520 won, respectively. This means that the shift effect in both cases is negative, amounting to 4,408

[9] Even if we take the period 1954–1972 leaving out the years from 1973 to 1975, the results are basically the same.

[10] Figures in parenthesis are t-values.

won for per capita non-defense expenditure and 3,259 won for per capita total expenditure in 1965. In other words, the disruption during the period 1961–1964 had the effect of lowering the per capita non-defense expenditure and per capita total expenditure by 40 percent and 27 percent respectively, suggesting a downward displacement after the disruption. The *t* test[11] for the shift also shows that they were statistically significant at the 0.025 level or better, rejecting the null hypothesis that the downward shift was not associated with the disruption during 1961–1964.

The coefficients for the change in the slope in both equations are negative and statistically significant. The negative coefficient here implies a decline in income elasticity in the later period. The income elasticity during 1954–1960 was very high, 4.97 for non-defense and 2.36 for total per capita expenditure. However, it fell off markedly to 1.19 and 1.11 respectively, during the period 1965–1975.

The higher increase of per capita expenditure relative to per capita GNP during 1954–1960 seems attributable to both demand and supply factors. The period 1954–1960 is the reconstruction period of the war-damaged economy during which the demand for the public services increased very rapidly, especially, in the field of economic and social services. Between 1954 and 1960, for example, the per capita economic and social services increased at annual rates of 10.6 percent and 24.2 percent respectively, whereas the growth rate of per capita total expenditure averaged at 4.0 percent.

Although tax revenues increased rapidly through a series of tax reforms during this post war period, they were far from sufficient to finance both post war reconstruction expenditures and defense expenditures which did not decline in real terms until 1958.[12] We may say, therefore, that there was a great gap between the "desirable level" of government expenditure and a "tolerable burden" of taxation even after the war. This gap was financed largely by foreign aid and deficit financing. The counterpart fund revenue generated from foreign aid constituted the most important source of government revenues until 1958. The rapid increase in tax revenues combined with an inflow of foreign aid and deficit financing have resulted in a higher increase of per capita expenditure relative to per capita GNP between 1954 and 1960. GNP grew very slowly during this

[11] The significance of a shift was tested by using the following formula: $t = \text{shift}/\gamma$ where γ denotes the standard error of the regression. See S.P. Gupta (1967), p. 431.

[12] Since the Korean war ended in ceasefire the government continued to strengthen its defense power despite the end of war in 1953. As a result, the military forces were not reduced between 1954 and 1958. See Myung Yoon Kim (1967), p. 72.

period because of the severe destruction of industrial facilities during the war.

The role of counterpart funds as the major source of financing government expenditures suggests that the pattern of government expenditure could have been greatly influenced by the inflow of foreign aid. In order to eliminate the impact of foreign aid on the pattern of government expenditure, all the expenditures financed by the counterpart funds are excluded and regression equations[13] are reestimated as follows:

$$\log E_p^* = -14.8795 + 2.1898 \log Y_p + 7.6651 D$$
$$\qquad\qquad (1.32) \qquad\quad (2.07) \qquad\qquad (0.67)$$
$$- 0.7142\, D \log Y_p \ldots\ldots\ldots\ldots\ldots\ldots \text{(3)}$$
$$(0.67)$$
$$R^2 = 0.94$$
$$DW = 1.10$$

and

$$\log NE_p^* = -38.2635 + 4.3241 \log Y_p + 32.9497\, D$$
$$\qquad\qquad (2.68) \qquad\quad (3.24) \qquad\qquad (2.27)$$
$$- 3.0361\, D \log Y_p \ldots\ldots\ldots\ldots\ldots\ldots \text{(4)}$$
$$(2.25)$$
$$R^2 = 0.94$$
$$DW = 1.51$$

where E_p^* and NE_p^* denote per capita total and per capita non-defense expenditures excludin g the expenditure financed by counterpart funds.

The calculated values from the equations (3) and (4) indicate that there was a downward shift in both per capita total and per capita non-defense expenditure after 1965, even if the counterpart fund expenditure is excluded. However, the shift was much smaller, showing 11.1 percent for per capita total and 12.6 percent for per capita non-defense expenditure. Furthermore, when the test of significance is applied, the shift was statistically significant only at the level of 0.30 in both cases. It is also noted that in the case of per capita total expenditure the coefficients for both

[13] Figures in parenthesis are *t*-values.

dummy intercept and slope shift variables show a very low significance level. All this can be interpreted as suggesting that either no shift occurred after 1965, particularly for total government expenditure, or the shift, if any, was too small to exert a significant impact on the pattern of government expenditure. In other words, we may say that no significant downward shift in the level of government expenditure would have taken place had there been no counterpart fund expenditure. The counterpart fund expenditures which accounted for, on the average, more than 30 percent of total government expenditure declined drastically between 1962 and 1964 due to a sharp reduction in foreign aid, which continued to decline rapidly in the subsequent years.[14] This seems to support the above statistical result (See Appendix 7).

It is also interesting to observe that the rate of growth of government expenditure with respect to GNP declined after 1965 as in the case of government expenditure inclusive of counterpart fund expenditure, although the extent to which it declined was much smaller. This indicates that the direction of change in income elasticity of government expenditure was not much affected by the counterpart fund expenditure. In other words, the higher income elasticity of government expenditure between 1954 and 1960 seems largely attributable to a rapid increase in tax revenues relative to GNP growth[15] and to deficit financing which played an important role during the immediate post war years.

VI. Concluding Remarks

We have observed that the characteristic time pattern of government expenditure in Korea over the past quarter of a century was largely influenced by two major disruptions, namely the Korean war from 1950 to

[14] The United States aid to Korea declined from 165 million dollars in 1962 to 88 million dollars in 1964. See Suk Tai Suh (1976), p. 59.

[15] The rate of growth of central government tax revenues with respect to GNP is estimated at 1.5 during this period, while it is estimated at 1.2 during 1965–75. The higher income elasticity of taxation before 1954 was, however, largely due to a rapid increase in revenues from such taxes as foreign exchange tax, commodity tax and customs duties, which were mostly levied on the transaction of aid goods. Therefore, we may say that the higher increase in government expenditure relative to GNP between 1954 and 1960 was greatly influenced by the inflow of foreign aid. See Myung Yoon Kim (1967), p. 92.

1953 and the military revolution which was followed by a drastic decline in foreign aid in 1963 and 1964. The former tends to have had an upward shift effect on the level of government expenditure, while the latter had a downward shift effect which we found statistically significant. We also found that because of the different shift effect of these two disruptions, there is no clear evidence of an increasing expenditure share in GNP as income increases over the period under review.

It is remarkable that the expenditure shift took place in a downward direction after 1965 and that this downward shift was closely associated with the drastic decline in counterpart fund expenditures, which continued to decrease in the subsequent years due to diminishing foreign aid. There was also a substantial cut in the expenditures financed by other than foreign aid during these disruption years, but this did not likely exert a significant impact on the pattern of government expenditure over the entire period. As we have already indicated, we could not find any significant downward shift after 1965 if the counterpart fund expenditures were excluded from our consideration.

According to Peacock and Wiseman, displacement effect is always upward, although they do not exclude the possibility of downward displacement.[16] According to them, increase in government spending depends on revenue constraint which can be eased only through social upheaval such as war. If war is over, therefore, government expenditures do not return to their previous level but instead remain at a higher level, growing in discrete steps rather than continuously over time.

The fact that our expenditure shift was largely caused by the foreign aid component and moved in a downward direction seems, however, to suggest that displacement may occur not only as a result of war, as indicated by Peacock and Wiseman, but also as a result of political and economic characteristics peculiar to developing countries.[17] Accordingly, the nature of the expenditure shift may also differ from the one observed in developed countries. The Korean experience in the earlier part of the 1960s may be taken as an example of the type of disruption which appears to be more relevant to developing countries.

[16] See Alan T. Peacock and Jack Wiseman (1967), p. 28.
[17] See Irving J. Goffman and Dennis J. Mahar (1971), p. 70.

REFERENCES

1. Bank of Korea, *Annual Economic Review*, Seoul: various years.
2. ———, *Economic Statistics Yearbook*, Seoul: various years.
3. ———, *National Income Statistics Yearbook*, Seoul: various years.
4. Bonin, Joseph, B.W. Finch and Joseph Waters, Alternative Test of the "Displacement Effect" Hypothesis, *Public Finance/Finances publiques*, Vol. XXIV, No. 3, 1969.
5. Economic Planning Board, *Korea Statistical Yearbook*, Seoul: various years.
6. ———, *Summary of Budget*, Seoul: various years.
7. Goffman, Irving J., and Dennis J. Mahar, The Growth of Public Expenditures in Selected Developing Nations: Six Caribbean Countries 1940–65, *Public Finance/Finances Publiques*, Vol. XXVI, No. 1, 1971.
8. Gupta, Shibshankar P., Public Expenditure and Economic Growth-A Time Series Analysis, *Public Finance/Finances Publiques*, Vol. XXII, No. 4, 1967.
9. Kanesa-Thassan, S., "Stabilizing an Economy—A Study of the Republic of Korea," *IMF Staff Papers*, No. 16, 1969.
10. Kim, Myung Yoon, *Fiscal Structure of Korea*, Asia Research Institute, Korea University Press, 1967.
11. Korean Reconstruction Bank, *Economic Review* (1945–1955), Seoul: 1955.
12. Ministry of Finance, *Final Report on Revenues and Expenditures of Executed Budget*, Seoul: various years.
13. ———, *Summary of Financial Statistics*, Seoul: various years.
14. Musgrave, Richard A., *Fiscal Systems*, New Haven and London: Yale University Press, 1969.
15. Peacock, Alan T., and Jack Wiseman, *The Growth of Public Expenditure in the United Kingdom*, London: Allen and Unwin, 1967.
16. Suh, Suk Tai, *Statistical Report on Foreign Assistance and Loans to Korea (1945–1975)*, Seoul: Korea Development Institute, 1976.

APPENDIX

Appendix 1. Central Government Expenditures (at Current Prices)

(million won)

Year	GNP	Total Expenditures Including Defense	As % of GNP	Excluding Defense	As % of GNP
1949	—	88	—	64	—
1950	—	244	—	112	—
1951	—	772	—	442	—
1952	—	2,335	—	1,389	—
1953	48,180	5,680	11.8	2,420	5.0
1954	66,880	9,679	14.5	4,606	6.9
1955	116,060	14,877	12.8	8,380	7.2
1956	152,440	19,823	13.0	14,762	9.7
1957	197,780	32,603	16.5	21,310	10.8
1958	207,190	42,873	20.7	30,091	14.5
1959	221,000	42,977	19.4	29,003	13.1
1960	246,340	44,828	18.2	30,064	12.2
1961	297,080	59,988	20.2	43,326	14.6
1962	348,890	84,120	24.1	63,591	18.2
1963	488,530	79,550	16.3	59,069	12.1
1964	700,220	80,451	11.5	55,524	7.9
1965	804,410	102,433	12.7	72,558	9.0
1966	1,032,920	160,485	15.5	119,815	11.6
1967	1,269,970	207,823	16.4	157,823	12.4
1968	1,598,040	302,283	18.9	236,901	14.8
1969	2,081,520	423,272	20.3	338,409	16.3
1970	2,589,260	492,985	19.0	391,357	15.1
1971	3,151,830	600,850	19.1	464,794	14.7
1972	3,860,000	797,986	20.7	625,922	16.2
1973	4,928,670	756,453	15.3	574,296	11.7
1974	6,779,110	1,104,395	16.3	809,594	11.9
1975	9,051,780	1,695,990	18.7	1,301,730	14.4

Source: All the figures except GNP are estimated by the author.

Appendix 2. Central Government Expenditures (at 1970 Constant Prices)

(million won)

		Total Expenditures			
Year	GNP	Including Defense	As % of GNP	Excluding Defense	As % of GNP
1953	843,520	152,096	18.0	42,248	5.0
1954	890,180	134,082	15.1	52,949	5.9
1955	938,240	145,035	15.5	67,838	7.2
1956	942,210	169,965	18.0	97,723	10.4
1957	1,014,440	196,774	19.4	113,026	11.1
1958	1,067,150	224,149	21.0	145,395	13.6
1959	1,018,330	197,808	17.8	124,551	11.2
1960	1,129,720	184,947	16.4	113,103	10.0
1961	1,184,480	207,961	17.6	137,630	11.6
1962	1,220,980	253,186	20.7	184,777	15.1
1963	1,328,310	224,609	16.9	156,861	11.8
1964	1,441,990	190,789	13.2	124,538	8.6
1965	1,529,700	209,671	13.7	142,206	9.3
1966	1,719,180	268,113	15.6	193,857	11.3
1967	1,853,010	307,134	16.6	225,153	12.2
1968	2,087,120	392,155	18.8	303,540	14.5
1969	2,400,490	493,296	20.5	395,121	16.5
1970	2,589,260	492,985	19.0	391,357	15.1
1971	2,826,820	540,993	19.1	421,192	14.9
1972	3,023,630	608,683	20.1	482,760	16.0
1973	3,522,720	546,529	15.6	417,794	11.9
1974	3,825,500	586,339	15.4	426,692	11.2
1975	4,107,710	713,911	17.3	547,951	13.3

Source: All the figures except GNP are estimated by the author.

Appendix 3. Per Capita Expenditure and GNP
(at 1970 Constant Prices)

(won)

Year	Population (thousand persons)	GNP (million won)	Per Capita GNP	Per Capita Total Expenditure	Per Capita Non-Defense Expenditure
1953	21,440	843,520	39,343	7,094	1,971
1954	21,796	890,180	40,841	6,152	2,429
1955	21,502	938,240	43,635	6,745	3,155
1956	21,982	942,210	42,863	7,732	4,446
1957	22,329	1,014,440	45,432	8,812	5,062
1958	22,505	1,067,150	47,418	9,960	6,461
1959	22,866	1,108,330	48,471	8,651	5,447
1960	24,954	1,129,720	45,272	7,412	4,532
1961	25,498	1,184,480	46,454	8,156	5,398
1962	26,231	1,220,980	46,547	9,652	7,044
1963	26,987	1,328,310	49,220	8,323	5,812
1964	27,678	1,441,990	52,099	6,893	4,500
1965	28,327	1,529,700	54,001	7,402	5,020
1966	29,160	1,719,180	58,957	9,195	6,648
1967	29,541	1,853,010	62,727	10,397	7,622
1968	30,171	2,087,120	69,176	12,998	10,061
1969	30,738	2,400,490	78,095	16,048	12,854
1970	31,435	2,589,260	82,369	15,683	12,450
1971	31,828	2,826,820	88,816	16,997	13,233
1972	32,360	3,023,630	93,437	18,810	14,918
1973	32,905	3,522,720	107,057	16,609	12,697
1974	33,459	3,825,500	114,334	17,524	12,753
1975	34,708	4,107,710	118,350	20,569	15.787

Source: See Appendix 2.

Appendix 4. Central Government Expenditures Net of Counterpart Fund Expenditures (at Current Prices)

(million won)

	Total Expenditures					
Year	Including Defense	As % of GNP	Per Capita Expenditure (won)	Excluding Defense	As % of GNP	Per Capita Expenditure (won)
1953	5,513	11.4	257	2,420	5.0	113
1954	6,557	9.8	305	3,178	4.8	146
1955	10.078	8.7	469	5,781	5.0	269
1956	12,745	8.4	580	10.184	6.7	463
1957	17,366	8.8	778	10,906	5.5	488
1958	24,312	11.7	1,080	16,360	7.9	727
1959	29,390	13.3	1,285	20,716	9.4	906
1960	32,811	13.3	1,315	23,394	9.5	938
1961	37,908	12.8	1,487	37,349	12.6	1,465
1962	55,725	16.0	2,124	53,155	15.2	2,026
1963	54,740	11.2	1,029	49,391	10.1	1,883
1964	55,468	7.9	2,004	45,538	6.5	1,645
1965	74,538	9.3	2,631	63,163	7.9	2,230
1966	128,603	12.5	4,410	113,841	11.0	3,904
1967	179,607	14.1	6,080	154,178	12.1	5,219
1968	276,181	17.3	9,154	230,236	14.4	7,631
1969	403,686	19.4	13,133	334,433	16.1	10,880
1970	477,784	18.5	15,199	388,901	15.0	12,372
1971	591,135	18.8	18,573	462,849	14.7	14,542
1972	796,078	20.6	24,601	625,422	16.2	19,327
1973	756,453	15.3	22,989	574,296	11.7	17,453
1974	1,104,395	16.3	33,007	809,594	11.9	24,197
1975	1,695,990	18.7	48,865	1,301,730	14.4	37,505

Source: See Appendix 1 and 6.

Appendix 5. Central Government Expenditures Net of Counterpart Fund Expenditures (at 1970 Constant Prices)

(million won)

Year	Total Expenditures Including Defense	As % of GNP	Per Capita Expenditure (won)	Excluding Defense	As % of GNP	Per Capita Expenditure (won)
1953	146,257	17.3	6,822	42,248	5.0	1,971
1954	88.650	10.0	4,067	38,703	4.4	1,776
1955	100.232	10.7	4,662	52,725	5.6	2,452
1956	121.713	12.9	5,537	77,243	8.2	3,514
1957	11,7904	11.6	5,280	69,996	6.9	3,315
1958	138,790	13.0	6,167	89,796	8.4	3,990
1959	139,329	12.6	6,093	93,857	8.5	4,105
1960	137,242	12.2	5,500	91,417	8.1	3,663
1961	122,471	10.3	4,803	120,111	10.1	4,711
1962	166,211	13.5	6,298	156,647	12.8	5,972
1963	150,753	11.4	5,586	133,060	10.0	4,931
1964	132,189	9.2	4,776	105,797	7.3	3,822
1965	152,700	10.0	5,391	127,013	8.3	4,484
1966	212,137	12.3	7,275	185,184	10.8	6,351
1967	262,084	14.1	8,872	220,390	11.9	7,460
1968	357,682	17.1	11,855	295,411	14.2	9,791
1969	470,682	19.6	15,313	390,566	16.3	12,706
1970	477,784	18.5	15,199	388,901	15.0	12,372
1971	532,342	18.8	16,726	419,383	14.8	13,177
1972	607,249	20.1	18,766	482,356	16.0	14,906
1973	546,529	15.6	16,609	417,794	11.9	12,697
1974	586,339	15.4	17,524	426,692	11.2	12,753
1975	713,911	17.3	20,569	547,951	13.3	15,787

Source: See Appendix 2 and 7.

*Appendix 6. Counterpart Fund Expenditures**
(at Current Prices)

(million won)

Year	Including Defense			Excluding Defense		
	Total Government Expenditures	Counterpart Fund Expenditures	As % of Total Government Expenditures	Total Government Expenditures	Counterpart Fund Expenditures	As % of Total Government Expenditures
1953	5,680	167	2.94	2,420	—	—
1954	9,679	3,122	32.26	4,606	1,428	31.00
1955	14,877	4,799	32,26	8,380	2,599	31.01
1956	19,823	7,078	35.71	14,762	4,578	31.01
1957	32,603	15,237	46.73	21,310	10,404	48.82
1958	42,873	18,561	43.29	30,091	13,731	45.63
1959	42,977	13,587	31.61	29,003	8,287	28.57
1960	44,828	12,017	26.81	30,064	6,670	22.19
1961	59,988	22,080	36.81	43,326	5,977	13.80
1962	84,120	28,395	33.76	63,591	10,436	16.41
1963	79,550	24,810	31.19	59,069	9,678	16.38
1964	80,451	24,983	31.05	55,524	9,986	17.99
1965	102,433	27,895	27.23	72,558	9,395	12.95
1966	160,485	31,882	19.87	119,815	5,974	4.99
1967	207,823	28,216	13.58	157,823	3,645	2.31
1968	302,283	26,102	8.63	236,901	6,665	2.81
1969	423,272	19,586	4.63	338,409	3,976	1.17
1970	492,985	15,201	3.08	391,357	2,456	0.63
1971	600,850	9,715	1.62	464,794	1,945	0.42
1972	797,986	1,908	0.24	625,922	500	0.08
1973	756,453	—	—	574,296	—	—
1974	1,104,395	—	—	809,594	—	—
1975	1,695,990	—	—	1,241,823	—	—

* Indicates net expenditures of counterpart fund special account.
Source: *Summary of Financial Statistics*, Ministry of Finance, Seoul: various years.

Appendix 7. *Counterpart Fund Expenditures (at 1970 Constant Prices)*

(million won)

Year	Including Defense			Excluding Defense		
	Total Government Expenditures	Counterpart Fund Expenditures	As % of Total Government Expenditures	Total Government Expenditures	Counterpart Fund Expenditures	As % of Total Government Expenditures
1953	152,096	5,839	3.84	42,248	—	—
1954	134,082	45,432	33.88	52,949	14,246	26.91
1955	145,035	44,803	30.89	67,838	15,113	22.28
1956	169,965	48,252	28.39	97,723	20,480	20.96
1957	196,774	78,870	40.08	113,026	43,030	38.07
1958	224,149	85,359	38.08	145,395	55,599	38.24
1959	197,808	58,479	29.56	124,551	30,694	24.64
1960	184,947	47,705	25.79	113,103	21,686	19.17
1961	207,961	85,490	41.11	137,630	17,519	12.73
1962	253,186	87,975	34.75	184,777	28,130	15.22
1963	224,609	73,856	32.88	156,861	23,801	15.17
1964	190,789	58,600	30.71	124,538	18,741	15.05
1965	209,671	56,971	27.17	142,206	15,193	10.68
1966	268,113	55,976	20.88	193,857	8,673	4.47
1967	307,134	45,050	14.67	225,153	4,763	2.12
1968	392,155	34,473	8.79	303,540	8,129	2.68
1969	493,296	22,614	4.58	395,121	4,555	1.15
1970	492,985	15,201	3.08	391,357	2,456	0.63
1971	540,993	8,651	1.60	421,192	1,809	0.43
1972	608,683	1,434	0.24	482,760	404	0.08
1973	546,529	—	—	417,794	—	—
1974	586,339	—	—	426,692	—	—
1975	713,911	—	—	547,951	—	—

Source: See Appendix 6.

A FORECASTING MODEL FOR REVENUE ESTIMATION OF DIRECT TAXES

*Chong Kee Park**

I. Introduction

Every budget includes an estimate of anticipated revenues during the prospective budget year, and forecasts of the expected tax revenues are needed to aid in the formulation of budget policies. Forecasting tax yield is a highly involved process, subject to many uncertainties. This is particularly so in developing countries, where adequate and reliable basic economic statistics are lacking. Nevertheless, an accurate projection of tax yields is an important part of the budgetary decision-making process. Advance information strengthens policy formulation, for it provides the decision-maker with more and better tools than otherwise. Errors both of over-estimating and of under-estimating the government revenues will undermine the efficient fiscal planning of the government.

Over-estimation of prospective tax revenues, for instance, may encourage the adoption of unrealistic public programs, and subsequently may result in inflationary methods of finance. The resulting crisis may also contribute to a greater conservative bias in the next estimating round. Under-estimation, on the other hand, may mean that the government program is being carried on at a level less than the optimum resources available. The major objective of short-run revenue forecasting is thus to determine the budget constraint of available revenues on expenditures in

* Senior Fellow at the Korea Development Institute. This paper was presented at the First International Symposium sponsored by KDI, Seoul, July 5–11, 1972.

order to maintain a desirable expenditure-revenue relationship. Reliable estimates of tax revenues are also essential for the analysis of the economic impact of the government budget.

In the past, revenue forecasts were often based on judgement and on simple extrapolation of a time trend. It is frequently assumed that the changes in tax revenues are roughly proportional to changes in GNP and the general price level.[1] But this method is obviously much too rough, and will doubtless yield erroneous results. The purposes of this study are to develop new methods of forecasting tax revenue yields and to present estimates of Korea's tax revenue for the budget years 1972 and 1973. Another purpose of this study is to present measures of the responsiveness of income taxes to changes in aggregate income. An attempt is made to develop a simple tax model that is consistent with the structural characteristics of the economy and the tax system. A primary use of this model is to prepare the tax revenue estimates required in budget and tax planning as well as to provide an efficient method of estimating the revenue effect of proposed legislative changes in the tax structure.

The second section of this study briefly reviews historical trends in the basic tax yield series used. The third section provides a general discussion of the tax forecasting method and statistical techniques. The fourth section discusses structural features and the estimated tax functions of individual tax components. The fourth and final section summarizes the estimated values of tax elasticity measures and of tax yields for 1972 and 1973 and discusses their implications.

II. Tax Performance in Korea: Historical Analysis

It is always important to look back before we look ahead. The decade of the 1960's has witnessed a phenomenal growth in the collection of tax revenues in Korea. A longer-range view of the performance of the major taxes is presented in Appendix Table 1. The total tax revenue of the central government increased in money terms from a mere 25.0 billion won in 1960 to almost 420 billion won in 1971. This represents a nominal growth of nearly seventeen times in tax revenue available for new and improved services provided by the government. In comparison, the gross national product increased by thirteen times during the same period. Thus, increases

[1] For a general description of the revenue forecasting methods used in Korean government, see Ted E. McHold (1971).

in the collection of tax revenue far out-stripped concurrent gains in GNP.

The modernization of the tax system and the improvements in the administrative enforcement process, especially since 1966 when the government set up a new Office of National Tax Administration, were mainly responsible for the sharp increases in tax revenues during this time period. As shown in Appendix Table 2, which exhibits the pattern of growth in tax collections since 1960, the most rapid growth in total tax revenue was recorded in 1966—an amazing 62 percent. Since then, however, the rate of growth has been slowing down steadily. In 1971 the rate of increase was only 27 percent. This observation appears to confirm the general feeling that the limits of increased tax revenue through administrative improvements are being reached.

A notable feature of the tax system in Korea is that income taxes (both personal and corporation income taxes) play a significant role in financing government outlays, currently providing 40 percent of the central government's total tax revenue. Revenue yields from these two sources increased by a factor of 55 during the 1960–1971 period and accounted for more than 40 percent of the total increase in central government tax revenue during this period. A close examination of data in Appendix Table 3 reveals that the most dramatic gain in relative importance among individual tax sources was registered in corporation tax yields, which grew from 3.5 percent in 1960 to 13.6 percent of total tax revenues in 1971. Receipts from personal income taxes as a share of the total also increased significantly—from 8.4 percent to almost 26 percent. This situation is contrary to that usually prevailing in most developing countries, where taxes on income and profits constitute only a small proportion of total tax receipts and indirect taxes such as commodity tax and customs duties tend to play a more important role.

In Korea the commodity tax is much less important. Although the largest single source of tax revenue up until 1962, it shows a gradual decline in its fraction of all taxes from over 17 percent in 1960 to less than 11 percent by 1971. Furthermore, it is of interest to note that customs duties in Korea account for only a small proportion of total tax revenue, in sharp contrast with most other developing countries which depend to a substantial extent for their tax revenue on customs duties. In Ecuador, to cite an example, customs duties account for almost one-half of the total tax revenue. They account for 30 percent or more in nine other countries, including Ceylon and Thailand.[2] In Korea the relative importance of

[2] Raja J. Chelliah (1971).

Table 1. Summary Tax Measures, 1960–1971 (Amount in Billion Won)

Year	Total Tax[1] (*T*) (1)	GNP (2)	$\frac{T}{GNP}$ (3)	$\frac{dT}{GNP}$ (4)	$\frac{dT}{T} / \frac{dGNP}{GNP}$ (5)
1960	29.47	246.69	11.9%		
1961	28.44	296.82	9.6		
1962	37.66	348.58	10.8	17.8%	1.86
1963	43.26	487.96	8.9	4.0	0.37
1964	50.68	696.79	7.3	3.6	0.46
1965	69.47	805.85	8.6	17.2	2.36
1966	111.92	1,032.04	10.8	18.8	2.17
1967	153.16	1,242.35	12.3	19.6	1.80
1968	230.55	1,575.65	14.6	23.2	1.88
1969	310.14	2,047.11	15.2	16.9	1.15
1970	402.05	2,545.92	15.8	18.4	1.21
1971	494.85	3,112.68	15.9	16.4	1.04
1962–66 Average (First Five-Year Plan)			9.3	12.3	1.43
1967–71 Average (Second Five-Year Plan)			14.8	18.9	1.42

Sources: Tax data from Office of National Tax Administration, *Statistical Yearbook of National Tax* (Seoul, November 1971), pp. 26–7; and GNP data from Economic Planning Board, *Major Economic Indicators:* 1960–1971 (Seoul, November 1971), p. 15.

Note: [1] Total tax revenue as used here refers to central government tax revenue including customs duties and monopoly profits plus local government tax revenue.

customs duties is much smaller and has declined from 21 percent in 1960 and 24 percent in 1962 to less than 13 percent by 1971.

Three aggregate measures are used to summarize Korea's tax behavior since 1960, and they are exhibited in Table 1. The summary measures are: 1) the average tax rate, which shows the "tax burden" measured by the ratio of total tax revenue to GNP; 2) the marginal tax rate, which measures the absolute *won* change in total tax revenue per *won* change in GNP; and 3) the tax elasticity, which shows the percent change in observed tax yields for a 1 percent change in GNP.[3] The latter two measures are mathematically related; the tax elasticity is the marginal tax rate divided by the average tax rate.

It can be seen from Table 1 that although the overall tax ratio has increased from almost 12 percent in 1960 to 16 percent in 1971, there has been some

[3] This value measures the total relative increase in tax yields, whether resulting from economic growth, or changes in tax parameters, or improvements in administrative enforcement.

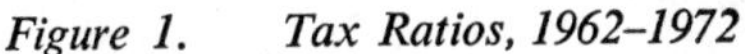

Figure 1. *Tax Ratios, 1962–1972*

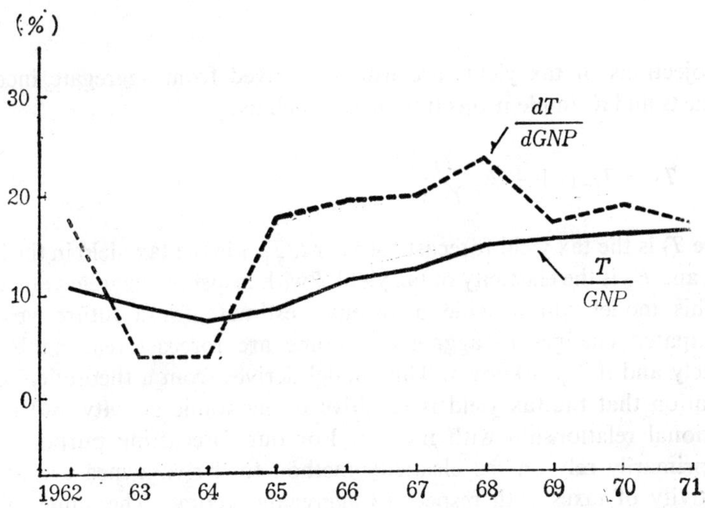

variation in the ratio during the early 1960's.[4] Since 1964, however, the ratio reveals a steady increase, but at a declining rate, until 1970. No increase in the ratio is shown for 1971. The marginal tax rate determines how fast the average tax rate (or tax burden) rises in the context of an increase in GNP over time. It gives us an idea of the proportion of an increment in GNP that the government has been able to divert to the public sector. In Korea the behavior of this ratio is seen to have varied from as high as 23.2 percent in 1968 to only 3.6 percent in 1964. Finally, the measures of tax elasticity are shown in the last column of Table 1. The overall elasticity of total tax yields with respect to GNP was only 0.37 in 1963, as compared with 2.36 in 1965 and 2.17 in 1966. This means that a 1 percent change in GNP yielded only 0.4 percent increase in total tax revenue in 1963 and nearly 2.2 percent increase in 1966. A close examination of the data reveals, however, that the tax elasticity tended downward since 1966, reaching about 1 by 1971.

[4] This instability in the tax ratio results from three temporary taxes in effect only during this period. They are land income tax, education tax, and foreign exchange tax.

III. Tax Revenue Estimation: an Elasticity Approach

Projections of tax yields are usually derived from aggregate income forecasts and a simple projection model such as:

$$T_t = T_{t-1}\left[1 + E_T \frac{dY}{Y_{t-1}}\right]$$

where T_t is the tax yield forecast for year t, T_{t-1} is the tax yield in the base year, and E_T is the elasticity of tax yield T with respect to aggregate income Y. This model will provide a revenue estimate for a future year if aniticipated changes in aggregate income are forecast reasonably accurately and if E_T is known. This model derives from a theoretical consideration that the tax yield is sensitive to economic activity and has a functional relationship with income. For our forecasting purposes, we will primarily rely on the elasticity method to derive a measure of the sensitivity of taxes with respect to aggregate income. The value of the elasticity coefficient E_T is implicitly estimated from an equation of the form

$$T = a + b\,(Y)$$

where b is the estimate of E_T in the logarithmic form of the above equation. Solving for the regression coefficient b in this equation yields an average revenue-income elasticity coefficient that reflects the percentage change in revenue yields per one percent change in aggregate income over the pertinent time period.[5]

In the following section we present an econometric analysis in which the Office of National Tax Administration (ONTA) quarterly series on component tax yields is related to aggregate income, policy variables, and

[5] The income elasticity of a given tax may also be determined by the relationship between the marginal yield per unit of income in a given period and the average yield-income ratio in the previous period:

$$E_T = \frac{dT_t}{T_{t-1}}\bigg/\frac{dY_t}{Y_{t-1}} = \frac{dT_t}{dY_t}\bigg/\frac{T_{t-1}}{Y_{t-1}} = \frac{Tm_t}{Ta_{t-1}}$$

It is obvious from the above equation that as the marginal ratio (T_m) rises in relation to the initial average ratio(T_a), the elasticity (E_T) increases. In other words, as long as T_m exceeds T_a, the value of E_T will be greater than 1. Similarly, the larger the T_a, the less the elasticity coefficient for a given marginal ratio.

other variables. The relation, based on the years 1965–1970, is estimated in each of three different ways: one relates the taxable base to aggregate income; the second relates tax yield to income; and the third, tax yields to average effective tax rates. Most empirical work has been done on income elasticity of tax yields. However, in this study we extend our analysis to the income elasticity of the tax base and the rate elasticity of tax yields. Since most taxes are levied on bases that respond to economic change, increases in aggregate income and business activity can be expected to produce automatic tax revenue increases without changes in tax parameters. Different tax bases vary widely in their response to changes in the level of economic activity. In most cases, however, a change in the tax base will have more impact on its yield than will a tax rate change.

The choice of the independent variables included in the equations is limited by several practical difficulties. Many types of national income statistics, such as personal income and corporate profits, are not available on a quarterly basis. Furthermore, the need to project the basic variables dictated that we limit the number of variables to be included in the equation. We had to rely on variables whose future course of variation can be projected with reasonable accuracy. In view of the fact that our primary concern is projection rather than establishing the relationship between revenue variables and other economic variables *per se*, we avoided including variables whose future courses of change are very difficult to foresee, even if they are theoretically quite relevant.[6]

The choice of the form of the estimating equation is determined in the light of two criteria. First, the choice is made according to the goodness of fit to the observed data. The goodness of fit is usually represented by the coefficient of determination denoted by R^2 and is given for each of the estimating equations shown. Secondly, the choice is made on the basis of theoretical justifications (or of empirically tested hypotheses). If the relationship to be examined is considered to be one of a given percentage change in one variable associated with a corresponding change in the other variable, logarithmic forms of the equation are preferred.

In discussing time series data, we need to separate the revenue effects of price changes from the effects of real changes in income and production. Whereas the real value of tax yield will rise if the growth of income is due to rising output, the real yield will fall or remain unchanged if the income change is due to a rise in price level. It is generally agreed that the ap-

[6] Estimates of independent variables used in the forecasting equations are based on forecasts derived from the quarterly projection model. See H. Song (1972).

preciation of taxable income that reflects an increase in the general price level must be excluded from the tax base.[7] In order to eliminate the effect of price increases from our analysis, all variables in the estimating equations are expressed in real terms. All tax revenue series were uniformly deflated by the wholesale price index.

IV. The Estimating Equations

1. Personal Income Tax

The personal income tax is the most productive revenue source of the government in Korea, currently providing over a fourth of total tax revenue. The growth has been steady and remarkable. On a per capita basis, tax yields increased from less than 90 won in 1960 to nearly 2,700 won in 1970. The tax absorbed over 4 percent of personal income in 1970, rising from only 1 percent in 1960.

The basic feature of Korea's personal income tax is the schedular tax system which provides the independent determination of taxable income and of the tax liability under each applicable rate schedule. Different income tax rates are applied to five separate groups of income: 1) wages and salaries, 2) business income, 3) real estate income, 4) dividend and interest, and 5) income from other miscellaneous sources. A graduated rate schedule is applied against wages and salaries, business income, and real property income. Table 2 presents the personal income tax rate schedule which became effective as a result of the tax reform of 1971, and Table 3 compares the wage and salary income tax rate structures in effect before and after the tax reform.

The projection of the personal income tax was achieved in two separate steps. Because of the complex and graduated nature of the rate structure and the frequent rate adjustments which took place in the past, we chose for our estimating equation the volume of the taxable base rather than tax yields as the dependent variable. Thus we first projected the tax base separately for different income schedules using the time-series quarterly data from the first quarter of 1965 to the fourth quarter of 1970 as a frame of reference. Effective tax rates for each income group were also derived from relating tax revenues to their respective tax base. Applying such a

---

[7] Richard A. Musgrave (1959).

Table 2. Personal Income Tax Rates, by Types of Income (Effective 1972)

Income Bracket (Annual Income in Thousand Won)	Taxable Income[1]			
	Wage & Salary(%)	Real Estate & Business(%)	Dividend & Interest	Other Income[2]
120 or less	7	—		
In Excess of 120	9	—		
In Excess of 240	12	—		
300 or less	—	15		
In Excess of 300	—	20		
In Excess of 480	15	—		
In Excess of 600	—	28		
In Excess of 720	19	—		
In Excess of 960	25	—		
In Excess of 1,200	32	—		
In Excess of 1,400	—	38		
In Excess of 1,800	40	—		
In Excess of 2,400	48	—		
In Excess of 3,000	—	48		
Flat Rate			20%	20%

Notes: [1] In addition, a global income tax is levied on top of the schedular structure if income from all sources combined exceeds 3 million won a year.
[2] Refers to miscellaneous income such as bonuses, prizes, and rewards.

Table 3. Personal Income Tax Rates for Wage and Salary Income, 1971 and 1972

Income Bracket (Annual Income in Thousand Won)	1971 (%)	1972 (%)
120 or less	7.7	7
In Excess of 120	9.9	9
In Excess of 240	12.1	12
In Excess of 360	15.4	—
In Excess of 480	—	15
In Excess of 720	22.0	19
In Excess of 960	29.7	25
In Excess of 1,200	37.4	32
In Excess of 1,800	46.2	40
In Excess of 2,400	55.0	48

tax rate for a current year to the associated tax base for the next year resulted in an estimate of tax revenue due primarily to changes in the tax base.[8] In projecting the tax revenue for the next year, it was assumed that the tax rate structure effective in 1972 will be maintained through the next budget year. We thus concentrate on the changes in tax yield that result while the tax parameters (statutory rates of tax) are held constant. The general procedure may be outlined as follows:

$$r_{t-1} = T_{t-1}/TB_{t-1}$$

$$T_t = TB_t \cdot r_{t-1}$$

where r = implicit tax rate
T = tax yield
TB = taxable income (or base)

List of Variables

E_{NA} = Number of non-agricultural employment
r_P = Average effective tax rate for personal income tax
r_{PW} = Average effective tax rate for wage and salary income
r_C = Average effective tax rate for corporation income tax
T_P = Tax yield from personal income tax
T_{PW} = Tax yield from wage and salary income tax
T_C = Tax yield from corporation income tax
T_{AR} = Tax yield from assets revaluation tax
T_{GII} = Tax yield from gift and inheritance tax
T_R = Tax yield from registration tax
TB_P = Taxable base of personal income tax
TB_{PW} = Taxable base of wage and salary income
TB_{PBR} = Taxable base of business and real property tax
TB_{PDI} = Taxable base of dividend and interest income
TB_C = Taxable base of corporation income tax
Y_{NA} = Amount of non-agricultural GNP

Values of T, TB, and Y_{NA} in estimating equations are all measured in 1965 constant prices.

The relation between taxable base and aggregate income was measured by log linear regressions of the following type:

[8] The tax base as defined here refers to the net taxable income which is the difference between gross income and statutory allowances.

1. $\text{Log } TB_P = -12.8488 + 1.9721 \log Y_{NA}$
$$\quad\quad(0.0625)$$
$$R^2 = .977 \qquad DW = 2.44$$

2. $\text{Log } TB_{PW} = -14.6281 + 1.7828 \log Y_{NA} + 0.4519 \log E_{NA}$
$$\quad(0.1233) \qquad\qquad (0.2745)$$
$$R^2 = .980 \qquad DW = 1.71$$

3. $\text{Log } TB_{PBR} = -12.1322 + 1.7675 \log Y_{NA}$
$$\quad(0.2374)$$
$$R^2 = .705 \qquad DW = 3.53$$

4. $\text{Log } TB_{PDI} = -22.6640 + 2.5750 \log Y_{NA}$
$$\quad(0.1834)$$
$$R^2 = .895 \qquad DW = 1.32$$

As is evident from the equations shown above, all of the tax base elasticity coefficients (E_b) are very high and most equations indicate a rather good fit to the observed data. The numbers in parentheses under the estimated elasticity coefficients are their respective estimated standard errors. R^2 is the coefficient of determination adjusted for degrees of freedom, and DW is the Durbin-Watson test statistic for serial correlation in the residuals.

It is to be noted that a regression coefficient in our equations measures the percentage change in tax base for each percentage change in the independent variable, i.e., non-agricultural GNP (Y_{NA}). The regression coefficient of 1.7828 in equation (2), for instance, demonstrates that during the 1965–1970 period, the taxable base for wages and salaries increased an average of approximately 18 percent for each increase of 10 percent in Y_{NA}.[9] It may be concluded from such an estimate that the personal income tax base has a high degree of responsiveness to changes in aggregate income as one should expect. In particular, the value of E_b in the case of dividend and interest income (TB_{PDI}) in equation (4) is very high. The results obtained conform to an established theoretical view that as aggregate income rises the taxable income of the tax rises more rapidly. The faster rise in taxable income is due to the fact that when incomes are rising, more persons are moving from exempt status (a zero-rate bracket) to

[9] It is quite interesting to note that this estimate of $E_b = 1.8$ for Korea is somewhat higher than the base-elasticity coefficient of personal income tax of 1.5 for Japan. See Hiromitsu Ishi (1968).

Figure 2. Taxable Income of Personal Income Tax (Based on Equation 1) Actual and Estimated

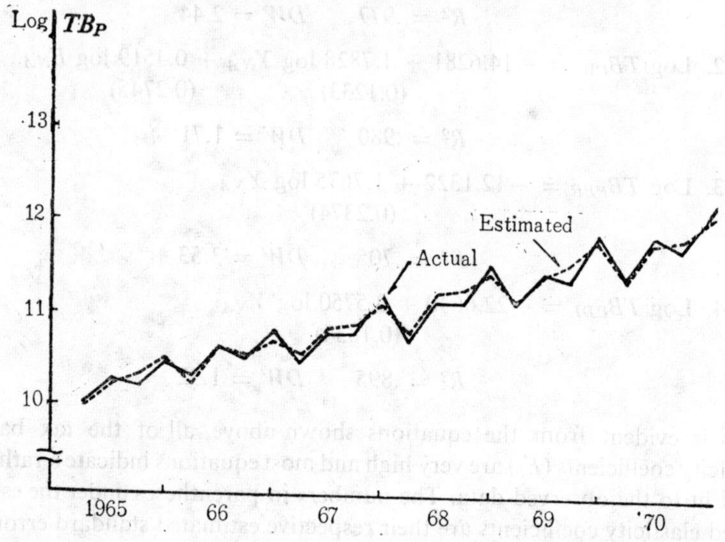

Figure 3. Taxable Income of Wage and Salary Income Tax (Based on Equation 2) Actual and Estimated

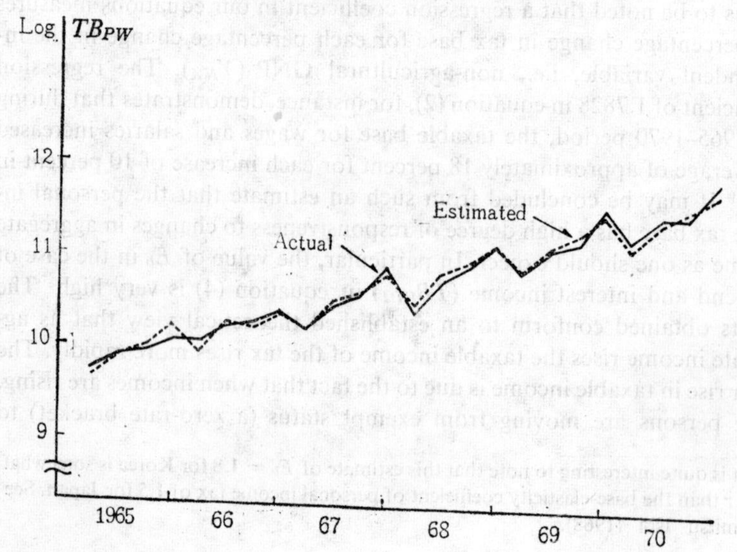

taxable status (a positive-rate bracket). Under the personal income tax with a graduated rate structure like Korea, the increase in income would push many persons into higher-rate brackets. Hence more aggregate income moves into the taxable base.

The values of the tax base thus derived from these elasticity coefficients combined with an effective tax rate for 1972 yields the forecast of future tax yields. It should be noted, however, that since the elasticity coefficients derived from our estimating equations represent an average of the E_b's for the 24 observations selected from the first quarter of 1965 to the fourth quarter of 1970 period reflecting the exceptionally high values of E_b for the mid-1960's, we needed in certain cases, to make downward adjustments to estimated tax yields. In order to check the reasonableness of our initial estimate of total taxable income derived by aggregating values of the *TB* of individual component income groups, we have also estimated independently the total tax base of personal income tax using equation (1) above. The result shows two totals differing by about 2 percent.[10]

As a final step, tax yields thus derived have been modified to take account of revenue effects of the new tax law which became effective beginning in 1972. Major changes in the tax provision include increases in the basic exemption levels for business and employment income (from 10,000 won per month in 1971 to 15,000 won per month in 1972) and reductions in the statutory tax rate (See Table 3). The Ministry of Finance has estimated that the revenue loss resulting from these changes in the tax code would amount to about 22 billion won for 1972. Since 1969, a global income tax has also been levied, on top of the schedular structure, if income from all sources combined exceeds a specified amount per year—3 million won in 1972. For our purpose of revenue estimation, this tax component plus miscellaneous income such as bonuses, prizes, and rewards has been derived as a residual.[11] In other words, it has been estimated as a function

---

[10] The following alternative equation gives the elasticity coefficients of the personal income tax yield using non-agricultural GNP and tax rate changes as the explanatory variables:

$$\underset{}{\text{Log } T_p} = -17.5301 + \underset{(0.0659)}{1.9636} \log Y_{NA} + \underset{(0.1514)}{1.0735} \log r_p$$

$$R^2 = .980 \qquad D.W. = 2.25$$

This equation indicates that the overall personal income tax yield is highly responsive to changes in the level of aggregate income ($E_T = 1.9636$) and the rate-revenue elasticity coefficient at 1.0735 equals unity. The estimated values of coefficients seem consistent with theoretical knowledge on the subject.

[11] The tax yield from these two sub-groups amounted to only 5.8 billion won in 1971, representing less than 5 percent of total personal income tax revenue.

of total tax yield from the schedular system

$$T_G = T_P - (T_{PW} + T_{PBR} + T_{PDI})$$

where T_G = global income tax yield
T_P = total personal income tax yield
T_{PW} = tax yield from wages and salaries
T_{PBR} = tax yield from business and real property income
T_{PDI} = tax yield from dividend and interest income

2. Corporation Income Tax

The corporation income tax is the third largest source of central government tax revenue in Korea, currently providing about 14 percent of total tax revenue. Until 1960, however, the tax on corporation income provided less than 4 percent of total tax revenue. In an absolute amount, the tax intake rose from 0.9 billion in 1960 to 56.7 billion by 1971.

The tax is levied on the regular income earned by corporate taxpayers during each accounting period as well as on liquidation income. The corporation tax law provides three stages of tax rates in order to give small and medium size firms a lighter tax burden. In addition, a reduced rate applies to the income of non-profit corporations and open corporations.

Table 4. Corporation Income Tax Rate, Effective 1972

Income Bracket	Profit-Making Corporation (%)	Open Corporation (%)	Non-Profit Corporation (%)
One Million Won or Less	20	16	20
In Excess of One Million Won	30	20	30
In Excess of Five Million Won	40	27	35

Although the tax rate varies considerably according to the level of income and the type of corporation, over 90 percent of corporate taxable income is subject to the top rate bracket of 5 million won or more.

Because of the volatility of corporate profits, the corporate income tax is the most difficult component of government revenues to estimate. Payment of the tax rarely coincides with the timing of tax liability. The question of time lags is thus very important in the collection of corporate income tax. Because of the collection lags, the tax behavior reveals a slower response to income accruals and tax yields usually lag a few months behind the variation in income. This factor has been taken into account in the equation for corporation income tax, using an average lag of one-quarter of a year.

A forecasting procedure suggested for corporation income tax is to make our estimating equation a multiple regression equation in which non-agricultural GNP and the average tax rate are independent variables. The rate variable is inserted into the estimating equation in order to test the revenue effects of changes in tax rates.[12]

$$4.\ \text{Log}\ T_{C(t)} = -13.5204 + \underset{(0.3944)}{1.6402} \log Y_{NA(t-\frac{1}{4})} + \underset{(0.6440)}{0.5257} \log r_C$$

$$R^2 = 0.858 \qquad DW = 2.46$$

As equation (4) above indicates, tax yields from corporate profits depend on aggregate income and the average tax rate. It will be seen from the equation that the value of the income elasticity for the corporation income tax at 1.6402 is quite high, and that the fit, as indicated by the coefficient of determination, is fairly good.[13] However, the rate elasticity coefficient of corporation income tax at 0.53 is very low and not significant. This seems to suggest that increases in tax yields from Korea's corporation income tax are a consequence primarily of increases in aggregate income rather than of changes in the tax rate. This result is consistent with the established view regarding the effect of broadening the tax base. As Professor Richard A. Musgrave stated:

> The primary need is for measures which will secure a fuller coverage in assessment of the tax bases (be it income, sales or property values) under the various taxes. As compared to this, increases in tax rates are less important. Not only are they less significant from a revenue point of view, but primary attention to fuller coverage of the base comes first.[14]

3. *Other Direct Taxes*

Direct taxes other than income taxes (both personal and corporate

[12] For a general discussion of the method of estimating rate elasticity, see, among others, Walton Terry Wilford (1965).

[13] This value of $E_T = 1.6402$ for Korea's corporate income tax compares with an income elasticity of 1.4619 for the corporation tax in Japan, see Ishi (1968), p. 54.

[14] Richard A. Musgrave (1965).

income taxes) accounted for only 3.7 percent of total tax revenue of the Korean government in 1971, and is thus insignificant from a revenue point of view. These taxes include registration tax, gift and inheritance tax, assets revaluation tax, and real estate speculation control tax. Among these the registration tax is by far the most important, and tax yields from this source have been rising steadily over the past decade and currently account for 2.7 percent of all central government tax receipts. This proportion of 2.7 percent compares with a little over 1 percent in early 1960's.

The registration tax is levied on the registration of official books or documents relating to acquisition, creation, transfer, alteration, etc., of rights. The tax is also imposed on the registration of certain professional workers in connection with their qualification for general practice. Tax receipts from this source are, therefore, a conglomerate of various sources. However, the taxable registration of real properties account for the major portion of the tax base.

The following equation gives the results of regressing changes in the yield of the registration tax on changes in non-agricultural GNP:

$$5.\ \text{Log } T_R = -15.9596 + \underset{(0.1149)}{1.8544} \log Y_{NA}$$

$$R^2 = .919 \qquad DW = 2.04$$

The above equation shows an income elasticity of 1.8544 for the registration tax. This means that if Y_{NA} (non-agricultural GNP) increases by one percent, registration tax yield increases an average of roughly 1.8 percent. The coefficient of determination (R^2) at .919 is also very high. The estimate of the intercept is negative, as should be expected since tax yield is always less than Y_{NA}. Estimating equations for gift and inheritance tax and assets revaluation tax are shown below. Because of a recent change in the provision of basic deductions for the real estate speculation control tax, the prospect of tax yield from this source is very uncertain. Consequently, this tax revenue source is determined outside the model.

$$6.\ \text{Log } T_{GH} = -28.7138 + \underset{(0.4253)}{2.7374} \log Y_{NA}$$

$$R^2 = .637 \qquad DW = 2.22$$

$$7.\ T_{AR} = -262.7212 + \underset{(0.00017)}{0.00094}\, Y_{NA}$$

$$R^2 = .742 \qquad DW = 1.03$$

V. Summary and Conclusion

Accurate forecasts of the prospective growth of tax revenue are needed to aid in the formulation of tax and expenditure policies. They are also essential for the analysis of the economic impact of the government budget. Advance information on tax revenues thus strengthens fiscal policy formulation. One method of making such forecasts is the income elasticity approach. In this paper an attempt was made to make quantitative assessment of the short-run revenue outlook of Korea's direct taxes through an income elasticity method. This approach generally assumes that the tax law and the quality of tax administration remain constant. However, our interest in this study lies more in the total relative increase in tax yields, whether due to economic growth, or changes in tax parameters, or improvements in administrative enforcement.

Table 5 summarizes the constant price forecasts of direct tax revenues for 1972 and 1973. With a considerable slowdown in the nation's economic activity combined with the effects of a new tax law, the total tax yield from direct taxes is expected to decline in 1965 constant price by about 8 percent. As shown in Appendix Table V, the growth of non-agricultural GNP is anticipated to decline sharply from 13 percent in 1971 to 8.2 percent in 1972. Furthermore, an enactment of a new tax law which became effective beginning in 1972 is expected to result in a revenue loss of about 28 billion won in 1972.

Looking ahead to 1973, with a gradual recovery of the general economic activity, the growth of tax yields is anticipated to accelerate during the year. Real yields from direct taxes are projected to increase by about 15 percent in 1973. The nominal increase, however, will be much bigger—22 percent. Table 6 presents the current price forecasts of direct tax revenue.

Table 5. ***Projection of Direct Tax Revenue for 1972 and 1973***

(billion won at 1965 prices)

	1971 Actual	1971 Adjusted[1]	1972 Projection	1973 Projection
Income Tax	70.7	70.2	63.0	72.0
Corporation Tax	37.3	31.8	28.6	34.0
Registration Tax	5.5	5.5	7.5	8.8
Gift and Inheritance	1.3	1.4	1.4	1.7
Assets Revaluation	0.9	0.9	1.0	1.1
Real Estate Speculation Control Tax	1.6	1.6	0.8[2]	—
Total Direct Tax	117.3	111.4	102.3	117.6

Source: 1971 base year figures are from the Office of National Tax Administration, Seoul.

Notes: [1] 1971 actual figures have been adjusted for the amount of precollection this year of the tax liability to be incurred next year.

[2] Forecast figure from the Ministry of Finance.

Table 6. ***Projection of Direct Tax Revenue for 1972 and 1973***

(billion current won)

	1971 Actual	1971 Adjusted[1]	1972 Projection	1973 Projection
Income Tax	107.6	106.7	104.7	127.1
Corporation Tax	56.7	48.3	47.5	60.1
Registration Tax	8.4	8.4	12.4	15.6
Gift and Inheritance	2.0	2.1	2.4	3.0
Assets Revaluation	1.3	1.3	1.6	1.9
Real Estate Speculation Control Tax	2.5	2.5	1.3[2]	—
Total Direct Tax	178.5	169.3	169.9	207.7

Source: 1971 base year figures are from the Office of National Tax Administration, Seoul.

Notes: [1] 1971 actual figures have been adjusted for the amount of precollection this year of the tax liability to be incurred next year.

[2] Forecast figure from the Ministry of Finance.

REFERENCES

1. Chelliah, Raja J., "Trends in Taxation in Developing Countries," *IMF Staff Papers*, XVIII, July 1971, pp. 254–331.
2. Economic Planning Board, *Major Economic Indicators*, 1960–1971, Seoul, 1971.
3. Ishi, Hiromitsu, "The Income Elasticity of the Tax Yield in Japan," *Hitotsubashi Journal of Economics*, IV, June 1968, pp. 45–63.
4. McHold, Ted E., "Forecasting Tax Revenues in the Republic of Korea," *Korean Economist*, September 1971, pp. 47–52.
5. Musgrave, Richard A., *Revenue Policy for Korea's Economic Development*, Seoul: Ministry of Finance, 1965.
6. _______. *The Theory of Public Finance*, McGraw-Hill Book Co., New York: 1959.
7. Office of National Tax Administration, *Statistical Yearbook of National Tax, 1971*, Seoul, November 1971.
8. Park, Chong Kee, "An Analysis of Income Elasticity of the Tax Yield in Korea," Unpublished Doctoral Dissertation, The George Washington University, 1970.
9. Song, Heeyhon, "A Quarterly Forecasting Model of the Korean Economy," Seoul: The Korea Development Institute 1972.
10. The Bank of Korea, *National Income Statistics Yearbook, 1971*, Seoul, November 1971.
11. The Korea Development Institute, *Growth Strategy for Overall Resources Budget Plan*, Seoul, 1972.
12. Wilford, Walton Terry, "State Tax Stability Criteria and the Revenue-Income Elasticity Coefficient," *National Tax Journal*, XVIII September 1965, pp. 304–12.

Appendix 1. National Tax Revenue in Korea

(billion current won)

	1960	1962	1964	1965	1966	1967	1968	1969	1970	1971
Internal Tax	19.8	21.4	28.9	41.8	70.5	104.0	156.9	208.5	286.9	364.2
1. Direct Tax	11.8	7.6	13.8	18.9	33.8	51.1	77.7	110.4	139.6	178.5
Personal Income	2.1	4.6	8.6	11.7	20.3	31.0	47.6	69.6	84.5	107.6
Corporation	0.9	2.0	4.1	5.7	10.9	15.9	24.6	33.1	42.4	56.7
Others[1]	8.8	1.0	1.1	1.5	2.6	4.2	5.5	7.7	11.7	14.2
2. Indirect Tax	7.5	12.9	14.1	21.9	34.2	49.3	75.7	96.8	135.9	172.6
Business	1.0	1.9	3.2	4.4	7.3	11.6	17.5	23.0	31.0	37.9
Liquor	1.2	2.5	2.9	3.8	6.3	8.1	11.1	16.0	21.6	27.7
Commodity[2]	4.3	4.7	3.3	7.0	10.3	15.4	22.2	24.8	36.9	45.0
Others[3]	1.0	3.8	4.7	6.7	10.3	14.2	24.9	33.0	46.4	62.0
3. Others[4]	0.5	0.9	1.1	1.0	2.4	3.6	3.5	1.3	12.4	13.1
Customs Duties	5.2	6.8	8.5	12.8	18.0	25.4	37.9	47.6	51.8	53.1
Total Tax	25.0	28.2	37.4	54.6	88.5	129.4	194.8	256.1	338.7	417.3

Sources: Government of Korea, Office of National Tax Administration, *Statistical Yearbook of National Tax* (Seoul, November 1971), pp. 26–7, and unpublished data for 1971.

Notes: [1] Included are receipts from inheritance and gift tax, registration tax, assets revaluation tax, real estate speculation tax, and land income tax and education tax for 1960.

[2] Includes textile tax.

[3] Includes petroleum products tax, transportation tax, electricity and gas tax, and admission tax.

[4] Includes stamp revenue.

Appendix 2. National Tax Revenues in Korea: Annual Growth Rates

(unit: percent)

	1960	1962	1964	1965	1966	1967	1968	1969	1970	1971
Internal Tax	7	19	18	44	68	48	50	32	37	27
1. Direct Tax	2	−14	40	37	78	51	52	42	25	29
Personal Income	−3	86	45	35	74	52	54	46	21	27
Corporation	28	19	37	39	91	47	54	35	28	34
Others	1	−78	24	49	63	62	31	40	52	21
2. Indirect Tax	20	53	4	56	56	44	53	28	40	27
Business	−5	84	27	35	67	59	52	32	35	22
Liquor	13	73	6	28	68	28	38	43	35	28
Commodity	33	−4	−13	113	47	49	45	11	49	22
Others	4	217	2	46	54	38	75	33	41	34
3. Others	−12	25	5	−9	149	47	−1	−64	875	6
Customs Duties	45	29	27	51	40	41	49	25	9	3
Total Tax	13	22	20	46	62	46	50	31	32	23

Sources: Government of Korea, Office of National Tax Administration, *Statistical Yearbook of National Tax* (Seoul, November 1971), pp. 26–7, and unpublished data for 1971.

Notes: [1] Included are receipts from inheritance and gift tax, registration tax, assets revaluation tax, real estate speculation tax, and land income tax and education tax for 1960.

[2] Includes textile tax.

[3] Includes petroleum products tax, transportation tax, electricity and gas tax, and admission tax.

[4] Includes stamp revenue.

Appendix 3. *Composition of National Tax Revenue in Korea (Percent of Total)*

(unit: percent)

	1960	1962	1964	1965	1966	1967	1968	1969	1970	1971
Internal Tax	79.2	75.9	77.3	75.6	79.7	80.4	80.5	81.4	84.7	87.3
1. Direct Tax	47.2	27.0	36.9	34.6	38.2	39.5	39.9	43.1	40.9	42.8
Personal Income	8.4	16.3	23.0	21.4	22.9	24.0	24.4	27.2	24.9	25.8
Corporation	3.6	7.1	11.0	10.4	12.3	12.3	12.6	12.9	12.5	13.6
Others	35.2	3.5	2.9	2.8	2.9	3.2	2.8	3.0	3.5	3.4
2. Indirect Tax	30.0	45.7	37.5	40.1	38.6	38.1	38.9	37.8	40.1	41.4
Business	4.0	6.7	8.6	8.0	8.2	9.0	9.0	9.0	9.2	9.1
Liquor	4.8	8.9	7.8	6.9	7.1	6.3	5.7	6.2	6.4	6.6
Commodity	17.2	16.7	8.8	12.9	11.6	11.9	11.4	9.7	10.9	10.8
Others	4.0	13.5	12.3	12.3	11.6	11.0	12.8	12.9	13.7	14.9
3. Others	2.0	3.2	2.9	1.8	2.8	2.8	1.8	0.5	3.7	3.1
Customs Duties	20.8	24.1	22.7	23.5	20.3	19.6	19.5	18.6	15.3	12.7
Total Tax	100.0	100.0	100.0	100.0	100.0	100.0	100.0	100.0	100.0	100.0

Sources: Government of Korea, Office of National Tax Administration, *Statistical Yearbook of National Tax* (Seoul, November 1971), pp. 26–7, and unpublished data for 1971.

Notes: [1] Included are receipts from inheritance and gift tax, registration tax, assets revaluation tax, real estate speculation tax, and land income tax and education tax for 1960.

[2] Includes textile tax.

[3] Includes petroleum products tax, transportation tax, electricity and gas tax, and admission tax.

[4] Includes stamp revenue.

Appendix 4. Method for Adjusting Actual Tax Revenue Data

In order to reach the revenue target set for a given year, the Office of National Tax Administration has been in the practice since 1969 of collecting in advance a certain amount of tax liability legally due in the following year. For our purpose of analyzing the functional relationship between tax yields and changes in aggregate income, actual tax revenue data for 1969–1971 have been adjusted to eliminate the effect of this distortion. The method of adjustment is illustrated below.

	1969	1970	1971
T_t	207.2	274.5	351.1
T_t^p	8.7	17.4	32.1
$T_t - T_t^p$	198.5	257.1	319.0
$AT_t = (T_t - T_t^p) + T_{t-1}^p$	198.5	265.8	336.4

T_t = Actual tax revenue in year t
T_t^p = Amount of tax collected in advance in year t
T_{t-1}^p = Amount of tax collected in advance in previous year
A_t = Adjusted tax revenue in year t

Appendix 5. Projected Major Economic Indicators

	1971	1972	1973
GNP[1]	1,566.9	1,681.7	1,827.6
Non-agricultural GNP[1]	1,190.5	1,288.3	1,418.4
Non-agricultural Employment[2]	5.0	5.2	5.3
Annual Growth Rate:			
GNP	10.2%	7.3%	8.7%
Non-agricultural GNP	12.8	8.2	10.1
Non-agricultural Employment	5.5	3.0	3.0
Wholesale Price Index	8.7	13.3	7.4

Source: Korea Development Institute, *Growth Strategy for Overall Resources Budget Plan,* Seoul, 1972.

Notes: [1] In billion won at 1965 prices.
[2] In millions won

THE EQUALIZING EFFECT OF FINANCIAL TRANSFERS: A STUDY OF INTERGOVERNMENTAL FISCAL RELATIONS

*Wan Soon Kim**

I. Introduction

With rapid industrialization and economic growth since 1962, the Korean economy has become more productive, but the inequalities in personal incomes and wealth among provinces have remained. This inequality is particularly evident between major urban areas and provinces. As shown in Table 1, the regional per capita gross product of Seoul and Pusan, the most prosperous and most urbanized areas in Korea, exceed, and the rest of nine provinces fail to reach, the national average.

These disparities among the local governments in their fiscal capacities create difficulties in supporting basic local needs. Table 1 shows that Seoul and Pusan together account for more than 60 percent of national tax and local tax revenue, respectively. Although the central government has provided a variety of subventions to the provincial governments to alleviate the divergency between need and capacity, provision has been inadequate. Indeed, the fiscal imbalances have been accentuated by the serious defects inherent in the method of intergovernmental fiscal adjustment.

In brief, in Korea's grant method, of which the principal type is revenue

* Professor of Economics at Korea University. This paper was written while the author was a Senior Fellow at the Korea Development Institute and was originally published in April 1974 as KDI Working Paper No. 7402.

Table 1. Indices of Provincial Differences in Korea

Province	Per Capita Gross Product(won) 1962	Per Capita Gross Product(won) 1968	Per Capita Wealth (won) 1968	National Internal Tax Revenue (billion won) 1970		Local Tax Revenue (billion won) 1970	
Seoul	28,157	80,130	211,750	139.8	(50.6%)	17.10	(51.5%)
Pusan	21,862	88,635	193,790	33.8	(12.2%)	3.20	(9.6%)
Kyonggi	17,932	45,012	106,450	21.8	(7.9%)	2.60	(7.8%)
Kangwon	15,762	40,131	174,520	5.5	(2.0%)	0.65	(1.9%)
Chungpuk	14,875	44,602	71,230	3.3	(1.2%)	0.65	(1.9%)
Chungnam	15,158	43,457	62,580	6.9	(2.5%)	1.56	(4.7%)
Chonpuk	16,513	37,239	62,900	7.0	(2.5%)	1.27	(3.8%)
Chonnam	13,533	31,966	64,200	16.4	(5.9%)	1.74	(5.2%)
Kyongpuk	15,413	40,101	73,180	15.8	(5.7%)	2.78	(8.4%)
Kyongnam	13,047	43,539	91,590	25.0	(9.1%)	1.43	(4.3%)
Cheju	14,438	48,355	120,170	1.0	(0.4%)	0.26	(0.8%)
Nation	17,018	48,832	103,810	276.3	(100.0%)	33.23	(100.0%)

Sources: Ministry of Home Affairs, *Annual Report of Gross Regional Product* (Seoul, 1972) (in Korean); Economic Planning Board, *Report on National Wealth Survey* (Seoul, 1973); Bank of Korea, *Regional Economic Statistics,* various issues, (in Korean); and Ministry of Finance, *Summary of Financial Statistics,* FY 1971.

sharing, the amount of local shared revenues was to be the difference between the amount needed for standard services defined by the central government, calculated on the basis of a system of unit costs,[1] and the amount yielded by 80 percent of the local taxes at the legal or standard rates[2] enumerated in the Local Shared Tax Law. While this method appeared to objectively recognize inequalities of financial capacity and need existing at the local level, the total grant disbursed was not the aggregate of the excess of total needs over total revenues, if any. Instead, the grant was pegged to a fixed percentage of estimated internal taxes,[3] and actual distribution procedures became subject to political negotiations between the central and local governments.

Other defects existed. The amount needed for standard services was computed only on the basis of the units of service enumerated in the Local Finance Law, which inadequately measured minimum public service

[1] See pp. 334–335.

[2] The legal or standard rates could differ slightly from the actual rates, when the local governments exercise some discretion given in the choice of local tax rates. But the permissible range is very narrow.

[3] Central government taxes excluding custom duties and monopoly profits.

levels. Adjustments made to expenditure requirements due to unforseen factors such as price increases were inadequate. Furthermore, a regionally differentiated unit-cost method without due regard to population size, for instance, was discriminatory among provinces.

The final defect in the grant formula stemmed from the fact that the provincial governments have neither their own kinds of tax nor the power to raise or lower tax rates in response to the needs of the local residents. In short, Korea's equalization scheme offered no opportunity for the provinces to exercise their own tax efforts.

In August, 1972, after more than twenty years of experience in the determination of the grant amount by the formula, the Emergency Decree on Economic Stabilization and Growth made the total size of the grant dependent on the policies of the central government at a given time. While the legal stipulation of the proportion of estimated internal taxes was eliminated, reckoning of basic local need and basic local revenue remains unchanged. There is no indication yet that this measurement is likely to be changed within the forseeable future.

Should the amount of shared taxes fluctuate year by year, depending on the demands of various national policies on the budget? Would it not be better for local governments to have some guarantee that their financial requirements for acceptable minimum levels of service, if specified, would be met? Should there not be a reasonable device to put the total grant on a more stable basis? These are some of the major issues raised in this paper in an attempt to propose a workable scheme of equalization, having due regard to the fiscal capacity, tax effort, and needs of the provinces. Specific-purpose subsidies, another means of transferring revenue to local governments in Korea, will be reviewed briefly because of their relatively small share in central government financial transfers.

The paper is divided into five sections. Section II is concerned with the structure of local governments and finances and offers a comprehensive picture of central-local financial relations. The essential feature emerging from this section is the existence of an overcentralized governmental structure and control of local expenditures and revenues by the national government. While this is the case, and while political pressure for further centralization of revenues and expenditures continues unabated, the point of view of this paper is that the local governments should be able to provide some local services at their own discretion.

Relevant statistical data are assembled and examined in Section III in order to provide a quantitative background for interprovincial fiscal comparisons. The construction of indices of provincial fiscal capacity, tax effort, and fiscal performance receives major attention.

In Section IV, analysis of the financial adjustment arrangements up to August 1972 is confined to central-provincial relations. Because of the limitation on data availability, intergovernmental transfers of central government funds from province to county and city governments are not examined. The period covered by this section dates from 1962 during which the Local Shared Tax Law, Law 931, came into effect, and ends on August 3, 1972. But frequent references are made to 1968 by way of illustration. It should be noted that assessment of Korea's intergovernmental financial relations and the existing grant method during this period is not meant to delve into the shortcomings of the past adjustment system but rather to reflect upon them in an attempt to propose an alternative grant method. This is the major task of the last section of this paper.

II. Korea's Local Finance System, 1962–1972

1. Structure of Local Governments

There are two subnational levels of government in Korea: eleven provincial governments consisting of nine provinces, one Direct Control City (Pusan), and one Special City (Seoul); and the governments of 140 counties and 30 cities (other than Seoul and Pusan). Fiscal relations between the lower levels of government and the central government are, however, hierarchical, because the latter controls the subordinate units of government.

The province holds an intermediary position in Korea's thoroughly centralized government structure. As an appointed national officer, the provincial governor supervises counties and the cities of less than 50,000 population. When a city reaches the population mark of 50,000, it ceases to belong to the county and enjoys an equal status with the county.

Within the central government, the supervisory organ for the province and, as a matter of fact, for the entire local government machinery is the Bureau of Local Administration in the Home Affairs Ministry. The Bureau controls not only the personnel of the local governments but also affects their budgets, accounting and auditing, tax collection, local borrowing, and the disbursements of shared revenues. Arrangements for Seoul are an exception, however. In 1962, the government promulgated a special law which transferred control of the Special City of Seoul from the Home Affairs Ministry to the Office of the Prime Minister.

But the control of the central government over local governments is not limited to the areas under the influence of the Home Affairs Ministry. It is broader and more extensive because a great number of special laws enable the various ministries to deal with their specific functions, issuing directives and instructions to the provincial governors. For instance, the Education Ministry assumes and supervises local education financing, and the distribution of specific subsidies to the local governments is not coordinated, but managed, by the concerned ministries.

Classified into types of budgetary accounts, local governments have three different accounts: a general account, some 80 odd special accounts (designed to run on a commercial basis) and the Education Special Account. The third category is, however, independent of local governments and is handled by special boards of education and controlled by the Ministry of Education. The general account covers functions that are assigned by the central government as well as those which a local government undertakes on its own initiative. Its expenditures are largely financed through local taxes, transfers, and subsidies. The special account expenditures, which include those associated with the management of hospitals, toll roads, sewage disposal, and the like, derive their financial resources from user and special charges, loans, and transfers from the general account.

Central controls tend to encompass all aspects of local finances. In the next section the degree of Korea's fiscal centralization is seen from the revenue as well as expenditure side. In a nutshell, much of the local revenue from which the expenditures are made does not come from local taxes. Where functions are largely assigned from above and revenue shortfalls are covered by transfers and subsidies from the central government, exercise of local autonomy is totally restricted.

2. *Revenue Centralization*

A local government, able to finance its needs through local taxes, does not require grants-in-aid from the central government. What is the situation in this regard in Korea? The order of magnitude of the types of the general account revenues is given in Table 2.[4]

Local taxes are divided into ordinary and special purpose taxes, the latter being used for specific undertakings and levied on persons who stand

[4] Normally, local general account revenues include contributions, carried-over, brought-forward, etc. These items are excluded in Table 2 because of their ambiguities.

to benefit from these undertakings. The most important local tax source is the acquisition tax, a transaction tax, imposed on the basis of acquisition of land, buildings, ships, vehicles, etc. Similar to it is the property tax, levied on the ownership of property such as dwelling houses and non-farming lands. Agricultural land taxes rank second, providing about 5.5 percent of the general account revenues. Its tax bases are either net harvest from, or value added by, the agricultural land, depending on the classification of the land. In total, local ordinary taxes contributed about 31 percent to the general account revenues. Non-tax revenues such as income from property and rents and fees provide about 9 percent; they are also of local origin.

Subject to the Local Finance Law, local governments are permitted to float loans for the financing of the special accounts and the Education Special Account expenditures. As Table 2 indicates, local loans amounted to less than 1 percent of the general account revenues. Usually, government-owned banks have extended credit to local governments to finance the budgetary gaps resulting from their inability to meet shared-cost programs out of current receipts.

Nevertheless, a major portion of the revenue with which local governments operate comes from the central government. Of the funds transferred from the central government, local shared tax accounted for more than 40 percent and subsidies for about 19 percent. Together these two sources, derived from the collection of national internal taxes, provided 59 percent of local general revenues.[5] The subject of intergovernmental financial transfers will be examined in Section IV.

The central government, relying on income taxes, has shown itself a much more efficient taxing unit than the local government, which depends largely on acquisition, agricultural land, and property taxes. Although the tax base of the local government has been responsive to over-all economic activity, it has fallen behind the growth of national internal tax revenue. Compared with the annual average growth rate of 37 percent during the period, 1962–1971, local tax revenue registered a growth rate of 25 percent over the same period.

The distribution of tax resources between the central and the local government draws our attention. Table 3 shows that in 1972 the central government collected about 91 percent of the total tax revenues; the remaining 9 percent was raised by local taxation. As Table 3 shows, the percentage

[5] In 1968, total grants-in-aid accounted for about 89 percent of the Educational Special Account receipts.

Table 2. Composition of Local Revenue of the General Account, 1968

Source of Revenue	Percentage (%)
Local Taxes	31.0
Ordinary Taxes	28.5
Acquisition Tax	8.3
Automobile Tax	4.0
Entertainment Tax	5.1
Butchery Tax	0.3
License Tax	1.4
Horse-race Tax	0.1
Property Tax	3.8
Agricultural Land Tax	5.5
Special Purpose Taxes	2.3
City Planning Tax	1.8
Fire-Fighting Facilities Tax	0.5
National Surtaxes	0.2
Non-tax Revenue	9.3
Income from Property	4.4
Rents and Fees	4.9
Local Loans	0.8
Local Shared Tax	40.3
Subsidies	18.6
Total	100.0%

Source: Ministry of Home Affairs, *Statistical Yearbook of Local Tax,* 1971.

was not always so small. Before 1967 surtaxes on national taxes were levied. Their discontinuance, as well as reduction in the rates and assessment base of the agricultural land tax, greatly reduced the amount of revenues which local governments raised from their own sources. The revenue loss from these changes is estimated to be 28.9 billion won in 1972, an amount almost equal to 38 percent of local shared tax in that year.

The situation could be rectified by transferring some national internal taxes to local governments. The kinds of internal taxes of the central government, and the contributions made by them, are shown in Table 4. There appears to be some support in the Ministry of Home Affairs for the transfer of registration, transportation, electricity and gas, and admission taxes to local governments in order to provide them with greater fiscal resources. The argument that the local governments are totally inefficient in handling national taxes is too general; some taxes which are now national seem suitable for local collection.

Table 3. Taxes and Tax Burden Ratios, 1962–1972

(billion won).

Fiscal Year	National Internal Tax	Local Tax	Custom Duties plus Monopoly profits	Total Tax Revenues	Local Tax Share (%)	Local Tax Burden (% of GNP)	National Internal Tax Burden (% of GNP)	Total Tax Burden (% of GNP)
1962	21.50	5.18	10.98	37.66	13.7	1.5	6.2	10.8
1963	24.69	7.35	11.22	43.26	17.0	1.5	5.1	8.6
1964	29.19	8.73	12.76	50.68	17.2	1.3	4.2	7.2
1965	42.06	11.21	16.17	69.44	16.1	1.4	5.2	8.6
1966	70.01	15.95	25.10	111.06	14.4	1.6	6.8	10.8
1967	103.83	13.79	35.41	153.03	9.0	1.1	8.2	12.1
1968	156.41	19.36	54.30	230.07	8.4	1.2	9.8	14.4
1969	218.10	26.58	69.00	313.68	8.5	1.3	10.5	15.1
1970	283.80	33.23	81.02	398.05	8.4	1.3	11.0	15.4
1971	355.50	39.81	97.56	492.87	8.1	1.3	11.3	15.6
1972	374.34	46.61	101.36	522.31	8.9	1.2	9.8	13.6

Sources: Ministry of Finance, *Summary of Financial Statistics*, FY 1971; Ministry of Home Affairs, *Statistical Yearbook of Local Tax*, 1972; and Office of National Tax Administration, *Statistical Yearbook of National Tax*, 1972.

Table 4. National Internal Tax Collections, 1970

	Amounts (billion won)	Percentage Distribution
Personal income tax	84.5	30.0
Corporation income tax	42.4	15.0
Registration tax	7.2	2.5
Business activity tax	31.0	11.0
Transportation tax	13.4	4.8
Liquor tax	21.7	7.7
Commodity tax	31.7	11.2
Textile products tax	10.7	3.8
Petroleum products tax	21.3	7.6
Electricity and gas tax	7.0	2.5
Admission tax	4.6	1.6
Others[1]	6.4	2.3
Internal tax Revenue Total	281.8	100.0 %

Source: Office of National Tax Administration, *Statistical Yearbook of National Tax*, 1973.

Note: [1] Others include inheritance, assets revaluation, real estate speculation control, and securities transaction taxes, and stamp revenue.

Additionally, the fiscal situation could be improved if local governments had some freedom to change rates in response to local needs. At present, however, the central government determines, uniformly, the rates of local taxes, permitting no diversity, despite the diversity of local entities. This revenue centralization has led to a situation where one locality lacks certain tax resources while another has an excess of them.

In an attempt to increase the revenue from local taxes, the central government has instituted a new additional local tax: the provincial and municipal Resident Tax on Households and corporations. It is a hybrid tax, consisting partly of a per capita tax and partly of a percentage (5 percent) of the income and agricultural land taxes. The per capita element of the Resident Tax varies for both households (from 300 won to 2,000 won) and corporations with the size of city. For example, a Seoul resident has to pay 2,000 won for his household, and he is additionally levied a tax of 5 percent on his income taxes. By the end of 1973, the resident tax, which began on June 1973, was expected to bring a sum of about 9.4 billion won.

3. Expenditure Centralization

A look at overall governmental expenditures since 1962 provides a preliminary base from which the degree of central direction of local expenditures may be discerned. Table 5, constructed on the basis of the national income accounts, gives useful indications of expenditure patterns. The share of total government spending of the GNP reached about 20 percent in 1962, fell to 17 percent in 1970, and is estimated, according to the Third Five-Year Economic Development Plan (1972–76), as going up to 25 percent in 1976. During the period 1962–71, the average share of defense expenditures in total government spending remained nearly 29 percent. By the end of the Third Five-Year Economic Development Plan (1972–76), the defense share is estimated to fall by 10 percentage points.[6]

Table 6 shows two sets of figures for government spending in 1962, 1970 and 1976. One counts the financial transfers from the central government as expenditures made by the local governments (final level); and the other counts them as spent by the originating level of government. On the basis of the originating level, it can be seen that the relative shares of the levels of government—87 percent for central versus 13 percent for local—has changed little since 1962. But this does not take into consideration that the various central government transfers—largely of shared taxes—are ultimately expended on the local level. On this basis the local share of government spending is larger. In 1962, financial transfers by the central government amounted to about 22 percent of its expenditures, and increased to 36 percent in 1970. The share of financial transfers in central government expenditures in 1976 is estimated to be 23 percent.

In theory, expenditures made at the local level, but centrally financed, need not necessarily be centrally directed. What is the real extent to which local governments are subject to the central government in determination of the size and composition of their expenditures?

Table 7 shows a crude functional classification of expenditures for which local governments are responsible: general services, community services, economic services, and social services. What portion of these represents an area of independent local action? An unpublished report indicates that more than 84 percent of local taxes and shared revenues are allocated for "obligatory" expenses,[7] *i.e.* those specified by the central government;

[6] Economic Planning Board, *Third Five-Year Economic Development Plan (1972–76)*.

[7] Some of these include expenditures required for the "new village movement," local construction, interprovincial projects, shared-cost programs, etc.

Table 5. *Government Expenditures, 1962–1971*

(billion won)

	1962	1963	1964	1965	1966	1967	1968	1969	1970	1971
1) Current Expenditures	65.16	71.85	80.61	96.86	138.49	185.78	250.33	329.56	425.55	541.09
Exhaustive	47.36	51.40	58.41	71.45	99.10	124.29	164.15	210.21	268.51	340.52
(a) Central gov't	31.56	32.80	37.64	46.07	65.07	77.58	102.46	131.87	165.92	290.61
(b) Local gov't	15.80	18.60	20.77	25.38	34.03	46.71	61.69	78.34	102.59	130.91
Non-Exhaustive	17.80	20.45	22.20	25.41	39.39	61.49	86.58	119.35	157.04	200.57
(c) Central gov't	17.09	19.64	21.51	24.30	37.72	59.16	82.29	112.35	149.80	187.78
(d) Local gov't	0.71	0.81	0.69	1.11	1.67	2.33	4.29	7.00	7.24	12.79
2) Gross Capital Formation	19.21	17.55	24.10	31.25	49.31	61.92	106.63	168.27	169.07	194.42
(e) Central gov't	13.34	11.97	17.46	20.61	32.31	37.43	60.65	94.79	77.67	83.22
(f) Local gov't	5.87	5.58	6.64	10.64	17.00	24.49	45.98	73.48	91.40	111.20
3) Central gov't (a + c + e)	61.99	64.41	76.61	90.98	135.10	174.17	245.40	339.01	393.39	480.61
4) Local gov't spending (b + d + f)	22.38	24.99	28.10	37.13	52.70	73.53	111.96	158.82	201.23	254.90
5) Local gov't spending (Excluding grants-in-aid)	8.76	8.94	11.40	15.05	18.34	19.85	32.30	51.41	59.40	80.90
6) Total gov't spending (3 + 5)	70.75	73.35	88.01	106.03	153.44	194.02	277.70	390.42	452.79	561.51
7) (4)/GNP (%)	6.4	5.1	4.0	4.6	5.1	5.8	7.0	7.6	7.8	8.1
8) (5)/GNP (%)	2.5	1.8	1.6	1.9	1.8	1.6	2.0	2.5	2.3	2.6
9) (6)/GNP (%)	20.3	15.0	12.6	13.2	14.9	15.3	17.4	18.7	17.5	17.8

Source: Bank of Korea, *National Income Statistics Yearbook*, 1972.

Notes: [1] "Exhaustive" current expenditures refer to those excluding transfer payments, subsidies, and interest on public debt.

[2] "Non-exhaustive" expenditures include transfer payments, subsidies, and interest on public debt.

[3] The share of local government spending in GNP would be larger, if central government transfers are included. See Table 5 for the level of government to which intergovernmental payment is charged.

Table 6. Current and Capital Expenditures by Final Disbursing Level and Originating Level of Government 1960, 1970 and 1976

Level of Government	Final Level	Originating Level
A) 1962 Current Expenditures	55.60 (100%)	55.60 (100%)
Central	39.08 (70.3)	48.65 (87.5)
Local	16.51 (29.7)	6.95 (12.5)
Gross Capital Formation	15.16 (100%)	15.16 (100%)
Central	9.29 (61.3)	13.34 (88.0)
Local	5.87 (38.7)	1.82 (12.0)
Total Expenditures	70.75 (100%)	70.75 (100%)
Central	48.37 (68.4)	61.99 (87.6)
Local	22.38 (31.6)	8.76 (12.4)
B) 1970 Current Expenditures	317.2 (100%)	317.2 (100%)
Central	207.4 (65.4)	315.7 (99.5)
Local	109.8 (34.6)	1.4 (0.5)
Gross Capital Formation	135.6 (100%)	135.6 (100%)
Central	44.2 (32.6)	77.7 (57.3)
Local	91.4 (67.4)	57.9 (42.7)
Total Expenditures	452.8 (100%)	452.8 (100%)
Central	251.6 (55.6)	393.4 (86.9)
Local	201.2 (44.4)	59.4 (13.1)
C) 1976 Current Expenditures	650.5 (100%)	650.5 (100%)
Central	446.7 (68.7)	623.6 (95.9)
Local	203.8 (31.3)	26.9 (4.1)
Gross Capital Formation	407.7 (100%)	407.7 (100%)
Central	262.6 (64.4)	294.7 (72.3)
Local	145.1 (35.6)	113.0 (27.7)
Total Expenditures	1,058.2 (100%)	1,058.2 (100%)
Central	709.3 (67.0)	918.3 (86.8)
Local	348.9 (33.0)	139.9 (13.2)

Sources: Bank of Korea, *National Income Statistics Yearbook*, 1972, and Economic Planning Board, *Third Five-Year Economic Development Plan (1972–1976)*.
Note: Data relating to 1976 are in 1970 prices.

only the remaining 16 percent is available to be used at local discretion for some local-type services.

Another evidence of expenditure centralization is the system for financing public education. As can be verified by Table 7, public education financing is one of Korea's most important items of local government spending, absorbing about 33 percent of total local expenditures. But the local contribution to the financing of public education is negligible.

Table 7. *Broad Functional Classification of Gross Local Government Expenditures by Accounts, 1968*

(billion won)

	General Account	Education Special Account	Other Special Account	Total	Percentage
General Services	16.75	—	0.05	16.79	12.5
Community Services	18.31	—	27.20	45.51	34.0
Economic Services	12.88	—	4.24	17.12	12.8
Social Services	9.05	44.46	0.84	54.35	40.6
Education	—	44.46	—	44.46	33.2
Others	0.20	—	—	0.20	0.1
Total	57.19	44.46	32.32	133.97	100.0%

Source: Ministry of Home Affairs, *Financial Abstract of Local Government*, 1971.

The major burden for the primary and public education program is left with the central government.

Provision of financial aid to, and assertion of control over, major expenditure programs by the central government is not to be condemned in general. It would be inefficient and uneconomical to have these functions carried out by a host of local governments without some degree of national control or a nationally established basis for cooperation in the performance of such functions as health, education, construction and maintenance of roads and rivers where the benefits extend beyond the boundaries of a single province. In particular, Korea, setting out on a course of rapid industrialization, could entrust only limited functions to local governments which lack personnel of sufficient ability and knowledge to assist in the implementation of developmental expenditures.

While centralization may be justifiable during the initial period of economic development, the issue really is whether Korea has more centralization than is needed. What is true is that important governmental functions such as education, construction of highways, and rural electrification are entirely relegated to the central government. Local entities exercise a small number of minor functions. If economic development is ever really to take root in a county, local leadership and local involvement will help in modernization and industrialization. Some serious efforts should be directed to the wider use of conditional grants or specific-purpose grants to the local governments so that they could participate in overall economic development.

III. Fiscal Performance and Revenue Effort

1. Diversity in Per Capita Expenditure

In Section II, the distribution of tax revenues and aggregate governmental expenditures between the central and the local government were analyzed. If the share of gross governmental expenditures is considered for the subordinate levels of local government, excluding Seoul and Pusan, province spending accounted, in 1970, for 16 percent and city and county together for about 54 percent.[8] What draws our attention is, however, the skewed regional distribution of some governmental expenditures. To take as an example, social and welfare expenditures, Seoul and Pusan accounted for about 69 percent of them. With respect to local taxes collected, provinces accounted for 10 percent, cities for 11 percent, and counties for 15 percent.[9]

Because of Korea's thoroughly centralized government structure, however, the division of expenditure and revenue by the different levels of local government may be meaningless. Furthermore, since data on intergovernmental transfers, except for the flows from central to province, are not classified according to the level which receives or pays the grant, double-counting is unavoidable. Hence, inter-province, inter-county or inter-city comparisions of expenditures may be quite misleading with regard to the relative levels of services provided by each of the three levels of local government.

Table 8 shows that, according to the data gathered from local government sources in 1968, province-city-county expenditures for the nation averaged 5,058 won per capita. Since column (1)—per capita expenditure—includes intergovernmental transfers without separating the level of government that pays the grant from the one that gets it, these figures are subject to double-counting. In order to secure figures of per capita expenditure by entire local entities from their own sources, intergovernmental transfers must be deducted. For 1968, the national per capita province-city-county expenditure, less intergovernmental transfers, was

[8] As indicated, the three levels of local government consist of province, city, and county. Unless specified, however, (province) will represent the totality of local entities. For example, Chungnam Province includes provincial, city, and county governments.

[9] The balance of 64 percent came from Seoul and Pusan.

Table 8. *Per Capita Gross Local Government Expenditure and Financial Transfers from Central Government, 1968* (won)

Province	Per capita[1] expenditure (1)	Per capita educational expenditure (2)	Per capita[2] financial transfers (3)	Per capita financial transfers for education (4)
Seoul	6,687	1,347	1,551	957
Pusan	9,175	1,575	1,996	1,221
Kyonggi	4,377	1,424	2,634	1,290
Kangwon	4,653	1,772	3,700	1,588
Chungpuk	3,970	1,649	3,123	1,495
Chungnam	3,547	1,469	2,615	1,319
Chonpuk	4,116	1,484	3,224	1,359
Chonnam	4,999	1,523	3,974	1,418
Kyongpuk	4,551	1,403	2,705	1,287
Kyongnam	5,106	1,580	3,439	1,406
Cheju	5,362	1,695	4,316	1,486
Nation	5,058	1,493	2,882	1,307

Sources: Ministry of Home Affairs, *Financial Abstract of Local Government*, 1971, and data provided by the Ministry of Education.

Notes: [1] This is the sum of local government spending through the general account, special accounts, and education special account.

[2] This is the sum of central government transfers effected to the three budget accounts.

2,176 won.[10] In order to measure the variation in per capita province-city-county expenditures from their own sources, the value of 100 is assigned to the national average to see how much each local government spends in relation to this national average. Table 9 shows that Pusan has a relative expenditure of 330, and is thus spending 230 percent more than the national average; Chungpuk Province, with a relative expenditure of 39, spends 61 percent less than the average. It can easily be seen that wide disparities in per capita expenditure exist largely between provinces and the two major urban areas; variations among the nine provinces are less pronounced.

Income and wealth appear to be the most important factors which account for the diversity existing between the two urban areas and the nine provinces. In relation to per capita gross domestic product, Seoul and Pusan exceed,and the rest of the nine provinces fail to reach, the national average.

[10] Column (1)-Column (3)

Table 9. Some Indicators of Regional Differences in Korea, 1968

Province	Index of per capita expendi-ture	Index of per capita expendi-ture (less transfers)	Index of per capita gross product	Index of per capita wealth	Index of[1] tax "effort"	Index of[2] tax "effort"
	(1)	(2)	(3)	(4)	(5)	(6)
Seoul	132.2	236.0	164.1	204.0	191.7	154.8
Pusan	181.4	329.9	181.5	186.7	97.0	93.6
Kyonggi	86.5	80.1	92.2	102.5	87.1	80.7
Kongwon	92.0	39.2	82.2	168.1	44.7	40.3
Chungpuk	78.5	38.9	91.3	68.6	62.1	82.3
Chungnam	70.1	42.8	89.0	60.3	69.7	104.8
Chonpuk	81.4	41.0	76.3	60.6	70.5	88.7
Chonnam	98.8	47.1	65.5	61.8	53.8	56.5
Kyongpuk	90.0	84.8	82.1	70.5	84.1	96.8
Kyongnam	101.0	76.6	89.2	88.2	58.3	59.7
Cheju	106.0	48.1	99.0	115.8	50.0	41.9
National	100.0	100.0	100.0	100.0	100.0	100.0

Sources: Ministry of Home Affairs, *Annual Report of Gross Regional Product*, 1972; Economic Planning Board, *Report on National Wealth Survey*, 1973; and Ministry of Home Affairs, *Statistical Yearbook of Local Tax*, 1971.

Notes: [1] Computed by dividing local tax collections by gross domestic product.
[2] Computed by dividing local tax collections by wealth.

Ranking of local governments according to their relative standing in per capita wealth shows a slightly different pattern. As usual, while Seoul and Pusan exceed the national average, Kyonggi, Kangwon, and Cheju Provinces have relative wealth of 103, 168, and 116, respectively.

With respect to the expenditure variation among the nine provinces no conclusive relationship emerges between per capita income and per capita government expenditure. Because local tax bases consist largely of wealth components, variation in per capita expenditure has been examined in relation to per capita wealth. The wealth factor appears to explain the intergovernmental expenditure diversity slightly better than the income variable.

It is interesting to observe that provinces that rank low in per capita gross domestic product and/or in per capita wealth, have a higher rank in per capita expenditure; conversely, provinces that rank high in income and wealth have a lower rank in per capita government expenditure. Kangwon, Chungpuk, and Cheju Provinces, which ranked third, eighth, and fourth in terms of per capita wealth, ranked tenth, eleventh, and sixth in terms of per capita expenditure.[11] Kyongpuk Province, which ranked seventh in terms of per capita wealth and ninth in terms of per capita gross domestic product ranked third in terms of per capita expenditure.

2. *Functional Distribution of Expenditure*

The per capita expenditure classified by major functions, and the percentage spent for each, are given in Table 10. For 1968, local expenditures for the nation averaged 5,058 won per capita. These figures include funds provided from their own sources as well as from intergovernmental transfers. The data on local finances in Korea do not provide figures of per capita expenditure by both functions and provinces, less intergovernmental transfers.

Per capita expenditure for education, as shown in Table 10, is the largest single expenditure item. Education was by far the most important type of spending by local governments in 1968, absorbing 1,493 won per capita, or about 30 percent of total local expenditures. As mentioned earlier, the central government assumes the major burden of financing local public

Table 10. Per Capita and Percentage Distribution of Local Expenditure for Selected Functions, 1968

Function	Per Capita Expenditure	Percentage of total spending
General administration	577 won	11.4 %
Highways	780	15.4
Housing	561	11.1
Waterworks	300	6.0
Agriculture and livestock	293	5.8
Education	1,493	29.5
Health and sanitation	203	4.0
Other functions	851	16.8
Nation	5,058	100.0 %

Sources: Ministry of Home Affairs, *Financial Abstract of Local Government*, 1971, and data provided by the Ministry of Education.

[11] In terms of per capita gross domestic product, they ranked eighth, fifth, and third.

education.

3. Revenue Effort

A similar range of variation is found in Table 9 for indices of tax "effort" in which the local tax revenues collected by provinces, counties, and cities are compared to gross domestic product and to national wealth.[12] Wealth as a denominator may be suitable in Korea, because local governments have relied heavily on the type of taxes that have wealth bases. Table 9 shows that while Seoul exerts the greatest tax effort on both bases, the effort index for Kangwon Province is lowest.

But a caution is in order here. The reason that Kangwon Province shows the lowest tax effort despite its relative wealth of 168 may be that its wealth is largely non-taxable. In 1970, Kangwon Province accounted only for 1.8 percent of total acquisition tax collections, 2.4 percent of agricultural land tax collections, and 2.2 percent of property tax collections.

IV. Inter-governmental Financial Transfers in Korea

In Korea, the financial arrangements between the central and provincial governments are subject to the Local Finance Law, the Local Shared Tax Law, and the Subsidy Administration Law.[13] These laws provide for a variety of subventions to the local governments, as shown in Table 11, in the form of grants-in-aid for education, local shared taxes, and subsidies of various types. Between 1962 and 1972, total central government transfers to local governments increased more than fifteen times, from about 14 billion to 202 billion won. The importance of grants-in-aid for education in total resources transferred by the central government to local governments can be easily seen in Table 11, they accounted for more than 50 percent of total central government transfers during the period, 1962–

[12] Since the kinds and legal rates of local taxes are uniform throughout Korea, the concept of the representative tax system is not relevant. Ideally, tax effort should be measured in terms of tax collections per won of income above the subsistence level or the basic exemption amount.

[13] Because of the lack of information on how the grant money flows from the central government to the provincial government and to the city or county governments, the grantor and the recipient governments are identified here as the central and local governments, respectively.

Table 11. *Intergovernmental Financial Transfers by Types and Regions, 1968*

(In millions won)

	Local shared taxes distributed by Home Affairs Ministry[1] (1)	Local shared taxes for education distributed by Education Ministry[2] (2)	Primary education treasury grant[3] (3)	
			current	capital
Seoul	2,130	345	2,117	1,637
Pusan	1,111	41	960	718
Kyonggi	2,645	251	2,675	769
Kangwon	3,293	184	1,971	507
Chungpuk	1,641	162	1,554	386
Chungnam	2,121	216	2,592	678
Chonpuk	2,236	162	2,365	566
Chonnam	3,483	239	3,967	1,104
Kyongpuk	3,650	262	4,043	1,160
Kyongnam	3,164	250	3,081	709
Cheju	628	63	318	84
Total	25,102	2,175	26,043	8,318

Sources: Ministry of Finance, *Summary of Financial Statistics*, 1970, and Ministry of Home Affairs, *Financial Abstract of Local Government*, 1969.

Notes:[1] Local shared taxes to be distributed by the Home Affairs Ministry are equivalent to 17.60 percent of estimated internal taxes.

[2] Local shared taxes for education to be distributed to provinces by the Education Ministry are equivalent to 1.43 percent of estimated internal taxes.

[3] Primary education treasury grant to be distributed to city and county governments by the Education Ministry are equivalent to 11.55 percent of estimated internal taxes.

1972. Under the Local Education Shared Tax Law and Primary Education Treasury Grant Law, the central government supports school boards directly, so that resources for local education would be provided to all schools.

1. Tax Sharing

As already indicated, Seoul, Pusan, and the nine provinces do not have the same fiscal capacity. Because of the uneven distribution of resources and income, per capita tax yields differ between provinces. As a result, cer-

Table 11. (Continued)

	Other education subsidies (4)	Grant-in-aid for education: Total[4] (5)	Subsides[5] (6)	Total central government financial transfers[6] (7)
Seoul	49	4,148	456	6,734
Pusan	177	1,896	93	3,100
Kyonggi	312	4,007	565	8,217
Kangwon	235	2,897	785	5,975
Chungpuk	196	2,298	415	4,354
Chungnam	340	3,826	875	6,826
Chonpak	284	3,377	1,370	6,983
Chonnam	557	5,867	4,377	13,727
Kyongpuk	394	5,859	1,321	10,830
Kyongnam	406	4,446	1,603	9,213
Cheju	67	532	256	1,416
Total	3,017	39,553	13,121	77,776

Notes: [4] Total grants-in-aid for education are, therefore, 12.98 percent of estimated internal taxes, plus other education subsidies.

[5] Subsidies here refer to those other than the subsidies given for educational purposes, composed of national treasury shares, specific outright subsidies, and promotional subsidies. There is a discrepancy between the amount of subsidies reported by the Home Affairs Ministry and that by the Bank of Korea. See Table 14.

[6] In 1968, total central government financial transfers amounted to 77,776 million won, according to the data sources used here, whereas the Bank of Korea's *Economic Statistics Yearbook* reports 79,656 million won. The major discrepancy stems from the differences in the amount of subsidies reported.

tain provincial governments are unable to provide their citizens with the nationally acceptable level of services. In such circumstances, an allocation of tax revenues by means of equalization payments enables the lower income provinces to provide a higher level of services than their own resources would enable them to provide.

In Korea the system of shared taxes, aimed at providing equalization effects, has its origin in the provisional shared tax system under Law 192, declared on April 1, 1951. But it was not until the end of 1961 that some rationalization of tax-sharing arrangements began in earnest.[14] Although

[14] By the Local Shared Tax Law, promulgated and enforced as Law No. 931 on December 31, 1961.

there were changes in the revenue-sharing arrangements during the period 1962–1972, its essential feature was the determination of the grant amount by the formula. As mentioned previously, on August 3, 1972, the Emergency Decree abolished the existing grant method and made the grant amount dependent on the budgetary conditions of the central government at a given time. A new system is being planned. Therefore, a review of the tax sharing arrangements which prevailed, in particular, from 1969 to 1972, is of great importance in considering an alternative equalization payment scheme.

The 1969–1972 tax-sharing arrangement was based on a method whereby the Economic Planning Board set aside each year for distribution to the local governments revenue equivalent to 17.60 percent of estimated national internal tax collections (see Table 11).[15] Based on a fixed percentage of revenue, the grant money fluctuated with the rate and yield of tax revenue.

As to the method of actual allocation of shared taxes, the Home Affairs Ministry took into account differences in provincial revenue-raising capacity and in expenditure requirements. Provincial service requirements (legally designated the basic financial need) were reckoned by three factors: categories of expenditure, measurement units, and unit costs.[16] During the period under consideration, there were 33 categories of expenditure with their measurement units and costs differentiated by Seoul, Pusan, province, city, and county. A few examples are indicated in Table 12.

The basic financial need for each provincial government was then computed by first identifying, among 33 items, the units of service to be performed by each provincial government, multiplying them by the unit cost, and adding the subtotals together. To cite a few examples, the unit of service for road pavement was the length of road to be paved; for local council expenses it was the number of local council personnel.

The unit cost could be adjusted upward whenever an annual price increase exceeded 15 percent. Additionally, the basic amount of financial needs could be supplemented, should the cost of services borne by the local governments increase. Some remote off-shore and war-damaged areas were also entitled to additional allowances for the cost of providing public services such as communication and medical care.

---

[15] Strictly speaking, the total shared taxes to be distributed consisted of ordinary shared taxes—16 percent, and special shared taxes—1.6 percent.

[16] The administrative orders governing the Local Shared Law determined the bases for the measurement.

Table 12. ***Measurement Units and Unit Costs Required for Reckoning of Basic Financial Need***

Categories of expenditure	Measurement units	Claimant entities	Unit costs (won)
Local Council	per head	Seoul	106,039
		Pusan	106,039
		Province	81,569
		City	32,959
		County	32,959
Road Pavement	length of road (per meter)	Seoul	924
		Pusan	462
		Province	154
		City	308
		County	154
Land Improvement	land acreage (per cheongbo)[1]	Seoul	258
		Pusan	258
		Province	128
		City	130
		County	130
Rural Development	number of houses (per house)	Seoul	335
		Pusan	335
		Province	126
		City	209
		County	209
Livestock	number of cows, pigs and horses (per animal)	Seoul	72
		Pusan	72
		Province	36
		City	36
		County	36

Source: *Local Shared Tax Law.*
Note: [1] *Cheongbo* is equivalent to about 2.45 acres.

The basic financial revenue was computed as 80 percent of the local taxes at the standard rates of the Local Shared Tax Law. Thus, the law based the distribution of shared taxes on fairly objective criteria. However, the total grant disbursed was not the aggregate of the excess of total needs over total revenues. In other words, each local government did not receive the difference between its fiscal capacity and needs, if any. The Home Affairs Ministry selectively trimmed the amount applied by the provincial governments in order to keep the total within the revenue provided by the prescribed percentage of estimated national internal taxes.

Table 13. Allocation of Shared Taxes, 1963, 1965, and 1966

(million won)

	Basic financial need	Basic financial revenue	Revenue shortage	Local shared tax	Budgetary gap
1963					
Pusan	185	115	−70	1	−69
Provinces	1,495	391	−1,105	935	−170
Total	4,937	2,170	−2,767	2,123	−644
1965					
Pusan	531	475	−55	2	−53
Provinces	2,254	628	−1,626	608	−1,018
Total	10,733	4,804	−5,929	2,821	−3,108
1966					
Pusan	950	712	−238	53	−185
Provinces	2,711	1,080	−1,631	1,300	−331
Total	14,717	6,845	−7,872	5,625	−2,247

Source: *The Structural Analysis of Local Government Finances and Policy Recommendations,* The Politics and Economics Research Institute of Korea, 1966, pp. 453–455.

Because no published data are available after 1967, on the calculation of basic financial need and revenue for each local government, there is no way of knowing the extent to which the distribution of shared taxes financed the total excess of need over revenue. However, on the basis of some available past data on fiscal capacity and needs of the local governments and the distribution of total shared revenue by province, the effect of recent tax sharing programs could be evaluated. In 1970, Seoul and Pusan, which accounted for more than 62 percent of national internal tax revenue, received less than 12 percent of total shared revenue. Relatively speaking, the richer Seoul and Pusan governments supported the poorer provinces, and there was some interprovincial redistribution of income. In other words, equalization money from the central government had the effect of somewhat reducing the disparity between basic local need and basic local revenue. But it did not come close to eliminating it, as the absolute data on the budgetary gap in Table 13 indicate.

Korea's 1969–1972 tax sharing arrangement had a number of defects. First, the revenue to be shared with the local governments was in theory a block grant, to be used by the local governments for local needs without further central government control. In practice supervision was not usually kept to this minimum level. Because the actual grant was not the sum of the excess of total needs over total revenues, contrary to the provisions of the Local Shared Tax Law, actual distribution procedures were affected by the statutory earmarking of estimated national internal tax revenues. The budgetary data submitted by the provincial governments were often inflated to serve as better starting points for the negotiations with the Home Affairs Ministry. In turn, the Ministry usually made adjustments to the local estimates of basic financial revenue and need in order to keep the total within the limit. Also, in the allocation of shared taxes, it was likely that the Home Affairs Ministry distributed shared taxes in accord not with national priorities but with ministerial priorities and took scant notice of the needs of local governments.

Secondly, the regionally differentiated unit-cost method was applied to categories of expenditure or service. Instead of looking simply at aggregate corrected *per capita* levels, different denominators such as the length of road, and land acreage were used, as shown in Table 11. A critical issue is whether these denominators were equitable bases for distribution. What was the reason for Seoul requiring the unit cost of paving road per meter to be 924 won, while an identical unit cost was applied to 30 different cities without further differentiation? In arriving realistically at the measurement of expenditure requirements, the administrative orders governing the Local Shared Tax Law did not take into account such factors as a decrease in unit cost due to economies of scale, or an increase in unit cost in the case of larger areas to be serviced. Furthermore, looking at the 33 categories of expenditure, it is questionable that they constitute adequate minimum public service levels, reflecting a national judgment.

Thirdly, the basic amount needed for standard services was computed on the basis of the categories of expenditure fixed by the local Shared Tax Law. Two faulty consequences emerged from this feature. For one, a new item of service had to be legislated before it could be provided, despite the obvious need for the expenditure. The other was that in general each local government could only submit to the Home Affairs Ministry the budgetary needs on the basis of the existing expenditure items. In other words, a local government which had not provided hospital services could not draw up its budget requirements for the construction of hospitals. It was entirely left to the discretion of the Home Affairs Ministry to meet the deficiency through some special allowances.

Lastly, the tax rates at which ordinary local taxes were computed were uniform, and the kinds of tax which could be imposed were set rigidly by the Local Finance Law. Hence, any regional differences in revenue-raising capacity were entirely due to the size of taxable bases and efficiency in tax collection. In other words, the amounts of tax collected were larger in "rich" Seoul and Pusan and smaller in the "poor" provinces.

On August 3, 1972, determination of the grant amount by the formula was officially abolished. The central government explained that such a policy shift was prompted because of the budgetary inflexibility brought about by statutory revenue earmarking. It added that the size of the grant would be dependent now on the policy decisions of the national government, taking into account its overall financial needs, resources, and administrative convenience. But no indication yet has been given of how basic local needs and revenues are to be reckoned. In all probability, the existing arrangement is likely to stay for a time. The 1973 budget document shows that the central government decreased the percentage of estimated national internal taxes by 0.93 percentage points to 16.67 percent from 17.60 percent. It is planned that the percentage would be further reduced to 15 percent by the end of 1980.

2. *The Subsidy System*

The major task of this paper is to propose an alternative revenue sharing arrangement. But something has to be said about specific-purpose subsidies, another means of transferring revenue to local governments in Korea. Despite the feasibility and desirability of introducing decentralization by relegating some governmental services to provinces, the central government has largely taken over those programs in which there is significant national interest. Indeed, according to the Bank of Korea's data, specific-purpose subsidies accounted for just about 18 percent of total central government financial transfers in 1968.

Since an economic classification of Korea's subsidy system, acceptable in public finance language, is difficult because of the overlapping objectives of the subsidies, let us follow the listing by the Local Finance Law. There are three types of subsidies: national treasury shares, specific outright subsidies, and promotional subsidies. No figures are available for them yet. Only a functional breakdown of subsidies exists. Table 14 shows that in 1968 the major recipient of subsidies was economic services, of which agriculture and forestry accounted for the most.

The distribution of the cost of services between the central government and recipient units is made rather vaguely on the assumption that certain services are in the local or in the national interest, while others are partly in the national and partly in the local interest. Thus, according to the

Table 14. Functional Classification of Subsidies, 1968

(million won)

	Current Transfers	Capital Transfers	Total	Percentage Distribution
General Services	2,155	17	2,172	14.8
Community Services	3	3,389	3,392	23.1
Roads	—	2,726	2,726	18.5
Waterways	—	297	297	2.0
Water Supply and Sewerage	—	340	340	2.3
Social Services	511	2,827	3,338	22.6
Health	499	137	636	4.3
Economic Services	1,061	4,755	5,816	39.5
Agriculture and Forestry	958	4,129	5,087	34.6
Manufacturing	—	238	238	1.6
Total	3,730	10,988	14,718	100.0

Source: Bank of Korea, *Economic Statistics Yearbook*, 1970.

Notes: [1] Subsidies here refer to those other than for educational purposes. See Table 11 for total grants-in-aid for education, which amounted to nearly 40 billion won in 1968.

[2] There is a discrepancy between the amount of subsidies reported by the Home Affairs Ministry and that by the Bank of Korea. See Table 11. The latter reports only a functional classification of subsidies.

Local Finance Law, specific outright subsidies are defined to be those for which the central government assumes one hundred percent of the burden because these functions, even though performed by local governments, are in the national interest.

The Primary Education Treasury Grant, which is given to the local school boards, is one typical example of specific outright subsidies. Its amount was "closed-end;" the Economic Planning Board set aside each year 11.55 percent of estimated national internal taxes to be distributed as subsidies. (see column (3), Table 11) Transferred to the Education Special Account, the grant money was spent for the purpose of defraying the entire current and capital costs of running primary education (compulsory) and half of salaries and wages paid to the teachers at public schools beyond the primary level.[17]

During the period, 1969–1972, besides the specific outright subsidy for local education, there were two more kinds of grant-in-aid for education in Korea: tax sharing for local education (See Table 11), which could have been discussed with "general" tax sharing, and the small amount of promotional subsidies for education. Similar to the determination of "general" shared taxes, the Economic Planning Board set aside each year 1.43 percent of estimated national internal taxes in order to finance administrative and management expenses for general local education (other than compulsory education). In sum, therefore, the Economic Planning Board earmarked 12.98 percent of national internal taxes to pay local public education.[18] But, on August 3, 1972, the central government abolished the formula. The 1973 budget indicates that the central government reduced the percentage by 1.39 percent to 11.59 percent.

For the projects that are considered to be in the joint national-local interest, provision of national treasury shares which are a type of variable matching grant, is justified. Since there are so many different types of national treasury shares programs, however, a few examples may suffice to illustrate their diversities. These include important city planning enterprises and other public works designated by national laws or ministerial orders, disaster prevention facilities, health prevention, etc. With respect to the sharing of expenses, except that the Subsidy Administration Law determines the eligibility of a province for the national treasury shares, the percentage of the national share was, in general, fixed by the concerned ministries without any reference to the degree of national interest. Only in a few cases, did the Subsidy Administration Law specify the maximum annual amount to be provided by the central government.[19]

Those programs which are entitled to national treasury shares are typically administered as follows: within the limit of budget appropriations made to a national ministry for subsidy payments, the concerned ministry

[17] Others include expenditures incurred for national election, management of national property, census, recruitment, etc.

[18] As in the case of the Home Affairs Ministry, which directed the allocation of "general" shared taxes, the Education Ministry was responsible for the distribution of shared taxes and specific outright subsidies for education to the local entities. Discussions on the measurement of needs for educational service and financial requirements for it are omitted here because they constitute separate chapters.

[19] The maximum annual amount, payable by the central government, is determined by specifying its aid ratio. Usually, the ratio is two-thirds or one half of the total cost, depending on particular programs.

secured passage of a law that assigned a new program, supposedly of joint national-local interest, to the local governments. It then determined the share of the expenses to be borne by the central government and paid for by subsidies, and the local governments to which the program was assigned has to bear the remainder of the expenses. In 1968, the average central government aid ratio was about 80 percent. And the richest and the poorest provinces received exactly the same ratio for the program under question.

Once the national government delegated its functions to local governments, they had no choice but to carry them out; and the required financial resource had to be secured. Hence, national treasury shares programs in many instances required the local governments to raise the money required only by sacrificing programs they considered more beneficial or where an additional financial burden was placed upon the local residents. The central-provincial cost sharing of the land adjustment program between the Ministry of Agriculture and Forestry and Chungnam Province could be one example. The matching ratio for this was set at 50/50 percent. Since the province could afford to bear only 5 percent of the assigned share, Chungnam Province obligated its residents to assume 45 percent in the next fiscal year.[20]

Promotional subsidies are designed to encourage local governments to undertake particular functions that they would otherwise not assume or induce them to improve the quality of local services. Excluding subsidies for education, only small amounts were in the form of promotional subsidies for general purposes, accounting for about 4 percent of the total amount of subsidies.

In order to consider what changes need to be made in the existing intergovernmental financial relations, the 1969–1972 subsidy system ought to be appraised. First, there were no explicit principles governing the allotment of subsidies. Specific outright subsidies for primary education were exceptions. As already indicated, in determining the proportion of the expenses to be shared by the central and recipient governments, *ad hoc* ministerial orders determined matching ratios without any clear reference to the degree of national or local interest involved. In addition, the administration of the subsidy system was too extensive; some ten different ministries administered the various subsidies. As a result, there were instances where local governments received subsidies twice for an identical program. Also, the concerned ministries imposed an excessive degree of

[20] Data provided by Chungnam Province.

administrative control on the local governments receiving subsidies. But no serious review is made by them by looking into whether or not the subsidies granted had produced their intended effects.

Secondly, there were too many fragmented subsidies. In 1971, for example, about 350 different subsidies existed. As a result of this fragmentation, there were small counties that received as little as 150,000 won for one government purpose or another.

Lastly, in the case of national treasury shares, a strain was placed on local resources by the requirement that central government aids be matched locally. A serious study ought to be undertaken to see if use of shared-cost programs had led to a weakening of the fiscal responsibility of the local governments.

V. An Alternative Revenue Sharing Method

In order to relieve the fiscal pressure on local governments, two major intergovernmental fiscal devices could be applied. For one, conditional or specific-purpose grants are needed to optimize the allocation of resources to local spending programs which yield significant externalities. Some of the benefits of economic goods, such as education, are consumed in areas which do not bear the financial costs of supplying the benefits. Hence, without central government intervention through the conditional grant, an undersupply of public goods might result within the government sector as a whole.

A case for unconditional grants stems from the need to equalize (although not completely) differences in fiscal capacity among local governments. A high concentration of low-income families, for instance, tends to make the cost of providing even an ordinary level of public services quite difficult. Through an unconditional grant, the revenue capacity of poorer governments could be raised to a certain equalizing level.[21]

Some elements of such intergovernmental fiscal devices already exist in Korea in the form of shared taxes and various subsidies. But, as shown in the previous section, they are deficient in that their allocation methods have insufficient and arbitrary regard for measurement of fiscal capacity, tax effort, and needs of the local governments. Before the proposed scheme

[21] Efficiency criteria should be an overriding factor in the allocation of specific-purpose grants. But through the application of variable matching requirements some geographical equalization could be achieved.

of equalization is appraised, however, some related issues ought to be resolved.

It has been indicated that, although revenue sharing is in theory an unconditional grant, the distribution of shared taxes and the use made of them has been subject, in practice, to central government direction and control. But this is not really surprising in view of the fact that South Korea has an underdeveloped economy with a unitary form of government. In a unitary nation, local governments are the creatures of the central government which alters and manipulates their duties and revenues. Moreover, in South Korea, local preferences, needs, and priorities are very similar; hence, a uniform set of central government requirements could be appropriate. Such a tendency to subjugate performance of governmental services to a uniform standard is further strengthened by Korea's rapid industrialization policies which demand a considerable degree of national control. There is still another factor which reinforces the centralizing tendency in a developing nation like Korea. Even if external benefits were only 10 percent of total benefits, all the local governments except for Seoul and Pusan would find it unable to finance their own 90 percent shares.

But if direct central government take-over is not desirable, a compromise is to let the central government define an acceptable minimum level of governmental services of which every citizen should be assured. This minimum would include not only purely local services but also spending programs with considerable spillover benefits (e.g., less than 50 percent).

The proposed formula defines the shared taxes to be distributed to a given province as:[22]

$$S_i = \frac{P_i\left(\frac{T_i}{Y_i}\right)\left(\frac{E}{E_i}\right)}{\sum_{i=1}^{11}\left[P_i\left(\frac{T_i}{Y_i}\right)\left(\frac{E}{E_i}\right)\right]} \cdot R$$

where S_i = amount of shared taxes to be distributed to the i–th local government,

[22] In arriving at this formulation, I benefited from discussions with Dr. Hyo Koo Lee. A similar presentation is also found in Professor Break's *Intergovernmental Fiscal Relations in the United States,* pp. 129–130. But the latter does not deal specifically with equalization problems in a developing country with a unitary form of government.

P_i = population in the i–th province,
T_i = local tax collection in the i–th province,
Y_i = regional gross domestic product in the i–th province,
$\bar{E}_i$ = nationally acceptable minimum level of governmental services,
E_i = actual expenditure in the i–th province,
R = total shared taxes to be distributed in a given year.

In a number of aspects, the proposed method contains definite improvements over the current grant method. First, representation of the general need for public services by population size (P_i) is simple and certain, compared with the unit cost method applied to a fixed number of expenditure items. The cumbersome and often arbitrary measures of the amount needed for standard services can be circumvented. Secondly, it combines a population-size factor with a tax-effort factor T_i/Y_i, in order to discourage some provinces from relaxing their won revenue-raising efforts. With wide differences in the fiscal strength among the individual provinces, particularly between urban areas such as Seoul and Pusan and the rural local governments, however, population and tax effort factors alone are not adequate for distributing funds to the poorest government. As shown in column (3) of Table 15, since Seoul is a high-income as well as densely populated area, a per capita allocation would not redistribute resources in favor of the poorest provinces. Indeed, the allotment percentage for Seoul is about 32 percent.

Therefore, thirdly, in order to bring about some distributional effects, the equal per capita payments to each province are adjusted by the reciprocal of an equalization factor, as illustrated in column (5) of Table 15. The average local expenditure without central government transfers is used as an equalization factor representing a nationally acceptable minimum level of governmental services. It is, however, to be understood that the use here of the average local expenditure is only an approximation of the nationally acceptable minimum level of governmental services.[23] Compared with column (3), column (5) demonstrates that equalization adjustment modifies the per capita allocation weighted by the relative tax effort. In other words, the poorer province's allotment percentage of shared taxes is boosted in so far as its own relative expenditure falls short of the national average.

The equalization effects brought about by the proposed method are also

[23] The reciprocal of per capita gross domestic product or per capita revenue could be alternative equalization factors.

B. Secondary Sources in Korean

17. Cha, B.K., "Analysis of Local Shared Tax and Subsidy System in Korea, and Fiscal Equity," *Economic Review* (publication of Seoul National University), June 1965, pp. 31–69.
18. Cha, B.K., *Local Finances in Korea—History, Nature and Development*, publication of the Korean Academy of Social Sciences, 1968/4.
19. Korea Development Association, *Research on the Finances of Seoul Special City*, 1971/11.
20. Korea University, Business Management Institute, *Research Report on Korea's Subsidy System*, 1971/12.
21. Politics and Economics Research Institute of Korea, *The Structural Analysis of Local Government Finances and Policy Recommendations*, 1966.

C. Secondary Sources in English

22. Johnson, Robert H., *A Survey of Korea's Fiscal System in Relation to the Third Five-Year Economic Development Plan*, Prepared for the Ministry of Finance, Republic of Korea and USAID/Korea by Robert R. Nathan Associates, Inc., Washington, D.C., September 1970.
23. Johnson, Robert H., *Proposed Tax Reforms for 1972 and Revenue Requirements for the Third Five-Year Plan*, Prepared for the Ministry of Finance, Republic of Korea and USAID/Korea by Robert R. Nathan Associates, Inc., Washington, D.C., July 1971.
24. Maxwell, James A., "Intergovernmental Financial Transfers in Korea," Seoul, Korea: Korea Development Institute, January 1973. (Typewritten.)
25. Musgrave, Richard A., *Revenue Policy for Korea's Economic Development*, 1965.
26. Musgrave, Richard A., *Suggestions for The 1967 Tax Reform*, Submitted to the Finance Ministry, Republic of Korea, 1967.
27. Robert R. Nathan Associates, Inc., *Local Government Finance in Korea*, Prepared for the Government of Korea and USAID/Korea, Washington, D.C., 1971.

D. Other References

28. Advisory Commission on Intergovernmental Relations, *Measuring*

support of flexibility in budgeting. But this has left local governments uncertain of any guarantee that their minimum financial requirements could be met. Being subject to the demands of various national policies on the budget, the grant amount would fluctuate year by year. Certainly, it would be more variable than when it is being pegged to a fixed percentage of central government taxes. There is an element of persuasiveness in the argument that the local government should be entitled to revenue growth linked to the growing economy. If some local autonomy is still desirable, it is important to put the grant amount on a more stable and objective basis.

REFERENCES

A. Official Sources

1. Bank of Korea, *Economic Statistics Yearbook*, 1970.
2. Bank of Korea, *National Income Statistics Yearbook*, 1972.
3. Bank of Korea, *Regional Economic Statistics*, various issues.
4. Economic Planning Board, *Long-Term Government Finance Data (1972–1981)*, 1973/6/12.
5. Economic Planning Board, *Third Five-Year Economic Development Plan (1972–1976): Planning Data*, 1972/12.
6. Economic Planning Board, *Report on National Wealth Survey*, 1973.
7. Government of Korea, *Local Shared Tax Law*, 1972.
8. Ministry of Finance, *Summary of Financial Statistics*, 1970 and 1971.
9. Ministry of Home Affairs, *Annual Report of Gross Regional Product* 1972.
10. Ministry of Home Affairs, *Financial Abstract of Local Government*, 1969 and 1971.
11. Ministry of Home Affairs, *Local Finance Adjustment System of Korea* 1973.
12. Ministry of Home Affairs, *Local Finance in Korea*, 1973.
13. Ministry of Home Affairs, *Local Tax System in Korea*, 1972.
14. Ministry of Home Affairs, *Statistical Yearbook of Local Tax*, 1971 and 1972.
15. Ministry of Home Affairs, *Summary of Local Tax*, 1971.
16. Office of National Tax Administration, *Statistical Yearbook of National Tax*, 1972 and 1973.

Table 15. Shared Taxes Allocated to Provinces by the Proposed Method

	Population (P_i) (1,000)	Tax Effort $\left(\frac{T_i}{Y_i}\right)$ Local Tax Collections to Regional GDP	$P\left(\frac{T_i}{Y_i}\right)$	Equalization Factor $\left(\frac{E}{E_i}\right)$	$P_i\left(\frac{T_i}{Y_i}\right)\left(\frac{E}{E_i}\right)$	Percentage of Actual Shared Taxes
	(1)	(2)	(3)	(4)	(5)	(6)
Seoul	4,335	0.0253	31.8%	0.424	10.7%	8.5%
Pusan	1,552	0.0128	5.8	0.303	1.4	4.4
Kyonggi	3,106	0.0115	10.3	1.250	10.3	10.5
Kangwon	1,824	0.0059	3.1	2.551	6.3	13.1
Chungpuk	1,537	0.0082	3.7	2.571	7.5	6.5
Chungnam	2,901	0.0092	7.7	2.336	14.3	8.4
Chonpuk	2,485	0.0093	6.7	2.439	13.0	8.9
Chonnam	4,138	0.0071	8.5	2.123	14.4	13.9
Kyongpuk	4,553	0.0111	14.6	1.179	13.7	14.5
Kyongnam	3,163	0.0077	7.1	1,306	7.3	12.6
Cheju	358	0.0066	0.7	2.079	1.1	2.5

Source: Table 8 and 11

compared in column (6) with these under the existing system. It can be seen that despite its simple properties the proposed method achieves equalization effects as decidedly as the existing system. What is noteworthy, however, is that the allotment percentage for Seoul under the proposed scheme is reduced because of the equalization to the average. In the case of Pusan, a smaller population size as well as an equalization factor have dampening effects. Both Kangwon and Kyongnam provinces are penalized for their relatively low tax effort.

Up to now, the grant distribution method has only been discussed. Nothing has been said yet about the determination of the total amount of shared revenue to be allocated. The example illustrated in Table 15 is taken as if the total amount of shared revenue (R) were already determined. In order to place the grant money on a more stable basis, the proposed formula does not intend to alter the determination of the total amount of shared revenue, as in the past method, by pegging it to a fixed percentage of estimated internal taxes.

As explained already, the Korean government abolished, on August 3, 1972, a precise formula for the determination of the grant amount in *the Fiscal Capacity and Effort of State and Local Areas*, Information Report, Washington, D.C., U.S.A., March 1971.

29. Break, George F., *Intergovernmental Fiscal Relations*, Washington, D.C.: Brookings Institution, 1967.
30. Levy, Michael E., and de Torres, Juan, *Federal Revenue Sharing with the States: Problems and Promises*, New York: The Conference Board, 1970.
31. Maxwell, James A., *Financing State and Local Governments* (Revised ed.), Washington, D.C.: Brookings Institution ,1969.
32. Maxwell, James A., and J. Richard Aronson, "Federal Grants and Fiscal Balance: the Instrument and Goal, "*Public Policy*, Vol. XX, No. 4 (Fall 1972), pp. 577–593.
33. Musgrave, Richard A., "Approaches to a Fiscal Theory of Political Federalism" in *Public Finances: Needs, Sources, and Utilization*, New York: National Bureau of Economic Research, 1961, pp. 97–133.
34. Musgrave, Richard A., and M. Gillis, *Fiscal Reform for Colombia*, Cambridge, Mass: Harvard Law School, 1971.

PART IV

FOREIGN EXCHANGE AND TRADE POLICIES

GROWTH AND TRADE PATTERN

*Wontack Hong**

I. Growth and Trade

1. Colonial Period

Korea was developed as a colonial economy by the Japanese during 1910–45, mainly exporting rice and other primary products to Japan and importing all kinds of manufactures from Japan. In the latter years of the colonial period, Japan tried to convert the Korean peninsula into a logistic base for the creation of the so-called Greater East Asian Co-prosperity Sphere.[1] As a result, some light and heavy industries as well as extended social overhead capital facilities were begun.

Per capita GNP of Korea is estimated to have been around $100 in 1911–20 (in 1970 prices), around $110 in 1921–30 and $120–$150 in 1931–40.[2] That is, the per capita GNP seems to have increased by more than 40 percent during the colonial period. In terms of gross output values, the share of agriculture in total commodity sectors (agriculture, forestry, fishery, mining and manufacturing) declined from about 85 percent in 1912 to around 50 percent in 1936, while the share of manufacturing increased

* Senior Fellow at the Korea Development Institute.

[1] This section is excerpted from my *Trade and Subsidy Policy and Employment Growth in Korea,* mimeographed (Seoul: KDI, 1976).

[2] We took the wholesale price index of Korea and deflated the output (or trade) statistics on a 1970 basis, and then converted the resulting estimates to 1970 dollars at the official exchange rate of 310.6 won per dollar.

Table 1. Industrial Structure of Korea in Colonial Period

Gross Output Values (Million Yen)	1912	1921	1930	1936
	(%)	(%)	(%)	(%)
Agriculture	378 (85)	877 (76)	598 (59)	1,107 (52)
Forestry	20 (4)	57 (5)	63 (6)	118 (5)
Fishery	13 (3)	45 (4)	50 (5)	80 (4)
Mining	7 (2)	16 (1)	35 (3)	110 (5)
Manufacturing	29 (6)	166 (14)	263 (26)	731 (34)
Total	447(100)	1,161(100)	1,009(100)	2,146(100)
Manufacturing	**1911**	**1920**	**1931**	**1939**
	(%)	(%)	(%)	(%)
Food Products	15.8 (51)	85.0 (37)	81.0 (34)	328.4 (22)
Textiles	5.2 (17)	20.6 (9)	32.9 (14)	201.4 (13)
Wood & Products	0.5 (2)	4.4 (2)	4.8 (2)	21.1 (1)
Nonmetallic Mineral Products	1.2 (4)	10.0 (4)	9.0 (4)	43.3 (3)
Chemical Products	0.7 (2)	17.2 (7)	42.6 (18)	501.8 (33)
Metal Products	1.2 (4)	12.1 (5)	6.6 (3)	136.1 (9)
Machinery	0.6 (2)	4.1 (2)	7.9 (3)	53.2 (4)
Misc. Goods	5.8 (19)	78.6 (34)	52.0 (22)	213.1 (14)
Total[1]	31.0(100)	232.0(100)	236.8(100)	1,498.4(100)
(Repairing Fee)	(—)	(—)	(1.5)	(24.1)
(Electricity & Gas)	(—)	(—)	(16.1)	(40.1)[2]
Employment (1,000)	**1917**	**1921**	**1930**	**1937**
	(%)	(%)	(%)	(%)
Agr. & Forestry	6,949 (90)	7,196 (90)	7,772 (87)	7,413 (84)
Fishery (Incl. Salt)	76 (1)	85 (1)	113 (1)	110 (1)
Manufacturing	116 (1)	115 (1)	143 (2)	203 (2)
Others	574 (7)	595 (7)	940 (10)	1,145 (13)
Total	7,175(100)	7,991(100)	8,968(100)	8,871(100)
Trade	**1917**	**1926**	**1932**	**1936**
Export/Commodity-Output	11%	24%	28%	28%
Exports/GNP Ratio	9%	21%	25%	28%
Population (1,000)	16,969	19,104	20,600	22,048
GNP (Million 1970 Dollars)	1,600	2,179	2,474	3,274
Per Capita GNP (1970$)	$94	$114	$120	$149

Sources: Government General of Chosen, *Chosen Sotokufu Tokei Nenpo* (Statistical Yearbook); H. Ouchi, ed., *Nihon Keizai Tokei Shu* (Japan Economic Statistics: Meiji, Taisho and Showa Eras) (Tokyo: Nihon Tokei Kenkyujo, 1958); and Hong, *op. cit,* Chapter 2.

Notes: [1] Output values of rice cleaning, sawing and cotton ginning are not included. The miscellaneous manufactures in 1911 and 1920 seem to have included the output value of rice cleaning. The miscellaneous sectors include footwear, wearing apparel, finished textile products, paper products, leather products and tobacco products.

[2] 1937 output value.

from about 6 percent in 1912 to about 34 percent in 1936. Among the manufacturing industries, the relative share of chemical and metal product sectors more than doubled during 1930–40, while that of the food product sector had decreased significantly.

The proportion of employed persons in agriculture, of total employed persons, had steadily declined from 90 percent in 1917 to 84 percent in 1937, while the share of employed persons in social overhead and service sectors increased from 7 percent in 1917 to 13 percent in 1937. The share of employed persons in manufacturing did not increase much but the absolute number of persons employed in manufacturing had almost doubled from 116 thousand persons in 1917 to 203 thousand persons in 1937.

The volume of Korea's commodity exports started to increase rapidly since the nineteen-eighties. However, the annual commodity exports amounted to less than 10 million yen (approximately less than $30 million in 1970 prices) at the dawn of the twentieth century. During the last decade of the Yi dynasty (1901–10) prior to the formal annexation to Japan, the annual export volume almost doubled to become about 20 million yen in 1910 (approximately $52 million in 1970 prices) which was equivalent to roughly 3–4 percent of GNP in value terms, and more than three-quarters of total exports went to Japan proper.[3] During the Japanese occupation, the volume of commodity exports almost tripled every ten year period to become about one billion yen in 1939 (approximately one billion dollars in 1970 prices). The total value of commodity exports was equivalent to 5–10 percent of GNP during 1910–20, but it increased to 15–25 percent in 1921–30 and to 25–30 percent of GNP since 1930. The portion of Korea's exports which went to Japan proper consistently increased to about 90 percent of total exports since 1920, and the rest of

[3] "Japan proper" represents Japan itself, Taiwan and South Pacific colonial islands.

Korea's exports went mostly to China and other Asian countries. On the other hand, more than two-thirds of total imports were from Japan proper during 1900–29, and Japan's share further increased to 80–90 percent of Korea's imports during 1930–39.

The balance of payments was always in deficit during 1886–1939, with the exception of 1924 and 1925. The deficit was financed by exports of gold and silver bullion and coins, and net capital inflow. Significant capital inflow from Japan occurred during 1904–1914 (amounting to nearly half of the import value), 1917–22 (about 13 percent of import value), 1927–30 (about 14 percent of import value), and during 1935–39 (about 20 percent of import value).[4] Net capital inflow in other years was insignificant.

During 1910–39, about 50–60 percent of Korea's commodity exports consisted of agricultural products, rice and some beans, and about 6 percent was fresh, dried and salted fish. Mineral products such as graphite, coal, iron and gold ore, lead, copper, pig iron, etc. took about 5–10 percent of total exports. There was a remarkable increase in exports of textile products such as silk and cotton fabrics which took about 10–15 percent of total exports during 1921–39. A significant amount of foodstuffs such as sugar, wheat flour, sea weed, dried laver, apples, etc. was also exported.

Exports of manufactured goods were negligible before 1920, but they increased steadily in the twenties and thereafter so that nearly 20 percent of Korea's exports during 1930–39 became manufactured goods.[5] The major manufactured exports were silk and the rest consisted of cotton fabrics, pig iron, pulp and paper, sugar, wheat flour, cement, leather, ammonium sulphate, miscellaneous crude chemicals, etc.

Being a Japanese colony, about one-third of Korea's imports during 1911–39 were various textile products. Machinery and equipment took less than 10 percent of total imports. Metals, chemical products and pulp and paper took about 20 percent of total imports, and the imports of processed foods amounted to nearly 10 percent. Furthermore, agricultural products took about 10–20 percent of total imports during 1919–39.

The most remarkable fact was that exports of rice (almost entirely to Japan) amounted to about 13 percent of total rice production in Korea during 1915–19, about 22 percent during 1920–24 and about 40 percent of total output during 1925–39. As a result, although the production of rice

---

[4] However, except for the period of 1904–14, the capital inflow from Japan was almost entirely through the so-called "foreign countries" which imply China, Manchuria, etc.

[5] Exports of manufactures from Korea included re-exports of Japanese-made products which seem to have amounted to around 5 percent of total manufactures' exports.

in Korea increased by nearly 50 percent during 1915–39, the increase in domestic consumption of rice was negligible.[6] Therefore, one may say that Korea mainly supplied rice to Japan, and it was only at the end of the Japanese occupation that some light and heavy industries as well as electricity, transportation and communication facilities began to be emphasized.

In 1939, about 28 percent of total gross output value of the manufacturing industry was contributed by processed food, beverages and tobacco sectors, about 16 percent by fibre spinning, textile fabrics and textile product sectors, about 32 percent by chemicals, fertilizer, coal products, rubber products and paper products sectors, and about 13 percent by metal and machinery sectors.[7] About two-thirds of food and kindred products and about three-quarters of textiles were produced in the southern part of Korea, while more than three-quarters of chemicals, fertilizer, coal products, paper products, nonmetallic mineral products, iron and steel, and metal products were produced in the northern part of Korea in 1939. Printing and publishing, leather products, rubber products, and machinery and transport equipment were mostly produced in South Korea. However, the machinery and transport equipment produced in the thirties was not only small in an absolute amount (4 percent of total gross manufactures output value) but was also not very sophisticated.

Heavy industries, electricity power resources and mineral deposits were mostly located in the northern part of Korea and the industries in the southern part consisted mainly of agriculture and light industries such as textiles and food manufacturing. However, the Korean economy, which was initially designed as a colonial economy dependent on Japan and then further crippled by the separation of the North from the South, had to industrialize out of the ruins left in the wake of the Korean War (1950–53).

2. *Post Korean War Era*

In 1953, which was the year the Korean War ended in a ceasefire, the gross national product amounted to about $2.7 billion in 1970 dollar

---

[6] H. Ouchi, ed., *Nihon Kezai Tokei Shu* (Tokyo: Nihon Tokei Kenkyujo, 1958), p.358. The increased demand for grain was satisfied by imports of millet and beans from China.

[7] Due to differences in classification, the sectoral output values presented here (which are based on I-O sectoral classification) do not agree with those presented in Table 1.

prices.[8] About 46 percent of the GNP was generated by the agricultural sector and about 43 percent by such service sectors as construction, wholesale and retail trade, public administration and defense, ownership of dwellings, eduation, etc. The manufacturing sector contributed only about 6 percent of the GNP and the social overhead sectors such as electricity, water and sanitary services, transportation and communication contributed about 2 percent. Commodity exports amounted to less than $0.06 billion while imports amounted to $0.53 billion in 1953 (all in 1970 prices), and the difference was financed by foreign savings, mostly U.S. grants-in-aid.

The average annual growth rate of GNP during the nine year period following the war (1953–61) was approximately 4 percent, and the agricultural and service sectors together still contributed about 83 percent of the GNP in 1962. Commodity exports remained negligible throughout the period, usually amounting to less than 1 percent of GNP, while most of the imports, which averaged about 15 percent of GNP, were mostly financed by U.S. grants-in-aid. Persistently overvalued domestic currency effectively eliminated the export potential of the economy. The industrialization policy pursued during this post-war period can be loosely characterized as a policy of import substitution of non-durable consumer goods with foreign aid funds under the protection of tariffs and quotas, but any kind of whole-hearted and systematic government effort for rapid economic growth was conspicuously absent during most of this era.

The military coup in mid-1961 provided a turning point. The military government started to make systematic efforts to achieve rapid economic growth, and its vigor was maintained by the formulation and energetic execution of a series of ambitious five-year economic development plans (1962–66; 1967–71; 1972–76). The average annual growth rate of GNP rose to about 9 percent during the decade 1962–71, and in 1973 the growth rate hit an all time high of 17 percent. Even in the midst of the oil crisis (1974–5), Korea could maintain about 8 percent growth rate of GNP.

---

[8] In this paper, we applied the exchange rate of 310.6 won per dollar in order to convert the (national income) figures in constant 1970 won values into those of 1970 dollar values, and also applied the GNP deflator of the United States to convert the (trade) figures in current dollar values during 1953–72 into those of 1970 constant dollar values. However, we applied the export or import unit value index constructed by the Bank of Korea to the trade data of 1973–75 because of the extremely high rates of price inflation in tradable commodities since 1973. This section is excerpted from my *Factor Supply and Factor Intensity of Trade in Korea* (Seoul: KDI Press, 1976).

Table 2. Growth and Changes in Industrial Structure, 1953–75

	1953	1957	1962	1967	1972	1975
Agriculture & Forestry	46%	42%	39%	32%	23%	19%
Fishery	2	2	2	2	2	3
Mining & Quarrying	1	1	2	1	1	1
Manufacturing	6	9	12	17	25	32
Electricity & Water	0	0	1	1	2	2
Transport & Comm.	2	2	3	5	6	7
Construction	2	2	3	4	5	5
Wholesale & Retail	11	13	15	15	18	18
Other Services	8	8	9	8	8	5
Education & Public Ad.	17	14	12	10	8	6
Ownership of Dwellings	5	4	4	3	2	2
GNP (billion 1970 dollars)	2.7	3.3	3.9	6.0	9.7	13.2
Per Capita GNP (1970 dollars)	129	143	150	201	299	381
				(billion current dollars)		
Commodity Imports	0.35	0.44	0.42	1.00	2.52	7.27
Service Imports[1]	0.01	0.01	0.03	0.08	0.19	0.59
Commodity Exports	0.04	0.02	0.06	0.32	1.62	5.08
Service Exports[1]	0.12	0.04	0.10	0.30	0.49	0.80
Official Aid[2]	0.19	0.37	0.22	0.15	0.07	0.04
Foreign Loans	—	—	0.00	0.17	0.63	0.89

Source: The Bank of Korea, *National Income Statistics Yearbook* and *Economic Statistics Yearbook*.

Notes: [1] Total invisible payments or receipts minus investment income and donations.

[2] Including imports financed by properties and claims funds from Japan.

The initiation of the ambitious First Five-Year Plan (1962–66) necessitated the acquisition of a large amount of foreign exchange as well as increased domestic savings in order to finance various planned investment projects for import-substitution, social overhead capital formation, etc.[9] The inflow of U.S. aid funds which peaked in 1957 at nearly $0.4 billion had already started its irreversible decline. As a result the government had to turn to such alternative sources of foreign exchange as foreign loans and export expansion, along with increased taxation and higher interest rates on time and savings deposits to mobilize domestic investment funds.[10]

The government was able to achieve particularly dramatic gains in the area of export expansion. Commodity exports increased at the average annual rate of about 35 percent during the period 1962–71, amounting to $0.25 billion in 1966 and $1.07 billion in 1971. By efficient exploitation of the opportunity provided by the repeated yen appreciations during 1972–73, Korea further expanded its exports by about 50 percent in 1972 and 100 percent in 1973, mostly to Japan itself and to other markets in which Korean goods were in competition with those of Japan. Total commodity exports amounted to about $5 billion in 1975.

During 1953–61, non-commodity exports, which amounted to more than twice the value of commodity exports, were dominated by the sales of goods and services to the U.S. Army detachments stationed in Korea. The annual sales to the U.S. Army steadily increased from less than $0.1 billion during 1953–61 to more than $0.2 billion after 1967, but their magnitude started to decline after 1973. On the other hand, the receipts from exports of transportation, construction, insurance, travel and

---

[9] The First Five-Year Plan emphasized investments for import substitution of cement, fertilizer, iron and steel, and refined petroleum, and investments for electricity, coal mining, transportation and other social overhead capital formation. See the Government of Korea, *First Five-Year Economic Development Plan* (1962–66), Seoul, January 1962.

[10] The annual inflow of foreign loans increased from zero in 1961 to more than $0.1 billion in 1966 and to as high as $0.9 billion in 1975. The direct and indirect tax revenue of the government, which amounted to less than $0.4 billion before 1962, increased to about $0.6 billion in 1966 and to about $1.5 billion by 1973 (all in 1970 prices). The existing interest rates on time and savings deposits and loans (except export credits) were almost doubled in 1965, and as a result the share of time and savings deposits in the rapidly expanding total loan funds of the deposit money banks increased from less than 20 percent before 1965 to nearly half in 1971. (Data from the Bank of Korea, *National Income Statistics Yearbook* and *Monetary Statistics of Korea: 1960–73*.)

miscellaneous services increased very rapidly from almost negligible amounts during 1953–61 to $0.25 billion by 1972. In 1973, these receipts from invisible trade amounted to $0.6 billion while sales to the U.S. Army amounted to less than $0.2 billion. The rapidly increasing tonnage of domestic vessels, tourist services, remittances of Korean workers abroad and revenues from overseas construction projects made the greatest contribution to the remarkable increase in non-commodity exports.

Until early in the sixties, the major export items were such primary products as metal ores and concentrates, raw materials of vegetable or animal origin, fish, swine and raw silk. By the mid-sixties, however, plywood, clothing and miscellaneous manufactures emerged as the principal export commodities. In 1973, electronic products (thermionic valves, tubes and transistors), footwear, plates and sheets of iron or steel, and woven fabrics of synthetic fibres joined the list of major export commodities.[11]

Machinery and transport equipment made up roughly 10–15 percent of total imports during 1953–61, but their share steadily increased to the 30 percent level during the ten year period 1962–71. Significant changes in the list of major manufactured imports resulting from import substitution and changing demand patterns can also be observed. During 1953–61, large amounts of such manufactured products as chemical fertilizers, synthetic fiber yarns and thread, yarn of regenerated fibers, petroleum products, printing papers, cement, iron or steel plates, plastic materials, etc., were imported. By 1971, however, the progress in import substitution eliminated all these items but synthetic fiber yarn and thread and plastic materials from the list of major import commodities. For instance, the remarkable progress of import substitution in the production of chemicals resulted in a sharp decrease in the share of chemical products in total commodity imports from more than 20 percent in 1962 to less than 10 percent by 1973. We can also observe the emergence of a new generation of manufactured imports such as woven fabrics of synthetic fibers, iron and steel coils, thermionic valves and transistors, chemical pulp, synthetic fibers, etc. which were mostly used as raw materials for export production.

The major imported materials for export production were basic chem-

[11] In 1961, for example, the only manufactured goods which could be exported in sizable quantities were raw silk, plywood and cotton fabrics. Beginning in the seventies, however, Korea could list as important export commodities such diversified items as: clothing, thermionic valves, tubes and transistors, footwear, cotton yarn, synthetic fibre yarn, iron and steel plates, twine and rope, synthetic fibre fabrics, silk fabrics, leather products, knitted fabrics, cement, TV sets, tape recorders, radio receivers, toys, trunks and suitcases, etc.

icals and other chemical products, forestry products (timber), steel products, textile fabrics, fibers and miscellaneous tetxtile products, various agricultural products, and electronic products. The share of imports for export production in total commodity imports steadily increased from about 14 percent in 1966 to 38 percent in 1973. Their import value was equivalent to about 40–50 percent of the total value of commodity exports during 1966–75. This implies that the apparent value added content of exports was less than 60 percent, although the actual import content of exports might have been smaller due to the official wastage allowances which leaked out large amounts of duty-free imported raw materials to domestic markets.[12]

A notable fact is that during 1967–74 about 70 percent of Korea's total trade was conducted with the U.S. and Japan and 13 percent was with other developed countries. The share of developing countries in total trade was less than 20 percent. Most of the imports from developing countries consisted of crude oil, crude rubber and timber. Hence it appears that Korea had very little to offer other developing countries and *vice versa*, with the exception of natural-resource intensive goods.

Korea started to intensify its promotion of import substitution systematically in the early sixties, but being faced by a balance of payments problem in financing the various investment projects it had to promote export expansions. The export subsidy policies were not purposely designed to discriminate among industries. However, due to the limited export potential of the primary sector, the share of manufactured products in total commodity exports, which never exceeded the 20 percent level before 1961, steadily increased to about 80 percent in 1966 and to more than 90 percent of total commodity exports by 1973.[13] We may say that, as one of the most densely populated countries in the world, Korea possessed strong potential for the production of labor-intensive manufactures for export, and this latent potential has been effectively realized by positive government policies. Export promotion policies gathered momentum of their own as time passed, and as a result people started to identify the

[12] The most remarkable fact seems to be that about half of the imported materials for export production were those items classified by the Bank of Korea as "competitive" imports. This perhaps overlooks some intrinsic (quality) differences between the competitively imported products and the so-called "competing" domestic products. However, it still suggests the existence of large potential increases in the value added content of total commodity exports.

[13] The First Five-Year Plan (1962–66) set up the target of achieving 33 percent of total commodity exports ($138 million) to be manufactured goods by 1966.

period after 1962 as the export-oriented growth phase in Korea's development. However, Korea also achieved a very significant level of import substitution in cement, fertilizer, refined petroleum, textile yarn and fabrics, etc. during this period, which in due course started to emerge as a new generation of exportables. Import substitution and export expansion seem to go side by side although understandably with some time lag.[14]

In 1975, the modernized manfacturing sector contributed about 32 percent of the GNP while the social overhead sectors contributed nearly 10 percent. The once dominant agricultural sector declined to merely 19 percent of GNP by 1975, and even the share of the service sectors was reduced to about 36 percent.

II. Factor Supply and Factor Intensity of Trade

Korea achieved one of the highest growth rates in the world during 1962–75 period. Over that period, per capita GNP in 1970 dollars rose from $150 to $387, for an average annual growth rate of 7.5 percent. The annual commodity exports of Korea, which amounted to less than $ 0.1 billion before 1962, increased at the average annual rate of about 40 percent (35 percent in 1970 constant prices) during the period 1962–75, and the ratio of commodity exports to GNP increased from about 2 to 25 percent.[15] By 1975, 32 percent of GNP originated in manufacturing, and manufactured products constituted more than 90 percent of total commodity exports which had never exceeded the 20 percent level during 1953–61. In 1973, about one third of total workers in manufacturing were employed for export production.

During 1963–73, commodity exports increased about 23 times (in 1970 constant prices) and the number of persons employed directly and indirectly in export production increased about 7 times (from 0.15 million to 1.01 million), implying average annual growth rates of about 37 percent

[14] Having enjoyed such positive effects of export-oriented growth as expanded market size, and improved skills, technological transfers and the over-all spur to efficiency which result from international competition, it does not seem likely that Korea will abruptly reverse its "outward-looking" industrialization policy in the seventies.

[15] The share of commodity exports in GNP, taking account of the import content of exports which has usually been equivalent to around 40 percent of total export value, was about 15 percent in 1975. This section is also excerpted from Hong, *op. cit.* The data are updated.

Table 3. Major Indicators of Growth and Trade

	Commodity Exports (billion current dollars)	Commodity Imports (billion current dollars)	Total Fixed Capital Stock (billion 1970 dollars)	Total Population (million persons)	Total Employed Persons (million persons)	Per Capita Capital Stock (1970 dollar)	Capital Per Employed Person (1970 dollar)	Per Capita GNP (1970 dollar)
1953	0.04	0.35	3.29	21.05		157		129
1954	0.02	0.24	3.36	21.27		158		135
1955	0.02	0.34	3.47	21.50		161		141
1956	0.03	0.39	3.59	22.15		162		137
1957	0.02	0.44	3.73	22.82		164		143
1958	0.02	0.38	3.86	23.51		164		146
1959	0.02	0.30	3.99	24.22		165		147
1960	0.03	0.34	4.11	24.95		165		146
1961	0.04	0.32	4.27	25.61		167		149
1962	0.06	0.42	4.50	26.28		171		150
1963	0.09	0.56	4.78	26.98	7.66	177	624	159
1964	0.12	0.40	5.00	27.69	7.80	181	641	168
1965	0.18	0.46	5.32	28.41	8.21	187	649	173
1966	0.25	0.72	5.91	29.16	8.42	203	702	190
1967	0.32	1.00	6.64	29.71	8.72	224	761	201
1968	0.46	1.46	7.67	30.28	9.16	253	837	222
1969	0.62	1.82	9.06	30.85	9.41	294	962	251
1970	0.84	1.98	10.38	31.44	9.75	330	1.065	265
1971	1.07	2.39	11.71	31.97	10.07	366	1,163	285
1972	1.62	2.52	12.82	32.51	10.56	394	1,214	299
1973	3.23	4.24	14.25	33.07	11.14	431	1,280	343
1974	4.46	6.85	15.73	33.63	11.59	468	1,357	366
1975	5.08	7.27		34.20*	11.82			387*

Sources: Wontack Hong, *Factor Supply and Factor Intensity of Trade in Korea* (Seoul, KDI Press, 1976), Table 5.1. and Table A.9. Data are updated.
* See footnote to Table 13.

Table 4. ***Contribution of Exports to Sectoral Employment and Sectoral Capital Use, 1963–73***

(million 1970 dollars & thousand persons)

Sectoral Employment	1963	1968	1973
Primary Sector			
(A) Total Employment	4,894	4,907	5,616
(B) Directly Employed for Exports	40	66	118
(C) Indirectly Employed for Exports	46	66	144
(B + C)/(A)	(2%)	(3%)	(5%)
Manufacturing Sector			
(A) Total Employment	610	1,176	1,774
(B) Directly Employed for Exports	32	182	471
(C) Indirectly Employed for Exports	16	44	108
(B + C)/(A)	(8%)	(19%)	(33%)
SOC & Service Sector			
(A) Total Employment	2,158	3,072	3,749
(B) Directly Employed for Exports	0	0	0
(C) Indirectly Employed for Exports	16	53	174
(B + C)/(A)	(1%)	(2%)	(5%)
Whole Industry			
(A) Total Employment	7,662	9,155	11,139
(B) Directly Employed for Exports	72	248	589
(C) Indirectly Employed for Exports	78	162	426
(B + C)/(A)	(2%)	(4%)	(9%)
Sectoral Capital Use	**1963**	**1968**	**1973**
Primary Sector			
(A) Total Fixed Capital Stock	601	928	1,568
(B) Directly Employed for Exports	27	65	140
(C) Indirectly Employed for Exports	20	49	130
(B + C)/(A)	(8%)	(12%)	(17%)
Manufacturing Sector			
(A) Total Fixed Capital Stock	936	1,682	2,809
(B) Directly Employed for Exports	26	143	982
(C) Indirectly Employed for Exports	21	97	433
(B + C)/(A)	(5%)	(14%)	(50%)
SOC & Service Sector			
(A) Total Fixed Capital Stock	3,247	5,057	9,877
(B) Directly Employed for Export	0	0	0
(C) Indirectly Employed for Exports	35	109	553
(B + C)/(A)	(1%)	(2%)	(6%)
Whole Industry			
(A) Total Fixed Capital Stock	4,784	7,667	14,253
(B) Directly Employed for Exports	53	208	1,123
(C) Indirectly Employed for Exports	75	254	1,116
(B + C)/(A)	(3%)	(6%)	(16%)

Source: Hong, *op. cit.,* Table 7.7. and Table 7.9. Data are updated.

and 21 percent, respectively, and an export expansion elasticity of employment of 0.6. The fixed capital stock directly and indirectly employed for export production increased about 17-fold (from $0.13 billion to $2.23 billion) during 1963–73 implying an average annual growth rate of 33 percent and an export expansion elasticity of capital absorption of about 0.9.

Total net fixed capital stock in Korea increased by an average annual rate of 3.5 percent during 1953–61, 6.7 percent during 1962–66, and a remarkable 13.0 percent during 1967–74. The net fixed capital stock of all industries amounted to about $15.7 billion in 1974. On the other hand, the total number of employed persons increased by about 50 percent during 1963–74, *i.e.*, from about 7.7 million in 1963 to 11.6 million persons in 1974.

Per capita capital stock in Korea increased by about 30 percent during the fourteen year period of 1953–66, and it was only after 1966 that per capita capital stock started to increase rapidly. Per capita capital stock increased by 130 percent during 1966–74 (from $203 to $468 in 1970 prices), but due to rapidly increasing employment (from 8.4 million to 11.6 million persons), the fixed capital stock per employed person increased by around 90 percent. However, this still implies that significant overall capital deepening occurred in Korea during 1966–74.

According to the manufacturing census data, the per worker capital stock in manufacturing has steadily and significantly increased since 1966, *i.e.*, from $1.8 thousand per worker in 1966 to $2.4 thousand in 1971 and to $3.2 thousand in 1973. However, according to the Han-BOK capital stock data, the increase in per worker capital stock was rather small, i.e., about 15 percent during 1966–71 (from about $1.53 thousand in 1966 to about $1.76 thousand in 1971) or about 19 percent during 1967–72.[16] The enormous difference between these two sets of data, especially since 1971, may be partly attributed to the fact that the census data covers only those establishments with five or more workers while those with less than five workers may use much more labor intensive production techniques. But it appears mainly due to the fact that the allowance for the consumption of fixed capital stock as estimated by the BOK, which takes about two-thirds of total gross capital formation in manufacturing, has

[16] Han-BOK sectoral annual fixed capital stock data were estimated by adding (or subtracting) BOK's estimation of net annual fixed capital formation (gross fixed capital formation minus allowance for the consumption of fixed capital stock) to the Han's capital stock data of 1968 which were computed on the basis of the 1968 National Wealth Survey.

Table 5. Capital Stock Per Worker and the Average Wage Rate in Manufacturing (Mining and Manufacturing Census Data)

	Total Number of Workers (1,000 persons)		Wage Rate for Employee	Per Worker Value Added	Total Output (million 1970 $)	Capital-Output Ratio (k)	Labor-Output Ratio (n)	Capital-Labor Ratio (k/n)	Per Worker Capital Stock[2] (Han-BOK, EPB Quarterly Data)
	M & M Census[1]	Quarterly Survey	(thousand 1970 dollars)						
1960	274	—	0.33	0.97	699	0.39	0.39	1.00	—
1961	—	—	—	0.71	—	—	—	—	—
1962	—	—	—	0.92	—	—	—	—	—
1963	402	610	0.33	1.19	1,227	0.33	0.33	1.00	1.53
1964	—	637	—	0.91	—	—	—	—	1.55
1965	—	772	—	1.06	—	—	—	—	1.39
1966	567	833	0.29	1.16	1,759	0.56	0.31	1.81	1.53
1967	649	1,021	0.36	1.32	2,274	0.47	0.29	1.62	1.43
1968	748	1,170	0.41	1.54	2,948	0.43	0.25	1.72	1.44
1969	829	1,232	0.47	1.82	3,708	0.41	0.22	1.86	1.56
1970	861	1,284	0.53	2.06	4,297	0.39	0.20	1.95	1.67
1971	848	1,336	0.61	2.53	5,183	0.39	0.16	2.44	1.76
1972	973	1,445	0.61	2.52	6,096	0.40	0.16	2.50	1.70
1973	1,158	1,774	0.69	2.98	9,209	0.41	0.13	3.15	1.58
1974	1,321	2,012	0.69	2.82	11,397	0.41	0.12	3.42	1.49

Sources: Economic Planning Board, *Report on Mining and Manufacturing Census (or Survey)*, and Hong, *op. cit.*, Table 6.3.

Notes: [1] Total number of workers at manufacturing establishments operating with five or more workers.

[2] Based on Han-BOK capital stock data and EPB's quarterly sample survey on economically active population.

Table 6. Capital Stock Per Worker and Average Wage Rate in Agriculture (Farm Household Survey Data)

	Total Number of Persons Employed in Agriculture[1] (thousand persons)	Wage Rate for Farm Employee (thousand 1970 dollars)	Per Worker Farm Income (thousand 1970 dollars)	Capital-Output Ratio (k)	Man-Year-Output Ratio (n)	Capital-Man-Year Ratio[2] (k/n)	Per Farmer Capital-Stock[3] (Han-BOK, EPB Quarterly Data)	Land-Output Ratio
1962	—	0.22	0.23	—	—	—	—	—
1963	4,644	0.21	0.26	—	1.15	—	0.11	3.48
1964	4,655	0.25	0.26	—	—	—	0.12	2.64
1965	4,603	0.19	0.22	—	—	—	0.13	3.10
1966	4,695	0.17	0.22	0.29	1.23	0.24	0.14	3.27
1967	4,598	0.20	0.23	—	—	—	0.16	3.16
1968	4,582	0.23	0.25	0.38	1.19	0.32	0.18	3.16
1969	4,687	0.26	0.27	—	—	—	0.19	2.72
1970	4,826	0.27	0.28	0.41	1.08	0.38	0.21	2.75
1971	4,758	0.30	0.35	—	—	—	0.24	2.38
1972	5,110	0.30	0.36	0.42	0.96	0.44	0.25	2.64
1973	5,260	0.35	0.40	0.51	0.91	0.56	0.27	3.64
1974	5,304	0.38	0.43	—	0.80	—	0.31	4.45

Sources: Ministry of Agriculture and Fisheries, *Reports on the Results of Farm Household Economy Survey*, and Hong, *op. cit.*, Table 6.3.

Notes: [1] Includes forestry.

[2] Man-year input per thousand 1970 dollar of output.

[3] Includes forestry and fishery.

Table 7. *Interest Rates on Loans and Time Deposits*

(billion won & percent)

	Interest Rates on Time Deposits (Over 1 Year)		Time & Savings	Weighted Av. Interest Rate of KDB & DMB Loans[1]		Total KDB & DMB	Av. Interest Rate of Curb Market Loans		Total Curb Market
	Nominal	Real	Deposits	Nominal	Real	Loans[1]	Nominal	Real	Loans[2]
1961	15.0%	1.8%	5	10.3%	−2.9%	50	—	—	—
1962	15.0	5.6	12	10.4	1.0	68	—	—	—
1963	15.0	−5.6	13	10.5	−10.1	77	52.5%	31.9%	—
1964	15.0	−19.6	15	10.6	−24.0	85	61.8	27.2	11.7
1965	26.4	16.4	31	13.3	3.3	107	58.9	48.9	20.4
1966	26.4	17.5	70	17.1	8.2	149	58.7	49.8	22.6
1967	26.4	20.0	129	18.5	12.1	229	56.5	50.1	38.9
1968	25.2	17.1	256	18.8	10.7	373	56.0	47.9	78.2
1969	22.8	16.0	452	18.5	11.7	626	51.3	44.5	112.1
1970	22.8	13.6	576	16.1	6.9	851	49.8	40.6	181.6
1971	20.4	11.8	709	15.2	6.6	1,077	46.4	37.8	218.4
1972	12.0	−2.0	921	16.4	2.4	1,437	39.0	25.0	204.2
1973	12.0	5.1	1,214	13.3	6.4	1,906	33.3	26.4	246.4
1974	15.0	−27.1	1,451	13.5	−28.6	2,853	40.6	−1.5	—
1975	15.0	−11.0	1,911			3,483			

Source: The Bank of Korea, *Economic Statistics Yearbook*.

Notes: [1] KDB represents Korea Development Bank and DMB represents Deposit Money Banks.

[2] Data from the preliminary draft of *The Unorganized Financial Sector in Korea*, 1945–75, KDI, 1976 by Y.C. Park.

led to serious under-estimation of the magnitude of net fixed capital formation in the manufacturing sector. It is often argued that the allowance for the consumption of fixed capital is simply a legal concept having little to do with actual depreciation.

According to the Farm Household Survey data, capital stock per man-year input in agriculture was estimated to be about $0.23 thousand before 1967 but has steadily increased during 1967–73 to become $0.55 thousand in 1973.[17] The per farmer (without taking account of underemployment) capital stock estimated on the basis of Han-BOK capital stock data has also doubled during 1966–74.

The per worker farm income started to rise significantly after 1967 (from $230 in 1967 to $430 in 1974 in 1970 prices), as did the wage rate for employees in the manufacturing sector (from $360 in 1967 to $630 in 1973). On the other hand, the weighted average real interest rates on all types of loans supplied by both banking institutions and curb markets reached their peak in 1967 and declined steadily and substantially thereafter. Hence, we can conclude that there has been rapid and significant capital accumulation and capital deepening in Korea since 1967 which was accompanied by the rapidly rising wage/rental ratio.

The factor intensity (i.e., capital/labor ratio) of Korea's export commodity bundle grew significantly in capital intensity during 1966–73. The ratio of capital to labor, required directly and indirectly for $100 million worth of export production, was about 0.9 in 1966 ($90 million/98 man-year) which became about 2.2 in 1973 ($88 million/40 man-year).[18] However, the factor intensity of competitive import replacement did not shift much in any specific direction. Consequently, although competitive imports were much more capital intensive than exports before 1966 (e.g., 1.8 versus. 0.9 in 1966), the difference became smaller subsequently and there seem to have been only slight differences in their factor intensities after 1970.

---

[17] The land per man-year input in agriculture was about $2.6–$3.0 thousand during 1962–72, but increased to about $4.0 thousand in 1973 and to $5.6 thousand in 1974 due to sharp rises in land price.

[18] The (direct plus indirect) labor-output ratios in export productions have been decreasing at the average annual rate of 13 percent during 1966–73 (about 10 percent during 1966–68, 12 percent during 1968–70 and 18 percent during 1970–73), and the labor-output ratios in import competing productions have been decreasing at the average annual rate of 5 percent (zero percent during 1966–68, 6 percent during 1968–70, and 9 percent during 1970–73). On the other hand, the capital-output ratios in most sectors did not decrease (and have rather increased in many cases) during 1966–73.

Table 8. Changing Factor Intensity of Trade, 1960–73
(Per $100 Million Commodity Exports or Import Replacements)

(million 1970 dollars & thousand persons)

	1966	1968	1970	1973
I. Direct Factor Intensity of Exports	(0.69)	(0.84)	(1.05)	(1.91)
Capital Directly Employed	41	41	41	44
Labor Directly Employed	59	49	39	23
II. Indirect Factor Intensity of Exports	(1.29)	(1.56)	(2.15)	(2.59)
Capital Indirectly Employed	49	50	58	44
Labor Indirectly Employed	38	32	27	17
III. Factor Intensity of Imported Inputs	(1.43)	(2.22)	(2.75)	(3.10)
Capital Content of Imported Inputs	10	20	22	31
Labor Content of Imported Inputs	7	9	8	10
IV. Aggregate Factor Intensity of Exports	(0.93)	(1.12)	(1.48)	(2.20)
Total Capital Employed (I + II)	90	92	98	88
Total Labor Employed (I + II)	97	82	66	40
I. Direct Factor Intensity of Imports	(1.45)	(1.20)	(1.05)	(1.33)
Capital Directly Required	58	49	45	44
Labor Directly Required	40	41	43	33
II. Indirect Factor Intensity of Imports	(2.14)	(1.80)	(2.60)	(3.46)
Capital Directly Required	60	45	52	45
Labor Indirectly Required	28	25	20	13
III. Factor Intensity of Imported Inputs	(2.09)	(2.00)	(2.25)	(3.56)
Capital Content of Imported Inputs	23	24	18	32
Labor Content of Imported Inputs	11	12	8	9
IV. Aggregate Factor Intensity of Imports	(1.78)	(1.51)	(1.62)	(2.24)
Total Capital Required (I + II + III)	141	118	115	121
Total Labor Required (I + II + III)	79	78	71	54

Source: Hong, *op. cit.*, Table 7.10. Data are updated.

Note: Factor intensity (figures in the parentheses) is the amount of capital (in million 1970 dollars) required divided by the amount of labor (in thousand persons) required per $100 million worth of exports or import replacements. ("Requirements" are rounded figures.) Competitive imports are competitive as of 1968.

Table 9. *Impact of Capital-Labor Substitution on Factor Intensity of Trade, 1966–73*
(Per $100 Million Commodity Exports or Import Replacements)

	1966	1968	1970	1973
Direct Factor Intensity of Exports, applying				
1966 Factor Coefficients	41/59 = **0.69**	43/57 = 0.75	43/57 = 0.75	45/49 = 0.92
1968 Factor Coefficients	43/51 = 0.84	41/49 = **0.84**	41/48 = 0.84	39/43 = 0.90
1970 Factor Coefficients	43/42 = 1.02	43/40 = 1.08	41/39 = **1.05**	41/34 = 1.21
1973 Factor Coefficients	44/29 = 1.52	45/28 = 1.61	43/27 = 1.59	44/23 = **1.91**
Direct Factor Intensity of Competitive Import Replacements, applying				
1966 Factor Coefficients	58/40 = **1.45**	42/49 = 0.86	37/57 = 0.65	41/60 = 0.68
1968 Factor Coefficients	66/33 = 2.00	49/41 = **1.20**	42/50 = 0.84	45/54 = 0.83
1970 Factor Coefficients	62/28 = 2.26	50/35 = 1.42	45/43 = **1.05**	48/46 = 1.04
1973 Factor Coefficients	63/19 = 3.32	49/24 = 2.04	44/31 = 1.42	44/34 = **1.29**
Total Factor Intensity of Exports, applying				
1966 A^d Matrix & Factor Coefficients	90/98 = **0.92**	92/97 = 0.95	95/98 = 0.97	98/89 = 1.11
1968 A^d Matrix & Factor Coefficients	93/84 = 1.11	92/82 = **1.12**	94/83 = 1.13	92/74 = 1.24
1970 A^d Matrix & Factor Coefficients	100/69 = 1.45	100/66 = 1.50	98/66 = **1.48**	100/60 = 1.67
1973 A^d Matrix & Factor Coefficients	93/49 = 1.90	92/46 = 2.00	90/46 = 1.96	88/40 = **2.20**
Total Factor Intensity of Competitive Import Replacements, applying				
1966 A Matrix & Factor Coefficients	141/79 = **1.78**	111/90 = 1.23	98/96 = 1.03	104/98 = 1.06
1968 A Matrix & Factor Coefficients	145/68 = 2.14	118/78 = **1.51**	105/85 = 1.24	109/88 = 1.24
1970 A Matrix & Factor Coefficients	139/55 = 2.53	123/65 = 1.89	115/71 = **1.62**	120/74 = 1.62
1973 A Matrix & Factor Coefficients	149/40 = 3.73	134/47 = 2.85	123/53 = 2.32	121/54 = **2.24**

Sources: Hong, *op. cit.*, Table 8.3. and 8.4. Data are updated.

Table 10. Factor Requirements per $100 Million Exports or Import Replacements: U.S.(1947), Japan(1951) and Korea(1970)

	Capital(K) (million 1970 $)	Labor(N) (1,000 persons)	Factor Intensity (K)/(N)
Korea(1970)			
Exports	98.2	65.7	1,495
Competitive-Imports	116.5	69.5	1,676
(1947 U.S. Coefficients)	(166.4)	(9.9)	(16,808)
(1958 U.S. Coefficients)	(153.0)	(8.5)	(18,000)
(1965 Japanese Coefficients)	(124.9)	(45.2)	(2,763)
(1970 Japanese Coefficients)	(117.9)	(38.6)	(3,054)
Non-Competitive Imports			
1947 U.S. Coefficients	178.6	9.7	18,466
1958 U.S. Coefficients	148.3	8.1	18,393
1965 Japanese Coefficients	143.0	34.9	4,102
1970 Japanese Coefficients	137.5	28.0	4,918
Japan (1951)			
Exports	138.6	125.8	1,102
Competitive Imports	133.1	187.6	710
U.S.(1947)			
Exports	255.1	10.1	25,258
Competitive Imports	309.1	9.4	32,883

Source: Hong, *op. cit.*, Table 9.4. Data are updated.

Note: The U.S. GNP deflator was applied to both Leontief's and Ichimura's data in order to get 1970 dollar figures. If we apply the GNP deflator of Japan (1970 = 100) and its official exchange rate of 360 yen per dollar in 1970 to Ichimura's data, we get about $1,400/worker for the capital intensity of Japan's exports and $900/worker for that of Japan's competitive imports in 1951. Rice and wheat imports were excluded when the U.S. coefficients were applied to Korea's competitive imports.

The increase in the factor intensity of Korea's exports during 1966–73 was partly due to shifts in the composition of exports, but was predominantly due to labor-saving factor substitutions in the production process.[19]

[19] For instance, the direct capital intensity of exports increased by about 5 percent due to shifts in composition of exports but increased by about 11 percent due to capital-labor substitutions during 1966–68. The direct plus indirect capital intensity of commodity exports increased by about 0.2 percent due to shifts in composition of exports but increased by about 33 percent due to capital-labor substitutions during 1968–70. Although we can observe a significant increase in the capital intensity of Korea's commodity exports due to shifts in composition of exports (12 percent) during the period 1970–73, our impression is that it was factor substitution which dominated the changes in the factor intensity of Korea's exports. See Table 11.

Table 11. Changes in Factor Intensity of Commodity Exports Due to Factor Substitutions and Shifts in Composition of Exports, 1966–73

		Average	1966	1968	1970	1973	Due to Changes in Export Composition		
							1966–68	1968–70	1970–73
Direct Factor Intensity of Exports (Capital/Labor Ratios)									
		Average					**(5.1%)**	**(−1.0%)**	**(16.3%)**
Applying 1966 Coefficients			**0.69**	0.75	0.75	0.92	8.7%	0.0%	22.7%
Applying 1968 Coefficients			0.84	**0.84**	0.84	0.90	0.0%	0.0%	7.1%
Applying 1970 Coefficients			1.02	1.08	**1.05**	1.21	5.9%	−2.8%	15.2%
Applying 1973 Coefficients			1.52	1.61	1.59	**1.91**	5.9%	−1.2%	20.1%
Due to Factor	1966–68	**(10.9%)**	21.7%	12.0%	12.0%	−2.2%	**21.7%**	—	—
Substitutions	1968–70	**(27.4%)**	21.4%	28.6%	25.0%	34.4%	—	**25.0%**	—
	1970–73	**(51.9%)**	49.0%	49.1%	51.4%	57.9%	—	—	**81.9%**
Direct plus Indirect Factor Intensity of Export (Capital/Labor Ratios)									
		Average					**(3.0%)**	**(0.2%)**	**(12.0%)**
Applying 1966 Coefficients			**0.93**	0.95	0.98	1.11	2.2%	3.2%	13.3%
Applying 1968 Coefficients			1.11	**1.12**	1.13	1.24	0.9%	0.9%	9.7%
Applying 1970 Coefficients			1.45	1.50	**1.48**	1.67	3.4%	−1.3%	12.8%
Applying 1973 Coefficients			1.90	2.00	1.96	**2.20**	5.3%	−2.0%	12.2%
Due to Factor	1966–68	**(16.1%)**	19.4%	17.9%	15.3%	11.7%	**20.4%**	—	—
Substitutions	1968–70	**(32.6%)**	30.6%	33.9%	31.0%	34.7%	—	**32.1%**	—
	1970–73	**(32.1%)**	31.0%	33.3%	32.4%	31.7%	—	—	**48.6%**

Source: Hong, *op. cit.*, Table 8.5. Date are updated.

On the other hand, the factor intensity of Korea's competitive import replacements became less capital intensive due to shifts in the import pattern, but because of offsetting increases in sectoral labor saving factor substitutions we could not find any consistent decline in the capital intensity of competitive import replacements. Instead, the increase in capital intensity of competitive import replacement sectors seems to have been more than offsetting the shifts in the import pattern since 1968.

The capital intensity of Korea's non-competitive imports as estimated by using the U.S. and Japanese sectoral factor coefficients was much higher than that of either exports or competitive imports. Therefore, Korea's trade appears to have been consistent with the comparative advantage doctrine of Heckscher-Ohlin principally with regard to exports versus non-competitive imports and exports versus natural resource intensive imports.

It appears that exports were significantly more labor-intensive than competitive imports in the sixties, but that significant changes in Korea's trade pattern, as well as increasing labor-saving factor substitutions in production processes, led to the employment implications of export promotion and import substitution being approximately equal in the early seventies. Therefore, attention will have to be focused on those aspects of the trade regime and factor markets that affected employment in exports and in import-substitution.

Government trade and subsidy policies can directly influence the composition of the various subcategories of tradable goods. Such policies can also affect the prices of factors of production, and thus alter the profitability of alternative activities and the factor proportions used in them. Part of the capital-labor substitutions in Korea may be attributed to the increase in per capita capital stock and the associated rise in the wage-rental ratio, but most of the factor substitutions might have to be attributed to the subsidy on capital use. For example, the estimated annual interest subsidy associated with bank loans to the manufacturing sector was, in value terms, equivalent to more than 10 percent of total fixed capital stock in the manufacturing sector during 1967–71.[20]

Korea's exports might have been less capital intensive if there had been no subsidy on capital use, but it is questionable whether Korea could have expanded its exports so rapidly if it had insisted upon using less capital-intensive production techniques in order to maximize employment. This is because capital and labor might not be good susbtitutes for each other in

[20] See my *Trade and Subsidy Policy and Employment Growth in Korea,* mimeographed (Seoul: KDI, 1976).

terms of product quality and there might have been limited foreign demand for extremely labor-intensive goods. One might also argue that once a developing country becomes successful in exporting large amounts of labor-intensive goods, the developed countries will erect sufficiently high barriers against these imports so that the developing country has no other choice but to expand capital intensive exports.[21]

III. A Projection of Korea's Export Pattern (1975–81)[22]

1. Forecast, Target and Projection

Maizels expounds three different ways of considering future developments, each of which is useful for a particular purpose.[23] "Forecasting" takes account, as far as possible, of likely future changes that might influence the trade and growth of a country and then makes a prediction. Economic forecasting of this type is inevitably confined to the short-run future; predicting medium or long-term changes is subject to so much error that it is of little value in practice. Establishment of a "target" rate of growth (or future level) of trade or production is essentially a policy-oriented approach, since the target will imply policy changes in many directions in order to achieve it. A "projection" of the future growth rate of exports, the future pattern of outputs, or any other economic magnitude, is based on specific assumptions concerning the variables, both structural and governmental policies, which are likely to influence the outcome. The explicit statement of assumptions is an essential part of the concept of a "projection", since it allows for an evaluation of the probable impact of any given variation in the assumptions on the projected levels of production and trade. Thus, projections are essentially neutral regarding alternative policies; their function is rather to present the contrast between the probable results of each alternative.

---

[21] The quantitative import restrictions can partly be circumvented by quality improvements. As far as long-run improvements in production technology and management efficiency are concerned, Korea seems to benefit from such restrictions against simple quantitative export expansions.

[22] A preliminary version of this section (with detailed data sets) was published, in Korean, as *A Projection of Korea's Trade Pattern: 1977–86* (Seoul: KDI Press, 1975).

[23] A. Maizels, *Exports and Economic Growth of Developing Countries* (London: Cambridge University Press, 1968).

Although projections can be made without postulating targets, the reverse does not hold. Every economic development plan is based, explicitly or implicitly, on a target or a set of interrelated targets; but government policies can be rationally set out only on the basis of "projections" as defined above. For instance, if projections reveal unfavorable tendencies which are likely to develop in the future, they clearly have policy implications. Indeed, the adoption of appropriate new policies designed to prevent such unfavorable results from arising would in itself be a justification for making the projection, though such policy changes would be expected to "invalidate" the projection, in the sense that the basic assumptions relating to government policies would themselves be changed.

The government export plan in Korea—the product of experiences, common sense, intuition, dreams and simple logic of government officials and their consultants—has not been a simple forecasting exercise or just a harmless guideline for businessmen in Korea. Past experience shows that government export plans heavily influence the flow of bank loans, government subsidies, government direct investments, foreign loans and investments, and other government incentive measures. Although the government export plan is revised each year with up-to-date information, any irrational elements in the initial plan would still result in a significant waste of resources. In order to reduce the extent of resource misallocation and to avoid the costly trial and error process, we have to carefully examine the government export plan and revise it if we find obvious irrational elements in it.

However, since a comprehensive government export plan for the period of 1977–81 does not exist yet, the main purpose of this section is not to examine some existing export plans on a piecemeal basis but to "project" an efficient (and comprehensive) commodity trade pattern for Korea on the basis of a cross-sectional analysis. The objective is to provide a basis, or a starting point, to formulate a rational government export plan.

2. A Typical Pattern of Export: Chenery Type Cross-Section Analysis

As capital accumulates and as the skill composition of labor changes, the comparative advantage position of a country changes, and as a result the optimum trade pattern (which can generate maximum growth and employment) of a country changes. One way to project such changes in the optimal trade pattern of a country is to project factor supplies, technical progress and international market conditions in the future and then theoretically deduce the optimal path of the changing trade pattern. Unfortunately, however, there has been no workable methodology developed for this purpose yet.

Another way to project an optimal path of changing trade patterns is to analyze the actual experiences of many different countries in terms of changing factor endowment, income level, market sizes, etc., and then empirically deduce an efficient path of changing the trade pattern for a country, taking account of its own specific characteristics. In this section, we adopted the Chenery type methodology of projecting the typical commodity export pattern on the basis of the world-wide cross-country analysis as a first step to deduce an efficient path of changing the export pattern.[24] We then modified this initially projected pattern taking account of government policies and other specific characteristics of the Korean economy. We also examined the investment and employment implications of the projected export pattern.

In our cross-section analysis, we did not include every country in the world which happened to possess trade statistics. Since the objective of our projection is to provide a directional guide-line for Korea's commodity export expansion during the period 1977–81, we included, in principle, only those countries which could achieve above (world) average performance in per capita income growth and export expansion during 1960–70. That is, we tried to select only those countries which seem to have accomplished efficient resource allocation and successful growth with significant export expansion, and therefore may provide reference data

[24] H. B. Chenery and L. Taylor, "Development Patterns: Among Countries and Over Time" *The Review of Economics and Statistics,* November 1968, and H. B. Chenery, "Patterns of Industrial Growth," *American Economic Review,* September 1960. If growth of a country takes place mainly through capital accumulation, without much change in tastes, technology, economic organization, or international market conditions, we may observe common features between a country's growth and trade pattern and cross-country patterns. The impacts of varying natural resource endowment among countries may be measured by the intercountry variations. Furthermore, the systematic effects of changes in technology and other factors may be measured by changes in the cross-country patterns over time. Two procedures have been suggested for quantitative comparisons of growth and trade patterns. One is to use the value of some of the variables as a basis for subdividing the sample into groups of countries that are expected to have more homogeneous patterns. The other is to utilize all the explanatory variables in a single multiple regression equation. This method assumes that the effect of each variable is additive in logarithms and independent of the values taken by the others. The former approach is preferable when there are complex interactions among the explanatory variables that may require different functional forms for each groups.

for Korea's future growth path. Twenty-one countries (Korea, Turkey, Taiwan, Portugal, Singapore, Spain, Greece, Ireland, Italy, Israel, Japan, Austria, the Netherlands, Finland, Belgium, West Germany, France, Denmark, Norway, Canada and Sweden) were included in the sample. The data used were mostly from 1971 and some from 1970.

We took three explanatory variables for per capita sectoral exports: (1) per capita income to measure the "growth elasticity" associated with increasing income level and per capita capital accumulation, (2) per capita land to measure the "resource elasticity" associated with a country's natural resource endowment[25] and (3) population to measure the "size elasticity" associated with a country's domestic market size.

We estimated two logarithmic equations from cross-country data:

$$\text{(A)}\ ln\ X_i = \alpha + \beta\ ln\ Y + \gamma\ ln\ L + \delta\ ln\ N$$

$$\text{(B)}\ ln\ X_i = \alpha + \beta_1\ ln\ Y + \beta_2\ (ln\ Y)^2 + \gamma\ ln\ L + \delta\ ln\ N$$

where X_i represents per capita exports in i-sector, Y per capita GNP, L per capita land and N represents the size of population. The non-linear income term (log $Y)^2$ allows for the changes in elasticities with rising income, which avoids the necessity of subdividing the sample by income level. However, we decided to use type A estimate without (log $Y)^2$ term for our projection, because β_2's were not significantly different from zero in most cases.

All the growth elasticities (β's) had positive signs while almost all the resource and size elasticities (γ's & δ's) had negative signs. The result seems to reflect a general tendency of less need for manufactures exports from a country the larger the natural resource endowment of the country on the one hand, and the smaller the trade volume of a country the larger the domestic market size of the country which allows more self-sufficient production on the other. Machinery, steel and metal products and chemicals had very high growth elasticities of exports, while primary products and textile products had very low growth elasticities. A notable fact seems to be that electrical and non-electrical machinery, electronics and nonmetallic mineral products had very low size elasticities of exports (in absolute

[25] Share of primary outputs or exports in GNP may also be used as an index to reflect natural resource endowment of a country. However, a previous study of mine suggests that per capita land can serve best as such an index in a cross-country analysis. See "Industrialization and Trade in Manufactures: The East Asian Experience", in *The Open Economy: Essays on International Trade and Finance,* ed. by P. B. Kenen (New York: Columbia University Press, 1968).

Table 12. Estimates of Typical Export Patterns

$(ln\ X = \alpha + \beta\ ln\ Y + \gamma\ ln\ L + \delta\ ln\ P)$

Commodity & Equation	Regression Coefficients with Respect to: Intercept α	*ln Y* (β)	*ln L* (γ)	*ln P* (δ)	R^2
1. Agricultural Products	0.31 (0.12)	0.56 (1.57)	−0.24 (1.29)	−0.46 (1.92)	0.30
2. Fishery Products	−5.51 (1.35)	0.71 (1.39)	0.02 (0.06)	−0.10 (0.28)	0.12
3. Mining Products	−3.68 (1.22)	0.92 (2.26)	0.13 (0.64)	−0.70 (2.56)	0.49
4. Primary Products (1–3)	−0.08 (0.04)	0.70 (2.62)	−0.11 (0.77)	−0.61 (3.37)	0.55
5. Food Products	−2.14 (1.15)	0.99 (3.97)	−0.18 (1.38)	−0.63 (3.77)	0.66
6. Textile	−1.92 (1.45)	0.80 (4.51)	−0.53 (5.77)	−0.17 (1.42)	0.72
7. Wearing Apparel	−2.02 (1.08)	0.85 (3.42)	−0.40 (3.14)	−0.34 (2.01)	0.55
8. Textile Products (6–7)	−1.12 (0.78)	0.81 (4.20)	−0.45 (3.49)	−0.26 (2.01)	0.66
9. Footwear	−0.05 (0.02)	0.11 (0.35)	−0.10 (0.66)	0.07 (0.36)	0.04
10. Leather & Products	−10.58 (4.89)	1.60 (5.52)	−0.27 (1.80)	−0.29 (1.50)	0.67
11. Rubber & Products	−10.69 (6.55)	1.73 (7.92)	−0.43 (3.83)	−0.20 (1.35)	0.80
12. Wood Products	−2.95 (0.84)	0.78 (1.65)	0.09 (0.04)	−0.53 (1.69)	0.29
13. Furniture	−13.55 (5.41)	1.99 (5.76)	−0.28 (1.72)	−0.20 (1.01)	0.69
14. Printing	−12.91 (7.41)	2.03 (8.73)	−0.49 (4.07)	−0.33 (2.11)	0.84
15. Plastic Products	−7.43 (3.09)	1.30 (3.91)	−0.41 (2.61)	−0.34 (1.76)	0.54
16. Pottery & China	−10.32 (3.19)	1.24 (2.76)	−0.25 (1.23)	0.15 (0.64)	0.38
17. Paper & Products	−12.97 (3.78)	2.06 (4.34)	0.24 (1.07)	−0.52 (1.85)	0.69
18. Precision Instruments	13.38 (4.79)	2.08 (5.38)	−0.56 (3.09)	−0.03 (0.14)	0.65
19. Other Manufactures	−5.61 (3.02)	1.29 (5.19)	−0.47 (3.63)	−0.31 (1.83)	0.68
20. Misc. Manufactures (9–19)	−5.67 (2.68)	1.45 (5.13)	−0.15 (1.05)	−0.39 (2.04)	0.67

Table 12. (Continued)

Commodity & Equation	Regression Coefficients with Respect to				R^2
	Intercept α	*ln Y* (β)	*ln L* (γ)	*ln P* (δ)	
21. Industrial Chemicals	−10.84 (8.82)	1.94(11.77)	−0.32 (3.78)	−0.21 (1.87)	0.90
22. Other Chemicals	−13.34 (7.79)	2.28 (9.93)	−0.57 (4.82)	−0.19 (1.22)	0.86
23. Petroleum & Coal Products	−9.61 (2.40)	1.69 (3.15)	−0.56 (2.03)	−0.17 (0.47)	0.40
24. Chemicals (21–23)	−9.78 (7.26)	2.02(11.19)	−0.54 (5.77)	−0.33 (.269)	0.89
25. Glass & Products	−9.37 (3.81)	1.47 (4.48)	−0.45 (2.64)	−0.15 (0.69)	0.57
26. Cement	−3.32 (1.52)	0.31 (1.06)	0.17 (1.12)	−0.13 (0.65)	0.22
27. Other Non-Metallic Minerals	−13.44 (6.45)	2.02 (7.26)	−0.38 (2.66)	−0.17 (0.88)	0.77
28. Non-Metallic Products (25–27)	−7.06 (4.13)	1.24 (5.42)	−0.26 (2.16)	−0.11 (0.71)	0.65
29. Iron & Steel	−12.95 (4.95)	2.08 (5.94)	−0.37 (2.03)	−0.20 (0.85)	0.68
30. Non-Ferrous Metal Products	−13.08 (5.94)	2.04 (6.91)	0.03 (0.21)	−0.28 (1.39)	0.78
31. Metal Products	−11.64 (7.36)	2.04 (9.63)	−0.44 (3.99)	−0.23 (1.62)	0.85
32. Steel & Metal (29–31)	−10.96 (6.64)	2.02 (9.14)	−0.25 (2.19)	−0.11 (0.75)	0.84
33. Machinery	−16.19 (6.13)	2.67 (7.55)	−0.48 (2.62)	−0.02 (0.07)	0.77
34. Electrical Machinery	−12.53 (6.03)	2.19 (7.85)	−0.55 (3.81)	−0.18 (0.98)	0.79
35. Electronics & Comm. Equip.	−5.86 (2.28)	1.21 (3.40)	−0.38 (2.28)	−0.11 (0.55)	0.44
36. Shipbuilding	−15.22 (4.27)	2.27 (4.67)	0.03 (0.10)	−0.23 (0.78)	0.67
37. Transport Equipment	−18.50 (8.07)	2.82 (9.19)	−0.41 (2.60)	0.27 (1.32)	0.83
38. Machinery (38–37)	−12.93 (5.27)	2.39 (7.29)	−0.43 (2.55)	−0.07 (0.03)	0.76
All Commodities	−3.02 (3.18)	1.34(10.52)	−0.24 (3.71)	−0.27 (3.12)	0.88

Note: Figures in the parentheses are t-values.

magnitude).

The actual commodity exports of Korea in 1975 were used as base figures for the projection of Korea's trade pattern. We computed the growth rate of each commodity export in the period 1976–81 on the basis of the above sectoral elasticities, projected per capita income growth rates (7 percent a year), projected population growth rates and the rate of decrease in per capita land endowment of Korea during 1975–81. Per capita sectoral exports were computed in terms of 1970 constant dollar prices first and then they were coverted into 1975 dollar prices by applying the BOK's unit export price index.

We use the estimated sectoral growth rates instead of the estimated sectoral export values themselves. That is, we do not assume that the

Table 13. Projection of Population, Per Capita GNP and Per Capita Land, 1975–81

	Total Population (million)	Per Capita GNP (1970 $)	Per Capita Land (Km²/1,000)	Total GNP (billion 1970 $)
1975	34.68	381(538)*	2.84	13.2
Av. Annual Growth Rate	1.7%	7.0%	−1.6%	8.7%
Net Increase During 1975–77	3.4%	14.4%	−3.2%	18.2%
1977	35.87	436(616)*	2.75	15.6
Av. Annual Growth Rate	1.6%	7.0%	−1.5%	8.6%
Net Increase During 1977–81	6.6%	31.2%	−6.2%	40.4%
1981	38.22	572(807)*	2.58	21.9

Sources: Economic Planning Board, *1975 Population and Housing Census Report* (preliminary) 1976, and the Bank of Korea, *Monthly Economic Statistics* (January, 1976).

* At 1975 current market price and official exchange rate of 485 won per U.S. dollar.

Note: According to the published 1970 Population Census Report, the total population of Korea (excluding foreigners) was 31,435,000 on October 1, 1970 and the growth rate of population was 1.9 percent per annum during 1966–70. (EPB, *op. cit.*, p. 404). On the basis of a population sample survey conducted in 1973, the EPB officially announced that total population on March 31, 1974 was 33,333,333 and the population growth rate during 1970–73 was 1.7 percent. Hence we applied 1.7 percent to 1970–75 period implying total population of 34,200,000 in 1975. However, the 1975 Population Census reported total population to be 34,681,000 on October 1, 1975, implying a growth rate of 2 percent per annum during 1970–75.

Table 14. Commodity Export Pattern: Actual, Projected and Modified

Base Year: 1975 (million 1975 dollars & percent)

	Actual				1981 (Original Projection)	1981 (Modified Projection)
	1962[1]	1967[1]	1972[1]	1975		
	(%)	(%)	(%)	(%)	(%)	(%)
Primary Products[2]	55 (53)	83 (17)	270 (11)	487 (10)	694 (7)	700 (5)
Processed Foods	17 (17)	43 (9)	72 (3)	283 (6)	447 (5)	450 (3)
Textile Products	15 (15)	187 (39)	990 (39)	1,817 (36)	2,839 (31)	3,600 (28)
Misc. Manufactures	8 (8)	124 (26)	612 (24)	1,069 (21)	1,889 (20)	2,400 (18)
Sub-Total	95 (92)	437 (91)	1,944 (77)	3,656 (72)	5,869 (63)	7,150 (55)
Nonmetallic Mineral	0 (0)	2 (0)	35 (1)	101 (2)	154 (2)	170 (1)
Petro-chemical	2 (2)	4 (1)	95 (4)	188 (4)	459 (5)	460 (4)
Steel & Metal Products	3 (3)	16 (3)	183 (7)	367 (7)	969 (10)	1,300 (10)
Electronics	0 (0)	6 (1)	177 (7)	409 (8)	759 (8)	1,600 (12)
Shipbuilding	0 (0)	2 (1)	1 (0)	138 (3)	368 (4)	1,000 (8)
Other Machinery	3 (3)	13 (3)	91 (4)	222 (4)	702 (8)	1,300 (10)
Sub-Total	8 (8)	43 (9)	582 (23)	1,425 (28)	3,411 (37)	5,830 (45)
All Commodities	103(100)	479(100)	2,526(100)	5,081(100)	9,280(100)	12,980(100)

Notes: [1] Current dollar figures were converted into 1975 dollar figures by multiplying 1.9(1962) and 1.5(1967 & 1972).
[2] Including deep-sea fishery products.

magnitude of Korea's sectoral trade will converge toward the average cross-sectional pattern. We assume rather that Korea will move parallel to the cross-country pattern implying that long-term differences in comparative advantage and factors other than short-term disequilibrium are typically responsible for the initial departures from the predicted values.

Total commodity exports of Korea were projected to increase by about 83 percent during 1975–81, i.e., from $5.1 billion in 1975 to $9.3 billion in 1981 (in 1975 dollar prices) implying an average annual growth rate of about 11 percent. Exports of textiles and wearing apparel which amounted to about 36 percent of total exports ($1.8 billion) in 1975 were projected to become about 31 percent of total exports ($2.8 billion) in 1981. The share of primary products in total exports was projected to decrease from about 10 percent ($0.49 billion) in 1975 to about 7 percent ($0.69 billion) in 1981. On the other hand, the share of electrical and nonelectrical machinery and transport equipment in total exports was projected to increase from about 4 percent ($0.2 billion) in 1975 to about 8 percent ($0.7 billion) in 1981, and the share of steel and metal products was projected to increase from about 7 percent ($0.37 billion) in 1975 to about 10 percent ($0.97 billion) in 1981. In general, the export pattern gradually shifts from the so-called light industrial products to heavy industrial products.

3. *A Modification of the Projected Trade Pattern*

The least developed country (in terms of per capita GNP) in our sample countries was Korea itself, and we included many of the very advanced countries in our cross-section analysis. As a result, our projection ignores possible ups and downs in the expansion of certain sectors in the long-run growth process. In any case, our projection emphasizes the aspect of a long-run "directional guide-line" at the starting point of formulating an economic development plan, and does not implicate the exactness of the magnitude of projected sectoral exports themselves as optimal figures for the Korean economy.

In this section, we will make a modification of those initially projected figures of sectoral exports, more or less on the basis of intuitive feelings, in order to take account of the peculiar characteristics of the Korean economy and the plan of the Korean government.

The growth rate of (total) textiles and clothing exports was projected to be about 8 percent per annum. Considering the past trend of expansion of their exports (which amounted to about 28 percent per annum in real value even during 1972–75) and also the available labor supply in Korea, we revised the annual (aggregate, not per capita) growth rate to 21 percent during 1975–77 and then applied the projected annual growth rate of 8 percent for the 1978–81 period. Since the textile quota system of either the U.S. or EC allows about 6 percent (quantitative) increases each year, we are assuming significant quality improvements and expansion of new markets for textiles and clothing exports during 1975–77 to make the 21 percent average annual (aggregate) growth rate. However, we do expect not only severe competition in textiles exports with other developing countries (such as Communist China) but also a somewhat declining comparative advantage in textiles and clothing production after 1978. Furthermore, we may expect a full scale world-wide quota restriction against Korea's textile exports after 1978. To be on the conservative side, we adopted the projected 8 percent for the average annual growth rate of textiles and clothing exports after 1978.

On the basis of the investment schedule, already started or firmly planned, Ministry of Commerce and Industry (MCI) estimated the expected annual shipbuilding capacity of Korea to be about 3.97 million DWT in 1976 and 4.25 million DWT in 1981 which includes 2 million DWT capacity Hyundai shipyard and 1.2 million DWT capacity Okpo Shipyard.[26] Since the maximum shipbuilding capacity of the two giant shipyards was based on oil tanker production, the estimated capacity has to be reduced approximately by 50 percent should we assume absolutely no demand for oil tankers in the near future. Assuming that Korea builds mostly 20–30 thousand DWT cargo vessels, the maximum annual shipbuilding capacity of Korea will be about 2.6 million DWT in 1981. If we further assume that production for domestic demand will amount to about 0.6 million DWT in 1981, the capacity available for export production becomes about 2 million DWT in 1981. Since the average unit price of ships exported from Korea has amounted to approximately $500 per DWT (in 1975 prices), the projected exports of ships in 1981 were modified from $368 million to $1 billion. Since the demand for cargo vessels is usually proportional to world trade volume, since the Japanese exports of non-tanker vessels exceeded 6 million DWT annually in the mid-seventies, since the average unit price of ships exported from Korea is expected to increase with quality improvements, and since shiprepairing capacity is expected to exceed 10 million DWT by 1981, the modified figure of $1 billion ship exports in

[26] Ministry of Commerce and Industry, *Plan to Promote Shipbuilding Industry, 1976* (mimeographed).

1981 may be regarded as a very conservative estimate.

Due to the world-wide depression, exports of iron and steel products, nonferrous metal products and metal products were relatively small in 1975. Hence we shifted the base year of projection to 1973 for iron and steel products and nonferrous metal products and to 1974 for metal products. As a result the projected exports of steel and metal products in 1981 were revised from about $9.7 billion to $1.3 billion. Similarly, the base year for glass products was also shifted to 1973, resulting in the revision of projected glass product exports in 1981 from $11 million to $28 million and raising the projected total nonmetallic mineral products exports in 1981 by about 10 percent.

Taking account of the vigorous promotive government policies for machinery and electronics industries, we replaced our projected export figures for these sectors with MCI's planned export figures which were approximately double the originally projected figures. Similarly, we took MCI's planned export figures for footwear, leather products, rubber products, plywood and wood products, furniture and pottery (which exceed our projected figures by 76 percent, 435 percent, 26 percent, 43 percent, 92 percent and 82 percent respectively) because MCI's figures seem to reflect recent changes in market conditions of these products much better than our projection. As a result, the projected exports of miscellaneous manufactures in 1981 were revised from about $1.9 billion to $2.4 billion.

On the other hand, we did not revise the initially projected export figures of primary products, processed foods and chemical products. The Korean government has been emphasizing development of petro-chemical industries not only for import substitution but also as a major export industry. However, petro-chemical industries are usually very capital-intensive and furthermore depend on imported crude oil. These are the industries in which the oil-producing countries have a strong comparative advantage in production. Considering the possible linkage effects, Korea may develop selected petro-chemical industries and may end up exporting some of their products if excess capacity occurs at the optimum scale of operation. However, Korea should not consciously try to develop petro-chemical industries as a major export industry unless it discovers vast crude oil deposits in the country. In order to emphasize this aspect, we did not revise the initially projected export figure for chemical products which allowed only moderate expansion of their exports.

The rationale for accepting MCI's planned export figures for electronics, electrical and nonelectrical machinery and transport equipment and taking for granted the current investment in shipbuilding facilities is that quite a few of these industries are relatively skilled-labor intensive, though moderately more capital intensive than the so-called light manufacturing industries, and hence Korea has, or is expected to develop in the near future, strong comparative advantages in their production. So long as Korea avoids excessively capital intensive projects among those industries, the strategy of promoting so-called heavy industries as major export industries will be consistent with the expected shifts in the comparative advantage position of Korea associated with continued capital accumulation and the rising wage-rental ratio. Even the emphasis on promoting exports of steel and metal products may not be regarded as irrational, so long as the emphasis is on exports of relatively labor intensive processed steel products and metal products. Furthermore, these so-called heavy industrial products have a vast international market and are subject to much fewer (almost negligible) quantitative import restrictions in advanced countries compared to other light industrial products.

The basic rationale of our modifications to the initially projected export figures are first that, considering the existence of a massive potential labor force (especially in rural areas), the ever increasing rate of female labor force participation, and the expected high natural growth rate of population over 14 years of age during 1976–81, Korea has to continue exporting large amounts of (skilled) labor intensive products, and second that, considering international market conditions and the ever increasing wage-rental ratio associated with rapid capital accumulation, Korea has to develop so-called heavy industries as major export industries but should concentrate on the relatively (skilled) labor intensive type and avoid excessively capital intensive products. Therefore, Korea should not insist on complete import substitution of every component of heavy industrial products. Rather, it should concentrate on the relatively (skilled) labor intensive portion of these heavy industrial production processes, importing significant amounts of extremely capital intensive components for the time being.

On the other hand, the rationale for using a Chenery type typical pattern as a point of departure is that the projected pattern is a kind of average pattern of successfully growing countries (in terms of GNP and exports) and hence the pattern of resource allocation would not become excessively wasteful even if Korea had duplicated such a typical pattern. Another justification can be the fact that the various elasticities derived from our cross-section analysis were more or less consistent with common sense expectations.

Our modifications resulted in a 40 percent increase in total export value in 1981, i.e., increase from $9.3 billion of originally projected value to $13.0 billion (in 1975 dollar prices). This implies the commodity-exports-to-GNP ratio of 42 percent in 1981 and an average annual export growth rate of about 17 percent during 1975–81.

The share of primary products and processed foods in total exports is projected to decrease by 50 percent during 1975–81, and the share of textiles and clothing and miscellaneous manufactures is projected to decrease by 14–22 percent. As a result, the share of these commodities (the so-called light manufactures) in total exports will decline from 72 percent in 1975 to 55 percent in 1981.

On the other hand, the share of ships, electrical and nonelectrical machinery and transport equipment in total exports is projected to more than double during 1975–81, and the share of electronics and processed steel and metal products is projected to increase by around 50 percent. The share of chemicals and nonmetallic mineral products is not projected to increase. Hence our modified projection increases the share of the so-called heavy industrial products in total exports from 28 percent in 1975 to 45 percent in 1981.

4. Employment and Investment Implications of the Projected Export Pattern

Korea has detailed input-output tables and reports on population census, census (or survey) of mining and manufacturing and the national wealth survey of 1968. Therefore, we can estimate the sectoral labor and capital coefficients and approximate the factor requirements of a projected export pattern so that one may examine the implication of the various possible modifications of the projected export pattern in terms of capital and labor requirements.

However, if we use a set of fixed factor coefficients of a certain past time period, the estimates of capital and labor requirements of the projected future export pattern can be very much biased. For instance, due to the significantly decreasing trend in sectoral labor-output ratios, the employment effect of a given export pattern of 1975–81 may be very much exaggerated. Furthermore, the capital-output ratios of some heavy industrial sectors in Korea might have been unduly small before, reflecting the relatively backward nature of their products, and hence lead to underestimation of their capital requirements in the future. Hence, we have to examine the past trend of changes in sectoral factor-output ratios in Korea as well

Table 15. *Total Factor Requirements for Export Production, 1975 & 1981*

Direct plus Indirect Factor Coefficients	Capital-Output Ratio Korea (1970)	Capital-Output Ratio Japan (1965)	Labor-Output Ratio Korea (1970)	Labor-Output Ratio Korea* (1975/1981)	Labor-Output Ratio Japan (1965)
Primary Products	0.91	0.93	1.26	0.99/0.74	0.79
Processed Foods	0.76	0.91	0.65	0.51/0.38	0.56
Textile Products	1.77	1.10	1.03	0.81/0.60	0.66
Misc. Manufactures	1.08	1.09	0.77	0.60/0.45	0.35
Nonmetallic Mineral	2.31	1.30	0.44	0.35/0.26	0.29
Chemicals	1.23	1.26	0.45	0.35/0.26	0.28
Steel & Metal	1.26	3.11	0.59	0.46/0.35	0.27
Electronics	1.02	1.04	0.40	0.31/0.23	0.30
Shipbuilding	1.38	1.41	0.68	0.53/0.40	0.29
Other Machinery	1.10	1.24	0.62	0.49/0.36	0.29
Factor Requirements for 1975 Exports	**Capital (In Million 1970 Dollars)**		**Labor (In Thousand Persons)**		
Primary Products	296	302	410	322	257
Processed Foods	144	172	123	96	106
Textile Products	2,144	1,332	1,247	981	799
Misc. Manufactures	770	777	549	428	250
Nonmetallic Mineral	155	87	30	24	19
Chemicals	154	158	56	44	35
Steel & Metal	309	762	145	113	66
Electronics	279	284	109	85	82
Shipbuilding	127	130	63	49	27
Other Machinery	163	184	92	73	43
All Commodities	4,541	4,188	2,824	2,215	1,684
Factor Requirements for 1981 Exports	**Capital (In Million 1970 Dollars)**		**Labor (In Thousand Persons)**		
Primary Products	425	434	588	346	369
Processed Foods	228	273	195	114	168
Textile Products	4,248	2,640	2,472	1,440	1,584
Misc. Manufactures	1,728	1,744	1,232	720	560
Nonmetallic Mineral	261	147	50	29	33
Chemicals	378	387	138	80	86
Steel & Metal	1,092	2,696	512	304	234
Electronics	1,088	1,110	427	245	320
Shipbuilding	921	941	454	267	193
Other Machinery	954	1,075	538	312	251
All Commodities	11,323	11,447	6,606	3,857	3,798
Net Factor Requirements (1975–81)	6,782	7,259	3,782	1,642	2,114

* Modified (to take account of increasing labor productivity) by assuming 5 percent average annual rate of decrease in labor-output ratios.

as the factor coefficients of some other countries such as Japan in order to obtain a more reasonable approximation of the factor requirements.

Using the 1970 set of sectoral direct factor coefficients and 1970 input-output table (A matrix), we could estimate the 1970 set of sectoral direct plus indirect factor-output ratios in Korea. According to these coefficients, the total amount of capital required for export production in 1975 was about $4.5 billion and that required to produce projected exports of 1981 was about $11.3 billion, implying a net investment requirement of about $7 billion (in 1970 dollars) during the period of 1975–81.

The amount of labor employed for export production in 1975 was estimated to be about 2.8 million persons and that required to produce projected exports in 1981 was estimated to be about 6.6 million persons, implying an increase of employment by about 4 million persons. However, past experience shows that the sectoral labor-output ratios decrease at the average annual rate of about 5 percent. If we discount the labor requirements by taking account of such improvements in labor productivity, the increase in employment in export production during 1975–81 amounts to about 1.6 million persons.[27]

If we apply the 1965 set of Japanese sectoral direct plus indirect factor coefficients, we again get a similar result, i.e., a net extra investment requirement of $7 billion and an increase of employment of about 2 million persons for export expansion during 1975–81.

From the set of sectoral factor coefficients presented in Table 16, we may safely deduce that primary products, processed foods, textile products, miscellaneous manufactures, and electronics will stay as relatively labor intensive sectors in Korea in the foreseeable future. Therefore, increased exports of these products would not contradict the objective of rapid growth with maximum employment expansion.

However, it seems that the other sectors producing such commodities as steel and metal products, chemicals, nonmetallic minerals, shipbuilding, machinery and transport equipment can be very much capital intensive depending on the type of commodities produced. That is, the factor coefficients of so-called heavy and chemical product industries can be made extremely capital intensive or only moderately capital intensive depending on the chosen development strategy. Without government subsi-

[27] Since we applied A matrix (domestic plus imported input coefficients) in computing the sectoral direct plus indirect factor coefficients, we are assuming that those imported inputs used in export production which were competitive as of 1970 will be completely replaced by domestic production by 1981.

Table 16. *Sectoral (Direct plus Indirect) Factor Requirements: Korea (1970) and Japan (1965)*

	Capital-Output Ratio				Labor-Output Ratio				Capital-Labor Ratio			
	Korea (1970)		Japan (1965)		Korea (1970)		Japan (1965)		Korea (1970)		Japan (1965)	
	Direct	Total	Direct	Total	Direct	Total	Direct	Total	Direct	Total	Direct	Total
Primary Products	0.51	0.91	0.48	0.93	1.01	1.26	0.64	0.79	0.50	0.72	0.75	1.18
Processed Foods	0.18	0.76	0.21	0.91	0.12	0.65	0.08	0.56	1.50	1.17	2.63	1.63
Textile Products	0.53	1.77	0.24	1.10	0.33	1.03	0.15	0.66	1.61	1.72	1.60	1.67
Misc. Manufactures	0.32	1.08	0.27	1.09	0.28	0.77	0.13	0.35	1.14	1.40	2.08	3.11
Nonmetallic Mineral	1.18	2.31	0.51	1.30	0.21	0.44	0.12	0.29	5.62	5.25	4.25	4.48
Chemicals	0.46	1.23	0.42	1.26	0.09	0.45	0.05	0.28	5.11	2.73	8.40	4.50
Steel & Metal	0.33	1.26	0.39	3.11	0.19	0.59	0.08	0.27	1.74	2.14	4.88	11.52
Electronics	0.27	1.02	0.21	1.04	0.21	0.40	0.12	0.30	1.29	2.55	1.75	3.47
Shipbuilding	0.59	1.38	0.20	1.41	0.29	0.68	0.08	0.29	2.03	2.03	2.50	4.86
Other Machinery	0.30	1.10	0.26	1.24	0.22	0.62	0.10	0.29	1.36	1.77	2.60	4.28

Sources: Ministry of Commerce and Industry (Korea), *Report on Mining and Manufacturing Census,* Ministry of International Trade and Industry (Japan), *Census of Manufactures, and input-output tables of Korea (1970) and Japan (1965).*

dies on capital-use, these sectors will not become excessively capital intensive in Korea during 1975–81. However, the very existence of an extensive subsidy system will make such development a good possibility. Therefore, if the government decides to develop heavy industries as a major export industry during 1975–81, the utmost attention should be given to the employment implication of the selected industries to be promoted.

5. *Comparison of Korea's Export Pattern with Japanese Pattern*

In terms of per capita GNP, the period 1975–81 in Korea ($381–$572 in 1970 dollar) may correspond to the period 1951–58 in Japan ($379–$594), but in terms of per capita export value, the period 1975–81 in Korea ($98–$227 in 1970 dollar) may correspond to the period 1965–71 in Japan ($105–$218).

We made a comparison of Japanese export patterns in the period 1955–72 with the actual and projected trade pattern of Korea in the period 1967–81. We could observe a close similarity between these two countries in the export pattern of electronics and shipbuilding, whose exports have been steadily expanding absolutely as well as relatively, and nonmetallic mineral products whose exports did not exhibit any such trend. Both in Korea (1967–81) and Japan (1955–72), the share of primary products, processed foods, textiles and clothing and miscellaneous products in total commodity exports is declining. However, the exports of these commodities from Korea are still much larger than those from Japan in terms of an absolute amount as well as in terms of a relative share. The share of machinery and transport equipment in total commodity exports is rising both in Korea (1967–81) and Japan (1955–72), but Japan's exports of these products are much larger than those of Korea in an absolute amount as well as in a relative share.

Exports of steel and metal products have steadily increased in Korea and are projected to continue increasing absolutely and relatively during 1975–81. However, in Japan, the relative share of steel and metal products in total exports stopped increasing at the beginning of the seventies although the absolute amount of their exports kept increasing. The share of chemical products was more or less stabilized in Japan and is also projected to stay at a constant level in Korea but the exports of these products from Japan in the seventies were much larger than those projected for Korea in 1975–81.

It seems that the actual and projected changing pattern of exports of Korea (1967–81) is more or less similar to the actual changing pattern of

Table 17. *Commodity Export Pattern: Korea & Japan*

(1975 dollars & percent)

Korea	Per Capita Exports (1975$)					Composition of Exports (%)				
				1981 (Projected)					1981 (Projected)	
	1967	1972	1975	Original	Modified	1967	1972	1975	Original	Modified
Primary Products	3	8	14	18	18	17%	11%	10%	7%	5%
Processed Foods	1	2	8	12	12	9	3	6	5	3
Textile Products	6	30	52	74	94	39	39	36	31	28
Misc. Manufactures	4	19	31	49	63	26	24	21	20	18
(Sub-Total)	(14)	(60)	(105)	(154)	(187)	(91)	(77)	(72)	(63)	(55)
Nonmetallic Mineral	0	1	3	4	4	0	1	2	2	1
Chemicals	0	3	5	12	12	1	4	4	5	4
Steel & Metal	1	6	11	25	34	3	7	7	10	10
Electronics	0	5	12	20	42	1	7	8	8	12
Shipbuilding	0	0	4	10	26	1	0	3	4	8
Other Machinery	1	3	6	18	34	3	4	4	8	10
(Sub-Total)	(2)	(18)	(41)	(89)	(153)	(9)	(23)	(28)	(37)	(45)
Total Exports	16	78	147	243	340	100	100	100	100	100
Japan	1955	1960	1965	1970	1972	1955	1960	1965	1970	1972
Primary Products	2	3	2	4	4	4%	3%	2%	2%	1%
Processed Foods	2	3	5	5	6	3	4	3	2	2
Textile Products	18	25	25	29	34	38	31	17	11	9
Misc. Manufactures	6	12	22	33	45	13	16	15	13	12
(Sub-Total)	(28)	(43)	(54)	(71)	(89)	(58)	(54)	(37)	(28)	(24)
Nonmetallic Mineral	2	3	2	3	3	4	4	1	1	1
Chemicals	3	4	12	21	30	6	5	8	8	8
Steel & Metal	9	11	29	51	64	19	14	20	20	17
Electronics	—	—	9	26	40	—	—	6	10	11
Shipbuilding	2	5	13	19	32	4	7	9	7	8
Other Machinery	4*	13*	25	66	117	9*	16*	17	26	31
(Sub-Total)	(20)	(36)	(90)	(186)	(286)	(42)	(46)	(61)	(72)	(76)
Total Exports	46	78	145	257	376	100	100	100	100	100

Sources: United Nations, *Yearbook of International Trade Statistics*, and Hong *op. cit.*
*Includes electronics products.

exports of Japan (1955–72). However, there do exist significant differences in the absolute and relative magnitude of each export commodity group in total exports. For instance, Korea has to cut the exports of primary products, processed foods and textiles and clothing very drastically and increase the exports of machinery and transport equipment more rapidly in the late seventies in order to make the changing export pattern of Korea look more similar to that of Japan in the period 1955–72. Of course, Korea does not have to encourage more rapid expansion of machinery and discourage exports of textiles simply to copy the Japanese export pattern. The policy decision should be based on the peculiar characteristics of the Korean economy itself.

6. Some Policy Issues Related to Korea's Trade Pattern

Korea's current export pattern is characterized by (1) the concentration on a limited number of simple labor intensive products, (2) the concentration on Japanese and U.S. markets, (3) the relatively low net value added content of exported commodities, and (4) the increasing export dependency of the Korean economy. Therefore, Korea first has to try to diversify its exportable commodities, and avoid continuous simple quantitative expansion of current major export items such as textiles, plywood, footwear, etc. which are subject to various quantitative import restrictions in developed countries and are facing ever-increasing competition from other developing countries. It should try to develop new export items, especially such skilled-labor intensive (and moderately capital intensive) products as ships, electronics, machinery, metal products, etc. Second, Korea must try to reduce its dependence on Japanese and U.S. markets through diversification of its export markets. It has to promote the development and expansion of its own world-wide marketing network. Third, Korea has to increase the value added content of its exports through increased import substitution of selected intermediate inputs and improvements of the quality of products exported from Korea. The fourth problem is to find the optimum rate of trade dependence for the Korean economy. Excessive trade dependency not only makes the Korean economy extremely vulnerable to international business fluctuation, but can also result in the waste of resources. Korea has to try to reduce its overall trade dependency by promoting industries which depend less on imported raw materials, and by promoting selected import-substituting industries on the basis of its (changing) comparative advantage position. Finally, the government has to improve current export promotion policies in order to realize the projected (or planned) trade pattern more efficiently.

REFERENCES

1. Bank of Korea, *Economic Statistics Yearbook* (various issues), Seoul.
2. Chenery, H.B., "Patterns of Industrial Growth", *American Economic Review*, September 1960.
3. Chenery, H.B. and Taylor, L., "Development Patterns: Among Countries and Over Time," *Review of Economics and Statistics*, November 1968.
4. Economic Planning Board, *Report on Mining and Manufacturing Census or Survey*, Seoul.
5. Government General of Chosen, *Chosen Sotokufu Tokei Nenpo*, Seoul.
6. Hong, Wontack, *A Projection of Korea's Trade Pattern: 1977-86*, Seoul: KDI Press, 1975 (in Korean).
7. ———, *Factor Supply and Factor Intensity of Trade in Korea*, Seoul: KDI Press, 1976.
8. ———, "Industrialization and Trade in Manufactures: The East Asian Experience", in *The Open Economy: Essays on International Trade and Finance*, ed. by P.B. Kenen, New York: Columbia University Press, 1968.
9. ———, *Trade and Subsidy Policy and Employment Growth in Korea,* Seoul: Korea Development Institute, 1976 (mimeographed).
10. Maizels, A., *Exports and Economic Growth of Developing Countries*, London: Cambridge University Press, 1968.
11. Ministry of Agriculture and Fisheries, *Reports on the Results of Farm Household Economy Survey*, Seoul.
12. Ministry of Commerce and Industry, *Plan to Promote Shipbuilding Industry*, 1976 (mimeographed).
13. Ministry of International Trade and Industry, Japanese Government, *Census of Manufactures*, Tokyo.
14. Ouchi, H., ed., *Nihon Keizai Tokei Shu*, Tokyo: Nihon Tokei Kenkyujo, 1958.
15. United Nations, *Yearbook of International Trade Statistics* (various issues).

GROWTH CONTRIBUTION OF TRADE AND THE INCENTIVE SYSTEM

*Suk Tai Suh**

I. Introduction

The true industrialization process of the Korean economy started only after the end of the Korean war (1950–53), and industrial growth was necessarily preceded by a period of reconstruction in the 1950's. The post-war Korean reconstruction period was characterized by a heavy influx of various imported goods and raw materials financed by foreign aid. The period also saw the gradual recovery of light manufacturing sectors, producing consumer goods which were previously imported, as domestic productive capacity was restored and new investments made in consumer goods as well as essential raw material sectors such as fertilizer and electricity. Therefore, the period of the 1950's is regarded as a period of import substitution in light manufacturing sectors.

In the 1960's, export incentive policies and industrial promotion policies were pursued throughout the three consecutive five-year economic plan periods. Exports grew in response to various promotional incentives and the much pronounced export-led economic growth was realized by the mid-1960's. Import substitution in many of the manufacturing sectors occurred at the same time although its contribution to growth was much less pronounced than export growth.

---

* Senior Fellow at the Korea Development Institute. This paper is a revised version of a part of the author's paper, *Import Substitution and Economic Development in Korea,* KDI Working Paper No. 7519, Dec. 1975.

Few studies have dealt with the subject of import substitution in Korean economic growth. Therefore in this study we will attempt to deal with the role of import substitution in the growth process of the Korean economy from the 1960's to the early 70's.

In this study we find that import substitution was an important element in Korean economic growth although governmental promotional policies for import substitution were much less pronounced than for export growth. Thus, it is interesting to ask whether the import substitution realized during the later period may be regarded as a mere natural offspring of economic development or as a result of deliberate protectionist policies of the government. These are the basic questions which we hope to raise and answer in this study.

In Chapter 2, we deal with the methodological outline on the concept of import substitution and its measurement. For instance, import substitution in a nutshell implies a phenomenon associated with the lowering of the ratio of imports to total domestic demand. However, the ratio of total imports to the Korean GNP increased continuously from 16 percent in 1962 to 43 percent in 1975. Then, a question arises as to how import substitution could have taken place in the Korean economy without really having reduced the overall import coefficient. This is an interesting question since the concept of import substitution on a detailed sectoral level may be different from that for the economy as a whole because import substitution in the latter case implies a reduction in the import to GNP ratio while import substitution in the former case may be related to a phenomenon of inter-sectoral resource shift from one sector to another. This intersectoral resource shift may be an efficient one or an inefficient one, depending on whether the shift of resources is motivated by a market mechanism or deliberate protectionist policy. This question is dealt with in Chapter 3.

In Chapter 3, we also analyze the relationship between changes in the trade structure and changes in the production structure. When one sector achieves import substitution or export growth, other sectors may or may not experience an import deepening structural change, depending on the relative change in the demand for raw material imports. In general, changes in the pattern of trade largely reflect two underlying causes; a change in the pattern of import substitution and export growth on the one hand and a change in the pattern of consumer preference on the other. In this study consumer preferences are assumed constant. In this case changes in the production structure mainly reflect changes in the trade structure, and we consider the governmental incentive policies for export growth and import substitution to have played an important role in the relative efficiency of resource allocation.

Therefore, in Chapter 4, we introduce the Korean incentive system for export promotion and import substitution. We ascertain whether the import substitution that occured in many of the Korean manufacturing sectors in the 1960's is a result of an efficient resource allocation through market mechanism or of an inefficient resource allocation through governmental protectionist policies.

In Chapter 5, concluding remarks discuss the efficiency of the growth strategy pursued by Korea and its usefulness as a strategy for economic development for developing countries today.

II. Methodological Outline

The existing literature on import substitution illustrates various concepts and measures of import substitution. In this study, following the Chenery-Hirschman type measure, we employed two concepts of import substitution: one is a forward import substitution (*FIS*), which measures an activity associated with lowering the ratio of imports to domestic demand in the intermediate and final demand through a forward linkage effect, and the other is a backward import substitution (*BIS*), a concept associated with lowering the ratio of intermediate inputs imported to total intermediate input (domestic plus imported) in the sense of a backward-linkage effect. The measure we employed here is based on the most commonly used concept, the deviation of actual domestic production from expected production based on the constant supply proportion of the previous period.

Consider the following activity relationship of industry i:

$$X_i = W_i^d + Y_i^d = \sum_j^n W_{ij}^d + \sum_s^m Y_{is}^d \quad \cdots\cdots\cdots\cdots (1)$$

where X_i : industry i gross output

W_i^d : total intermediate demand of ith good supplied by domestic production

Y_i^d : total final demand of ith good supplied by domestic production

W_{ij}^d : the intermediate demand for ith good by jth sector supplied by domestic production ($j = 1 \ldots\ldots. n$)

Y_{is}^d : the final demand for ith good consumed by sth consuming sector ($s = 1 \ldots\ldots. m$) (For instance, private consumption, government consumption, and etc.), domestically supplied.

$$X_i = k_i \cdot W_i + f_i \cdot Y_i = \sum_j k_{ij} \cdot W_{ij} + \sum_j f_{is} \cdot Y_{is} \quad \ldots\ldots.(1)'$$

Take a total differential of (1)′ and rearranging gives the following relation:

$$dX_i = dk_i \cdot W_i + k_i \cdot dW_i + dk_i \cdot dW_i + df_i \cdot Y_i + f_i \cdot dY_i + df \cdot dY_i$$
$$\doteqdot \sum_j dk_{ij} \cdot W_{ij} + \sum_j k_{ij} \cdot dW_{ij} + \sum_i dk_{ij} \cdot dW_{ij} + \sum_s df_{is} \cdot Y_{is}$$
$$+ \sum_s f_{is} \cdot dY_{is} + \sum_s df_{is} \cdot dY_{is} \quad \ldots\ldots\ldots\ldots\ldots\ldots\ldots.(2)$$

where $kij = \frac{W_{ij}{}^d}{W_{ij}}$, $W_{ij}{}^d = W_{ij} - W_{ij}^m$

W_{ij}^m denotes intermediate input imports of *i*th good used in *j*th sector.

$K_i = \frac{W_i{}^d}{W_i}$, $W_i{}^d = W_i - W_i^m$

W_i^m denotes total intermediate input imports of *i*th good

$f_{is} = \frac{Y_{is}{}^d}{Y_{is}}$, $Y_{is}{}^d = Y_{is} - Y_{is}^m$

Y_{is}^m denotes final imports of *i*th good consumed by *s*th group

$f_{is} = \frac{Y_i{}^d}{Y_i}$, $Y_i{}^d = Y_i - Y_i^m$

Y_i^m denotes total final imports of *i*th good in (2), *and* $\doteqdot$ denotes near equality due to composition bias.

In equation (2), there are *m* different $df_{is} \cdot Y_{is}$ values ($s = 1 \ldots\ldots m$), which represent output growth due to forward import substitution of *i*th good in *s*th final consuming sector, *m* different $f_{is} \cdot dY_{is}$ values ($s = 1 \ldots m$), which represent output growth due to final demand expansion of *i*th good in *s*th final consuming sector, *m* different $df_{is} \cdot dy_{is}$ values, the term of which is attributable to both import substitution and demand expansion of *i*th good in *s*th consuming sector. This interaction term is also dumped into import substitution for the same reasons stated below.

There are also *n* different $dk_{ij} \cdot W_{ij}$ (*for* $j = 1 \ldots. n$), which represent output growth due to import substitution of ith intermediate good by jth sector, and n different $kij \cdot dwij$ which represent output growth due to intermediate demand growth, and n different $dk_{ij} \cdot dW_{ij}$ due to both forward import substitution and intermediate demand growth of the ith good in the jth sector. We call this an interaction term. There seems, however, to be no way to define this interaction term in any definite and indisputable way. We followed the Chenery method of dumping this interaction term in the import substitution term.[1]

Therefore, we have used three different sources for output growth: (i) output growth due to forward import substitution *(FIS)*, (ii) due to domestic demand expansion *(DDE)*, and (iii) due to export expansion *(EE)*, *i.e.*,

$$\sum_j dk_{ij} \cdot W_{ij} + \sum_j dk_{ij} \cdot dW_{ij} + \sum_s df_{is} \cdot Y_{is} + \sum_s df_{is} \cdot dY_{is}$$
$$(\text{for } j = 1 \ldots\ldots\ldots n) \quad \ldots\ldots\ldots\ldots\ldots\ldots\ldots\ldots\ldots\ldots \text{(2)–(i)}$$

$$\sum_j k_{ij} \cdot dW_{ij} + \sum_s f_{is} \cdot dY_{is} \text{ (s excludes exports)}$$
$$(\text{for } s = 1 \ldots\ldots\ldots m) \ldots\ldots\ldots\ldots\ldots\ldots\ldots\ldots\ldots\ldots \text{(2)–(ii)}$$

$$f_{ie} \cdot dY_{ie} \text{ (e denotes exports)} \ldots\ldots\ldots\ldots\ldots\ldots\ldots\ldots \text{(2)–(iii)}$$

Consider the following intermediate input relationship of industry i:

$$U_i = U_i{}^d + U_i{}^m, \text{ and}$$
$$U_i = \sum_j U_{ji}{}^d + \sum_j U_{ji}{}^m \quad \ldots\ldots\ldots\ldots\ldots\ldots\ldots\ldots \text{(3)}$$
$$U_i^d = h_i \cdot u_i = \sum h_{ji} u_{ji} \quad \ldots\ldots\ldots\ldots\ldots\ldots\ldots\ldots \text{(3)}'$$

where $U_i = X_i - V_i$

V_i = value-added of ith good, (for $j = 1 \ldots\ldots\ldots\ldots n$)

X_i = gross input = gross output, (for $j = 1 \ldots\ldots\ldots\ldots n$)

$U_{ji}{}^d = U_{ji} - U_{ji}{}^m$, (for $j = 1 \ldots\ldots\ldots\ldots n$)

$U_{ji}{}^m$ = the intermediate input imports of jth good used in ith sector.

Take total differential of (3)′ and rearranging gives the following relation:

$$dU_i^d = dh_i \cdot U_i + hi \cdot dU_i + dh_i \cdot dU_i \text{ or}$$

[1] This interaction term has caused some controversy as in Eysenbach, M. L. "A Note on Growth and Structural Change in Pakistan's Manufacturing Industry, 1954–64," *Pakistan Development Review*, Spring 1965, and in Fane, George, "Import Substitution and Export Expansion: their measurement and an example of their application," *Pakistan Development Review*, Spring 1971.

$$dU_i^d \doteqdot \sum_j dh_{ji} \cdot U_{ji} + \sum_j h_{ji} \cdot dU_{ji} + \sum_j dh_{ji} \cdot dU_{ji} \quad \ldots\ldots\ldots\ldots (4)$$

$$\text{where } h_i = \frac{U_i^d}{U_i} \qquad (\text{for } i, j = 1 \ldots\ldots\ldots n)$$

$$h_{ji} = \frac{U_{ji}^d}{U_{ji}}$$

In equation (4), there are there n different sectoral sources of intermediate input growth. This paper classified two different kinds of intermediate input growth as in the following:

$$\sum_j dh_{ji} \cdot U_{ji} + \sum_j dh_{ji} \cdot dU_{ji} \quad \ldots\ldots\ldots\ldots (4)\text{–(i)}$$

and

$$\sum h_{ji} \cdot dU_{ji} \quad \ldots\ldots\ldots\ldots (4)\text{–(ii)}$$

where (i) represents the growth due to backward input import substitution in the ith sector, and (ii) the growth due to intermediate input expansion.[2]

We have, therefore, the following two conditions for import substitution in industry i:

$$\sum_j dk_{ij} W_{ij} + \sum_j dk_{ij} dW_{ij} + \sum_s df_{is} Y_{is} + \sum_s df_{is} dY_{is} > 0 \qquad \text{(a)}$$

$$\sum dh_{ji} U_{ji} + \sum dh_{ji} dU_{ji} > 0 \qquad \text{(b)}$$

If condition (a) is satisfied, a forward import substitution in sector i has occurred and its measure is given by the summation of the four terms in (a). If condition (b) is satisfied, backward import substitution has occurred in sector i, and its measure is given by the summation of the two terms in (b). If condition (a) is satisfied but condition (b) is not, positive *FIS* in sector i is associated with a negative (import deepening) *FIS* in sector i. This implies that *FIS* in sector i induced an import-deepening change in the production structure of sector i. If conditions (a) and (b) are both satisfied, *FIS* in sector i induced an import-saving change in the production structure of sector i.

In a Hirschman-Chenery type economy in which imports play an important role, forward import substitution in the intermediate demand for

[2] The interaction term, *dh dU* is dumped into the backward import substitution for the same reason as in the previous case of forward import substitution.

ith good may contribute to backward import substitution in the jth sector if the jth sector uses the ith output as an intermediate input. The greater the forward-linkages of industry i are, the more a given amount of forward import substitution of ith good may contribute to backward import substitution in other sectors.

Import substitution, whether planned or natural, should start from forward import substitution in a given sector, which in turn will induce backward import substitution in other sectors if ith good is an intermediate input used in other sectors. Therefore, backward import substitution is a result of forward import substitution, and not vice versa. Consequently, the cause of backward import substitution may be regarded as an effect of forward import substitution, and consequently, we cannot achieve one without the other. However, forward import substitution does not always imply backward import substitution due to the existence of forward import substitution in the final demand sectors only.

III. Quantitative Analysis of Import Substitution

In this Chapter we summarize the results of our sectoral analysis of *FIS* and *BIS* by applying the concepts of measurement introduced in the previous chapter to the 38 sector input-output data of the Korean economy for the period of 1960 to 1973.

As shown in Table 1, we summarize the growth contribution of the 7 sector economy by sources, aggregated from the 38 sectoral estimations of (2)-(i), (2)-(ii), and (2)-(iii) for the five sub-periods. (+) refers to the total sum of positive contributions aggregated from the 38 sector estimations and (−) to the total sum of negative contributions aggregated from the 38 sector estimations.

One must consider, however, that the relative contribution of *FIS* and *DDE* is over-estimated while that of *EE* is underestimated because *FIS* and *DDE* include not only the final demand sector but also the intermediate demand sector whereas *EE* includes only the final demand sector, not the intermediate sector induced by export growth. However, the Korean I–0 data do not distinguish between the input-output structure for domestic demand and that for export demand. This is a serious weak point of the I–0 analysis particularly for an economy like Korea's composed of large export production sectors which heavily depend on imported raw materials and the domestic production sector which does not depend as much

Table 1. *Growth Contribution by Source and Year*

(million won)

		1960–63				1963–66			
		F.I.S.	*D.D.E.*	*E.E.*	Total	*F.I.S.*	*D.D.E.*	*E.E.*	Total
1. Agriculture	(+)	1,661	140,011	469	142,141	18,251	216,458	2,188	236,897
	(−)	9,065	—	375	9,440	500	—	—	500
2. Forestry	(+)	—	2,763	32	2,795	81	18,352	—	18,433
	(−)	350	—	—	350	246	—	69	315
3. Fishery	(+)	9	4,121	166	4,296	—	14,581	1,806	16,387
	(−)	—	—	—	—	—	—	—	—
4. Mining	(+)	152	5,724	746	6,622	575	12,517	4,379	17,417
	(−)	446	—	—	446	5	171	—	176
5. Light Manufacturing	(+)	9,817	81,840	4,235	95,892	4,113	203,594	42,593	250,300
	(−)	3,520	—	108	3,628	10,314	2,589	—	12,903
6. Heavy & Chemical Industry	(+)	6,699	45,690	2,198	54,587	19,448	93,067	6,236	118,751
	(−)	16,456	691	77	17,224	12,741	—	9	12,750
7. Services	(+)	4,372	112,273	4,544	121,189	2,595	328,298	35,115	366,008
	(−)	524	5,066	527	6,117	4,787	3,443	72	8,302
8. Total Positive Effect	(+)	22,710	392,422	12,390	427,522	45,063	886,867	92,317	1,024,247
9. Total Negative Effect	(−)	30,361	5,757	1,087	37,205	28,593	6,203	150	34,946
10. Total (8 + 9)		−7,651	386,665	11,303	390,317	16,470	880,664	92,167	989,301
11. Percentages to Total Growth (%)		−2.0	99.0	3.0	100.0	1.7	89.0	9.3	100.0

Table 1. *(Continued)*

		1966–68				1968–70			
		F.I.S.	*D.D.E.*	*E.E.*	Total	*F.I.S.*	*D.D.E.*	*E.E.*	Total
1. Agriculture	(+)	28	121,658	1,048	122,734	2,668	311,471	5,917	320,056
	(−)	12,349	—	1,614	13,963	62,543	—	103	62,646
2. Forestry	(+)	821	8,612	146	9,579	16,991	51,431	—	68,422
	(−)	346	993	—	1,339	38,283	271	85	38,639
3. Fishery	(+)	—	19,694	352	20,046	751	9,944	13,053	23,748
	(−)	242	—	—	242	9	2,206	—	2,305
4. Mining	(+)	—	13,307	2,221	15,528	694	38,136	3,566	42,396
	(−)	646	1,129	—	1,775	25,215	—	—	25,215
5. Light Manufacturing	(+)	6,204	254,946	54,312	315,462	37,585	367,135	91,912	496,632
	(−)	15,945	5,572	14	21,531	4,162	18,567	2,254	24,983
6. Heavy & Chemical Industry	(+)	80,880	156,162	5,264	242,306	89,748	263,699	28,133	381,580
	(−)	18,631	52,951	2,139	73,721	66,752	3,932	—	70,684
7. Services	(+)	2,191	450,870	43,737	496,798	61,298	927,397	27,379	1,015,984
	(−)	11,243	—	—	11,243	1,031	241	8,764	10,036
8. Total Positive Effect	(+)	90,124	1,025,249	107,080	1,222,453	209,735	1,969,123	169,960	2,348,818
9. Total Negative Effect	(−)	59,402	60,645	3,767	123,814	198,085	25,217	11,206	234,508
10. Total (8 + 9)		30,722	964,604	103,313	1,089,639	11,650	1,943,906	158,754	2,114,310
11. Percentages to Total Growth (%)		2.8	87.8	9.4	100.0	0.6	91.9	7.5	100.0

Table 1. (*Continued*)

		1970–1973			
		F.I.S.	*D.D.E.*	*E.E.*	Total
1. Agriculture	(+)	24,078	598,121	16,126	638,325
	(−)	90,612	—	—	90,612
2. Forestry	(+)	—	60,015	2,388	62,403
	(−)	42,478	—	—	42,478
3. Fishery	(+)	—	74,593	34,256	108,849
	(−)	2,210	—	—	2,210
4. Mining	(+)	439	58,538	979	59,956
	(−)	22,302	2,012	83	24,397
5. Light Manufacturing	(+)	10,989	973,260	626,043	1,610,292
	(−)	70,250	8,412	—	78,662
6. Heavy & Chemical	(+)	100,367	754,045	271,371	1,125,783
Industry	(−)	141,741	19,529	—	161,270
7. Services	(+)	578	1,707,481	250,497	1,958,556
	(−)	31,699	46,451	1,637	79,887
8. Total Positive Effect	(+)	136,451	4,226,053	1,201,660	5,564,164
9. Total Negative Effect	(−)	401,292	76,404	1,720	479,416
10. Total (8 + 7)		−264,841	4,419,649	1,199,940	5,084,748
11. Percentages to Total Growth(%)		−5.2	81.6	23.6	100.0

Sources: [1] Bank of Korea *I-O Tables 1960, 1963, 1966, 1968, 1970, 1973,* and [2] Suk Tai Suh, *Import Substitution and Economic Development in Korea* (KDI Press, 1975).

Notes: [1] (+) and (−) refer to summation of positive and negative contributions from 38 sector estimations.

[2] *F.I.S.*, *D.D.E.*, and *E.E.* refer to estimation of equation (2)-(i), (2)-(ii) and (2)-(iii), respectively.

on imported raw materials.

We find that for 1960–63 negative *FIS* occurred in agriculture, forestry, mining and heavy and chemical manufacturing sectors, and positive *FIS* in light manufacturing sectors while the overall *FIS* is negative for this period, contributing to −2 percent of the total growth. The main contribution came from domestic demand expansion in the service sector, agriculture, light manufacturing, and heavy and chemical manufacturing. The manufacturing exports and service exports accounted for most of the export growth.

For 1963–66, positive *FIS* was realized in agriculture, and heavy and chemical manufacturing sectors, and negative *FIS* in light manufacturing while *DDE* and *EE* accounted for most of the growth in the service, agriculture and light manufacturing sectors.

For 1966–68, negative *FIS* was realized in agriculture and light manufacturing while positive *FIS* was realized in heavy and chemical manufacturing sectors. *DDE* accounted for most of the growth in most sectors while export growth in the light manufacturing and service sectors accounted for most of the export growth.

For 1968–70, negative *FIS* was realized in the agriculture, forestry, and mining sectors while there was positive *FIS* in light manufacturing and heavy and chemical manufacturing sectors. *DDE* in the service, and manufacturing sectors and in agriculture accounted for most of the *DDE* while export growth in the manufacturing, fishery and service sectors accounted for most of the export growth.

For 1970–73, negative *FIS* dominates all sectors, contributing to –5.2 percent of total growth. *DDE* in the service sector, manufacturing sectors and agriculture accounted for most of *DDE* while export growth in the manufacturing sectors, the service sector, and fishery sector accounted for most of the export growth.

No simple characterization of the pattern of import substitution seems to be readily available from Table 1. Within a given sector, *FIS* is positive in some periods and negative in others although *DDE* accounts for most of the growth in some periods and *EE* accounts for a growing share of the total growth as the time period changes.

However, a certain consistent behavior of *FIS*, *DDE* and *EE* can be drawn from the analysis of the table. *FIS* in the primary sector as a whole (including agriculture, forestry and fishery) declined in importance in contributing to total growth, oftentimes characterized by negative *FIS* although some positive *FIS* was realized in some sectors for some periods. This declining importance of *FIS* in the primary sector is consistent with the changing pattern of trade exhibited by a growing dependency of the primary sector on imports.

The pattern of *FIS* in manufacturing is interesting. The light manufacturing sector exhibited a positive *FIS* in 1960–63 and then a continuously negative *FIS* for the rest of the periods. Furthermore, the level of the negative *FIS* increased since the 1963–66 period. However, the heavy and chemical manufacturing sector exhibited a negative *FIS* in 1960–63 and then a continuously positive *FIS* for the rest of the periods except for 1970–73. Even the magnitude of negative *FIS* for the heavy and chemical manufacturing sector is rather small compared with that of negative *FIS* in the light manufacturing and other sectors. The late 1960's and early 70's are characterized by negative *FIS* in the light manufacturing sector and positive *FIS* in the heavy and chemical manufacturing sectors.

An interesting question arises as to whether the negative *FIS* in the light manufacturing sector indicates that the light manufacturing sector has become rather an inefficient sector relative to other sectors. This implication is, however, contradictory to the fact that Korea experienced superb export growth in the light manufacturing sector for the whole period.

This seemingly contradictory result is mainly due to the fact that the Korean input-output data do not distinguish the imports for domestic demand from the raw material imports for export production. Korean manufacturing exports have been of high import content and, therefore, of low value-added ratio, requiring imports of about 40 percent of total value of exports. This high import content ratio has not declined for the entire period due to the export incentive system that allowed unlimited duty-free imports for export production. Therefore, the negative *FIS* in the light manufacturing sector is caused by the built-in bias in our input-output data that includes the imports for domestic demand as well as the imports for export production in computing the ratio of imports to domestic demand, *i.e.*, k and dk.

Although negative *FIS* characterized the overall pattern of forward import substitution in the manufacturing sector, the magnitude of positive *FIS* in the manufacturing sectors is nonetheless significant to indicate that many sub-sectors in the light and heavy and chemical manufacturing sectors experienced positive *FIS*. In other words, some sub-sectors experienced positive *FIS* and some other sub-sectors negative *FIS* although positive *FIS* is outweighed by negative *FIS* in most periods. Therefore, positive forward import substitution has been an important element in some sub-sectors contributing to the total growth for the entire period. However, the overall contribution of *FIS* to the total growth has been negative as indicated by −2.0 percent for 1960–63, 1.7 percent for 63–66, 2.8 percent for 66–68, 0.6 percent for 68–70, and −5.2 percent for 70–73 in Table 1.

In Table 2, we summarize the results of our estimation of *BIS* for the seven sector Korean economy aggregated from the 38 sectoral estimations. For the entire period of 1960–73, a consistent pattern of *BIS* is found for the forestry, fishery, mining and service sectors. Agriculture stands out as a single sector that shows a continuous positive *BIS* for the entire period while the light manufacturing, and heavy and chemical manufacturing sectors show a continuous negative *BIS* for the entire period except for the period 1960–63 in the light manufacturing sector.

Comparing the *BIS* with the *FIS*, we note that the negative *FIS* and

Table 2. *Backward Import Substitution by Sector*

(current million won & percent)

		1960–63	1963–66	1966–68	1968–70	1970–73
1. Agriculture						
Backward Import	(+)	821 (.60)	3,036 (.93)	2,996 (.67)	21,282 (2.61)	6,514 (.35)
Substitution	(−)	−168(−.12)	—	−1,105(−.25)	—	−2,819(−.15)
Intermediate Input	(+)	23,381(17.01)	45,394(13.89)	48,367(10.88)	54,546 (6.17)	125,730 (6.85)
Expansion	(−)	—	—	—	—	—
Sub-total	(+)	24,202(17.61)	48,430(14.82)	51,363(11.55)	75,828 (9.32)	132,244 (7.20)
	(−)	−168(−.12)	—	−1.105(−.25)	—	−2,819(−.15)
Sum		24,034(17.49)	48,430(14.82)	50,258(11.30)	75,828 (9.32)	129,425 (7.05)
2. Forestry						
Backward Import	(+)	473 (.34)	—	—	1,066 (.13)	—
Substituion	(−)	—	−287(−.09)	−31(−.01)	—	−1,643(−.09)
Intermediate Input	(+)	530 (.39)	3,082 (.94)	1,017 (.23)	2,645 (.33)	2,791 (.15)
Expansion	(−)	—	—	—	—	—
Sub-total	(+)	1,003 (.73)	3,082 (.94)	1,017 (.23)	3,711 (.46)	2,791 (.15)
	(−)	—	−287(−.09)	−31(−.01)	—	−1,643(−.09)
Sum		1,003 (73.)	2,795 (.85)	986 (.22)	3,711 (.46)	1,148 (.06)
3. Fishery						
Backward Import	(+)	197 (.14)	—	—	5,098 (.63)	—
Substitution	(−)	—	−195(−.06)	−1,658(−.37)	—	−1,900(−.10)
Intermediate Input	(+)	772 (.56)	3,599 (1.10)	3,554 (.80)	10,974 (1.35)	41,829 (2.28)
Expansion	(−)	—	—	—	—	—
Sub-total	(+)	969 (.70)	3,599 (1.10)	3,554 (.80)	16,072 (1.98)	41,829 (2.28)
	(−)	—	−195(−.06)	−1,658(−.37)	—	−1.900(−.10)
Sum		969 (.70)	3,404 (1.04)	1,896 (.43)	16,072 (1.98)	39,929 (2.18)

4. Mining						
Backward Import	(+)	118 (.09)	240 (.07)	—	404 (.05)	—
Substitution	(−)	−98 (−.07)	−46 (−.01)	−408 (−.09)	−91 (−.01)	−2,647 (−.14)
Intermediate Input	(+)	2,149 (1.56)	4,288 (1.31)	9,963 (2.24)	438 (.05)	13,309 (.73)
Expansion	(−)	—	—	—	−4,192 (−.50)	—
Sub-total	(+)	2,267 (1.65)	4,528 (1.39)	9,963 (2.24)	842 (.10)	13,309 (.73)
	(−)	−98 (−.07)	−46 (−.01)	−408 (−.09)	−4,192 (−.51)	−2,647 (−.14)
Sum		2,169 (1.57)	4,462 (1.38)	9,555 (2.15)	−3,350 (−.41)	10,662 (.59)
5. Light Manufacturing						
Backward Import	(+)	4,279 (3.11)	12,116 (3.71)	181 (.04)	8,680 (1.07)	3,107 (.17)
Substituion	(−)	−2,480(−1.80)	−10,916(−3.34)	−20,096(−4.52)	−39,324(−4.83)	−143,670(−7.83)
Intermediate Input	(+)	45,408 (33.04)	128,670 (39.36)	171,409 (38.56)	253,418 (31.44)	796,482 (43.39)
Expansion	(−)	—	—	—	−61 (−.01)	—
Sub-total	(+)	49,687 (36.15)	140,786 (43.07)	171,590 (38.60)	262,098 (32.21)	799,589 (43.56)
	(−)	−2,480(−1.80)	−10,926(−3.34)	−20,096(−4.52)	−39,385(−4.84)	−143,670(−7.83)
Sum		47,207 (34.35)	129,860 (39.73)	151,494 (34.08)	222,713 (27.37)	655,919 (35.73)
6. Heavy & Chemical Industry						
Backward Import	(+)	380 (.28)	2,757 (.84)	4,614 (1.04)	9,108 (1.12)	14,990 (.82)
Substitution	(−)	−2,055(−1.50)	−4,933(−1.51)	−6,566(−1.48)	−61,878(−7.60)	−89,710(−4.89)
Intermediate Input	(+)	19,995 (14.55)	46,866 (14.34)	83,603 (18.81)	151,247 (18.58)	407,723 (22.21)
Expansion	(−)	—	—	—	—	—
Sub-total	(+)	20,375 (14.83)	49,623 (15.18)	88,217 (19.84)	160,355 (19.70)	422,713 (23.03)
	(−)	−2,055(−1.50)	−4, 933(−1.51)	−6,566(−1.48)	−61,878(−7.60)	−89,710(−4.89)
Sum		20,320 (13.33)	44,690 (13.67)	81,651 (18.36)	98,477 (12.10)	333,003 (16.14)

Table 2. *(Continued)*

		1960–63	1963–66	1966–68	1968–70	1970–73
7. Services						
Backward Import	(+)	4,734 (3.44)	7,614 (2.38)	3,542 (.80)	50,556 (6.21)	2,384 (.13)
Substitution	(−)	−379 (.28)	−5,287 (−1.62)	−12,850 (2.89)	−9,678 (−1.19)	−13,569 (−.74)
Intermediate Input	(+)	39,373 (28.65)	90,912 (27.81)	158,019 (35.55)	359,583 (44.18)	711,882(38.78)
Expansion	(−)	−6 (0)	—	—	—	−35,081(−1.91)
Sub-total	(+)	44,107 (32.09)	98,526 (30.14)	161,561 (36.35)	410,139 (50.39)	714,266(38.91)
	(−)	−385 (−2.8)	−5,287 (−1.62)	−12,850 (−2.89)	−9,678 (−1.19)	−89,710(−2.65)
Sum		43,722 (31.81)	92,239 (28.52)	148,711 (33.46)	400,461 (49.20)	624,556(36.26)
8. Total Positive Effect						
Backward Import Substitution	(+)	11,022 (8.01)	25,763 (7.88)	11,333 (2.55)	96,194 (11.82)	26,995 (1.47)
Intermediate Input Expansion	(+)	131,608 (95.76)	322,811 (98.75)	475,932(107.06)	832,851(102.33)	2,099,746(114.38)
Sub-total	(+)	142,610(103.77)	348,574(106.62)	487,265(109.61)	929,045(114.15)	2,126,741(115.85)
9. Total Negative Effect						
Backward Import Substitution	(−)	−5,180 (−3.70)	−21,674 (−6.63)	−42,714 (−9.61)	−110,971(−13.64)	255,958(−1[illegible].94)
Intermediate Input Expansion	(−)	−6 (0)	—	—	−4,162 (−.51)	−35,081 (−1.91)
Sub-total	(−)	−5,186 (−3.77)	−21,674 (−6.63)	−42,714 (−9.61)	−115,133(−14.15)	291,039(−15.85)

10. Total(8 + 9)					
Backward Import Substitution	5,822 (4.24)	4,089 (1.25)	−31,381 (−7.06)	−14,777 (−1.82)	−228,963(−12.47)
Intermediate Input Expansion	131,602 (95.76)	322,811 (98.75)	475,932(107.06)	828,689(101.82)	2,064,665(112.47)
Sub-total	137,424(100.00)	326,900(100.00)	444,551(100.00)	813,912(100.00)	1,835,702(100.00)

Sources: Bank of Korea ,*Korean I-0 tables.*

Notes: [1] Backward Import Substitution refers to $\sum_j dh_{ji}U_{ji} + \sum_j dh_{ji}dU_{ji}$

[3] Intermediate Imput Expansion refers to $\sum_j h_{ji}dU_{ji}$

[2] (+) refers to summation of positive effects aggregated from 38 sector estimations, and (−) refers to summation of negative effects aggregated from 38 sector estimations

positive *BIS* that occurred simultaneously in the agricultural sector for the period of 1960–73 indicates a structural change that reduced the import dependency in agricultural production and at the same time increased the import dependency on the demand side. It implies that the Korean economy has been losing its comparative advantage in the agricultural sector, increasing the import demand of agricultural commodities while agricultural production has depended less on imported intermediate goods.

Apparently, the positive *FIS* that occurred in the other sectors including some of the manufacturing sectors contributed to the *BIS* of the agricultural sector as we would expect from our *a priori* reasoning that *BIS* can occur only when the *FIS* of the other sectors, with the forward linkages, can contribute to *BIS* of the linkage sectors. For the light manufacturing sector, a consistent negative *BIS* characterized the whole period, indicating that the overall negative *FIS* in the light manufacturing sector also accompanied an overall import deepening structural change in the production structure. For the heavy and chemical manufacturing sector, negative *BIS* and positive *FIS* indicate that the positive *FIS* accompanied an import deepening structural change in the production structure.

In terms of the 38 sector analysis as shown in Appendices 1 and 2 the *FIS* and *BIS* are analyzed with the export expansion (*EE*) as in the following:

(1) rice, barley & wheat
FIS: negative
BIS: some positive
EE: not significant

(2) other agriculture
FIS: negative
BIS: positive
EE: increasing

(3) forestry
FIS: negative
BIS: negative
EE: not significant

(4) fishery
FIS: negative
BIS: negative and positive
EE: increasing

(5) coal
FIS: negative
BIS: negative
EE: not significant

(6) other minerals
FIS: negative
BIS: negative
EE: not significant

(7) processed food
FIS: negative
BIS: negative
EE: increasing

(8) beverage & tobacco
FIS: negative
BIS: negative
EE: not significant

(9) fibre spinning & textile
FIS: negative
BIS: negative
EE: increasing

(10) finished textile products
FIS: negative
BIS: negative
EE: increasing

(11) lumber, plywood & wood products
FIS: negative
BIS: negative
EE: increasing

(12) paper products
FIS: negative
BIS: negative
EE: increasing

(13) printing & publishing
FIS: negative
BIS: negative
EE: increasing

(14) leather & leather products
FIS: negative
BIS: negative
EE: increasing

(15) rubber products
FIS: negative
BIS: negative
EE: increasing

(16) basic chemicals
FIS: negative
BIS: negative
EE: increasing

(17) other chemical products
FIS: positive
BIS: positive
EE: increasing

(18) chemical fertilizer
FIS: positive
BIS: negative
EE: not significant

(19) petroleum & coal products
FIS: negative
BIS: negative
EE: increasing

(20) glass, clay & stone products
FIS: negative
BIS: negative
EE: increasing

(21) iron & steel
FIS: negative
BIS: negative
EE: not significant

(22) steel products
FIS: negative
BIS: negative
EE: increasing

(23) non-ferrous metal products
FIS: negative
BIS: negative
EE: increasing

(24) finished metal products
FIS: positive
BIS: negative
EE: increasing

(25) machinery except electrical machinery
FIS: negative
BIS: negative
EE: increasing

(26) electrical machinery
FIS: negative
BIS: negative
EE: increasing

(27) transportation equipment
FIS: negative
BIS: negative
EE: not significant

(28) miscellaneous manufacturing
FIS: negative
BIS: positive
EE: increasing

From the above pattern of *FIS*, *BIS* and *EE*, we find an interesting relationship between *BIS* and *EE*. Most of the sectors that showed an increasing export expansion experienced negative *BIS*. This suggests that export performance is positively correlated to negative *BIS*, indicating the importance of raw material imports for export production, which may be called an import-intensive export growth. Korean exports have not only been labor-intensive but also import-intensive due to the export incentive system that allowed duty-free intermediate imports for export production.

Another interesting finding is that the occurrence of negative *FIS* alone does not tell anything about the comparative advantage of the sector since most sectors with superb export performance showed negative *FIS*. Rather, it should be construed as an effect of aggregation bias associated with an inter-sectoral resource shift among the many sub-sectors of a given sector. For instance, the leather and leather products sector (14) is composed of 3 sub-sectors: leather and fur with no export but significant import increase, leather footwear with significant export growth but no import, and other leather products with no export but increasing imports. The leather footwear sector achieved a superb export expansion which outweighed the other two sub-sectors' lagging exports so that the whole sector has become a superb export sector. At the same time the leather footwear sector had only meager imports although the sub-sector's meager imports are overshadowed by the heavy imports of the other two sub-sectors so that the whole sector has become a negative *FIS* sector.

This kind of aggregation bias is prevalent in economic data analysis as indicated by the previous work.[3] The apparent negative *FIS* and *BIS* tend to overstate the extent of negative import substitution for the whole period in the Korean economy.

Therefore, import substitution was an important element, contributing

[3] Suk Tai Suh, *Import Substitution and Economic Development in Korea* (Seoul: Korea Development Institute, Dec. 1975).

to rapid economic growth in this later period although it is much less pronounced than export growth.

IV. Korean Incentive System for Import Substitution and Export Promotion

As specified in the three consecutive five-year economic plans (1st plan for 1962–66, 2nd for 1967–71, and 3rd plan for 1972–76), rapid economic growth through rapid export promotion and achievement of a self-sufficient economy through import substitution in the light and heavy, and chemical manufacturing sectors were the two most important objectives, among other important goals such as the development of agriculture, fishery and mining industries as well as the development of Social Overhead Capital service (SOC) sectors, of the plans.

However, the goals of achieving rapid export growth and promoting import substitution could be conflicting in terms of the policy instruments pertaining to resource allocation. For instance, the foreign trade and foreign exchange regime for rapid import substitution may require a protectionist policy which may not be conducive to rapid export growth, and vice versa. Conventionally viewed, policies for rapid import substitution require protection of the domestic infant industries although protectionist policies may not be the only alternative instrument available for import substitution.

The fact that Korea achieved both rapid export growth and import substitution in many sectors suggests two possible policy regimes that might have been effective for the plan periods. One is an export-oriented policy regime to promote export growth by providing financial and fiscal incentives to the export sectors, and the other is an inward-looking policy.

In the former case significant import substitution that occurred in the past decade may be attributable to a spontaneous offspring of rapid economic growth through the market mechanism, and in the latter case import substitution may have occurred in response to a deliberate protectionist policy designed to foster infant industries. Or, it may have occurred in response to a policy regime which may be some combination of the two extreme regimes.

Therefore, we analyzed the tariff structure to see to what extent the protectionist regime in the three plan periods was conducive to export growth and import substitution, respectively. We also analyzed the internal tax system to find out whether export sectors received more fiscal incentives than import substitution sectors. Our final analysis included the financial incentives for export promotion and import substitution to see whether there was any allocative mechanism in the financial incentive system.

The incentives for export promotion include, (1) the duty-free entry of raw material imports for export production, (2) the wastage allowance system that allows some portion of the raw material imports for export to be used for the domestic market, (3) short-term (usually 90 days) low interest financing up to 90 percent of the value of L/C, (4) other short-term and long-term preferential loans as shown by Tables 5, 6 and 7, (5) a low advance deposit rate for raw material imports for export production, (6) an income tax reduction (ceased in 1973) and an indirect tax exemption for exports, and (7) other institutional promotional activities such as opening of trade fairs, providing information channels through such institutions as the Korea Trade Association and the Korea Trade Promotion Corporation and the monthly Export Expansion Meeting.

The incentives for import substitution include (1) duty-free entry of machines and equipment for selected industries, (2) an income tax reduction provision for the newly established industries, (3) long-term low interest loans for selected industries, including the foreign loan guarantee programs, and (4) tariff protection for domestic industries competing with foreign industries, and some over-generous depreciation allowances.

For tax incentives, there are seven different exemptions and reduction provisions that affect resource allocation among different industries. At the moment we do not have the exemptions and reductions data by industry but only the economy-wide data. As shown in Table 3, the tax credit for foreign exchange earnings decreased from 85.7 percent in 1969 to 70.2 percent in 1975 while reduction by exemption control law increased from 4.2 percent in 1969 to 14.3 percent in 1975. Other categories remain more or less the same and insignificant. The rate of increase of the reductions and exemptions fluctuated from a high of 70 percent to a low of 12.0 percent in 1975. However, the ratio of total exemptions and reductions to total tax collections increased from 11.0 percent in 1969 to 23.8 percent in 1975, indicating that the fiscal incentives governing the allocation of resources have become more important in recent years. However, for the whole period the fiscal incentives for export promotion represent an annual average of over 70 percent of total incentives, this suggests that the Korean fiscal incentive system favors the export sectors more than any other sectors.

In Table 4, we find that the tariff exemption and reduction increased from 193 percent of the ratio of exemption to collection in 1969 to 230.5

Table 3. Annual Trends of Reduction & Exemption of Internal Tax

(million won)

By Type	1969				1970				1971			
	D.T.	*I.T.*	Total	Ratio	*D.T.*	*I.T.*	Total	Ratio	*D.T.*	*I.T.*	Total	Ratio
Foreign-route Navigation Income Exemption	215	21	236	1.0	293	300	593	1.5	65.3	726	1,579	3.0
Credit for Foreign Exchange Earnings	2,431	18,049	20,480	85.7	3,044	23,784	26,828	70.0	5,401	36,450	41,851	78.6
Investment Credit	164	—	164	0.7	1,883	—	1,883	4.9	1,942	—	1,942	3.6
Reduction by Emergency Decree	—	—	—	—	—	—	—	—	—	—	—	—
Reduction for Loss of Financing Resources	29	6	35	0.1	41	13	54	0.1	16	7	23	0
Reduction by Exemption Control Law	644	349	993	4.2	547	340	887	2.3	1,687	255	1,942	3.6
Other Reduction	1,014	891	1,905	8.0	4,022	4,071	8,093	21.1	2,996	2,929	5,925	11.0
Total	4,572	19,315	23,887	100.0	9,830	28,508	38,338	100.0	12,695	40,567	53,262	100.0
Value of Increase	1,932	7,745	9,677		5,258	9,193	14,451		2,865	12,059	14,924	
Increase Rate	73.2	66.9	68.1		125.0	47.6	60.5		29.1	42.3	38.9	
Collection of Internal Tax			218,099				283,799				355,496	
Ratio to Collection (%)			11.0				13.5				15.0	

Table 3. (Continued)

By Type	1972				1973			
	D.T.	I.T.	Total	Ratio	D.T.	I.T.	Total	Ratio
Foreign-route Navigation Income Exemption	1,599	2,042	3,641	5.7	1,543	2,996	4,539	4.6
Credit for Foreign Exchange Earnings	3,255	44,197	47,452	73.9	4,503	68,689	73,192	73.7
Investment Credit	2,290	—	2,290	3.6	4,009	—	4,009	4.0
Reduction by Emergency Decree	—	—	—	—	188	—	188	0.2
Reduction for Loss of Financing Resources	26	29	55	0.1	69	116	185	0.2
Reduction by Exemption Control Law	842	5,428	6,270	9.7	3,992	7,755	11,747	11.8
Other Reduction	1,338	3,152	4,490	7.0	2,619	2,796	5,415	5.5
Total	9,350	54,848	64,198	100.0	16,923	82,352	99,275	100.0
Value of Increase	−3,345	14,281	10,936		7,573	27,504	35,077	
Increase Rate	−26.3	35.2	20.5		81.0	50.1	54.6	
Collection of Interal Tax			374,340				439,121	
Ratio to Collection(%)			17.1				22.6	

Table 3. *(Continued)*

By Type	1974				1975			
	D.T.	*I.T.*	Total	Ratio	*D.T.*	*I.T.*	Total	Ratio
Foreign-route Navigation Income Exemption	2,986	5,586	8,572	5.1	1,435	7,624	9,059	3.8
Credit for Foreign Exchange Earnings	0	101,763	101,763	60.0	—	169,129	169,129	70.2
Investment Credit	540	0	540	0.3	4,885	—	4,885	2.0
Reduction by Emergency Decree	4,230	13,235	17,465	10.3	1.960	—	1,960	0.8
Reduction for Loss of Financing Resources	45	40	85	0.1	155	93	248	0.1
Reduction by Exemption Control Law	4,266	18,532	22,798	13.4	3,248	31,193	34,441	14.3
Other Reduction	12,980	5,399	18,379	10.8	15,464	5,732	21,196	8.8
Total	25,047	144,555	169,602	100.0	27,147	213,771	240,918	100.0
Value of Increase	8,124	62,208	70,327		2,100	69,216	71,316	
Increase Rate	48.0	75.5	70.8		8.4	47.9	12.0	
Collection of Interal Tax			717,976				1,012,291	
Ratio to Collection(%)			23.6				23.8	

Source: Ministry of Finance
Notes: The amount of business tax is included in indirect tax.
D.T. — Direct Tax
I.T. — Indirect Tax

Table 4. *The Trends of Reduction & Exemption of Tariff*

(million won)

By Type	1969 Amount	1969 Increase Rate	1969 Ratio	1970 Amount	1970 Increase Rate	1970 Ratio	1971 Amount	1971 Increase Rate	1971 Ratio	1972 Amount	1972 Increase Rate	1972 Ratio
Export	22,551	36.7	26.1	35,613	39.3	33.2	54,333	52.6	38.0	111,208	104.7	51.8
Major Industry	33,036	38.3	38.3	33,830	12.7	31.5	37,312	10.3	26.1	45,797	22.7	21.3
Import of Foreign Capital	1,741	2.0	2.0	1,350	−22.5	1.3	2,383	76.5	1.7	4,160	74.6	2.0
Other	29,015	21.7	33.6	36,612	26.2	34.0	49,015	33.9	34.2	53,395	8.9	24.9
Total	86,343	30.0	100.0	107,405	24.4	100.0	143,043	33.2	100.0	214,560	50.0	100.0
Value of Increase	19,932			21,062			35,638			71,517		
Increase Rate	30.0			24.4			33.2			50.0		
Tariff Collection	44,724			50,924			52,187			59,106		
Ratio of Collection(%)	193.1			210.9			274.1			363.0		

Table 4. *(Continued)*

By Type	1973			1974			1975		
	Amount	Increase Rate	Ratio	Amount	Increase Rate	Ratio	Amount	Increase Rate	Ratio
Export	210,788	89.5	65.9	248,998	18.1	82.2	171,553	31.1	77.0
Major Industry	55,825	21.9	17.5	31,267	−44.0	10.3	25,487	−18.5	11.5
Import of Foreign Capital	6,919	66.3	2.2	6,615	−4.4	2.2	3,170	−52.1	1.4
Other	46,077	−13.7	14.4	15,941	−65.4	5.3	22,518	41.3	10.1
Total	319,609	49.0	100.0	302,821	−5.3	100.0	222,728	−26.4	100.0
Value of Increase	105,049			−16,788			−80,093		
Increase Rate	49.0			−5.3			−26.4		
Tariff Collection	82,371			126,697			181,004		
Ratio to Collection(%)	388.0			239.0			230.5		

Source: Ministry of Finance

Table 5. *Preferential Loans for Exports, 1961–1975*
(Year-end figures)

(million won)

	1961	1962	1963	1964	1965	1966	1967	1968
I. Short-term	826	1,772	3,893	9,834	11,366	16,273	28,561	32,813
1. Export Credit	826	1,772	1,817	1,857	3,867	3,636	6,618	8,072
2. Loans for advance export	—	—	—	—	—	—	—	17
3. Loans for production of raw materials	—	—	—	—	—	—	—	—
4. Loans for suppliers of U.S. offshore procurement	—	—	861	526	655	1,190	3,400	3,567
5. Credit for imports of raw materials for exports	—	—	1,215	6,684	6,325	10,975	17,835	20,239
(Payment guarantee)	—	—	(1,215)	(4,101)	(4,005)	(5,417)	(11,292)	(8,859)
(Domestic Use-foreign exchange)	—	—	—	(2,583)	(2,320)	(5,558)	(62)	(29)
(Import Loans)	—	—	—	—	—	—	(6,481)	(11,351)
6. Export Use	—	—	—	690	456	431	652	550
7. Loans for preparing agricultural and fishery products for exports	—	—	—	—	—	—	—	—
8. Export industry promotion loans	—	—	—	77	63	41	56	368

II. Long-term	—	—	—	368	773	1,293	3,865	10,602
1. Loans for deferred payment exports	—	—	—	—	—	—	—	—
2. Foreign exchange loans for import of capital goods for export industries	—	—	—	—	—	—	1,849	7,802
3. Equipment of export industry	—	—	—	—	—	—	—	—
4. Equipment loans for conversion into export industry	—	—	—	178	603	1,014	1,531	2,237
5. Loans for export specializing industries	—	—	—	—	—	93	292	563
6. Priority loans for export producing industry	—	—	—	—	—	—	—	—
7. Loans for export promotion of sundry goods manufacturing	—	—	—	—	—	—	—	—
8. Export industry operating loans (Counterpart Fund)	—	—	—	190	170	186	193	—
Total (I + II) (A)	826	1,772	3,893	10,202	12,139	17,566	32,426	43,415
Total domestic loans (B)	—	—	—	—	—	—	221,000	431,700
A/B(%)	—	—	—	—	—	—	14.7	7.5

Table 5. *(Continued)*

	1969	1970	1971	1972	1973	1974	1975
I. Short-term	56,009	83,098	113,618	134,727	313,568	489,683	609,520
1. Export Credit	11,866	19,129	29,168				
2. Loans for advance export	35	154	248	51,106	112,418	126,936	232,873
3. Loans for production of raw materials	134	853	4,290				
4. Loans for suppliers of U.S. offshore procurement	5,291	4,510	6,852	9,060	10,170	50,203	96,998
5. Credit for imports of raw materials for exports	33,256	49,981	68,237	68,509	183,428	271,190	238,299
(Payment guarantee)	(15,001)	(21,244)	(33,481)	(27,913)	(91,333)	(130,222)	(146,331)
(Domestic Use foreign exchange)	(589)	—	—	—	—	—	—
(Import Loans)	(17,666)	(28,737)	(34,756)	(40,596)	(92,095)	(140,968)	(91,968)
6. Export Use	1,986	4,463	—	—	—	—	—
7. Loans for preparing agricultural and fishery products for exports	3,413	4,001	4,823	6,052	7,552	41,354	41,420
8. Export industry promotion loans	28	7	—	—	—	—	—

II. Long-term	13,569	25,594	57,106	72,246	153,948	246,992	286,086
1. Loans for deferred payment exports	—	—	388	1,448	2,908	4,338	27,088
2. Foreign exchange loans for import of capital goods for export industries	10,291	21,372	51,740	65,610	100,219	166,597	178,596
3. Equipment of export industry	—	—	—	—	44,218	66,294	71,504
4. Equipment loans for conversion into export industry	2,536	2,826	2,702	2,406	2,565		
5. Loans for export specializing industries	742	807	925	681	437		
6. Priority loan for export producing industry	—	385	924	1,433	3,009	9,763	8,898
7. Loans for export promotion of sundry goods manufacturing	—	204	332	591	561		
8. Export industry operating loans (Counterpart Fund)	—	—	95	77	31		
Total (I + II) (A)	68,836	108,672	170,724	206,973	467,516	736,741	895,540
Total domestic loans (B)	706,300	919,400	1201,200	1463,000	1899,800	2862,500	3520,900
A/B (%)	9.8	11.8	14.2	14.2	24.6	25.7	25.4

Sources: Bank of Korea and Medium Industry Bank.

Notes: [1] Aggregated under the heading, "export credit" since March 2, 1972.

[2] Abolished since July 4, 1969.

[3] Included in the loans for export specializing medium industry since March 18, 1974.

[4] The data total domestic loan from 1967 to 1975 refer to Kwang Suk Kim and Larry E. Westphal, *The Exchange and Trade Policy in Korea,* 1976, P. 107.

Table 6. *Gross Interest Subsidies for Export, 1961–1975*
(Annual Average Figure)

(million won)

	1961	1962	1963	1964	1965	1966	1967	1968
I. Short-term	69	124	160	504	1,389	2,095	3,442	4,529
1. Export Credit	69	124	109	149	754	709	1,323	1,550
2. Loans for advance export	—	—	—	—	—	—	—	3
3. Loans for production of raw materials	—	—	—	—	—	—	—	—
4. Loans for Suppliers of U.S. offshore procurement	—	—	51	42	128	232	680	685
5. Credit for imports of raw materials for export	—	—	—	258	464	1,113	1,279	2,185
(Domestic use-foreign exchange)	—	—	—	(258)	(464)	(1,113)	(12)	(6)
(Import loans)	—	—	—	—	—	—	(1,267)	(2,179)
6. Export Use	—	—	—	55	43	41	130	106
7. Loans for preparing agricultural and fishery products for exports	—	—	—	—	—	—	—	—
8. Export industry promotion loans								

II. Long-term	—	—	—	7	107	181	541	1,423
1. Loans for export on credit	—	—	—	—	—	—	—	—
2. Foreign exchange loans for import of capital goods for export industries	—	—	—	—	—	—	259	1,030
3. Equipment of export industry								
4. Equipment loans for conversion into export industry	—	—	—	7	84	142	214	295
5. Loans for export specializing industries	—	—	—	—	—	13	41	98
6. Priority loans for export producing industry	—	—	—	—	—	—	—	—
7. Loans for export promotion of sundry goods manufacturing	—	—	—	—	—	—	—	—
8. Export industry operating loans (Counterpart Fund)	(—)	(—)	(—)	(—)	(—)	(—)	(—)	(—)
Total (I + II) (A)	69	124	160	511	1,496	2,276	3,983	5,942

Table 6. *(Continued)*

	1969	1970	1971	1972	1973	1974	1975
I. Short-term	6,741	10,409	12,050	9,571	19,270	27,541	36,826
1. Export Credit	2,136	3,443	4,667				
2. Loans for advance export	6	28	40	4,855	9,555	10,790	19,794
3. Loans for production of raw materials	24	150	686				
4. Loans for Suppliers of U.S. offshore procurement	952	812	1,096	860	966	4,769	9,215
5. Credit for imports of raw materials for export	3,286	5,173	5,561	3,856	8,749	11,982	7,817
(Domestic use-foreign exchange)	(106)	(—)	(—)	(—)	(—)	(—)	(—)
(Import loans)	(3,180)	(5,173)	(5,561)	(3,856)	(8,749)	(11,982)	(7,817)
6. Export Use	357	803	—	—	—	—	—
7. Loans for preparing agricultural and fishery products for exports	—	—	—	—	—	—	—
8. Export industry promotion loans							

II. Long-term	1,628	3,071	5,734	2,616	4,015	6,585	9,135
1. Loans for export on credit	—	—	62	138	276	412	2,573
2. Foreign exchange loans for import of capital goods for export industries	1,235	2,465	5,174	2,296	3,508	5,831	6,251
3. Equipment of export industry							
4. Equipment loans for conversion into export industry	304	339	270	84	90		
5. Loans for export specializing industries	89	97	93	24	15		
6. Priority loans for export producing industry	—	46	92	50	105	342	311
7. Loans for export promotion of sundry goods manufacturing	—	24	33	21	20		
8. Export industry operating loans (Counterpart Fund)	—	—	10	3	1		
Total (I + II) (A)	8,369	13,480	17,784	12,187	23,285	34,126	45,961

Sources: Bank of Korea and Medium Industry Bank.
Note: The interest rate structure for export financing is shown in a separate table.

Table 7. *Comparison of Interest Rates on Loans and Discounts*

(percent per annum)

	1961	1962	1963	1964	1965	1966	1967	1968	1969	1970	1971
Discounts on bills[1]	17.52	16.43	14.00	16.00	26.00	26.00	26.00	25.20	24.00	24.00	22.00
Export Credit[2]	—	9.13	8.03	8.00	6.50	6.50	6.00	6.00	6.00	6.00	6.00
Loans for suppliers of offshore procurement	—	9.13	8.03	8.00	6.50	6.50	6.00	6.00	6.00	6.00	6.00
Credit for imports of raw materials for export[3]	—	—	6.00	6.00	6.00	6.00	6.00	6.00	6.00	6.00	6.00
Export Usance	—	—	—	8.00	6.50	6.50	6.00	6.00	6.00	6.00	6.00
Loans for preparing agricultural & fishery products for exports	—	—	—	—	—	—	—	—	24.00	24.00	22.00
Export industry promotion loans	—	—	14.00	16.00	26.00	26.00	26.00	25.20	24.00	24.00	—
Loans for export on credit	—	—	—	—	—	—	—	—	—	—	6.00
Foreign exchange	—	—	—	—	—	—	12.00	12.00	12.00	12.00	12.00
Loans for export specializing medium industries	—	—	—	12.00	12.00	12.00	12.00	12.00	12.00	12.00	12.00
Equipment loans for export industry	—	—	—	—	—	—	—	—	—	—	—
Export industry operating loans	—	—	—	10.00	10.00	10.00	10.00	—	—	—	—

Table 7. (Continued)

	1972 1.17	1972 3.2	1972 8.3	1972 10.2	1973 2.9	1973 5.14	1974 1.24	1974 11.12	1974 12.7	1975 2.15	1975 4.17
Discounts on bills [1]	19.00	15.50	15.50	15.50	15.50	15.50	15.50	15.50	15.50	15.50	15.50
Export Credit [2]	6.00	6.00	6.00	6.00	6.00	7.00	7.00	7.00	7.00	7.00	7.00
Loans for suppliers of offshore procurement	6.00	6.00	6.00	6.00	6.00	7.00	7.00	7.00	7.00	7.00	7.00
Credit for imports of raw materials for export [3]	6.00	6.00	6.00	6.00	6.00	7.00	7.00	7.00	7.00	7.00	7.00
Export Usance	6.00	6.00	6.00	6.00	6.00	7.00	7.00	7.00	7.00	7.00	7.00
Loans for preparing agricultural & fishery products for exports	19.00	19.00	15.50	15.50	15.50	15.50	15.50	15.50	15.50	15.50	15.50
Export industry promotion loans	—	—	—	—	—	—	—	—	—	—	—
Loans for export on credit	6.00	6.00	6.00	6.00	6.00	6.00	6.00	6.00	6.00	6.00	6.00
Foreign exchange	12.00	12.00	12.00	12.00	12.00	12.00	15.00	12.00	12.00	10.75	10.25
Loans for export specializing medium industries	12.00	12.00	12.00	12.00	12.00	12.00	12.00	13.15	12.00	12.00	12.00
Equipment loans for export industry	—	—	—	—	—	12.00	12.00	12.00	12.00	12.00	12.00
Export industry operating loans	—	—	—	—	—	—	—	—	—	—	—

Sources: Bank of Korea, Medium Industry Bank, and Export-Import Bank of Korea.

Notes: [1] Figure is the interest rates on loans and discounts of local banks.

[2] The interest rate changed for the export credit, loans for suppliers of offshore procurement and the credit for imports of raw materials for export was decreased from 9 percent per annum to 7 percent by the resolution of the Monetary Board on Jan. 24, 1974 and 7 percent is to remain effective until Sep. 30, 1976.

[3] Aggregated into the rule of export credit since March 2, 1972.

percent in 1975. Exemption for raw material imports for export production increased from 26.1 percent in 1969 to 77 percent in 1975 while that for major industries (Article 28 of Tariff Law) decreased from 38.3 percent in 1969 to 11.5 percent in 1975 and other exemptions also declined rapidly. This suggests that the tariff exemption system has favored the export industries more than any of the other sectors, and the tariff incentives have increased over time.

As shown in Tables 5, 6 and 7 export financing has been not only an important source of low interest loans which would otherwise not be available, but also an increasing portion of the total domestic loans. Total export financing increased from 826 million won in 1961 to 895,540 million won in 1975, and the proportion of export financing in total domestic loans increased from 14.7 percent in 1967 to 25.4 percent in 1975 as shown in Table 5. Therefore, the financial incentive has increasingly favored the export sectors and at the same time the interest subsidies increased from won 2.0 per dollar export in 1962 to won 9.0 per dollar export in 1975.

As shown in the above tables, fiscal, financial and tariff incentives for export promotion have dominated the Korean incentive system. However, more export incentives do not mean negative incentives for import substitution because there was clearly positive protection of the domestic sectors from foreign competition. Export sectors received more exemptions than domestic sectors, implying that fewer tariff exemptions were applied to domestic import substitution sectors. Low tariff rates were applied to imports of raw materials and necessities, and oftentimes tariffs were exempted for imports of capital equipment which was unavailable domestically. High tariff rates were applied to the final, manufactured goods including the final consumption goods, which protected domestic industries at the final product stage rather than at the raw material and intermediate product stage. The consequence was a remarkable growth of the final goods producing industries with low value-added and high import content industries for domestic as well as export sectors. Therefore, a significant amount of import substitution has occurred already in the final goods sectors although import dependency has not declined. The simultaneous occurrence of remarkable *EE* and negative *FIS* as well as negative *BIS* shows an underlying incentive system that encouraged an import-intensive export promotion and a low domestic value-added import substitution, both of which increased the economy's overall import to GNP ratio.

We may conclude that the Korean incentive system is composed of incentives for export and incentives for import substitution although the former outweighs the latter in the fiscal, tariff, financial and other institu-

Table 8. *Won Incentives per Dollar Exported*

(million won)

	1962	1963	1964	1965	1966	1967	1968
I. Total tax reduction & exemption	310	527	992	2,838	5,021	7,724	11,127
II. Total tariff reduction & exemption	255	571	1,197	2,692	5,333	8,224	19,261
III. Total interest subsidies	124	160	511	1,496	2,276	3,983	5,942
IV. Total subsidies	689	1,258	2,700	7,026	12,630	19,931	36,330
V. Total exports (million dollars)	54.8	86.8	119.1	175.1	250.3	320.2	455.4
VI. Won subsidies per dollar exported (IV/V) (won)	12.6	14.5	22.7	40.1	50.5	62.2	79.8
	1969	**1970**	**1971**	**1972**	**1973**	**1974**	**1975**
I. Total tax reduction & exemption	20,480	26,828	41,851	47,452	73,192	101,763	169,129
II. Total tariff reduction & exemption	22,551	35,613	54,333	111,208	210,788	248,998	171,553
III. Total interest subsidies	8,369	13,480	17,784	12,187	23,285	34,126	45,961
IV. Total subsidies	51,400	75,921	113,968	170,847	307,265	384,887	386,643
V. Total exports (million dollars)	622.5	835.2	1,067.6	1,624.1	3,225.0	4,460.4	5,081.0
VI. Won subsidies per dollar exported (IV/V) (won)	82.6	90.9	106.8	105.2	95.3	86.3	76.1

Sources: The Bank of Korea; Ministry of Finance; C. R. Frank, Jr., Kwang Suk Kim & L. E. Westphal, *Foreign Trade Regimes & Economic Development: South Korea* (New York: NBER, 1975); and Suk Tai Suh, *Import Substitution and Economic Development in Korea* (Seoul: Korea Development Institute, Dec. 1975).

tional incentives. The efficiency of export incentives may be judged in terms of the won subsidies per dollar exported as shown in Table 8. Export incentives were effective in promoting rapid export growth because the incentives per dollar exported have actually declined although exports have grown at the same remarkable rate as shown in Table 10.

Therefore, the remarkable import substitution that occurred in many of the sub-sectors may in part have been a natural offspring of the rapid economic growth as the domestic market size expanded and the profitability of the industries increased. However, it is a non sequitur that the most efficient sectors achieved import substitution most rapidly since there were still some incentives for import substitution and the positive protection of the domestic industries from foreign competition. Import substitution of the final goods producing industries may have occurred in part in response to the high tariff protection afforded to the final goods sectors, thus encouraging the low value-added (high import-content) industrial development.

V. Concluding Remarks

Import substitution and export growth both can release the external bottleneck of an *LDC*, and therefore, an appropriate incentive system for import substitution or export growth or some effective combination of the two can help allocate resources in such an efficient way that the growth rate may be maximized and the resource cost may be minimized.

In the Korean economy more incentives were given to export sectors and fewer incentives to domestic infant industries. The export incentive system has been effective since the real budgetary cost to the government of each dollar exported decreased over time. The incentive for import substitution included promotion of such intermediate goods productions as fertilizer, petro-chemicals, iron and steel products, transport equipment, electronics, building materials, and metals. If there were no serious protective tariffs for any particular sector, the inter-sectoral resource shifts among the many sub-sectors may have followed an efficient growth path so that an inefficient sub-sector may have experienced a negative *FIS* while an efficient sub-sector a positive *FIS* although the sector's overall effect may be a negative *FIS* due to aggregation bias. However, high tariff protection for the final goods sectors and low tariffs for raw materials exerted an effect aimed at promoting the final goods production of low domestic value-added and neglecting the intermediate goods production. Therefore, the protective tariff structure may have caused some distortions in the efficient growth path of the Korean economy.

Going back to the initial question of whether the Korean incentive system is an export-oriented system, or an import substitution system or some combination of the two, we may in a nutshell, conclude that it is a combination of the two although it is overshadowed by export incentives. Nevertheless, the incentives for import substitution may have caused some inefficient growth of domestic infant industries in the inefficient sectors including the intermediate and final goods sectors. However, most of the positive import substitution which occurred in many of the sub-sectors may have occurred as a result of efficient allocation of resources through market mechanisms rather than in response to a deliberate protectionist policy. Efficiency in the distribution of scarce resources seems to be one of the most essential elements in the process of Korean economic growth which contributed to a superb export performance and rapid economic growth. There seems to be a relationship which is more than a mere coincidence, between the trade liberalizing reform in the mid 1960's and the rapid economic growth in the latter half of 1960's.

REFERENCES

1. Balassa, B., "Trade Policies in Developing Countries," *American Economic Review Proceedings*, May 1971.
2. Chenery, H.B., "Patterns of Industrial Growth," *American Economic Review*, May 1960.
3. Eysenbach, M.L., "A Note on Growth and Structural Change in Pakistan's Manufacturing Industry, 1954–64," *Pakistan Development Review*, Spring 1965.
4. Fane, George, "Import Substitution and Export Expansion: Their measurement and an Example of Their Application," *Pakistan Development Review*, Spring 1971.
5. Frank, Charles, Kwang Suk Kim, & Larry E. Westphal, *Foreign Trade Regimes and Economic Development: South Korea*, New York: N.B.E.R., 1975.
6. Healey, Derek, "Development Policy: New Thinking about an Interpretation," *Journal of Economic Literature*, Vol. X., No. 3 (Sept 1972), pp. 757–795.

7. Hirschman, A.O., *The Strategy of Economic Development*, New Haven: Yale University press 1958.
8. Hong, Wontack, Alternative Trade Strategies and Employment: The case of Korea, Seoul: Korea Development Institute, December 1975.
9. Krueger, A.O., "Evaluating Restrictionist Trade Regimes: Theory and Measurement," *Journal of Political Economy*, 80, 1972.
10. Little, I., T. Scitovsky and M. Scoff, *Industry and Trade in Some Developing Countries*, London: Oxford University Press, 1970.
11. Rader, T., "International Trade and Development in a Small Country I & II," in A. Zarley (ed.), *Papers in Quantitative Economics I & II*, Lawrence: University of Kansas Press, 1971.
12. Suh, Suk Tai, *Import Substitution and Economic Development in Korea*, Seoul: Korea Development Institute, Dec. 1975.
13. Economic Planning Board, *Statistical Yearbook of Korea*, 1960–74. Office of Customs Administration, *Korea Trade Statistical Yearbook*, 1969–74.
14. Bank of Korea, *Korean I-O Tables for 1960, 1963, 1966, 1968, 1970, 1973*. Bank of Korea, *Economic Statistics Yearbook: 1955, 1960, 1966, 1968, 1970, 1974.*
15. Economic Planning Board and The Korea Development Bank, *Report on Mining and Manufacturing Survey: 1963, 1966, 1970, 1972.*
16. Bank of Korea, *National Income Statistics Yearbook* 1971–74.
17. Ministry of Finance, *Foreign Trade of Korea.*

APPENDIX

Appendix 1. Composition of Demand Expansion By Sectors

(million won)

	1960–63	63–66	66–68	68–70	70–73
1. Rice, Barley and Wheat					
Intermediate Demand					
I.S.	−2,135	1,913	−3,323	2,668	−61,420
D.D.E.	6,487	26,392	35,052	8,183	51,974
Final Demand					
I.S.	−6,930	6,009	−8,010	−33,306	24,078
D.D.E.	84,284	102,604	7,023	179,749	283,528
E.E.	−375	1,594	−1,614	−103	3,207
Total	81,331	138,512	29,128	157,191	301,367

Appendix 1. (Continued)

	1960–63	63–66	66–68	68–70	70–73
2. Other Agriculture					
Intermediate Demand					
I.S.	1,320	10,329	28	−27,445	−21,560
D.D.E.	18,225	26,268	39,163	48,775	150,799
Final Demand	341	−500	−1,016	−1,792	−7,632
D.D.E.	31,015	61,194	40,420	74,764	111,820
E.E.	469	594	1,048	5,917	12,919
Total	51,370	97,885	79,643	100,219	246,346
3. Forestry					
Intermediate Demand					
I.S.	−339	81	821	−38,283	−41,243
D.D.E.	1,297	14,015	8,612	51,431	52,042
Final Demand					
I.S.	−11	−246	−346	16,991	−1,235
D.D.E.	1,466	4,337	−993	−271	7,973
E.E.	32	−69	146	−85	2,388
Total	2,445	18,118	8,240	29,783	19,925
4. Fishery					
Intermediate Demand					
I.S.	6	0	−242	751	−1,942
D.D.E.	1,107	5,073	4,732	−2,206	13,467
Final Demand					
I.S.	3	0	0	−99	−268
D.D.E.	3,014	9,508	14,962	9,944	61,126
E.E.	166	1,806	352	13,053	34,356
Total	4,296	16,387	19,804	21,443	106,739
5. Coal					
Intermediate Demand					
I.S.	86	−5	−6	−89	−5,500
D.D.E.	3,310	7,886	7,229	1,935	23,010
Final Demand					
I.S.	0	0	0	−10	−30
D.D.E.	261	−171	−445	479	−2,012
E.E.	172	11	197	337	−83
Total	3,829	7,721	6,975	2,652	15,385
6. Other Minerals					
Intermediate Demand					
I.S.	−446	65	570	−25,116	−16,772
D.D.E.	1,803	4,609	6,078	34,814	30,123

Appendix 1. (Continued)

	1960–63	63–66	66–68	68–70	70–73
Final Demand					
I.S.	66	510	−70	694	439
E.E.	574	4,368	2,024	3,229	979
Total	2,346	9,574	6,778	14,529	20,174
7. Processed Food					
Intermediate Demand					
I.S.	2,274	628	−3,505	523	−9,220
D.D.E.	7,298	8,493	20,203	37,149	138,434
Final Demand					
I.S.	−31	−2,108	4,760	851	4,892
D.D.E.	13,751	38,504	45,176	79,084	183,280
E.E.	1,058	5,420	5,259	4,039	40,563
Total	24,350	50,937	71,893	121,646	357,949
8. Beverage and Tobacco					
Intermediate Demand					
I.S.	334	−21	31	40	2,228
D.D.E.	4,860	−2,589	4,467	34,985	24,839
Final Demand					
I.S.	928	−63	96	−89	−122
D.D.E.	8,342	16,348	27,908	49,174	114,345
E.E.	−58	2,156	409	−2,118	852
Total	14,406	15,831	32,911	81,992	137,686
9. Fibre Spinning and Textile Fabrics					
Intermediate Demand					
I.S.	732	−4,123	−2,671	20,775	−27,592
D.D.E.	8,778	36,047	23,938	26,817	166,544
Final Demand					
I.S.	810	−1,109	25	2,820	771
D.D.E.	1,828	10,902	18,857	−14,752	15,258
E.E.	1,344	8,450	6,589	12,308	114,958
Total	13,492	50,167	46,738	47,968	269,939
10. Finished Textile Products					
Intermediate Demand					
I.S.	78	−366	366	−607	−3,819
D.D.E.	2,855	2,159	3,519	13,861	20,088
Final Demand					
I.S.	1,256	−106	−355	1,388	−9,759
D.D.E.	10,561	27,132	20,320	52,238	87,446

Appendix 1. (Continued)

	1960-63	63-66	66-68	68-70	70-73
E.E.	619	10,609	23,967	35,581	252,922
Total	15,369	39,428	47,817	102,461	346,878
11. Lumber, Plywood and Wood Products					
Intermediate Demand					
I.S.	−3,068	−1,989	−2,552	6,569	−318
D.D.E.	6,496	11,300	12,980	10,877	20,572
Final Demand					
I.S.	−136	334	−202	61	165
D.D.E.	820	1,895	3,254	−1,250	−5,613
E.E.	858	7,127	10,158	10,017	98,123
Total	4,970	18,667	23,638	26,274	112,929
12. Paper Products					
Intermediate Demad					
I.S.	2,111	793	−1,806	140	−4,206
D.D.E.	3,008	9,396	12,008	14,184	61,808
Final Demand					
I.S.	3	−69	−171	2,433	162
D.D.E.	1,274	527	80	−941	3,575
E.E.	2	294	280	517	8,260
Total	6,398	10,941	10,391	16,333	69,599
13. Printing and Publishing					
Intermediate Demand					
I.S.	41	−137	−626	151	1,655
D.D.E.	622	4,712	8,333	3,281	15,070
Final Demand					
I.S.	−58	328	34	−227	42
D.D.E.	1,317	4,444	8,842	−1,624	12,933
E.E.	−6	118	−14	281	9,443
Total	1,916	9,465	16,569	1,862	39,143
14. Leather and Leather Products					
Intermediate Demand					
I.S.	3	−223	191	−461	−2,984
D.D.E.	755	1,500	1,498	167	17,396
Final Demand					
I.S.	4	10	−140	3	−531
D.D.E.	1,195	2,860	2,523	455	2,745
E.E.	−27	379	611	−136	9,291
Total	1,930	4,526	4,683	28	25,917

Appendix 1. *(Continued)*

	1960–63	63–66	66–68	68–70	70–73
15. Rubber Products					
Intermediate Demand					
I.S.	164	59	−99	998	−298
D.D.E.	1,048	3,358	2,336	4,051	10,139
Final Demand					
I.S.	−78	126	178	16	246
D.D.E.	1,456	2,513	−664	1,755	11,281
E.E.	−15	2,349	1,307	2,367	32,787
Total	2,575	8,405	3,058	9,187	54,155
16. Basic Chemicals					
Intermediate Demand					
I.S.	−537	−105	484	−7,586	7,107
D.D.E.	2,516	3,033	5,741	13,781	30,543
Final Demand					
I.S.	−10	−93	−511	4,660	2,546
D.D.E.	−418	549	−283	−2,966	−3,522
E.E.	−32	148	28	262	6,619
Total	1,519	3,532	5,459	8,151	43,293
17. Other Chemical Products					
Intermediate Demand					
I.S.	1,305	121	−4,246	26,332	10,933
D.D.E.	1,989	8,354	10,141	24,543	94,529
Final Demand					
I.S.	1,643	−699	223	983	2,978
D.D.E.	3,089	5,532	13,498	21,989	49,107
E.E.	29	−9	95	2,947	20,078
Total	8,055	13,299	19,711	76,794	177,625
18. Chemical Fertilizer					
Intermediate Demand					
I.S.	−7,401	2,696	5,359	12,450	−5,389
D.D.E.	8,240	1,066	216	6,690	17,004
Final Demand					
I.S.	699	−863	869	−145	396
D.D.E.	−65	293	969	−150	−2,271
E.E.	0	0	0	1,299	84
Total	1,473	3,192	7,413	20,144	9,824
19. Petroleum and Coal Products					
Intermediate Demand					

Appendix 1. (*Continued*)

	1960–63	63–66	66–68	68–70	70–73
I.S.	−150	11,667	5,631	11,962	−6,112
D.D.E	808	5,509	16,950	31,975	136,386
Final Demand					
I.S.	313	1,453	61,728	−941	889
D.D.E.	4,711	6,427	−51,653	9,842	37,198
E.E.	0	1,687	282	6,664	5,936
Total	5,682	26,743	32,938	59,502	174,297
20. Glass, Clay and Stone Products					
Intermediate Demand					
I.S.	−65	1,519	523	759	−3,292
D.D.E.	4,201	10,921	27,254	22,634	52,487
Final Demand					
I.S.	−84	68	−1,157	−506	1,691
D.D.E.	487	536	−4,908	6,844	−2,799
E.E.	35	1,176	563	1,060	14,799
Total	4,574	14,220	22,275	30,791	62,886
21. Iron and Steel					
Intermediate Demand					
I.S.	−935	−353	−741	10,244	−36,786
D.D.E.	2,226	5,703	4,366	1,738	81,357
Final Demand					
I.S.	−345	475	−216	−2,028	−693
D.D.E.	342	28	−521	1,836	638
E.E.	−42	19	−20	944	256
Total	1,246	5,872	2,868	12,734	44,772
22. Steel Products					
Intermediate Demand					
I.S.	−307	1,473	2,194	−4,225	−29,460
D.D.E.	2,867	7,163	17,028	32,930	101,163
Final Demand					
I.S.	45	155	−239	−5,475	3,320
D.F.E.	11	90	−491	12,686	10
E.E.	1,847	236	−1,681	2,488	64,141
Total	4,463	9,117	16,811	38,404	139,262
23. Non-Ferrous Metal Products					
Intermediate Demand					
I.S.	414	341	−1,731	3,631	−12,759
D.D.E.	1,233	2,301	2,383	3,868	23 654

Appendix 1. (Continued)

	106–63	63–66	66–68	68–70	70–73
Final Demand					
I.S.	51	−380	−83	−593	598
D.D.E.	−208	327	−3	534	390
E.E.	98	523	639	374	1 223
Total	1,588	3,112	1,205	7,814	13,106
24. Finished Metal Products					
Intermediate Demand					
I.S.	−353	−2,884	267	−6,622	5,398
D.D.E.	1,727	6,897	2,418	15,092	11,418
Final Demand					
I.S.	−177	−738	403	2,373	1,753
D.D.E.	464	2,565	373	428	4,440
E.E.	70	1,141	598	2,368	25,957
Total	1,731	6,981	4,059	13,639	48,966
25. Machinery Except Electrical Machinery					
Intermediate Demand					
I.S.	−529	−1,235	−3,596	2,277	−3,018
D.D.E.	3,365	1,120	8,134	−70	8,775
Final Demand					
I.S.	−4,344	−945	−5,263	750	16,552
D.D.E.	5,434	5,259	11,728	−746	3,554
E.E.	151	806	−438	300	17,409
Total	4,077	5,005	10,565	2,511	43,272
26. Electrical Machinery					
Intermediate Demand					
I.S.	475	−85	2,260	−12,449	−22,375
D.D.E.	1,207	4,436	12,249	18,877	93,766
Final Demand					
I.S.	1,158	1,067	1,000	−7,209	38,660
D.D.E.	429	4,220	8,676	14,079	−13,736
E.E.	−3	1,425	3,618	9,170	121,569
Total	3,266	11,063	27,803	22,468	217,884
27. Transportation Equipment					
Intermediate Demand					
I.S.	596	−127	−848	−19,479	9,237
D.D.E.	1,900	5,651	17,712	21,560	5,034
Final Demand					
I.S.	−1,368	−4,234	462	14,086	−25,149

Appendix 1. (Continued)

	1960–63	63–66	66–68	68–70	70–73
D.D.E.	3,132	16,544	23,580	31,251	55,079
E.E.	3	251	4	1,317	8,099
Total	4,263	18,085	40,910	48,735	52,300
28. Miscellaneous Manufacturing					
Intermediate Demand					
I.S.	353	79	−2,084	58	−5,881
D.D.E.	631	4,742	4,102	4,828	5,233
Final Demand					
I.S.	726	169	−577	−2,272	1,365
D.D.E.	257	5,305	7,348	4,751	9,787
E.E.	319	4,515	5,169	25,742	44,045
Total	2,286	14,810	13,958	33,107	54,549
29. Building and Maintenance					
Intermediate Demand					
I.S.	0	0	0	0	0
D.D.E.	2,074	9,623	9,749	7,170	17,105
Final Demand					
I.S.	0	0	0	0	0
D.D.E.	6,050	48,328	50,540	123,137	189,376
E.E.	−475	0	0	0	0
Total	7,649	57,951	60,289	130,307	206,481
30. Other Construction					
Intermediate Demand					
I.S.	0	0	0	146	0
D.D.E.	0	0	0	0	28
Final Demand					
I.S.	0	0	0	0	0
D.D.E.	11,428	29,843	58,332	91,794	57,126
E.E.	725	2,635	4,530	−340	−417
Total	12,153	32,478	62,862	91,600	56,737
31. Electricity					
Intermediate Demand					
I.S.	0	0	0	0	0
D.D.E.	1,679	9,306	11,010	16,999	41,325
Final Demand					
I.S.	0	0	0	−64	105
D.D.E.	327	2,655	3,540	5,767	12,135
E.E.	−8	576	121	2,201	−1,204
Total	1,998	12,537	14,671	24,903	52,361

Appendix 1. (Continued)

	1960–63	63–66	66–68	68–70	70–73
32. Banking, Insurance and Real Estate					
Intermediate Demand					
I.S.	82	50	−2,563	4,124	−820
D.D.E.	2,819	5,198	11,696	30,301	30,911
Final Demand					
I.S.	0	2,273	0	−37	73
D.D.E.	8,660	21,470	19,403	48,069	110,962
E.E.	60	−25	3,863	−3,203	5,857
Total	11,621	28,966	32,399	79,254	146,983
33. Water and Sanitary Services					
Intermediate Demand					
I.S.	0	0	0	0	−20
D.D.E.	−909	1,276	2,336	867	3,379
Final Demand					
I.S.	0	0	0	−38	59
D.D.E	−4,157	441	1,521	1,132	5,755
E.E.	−44	−38	87	17	−16
Total	−5,110	1,679	3,944	1,978	9,157
34. Communication					
Intermediate Demand					
I.S.	2,093	151	−81	308	−330
D.D.E.	0	4,541	6,670	4,773	14,379
Final Demand	1,456	0	0	−441	341
D.D.E.	0	2,767	2,180	5,082	9,953
E.E.	0	−9	6	649	600
Total	3,549	7,450	8,775	10,371	24,943
35. Transportation and Storage					
Intermediate Demand					
I.S.	−205	−81	−149	1,185	−8,520
D.D.E.	3,591	14,338	20,564	59,585	97,212
Final Demand					
I.S.	−185	−117	−148	628	−7,789
D.D.E.	6,381	27,232	26,906	65,281	117,345
E.E.	1,207	7,847	19,372	11,291	104,644
Total	10,789	49,219	66,545	137,970	302,892
36. Trade					
Intermediate Demand					
I.S.	0	0	0	−451	−485

Appendix 1. (Continued)

	1960–63	63–66	66–68	68–70	70–73
D.D.E.	17,630	34,029	51,286	95,312	272,050
Final Demand					
I.S.	0	0	−332	719	0
D.D.E.	20,131	66,858	68,019	94,523	214,120
E.E.	761	5,135	3,740	8,770	62,372
Total	38,522	106,022	122,713	198,873	548,057
37. Other Services					
Intermediate Demand					
I.S.	165	−273	207	1,730	−3,029
D.D.E.	11,823	−3,443	13,561	55,803	252,553
Final Demand					
I.S.	352	121	−103	4,846	−2,578
D.D.E.	17,758	39,349	70,764	166,161	261,767
E.E.	120	2,169	1,861	4,451	30,925
Total	30,218	37,923	86,290	232,991	539,638
38. Scrap and Unclassifiable					
Intermediate Demand					
I.S.	−134	−4,104	−7,867	44,737	−7,550
D.D.E.	1,825	10,664	19,603	55,551	−36,423
Final Demand					
I.S.	224	−212	1,984	2,875	−578
D.D.E.	97	380	3,190	−241	−10,028
E.E.	1,671	16,753	10,157	−5,221	46,099
Total	3,683	23,481	27,067	97,701	−8,480

Source: I-O Tables, 1960, 1963, 1966, 1968, 1970, 1973, The Bank of Korea.
Notes: *I.S.*; Import Substitution.
D.D.E.; Domestic Demand Expansion.
E.E.; Export Expansion.

Appendix 2. Intermediate Input Expansion by Import Substitution and Domestic Input Expansion

(million won)

	1960–63	63–66	66–68	68–70	70–73
1. Rice, Barley and Wheat					
Import Substitution	821	1,656	2,996	10,167	−2,819
Domestic Input Expansion	7,814	14,594	10,688	22,818	34,269
Total	8,635	16,250	13,684	32,985	31,450
2. Other Agriculture					
Import Substitution	−168	1,380	−1,105	11,115	6,514
Domestic Input Expansion	15,567	30,800	37,679	31,728	91,461
Total	15,395	32,180	36,574	42,843	97,975
3. Forestry					
Import Substitution	473	−287	−31	1,066	−1,643
Domestic Input Expansion	530	3,082	1,017	2,645	2,791
Total	1,003	2,795	986	3,711	1,148
4. Fishery					
Import Substitution	197	−195	−1,658	5,098	−1,900
Domestic Input Expansion	772	3,599	3,554	10,974	41,829
Total	969	3,404	1,896	16,072	39,929
5. Coal					
Import Substitution	−98	240	−305	−91	−2,411
Domestic Input Expansion	1,437	2,301	6,065	−4,101	6,664
Total	1,339	2,541	5,760	−4,192	4,253
6. Other Minerals					
Import Substitution	1.8	−46	−103	404	−236
Domestic Input Expansion	712	1,978	3,898	438	6,645
Total	830	1,941	3,795	842	6,409
7. Processed Food					
Import Substitution	−459	5,623	−6,975	−1,838	−69,456
Domestic Input Expansion	14,977	25,778	50,636	68,482	247,640
Total	14,518	31,401	43,661	66,644	178,184
8. Beverage and Tobacco					
Import Substitution	1,367	1,187	−34	−1,575	−3,248
Domestic Input Expansion	6,060	16,057	23,774	11,375	49,390
Total	7,427	17,244	23,740	9,800	46,142

Appendix 2. (*Continued*)

	1960–63	63–66	66–68	68–70	70–73
9. Fibre Spinning and Textile Fabrics					
Import Substitution	1,056	−7,821	−5,037	6,532	−15,655
Domestic Input Expansion	5,293	28,271	17,179	34,687	127,211
Total	6,349	20,450	12,142	41,219	111,556
10. Finished Textile Products					
Import Substitution	−692	3,335	−1,651	−10,033	−21,897
Domestic Input Expansion	9,910	21,796	32,632	62,569	193,273
Total	9,218	25,131	30,981	52,536	171,376
11. Lumber, Plywood and Wood Products					
Import Substitution	−1,291	−1,726	−1,249	−24,505	−17,825
Domestic Input Expansion	1,302	7,724	6,775	30,394	30,679
Total	11	5,998	5,526	5,889	12,854
12. Paper Products					
Import Substitution	991	688	−1,542	−319	−6,017
Domestic Input Expansion	1,688	4,492	4,767	8,429	28,752
Total	2,679	5,180	3,225	8,110	22,735
13. Printing and Publishing					
Import Substitution	414	363	−705	966	−405
Domestic Input Expansion	696	5,525	10,113	260	25,994
Total	1,110	5,888	9,408	1,226	25,589
14. Leather and Leather Products					
Import Substitution	−38	60	−690	−679	−5,301
Domestic Input Expansion	1, 96	2,585	2,945	−61	14,841
Total	1,358	2,645	2,255	−740	9,540
15. Rubber Products					
Import Substitution	210	−98	−1,876	−375	· 463
Domestic Input Expansion	767	2,991	814	7,387	24,228
Total	977	2,893	−1,062	7,012	24,691
16. Basic Chemicals					
Import Substitution	35	−387	−507	1,169	−3,422
Domestic Input Expansion	702	1,451	1,438	4,909	18,985
Total	737	1,064	931	6,078	15,563
17. Other Chemical Products					
Import Substitution	2	820	−1,311	−254	11,041
Domestic Input Expansion	3,793	3,010	7,365	26,298	63,746
Total	3,795	3,830	6,054	2,6044	74,787

Appendix 2. (Continued)

	1960–63	63–66	66–68	68–70	70–73
18. Chemical Fertilizer					
Import Substitution	−26	315	269	−635	−94
Domestic Input Expansion	628	1,563	3,211	10,335	5,195
Total	602	1,878	3,480	9,700	5,101
19. Petroleum and Coal Products					
Import Substitution	−22	−4,033	1,820	−39,625	−7,176
Domestic Input Expansion	4,658	11,728	14,678	49,966	63,009
Total	4,636	7,695	16,498	10,341	55,833
20. Glass, Clay and Stone Products					
Import Substitution	225	860	181	1,061	−3,866
Domestic Input Expansion	1,738	6,405	14,408	15,834	28,473
Total	1,963	7,265	14,408	15,834	28,473
21. Iron and Steel					
Import Substitution	−160	466	−268	−1,652	−2,441
Domestic Input Expansion	526	2,794	553	5,421	11,425
Total	366	3,260	285	3,769	8,984
22. Steel Products					
Import Substitution	−1,107	266	2,318	−9,715	−21,604
Domestic Input Expansion	2,900	4,697	9,924	24,529	66,136
Total	1,793	4,963	12,242	14,814	44,532
23. Non-Ferrous Metal Products					
Import Substitution	−141	−13	−1,177	1,563	−911
Domestic Input Expansion	833	2,025	686	2,672	6,316
Total	692	2,012	491	4,235	5,405
24. Finished Metal Products					
Import Substitution	−599	563	−12	2,599	−1,733
Domestic Input Expansion	826	2,739	1,696	6,889	27,331
Total	227	3,302	1,684	9,488	25,598
25. Machinery Except Electrical Machinery					
Import Substitution	79	−383	−2,130	3,777	−4,709
Domestic Input Expansion	1,484	2,835	5,155	1,408	27,891
Total	1,563	2,452	3,025	5,185	23,181
26. Electrical Machinery					
Import Substitution	47	327	−1,161	−3,460	−47,620
Domestic Input Expansion	1,495	4,939	14,490	9,576	93,073
Total	1,542	5,266	13,329	6,116	45,453

Appendix 2. (*Continued*)

	1960–63	63–66	66–68	68–70	70–73
27. Transportation Equipment					
Import Substitution	217	−117	207	−6,537	3,949
Domestic Input Expansion	2,150	9,085	24,407	9,244	24,616
Total	2,367	8,968	24,614	2,707	28,565
28. Miscellaneous Manufacturing					
Import Substitution	16	−1,281	−337	121	2,644
Domestic Input Expansion	1,581	7,046	7,366	14,001	26,001
Total	1,597	5,765	7,029	14,122	28,645
29. Building and Maintenance					
Import Substitution	539	−1,493	3,542	−9,490	−2,118
Domestic Input Expansion	5,202	31,252	39,005	75,882	127,274
Total	5,741	29,759	42,547	66,392	125,156
30. Other Construction					
Import Substitution	−159	1,695	−4,298	10,010	−2,444
Domestic Input Expansion	5,435	11,198	25,381	45,849	28,750
Total	5,276	12,893	21,083	55,859	26,306
31. Electricity					
Import Substitution	−17	1,537	−238	176	697
Domestic Input Expansion	−6	2,020	7,555	5,328	30,053
Total	−23	,3557	7,317	5,504	30,750
32. Banking, Insurance and Real Estate					
Import Substitution	62	−81	−400	965	−381
Domestic Input Expansion	1,375	5,473	4,449	13,856	22,964
Total	1,437	5,392	4,049	14,821	22,583
33. Water and Sanitary Services					
Import Substitution	92	3	−43	191	−136
Domestic Input Expansion	321	620	1,497	1,056	2,403
Total	413	623	1,454	1,247	2,267
34. Communication					
Import Substitution	136	270	−67	−188	−852
Domestic Input Expansion	222	782	1,315	1,912	6,160
Total	358	1,052	1,248	1,724	5,308
35. Transportation and Storage					
Import Substitution	1,083	4,109	−2,297	12,291	85
Domestic Input Expansion	2,193	11,557	20,991	39,329	147,692
Total	3,276	15,666	18,694	51,620	147,777

Appendix 2. (*Continued*)

	1960-63	63-66	66-68	68-70	70-73
36. Trade					
Import Substitution	−203	−735	−2,029	6,783	−3,904
Domestic Input Expansion	7,030	7,995	17,774	38,150	77,708
Total	6,827	7,260	15,745	44,933	73,804
37. Other Services					
Import Substitution	1,739	−2,040	−2,521	6,963	1,602
Domestic Input Expansion	15,860	3,532	23,556	56,167	268,878
Total	17,599	1,492	21,035	63,130	270,480
38. Scrap and Unclassifiable					
Import Substitution	1,083	−938	−957	13,177	−3,734
Domestic Input Expansion	1,735	16,483	16,496	82,054	−35,081
Total	2,818	15,545	15,539	95,231	38,815

FOREIGN EXCHANGE POLICIES: AN EVALUATION AND PROPOSALS

*Bon Ho Koo**

I. Introduction

As in many other underdeveloped economics, Korea's foreign trade has been particularly vulnerable to a variety of restrictions and subsidies on both imports and exports. Modern trade theory tells us that unified exchange rates are theoretically suboptimal in the presence of factor market imperfections, externalities, monopoly, and "infant stage". In practice, however, government administrators may lack the ability to correctly estimate the magnitudes of "imperfections" or "externalities".

Since 1965 the Korean government has nominally adopted a unified floating exchange rate but effectively practiced a multiple exchange rate system. Many of the adverse effects resulting from Korea's *defacto* multiple exchange rate system will be indicated and explained. We will then propose that a realistic adjustment of the exchange rate should lead to other measures being utilited to stimulate exports and to restrict imports. In the final chapter, various approaches will be taken to estimate a proper level of Korea's foreign exchange rate. In contrast with the gap theory and other pessimistic views on the potency of exchange rates in restoring both internal balance and external balance, the purpose of this paper is to show that an adjustment of exchange rates can serve as a powerful policy measure in restoring both internal and external balance even in developing

* Vice President of the Korea Development Institute. This paper was presented at the First International Symposium sponsored by KDI, Seoul, July 5–11, 1972.

economies.

II. A Survey of Korea's Foreign Exchange System

1. Korea's Nominal Exchange Rates

Following the foreign exchange crisis of 1963–64 an exchange rate reform was announced in early May 1964, when the official rate was raised from 130 won to 255 won per U.S. dollar. The reform also involved transformation of the multiple, fixed-rate system to a fluctuating, unitary rate for all transactions. The actual implementation of the unitary fluctuating exchange rate was, however, announced later on March 22, 1965. Under this "floating" system the Bank of Korea (BOK) posted daily buying and selling rates with an eye to the free market. Immediately after the announcement of the new floating system, the first market exchange rate was formed at 270 won to the dollar. The exchange rate, however, declined gradually to 256 won to the dollar at the end of April 1965. The rate began to rise in May and the market exchange rate was quoted at 280 won per dollar by the end of May. On June 22, 1965, the Bank of Korea started to intervene in the market by increasing the supply of exchange certificates, but in the beginning the BOK intervention was limited and allowed the market exchange rate to fluctuate to a certain extent. From August 22, 1965 through 1967 the exchange rate was, however, completely pegged at around 272 won to the dollar by the BOK, while Korea's wholesale price index increased from 100 to 115.8 between 1965 and 1967. Although from 1968 to 1970 the exchange rate was allowed to depreciate, the degree of depreciation was limited by intervention from the BOK. In June 1971, the won was devalued by about 13 percent from 326.4 to 370.8 won to the dollar. After the June devaluation, the exchange rate was again pegged by BOK intervention in the foreign exchange market until early December 1971. After December 3, 1971, the exchange rate was allowed to devalue in the foreign exchange market, reaching 373.3 won per dollar at the end of 1971 and 392.90 won per dollar on April 30, 1972 (See Table 1).

2. Korea's Purchasing-Power-Parity Exchange Rate

The purchasing power parity theory has been developed almost exclusively with respect to changes on the monetary side in the form of differential rates of inflation between countries. Hence the purchasing power parity theory has the obvious limitation of partial equilibrium analysis. Neither changes on the real side in the form of unequal rates of technical change, output, and productivity, nor capital movements are accounted for in measuring the purchasing power parity. The purchasing power parity theory has, however, survived as an approximate way of measuring international competitiveness, especially in the short run.

Table 1, shows Korea's purchasing power parity exchange rates in relation to Korea's major trading countries between 1965 and 1971. Korea's purchasing-power-parity rate showed a continuous decline between 1965 and 1968 and a slight increase in both 1969 and 1970. Although Korea's purchasing-power-parity rate increased sharply in 1971, the rate still lagged below the 1965 level.

3. *"Adjusted" Parity Exchange Rates*

One conceptual difficulty with the purchasing power parity theory is that prices of many items which cannot enter foreign trade are included. Hence, it fails as an indicator of price movements in traded goods. In other words, wholesale price indices are weighted so heavily with standard goods of domestic consumption that they cannot be truly representative of any country's traded sectors. To moderate such biases, we have adjusted the parity rates using the import and export price indices in place of the wholesale price indices of Korea's major trading countries. These adjusted rates are also illustrated in Table 1. The trend of Korea's "adjusted" parity rates, although there are mild differences, shows similarity to the trend of Korea's purchasing power parity rates with the adjusted parity rate of 1971 still below the 1965 level.

4. *Korea's Effective Exchange Rates*

Korea adopted various policy measures to promote exports and to restrict imports. In addition to the consideration of foreign exchange rates and relative price stability, various policy measures should therefore be accounted for when measuring the effective exchange rates.

The concept of effective exchange rates can be easily defined as follows: R_m stands for the effective exchange rate for imports, R_x the effective exchange rate for exports, N the official (nominal) exchange rate, t_m and t_x the *ad valorem* rates of tariffs and other taxes and/or subsidies on imports and exports respectively. We then have the following relationships: $R_m =$

Table 1. Korea's Foreign Exchange Rates

won per U.S. dollar (the year-end base)

	1965	1966	1967	1968	1969	1970	1971
1. Nominal Exchange Rates	271.78	271.18	274.60	281.50	304.45	316.65	373.30
2. Purchasing Power Parity Rates (1965 base)[1]	271.78	254.50	243.68	235.47	247.49	238.88	252.69
3. Adjusted Parity Rates (1965 base)							
(a) Exports[2]	270.96	250.14	243.02	236.71	249.55	243.21	258.33
(b) Imports[3]	272.60	256.01	239.33	237.75	249.71	239.99	252.82
4. Real Effective Exch. Rates (1965 base)							
(c) Exports[4]	318.24	301.70	311.57	308.84	321.44	324.18	336.38
(d) Imports[5]	305.42	284.46	271.35	265.24	277.31	266.12	273.87
2A. Purchasing Power Parity Rates (1971 base)	399.16	373.17	358.60	345.03	363.12	354.55	373.30
3A. Adjusted Parity Rates (1971 base)							
(a') Exports	390.75	360.74	350.46	341.37	358.85	350.52	372.50
(b') Imports	403.39	378.87	354.12	351.84	369.51	355.14	374.10
4A. Real Effective Exch. Rates (1971 base)							
(c') Exports	458.93	435.10	449.30	445.38	463.52	467.22	485.04
(d') Imports	451.96	420.98	401.54	392.51	410.34	393.82	405.26

1. Nominal buying rate	270.96	270.36	274.20	281.10	303.70	315.90	372.50
2. Subsidies per dollar export (a + b + c + d + e)	47.28	55.73	77.34	85.65	87.49	105.17	112.54
a. Interest subsidy	10.10	11.42	17.29	13.16	14.97	17.33	12.55
b. Tariff exemptions	15.37	18.21	22.58	36.24	35.23	42.64	50.89
c. Internal tax concessions	10.77	13.43	19.92	20.07	21.93	28.76	35.86
d. Liberal wastage allowance	9.25	10.00	12.35	12.35	12.35	12.35	9.66
e. Other subsidies	1.79	2.67	4.70	3.83	2.01	4.09	3.58
3. Nominal effective exchange rate of exports (1 + 2)	318.24	326.09	351.04	366.75	391.19	421.07	485.04
4. Real effective exch. rate of exports							
f. Adjusted parity index on exports							
(1965 base)	100.00	92.52	88.63	84.21	82.17	76.99	69.35
(1971 base)	144.21	133.43	127.81	121.44	118.49	110.96	100.00
g. Real effective exch. rate on exports (3 × f, 1965 base)	318.24	301.70	311.13	308.84	321.44	324.18	336.38
h. Real effective exch. rate on exports (3 × f, 1971 base)	458.93	435.10	448.66	445.38	463.52	467.22	485.04

Table 1. (Continued)

	1965	1966	1967	1968	1969	1970	1971
1. Nominal selling rate	272.60	272.00	275.00	281.90	305.20	317.40	374.10
2. Effective cost per dollar import (a + b)	32.82	30.23	30.61	32.59	33.73	34.57	31.16
a. Effective tariff per dollar import	27.72	25.13	25.51	25.89	24.53	25.67	22.16
b. Interest cost of predeposit per dollar import	5.1	5.1	5.1	6.7	9.2	8.9	9.0
3. Nominal effective exch. rate of imports (1 + 2)	305.42	302.23	305.61	314.49	338.93	351.97	405.26
4. Real effective exch. rate on imports							
c. Adjusted parity index on imports							
(1965 base)	100.00	94.12	88.79	84.34	81.82	75.61	67.58
(1971 base)	147.98	139.29	131.39	124.81	121.07	111.89	100.00
d. Real effective exch. rate on imports (3 × c, 1965 base)	305.42	384.46	271.35	265.24	277.31	266.12	273.87
e. Real effective exch. rate on imports (3 × c, 1971 base)	251.96	420.98	401.54	392.51	410.34	393.82	405.26

Sources: Bank of Korea, Ministry of Finance, and Economic Planning Board.

Notes: [1] Ratio of weighted wholesale price index of major trading partners to Korea's WPI is multiplied by Korea's nominal exchange rates:

1965	1966	1967	1968	1969	1970	1971
100	93.85	88.74	83.65	81.29	75.44	67.69

[2] Instead of using WPI of major trading partners, weighted unit value of major trader's imports is used.

[3] Conversely weighted unit value of major trader's exports is used.

[4] Real effective exchange rates of exports are computed in the following way.

[5] Real effective exchange rates of imports are computed in the following way.

$N(1 + t_m)$, $R_x = N(1 + t_x)$. However, the actual computation of effective exchange rates is subject to severe constraints. Firstly, some of the export-measures and import-restriction measures are hard to quantify. Government persuasion or pressure to expand exports, government-sponsored market research and other export promotion activities, encouragement of direct foreign investment, and import quotas are a few examples. These are omitted in our computation of effective exchange rates. Secondly, different commodities are subject to different rates of export subsidy or import duty. Various tax provisions and credit incentives in Korea imply different rates of benefit and/or cost for different commodities.

Two methods are used in our computation of effective exchange rates. The first method is to compute an average effective exchange rate based on aggregate data for the selected period. In the other method we select some major exports and compute different effective exchange rates for different commodities during the selected years.

A. Average Effective Exchange Rates

When the value of aggregate international trade is recorded in terms of foreign currency, and the aggregate value of various export subsidies and import duties is recorded in terms of local currency, an aggregate effective exchange rate can be easily computed. In Table 1, nominal and various real effective exchange rates are illustrated.

B. Different Effective Exchange Rates for Different Commodities

(i) Different effective exchange rates of exports

Various incentives to promote export activities effectively resulted in differential subsidies and thus *de facto* multiple exchange rates. Differential export subsidies were intensified partly as a result of the proliferation of various forms of subsidies which were established to offset the adverse effect on exports of the overvaluation of Korea's exchange rate resulting from inflation. The government subsidy for earning one dollar through exports (by means of tax remissions or rebates, preferential loans and other subsidies) varied widely among the major commodities. It ranged from an effective subsidy of 125 won per dollar export of nylon fabrics to 5 won per dollar of fresh fish exports in 1969 (See Appendix 1).

(ii) Different effective rates of protection for different commodities

Although the tariff reform of 1967 slightly reduced the differentials of legal tariff rates, the rate structure remained widely varied from 13.5 percent of mining and energy to 106.3 percent of tobacco and beverages. In addition, various policy measures to promote export expansion and import substitution made effective rates of protection vary widely among different commodities (See Appendix 2).

5. Some Modifications

The method used in computing Korea's average effective exchange rates in Table 1 is basically similar to works of the Bank of Korea and Professor Balassa. In our opinion, however, two important points are not allowed in this computation. Firstly, the Big Ten agreement on new exchange rates, on December 17, 1971, is not considered at all. Secondly, tariff exemptions, as an export subsidy in the above computation of effective exchange rates, are quite exaggerated. These viewpoints will be explained now and the above computation of effective exchange rates will be accordingly modified.

A. An estimated impact of the Big Ten Agreement on the value of Korean won

When the Big Ten countries agreed on new exchange rates on December 17, 1971, the U.S. dollar was relatively devalued as shown in Table 2. Since the exchange rate of the Korean won is fixed in terms of the U.S. dollar, the Big Ten Agreement meant the effective devaluation of the Korean won. However, the impact of the new agreement on the Korean won must be independently computed because the composition of Korea's trading countries is different from that of the U.S. The implicit devaluation of the Korean won which resulted from the Big Ten Agreement is computed in Tables 3 and 4 below. That is, Korea's exchange rates of imports and exports and its average rate were respectively devalued by about 7.83 percent, 5.02 percent and 6.96 percent, or by 29.33 won, 18.74 won and 25.98 won.

B. Is tariff exemption for imported inputs for exports an export subsidy?

In the Table 1, tariff exemptions for imported inputs for exports are counted as export subsidies. In the 1971 example of Table 1, the 50.89 won tariff exemption per dollar export is computed in the following way:

$$\sum_{i=1}^{n} M_i \times x\, t_i \,/\, \text{value of 1971 exports}$$

where M_i and t respectively stand for C.I.F value of imports for export production in terms of Korean currency and the *ad valorem* nominal rate of tariff. In Table 1, the weighted average rate of nominal tariff for imported

Table 2. New Exchange Rates Agreed by Big Ten Countries (Dec. 17, 1971)

Countries	Relative appreciation to the U.S. dollar(%)	Countries	Relative appreciation to the U.S. dollar (%)
U.S.A.	—	Netherlands	+11.57
Switzerland	+ 6.35	France	+ 8.57
Germany	+13.75	U.K.	+ 8.57
Japan	+16.88	Sweden	+ 7.49
Belgium	+11.57	Italy	+ 7.49

Table 3. An Estimated Impact of the Big Ten Agreement on Effective Exchange Rates of Korea's Imports

Countries	1971 Korea's Imports		As a result of the Big Ten Agreement	
	Total imports (1,000$)	Share of imports (%) (1)	Induced nominal devaluation of Korean won (%) (2)	Devaluation of Korea's average effective exchange rates (%) (3) = (1) × (2)
Japan	953,778	39.84	16.88	6.73
EEC[1]	257,743	10.74	10.25	1.10
U.S.A. and others	1,182,799	49.42	0	0
Total	2,394,320	100.00		7.83

Notes: [1] Includes U. K. and Sweden
[2] Won devaluation on imports 0.0783 × 373.30 = 29.23 (won)

inputs for exports amounted to about 38 percent. It is true that such tariff exemptions are export-subsidies if these imports, and/or their products from using these imports, were allowed to sell in the domestic market. But, the tariffs are exempted on the basis that the imports are used for the production of exports. On this matter, we cannot expect perfect honesty from the producer-cum-exporter. Technically and in practice, the producer-cum-exporter manages to divert some of his products into the domestic market

Table 4. An Estimated Impact of the Big Ten Agreement on Effective Exchange Rates of Korea's Exports.

As a result of the Big Ten Agreement

Countries	1971 Korea's Exports		Induced nominal devaluation of Korean won (%)	Devaluation of Korea's average effective exchange rates (%)
	Total exports (1,000$)	Share of exports (%) (1)	(2)	(3) = (1) × (2)
Japan	261,988	24.54	16.88	4.14
EEC[1]	82,506	7.73	11.35	0.88
U.S.A. and others	723,113	67.73	0	0
Total	1,067,607	100.00		5.02

Notes: [1] Includes U. K. and Sweden

[2] Won devaluation on exports 0.0502 × 373.30 = 18.74 (won), Average won Devaluation; 1,067,607/3,461,927 × 5.02 + 2,394,320/3,461, 927 × 7.83 = 6.96(%), 0.0696 × 373.30 = 25.98 (won)

instead of for exports. This must be, however, separately imputed as an export-subsidy in the category of "leakage to domestic markets." If we assume the perfect honesty of the producer-cum-exporter, these tariff exemptions are not export subsidies from the viewpoint of the producer-cum-exporter who has to sell at world market prices. In other words, the producer-cum-exporter who had to pay the tariff for imported inputs for the production of exports is effectively getting negative protection if competitors of Korean exporters in the world market do not pay tariffs or taxes for such inputs. This view is adopted in computing the "modified" effective exchange rates of exports in Table 5 below. Two alternative assumptions are used. In one case we assume that competitors of Korean producer-cum-exporters in the world market do not pay tariffs or taxes for equivalent inputs and that Korean producer-cum-exporters do not leak their imported inputs and/or their products for domestic sale in an illegal way. This assumption is used in computing row 3 of Table 5. Alternatively, we assume that competitors of Korean producer-cum-exporters in the world market pay certain *ad valorem* tariffs or taxes for equivalent inputs, and that Korean producer-cum-exporters leak a certain portion of their imported inputs and their products for domestic sale. On the basis of this latter assumption, tariff exemptions for imported inputs for exports are

Table 5. *Modified Effective Exchange Rates of Exports*

	1965	1966	1967	1968	1969	1970	1971
1. Nominal Effective Exch. Rate of Export	318.24	326.09	351.04	366.75	391.19	421.07	485.04
2. Tariff Exemptions per Dollar Export	15.37	18.21	22.58	36.24	36.23	42.64	50.89
3. "Ideally Modified" Nominal Effective Exchange Rates by Assuming Tariff Exemptions Not As Export Subsidies	302.87	308.88	328.46	330.51	354.96	378.43	434.15
4. Imputed Export Subsidies per Dollar Export by the Alternative Assumption	8.51	8.54	8.49	9.12	9.83	10.57	13.31
5. "Crudely Modified" Nominal Effective Exchange Rates by the Alternative Assumption (3 + 4)	311.38	316.52	336.95	339.63	364.79	389.00	447.46

effectively partial export subsidies. In row 5 of Table 3, the amount of these effective subsidies is crudely assumed to be about 10 percent of C.I.F. value of imported inputs for exports. In short, Korea's effective exchange rate of exports at the end of 1971 would be around 447.46 instead of about 485.04 on the basis of the latter assumption.

6. *Summary and Characteristics of the Present System*

From the above survey, we can sum up the following characteristics.

(1) Although the Korean won was devalued several times after 1965, Korea's parity exchange rates continuously lagged below the 1965 level, in spite of a small increase in 1969 and 1971 (See Table 1).

(2) To offset the adverse effect on exports of the overvaluation of Korea's exchange rates resulting from inflation, various export-promotion measures were adopted. As a result the real effective exchange rates on exports had not been lagged much below the parity rate of 1965 and in fact became

even more favorable for exports after 1969.

(3) On the other hand, the real effective exchange rates on imports had been decreasing generally although a slight reversing trend was indicated after 1969.

(4) As a result real effective exchange rates diverged between exports and imports. In addition, effective exchange rates varied widely for different commodities. Thus, *de facto* multiple exchange rates were in practice.

III. An Evaluation of the Present System

Korea's export expansion and impressive economic growth could not have been achieved without adopting export-oriented policies. But these export-oriented policies, coupled with Korean inflation, have brought about a *de facto* multiple exchange rate system and the nominal overvaluation of the Korean won.

1. Adverse Effects Resulting from the Present System

Modern trade theory contends that unified exchange rates are suboptimal in the presence of factor market imperfections, externalities, monopoly, and "infant export industries." Under these circumstances a tax-cum-subsidy and/or a tariff-cum-subsidy are theoretically optimal. However, in practice, the efficient administration of these measures is not easy. Tax-cum-subsidy and/or tariff-cum-subsidy interventions require an ability to estimate correctly the magnitudes of the "imperfections" or "externalities." In view of the uncertainties regarding the parameters of the systems which are candidates for adjustment, together with a lack of expertise among the administrators making the adjustments, and the temptations to subject the adjustments to political manipulation, it may well be that distortions and imperfections are likely to be accentuated rather than offset by public intervention, Korea's *de facto* multiple exchange rates, with the nominal overvaluation, contributed many adverse effects. Although relatively high effective exchange rates on exports through various export subsidy measures contributed to the continuous expansion of Korea's exports, tariff exemptions for the import of raw materials for exports with a nominal overvaluation made effective exchange rates on imported inputs asymmetrically low. This asymmetrical cheapening of imported inputs is defended in order to channel needed imports of capital goods and raw materials for export expansion and industrialization. This has, however, misallocated resources in the following ways. Firstly, the cheapening of imported inputs penalizes domestic producers (existing and potential) of capital goods and raw materials, with respect to foreign competitors. It discourages the development of domestic resources and of new skills at earlier stages of the production of exports. Thus it discourages the development of backward linkages and provides additional bias against the learning process (and it may even contribute to the inferiority complex of domestic producers). Secondly, a mix of low exchange rates on imported inputs and high exchange rates on exports may encourage "finishing-touch" type industries which use a large proportion of imported inputs. Average rates of net foreign exchange earnings in Korea's exports had been decreased from 70.1 percent in 1966 to 56.7 percent in 1970.[1] Thirdly, the cheapening of imported capital goods may accelerate overinvestment and contribute to excess capacity. Korea's level of capital utilization rates in the 1960's was lower than that in advanced countries, according to the recent studies of Professors Kim and Kwon.[2] In addition the present system of *de facto* multiple exchange rates creates complicated procedural work and red tape which mean greater implicit costs and administrative time lag from the viewpoint of an exporter. Further, it may invite government corruption and collusion between businessmen and governmental officials. Once adopted it is hard to terminate this "comfortable" collusion. In extreme cases it can lead to situations where more foreign exchange is devoted to purchasing imported inputs than is earned from the sale of the exported product.

In short, a tax-cum-subsidy or a tariff-cum-subsidy should not be substituted for a devaluation of the exchange rate. As a first step, exchange rate devaluation should precede a resort to other measures intended to stimulate exports and restrict imports. Devaluation has the advantage of being efficient with respect to the relative stimulus which it gives to production for export and import-competing productions.

There are, however, widespread criticisms against devaluation in Korea. These criticisms will now be reviewed.

---

[1] The Professorial Evaluation Team, *Evaluation Report of the Fourth Year of Second Five-Year Plan,* EPB, Korea, 1971.

[2] Young Chin Kim and Jene K. Kwon, *Capital Utilization in Manufacturing Industries in Korea,* Korean Industrial Development Research Institute, Seoul, Korea, 1971.

2. *An Evaluation of Views on Devaluation*

A. The Factor Proportions Problem

In relation to the so-called "gap model," there is growing support of the import minimum thesis which postulates a zero or very low substitutability between imported inputs and domestic resources in developing economies. Not only is a relatively fixed proportion of imported inputs to domestic resources needed to maintain the existing capacity in operation, but also a relatively fixed proportion of imported capital goods is required for net investment and growth in developing economies. Along this line of reasoning, some economists, including Vanek and Linder, hypothesize an import minimum thesis which cannot be solved by varying exchange rates.

In most developing countries, as in advanced countries, however, imports are not confined to raw materials and capital goods. Some imports are, in practice, for consumption. Further, in a strict sense, some advanced countries like the U.K. and Japan face a similar factor proportions question to that of developing countries. Hence, this is not an analytical problem but a quantitative question.

Professor Cooper studied the experience of twenty-four devaluations involving nineteen different developing countries during the 1955–1966 period.[3] In sixteen cases, absolute imports actually decreased in the year following devaluation. Further, imports may be assumed to rise with domestic imcome. Hence, the above figure has a serious bias toward underestimating the effectiveness of devaluation in reducing imports. He concludes that the currency devaluation seems to be successful in the sense of reducing imports.

Various quantitative studies have been made to estimate Korea's import function.[4] Although the exchange rate elasticity of the import of inter-

---

[3] R. N. Cooper, "An Assessment of Currency Devaluation in Developing Countries", in G. Ranis (ed.), *Government and Economic Development* (New Haven: Yale University Press, 1971).

[4] Korea's KFX import functions:
(Bank of Korea) $\text{Log } M_{kfx} = -5.03413 + 2.684 \text{ Log } Y - 0.80555 \text{ Log } R_m{}^*$
(KDI) $\text{Log } M_{kfx} = -2.260 + 1.039 \text{ Log } V - 0.6969 \text{ Log } R_m{}^*$ where Y, V, and $R_m{}^*$ respectively stand for gross national product, value-added, and real effective exchange rates of imports.

Korea's sectoral import functions (KDI studies):

$$M_i = 8.0 + 0.84\ V_m - 0.043\ R_m{}^*$$

mediate goods is lower than the exchange rate elasticity of imports of consumption goods, the exchange rate elasticity of Korea's aggregate imports is found to be around −0.7. This indicates that the level of imports is not insensitive to exchange rates and that the so-called import minimum thesis is not in this case empirically valid, although its argument is not insignificant in the sense that the exchange rate elasticity of imports of intermediate goods is found to be smaller than the elasticity of imports of consumption goods.

B. The Export Elasticity Pessimism and/or the Export Maximum Thesis

There has been growing pessimism about the potential for export expansion of developing countries among some economists. Analytically this pessimism is rooted either in so-called "elasticity pessimism" or in the so-called "export maximum thesis".

Primary exports, in which developing countries are traditionally adept, are subject to a low price elasticity and a low income elasticity of demand in advanced countries. Further, in overpopulated and poorly endowed countries such as Korea, the supply of primary goods might be too inelastic to provide export expansion. In addition, producers of simple industrial goods, such as textiles, face limited market outlets and administrative restrictions such as "voluntary" export quotas. In this case, the question arises, why do the developing countries not produce more advanced manufactures which face fewer institutional barriers and are demand-elastic in advanced countries? According to the pessimistic view, great differences in representative demand between advanced countries and developing countries mean that goods demanded in advanced countries are not typically produced for the home market of developing countries. Hence, workers in developing countries lack the skills for the production of these modern manufactures and thus their marginal contribution is very low or even negative in some cases. In addition, the entrepreneurs are unfamiliar with marketing these goods abroad. Thus, it is contended by the pessimists that in developing countries there may be an export maximum for both manufactures and primary commodities. With the former, the maximum is due to domestic-supply conditions resulting from their inexperience and thus low marginal productivity and/or possible

$$M_k = 11.3 + 0.87\ FL - 0.298\ R_m{}^*$$
$$M_d = 120.6 + 0.385\ V_m - 0.340\ R_m{}^*$$

where M_i, M_k, M_d, V_m and FL respectively stand for imports of intermediate goods, imports of machinery and equipment, and imports for domestic consumption, value added in manufacturing and foreign loans.

cases of negative value added. As for primary products, the exports maximum is determined by inelastic demand conditions for each of the individual commodities. For example, Linder argues that "no exchange rate at all can make the product more exportable."[5]

The export maximum thesis, however, seems to be exaggerated. Low productivity is a matter of training and education. If labor is available at a low cost and if competitive exchange rates provide incentives for some potentially profitable exports, the technology in use will be improved with the dissemination of knowledge, and productivity will thus be improved. Not all primary exports of the developing countries are subject to low income elasticities and low price elasticities. Oil, nonferrous metals, iron ore, and diamonds are a few examples. Hence, the effectiveness of devaluation for increasing export expansion is a quantitative question. According to Professor Cooper's study, nineteen of the twenty-four cases showed export increases in the year following devaluation.[6] Even in these five cases, however, one cannot write off the devaluation as a failure. In the case of India, for example, many exports were adversely affected by the drought, the closure of the Suez Canal, and other exogenous changes. Thus, Professor Cooper concludes that devaluation also seems to work for increasing overall exports in developing countries. A number of other recent studies including works of Devries, Balassa, Larry, and Little-Scitovsky-Scott also present some empirical evidence that total exports actually performed better in the countries where effective exchange rates were favorable to exports.[7]

Various quantitative studies have been made to estimate Korea's export function. These studies show that the coefficient of the effective exchange rate for exports seems positive and highly significant, although the sample period used for the regression is rather short and thus the reliability is limited.

C. A devaluation-inflation spiral

It has been contended by the pessimists that a devaluation will set off a

[5] S. B. Linder, *Trade and Trade Policy for Development* (New York: Praeger, 1967), p. 41.

[6] Cooper, *op. cit.*

[7] B. A. Devries, *Export Experiences of Developing Countries* (Baltimore: Johns Hopkins Press, 1967); B. Balassa, "Trade Policies in Developing Countries," *American Economic Review,* May 1971; H. B. Larry, *Imports of Manufactures from Less Developed Countries* (National Bureau of Economic Research, 1968); and I.M.D. Little, T. Scitovsky, and M. Scott, *Industry and Trade in Some Developing Countries* (New York: Oxford University Press, 1970).

devaluation-inflation spiral. Especially in developing economies where substitutability between imported inputs and domestic resources is limited, a devaluation will simply raise domestic prices of imported inputs, with little effect on quantity of imports. This will, in turn, cause a progressive rise of domestic prices and thus invite another devaluation. This is an exaggerated account, although the effect of devaluation-induced-inflation cannot be denied. In most of the theoretical literature on devaluation, it has been assumed that a devaluation will increase the domestic prices of importables and exportables not only relative to other prices in the economy but also in absolute amounts. Thus, a price index that includes importable and exportable commodities as well as nontraded goods is bound to show an increase. Indeed, this is the fundamental mechanism that triggers off the first effect of devaluation when we want to cut down real domestic absorption relative to output, that is, to reduce the trade balance deficit. Professor Harberger, in his recent studies of Argentina and other Latin American countries, concludes that a devaluation of about 50 percent will probably result in increases of the price level of between 24 and 30 percent, depending on the values of some key parameters.[8]

Various quantitative studies have been made to estimate the impact of Korea's devaluation on the domestic price level. In the case of a 10 percent devaluation, devaluation-induced increases in Korea's general price level are reported ranging from 2 percent (BOK studies) to 3.6 percent (KDI).[9]

D. Outstanding Foreign Loans and Political Pressure

Whenever there are large amounts of foreign loans outstanding, a devaluation substantially affects the asset position of firms and individuals who hold large foreign loan liabilities. Thus the firms and individuals who suffer financial losses from the devaluation are likely to exert political pressure against devaluation. The present situation in Korea is a case in point. Further, big firms holding large foreign loans are politically influen-

[8] A. C. Harberger, "Some Notes on Inflation", in W. Baer, I. Kerstenetzky, and R. D. Irwin (ed.) *Inflation and Growth in Latin America,* 1964.

[9] On the impact of devaluation on the price level in Korea; see (1) Bank of Korea and EPB; the elasticity of the WPI with respect to exchange rate is estimated as about 0.2. (2) Lee, Eric Y. (1971) .By using the equation $\Delta P/P = W_2 \times \Delta E/E$, where P is the WPI, W_2 the ratio of imports to GNP and E the exchange rate, the elasticity of the WPI to exchange rate in Korea is reported as about 0.22. (3) KDI Studies; $\Delta P_w/P_w = -0.704 - 0.165\ \Delta V_{na}/V_{na} + 0.232\ \Delta M_s/M_s + 0.363\ \Delta E/E + 0.121\ \Delta P_r/P_r + 0.20\ \Delta P_u/P_u$ where P_w is the WPI, V_{na} value added in non-agriculture-forestry-fishing, M_s money supply, E exchange rate, P_r price of rice, and P_u public utility price.

tial. Hence, devaluation becomes a difficult policy measure to implement in Korea. However, Korea's resource allocation should not be jeopardized because of the above transfer problems.

In short, the criticisms against a devaluation are analytically not sound. Empirically, in Korea both imports and exports are fairly elastic with respect to effective exchange rates, although the effect of devaluation on inflation is not insignificant.

3. A Summary Appraisal of the Present System

Insofar as particular subsidy or tax rebate incentives have been introduced as substitutes for a devaluation of the exchange rate, they are clearly unjustifiable.

As a first step, exchange rate devaluation should precede the resort to other measures used to stimulate exports and to restrict imports. Devaluation has the advantage of being efficient with respect to the relative stimulus which it gives to production for export and import-competing production. While a high exchange rate encourages the substitution of domestic inputs in place of imported inputs to the extent that the former can be produced at a lower opportunity cost, it does not otherwise discourage the use of imported inputs required in the production of more exports, since any given rise in the exchange rate increases the absolute margin measured in domestic currency, separating the gross price of the export product from the gross price of its imported input.

Reliance on control of the level of the exchange rate as the primary stimulus of export expansion possesses the further advantage of making it impossible for the foreign currency proceeds from exports to fall short of the foreign currency cost of the import content of those exports.

It would seem that the exchange rate should be sufficiently high to provide a prospective rate of profit from exports as high as could be provided by any alternative combination of particular subsidies. However, it is true that subsidies on a very large scale might provide a larger initial cash flow to export firms than could be provided by an exchange rate policy. For example, large subsidies might finance capital outlays for plant and equipment construction in advance of actual production of exports, whereas a high exchange rate provides rewards only following the acts of production and exportation. On the other hand, it is very doubtful whether subsidies of this magnitude and timing could be justified. They would amount to very large rewards in advance of the performance of the tasks which they were designed to encourage.

However, one valid argument against relying exclusively upon control over the level of the exchange rate is that a high exchange rate gives equal assistance to all export and import competing activities. It does not single out for special assistance those activities where the costs of training labor and management in new skills may fall upon the pioneering firms, but the benefits may be reaped by other firms which at a later date hire away the skilled personnel, or where potential economies of scale promise profits in the future but necessitate initial capital requirements larger than existing financial institutions can be expected to mobilize.

This rationale for selective subsidies would explain and justify all of the subsidy differentials tabulated in Appendix 2 if one could have confidence in the quality of the calculations which determine the size and duration of each subsidy, and in the quality of the bureaucracy which administers the subsidy programs.

If one lacks this confidence an alternative policy would be to substitute, in place of the selective subsidies, a higher exchange rate. This would over-expand in relative terms, those export and import-competing activities which are not in the abstract entitled to selective subsidies. In consideration of both trade theory and Korean practice, a reform of Korea's foreign exchange policies should be directed toward a greater reliance on foreign exchange rates for the realization of export-promotion and import restriction, while tax-cum-subsidy measures should be simplified and their applications clearly identified to externalities, factor market imperfections, or pioneering and new exporters.

IV. Proposals for Reform of Korea's Foreign Exchange Policies

1. Toward More Unified Effective Exchange Rates

As already indicated in this paper, there are substantial differences in effective rates between exports and imports and among different commodities. Such differences are hardly identified with respect to learning effects or new exports. Thus, such differentials cannot be theoretically justified and a reform toward more unified exchange rates is needed. For this purpose, we propose:

(1) To reduce the present level of export subsidies and to simplify the present export measures, and to make export subsidies more proportional

to net foreign exchange earnings rather than gross export earnings.

(2) To increase the present level of effective exchange rates on imports with a mix of an increased effective tariff and a reduction of differential tariff-rates for different commodities.

(3) To increase Korea's nominal exchange rate.

Our proposals, however, do not imply that the present tax-cum-subsidy measures should be completely replaced by an adoption of unified exchange rates. Proper tax-cum-subsidies are complementary to unified exchange rates for better resource allocation, internal balance, and external balance by decreased domestic absorption.

A. On Real Effective Exchange Rates of Exports and Export Subsidies

In consideration of Korea's balance of trade deficit and the perplexing balance of payments pressure, rapid export expansion must be continously pursued and maintained. For this purpose real effective exchange rates of exports must at least be maintained at the 1971 level. However, current export-subsidy measures must be simplified and the level of export-subsidies lowered, coupled with an increase in the nominal exchange rate. Further, different rates of export subsidy for different commodities should be moderated.

The Korean government has already made some progress in this direction. Since December 1971 the nominal exchange rate has been gradually increased by "floating". The rate was increased from 370.55 won in early December to 392.90 won at the end of April per U.S. dollar at an average annual rate of 14.47 percent. Bank loan interest rates were lowered from 24 percent to 22 percent in June 1971 and again in January 1972 from 22 percent to 19 percent. The lowered interest rates of bank loans means a reduction of effective export-subsidies per dollar export because the gap between interest rates of preferential loans and bank loans is reduced (See Table 6). Further the policy changes of February 14, 1972, including changes of preferential credit regulations in relation to export activities, effectively reduced the credit subsidy per dollar export (See Table 6). In addition, the change of preferential credit regulations made effective export subsidies more proportional to net foreign exchange earnings (See Table 7). More recently, rates of wastage allowance which are decided by the administrative discretion of the Ministry of Commerce, have been more strictly applied.

Table 6. *Comparative Data on Export Subsidies Per Dollar Export*

	1970	1971	Changes made in Jan.-Feb. 1972(imputed basis)		Proposals
1. Interest Subsidies (a + b + c + d)	**17.33**	**12.55**		**9.83**	(9.83)
a. Preferential Export Credit	6.06	6.65	9.62		
b. Preferential Import Credit	6.19	5.30	7.96		
c. Exemption of Predeposit Requirement	5.97	1.50	0.00	0.21	
d. Interest Cost of Predeposit for Import	0.89	0.90	7.75		
2. Internal Tax Concessions (e + f + g)	**28.76**	**35.86**		**35.86**	(30.60)
e. Corporation and Income Tax	3.53	5.25	5.25		To abolish
f. Business Taxes	3.60	3.12	3.12		
g. Commodity Taxes	21.63	27.49	27.49		
3. Liberal Wastage Allowance	12.35	9.66	lower than	9.66	To abolish
4. Other Subsidies Including Utility Discount, D/A, and Preferential Import Licensing	**4.09**	**3.58**	3.58	**3.58**	To abolish
5. Sub-total (1 + 2 + 3 + 4)	62.53	61.65	58.93		(40.43)
6. Tariff Exemptions					
h. Conventional Method[1]	42.64	50.89	50.89		
i. "Modified" Method[2]	10.57	13.31	13.31		
7. Total (1 + 2 + 3 + 4 + 6)					
j. Conventional Method[1] (5 + h)	105.17	112.54	109.82		
k. "Modified" Method[2] (5 + i)	73.10	74.69	72.24		

Sources: BOK, EPB, and MOF.
Notes: [1] See p. 456
[2] See p. 456

Table 7. Comparative Data on Export-Subsidies and Ratio of Net Foreign Exchange Earnings

Ratio of Net Foreign Earnings (%)	Preferential Export Credit[1]		Preferential Import Credit[2]		Exemption of Predeposit Requirement[3]		Interest Cost Predeposit for Import[4]		Total (1 + 2 + 3 − 4)	
α	1971	R^5	1971	R^5	1971	R^5	1971	R^5	1971	R^5
90	10.62	15.36	1.22	1.82	0.34	—	0.21	1.78	11.97	15.40
80	9.44	13.65	2.43	3.65	0.69	—	0.41	3.55	12.15	13.75
70	8.26	11.94	3.65	5.47	1.03	—	0.62	5.33	12.32	12.08
60	7.08	10.24	4.86	7.30	1.37	—	0.82	7.11	12.49	10.43
50	5.90	8.53	6.80	9.12	1.71	—	1.03	8.88	13.38	8.77
40	4.72	6.83	7.30	10.94	2.06	—	1.23	10.66	12.85	7.11
30	3.54	5.12	8.51	12.77	2.40	—	1.44	12.44	13.01	5.45
20	2.36	3.41	9.73	14.59	2.74	—	1.65	14.22	13.18	3.78
10	1.18	1.71	10.44	16.41	3.09	—	1.85	15.99	13.36	2.13
Average of Ratio of Net Foreign Earnings In 1971										
56.38	6.6529	9.62	5.3034	7.96	1.4958		0.8975	7.75	12.5546	9.83

Sources: BOK, EPB, and MOF

Notes: [1] $\begin{pmatrix}\text{Preferential}\\ \text{Export Credit}\end{pmatrix} = \alpha \times \begin{pmatrix}\text{won per dollar allowance}\\ \text{for preferential credit}\end{pmatrix} \times \begin{pmatrix}\text{Difference of}\\ \text{interest rate(\%)}\end{pmatrix} \times \begin{pmatrix}\text{Days allowed for}\\ \text{preferential loan}\end{pmatrix}$

$(1971) = \alpha \times 295 \times (22\text{–}6) \times (90/360)$

$(R) = \alpha \times 350 \times (19\text{–}6) \times (135/360)$

[2] $$\begin{pmatrix}\text{Preferential}\\ \text{import credit}\end{pmatrix} = (1-\alpha) \times \text{Selling rate} \times \begin{pmatrix}\text{Difference of}\\ \text{interest rate(\%)}\end{pmatrix} \times \begin{pmatrix}\text{Days allowed for}\\ \text{preferential loan}\end{pmatrix}$$

$$(1971) = (1-\alpha) \times 374.1 \times (22\text{–}9) \times 90/360$$

$$(R) = (1-\alpha) \times 374.1 \times (19\text{–}6) \times 135/360$$

[3] $$\begin{pmatrix}\text{Exemption of pre-}\\ \text{deposit requirement}\end{pmatrix} = (1-\alpha) \times \text{Selling rate} \times \begin{pmatrix}\text{Interest rate}\\ \text{on loans (\%)}\end{pmatrix} \times \begin{pmatrix}\text{Days allowed for}\\ \text{expredeposit}\end{pmatrix}$$

$$(1971) = (1-\alpha) \times 374.1 \times 22 \times 15/360$$

[4] $$\begin{pmatrix}\text{Interest cost of}\\ \text{predeposit for import}\end{pmatrix} = (1-\alpha) \times \text{Selling rate} \times \begin{pmatrix}\text{Interest rate}\\ \text{on loans (\%)}\end{pmatrix} \times \begin{pmatrix}\text{Rate of required}\\ \text{predeposit(\%)}\end{pmatrix} \times \begin{pmatrix}\text{Days required}\\ \text{for predeposit}\end{pmatrix}$$

$$(1971) = (1-\alpha) \times 374.1 \times 22 \times 10 \times 90/360$$

$$(R) = (1-\alpha) \times 374.1 \times 19 \times 100 \times 90/360$$

[5] The figures in *R* columns are based on reforms made in Jan.-Feb., 1972.

Table 8. *Comparative Parity Rates for 1965–1972*

	1965	1966	1967	1968	1969	1970	1971	1972[1]	1972[2]
1. Nominal Exchange Rates	271.78	271.18	274.60	281.50	304.45	316.65	373.30	—	—
2. Purchasing Power Parity (PPP)									
(a) PPP index (1965:100)	100.00	93.85	88.74	83.65	81.29	75.44	67.69	64.27	62.56
(b) Parity nominal rates[3]	271.78	289.59	306.27	325.01	334.33	360.26	401.51	422.87	434.31
(c) Parity nominal rates[4]	—	—	—	—	—	—	—	396.89	408.33
3. Adjusted Parity Rates (APR)									
(a) Adjusted parity index on exports[5]	100.00	92.52	88.63	84.21	82.17	76.99	69.35	—	—
(b) Adjusted parity index on imports[6]	100.00	94.12	88.79	84.32	81.82	75.61	67.58	—	—
(c) Average adjusted parity index (AAP)	100.00	93.32	88.71	84.27	82.00	76.30	68.47	68.47	63.07
(d) Parity nominal rates	271.78	291.23	306.37	322.51	331.44	356.20	396.93	419.54	430.92
(e) Parity nominal rates	—	—	—	—	—	—	—	393.56	404.94
4. Comparative Real Wages in Manufacturing									
(a) Real wage parity index[7]	100.00	93.54	96.89	99.63	86.03	83.38	—	—	—
(b) Real wage index(RWI) in manufacturing									
Korea (RWI^K)	100.00	114.44	116.96	124.02	158.58	176.82	208.59	—	—
Japan (RWI^J)	100.00	106.2	115.6	126.1	139.5	152.4	163.3	—	—
U.S.A. (RWI^U)	100.00	107.93	110.61	120.89	132.79	142.13	—	—	—

5. Per Capita Product Index in Manufacturing									
Korea	100.00	108.44	110.37	124.76	147.42	168.57	196.50	—	—
Japan	100.00	110.54	125.68	142.21	161.55	183.60	192.36	—	—
U.S.A.	100.00	101.50	100.14	105.07	106.16	106.28	—	—	—

Sources: Bank of Korea. *Monthly Economic Statistics:* U.S. Government, *Economic Report of The President,* Jan. 1972; Bureau of Statistics, Japan, *Monthly Statistics of Japan,* Feb. 1972.

Notes: [1] Projected inflation rates in 1972 are assumed as follows; Korea(10%), Japan(5.0%) U.S.A.(3.2%).

[2] Alternatively, Korea(13%), Japan(5.0%), U.S.A. (3.2%).

[3] The effective won depreciation resulting from the Big Ten Agreement last December *was not accounted.*

[4] The effective won depreciation resulting from the Group of Ten Agreement last December *was counted.*

[5] and [6] See Table 1.

[7] The formula used is $(RWI^{U} \times W^{U} + RWI^{J} \times W^{J})/RWI$, where *U,J,K,* and *W* respectively stand for U.S.A., Japan, Korea, and country's trade share to Korea's total trade.

However, in our opinion, such reforms should be further extended. In the near future we propose to abolish (i) preferential treatment of corporation and income taxes in relation to export activities, (ii) the wastage allowance, and (iii) other export subsidies including public utility discounts, D/A, and preferential import licensing of linkage benefits. The imputed results of these proposals are contrasted and summarized in Table 4. Eventually, however, export subsidies should be limited to the clear presence of externalities and "new" pioneering export activities.

B. On Real Effective Exchange Rates of Imports and Tariff Reform

Since 1965 Korea's real effective exchange rates have generally decreased due to the extended application of tariff exemptions and concessions. In 1971 the effective tariff rate was less than 6 percent. This rate is quite low compared to the rates of many other developing countries. To reduce Korea's balance of trade deficit and to increase government revenues which are much needed, Korea's effective tariff rate must be increased to a level of at least 10 percent. At the same time a tariff reform, including a sharp moderation of tariff exemptions currently in practice, coupled with narrowing differentials of tariff rates for different commodities, is needed. Such proposals are being made by the Ministry of Finance following recommendations made by McKinnon and Balassa.[10]

2. Practical Approaches to Estimate Korea's Proper Exchange Rates

Prior to discussing Korea's equilibrium exchange rates, crude but practical approaches will be used in estimating Korea's proper exchange rates in the context of international competitiveness and balance of trade.

A. Various Parity Rates

(1) Purchasing-power parity rate. Suppose we maintain the 1965 level of purchasing-power parity. Without considering the effective won depreciation resulting from the Big Ten Agreement last December, Korea's nominal exchange rate at the end of 1971 should be 401.50 won to the dollar and by the end of 1972 Korea's nominal exchange rate should be 422.87 won or 434.31 won depending on Korea's inflation rate in 1972 (See Table 8). Considering the effective won depreciation last December, Korea's parity exchange rates at the end of 1972 should be lower at 396.89

[10] R. I. McKinnon, "Tariff and Commodity Tax Reform in Korea: Some Specific Suggestions", USAID, Seoul, 1967, and B. Balassa, *The Korean Tariff Reform of 1971: An Evaluation* (Seoul: USAID, 1971).

won or 408.33 won depending on Korea's inflation rate (See also Table 8).

(2) Adjusted parity rates. If we use adjusted parity indexes instead of purchasing-power-parity indexes, nominal exchange rates to maintain the 1965 parity level are slightly lower as shown in Table 5.

(3) In terms of real wage and per capita products in manufacturing industries between 1965 and 1970, Korea's competitiveness has been relatively weakened compared to Japan while it has been relatively improved compared to the U.S. (See Table 8).

B. Real Effective Exchange Rates

For the continous export expansion which is vital for the Korean economy, the real effective exchange rate on exports must be at least maintained at the present level. To the extent that Korea's inflation rate is projected to be greater than that of its major trading countries, devaluation of Korea's nominal exchange rate is needed, preferably coupled with a reform of present export-subsidy measures. The effective exchange rate for exports by using our modified viewpoint, was about 447.46 won to a U.S. dollar in December 1971.[11] To maintain this level of the real effective exchange rate on exports, the nominal exchange rate in December 1972 is computed as follows: $R_n = (447.46 \times WPI_k/WPI_f) - W_d$ where R_n is the nominal exchange rate in December 1972, WPI_k wholesale price index in Korea, WPI_f weighted wholesale price index of major trading countries, and W_d effective won devaluation resulting from the Big Ten Agreement last December. That is, $R_n = 447.46 \times 110/104.1 - 25.98 = 446.84$.[12] Alternatively $R_n = 447.46 \times 113/104.1 - 25.98 = 459.74$.[13] The above figures, however, are computed assuming the adoption of our proposed reform of export-subsidy measures. If the proposed reform is delayed, the minimum level of the nominal exchange rate can be justified at a lower rate.

C. The Third Five-Year Plan

To meet the 1972 targets of the Third Five-Year Plan, however, the real effective exchange rate itself should be increased in 1972. This is illustrated in Table 9 below by using various assumptions.

---

[11] See p. 459 and Table 5 in this paper.

[12] Korea's inflation is assumed at 10 percent for 1972 and see Table 4 for 25.98 won.

[13] Alternatively Korea's inflation is assumed at 13 percent.

Table 9. Required Increase of Rural Effective Exchange Rates to Meet the Third Five-Year Plan

Target increasing rates		Required increase of exchange rates		Real effective exchange rates on exports in 1971 (won)	Required real effective exchange rates on exports in 1972 (won)	
$\Delta Y(\%)$	$\Delta X(\%)$	$\Delta R^*_{re}(\%)$[1]				
9	27	9.44[3]	4.42[4]	447.46	489.70[3]	467.24[4]
9	33	11.80	6.78	447.46	500.26	477.80
8	27	9.57	4.55	447.46	490.28	467.82
8	33	11.94	6.92	447.46	500.89	478.42
7	27	9.71	4.69	447.46	490.91	468.45
7	33	12.07	7.05	447.46	501.47	479.00

Target increasing rates		Required increase of exchange rates		Real effective exchange rates on imports in (won)	Required real effective exchange rates on imports in 1972 (won)	
$\Delta Y(\%)$	$\Delta M(\%)$	$\Delta R/pp(\%)$[2]				
9	3.4	8.2[3]	0.37[4]	405.26	438.49[3]	406.76[4]
9	0	13.8	5.97	405.26	461.19	429.45
7.3	0	11.2	3.37	405.26	450.65	418.92

Notes: [1] The formula used is $X = -1{,}003.6323 + 0.3400\ Y + 2.5367\ R^*_{re}$ (Frank-Kim-Westphal's formula)

[2] Imports function of KDI, $\text{Log}\ M_{kfx} = 2.260 + 1.039\ \text{Log}\ Y - 0.6968\ \text{Log}\ R/pp$, is used.

[3] The figures are computed without considering the effective won depreciation resulting from the Big Ten Agreement.

[4] The figures are computed considering the effective won depreciation resulting from the Big Ten Agreement.

3. *Transitional Problems-Devaluation by "Floating" or Once-and-for-all Devaluation*

Since there is abundant economic literature on the question of floating versus fixed rates,[14] our discussion will merely review some of the institutional and political constraints in Korea which would exist if we are to devalue the Korean won. If Korea's nominal exchange rate is in the neighborhood of its shadow rate, adjustment of exchange rates by floating is adequate and preferable. If the gap between the proper exchange rate and the actual rate is substantial, however, gradual devaluation by floating is subject to many constraints. First, the rate of devaluation by floating cannot exceed the Korean interest rate. Otherwise, Korean exporters may gain a greater rate of return by postponement of their exports. Suppose Korea were to devalue her currency by floating at an annual

Table 10. Projected Parity Exchange Rates by Floating

	1971	1972	1973	1974
Nominal Exchange Rates[1]	373.3	418.10	468.27	524.46
Purchasing-Power-Parity (PPP) Exchange Rates	373.3	395.69	419.38	444.53
(Purchasing Power Parity Index)[2]	(100)	(94.64)	(89.56)	(84.76)
The Gap between PPP Exchange Rates and Reference Exchange Rates of 447.46 won to the U.S. dollar[3]	74.16	51.77	28.08	2.93

Notes: [1] Projected Devaluation Rate of Korean Won

1972	1973	1974
12%	12%	12%

[2] Projected Annual Rate of Inflation

	1972	1973	1974
Korea	10%	10%	10%
Major Trading countries	4.1%	4.1%	4.1%
(U.S.)	3.2%	3.2%	3.2%
(Japan)	5.0%	5.0%	5.0%

[3] Reference exchange rate of 447.46 won to the U.S. dollar at the end of 1971 is based on the "modified" effective exchange rate of export at the end of 1971. (See Table 5).

[14] C. F. Bergsten, G. N. Halm, F. Machlup, and R. V. Rossa, (ed.), *Approaches to Greater Flexibility of Exchange Rates* (Princeton, N. J.: Princeton University, 1970).

rate of 15 per cent in consideration of the interest rate constraint. As shown in Table 10, it is difficult for Korea's nominal exchange rate to approach even our "reference" rate. Secondly, such a gradual devaluation is subject to political constraints. The firms and individuals who suffer financial loss from the devaluation will exert political pressure with increasing intensity. Especially when it comes near to election time, gradual devaluation becomes practically unthinkable in view of past experiences in Korea. Further, the transfer problem in relation to devaluation and repayment of foreign loans can be more easily tackled by once-and-for-all devaluation than through a gradual devaluation by floating. In consideration of these institutional and political constraints, once-and-for-all devaluation is preferable and more practical than a gradual devaluation by floating.

REFERENCES

1. Balassa,B., "Trade Policies in Developing Countries," *American Economic Review*, May 1971.
2. Balassa, B., *The Korean Tariff Reform of 1971: An Evaluation*, USAID, Seoul, 1971.
3. Bank of Korea, *Monthly Economic Statistics*, Jan. 1965–March 1972.
4. Bersten C.F., G.N. Halm, F. Machlup, and R.V. Rossa, (ed.), *Approaches to Greater Flexibility of Exchange Rates*, Princeton N. J., Princeton University Press, 1970.
5. Bhagwati, J.N., "The Generalized Theory of Distortions and Welfare", *Trade, Balance of Payments, and Growth,* ed. by Bhagwati, J.N., Jones, R.W., Mudell, R.A., and Vanek, J., Amsterdam and Oxford: North-Holland, 1971, pp. 69–90.
6. Bureau of Statistics, Japan, *Monthly Statistics of Japan* Feb. 1972.
7. Cooper, R.N., "An Assessment of Currency Devaluation in Developing Countries", *Government and Economic Development* ed. by Ranis, G., New Haven: Yale University Press, 1971.
8. Devries, B.A., *Export Experiences of Developing Countries*, Baltimore: Johns Hopkins Press, 1967.
9. Harberger, A.C., "Some Notes on Inflation", *Inflation and Growth in Latin America*, ed. by Baer, W., Kerstenetzky, I., and Irwin R.D., 1964.
10. Kim, Young Chin, and Jene K. Kwon, *Capital Utilization in Manu-*

facturing Industries in Korea, Seoul: Korean Industrial Development Research Institute, Korea, 1971.
11. Kreger, A.O., "The Role of Home Goods and Money in Exchange Rate Adjustments", University of Minnesota, 1969.
12. Larry, H.B., *Imports of Manufactures from Less Developed Countries*, National Bureau of Economic Research, 1968.
13. Lee, Eric Y., "Effects of Changes in the Exchange Rate on Domestic Price; The Case of Korea", AID, fall 1971.
14. Linder, S.B., *Trade and Trade Policy for Development*, New York: Praeger, 1967, p.41.
15. Little, I.M.D., Scitovsky, T., Scott, M., *Industry and Trade in Some Developing Countries*, New York: Oxford Univeristy Press, 1970.
16. McKinnon, R.I., "On Misunderstanding the Capital Constraint in LDCs: the Consequences for Trade Policy", *Trade, Balance of Payments, and Growth*, ed. by Bhagwati, J.N., Jones, R.W., Mundell, R.A., and Vanek, J., Amsterdam and New York: North-Holland, 1971, pp. 506–623.
17. McKinnon, R.I., "Tariff and Commodity Tax Reform in Korea: Some Specific Suggestions", Seoul: USAID, 1967.
18. Nippon Tokei Kenkyusha (ed.) *Collections of Japanese Statistics*, Nippon Hyronsha, 1958, p. 171.
19. Professorial Evaluation Team, *Evaluation Report of the Fourth Year of Second Five-Year Plan*, Seoul: EPB, 1971.
20. Schydlowsky, D.M., "On the Choice of a Shadow Price for Foreign Exchange", Cambridge, Mass: Economic Development Advisory Service Harvard University, 1968.
21. Taylor, L. and E. Bacha, "Foreign Exchange Shadow Prices; A Critical Review of Current Theories", Cambridge: Center for International Affairs, Harvard University, 1971.
22. U.S. Government, *Economic Report of the President,* Jan. 1972.